ECONOMICS
OF
DEVELOPMENT

To Accompany this Volume
Study Guide and Workbook, Third Edition,
by Bruce R. Bolnick and Jonathan Haughton

ECONOMICS OF DEVELOPMENT

Third Edition

Malcolm Gillis
DUKE UNIVERSITY

Dwight H. Perkins
HARVARD UNIVERSITY

Michael Roemer
HARVARD UNIVERSITY

Donald R. Snodgrass
HARVARD UNIVERSITY

W · W · NORTON & COMPANY
New York London

Copyright © 1992, 1987, 1983 by W. W. Norton & Company, Inc.

ALL RIGHTS RESERVED.

PRINTED IN THE UNITED STATES OF AMERICA.

The text of this book is composed in Times Roman,
with the display set in Optima.
Composition and Manufacturing by The Maple-Vail Book Group.

Library of Congress Cataloging-in-Publication Data
Economics of development / Malcolm Gillis . . . [et al.].—3rd ed.
     p.   cm.
   Includes bibliographical references (p.   ) and index.
   1. Developing countries—Economic policy. 2. Economic
development. I. Gillis, Malcolm.
HC59.7.E314 1992
338.9—dc20   91-17161

ISBN 0-393-96156-7

W. W. Norton & Company, Inc., 500 Fifth Avenue, New York, N.Y. 10110

W. W. Norton & Company Ltd., 10 Coptic Street, London WC1A 1PU

1 2 3 4 5 6 7 8 9 0

For Elizabeth, Julie, Linda, and Anne

Contents

Preface

Economic development often makes headlines. Long-established political and economic systems teeter or fall in Eastern Europe, China, and South Africa. Over one hundred thousand people die as floods devastate Bangladesh—yet again. Japan, in ruins after World War II, becomes an economic superpower 30 years later and challenges the primacy of American industry. South Korea, widely regarded as a hopeless case after the devastation of the Korean War, in turn challenges Japan for export markets along with Taiwan, Hong Kong, and Singapore. Within two decades, a pack of would-be industrializing countries contend for export markets. Oil-exporting countries, attempting to short-cut the normally slow accumulation of wealth by nations, extract unprecedented revenues from consumers around the world for a decade or so and then lose ground as the OPEC system weakens in the 1980s. Mexico, Brazil, Argentina, and many other nations go deeply into debt to finance their development and then create a crisis in the world financial system by being unable to repay. Public health makes such great strides that populations grow dramatically. World population surpasses five billion, and three out of four people live in developing countries. Sub-Saharan Africa faces multiple problems: drought, economic stagnation, political instability, and AIDS.

Television and the other news media bombard our senses daily with many stories about development. The developing countries no longer seem exotic or remote to North Americans and Europeans, and few now doubt that their struggle for development will have profound implications for the way people live in the industrial countries. Enhanced awareness about development creates an opportunity for those of us who write textbooks, but it also presents two challenges.

The first challenge is to keep up with the news. Development texts deal with recent history as well as tools of analysis and must be revised frequently to reflect current events. The third edition of *Economics of Development* utilizes data published as recently as 1990 by the World Bank, United Nations, and other sources. It also pays more attention to matters of greatest current interest.

An entirely new Chapter 5 examines one of the most far-reaching trends of our time, the march away from government intervention toward greater dependence on markets as a tool of development. Structural adjustment, the process by which countries shed controls and move toward market-based, export-oriented economies, is treated more extensively in this edition and appears in several chapters and a new technical appendix. Chapter 17 takes a fresh look at the differing means by which countries such as Japan, South Korea, and Taiwan have achieved the world's highest income growth through the unprecedented expansion of their manufactured exports.

Chapter 12 offers a critical analysis of the appropriate role of government in promoting development and describes the recent trends in tax policy, which stress lower tax rates, broad tax base, improved tax administration, and introduction of a value-added tax. The developing-country debt problem is treated more comprehensively in Chapter 14 than in previous editions; this reflects a decade of crises and countermeasures and a growing literature on debt and development, focused especially on Mexico and other Latin American countries.

Chapters 7 and 10 reflect the continuing debates on world population, nutrition, and health. They highlight the significant and widespread improvements in nutrition and life expectancy that have been achieved in recent years, even in the face of persistent problems such as famine and high fertility in Africa. The path to environmentally sound, self-sustaining development is explored in Chapter 19, which has been completely rewritten.

The second challenge is more difficult. News stories about third-world countries make development seem an exciting but ephemeral subject: it would appear necessary only to keep up with the latest events to capture the essence of the topic. But the reality is deeper. A textbook should distinguish between the merely evanescent and the truly enduring aspects of development. The forces underlying economic change may be barely perceptible, but they can be powerful and can radically alter a country's standard of living in two or three generations.

To meet these challenges, *Economics of Development* continues to rely on five distinguishing features: (1) It makes extensive use of the theoretical tools of classical and neoclassical economics, in the belief that these tools contribute substantially to our understanding of development. (2) It draws heavily on decades of empirical studies by economists and economic historians, studies that have uncovered and explained the structure of development, ot at least narrowed our zones of ignorance. (3) *Economics of*

Development deals explicitly with the political and institutional framework in which economic development takes place. (4) It presents many real-country examples to illustrate major points, drawing on the authors' collective experience of—hard as it is for us to believe—more than a century of work on development issues. (5) The book recognizes the diversity of development experience reflected in these country examples and acknowledges that the lessons of theory and history can only be applied within certain institutional and national contexts.

ORGANIZATION

The basic structure of the book remains as in earlier editions. Part 1 introduces the concept and measurement of development, some theories developed to explain it, and the body of data that has been amassed to recognize and define development when it takes place. Part 1 now includes a chapter on markets versus controls as the means of guiding development, in addition to one on planning models.

People make development happen and people benefit from it. Part 2 deals with the contribution of human resources to development and with the transformation of human lives as a consequence of development. It includes chapters on population, labor, education, and health.

Capital, the other major physical input in the growth process, is the subject of Part 3. Topics include domestic saving and investment, fiscal policy, financial policy, and foreign aid and investment.

International trade binds developing countries to industrial countries and offers opportunities for accelerating the development process. Part 4 explores strategies for realizing these opportunities.

In Part 5, the lessons of earlier chapters are applied and extended to help understand development in the major sectors: agriculture, natural resources and the environment, and industry.

SUPPLEMENTS

To help meet the needs of students and instructors, two supplements accompany the text. A *Study Guide and Workbook* by Bruce Bolnick and Jonathan Haughton of Northeastern University provides review material, self-tests, and problem sets that will help students to grasp the major points more firmly. An *Instructor's Manual,* also by Bolnick and Haughton, provides lecture and discussion topics along with answers to the problem sets in the workbook. Both of these supplements have been revised to match the third edition of the text.

ACKNOWLEDGMENTS

In the course of writing three editions, we have accumulated many debts to generous colleagues who have read chapters, reviewed the entire book, tested the manuscript in their classes, or otherwise encouraged us: Paul Albanese (Middlebury College), Ralph Beals (Amherst College), Richard Bird (University of Toronto), Bruce Bolnick (Northeastern University), Paul Clark (Williams College), David Dapice (Tufts University), Shantayanan Devarajan (Harvard University), James Duesenberry (Harvard University), Sebastian Edwards (University of Southern California), Alfred J. Field (University of North Carolina), Ira N. Gang (Rutgers University), Lester Gordon (Harvard University), Arnold Harberger (University of Chicago), Sue Horton (University of Toronto), John Isbister (University of California, Santa Cruz), Alan Kelley (Duke University), Anne Krueger (Duke University), David Lindauer (Wellesley College), Charles McLure (Stanford University), Malcolm McPherson (Harvard University), Stephen Radelet (Harvard University), Caroline Schwartz (Emory University), David Singer (University of Connecticut), Joseph Stern (Harvard University), Thomas Tushingham (Ryerson Polytechnic Institute), Yana van der Meulen (Harvard University), and Louis Wells (Harvard University). Although we cannot list their names, we would also like to thank the numerous teachers who responded to questionnaires circulated by the publisher.

Dedicated work on bibliography and data assembly for earlier editions by Ricardo Godoy and Kit Crowe was carried forward by Ali Agha and Hak Bin Chua. Christine Brake, Elizabeth Dyer, Jennifer Jordan, Sarah Potok, Susan Stewart, and Karen Turner gave support at various stages of revision. At W. W. Norton, Drake McFeely and Carol Loomis transformed the manuscript into the book you are reading now.

We have worked toward a book that meets the expectations of all these people, and we thank them for helping us.

Durham	M.G.
Cambridge	D.H.P.
Cambridge	M.R.
Cambridge	D.R.S.

June 1991

PART 1

THEORY AND PATTERNS

1

Introduction

In 1975, when she was 17 years old, Rachmina Abdullah did something no girl from her village had ever done before.[1] She left her home in a beautiful but poor part of the state of Kedah in Malaysia, where people grow rice in the valleys and tap rubber trees in the nearby hills, and went to work in an electronics plant in the busy city of Penang, 75 miles away. Rachmina's family was poor even by the modest standards of her village, and her parents welcomed the opportunity for their daughter to earn her own keep, and possibly even send money back to help the family feed and clothe themselves, deal with recurrent emergencies, and raise their five younger children. With these benefits in mind, they set aside their reservations about their unmarried daughter's unheard-of plan to go off by herself to work in the city.

Rachmina got a job assembling integrated circuits (ICs) along with 500 other young women in a factory owned by a Japanese company. Every day, she patiently soldered hundreds of tiny wires onto tiny chips of silicon. It was tedious, repetitive work, which had to be performed at high speed and, the management hoped and expected, with flawless accuracy. Each working day, Rachmina and her new colleagues rose very early and bicycled, walked, or bused to the factory. Being careful to arrive before the assigned hour of 7:00 a.m. to avoid being fined, the workers removed their shoes at the factory door, punched the time clock, and went to a room where they changed into spotless white uniforms and slippers. Then they

1. This narrative is loosely based on Fatimah Daud, *"Minah Karan." The Truth About Malaysian Factory Girls* (Kuala Lumpur: Berita Publishing, 1985) and Kamal Salih and Mei Ling Young, "Changing Conditions of Labour in the Semiconductor Industry in Malaysia," *Labour and Society* 14 (1989): pp. 59–80.

hurried to an assembly hall, where they heard a speech from the production supervisor about the day's production goals and sang the company song.

Except for one five-minute break, which most of the young women used to fill in forms showing how much they had produced, they worked without stopping until noon, when it was time for a 45-minute lunch break. Rachmina spent this period eating and chatting with her friends in the lunch hall, where the Malay, Chinese, and Indian workers clustered in separate areas. After lunch, the women resumed the morning's routine and stopped only when the quitting bell rang at 4:00 p.m. Then they reversed the morning's procedure; they returned to the assembly hall, sang the company anthem again, heard another speech from the production supervisor, lined up to clock out, changed to street clothes, and left for home. By the end of her long day of steady activity, Rachmina had earned the equivalent of $2.50.

Because their hourly wages were low, the workers welcomed opportunities to work overtime. Often they put in two or three extra hours in a day up to seven days a week. They particularly liked working Sundays and holidays, when double wages were paid. With overtime work and occasional bonuses, Rachmina was able to earn an average of $80 a month. She shared a small house in a squatter area with seven other factory workers. There was only one bedroom, so some of them slept in the lounge. By living simply and inexpensively, most of the young women managed to set aside $5 to $20 a month to send to their families in the villages. A few spent freely on clothes and cosmetics, and were criticized for it, but most led frugal lives. The young women enjoyed the unfamiliar freedom of living apart from their families.

In 1982 the electronics industry was hit by a recession. By this time Rachmina had become a line leader, responsible for supervising the work of a team of newer workers. Her factory reduced its work force, cut back on shift work, and virtually eliminated overtime. Rachmina, who was now 22 and had accumulated $400 in savings, decided it was time to return to her village, where she soon married a local man and settled down.

Rachmina's chance to work in an electronics factory came about because in the 1970s American and Japanese electronic manufacturers were moving into export processing zones (EPZs) established by the Malaysian government in several parts of the country. The government used the EPZs to tempt foreign investors to establish plants in Malaysia. The national unemployment rate was high, and the government was particularly anxious to find more urban, nonagricultural jobs for the indigenous Malay population, including Rachmina and her family. The Malays had long followed a rural life-style and were generally much poorer than the immigrants of Chinese and Indian stock. Now the government, which relied on Malay votes and had experienced terrifying race riots in 1969, was anxious to help Malays better their economic position.

Investors were drawn to Penang as a good place to set up semiconductor assembly plants. The electronics industry had originated in high-tech developing-country locations like Silicon Valley, California. By the mid-1970s, however, the demand for ICs and other electronic devices was growing by leaps and bounds and the firms were looking for overseas locations where they could carry out parts of their operations at lower cost. ICs are made in a four-step process. First, mask-making, the process of designing the circuit and reducing the artwork to an overlay version through high-resolution photography, is a high-skill operation. Second, wafer fabrication, the conversion of silicon into chips, is a capital-intensive process. Third, assembly, which includes mounting the chip on a frame, welding appropriate wires to it, and enclosing the completed chip in a resin, plastic, or ceramic covering, is very labor-intensive. Finally, testing, though also done by hand, requires some skill.

It was becoming too costly for electronic firms to meet the booming demand while carrying out all four operations in California, Japan, and similar locations. The firms decided to move their assembly and testing operations to countries where labor was cheap, compliant, and capable of learning the relatively simple skills involved. The first beneficiaries of this migration in electronics and other industries were the newly industrializing countries (NICs) of East Asia, South Korea, Taiwan, Hong Kong, and Singapore. In Malaysia, the city of Penang, with its good infrastructure and English-speaking work force, also attracted foreign investors, even though the electronic industry was forced to recruit thousands of farm women like Rachmina and introduce them to the disciplines of factory labor.

Factories making 64K chips and other electronic components flourished in Penang and other Malaysian cities in the 1970s and early 1980s. Malaysia, a middle-income country previously known mainly for the export of rubber, tin, and palm oil, became the second largest exporter of electronic components after Japan. The plants were almost all foreign-owned. They bought and sold few goods and services in Malaysia itself, and only the simpler parts of the manufacturing process were carried out in Malaysia. Drawn by generous tax exemptions and wages that averaged as little as $30 a month in 1971, the companies experienced cost increases as wages rose to $120 a month by 1980, an increase only partly offset by rising productivity. Meanwhile, advances in technology in the 1980s made ICs both more complex and smaller and thus reduced the amount of work that could be done by hand. These changes contributed to the industry shakeout that Rachmina experienced in 1982. Employment of unskilled workers dropped sharply for a while in Malaysia and other developing countries involved in electronic component assembly.

In time, however, technological advances and continuing cost pressures in the developed countries dictated that even some of the more complex parts of the manufacturing process be shifted to lower-wage countries. As wages rose in South Korea, Taiwan, Hong Kong, and Singapore, firms moved their labor-intensive operations from these NICs to the less-industrialized economies of Asia, such as Malaysia and Thailand. In this second wave of foreign investment, some of the migrating operations were owned by Korean, Taiwanese, Hong Kong, and Singaporean companies. The Penang electronic industry revived. It now uses less unskilled labor and more skilled workers than before, and it produces a wider range of products for both domestic and international markets. But it revived without Rachmina, happily engaged in raising a family in her Kedah village.

Rachmina Abdullah is a personification of the nearly 4 billion people of the developing countries whose lives have been profoundly affected, in many different ways, by economic changes in recent years. Her story raises many issues of development that are addressed in this book. How does industrialization affect the lives of the majority of people in developing countries who are still rural and still poor? Who benefits from foreign investment and who loses, in both the developing and the industrial countries? How do governments promote investment, industrialization, and exports? How do countries educate their people to become productive workers in more advanced industries? How do countries and their people cope with the disparities between urban industrial workers and the vast majority of still-poor farmers and marginal urbanites, and between the advances of some ethnic groups in contrast to the slow progress of others? This book explores the economics of these and other issues in an attempt to understand why some countries develop rapidly while others seem not to develop at all. We are concerned with both the characteristics of development and the policies that can be employed to improve development performance.

TERMINOLOGY: THE DEVELOPING WORLD

Before embarking on this complex task, we need to sort out some terms commonly used to describe developed and less-developed countries and to suggest some possible ways to measure where a country stands along the continuum from industrial to developing countries.

Rich and Poor Countries

The countries with which this book is concerned have been labeled with many different terms. All these terms are intended to contrast their state or rate of change with those of the more modern, advanced, developed countries, so that terms tend to be found in pairs. The starkest distinction is between **backward** and **advanced** economies, or between **traditional** and **modern** ones. The "backward" economy is traditional in its economic relationships, in ways that will be described in the next chapter. However precisely and neutrally the term can be defined, it retains perjorative connotations, a touch of condescension, and is therefore not much used today. In any case, the implication of stagnation is inappropriate, because in most countries economic and social relationships are changing in important ways.

The more popular classifications implicitly put all countries on a continuum based on their **degree of development.** Thus we speak of the distinctions between **developed** and **underdeveloped** countries, **more** and **less developed** ones, or, to recognize continuing change, **developed** and **developing** countries. The degree of optimism implicit in "developing countries" and the handy acronym LDCs for "less-developed countries" make these the two most widely used terms.[2] Developed countries are also frequently

---

2. The initials LDC have also been used, especially by the United Nations, to designate the least-developed countries, those with lowest incomes per capita (among other characteristics). In this book "LDC" is used to mean less-developed country (or countries).

called the **industrial countries,** in recognition of the close association between development and industrialization.

A dichotomy based simply on income levels, the **poor** versus the **rich countries,** has been refined by the World Bank[3] to yield a four-part classification that is useful for many analytical purposes. The developing countries are divided by income into **low-income economies** (less than $500 per capita in 1988) and **middle-income economies** (between $500 and $6,000 in 1988). The latter group is further divided into those with incomes below $2,200 per capita, the **lower-middle-income economies,** and the **upper-middle-income economies.** (A subset of upper-middle-income countries, mostly Asian and occasionally Latin American economies whose industrial output has been growing rapidly, is sometimes called the **newly industrializing countries or economies.**) The World Bank's classification is completed by the **high-income economies** (also called the **industrial countries**), mostly members of the Organization for Economic Cooperation and Development (OECD), with incomes over $6,000 per capita.

Three anomalous groups fit uneasily into this taxonomy. Five Middle Eastern petroleum exporters—Oman, Libya, Saudia Arabia, Kuwait, and the United Arab Emirates—whose incomes ranged from $5,000 to $16,000 per capita in 1988, have economies that are more traditional than the typical upper-middle income or industrialized country. Three other economies—Israel, Singapore, and Hong Kong—are considered by the United Nations (and many others) to be developing countries despite per capita incomes over $8,000 in 1988. And the economies of Eastern Europe, including the Soviet Union, have incomes that qualify them as middle incomes, though some of them may better be described as industrial economies in decline or in transition from controlled to market-oriented economies.

A term in vogue during the 1980s, especially in international forums, was the **third world.** Perhaps the best way to define it is by elimination. Take the industrialized (OECD) economies of Western Europe, North America, and the Pacific (the "first" world, though it was never called that) and the industrialized, formerly centrally planned economies of Eastern Europe (the "second" world); the rest of the countries constitute the third world. All third-world countries are developing countries, and these include all of Latin American and the Caribbean, Africa, the Middle East, and all Asia except Japan. The geographic configuration of this group has led to a parallel distinction, **north** (first and second worlds) versus **south,** which still has some currency. But the south or third world encompasses a wide variety of nations, from wealthy oil exporters to very low income, poorly endowed countries. Political motivations have created further exceptions: South Africa and Israel are usually not considered part of the third world;

3. World Bank, *World Development Report 1990* (New York: Oxford University Press, 1990), pp. 178–79. The World Bank, formally titled the International Bank for Reconstruction and Development (IBRD), borrows funds on private capital markets in the developed countries and lends to the developing countries, and, through its affiliate, the International Development Association (IDA), receives contributions from the governments of developed countries and lends to the low-income countries at very low interest rates with long repayment periods. The World Bank is perhaps the world's most important and influential development agency. See Chapter 14 for a more complete discussion.

nor are Spain and Portugal, former colonial powers, although in many respects they are developing countries.

It is necessary to be aware of these various terminologies and classifications and to recognize their exceptions and inconsistencies. But it is not wise to dwell too long over them. No system can capture all important dimensions of development and provide a perfectly consistent, manageable framework. Because there is no compelling selection of terms, we make none in this book. The less-developed countries will be called that, as well as developing or third-world countries. When one country or several do not fit a general observation, we will name the exceptions and desist from adding new terms to a field that is already awash in classification schemes.

Growth and Development

While the labels used to distinguish one set of countries from another can vary, one must be more careful with the terms used to describe the development process itself. The terms economic growth and economic development are sometimes used interchangeably, but there is a fundamental distinction between them. **Economic growth** refers to a rise in national or per-capita income and product.[4] If the production of goods and services in a nation rises, by whatever means, one can speak of that rise as economic growth. **Economic development** implies more. What has been happening in South Korea since 1960, for example, is fundamentally different from what has been happening in Libya as a result of the discovery of petroleum. Both countries experienced a large rise in per-capita income, but in Libya this rise was achieved by foreign corporations staffed largely by foreign technicians who produced a single product consumed mainly in the United States and Western Europe. Although the government and people of Libya have received large amounts of income from their oil, they have had little to do with producing that income. The effect of petroleum development has been much as if a rich nation had decided to give Libya large amounts of grant aid.

Libya's experience is not usually described as economic development. Economic development, in addition to a rise in per-capita income, implies fundamental changes in the structure of the economy, of the kind observed in South Korea since 1960. Two of the most important of these structural changes are the rising share of industry, along with the falling share of agriculture, in national product and an increasing percentage of people who live in cities rather than the countryside. In addition, countries that enter into economic development usually pass through periods of accelerating, then decelerating, population growth, during which the nation's age structure changes dramatically. Consumption patterns also change as people no longer have to spend all their income on necessities, but instead move on to consumer durables and eventually to leisure-time products and services.

A key element in economic development is that the people of the country must be major participants in the process that brought about these changes

---

4. Income per capita is measured as the gross national product (the value of all goods and services produced by a country's economy in a year) divided by the population.

in structure. Foreigners can be and inevitably are involved as well, but they cannot be the whole story. Participation in the process of development implies participation in the enjoyment of the benefits of development as well as the production of those benefits. If growth only benefits a tiny, wealthy minority, whether domestic or foreign, it is not development.

Modern economic growth, the term used by Nobel laureate Simon Kuznets, refers to the current economic epoch as contrasted to, say, the epoch of merchant capitalism or the epoch of feudalism. The epoch of modern economic growth is still going on, so all its features are not yet clear, but the key element has been the application of science to problems of economic production, which in turn has led to industrialization, urbanization, and even an explosive growth in population.

The widely used term **modernization** refers to much more than the economy. One can speak of the modernization of a society or of a political system, for example. But it is difficult to give the term a precise meaning. Too often there is a tendency to equate modernization with becoming more like the United States or Western Europe. Is it reasonable to say that the Soviet Union is not modern because it is not democratic or that Japan is not modern because it still maintains certain ways of organizing business based more on its own traditions than on practices in the West? Because of the vague and misleading nature of the term, we will not use it further here.

Finally, it should always be kept in mind that while economic development and modern economic growth involve much more than a rise in per-capita income or product, there can be no development without economic growth.

A DEVELOPMENT CONTINUUM

Much can be learned from a 10-minute perusal of Table 1–1 and Figures 1–1 to 1–4 about the nature of structural change during development and the many differences within the developing world. These data are from the World Bank's *World Development Report,* an annual publication that should become familiar to every student of development. The wide disparity of per-capita income among the groups of countries is not surprising because they are classified according to the World Bank's four-part scheme. The industrial (OECD) countries as a group have an average per-capita GNP 9 times that of the 54 middle-income countries, of which Mexico and the Philippines are typical examples, and more than 50 times that of the poorest 42 countries, of which India and Tanzania are examples.

In Chapter 3 we will discuss the shortcomings of using national income per capita to compare the well-being of country populations, but it remains the most useful single indicator. One of the major problems with income comparisons, the difference in national price structures, can be overcome by correcting for price differences, as explained in Chapter 3. A simpler, if less accurate, substitute for price corrections is to use a physical measure of economic welfare, of which per capita energy consumption has as much

TABLE 1–1   Development Characteristics of Groups and Selected Countries

	GNP per capita, 1988 (dollars)	Energy consumption per capita, 1988 (kg of oil equivalent)	Rural population share, 1988 (%)	Life expectancy at birth, 1988 (years)	Adult illiteracy rate, 1985 (%)
Low-income economies	320	322	65	60	44
(Excluding China, India)	(280)	(122)	(75)	(54)	(51)
Ethiopia	120	20	87	47	38
Tanzania	160	36	70	53	na
Bangladesh	170	50	13	51	67
Mali	230	21	81	47	83
Nigeria	290	150	66	51	58
China	330	580	50	70	31
India	340	211	73	58	57
Pakistan	350	210	69	55	70
Kenya	370	94	78	59	41
Ghana	400	15	67	54	47
Sri Lanka	420	162	79	71	13
Indonesia	440	229	73	61	26
Middle-income economies	1,930	1,086	42	66	26
Bolivia	570	249	50	53	26
Philippines	630	244	59	64	14
Senegal	650	155	62	48	72
Egypt, Arab Rep.	660	607	52	63	56
Honduras	860	203	58	64	41
Cameroon	1,010	152	53	56	44
Colombia	1,180	755	31	68	12
Peru	1,300	478	31	62	15
Mexico	1,760	1,305	29	69	10
Malaysia	1,940	784	59	70	27
Brazil	2,160	813	25	65	22
Hungary	2,460	3,068	40	70	*
Argentina	2,520	1,523	14	71	5
Korea, Rep. of	3,600	1,515	31	70	*
Saudi Arabia	6,200	3,098	24	64	*
OECD members	17,470	5,181	23	76	*
United Kingdom	12,810	3,756	8	75	*
Germany, Fed. Rep. of	18,480	4,421	14	75	*
United States	19,840	7,655	26	76	*
Japan	21,020	3,306	23	78	*

*Less than 5%.
Source: World Bank, World Development Report 1990, pp. 178–179, 186–187.

validity as any. Figure 1–1 shows how closely energy use per capita is correlated with GNP per capita.

A predominant structural characteristic of development is the growing share of both income produced and labor employed in industry. Table 1–1 and Figure 1–2 reflect this trend in the share of the population living in rural areas: 75 percent in the low-income countries other than China, contrasted with 42 percent in the middle-income countries, and only 23 percent in the OECD countries.

Rising income is not the only goal of development. People aspire to stay healthier and become better educated. Indicators for each of these aspects of well-being are included in Table 1–1, and they are correlated with per-

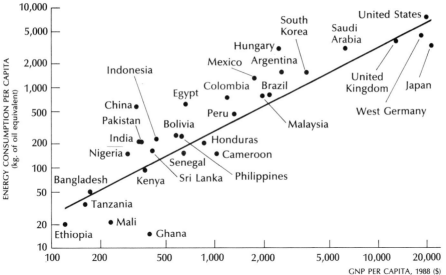

FIGURE 1–1   Energy Consumption per Capita. There is a strong tendency for energy consumption to rise with average income, though some countries use much less energy than others at the same average income.

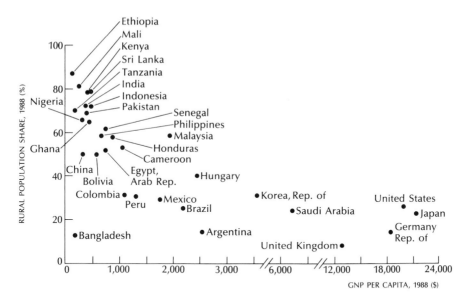

FIGURE 1–2   Rural Population. The share of the population living in rural areas declines as income grows.

capita income (Figures 1–3 and 1–4). Life expectancy, which is only 51 years in poor countries excluding China, is 76 years in the rich countries. But the most dramatic contrast is in adult illiteracy: 51 percent of the adult population are unable to read in low-income countries excluding China, compared with only 26 percent in the middle group; in industrial countries less than 5 percent of all adults are illiterate.

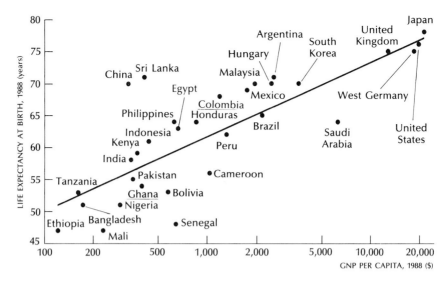

FIGURE 1–3   Life Expectancy. Although life expectancy rises with average income, there are large differences among countries with similar incomes.

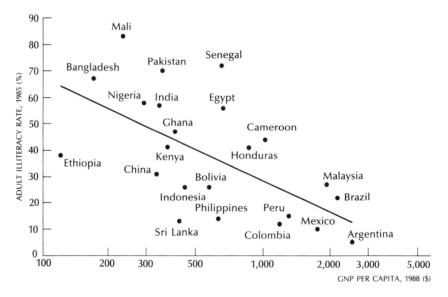

FIGURE 1–4   Adult Literacy. The rate of illiteracy among adults tends to fall as incomes rise, but some low-income countries have remarkably low rates of illiteracy.

In each category there is considerable variance and hence there are some interesting exceptions. China is a low-income country that consumes more energy per capita than many middle-income countries; while Ghana, with higher average income than China, has one of the lowest levels of energy consumption in the world (Figure 1–1). The rural population share in Malaysia is about twice that of Colombia, though Malaysia enjoys a higher income

(Figure 1-2). Chinese and Sri Lankans live as long as Koreans and Argen-

tineans (Figure 1-3). Almost 90 percent of Sri Lankan adults have learned
to read, more than in middle-income countries like Senegal, Egypt, and
Brazil (Figure 1-4). Behind these and other variations in development lie
many factors: different resource endowments, governments' varying ideologies and policies, cultural differences, colonial experience, war, and historical accident. In many cases variations suggest new theories of
development, and we will explore some of these in later chapters.

Development is inherently a dynamic process that cannot be completely
captured in Table 1-1. Most less-developed countries have experienced
growth in incomes since 1965 and many have enjoyed substantial growth,
as Table 1-2 shows. Even in the low-income countries, which account for
over half the world's population, per-capita GNP grew by 3.1 percent a
year, though without India and China the rate was only 1.5 percent a year.
Middle-income countries grew more slowly between 1965 and 1988, 2.3
percent a year. There were star performers in both groups: China, Sri Lanka,
Indonesia, Egypt, Cameroon, Malaysia, Brazil, Hungary, and Korea all
grew by 3 percent a year or more, enough to double their average incomes
over the period. However, over those 23 years there was not much change
in relative incomes between the rich and the poor: incomes in the developing countries as a group rose only 10 percent more than incomes in the
industrial countries. In developing countries as a group, manufacturing grew
more rapidly than gross national product; thus these economies moved
through the inevitable structural change that reduces the share of income
produced by, and labor employed in, agriculture.

Perhaps the most remarkable changes in the third world since 1965 have
been the virtually universal improvement in health conditions and the wide
spread of education, as documented in Table 1-3. The infant death rate in
low-income countries fell from 124 per thousand in 1965 to 72 per thousand
in 1988. Primary school enrollment became nearly universal in China, India,
Kenya, Sri Lanka, and Indonesia and rose dramatically in most other low-
income countries. These improvements have taken place in almost every
country in our list, regardless of their economic performance. That healthier populations have also meant greater population growth (Table 1-2) is
an important consideration, as discussed in Chapter 7. The spread of primary education, which now covers three-quarters of the eligible population
even in the low-income countries, is also shown in Table 1-3. Remarkable
strides have been made by countries like Tanzania, Kenya, Nigeria, and
Indonesia.

It is sometimes easy to become pessimistic about further progress in
developing nations, especially when confronted by gloomy predictions about
their future economic growth and by the myriad problems afflicting LDCs,
many of which will be catalogued in this book. As an antidote to discour-
agement, one needs to keep in mind the considerable economic development that has already taken place and the gratifying improvements in health
and education in even the poorest countries. There remains the question of
how these benefits have been distributed among the populace, a topic taken
up in Chapter 4 and in Part 2.

TABLE 1–2 Growth of Output and Population of Groups and Selected Countries, 1965–1988 (percent per year)

	Population[a]	GNP per capita	Manufacturing value-added per capita
Low-income economies	2.1	3.1	8.7
(Exc. China, India)	2.8	1.5	8.0
Ethiopia	3.1	−0.1	4.6
Tanzania	3.5	−0.5	2.7
Bangladesh	3.5	0.4	5.2
Mali	3.1	1.6	0.0
Nigeria	3.2	0.9	8.2
China	1.4	5.4	10.0
India	2.1	1.8	5.8
Pakistan	3.3	2.5	6.5
Kenya	3.6	1.9	8.4
Ghana	3.2	−1.6	2.7
Sri Lanka	1.6	3.0	4.2
Indonesia	1.9	4.3	12.4
Middle-income economies	2.1	2.3	6.6
Bolivia	2.8	−0.6	1.7
Philippines	2.4	1.6	4.7
Senegal	2.9	−0.8	3.5
Egypt, Arab Rep.	2.5	3.6	1.9
Honduras	3.1	0.6	5.5
Cameroon	3.2	3.7	6.7
Colombia	2.0	2.4	5.2
Peru	2.2	0.1	3.0
Mexico	2.3	2.3	4.8
Malaysia	2.5	4.0	2.5
Brazil	3.4	3.6	7.1
Hungary	−0.1	5.1	0.0
Argentina	1.2	0.0	1.7
Korea, Rep. of	1.0	6.8	16.9
Saudi Arabia	3.4	3.8	8.0
OECD members	0.4	2.3	3.5
United Kingdom	0.3	1.8	−0.3
Germany, Fed. Rep. of	0.0	2.5	2.5
United States	0.7	1.6	3.0
Japan	0.4	4.3	8.5

[a]Instantaneous growth rate in 1988, i.e., the rate of births less the rate of deaths per hundred.
Source: World Bank, _World Development Report 1990,_ pp. 180–181, 230–231.

FOCUS OF THE BOOK

Approaches to Development

This book is not for readers who are looking for a simple explanation of why some nations are still poor or of how poverty can be overcome. Library shelves are full of studies explaining how development will occur if only a nation will increase the amount it saves and invests or intensify its efforts to export. For two decades in the mid-twentieth century, industrialization through import substitution—the replacement of imports with home-produced goods—was considered by many as the shortest path to develop-

TABLE 1–3 Progress in Social Well-Being for Groups and Selected Countries, 1965–1988

	Infant mortality rate per 1,000		Percentage of age group enrolled in primary school	
	1965	1988	1965	1987
Low-income economies	124	72	73	104
(Exc. China, India)	165	135	11	37
Ethiopia	149	98	49	76
Tanzania	138	104	32	66
Bangladesh	144	118	49	59
Mali	207	168	24	23
Nigeria	177	103	32	77
China	90	31	89	132
India	150	97	74	98
Pakistan	149	107	40	52
Kenya	112	70	54	96
Ghana	120	88	69	71
Sri Lanka	63	21	93	104
Indonesia	128	68	72	118
Middle-income economies	98	52	92	104
Bolivia	160	108	73	91
Philippines	72	44	113	106
Senegal	126	78	40	60
Egypt, Arab Rep.	172	83	75	60
Honduras	128	68	80	106
Cameroon	143	92	94	109
Colombia	86	39	84	114
Peru	130	86	99	122
Mexico	82	46	92	118
Malaysia	55	23	90	102
Brazil	104	61	108	103
Hungary	39	16	101	97
Argentina	58	31	101	110
Korea, Rep. of	62	24	101	101
Saudi Arabia	148	69	24	71
OECD members	24	8	104	103
United Kingdom	20	9	92	106
Germany, Fed. Rep.	25	8	na	103
United States	25	10	100	100
Japan	18	5	100	102

Source: World Bank, *World Development Report 1990*, pp. 232–235.

ment. In the 1970s, labor-intensive techniques, income redistribution, and provision of basic human needs to the poor gained popularity as keys to development. Many economists now counsel governments to depend substantially on unfettered markets to set prices and allocate resources. Another school of thought once suggested that development is only possible if preceded by a revolution that eliminates existing elites and replaces the market with central planning. A different theme is that development will be possible if there is a massive shift of resources, in the form of foreign aid and investment, from the richest countries to the poorest.

No single factor is responsible for underdevelopment, and no single policy or strategy can set in motion the complex process of economic development. A wide variety of explanations and solutions to the development problem make sense if placed in the proper contexts and make no sense at all outside those sets of circumstances. Mobilization of saving is essential for accelerated growth in most cases, but sometimes may come second to a redistribution of income if extreme poverty threatens political stability or forestalls the mobilization of human resources. Import substitution has carried some countries quite far toward economic development, but export promotion has helped others when import substitution bogged down. Prices that are badly distorted from their free-market values can stifle initiative and hence growth, but removing those distortions leads to development only where other conditions are met as well. Moreover, some, but certainly not all, centrally planned economies achieved sustained periods of development with prices that bore little relation to those determined by market forces. Finally, where states are ruled by leaders backed by interests hostile to development, those leaders and their constituents must be removed from power before growth can occur. But more developing nations have governments that genuinely want to promote development.

This book is not neutral toward all issues of development. Where controversy exists, we shall point it out. Indeed, the authors of this book differ among themselves over some questions of development policy. But they do share a common point of view on certain basic points.

First of all, this text makes extensive use of the theoretical tools of classical and neoclassical economies in the belief that these tools contribute substantially to our understanding of development problems and their solution. The text does not rely solely or even primarily on theory, however. For three decades and more, development economists and economic historians have been building up an empircal record against which these theories can be tested, and this book draws heavily on many of these empirical studies. We try to give real-country examples for virtually all the major points made in this book. In part these examples come from the individual country and cross-country comparative studies of others, but they also draw extensively from our own personal experiences working on development issues around the world. Among the four of us, we have been fortunate enough to study and work over long periods of time in Bolivia, Chile, China, Colombia, Ghana, Indonesia, Kenya, Korea, Malayasia, Peru, Sri Lanka, and Tanzania. At one time or another, at least one from this group of nations has exemplified virtually all approaches to development now extant.

While this book draws extensively on the tools of classical and neoclassical economic theory, development involves major issues for which these economic theories do not provide answers or at best provide only partial answers. Economic theory tends to take the **institutional context** (the existence of markets, of a banking system, of international trade, etc.) as given. But development is concerned with how one creates institutions that facilitate development in the first place. How, for example, does a nation acquire a government interested in and capable of promoting economic growth? Can efficiently functioning markets be created in countries that currently lack them, or should the state take over the functions normally left to the market elsewhere? Is a fully developed financial system a precondition for growth, or can a nation do without at least some parts of such a system? Is

land reform necessary for development, and, if so, what kind of land reform?
These institutional issues and many others like them are at the heart of the development process and will reappear in different guises in the following chapters.

Organization

This book is divided into five parts. Part 1 examines the main factors that prevent development from taking place and the kinds of structural change, including changes in income distribution, that occur once growth is underway. Structural change, of course, does not just happen as a result of impersonal and uncontrolled forces. It is often the result of deliberate choices by governments, and the first part of the book also provides an introduction to issues of market-based *versus* command systems of development and to economic planning models.

Economic development is first and foremost a process involving people, who are the prime movers of development and its beneficiaries. Part 2 deals with how human resources are transformed in the process of economic development and how that transformation contributes to the development process itself. There are chapters on population, labor, education, and health.

The other major physical input in the growth process is capital, and Part 3 is concerned with how capital is mobilized and allocated for development purposes. Where, for example, do the savings come from and how are they transformed into investment? How does government mobilize resources to finance development? What kind of financial system is consistent with rapid capital accumulation? Will inflation enhance or hinder the process and what role is played by foreign aid and investment?

One of the most fundamental issues facing a developing nation is the degree to which that nation should integrate its economy with the economies of the rest of the world. These international trade and interdependence strategies are the subject of Part 4.

Finally, issues such as technological change and various kinds of institutional reform often differ significantly between sectors of the economy. The problems of agriculture are different from those of industry, natural resource development is different from either of the other two, and all impinge on the environment. In Part 5 problems of economic development are approached from the perspective of sectoral development and its sustainability.

2

Starting Modern Economic Growth

The era of modern economic growth is only two centuries old. Before the late eighteenth century there were individuals and families who became rich, but nations as a whole and most of the people in them were poor. An economy was seen as a pie of fixed size. One could cut oneself a bigger piece of the pie, but only by taking away a portion that originally belonged to someone else. Few saw the possibility of increasing the size of the pie so that all could have larger slices.

But the essence of modern economic growth is that, on average, the per-capita income of all people in a nation rises, not just the income of a select few. And as per-capita incomes rises, other fundamental changes occur that affect the way people live. The household as a production unit declines and is replaced by larger enterprises that find it economic to locate near each other. The result is that more people live in cities and work in facto-ries rather than on farms. As incomes rise and urbanization takes place, behavior within the household also changes. Families no longer want large numbers of children, and so the birth rate begins to fall. Modern economic growth, therefore, involves fundamental structural changes in the way both production and society are organized.

In the late eighteenth century England began to transform its economy, a process that would later be called the Industrial Revolution. By the middle of the nineteenth century other nations in Europe and North America had begun similar transformations, and toward the end of the century the first non-European population, the Japanese, had begun to industrialize. Two world wars and the Great Depression interrupted industrialization in the

already advanced nations and slowed the spread of economic advance to other parts of the globe. The Second World War, however, also undermined the strength of European colonialism and set the stage for a widespread effort to industrialize the large numbers of newly independent nations.

One of the key characteristics of modern economic growth, therefore, is that it did not begin everywhere in the world at the same time. Instead it spread slowly across Europe and North America, but did not break out of areas dominated by European culture (except for Japan) until the 1950s and 1960s. In parts of the world the process has yet to begin.

Between those parts of the world that have achieved sustained growth and those that have not, a gap in the standard of living has inevitably opened up. The average European, American, or Japanese enjoys a material way of life that is many times richer than that experienced by even large parts of the elites of India or Africa. But there is nothing inevitable or permanent about this gap. In the nineteenth century England was far ahead of the rest of the world, whereas today England is not even in the top 10 of the richest nations in terms of per-capita income. In the early 1950s Japan was poorer than such centers of European poverty as Spain or Greece, but by the mid-1980s Japanese income per capita was comparable to or above those of richer Western European nations such as France.

This chapter focuses on why these gaps in income between nations open up. Why is it that some nations began developing earlier than others? What has prevented some nations from entering into modern economic growth even today? Are the barriers that have inhibited development the result of conditions internal to the country affected, or is the lack of development in some nations today the result of externally imposed forces? A related question is whether the barriers to growth in nations are the same everywhere or whether particular conditions in one country act to inhibit growth while similar conditions elsewhere do little harm because the context is different. In much the same spirit, are there "prerequisites" that must be in place, such as a modern banking system, before growth can occur, or are there often substitutes available for particular prerequisites?

THE DEVELOPING NATIONS: A GLANCE AT HISTORY

The two features common to all traditional societies are a low per-capita income and an absence of modern economic growth. Beyond these simple common features is a great diversity of national experiences about which valid generalizations are difficult to make. The use of terms such as "third world," "less-developed countries," or "developing nations" tends to obscure this diversity by implying that all nations, except those already rich, have a common experience that transcends any differences in their backgrounds and current conditions. In fact the differences between developing nations are so great that one cannot really understand their development problems without taking these differences into account.

Even within Europe on the eve of industrialization there were great differences between societies, and these differences have much to do with why development began first in the West and spread only gradually to the East. In England, for example, laborers were free to change jobs and migrate to distant places, and commerce and banking had reached a high level of sophistication in the centuries preceding the Industrial Revolution. But Russia in the mid-nineteenth century was still feudal: Most peasants were tied to their lord's estate for life, and commerce, industry, and transport were still in a primitive state.

In Asia, Latin America, and Africa the range of political and cultural experience is more diverse than that which existed within Europe. Great empires, such as those of China and Japan, had over a thousand years of self-governing experience, and they thought of themselves as a single unified people, rather than as a collection of ethnically distinct tribes or regions. By premodern standards China and Japan also had high levels of urbanization and commerce, and they shared Confucian values, which emphasize the importance of education. Long years of comparative stability contributed to a population increase that resulted in the great shortage of arable land relative to population that still exists in the region today. Because of the comparative sophistication of premodern commerce in East Asia, European and American merchants were never able to play a significant role in the management of domestic commerce in the region. And as Chinese and Japanese merchants gradually acquired an understanding of foreign markets, they were able to compete successfully with representatives of the industrialized world in that sphere as well.

COLONIALISM AND INDEPENDENCE

At the other end of this spectrum with respect to self-government and commercial sophistications are several Southeast Asian and most African nations. Indonesia and Nigeria, for example, were really the arbitrary creations of Dutch and British colonialism, which brought together diverse groups of people who shared little in common and had no desire to maintain these externally imposed boundaries. Both Indonesia in 1958 and Nigeria in the late 1960s had to fight wars to keep their new nations together.

Experience with commerce in many parts of Southeast Asia and Africa was also quite limited and illiteracy was often nearly universal. Throughout the colonial era in Indonesia and many parts of sub-Saharan Africa, foreign trade and large-scale domestic commerce were almost entirely in the hands of Europeans. Small-scale commerce, particularly in the countryside, was sometimes controlled by local people, but usually it was in the hands of minorities who had immigrated from other poor but commercially more advanced nations. Thus local commerce in much of Southeast Asia was in the hands of Chinese, that in East Africa was mainly managed by Indians, while in West Africa Lebanese often played a central role. Because of inexperience the local people could not effectively compete with either these immigrant groups or the Europeans and because they could not compete, they did not gain much experience with trade or finance. This was one of the many vicious circles so common to the plight of poor nations.

Not all experiences with colonialism were the same. In India a tiny number of British ruled a vastly populated subcontinent. By necessity the British had to train large numbers of Indians to handle all but the very top jobs in the bureaucracy and army. At the time of independence in 1948, Indians were already running most of their own affairs because there were enough trained and experienced personnel to do so. But in Indonesia there were fewer than a thousand university or other postsecondary school graduates at the time of independence, and in Zaire there were hardly any. Prior to independence even the lower levels of the central bureaucracy in Indonesia had been manned by the Dutch and those in Zaire by Belgians. In comparison, India and China in the 1940s had hundreds of thousands of university graduates.

Latin America's historical heritage is different from that of either Asia or Africa. Independence in most of the region was achieved in the early nineteenth century, not after World War II as in Asia and Africa. Although there were local populations in the region when the Europeans first arrived, the indigenous populations were suppressed or enslaved. So to meet growing labor requirements, the elites turned to voluntary and forced immigration of Europeans and Africans. Spanish and Portuguese immigrants ruled; the Africans were enslaved until late in the nineteenth century. Ignored or pushed aside, the original population continued to exist, but in varying numbers: Peru and Bolivia maintained large indigenous populations, whereas in Argentina native peoples nearly disappeared.

North America above the Rio Grande was also peopled by immigrants who suppressed the local population. In both North and South America slavery existed in some regions and not in others, but there were important differences between the types of colonial rule. In the north the indigenous population was more thoroughly suppressed; hence, it was small and isolated and not a factor when economic development began. European immigrants were from the economically most-advanced parts of Europe, where feudal values and structures had already been partially dismantled. But Spanish and Portuguese immigrants came from an area that by the nineteenth century was one of the more-backward parts of Europe. The feudal values and structures that still dominated this region accompanied these colonists to the New World. Likewise, there were also great differences within Latin America. Argentina, for example, is largely a nation of European immigrants; Mexico, Peru, and Bolivia have large indigenous populations; a large minority of Brazilians and virtually all Haitians descended from former African slaves.

THE DEVELOPING NATIONS: A BRIEF TAXONOMY

It is impossible to summarize all the important differences between nations in the developing world, but those with the greatest bearing on the potential for modern economic growth in the region would include:

Differences between nations with a long tradition of emphasis on education and an elite that was highly educated, as contrasted with nations where illiteracy was nearly universal.

Countries with fairly highly developed systems of commerce, finance, and transport mainly run by local people versus countries where these activities were almost entirely in the hands of European or Asian immigrant minorities.

Nations peopled by those who shared a common language, culture, and sense of national identity versus nations where there was a great diversity of language, culture, and no common sense of national identity or shared common goals.

Nations with long traditions of self-government versus those with no experience with even limited self-government until the 1950s or 1960s.

This list could be extended but the point is made. Economic development requires both a government capable of directing or supporting a major growth effort and a people who can work effectively in and manage the enterprises and other organizations that arise in the course of development. Nations with people who have at least some relevant education and experience in economic affairs and which have governments able to support those people are better positioned for development than nations where the people have little relevant experience and where diverse groups within the nation are still arguing over their shares in what they believe, wrongly for the most part, to be a pie of fixed size.

THE CONCEPT OF SUBSTITUTES

Given the great diversity in developing-country experience, it would be a counsel of despair to suggest that the way to begin development is first to recreate the kinds of political, social, and economic conditions that existed in Western Europe or North America when those regions entered into modern economic growth. England prior to the Industrial Revolution had centuries of experience with merchant capitalism, but does it follow that Ghana or Indonesia must also acquire long experience with merchant capitalism before economic development would be feasible? If the answer were yes, these nations would be doomed to another century or more of poverty.

Fortunately there is no standard list of barriers that must be overcome or prerequisites that must be in place before development is possible. Instead, as the economic historian Alexander Gerschenkron pointed out, for most presumed prerequisites there are usually **substitutes.** The main point of this concept is best illustrated with an example from Gerschenkron's own work.[1]

Capital, like labor, is of course necessary for development, and much more will be said about both in later chapters. But Marx and others went a step further and argued that there must be an original or prior accumulation of capital before growth can take place. The basic idea came from looking at the experience of England where, Marx argued, trade, exploitation of colonies, piracy, and other related measures led to the accumulation of great wealth that in the late eighteenth century could be converted into

---

1. Alexander Gerschenkron, *Economic Backwardness in Historical Perspective* (Cambridge, Mass.: Harvard University Press, 1962), Chapter 2.

investment in industry. Is such an accumulation a *prerequisite* for development everywhere or at least for a large number of countries? In the absence of a prior accumulation of capital, does economic development become impossible?

In Europe the answer was clearly no. One did have to find funds that could be invested in industry, but they did not have to come out of the accumulated wealth of the past. Germany, for example, had little in the way of an original accumulation of capital when modern economic growth began there. But Germany did have a banking system that could create funds, which were then lent to industrialists. How banks create funds is not our concern here; the point is that banks can create accounts that investors can draw on, and the creation of those accounts depends in no significant way on long years of prior savings and accumulation by merchants or other wealthy individuals.

Russia in the nineteenth century had neither an original accumulation of wealth nor a banking system capable of creating large enough levels of credit. Instead Russia turned to the taxing power of the state. The government could and did tax funds away from people and use this tax revenue for investment in industry. Russia also imported capital from abroad. Thus the government's use of taxation was a *substitute* for an underdeveloped banking system, and elsewhere a modern banking system was a *substitute* for an original accumulation of capital.

Similar examples of substitutes in today's world abound. Latin American countries, for example, rely heavily on financial institutions to mobilize and allocate savings. Sub-Saharan African countries, in contrast, rely more on fiscal institutions (the government budget). Factories in advanced nations with well-developed commerical networks rely on central distributors to supply them with spare parts. Rural industries in China, where commerce is less developed, make spare parts in their own foundries. As already pointed out, a number of nations in the developing world today have substantial numbers of people with training and experience in areas relevant to economic development, while the number of such people in other nations is miniscule. The most common substitute for this lack of relevant experience is to import foreigners who have the required experience. For reasons that will become apparent in later chapters, foreigners are frequently not very good substitutes for experienced local talent, but where the latter is missing, they can fill the gap until local talent is trained.

Therefore, in the following discussion of political and social barriers to development and of what is required to initiate development, we shall not be looking for three or four universal causes of poverty or a similar number of prerequisites that must always be in place before growth is possible. Instead we shall attempt to identify some of the more common political and social barriers to development and recognize that the presence of these barriers or the absence of prerequisites does not guarantee the continuation of poverty. There are usually ways around, or substitutes for, any single barrier or prerequisite, but the existence of many of these barriers or the absence of a wide variety of desirable preconditions will at least make economic development more difficult and in some cases impossible.

The closest one can come to a single prerequisite without which economic development would be impossible lies not in the realm of politics or social structure but in whether or not a nation has access to the discoveries of modern science and innovators to adapt these discoveries for the marketplace. The industrial economy of the twentieth century would be inconceivable in the absence of the knowledge arising from such fields as chemistry, physics, and biology. A high percentage of the products in common use today, ranging from electric power to antibiotics, did not even exist prior to the advent of modern science.

While science is crucial to economic development, it is also clear that no nation today is really cut off from the main fruits of that science. Some of the great civilizations of the past probably were unable to expand beyond a certain level primarily from a lack of scientific discovery and technological advancement. It is also the case today that nations with educational and research capabilities of their own, such as South Korea and Mexico, can often make more and better use of many scientific discoveries. But even the most poorly endowed nations have access to much of what modern science has contributed since the fruits of scientific discovery are often embodied in products domestically manufactured by comparatively simple processes or imported as finished goods from more advanced nations. Developing countries do not have to rediscover the basic laws of thermodynamics. For many purposes they only need to understand those laws and how they can be usefully applied, or imitate others' applications of those laws, a much easier task than making the discovery in the first place. The issue of why some nations gained access to modern science earlier than others, therefore, is mainly of historical interest and will not be pursued further here.

In the eyes of some economists a failure to enter into modern economic growth is mainly the result of economic forces within the developing nation. Since the remainder of this book is concerned with these economic forces, we shall put them aside in this chapter. As the following chapters will make clear, however, there is no single economic barrier to development that accounts for why so few countries were able to initiate growth prior to the middle of the twentieth century. Savings rates in many of these countries were too low to pay for the investment needed to achieve development, but the crucial question is why were savings rates low. Poverty alone is not a cause of low savings rates. Even very poor nations, such as Japan in the late nineteenth century, were able to mobilize large amounts of savings. Japan could mobilize large amounts of savings in part because it had a strong governmental structure with a tradition of extracting large tax payments from the population.

Therefore, while there are economic causes for the prevalence of poverty in large parts of the world, economic explanations alone cannot account for why particular economic barriers exist. Economists are uncomfortable when they leave the realm of economic explanations, in part because the tools of economic analysis are of only limited help outside the sphere for which they were designed. But if one is seriously interested in understanding why some nations have had so much trouble initiating growth, there is little choice but to explore the relationship between economic development on the one hand, and political and social obstacles to development on the other.

POLITICAL OBSTACLES TO DEVELOPMENT

Economic development in England in the eighteenth century began with little direct assistance from the government, but since that time government's role in development has risen steadily to a point where successful growth is not really possible without the active support of a government. In subsequent chapters the role of many kinds of specific governmental policies in promoting economic development will be explained in detail. For our purposes here one mainly needs to know that an active, positive role for government is essential. It follows that if a government is unwilling or unable to play such a role, then the government itself can be considered a barrier to development or a fundamental cause of poverty.

Political Stability

To begin with, governments must be able to create and maintain a **stable environment** for modern enterprises, whether public or private. At a minimum, civil war, sustained insurrection, or invasion by hostile forces must be avoided. It is an obvious point but one frequently forgotten in discussions of the nature of development. Prolonged instability connected with civil war and foreign invasion goes a long way toward explaining why China failed to enter into modern economic growth prior to 1949. By extension, the creation of a stable environment after 1949 helps to explain why growth began then. More recently Vietnam with a civil war raging, was obviously not in a position to develop its economy on a sustained basis in the 1950s and 1960s and the same was true of Cambodia in the 1970s and 1980s. China, Cambodia, and Vietnam are extreme cases, but a much longer list of nations, including Bolivia, Pakistan, Ghana, Ethiopia, El Savador, and many others, have experienced prolonged domestic political instability of a kind that has inhibited growth. Bolivia, for example, has had 150 governments since independence in 1825. Investors will not put their money into projects that pay off only over the long run if, in the short run, a change of government could lead to the project's being confiscated or rendered unprofitable by new laws and other restrictions. Where instability is particularly rife, a common solution among the wealthy has been to stop investing in the local economy and to ship off a large part of their wealth to banks in Switzerland or to indulge in conspicuous consumption.

Political Independence

But a stable environment alone is not enough. Colonial governments were usually quite stable, often for very long periods of time. There were rebellions against British rule in India, French rule in North Africa, and Japanese rule in Korea, but these rebellions were generally short-lived or on the periphery of the colony. Furthermore, most colonial governments had a very specific interest in creating a stable environment for private business. Yet few, if any, European or Japanese colonies experienced anything that could be described as sustained economic development. Part of the explanation is that the stable environment created was often only for the benefit of a small number of traders and investors from the colonizing nation, whereas the citizens of the colonies themselves received little such support. Probably a more important part of the explanation, however, is that most colonial governments made only limited investments in training local people, in developing electric power resources, or in promoting industry. Thus, in most cases political independence was necessary before modern economic growth was possible. Conceivably, colonial governments could have promoted genuine development, but for the most part they did not. Later in this chapter we shall return to the question of whether relations between rich and poor countries today continue to possess some of the features that characterized the colonial era.

The Politics of Development Policy

Achieving independence and ending civil war and other threats to government stability are only the first step toward a political environment that is conducive to economic development. All governments, including stable independent ones, face numerous political constraints on their actions. An original meaning of the word "policy" was the art of government. Economic policy is thus concerned with the art of government in the economic sphere, with politics as well as with economic analysis.

Bad economic policy can prevent economic growth from getting underway, and it can bring growth to a halt after it has started. The concept of **takeoff** is seen frequently in the development literature and is at the center of economic historian Walt Rostow's analysis of the stages of economic growth.[2] Often the term means simply that a country has entered into a period of modern economic growth and it causes few problems when used that way. Frequently, however, the term has been used in ways that imply much more. Specifically, the term has been used to imply that development once started proceeds automatically along well-traveled routes until the country becomes a modern industrialized nation.

The problem with the concept is that, once started, economic development does not necessarily proceed without interruption. Economic development itself, particularly in its early stages, can create enormous social and political tensions that can undermine the stability so necessary for growth. The classic example from the early part of the twentieth century is in the case of Argentina. To many observers in the 1910s and 1920s, Argentina seemed well on its way to becoming a modern industrial state. At the time it was considered more advanced than Canada. But as urbanization

2. W. W. Rostow, *Stages of Economic Growth*, 2d ed. (New York: Cambridge University Press, 1971, 1st ed. 1960).

and industrialization progressed, the expanding Argentinian working class
became increasingly alienated from the nation's leadership. Juan Peron was able to use this alienation to build a political organization that brought him to power in 1946. To keep his support, however, Peron carried out measures that were popular with his constituents, such as price control of food grains and enlarged military expenditures, but that stifled growth and divided society into sharply contending classes. More importantly, long after Peron left office, the forces he unleashed prevented the nation from establishing a consensus behind any government that would maintain stability and promote growth.

More recent examples of similar connections between the early stages of economic development and political instability can be found in Pakistan and Iran. In the 1960s Pakistan experienced a decade of fairly rapid industrialization, but most of this industrialization was concentrated in the western half of the country. East Pakistan made few gains and the people there felt that the west was developing at their expense. It matters little now whether West Pakistan exploited East Pakistan: the people in the east perceived that they were the losers. The result was a civil war, the splitting of an already geographically divided country into two nations with the formation of Bangladesh, and subsequent instability and economic stagnation in Bangladesh.

Iran presents a variation on the same theme. Oil revenues in the 1950s and 1960s fueled rapid industrial development, which accelerated even more dramatically after the quadrupling of the price of oil in 1973. Oil revenues, however, were also used extravagantly in the purchase of weapons, in large capital-intensive projects such as the Teheran subway, and in fueling corruption among Iran's elite. Iran's new wealth, far from buying stability, increased the alienation of the great majority of the people, who felt that the nation's wealth was being monopolized by a corrupt few. When combined with other deeply felt grievances, such as those of the religious fundamentalists led by Ayatollah Khomeini, the result was a year of rioting and demonstrations, culminating in the fall of the Shah and his army.

Examples such as these have brought home to development economists as well as others that an understanding of the political context is an essential element in effective economic policy making. Understanding the political context in turn starts from a recognition that governments are led by politicians, not philosopher kings. Philosopher kings can ignore the special interests of various groups within the country and, with the help of competent engineers and economists, design development programs that maximize the benefits to society as a whole. Politicians must first take steps to ensure that the groups of people who put them into office will continue to support them. Or they must worry about avoiding policies that will create new opposition groups or invigorate old ones.

That politicians in a democracy must pay attention to the special interests of their supporters requires little elaboration. But authoritarian governments also have their constituencies. The power of President Park Chung Hee in the Korea of the 1960s and 1970s rested on the dual pillars of the Korean army and the conservative farmers of the southeastern provinces.

The political power of Argentina's Juan Peron rested on well-organized urban labor unions. The government bureaucracy can itself be a basis of authoritarian political power and government bureaucracies have their own special interests or goals.

These various constituencies come into play whenever difficult economic policy choices must be made. In fact, more often than not, it is the desires and goals of these constituencies that make the choices difficult in the first place. Economic growth may require improved management of state owned enterprises, for example, or the removal of large food subsidies causing a government budget deficit. Removal of food subsidies for urban workers frequently leads to widespread urban rioting. Such riots occurred in Egypt in 1977, in Zambia in 1990, and in numerous other countries before and since. Stopping inflation usually involves stopping the rapid rise in the money supply, which in turn requires the government to cut expenditures and increase revenues in order to eliminate the government deficit that is causing the rise in money supply. But in much of Latin America, as elsewhere, organized interest groups mobilize to prevent the government from cutting "their" expenditures or raising "their" taxes. The result is that the deficit is not cut and chronic inflation continues.

Currency devaluations can be a powerful tool for countries with severe balance-of-payments problems, a common phenomenon in developing countries. Devaluing the currency, as explained more fully in Chapters 16 and 17, raises the cost of imports and lowers the price of exports, this leads to a contraction of the former and an expansion of the latter. In Ghana in 1970 just such a devaluation was carried out for the purpose of closing a large unsustainable excess of imports over exports. But most imports were luxury goods consumed by the urban elite including the army. Two weeks later, using the sharp rise in the costs of luxury goods as an excuse, the army took over the government in a coup d'etat.

In recent years scholars and practitioners of economic policy reform have attempted to incorporate politics into their analysis in a more systematic way. One important issue has been whether or not to institute a full range of reforms all at once, what is sometimes referred to as the **big-bang approach** to economic reform. Poland in 1989–90 was the best example of the big bang approach. As part of an effort to end spiralling inflation, the Poles cut out virtually all subsidies to consumers, many of which had been in place for decades. Producer subsidies to state-owned enterprises were also sharply curtailed, and an effort was begun to privatize production as rapidly as possible.

Price stabilization is often best handled by the big-bang approach. After a long period of rapid price increases, the population is frequently in a mood for any change that will end them. Drastic action becomes politically acceptable. When the drastic action works to stop the price rise, the government's credibility as a good manager of the economy is enhanced and continued fiscal discipline gains critical support. A gradual approach, in contrast, does not really solve the problem, and the population quickly tires of halfway austerity measures that inflict some pain but seem to do little long-term good.

Structural adjustments such as privatization of state-owned enterprises, however, do not lend themselves so readily to the big-bang method. In a county such as Poland these enterprises have been used to following the dictates of planners who guaranteed inputs to the enterprise and sales by the enterprise. If the enterprise suddenly has to buy all of its inputs on a market and sell its output on that same market, it may not know how to do this. It takes time, perhaps years, for managers to learn how to behave in the new environment. If government support is withdrawn immediately and totally, the enterprise may go bankrupt before managers learn the new ways. Workers will be thrown out of work and political support for reform will erode.

Politics, therefore is central to what impedes development and what makes development possible. Politics is in turn deeply rooted in the culture of a society. The social structure and politics of East Africa have little in common with the social structure and politics of East Asia. The political and social systems of Central America differ significantly from each other even more from those of Africa or Asia. To understand why some countries have experienced sustained economic development and others have not, therefore, the scholar and policy analyst must understand the politics as well as the economies of those countries.

INTERNATIONAL OBSTACLES TO DEVELOPMENT

Up to this point our analysis of the obstacles to development has concentrated on political obstacles that are internal to the less-developed world. To the extent that these internal conditions are the main causes of a lack of economic growth in the past, successful development will depend on internal solutions. But many economists and others argue that the main barriers to development today lie with conditions external to the developing world. Specifically, the existence of already rich and industrialized nations, it is argued, creates international political and economic pressures that hamper the growth efforts of today's poor nations.

Before reviewing the various arguments that stress the negative political and economic aspects of the relations between rich and poor countries, it is useful to present a brief synopsis of some of the beneficial economic aspects for poor nations in a world where some nations are already rich. These positive economic elements are less controversial, and with them in mind, one can ask whether they are outweighed by the negative side of the ledger.

One important part of any argument about the positive side of rich-poor relations is based on the concept of the gains from trade. Since these gains are considered in some detail in Chapter 15, only a brief listing will be attempted here.

Gains from Trade: A Preliminary View

To begin with, the **theory of comparative advantage** states that nations with different endowments of capital, labor, and natural resources will gain by specializing in those areas where their relative costs of production are low and importing in those areas where their relative costs are high. Further, the greater the difference in endowments between countries—and the differences between rich and poor countries are great indeed—the greater these gains from trade are likely to be. In certain extreme cases, but ones that occur in the real world, a nation possesses one resource or factor, such as land or oil, in such abundance that it is impossible to make effective internal use of all of that resource. Trade makes it possible to use this surplus resource because the country can export what is not needed at home to purchase things that are needed. Saudi Arabia could not possibly use all the petroleum it is capable of producing, or Canada all the wheat from its great plains. Trade thus becomes what is sometimes referred to as a **vent for surplus.**

Developing countries also gain from trade because capital resources can only be transferred from rich to poor nations (and vice versa) through trade. In addition, some countries' export-producing enterprises are among their most progressive businesses because they have to be to survive international competition. The example set by these progressive firms then influences the operation of domestic enterprises.

Drawing on Experience

The gains from trade, however, encompass only a part of the economic advantages of poor nations that exist in a world where some countries have already achieved sustained development. The term used by Gerschenkron to describe this broader phenomenon is the **advantages of backwardness.** Developing countries are in a position to learn from the experience of already advanced nations. The most obvious area in which these advantages exist is the realm of science and technology. But the advantages are not confined to science and technology.

By the middle of the twentieth century, advanced nations had acquired a great deal of experience with management of enterprises, with national economic policymaking, and even with widely different kinds of economic systems. In the late eighteenth century, laissez-faire capitalism was probably the only system capable of achieving modern economic growth in England. During World War I, however, wartime conditions led Germany and others to experiment with close state management of the economy. In the 1930s the Soviet Union, building on the World War I experience of others, developed what we know today as the Soviet-type or socialist system of planned economy. When China opted for a fully socialized economy in the 1950s, Chinese planners were able to draw on Soviet experience, often to the extent of simply translating Soviet planning rules and regulations into Chinese and then putting them into effect. The Chinese later modified the Soviet planning system to make it more suitable to Chinese conditions, but the point is that without prior Soviet experience, China would have had to move much more cautiously in setting up a centrally planned economy. In a similar fashion, South Korea learned much from the experience of Japan about how to operate a privately owned but state-managed economy.

There are situations, of course, where having a wide range of choices
makes it possible for a country to make the wrong choice. Some nations would be better off if they had no range of options and instead had to follow a single optimal or at least feasible development path. But other nations have benefited from being able to make choices that took into account their own local economic, political, and social conditions.

Imperialism

While almost everyone acknowledges the potential advantages of learning from the experience of others, many have argued that this potential is seldom realized in practice because advanced nations create barriers to the progress of poor nations. Many economists and other scholars have attempted to explain the nature and sources of these barriers imposed on the less-developed world, but the largest group of theorists in one way or another owe an intellectual debt to Marx, the British economist Hobson, and Lenin, the architect of the Russian revolution.

Marxian Approaches to Development One of the centerpieces of Karl Marx's theory of capitalist development was the view that the rate of profits on capital inevitably declines as growth takes place.[3] These profits were produced by labor from the **surplus,** or the excess, of what was needed to meet the subsistence needs of that labor. Competition in the face of this declining rate of profit leads to stronger capitalists swallowing up the weaker, who then join the ranks of the proletariat or workers. Economic crises or depressions become more severe as development proceeds, and the wages of workers may actually decline as capitalists squeeze them harder in a desperate attempt to keep profits up. The end result is a revolution that overthrows the rule of the capitalist class.

By the late nineteenth and early twentieth century, there was little evidence to support the view that the rate of profit was declining, and it was clear that real wages were rising. At the same time, however, the capitalist powers of Europe were vigorously expanding their colonial empires. The question then became whether there was a connection between the two phenomena. Workers in the colony also produced a surplus. If the imperial power could drain off enough of that colonial surplus, it could maintain profits at home and perhaps have enough left over to raise the wages of workers so that they would not become restless.

Conversely, from the colonial country's point of view, its development was severely inhibited because its surplus was being drained off abroad. In the absence of this surplus, the colonial nation had few resources of its own to invest while at the same time it was receiving only small amounts of investment from abroad.

In this form the basic propositions of the theory can be tested empirically. The issue is mainly whether the flow of surplus, or profits and tax revenues, from the colonial to the imperialist nation was large enough to

3. Karl Marx, *Das Kapital,* the first volume of which was published in 1867.

keep the profit rate in the capitalist nation high or to keep the rate of investment in the colonial nation low. The issue is not whether this drain of surplus made a few people of England and others very rich, but whether it accounted for a large share of the total profits of the capitalist world. More important from the point of view of development, was the drain of surplus large enough relative to the national product of the colonial country to have a significant impact on the investment, and hence development, prospects of that country?

The end of colonialism in much of the world did not by itself necessarily change this situation. Capitalist nations could continue to accomplish much of what was achieved by colonialism through private investment activities abroad. Even many early proponents of this Marxian viewpoint, however, recognized that it was difficult to find quantitative data with which to support the argument in this form.

A different tack taken by other scholars is that what was lost was a potential, rather than actual, surplus. The drain of profits from the developing world might not be large, but measures taken by the capitalist nations prevented the developing nations from producing the surplus that would have existed in the absence of capitalist pressures from abroad. Some argued, for example, that free-trade policies imposed on the developing world made it impossible to protect infant industries, and hence those industries did not develop. The resources that would have gone to produce industrial output and funds for further investment instead lay idle. It is argued that free trade, leading to imports of manufactured cloth and the like, also destroyed local handicrafts and thereby further contributed to the unemployment of domestic resources. Still other scholars have argued that the drain of profits was real enough, but hidden by the way prices are set for goods transferred from the industrial to the developing nation. Multinationals, it is argued, charge much higher prices when they sell to developing countries than when they sell the same product at home.

Modern Theories of Imperialism Modern theories of imperialism or of the nature of relations between rich and poor nations continue to use many of these older themes, but there has been a definite shift of emphasis. There are also many differences in analysis and emphasis among scholars writing about imperialism. Broadly, however, these scholars share the view that slow growth, extreme inequality, and high levels of unemployment in developing nations arise out of unequal relations of power both between rich and poor nations and between classes within the poorer developing nations. Furthermore, a solution to these problems of poverty requires a fundamental change in these power relations usually involving the elimination of capitalist class structures and values.[4]

As to why capitalist nations are inherently imperialistic, the important point is not so much a declining rate of profit shored up by returns from abroad as it is the need of capitalist firms to secure a reliable supply of natural resources. Capitalist firms, therefore, are interested in protecting

4. Keith Griffin and John Gurley, "Radical Analyses of Imperialism, the Third World, and the Transition to Socialism," *Journal of Economic Literature* 23, no. 3 (September 1985): 1090–91.

their investments abroad, and to that end they want a large military force at home and abroad capable of providing that protection. But workers in capitalist societies also benefit from this large military force even though they gain nothing, or less than nothing, from foreign investments. In the absence of such military expenditures, scholars like Stanford economist Paul Baran have argued, there would be a great depression and large-scale unemployment in capitalist countries.[5] This belief is based on a Keynesian-like analysis of the sources of unemployment. In addition to avoiding unemployment, workers in the large defense industries benefit directly from military expenditures. Thus the presence of democracy in the capitalist world does not prevent imperialism because large numbers of voters in that world see imperialism, at least indirectly, as being in their interests.

For poor nations attempting to develop, the emphasis has shifted away from the role of a direct drain of surplus to collusion between advanced-nation capitalists and antigrowth forces within the developing nation. The issue is not so much the drain of surplus abroad as it is the misuse of that surplus at home.

There are many variations on this basic theme. Some scholars argue that it is in the interest of advanced-nation capitalists to keep raw materials from developing nations flowing. Industrial growth within the developing nation would be harmful to both goals since local industrial products would compete with imports and would also bid for local raw materials. The old ruling classes made up of landlords and other feudal elements also have no interest in promoting the rise of industrial capitalists who would compete with them for power, and who might find it in the interest of industry to advocate such measures as land reform. Although some commercial capitalists exist in such societies, it is argued that they too tend to side with foreign investors and the feudal ruling class because they make their living from the existing pattern of trade and do not want competition from newer patterns. Capitalists with this orientation are sometimes referred to as **compradores.** Even the workers in modern establishments share this viewpoint, because their wages are so much higher than the average. The end result is an alliance of foreign investors backed by their governments, feudal landlords, and merchant capitalists and their workers, who together keep a government in power that does little to promote development.

Income Inequality and the Demand for Luxury Products Another variation on this theme is that put forward by the prominent Brazilian economist Celso Furtado.[6] Furtado starts from the proposition, for which there is much evidence, that poor nations in the early stages of development tend to have a very unequal distribution of income. As a result demand for industrial products in these societies tends to be concentrated on luxury products such as automobiles, since the poor have little money left over after purchasing food and housing. It is precisely luxury goods such as automobiles that are usually either imported from abroad or produced

5. Paul Baran, *The Political Economy of Growth* (New York: Monthly Review Press, 1957).

6. Celso Furtado, "The Brazilian 'Model' of Development," in *The Political Economy of Development and Underdevelopment,* Charles K. Wilber, ed. (New York: Random House, 1979), pp. 324–333.

domestically by foreign firms. Local enterprises and investors lack the capital or know-how to produce such sophisticated products in the early stages of development. Foreign investors have an interest in keeping the distribution of income unequal because that is what keeps up demand for products only they can produce. The local ruling class has the same interest because they are the beneficiaries of this unequal distribution. Growth is slow because foreign investors only invest the minimum necessary to maintain control of the local market.

A key link in this argument is the connection between income inequality and the demand for luxury products. It is a link that can be tested empirically by observing what happens to demand in a given country when income is redistributed in a way to achieve greater equality. Although the tests are not conclusive because of the limitations of the data used, the results so far indicate that a major redistribution of income does not lead to large shifts in the structure of demand. The demand for a luxury good such as automobiles might fall, but there is little change in the demand for steel, cement, and machine tools, to mention only a few important items.

The common theme of these theories of imperialism, therefore, is that local elites combine with foreign capitalist powers to keep a government in power that pursues policies that put obstacles in the way of economic development. The differences among the theories are mainly over the reason why this collusion of antigrowth forces exists, not whether it exists.

There is also variation in emphasis about which policies, when forced on the poor of the developing world, most inhibit their prospects for a rise from poverty. Some continue to stress how in the developing world, the imposition of free-trade policies leads to an overemphasis on investment in natural resources and an underinvestment in industry. Others argue that foreign investment in developing nations, far from enriching those nations, is later returned to the industrialized world through repatriated profits, artificially low prices for developing-country exports, and high interest payments on developing-country debt. More will be said about these specific policies in later chapters.

While there are variations on how the imperialism of the industrialized world and the dependency of the developing world stifle growth and promote inequality, scholars who made these arguments used to share a common view that progress for a developing nation was possible only if its ties to the international capitalist system were severed. It is this claim for universality, however, that is the weakest point in these analyses of the relationship between rich and poor nations. It is simply too easy to demonstrate that some countries with close ties to the capitalist world-economic system have achieved rapid economic growth and, in a few cases, even a reduction in inequality. Taiwan is the clearest case in point, where both rapid growth and falling inequality have been achieved by increasing the island's integration into the international economic system, not by decreasing that involvement. A much longer list of nations has achieved rapid growth by exporting more to the capitalist world–growth in which most have shared in the benefits but not on an equal basis.

If the claim to universality is dropped and the argument is simply that some nations are hurt by becoming entangled in the capitalist economic system, few would object. The issue then becomes one of how, and under what circumstances, to become involved in world trade and capital movements, not whether to become involved at all. Few economists today, for example, would argue with the proposition that Mexico and Brazil would be better off if they had avoided becoming so dependent on loans from Western banks in the 1970s.

In a similar vein, Ethiopia under the rule of Emperor Haile Selassie was afraid of many key development-oriented reforms precisely because they would undermine the government's domestic sources of support. Certainly the Selassie government's ability to stay in power was also reinforced by continuing support from such countries as the United States. Similar situations involving external political support from France, Britain, and others can be found elsewhere. On the other hand, when Ethiopia overthrew Haile Selassie and switched its main international ties from the United States to the Soviet Union and Cuba, the nation's economy continued to stagnate and suffer from famine. Even in the case of Ethiopia, poverty was only in part the result of the nation's ties to the capitalist economic and political system.

Clearly international influences operating through politics as well as economics can have a profound impact on the course of a nation's development. Warfare is an extreme form of the negative influences that are possible, but there are many subtler effects on both the positive and negative side of the ledger. Which effects are likely to predominate in any given country depends on the particular historical circumstances in which that country finds itself.

The one clear conclusion is that there is no single cause for why some nations took longer to initiate growth than others or for why some have yet to enter into sustained modern economic growth even today. Nor is there any single set of explanations that applies to all countries. Instead there are a wide variety of reasons for the continued poverty of nations, some of which apply in certain cases but not in others. The list of elements, both internal and external, that may have some negative influence on the prospects for development is almost infinite. And yet a large number of countries have managed to enter into sustained periods of economic development, and the number of such nations is growing. The political and social barriers to development are being overcome among an ever-widening proportion of the world's people.

3

Growth and
Structural Change

Once started, economic development proceeds along paths that vary somewhat from country to country. The United States and Germany, for example,
did not follow slavishly the patterns of development set by England, the
first developing country. The economic growth strategies of China and India
were different from those of Europe or Japan.

There are some features of the development process that are common to
all nations, however. The next sections of this chapter introduce a framework of analyzing why some growth rates are higher than others and for
explaining what we know about the patterns of development that have
occurred in the past and are likely to occur in the future. Attempts to determine the basic sources and patterns of growth have followed two very different approaches—one empirical and the other theoretical. One group of
economists, best represented by Simon Kuznets of Harvard and Hollis B.
Chenery, formerly with the World Bank, has attempted to discern patterns
of development through an analysis of data on the gross national product
and the structure of that product for dozens of nations around the world
and through time. The search has been for patterns that are common to all
nations, or more realistically, to a large subgroup of nations.

The second approach has been to construct theories of how the structure
of a nation's economy could be expected to change given various assumptions about the conditions facing that nation. This theoretical approach has
a long tradition stretching back to Adam Smith and David Ricardo of the
eighteenth and nineteenth centuries, and in more recent decades includes

Lewis, John Fei, Gustav Ranis, and many others.

In economics the ultimate objective is to develop theories whose validity can then be tested with the data available. Therefore, the empirical or data-based approach and the theoretical approach are not two different ways of looking at a given problem, but are two parts of what is really a single approach. In the field of economic development, however, the process being studied is so complex and theorizing is at such an early stage in its own evolution that one can still speak of two quite different approaches to an analysis of the patterns of development.

ESTIMATING GROSS NATIONAL PRODUCT

Kuznets and Chenery approach the analysis empirically. Before we can talk about the empirical approach to an analysis of the sources of growth and of the patterns of development, however, it is important to understand both the strengths and particularly the weaknesses of the data used to measure those patterns. In essence the analysis of patterns of development involves relating trends in gross national product per capita to trends in the various components of gross national product. **Gross national product** (GNP) is the sum of the value of finished goods and services produced by a society during a given year and excludes **intermediate goods** (goods used up in the production of other goods, such as the steel used in an automobile or the chips that go into a computer). GNP counts only income earned by citizens of the country. **Gross domestic product** (GDP) is similar to GNP except that it counts all income produced within the borders of a country, including income earned by resident foreigners, but excludes income earned by citizens of the country who are resident abroad.

The share of a sector or component of GNP such as manufacturing or agriculture is measured by the **value-added** contributed by that sector. Value-added refers to the addition to the value of the product at a particular stage of production. Thus the value-added of the cotton textile industry is the value of the textiles when they leave the factory minus the value of raw cotton and other materials used in their manufacture. Value-added, in turn, is equal to the payments to the factors of production in the textile industry: wages paid to labor plus profits, interest, depreciation of capital, and rents for buildings and land.

The great advantage of the GNP concept is that it encompasses all a nation's economic activity in a few mutually consistent summary statistics. The alternative of describing growth in terms of tons of steel and kilowatt-hours of electricity either leaves out much economic activity or, in an effort to be inclusive, involves the hopelessly complex discussion of thousands of individual products. The analysis of individual products in physical terms can be misleading, particularly in the measurement of broad economic change over time. Cotton textile output, for example, may fall over time but textiles made from artificial fibers may be increasing by more than enough to offset that fall. Gross national product provides a consistent technique for adding these two different trends together.

If the concept of gross national product has certain advantages, it also has certain important limitations, particularly when comparing patterns of development in a wide variety of developing countries. One difficulty is that poor countries usually have poor statistical services; data from certain sectors of poor countries, such as agriculture and handicrafts, are the worst of all. Estimates of the gross national product of many developing nations are based on fairly reliable statistics on modern industrial and mining enterprises combined with estimates of rural-sector performance based on small samples or outright guesses.

In addition to data limitations, there are basic methodological issues that get in the way of reliable estimates.

What Is Included in GNP?

To begin with, there is a problem with the definition of gross national product. The proper way to calculate GNP is to add up all the goods and services which are produced by a country and then sold on the market. In adding up steel and mangos, one can use either the prices at which steel and mangos were sold on the market **(GNP at market prices),** or one can use the cost of all factor inputs (labor, capital, land) used to produce a ton of steel or a bushel of mangos **(GNP at factor cost).** Many valuable contributions to society are therefore excluded from gross national product. When housework and child care are performed by paid servants or day-care employees, for example, they are included in GNP, but when they are performed by unpaid members of the household, they do not enter GNP. In developing countries a very large number of activities do not enter the market. Much of what is produced by the agricultural sector, to take the most important example, is consumed by the farm household and never reaches the market. Strictly speaking, one cannot meaningfully discuss the changing share of agriculture in GNP but only the changing share of the marketed agricultural product in GNP. Because this strict definition of GNP would severely limit the usefulness of comparing structural change among nations where agriculture is the dominant sector, the usual practice is to include farm output consumed by the producer, with that produce valued at the prices of marketed farm produce. While making GNP a more meaningful indicator of the productive capacity of a developing economy, this procedure turns GNP into a somewhat arbitrary concept. If nonmarketed agricultural produce is included, for example, why not include household-provided child-care services? A related issue that works in an opposite way from subsistence agriculture is the treatment of nonrenewable resources such as petroleum or silver. The value-added of mining products includes the original value of the ore as well as the value-added of the labor and capital needed to mine that ore. But the original value of the ore was not produced by the economy and hence does not really belong in GNP. We shall return to the issue of nonrenewable resources in Chapter 19.

Exchange-Rate Conversion Problems

A second methodological problem arises when attempting to convert the GNP of several different countries into a single currency. To compare the changing economic structure of several countries as per-capita income rises, one must measure the per-capita income figures in a common currency. The shortcut to accomplishing this goal is to use the official exchange rate between dollars and each national currency. For example, to convert Pakistan's GNP from rupees into dollars, the official exchange rate between rupees and dollars (over 21 rupees per dollar in 1990) is used. One problem with this procedure is that exchange rates, particularly those of developing countries, are frequently highly distorted. Trade restrictions make it possible for an official exchange rate to be substantially different from a rate determined by free trade.

But even an accurate estimate of the exchange rate that would prevail under a free-trade regime would not eliminate the problem. A significant part of GNP is made up of what are called **nontraded goods** and **services,** that is, goods that do not and often cannot enter into international trade. Electric power, for example, can be imported only in rare cases from an immediate neighbor with a surplus to sell (the United States imports some electricity from Canada, for example). For the most part electric power must be generated within a country, and it makes little sense to talk about the international market or the international market price for electric power. By definition, internal transportation cannot be traded, although many transport inputs, such as trucks, can be imported. Wholesale and retail trade or elementary school teachers are nontraded services. The wages of workers in these nontraded services are less influenced by any international market.

The exchange rate that is calculated by comparing the prices in two countries of nontraded as well as traded goods is called the **purchasing power parity** exchange rate. In effect this purchasing power parity rate measures the amount in dollars it would take for an individual in, say, Pakistan to buy a market basket of goods and services that in Pakistan would cost 100 rupees. But the international foreign exchange markets do not determine purchasing power parity exchange rates; they set exchange rates based on traded goods.

Gross national product converted to dollars by exchange rates that are determined by the flow of traded goods alone will give misleading comparisons if the ratio of prices of nontraded goods to prices of traded goods is different in the countries being compared. The way around this problem is to pick a set of prices prevailing in one of the countries and use that set of prices to value the goods of all countries being compared. In effect what one is doing is calculating a purchasing power parity exchange rate. The essence of the procedure can be illustrated with the simple numerical exercise presented in Table 3–1. The two economies in the table are called the United States and India, and each economy produces one traded commodity (steel) and one nontraded service (measured by the number of retail sales people). The price of steel is given in dollars in the United States and rupees in India, and the exchange rate is based on the ratio of the prices of the traded good (in this case, steel). The value of the services of retail sales personnel is estimated in the most commonly used way, which is to assume the value of the service is equal to the wages of the service personnel. The two methods of converting Indian GNP into U.S. dollars are presented in

TABLE 3–1   **Exchange Rate versus Purchasing Power Parity Methods of Converting GNP into a Single Currency**

	United States			India		
	Quantity	Price (in U.S. dollars)	Value of output (in billion U.S. dollars)	Quantity	Price (rupees)	Value of output in billion rupees
Steel (million tons)	100	200 per ton	20	8	1,600 per ton	13
Retail sales personnel (millions)	2	5,000 per person per year	10	4	4,000 per person per year	16
Total GNP (in local currency)			30			29

Official exchange rate, based on steel prices, = 1,600/200 or Rs8 = U.S. $1.

1. Indian GNP in U.S. dollars calculated by using the official exchange rate:

$$\frac{29}{8} = \text{U.S. \$3.6 billion.}$$

2. Indian GNP in U.S. dollars calculated by using U.S. prices for each individual product or service and applying that price to Indian quantities:

Steel   8 million × $ 200 = $ 1.6 billion
Retail sales
  personnel   4 billion × $5,000 = $20   billion
GNP   = $21.6 billion.

3. Ratio of 2 to 1:

$$\frac{21.6}{3.6} = 6.0.$$

the table. Clearly, one gets very different results depending on which method is used.

The example in Table 3–1 exaggerates the differences in results obtained from the two methods mainly because the nontraded-services sector is larger relative to total GNP than would normally be the case. Systematic estimates using the two different methods on a select group of countries are presented in Table 3–2. While the differences in results between the two methods are not as great as in our numerical illustration, they are still substantial. Furthermore there is a reasonably systematic relation between the degree to which the exchange-rate conversion method understates GNP and the level of development of the country. For Germany and the United States, whose per-capita GNPs were not far apart in 1970, the exchange-rate conversion is a reasonable approximation of what is obtained when converting German GNP into dollars using the better method. For India, however, the ratio between the two results is 3.23 to 1. With differences of that magnitude, exchange-rate conversions are misleading. Although it would be desirable to use purchasing power parity converted GNP throughout this book, is is impractical to do so because such GNP data are not as widely available and current as data converted using official exchange rates.

TABLE 3–2 Gross Domestic Product[a] per Capita in 1975 in U.S. Dollars

	Using official exchange rate conversion (1)	Using dollar prices for each individual product (2)	Ratio 2 to 1 (3)
United States	7,176	7,176	1.00
West Germany	6,797	5,953	0.88
France	6,428	5,977	0.93
Japan	4,474	4,907	1.10
United Kingdom	4,134	4,588	1.11
Italy	3,440	3,861	1.12
Hungary	2,125	3,559	1.68
Colombia	568	1,609	2.83
South Korea	583	1,484	2.54
Kenya	241	470	1.95
India	146	470	3.22

[a]Gross domestic product (GDP) is similar to gross national product (GNP). GDP can be derived from GNP by subtracting payments to a country's own factors (labor and capital) from abroad and adding payments to foreign factors remitted abroad. In brief GDP includes everything produced within a country whoever receives the income, but excludes income received from abroad by residents of the country.

Source: World Bank, World Tables, Vol. 1, 3d ed., Economic Data (Baltimore: Johns Hopkins Press, 1983), p. 568.

Other Index-Number Problems

The issue being discussed here is part of a larger group of issues generally referred to as **index-number problems.** Index-number problems arise not only in the comparison of two countries using two different currencies, but also in the study of the growth of a single country over a long period of time. As growth occurs it usually happens that relative prices change; that is, the prices of some commodities fall while the prices of others rise. If the country is experiencing **inflation,** which is a sustained increase in the general price level, all prices are rising, but some rise faster than others so that relative prices still change. To eliminate the impact of inflation on the statistics, economists measure *real* increases (actual growth) rather than *nominal* increases (where the prices also grow) in GNP. The proper procedure is to recalculate GNP in each year using the prices of only one year. But which year does one pick? Estimates of the growth rate will differ as one uses the prices of different years, just as the ratio of Indian to United States GNP will vary if one uses Indian prices to value both countries' GNPs in one case and United States prices in another.

A hypothetical illustration of the impact of base-year versus current-year prices is presented in Table 3–3. In this example a higher growth rate is achieved using base-year rather than current-year prices. This happens because the relative price of the industrial product (television sets) is higher in the base year (when TV sets were scarce) than in the current year (when they are more abundant), and thus the faster-growing industrial product accounts for a larger share of total product when base-year prices are used. In most countries the industrial sector is growing faster than the agricultural sector, and hence a set of prices that gives the industrial sector a larger weight in national product will result in a higher GNP growth rate.

Data problems, therefore, are pervasive whenever one studies the aggregate performance of an economy as it evolves over time or compares the

TABLE 3–3 **Base-Year versus Current-Year Price Calculations of GNP**

Product per year	Base year (1960)		Current year (1982)	
	Quantity	Price (in U.S. dollars)	Quantity	Price (in U.S. dollars)
Television sets (millions)	1	300	50	100
Wheat (million tons)	100	200	200	300

1. GNP index using *base-year* prices:

$$100 \times \frac{(50 \times 300) + (200 \times 200)}{(1 \times 300) + (100 \times 200)} = 271.$$

2. GNP index using *current-year* prices:

$$100 \times \frac{(50 \times 100) + (300 \times 200)}{(1 \times 100) + (300 \times 100)} = 216.$$

aggregate performance of two different economies. When comparing the steel ingot output of two nations, it is possible to say precisely how many more tons of steel one of the nations produces when compared with the other. There is no comparable precision when one compares large aggregates such as GNP. A certain ambiguity is always present when these figures are used to measure the sources of growth or to search for similarities in the development patterns across countries or over time.

The emphasis here has been on data issues connected with the estimation of GNP, but it should also be noted that increases in GNP are not synonomous with improvements in the welfare of the population. Welfare, for example, may be raised markedly by improvements in public health, but those health advances may have only a modest impact on the level of GNP. These and related issued will be taken up at greater length in Chapter 4.

ONE-SECTOR GROWTH MODELS

In Parts 2 and 3 we shall analyze how the quality and quantity of labor and of savings and investment are mobilized and used to promote economic development. The theory explaining the relationship between these inputs and the growth in national product is based on the **production function.** At the individual firm or microeconomic level, the production function tells how much the output of a firm or factory, such as a textile mill, will increase if the number of workers or the number of spindles and looms rises by a given amount. These are mathematical expressions, often derived from engineering specifications, that relate given amounts of physical inputs to the amount of physical output that can be produced with those inputs. Often, for convenience, microeconomic production functions are expressed in money values rather than in physical quantities.

At the national or economy-wide level, production functions describe the relationship of the size of a nation's labor force and its stock of capital with the level of that nation's gross national product. These economy-wide relationships are called **aggregate production functions.** They measure increases in the value of output or national product, given the value of increases in such inputs as the stock of capital and the labor force. Because both inputs and outputs are measured in aggregate terms (national capital stock, GNP), index-number and other measurement problems of the kind just described do introduce some ambiguity into the interpretation of economy-wide production functions. Still, it is the one tool we have for relating inputs and output at the national level within a consistent framework. For that reason, it is useful to see what this aggregate production function can tell us about how inputs contribute to growth before turning in later chapters to how those inputs can be mobilized.

The Harrod-Domar Model

The simplest and best-known production function used in the analysis of economic development was developed independently during the 1940s by economists Roy Harrod of England and Evsey Domar of MIT, primarily to explain the relationship between growth and unemployment in advanced capitalist societies.[1] But the Harrod-Domar model has been used extensively in developing countries as a simple way of looking at the relationship between growth and capital requirements.

The underlying assumption of the model is that the output of any economic unit, whether a firm, an industry, or the whole economy, depends on the amount of capital invested in that unit. Thus if we call the output Y and the stock of capital K, then output can be related to capital stock by

$$Y = K/k, \qquad [3\text{--}1]$$

where k is constant, called the capital-output ratio. To convert this into a statement about the growth of output, we use the notation Δ to represent increases in output and capital, and write

$$\Delta Y = \Delta K/k. \qquad [3\text{--}2]$$

The growth rate of output g is simply the increment in output divided by the total amount of output, $\Delta Y/Y$. If we divided both sides of Equation 3–2 by Y, then

$$g = \Delta Y/Y = (\Delta K/Y) \cdot 1/k. \qquad [3\text{--}3]$$

For the whole economy, ΔK is the same as investment I, which must equal savings S. Hence, $\Delta K/Y$ becomes I/Y, and this is equal to S/Y, which can be designated by the savings rate s, a percentage of national product. Equation 3–3 can then be converted to

$$g = s/k, \qquad [3\text{--}4]$$

which is the basic Harrod-Domar relationship for an economy.

Underlying this equation is the view that capital created by investment in plant and equipment is the main determinant of growth and that it is

1. Roy F. Harrod, "An Essay in Dynamic Theory," *Economic Journal* (1939): 14–33; and Evsey Domar, "Capital Expansion, Rate of Growth, and Employment," *Econometrica* (1946): 137–147, and "Expansion and Employment," *American Economic Review* 37 (1947): 34–55.

savings by people and corporations that make the investment possible. The **capital-output ratio** is simply a measure of the productivity of capital or investment. If an investment of $3,000 in a new plant and new equipment makes it possible for an enterprise to raise its output by $1,000 a year for many years into the future, then the capital-output ratio for that particular investment is 3:1. Economists often use the term **incremental capital-output ratio,** abbreviated ICOR, because in studying growth, one is mainly interested in the impact on output of additional or incremental capital. The incremental capital-output ratio measures the productivity of additional capital while the (average) capital-output ratio refers to the relationship between a nation's total stock of capital and its total national product.

For economic planners, given this simple equation, the task is straightforward. The first step is to try to come up with an estimate of the incremental capital-output ratio (k in Equation 3–3) for the nation whose plan is being drawn up. There are two alternatives for the next step. Either planners can decide on the rate of economic growth (g) they wish to achieve, in which case the equation will tell them the level of saving and investment necessary to achieve that growth. Or planners can decide on the rate of saving and investment that is feasible or desirable, in which case the equation will tell planners the rate of growth in national product that can be achieved.

This procedure can be applied to the economy as a whole, or it can be applied to each sector or each industry. Incremental capital-output ratios, for example, can be calculated separately for agriculture and industry. Once planners decide how much investment will be allocated to each sector, the Harrod-Domar equations determine the growth rates to be expected in each of the two sectors.

Production Functions

At the heart of this kind of analysis is the explicit or implicit assumption that the incremental capital-output ratio is a fixed number. This assumption is consistent with a production function that employs fixed proportions of capital and labor and constant returns to scale, like that depicted in Figure 3–1. Output in this figure is represented by **isoquants,** which are combinations of inputs (labor and capital in this case), that produce equal amounts of output. Only two isoquants are shown in this diagram. The L-shape of the isoquants indicates production processes that use fixed proportions of capital and labor. For example, it takes capital (plant and equipment) of $10 million and 100 workers to produce 100,000 tons of cement. If more workers are added without investing in more capital, output will not rise above 10,000 tons per year. Because the diagram is also drawn with **constant returns to scale,** if capital in the cement industry is doubled to $20 million and labor is doubled to 200 workers, output also doubles to 200,000 tons per year.

Most economists, however, believe that the production function (often referred to as the **neoclassical production function**) for many industries, and for the economy as a whole, looks more like that depicted in Figure 3–2. In this figure, if one starts with output of 100,000 tons at point *a,* using $10

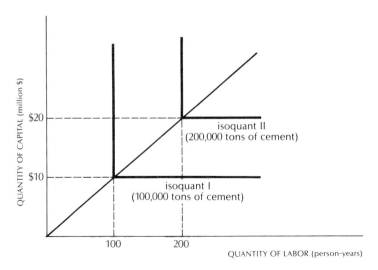

FIGURE 3–1   Production Function with Fixed Coefficients. With constant returns to scale, the isoquants will be L-shaped and the production function will be the straight line through their minimum-combination points.

million of capital and 100 workers (not shown in the figure), the industry could be expanded in any of three ways. If industry planners decide to expand at constant factor proportions and move to point *b* on isoquant II, the situation would be identical to the fixed proportions case of Figure 3–1. The capital-output ratio at both point *a* and point *b* would be 2:1. But production of 200,000 tons could be achieved by using more labor and less capital, a more *labor intensive* method, at a point like *c* on isoquant II. In

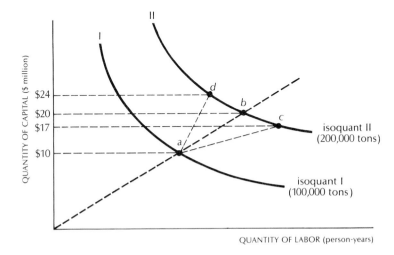

FIGURE 3–2   Neoclassical (Variable Proportions) Production Function. Instead of requiring fixed factor proportions, as in Figure 3–1, output can be achieved with varying combinations of labor and capital. This is called a **neoclassical** production function. The isoquants are curved, rather than L-shaped.

that case the incremental capital-output ratio (ICOR) falls to 1.4:1, if the price of cement is $50 a ton. Or if a more *capital-intensive* method is desired, such as the production technique given by *d* on isoquant II, the ICOR would rise to 2.8:1.

If the production function facing a nation is neoclassical, then the capital-output ratio becomes a variable that is to some extent under the control of policymakers in the government. Considering production functions like those in Figure 3–2 from the industry level, policymakers in developing countries in which capital is scarce can try to induce manufacturers and farmers to employ more labor-intensive technologies. Then, for a given amount of saving and investment, both growth and employment can be higher. At the level of the whole economy, policy will encourage labor-intensive technologies as well as encourage investment in the more labor-intensive industries, reducing the demand for investment and saving on both counts. The kinds of tools that policymakers may use to accomplish this reduction in the capital-output ratio are discussed in depth in several chapters of this text, especially Chapters 8, 13, and 17.

The appropriate incremental capital-output ratio will vary among countries and, for a single country, over time. Poor countries, with low savings rates and surplus (unemployed and underemployed) labor, can achieve higher growth rates by economizing on capital and utilizing as much labor as possible. As economies grow and per-capita income rises, savings rates tend to increase and the labor surplus diminishes. Thus the ICOR shifts upwards. In the more advanced countries it can be higher than in the developing countries without sacrificing growth. And resource-rich developing countries, such as those exporting petroleum, can afford more capital-intensive development than other LDCs. These shifts in the ICORs can come about through market mechanisms as prices of labor and capital change in response to changes in supplies. As growth takes place, savings become relatively more abundant and hence the price of capital falls while employment and wages rise. Thus all producers increasingly economize on labor and use more capital. Alternatively, in Soviet-type and other planned economies, the planners can allocate investment in ways that move the economy toward an appropriate ICOR. Finally, technological change and "learning by doing" can play important roles. Both can contribute to increased productivity of all factors of production, which reduces the ICOR. In Figures 3–1 and 3–2, increased factor productivity can be represented by a shifting inward of each isoquant toward the origin.

Data on incremental capital-output ratios for a few selected countries are presented in Table 3–4. These ratios vary from under 3:1 to 7:1 and even higher. Some of these differences can be explained by the point made earlier that richer nations such as the United States, Norway, and Japan tend to have higher ratios because capital is less expensive relative to labor than in poorer countries in the early stages of development. Other differences, however, such as those between Korea and India, have little to do with differences in the relative scarcity of capital. These differences are more likely to be the result of the differences between nations in the efficiency with which capital and other inputs are managed.

TABLE 3–4   Selected Incremental Capital-Output Ratios

Country	Incremental capital-output ratios[a]	
	1970–81	1978–87
United States	6.6	5.6
Japan	7.4	5.1
South Korea	3.3	4.0
Indonesia	2.6	5.5
India	6.0	5.7
Argentina	13.3	*
Brazil	2.8	4.8
Venezuela	6.8	*
Ivory Coast	4.2	8.2
Kenya	4.0	5.9
Tanzania	5.2	10.1

*Because there was little growth in these two countries during the decade, the incremental capital-output ratio was around 100.

[a]These ratios were derived by dividing the average share of gross domestic investment in gross domestic product by the rate of growth in gross domestic product.

Source: World Bank, World Tables, Vol. 1, Economic Data (1983), pp. 9, 23, 39, 85, 87, 95, 101, 103, 123, 175, 239, 247, and 257, and (1988), pp. 34–37, 62–65.

Sources of Growth

The simple Harrod-Domar production function, therefore, obscures some of the basic differences in growth performance between nations. One wants to know much more about why the capital-output ratio varies so much. To that end, economists such as Robert Solow and Edward Denison have attempted to explain the sources of growth with a different form of the production function, one that allows the analyst to separate out the various causes of growth rather than subsume all these other causes in the capital-output ratio.

The production function used in this analysis is neoclassical like that depicted in Figure 3–2. However, more factors of production are included. The function relates increases in output to increases in inputs of capital, skilled and unskilled labor, and other variables. This method also attempts to separate out the contribution made by rises in the efficiency with which inputs are used. The production function takes the following form:

$$Y = f(K, L, R, A), \qquad [3–5]$$

where

Y = output or national product
K = stock of capital
L = size of the labor force
R = stock of arable land and natural resources
and A = increases in the productivity or efficiency with which inputs are used.

The next step is to convert this production function into a form that makes measuring the contribution of each input possible. The deriviation of this new form of the equation involves calculus and so is presented in the appendix to this chapter. The resulting equation is

$$g_Y = a + W_K \cdot g_K + W_L \cdot g_L + W_R \cdot g_R \qquad [3\text{–}6]$$

where

g = growth rate of any variable
W = share in income of any input, (e.g., the share of wages)
Y = national product
K = capital stock
L = labor
R = arable land and natural resources

and a = variable measuring the shift in the production function resulting from greater efficiency in the use of inputs.

Data for each of these variables can be found in the statistical handbooks of many nations and the contribution of each of these variables to growth can thus be measured and identified.

A simple numerical example illustrates the way in which this equation is used. Assume the following values for the variables in the equation:

$g_Y = 0.06$ (GNP growth rate of 6 percent a year)
$g_K = 0.07$ (capital stock rises at 7 percent a year)
$g_L = 0.02$ (labor force increases at 2 percent a year)
$g_R = 0.01$ (arable land is rising by 1 percent a year).

The share of labor in national income is 60 percent ($W_L = 0.6$), the share of capital is 30 percent ($W_K = 0.30$), and the share of land is 10 percent ($W_R = 0.1$). By substituting these figures into Equation 3–6, we get:

$0.06 = a + 0.3 \cdot 0.07 + 0.6 \cdot 0.02 + 0.1 \cdot 0.01$. Solving for a, we get $a = 0.026$. What these figures tell us is that productivity growth is 2.6 percent a year and thus accounts for just under half the total growth of GNP of 6 percent a year.

Growth accounting or **sources of growth analysis,** as this method has been called, has been carried out for many nations. Because of variations in the way different economists carry out growth accounting, it is not possible to summarize the results of these calculations in a simple table. Two conclusions that have arisen from this empirical work, however, provide an important basis for much of the analysis in subsequent chapters.

First, most efforts to measure the sources of growth have indicated that increases in productivity or efficiency (a in Equation 3–6) account for a much higher proportion of growth than was believed to be the case before these calculations were made. Increases in the capital stock frequently account for less than half the increase in output, particularly in rapidly growing countries. Second, while capital does not contribute as much to growth as assumed in early growth models, capital does play a large role in growth in today's developing countries. Furthermore, some of the increases in efficiency or productivity involves advances in technology that are embodied in capital equipment. Thus mobilization of capital remains a major concern of policymakers in developing countries and is the subject of four chapters in this text (Chapters 11 to 14), but mobilization of labor and improvements in the quality of that labor are also important (Chapters 9 and 10).

Edward Denison, Dale Jorgenson, and others have attempted to measure in a more precise way the contribution of these and other elements to rising productivity. Thus labor is divided into different categories based on the amounts of formal education that that labor has received. A worker having a high school education and earning $20,000 a year is treated as the equivalent of two people having only primary school educations and earning $10,000 a year each. Similar procedures are used to measure the increase in productivity that occurs when workers shift from low-productivity occupations in rural areas to higher-productivity occupations in urban areas. Other methods are used to measure improvements in the quality of capital and increasing use of economies of scale. Price distortions and other data problems, however, cause difficulties in the calculation of some of these measures for developing countries. Few developing countries, for example, have reliable measures for differences in quality of alternative capital inputs.

Most measures of the sources of growth, for all of their limitations given the quality of developing-country data, make clear that productivity growth as well as capital formation are both critical to achieving high rates of growth in per-capita GNP. The sources of differences in productivity and capital formation that occur in the developing world are a recurring theme throughout this book.

THE CHANGING STRUCTURE OF OUTPUT

Structural change in the course of economic development thus involves rises in productivity and also increases in the capital stock relative to other inputs such as labor. Structural change also involves major shifts between the sectors that make up the output side of the production function equation. These shifts in the structure of output or national product are the subject of the remainder of this chapter. In this chapter we are mainly concerned with the relationship between these sectors as growth takes place. In later chapters (notably Chapters 18 to 20) we shall look at development within each of these sectors individually.

One clear pattern of changing economic structure in the course of economic development is that, as per-capita income rises, the share of industry in gross national product rises also. Although it is possible to conceive of a situation in which a nation moves from a condition of poverty to one of wealth while concentrating on agriculture, this kind of growth has yet to occur. Every country that has achieved a high per-capita income has also experienced a population shift, in which the majority moves from rural areas and farming to cities and industrial jobs. All have also experienced an increase in industrial value-added in gross national product.

There are two principal reasons for this. The first is **Engel's law.** In the nineteenth century Ernst Engel discovered that as incomes of families rose, the proportion of their budget spent on food declined. Since the main function of the agricultural sector is to produce food, it follows that demand for agricultural output would not grow as rapidly as demand for industrial products and services, and hence the share of agriculture in national product would decline. This relationship holds for all countries that have experienced sustained development.

A second reason has reinforced the impact of the first: productivity in the agricultural sector has risen as growth has progressed. People require food to survive, and if a household had to devote all of its energies to producing enough of its own food, it would have no surplus time to make industrial products or to grow surplus food that could be traded for industrial products. In the course of development, however, increased use of machinery and other new methods of raising crops have made it possible for an individual farmer in the United States, for example, to produce enough food to feed, and feed very well, another 70 to 80 people. As a result only 3 percent of the work force of the United States is in farming, while the others have been freed to produce elsewhere.

The rising share of industry also helps to explain why, as incomes rise, an increasing percentage of every country's population lives in cities rather than in the countryside. There are **economies of scale** in the manufacture of many industrial products. The existence of economies of scale implies that output per unit of input rises as the firm size increases; that is, a large industrial enterprise in an industry such as steel will produce more steel per dollar cost (made up from the cost of coal, iron ore, limestone, labor, plant machinery, and electricity) than will a smaller enterprise. Furthermore it makes sense for many different kinds of industrial enterprises to locate in the same place so that common support facilities, such as electric power stations, transport, and wholesalers, can also operate at an efficient level. The result is that industry leads to the growth of cities, and the growth of cities itself tends to increase the share of manufacturing and some services in gross national product. In the rural economies of most poor countries, for example, food processing is done in the home and is not usually included in gross national product calculations at all. In urbanized nations, in contrast, food processing is often done in large factories, and the value-added produced by these factories is included in the share of the manufacturing sector.

Even though the rising share of manufacturing in gross national product and the declining share of agriculture is a pattern common to all nations, it does not follow that the rates of change are the same in each country. In fact planners around the world have been plagued by the question of how much to emphasize agriculture versus industry during the course of development. The Chinese in the 1950s, for instance, tried to follow the Soviet example of putting most of their investment into industry, hoping that agriculture would somehow take care of itself. Disastrous harvests in 1959 through 1961 forced the government to put more resources, notably chemical fertilizer, into agriculture, but machinery, steel, and related industries continued to receive the lion's share of investment. Food production grew, but only just fast enough to hold per-capita consumption constant since population grew at 2 percent a year. When wages and farm incomes began to rise in the late 1970s, however, constant per-capita output was perceived as being insufficient, and the government once again greatly increased the share of investment going to agriculture. In the 1980s they took the even

more radical step of abandoning collectivized agriculture in what proved to
be a successful move to raise agricultural production at an accelerated rate.

For a decade and more after independence some African nations also felt
that agriculture required little help. Increased food requirements could be
met by the simple expedient of expanding the amount of land under cultivation. But population continued to grow, at rates over 3 percent a year in
many countries, and the supply of readily available arable land became
exhausted. On the edge of the Sahel desert the overuse of fragile land has
contributed to severe ecological damage that, together with a change in
weather patterns, has brought about widespread famine in the region.

In fact, virtually every government in the developing world has struggled
with the question of the proper relationship between agricultural and industrial development. Would a greater awareness of the historical relationship
between agriculture and industry in countries undergoing development
improve performance in these countries? If planners knew that the share
of agriculture in national product always remained above 40 percent until
per-capita income rose above $500, those planners would have a target to
aim at. Investment in agriculture could be kept at a level to ensure that the
share did not fall below 40 percent. But what if there were no consistent
patterns among countries at comparable levels of development?

Hollis Chenery and his coauthors, for example, found that there was no
single pattern for the changes in shares and that to talk meaningfully about
consistent patterns at all, the nations of the world had to be divided into
three subgroups: large countries, meaning countries with a population over
15 million in 1960; small countries that emphasize primary (agriculture plus
mining) exports; and small countries that emphasize industrial exports.[2]

Subsequent work in this same tradition has divided nations into very
large (with populations over 50 million in 1980), large (populations of 15 to
50 million in 1980), and small (under 15 million people). The patterns for
these three categories of countries are presented in Figure 3–3. The figure
also includes the individual country patterns for the years 1960 to 1982 or
1983 for 11 of the largest nations. As is apparent from this figure, the average performance of the very large, large, and small nations is similar although
the share of industry begins rising at a lower per-capita GNP in large countries than in small ones. An individual country's performance, however,
can deviate substantially from these average trends at least for a period of
two decades and longer. No one of the 11 very large countries in Figure 3–
3 is right on the average trend line for industry's share in GNP.

Chenery and his coauthors once spoke of the trends they estimated as
being the **normal pattern** of development for large (or small) countries. The
term has contributed to a good deal of misunderstanding and misuse of the
results. Planners have compared these estimated trends with the actual
performance of their country, and if their own industrial share has grown
more rapidly than the trend, they have congratulated themselves for a good

2. Hollis B. Chenery and Moises Syrquin, *Patterns of Development, 1950–1970* (London:
Oxford University Press, 1975), and Hollis B. Chenery and Lance J. Taylor, "Development
Patterns: Among Countries and over Time," *Review of Economics and Statistics* (November
1968): 391–416.

(A)

(B)

FIGURE 3–3 **Development Patterns.** In this figure the Chenery methodology for making cross-country comparisons is used to compare the patterns of the share of industry and agriculture in GNP for very large (over 50 million people), large (15 to 50 million people), and small (under 15 million people) countries. Part A depicts the share of agriculture and part B the share of industry. The very large countries for which individual country trends are given are China (CH), India (IN), Pakistan (PK), Brazil (BR), Mexico (ME), Japan (JA), West Germany (GE), Italy (IT), United Kingdom (UK), France (FR), and the United States (US).

Source: Dwight H. Perkins and Moshe Syrquin, "Large Countries: The Influence of Size," in *Handbook of Development Economics,* Vol. 2, Hollis B. Chenery and T. N. Srinivasan, eds.) (Amsterdam: North-Holland, 1989), pp. 1725–1726.

performance. Or if their share has grown at a rate below the general trend
line, they have concluded that something had to be done to correct a poor performance. In either case a deviation from the trend was seen as a cause for concern. But these patterns are nothing more than the average results obtained from comparing many diverse patterns. They are not a guide to what a country ought to do. Perhaps someday we shall be in a position to say that one trend makes more efficient use of a nation's resources than another or leads to a faster overall growth rate. Today all we have are data and estimates that give us a general idea of the trends to expect as economic development occurs. Under the circumstances it is better to drop the term "normal pattern" from the vocabulary and speak of **average pattern.** On the average the primary share (agriculture plus mining) of GNP in large countries falls from 32 percent at $600 per capita (in 1983 prices) to 19 percent at $1,600 per capita, but the variation around that trend is so great that these patterns provide only the crudest of guides for planners.

TWO-SECTOR MODELS

Long before the concept of GNP was invented or economists had many statistics of any kind to work with, they recognized the fundamental importance of the relationship between industry and agriculture. To better understand the nature of that relationship, they began to design simple models to explain the key connections between the two sectors. The best known of the earlier models appeared in David Ricardo's *The Principles of Political Economy and Taxation,* published in 1817. In his model Ricardo included two basic assumptions that have played an important role in two-sector models ever since. First, he assumed that the agricultural sector was subject to **diminishing returns:** given increases in inputs lead to continually smaller increases in output. The reason is that crops require land and land is limited. To increase production, Ricardo felt, farmers would have to move onto poorer and poorer land, and thus it would be more and more costly to produce a ton of grain. Second, Ricardo put forward the concept that today is called **labor surplus.** Britain in the early nineteenth century still had a large agricultural work force, and Ricardo felt that the industrial sector could draw away the surplus labor in the rural sector without causing a rise in wages in either the urban or rural areas.

The concept of labor surplus is closely related to concepts such as rural unemployment and underemployment or disguised unemployment. **Rural unemployment** is formally much the same as urban unemployment. When there are people who desire to work, are actively looking for work, and cannot find work, they are said to be **unemployed.** Very few people in rural areas of developing countries are unemployed in this sense. While most rural people have jobs, those jobs are not very productive. In many cases there is not enough work to employ the entire rural work force full time. Instead members of farm families all work part time and share what work there is. Economists call this **underemployment** or **disguised unemployment,** because some members of the rural work force could be removed entirely without a fall in production. Some remaining workers would simply change from part-time to full-time effort.

Underemployment and other features of developing-country labor markets will be discussed at greater length in Chapter 8. Here we are mainly interested in how an agricultural sector with diminishing returns and surplus or underemployed labor affects the development of the industrial sector. Put differently, if the industrial sector grows at a certain rate, how fast must the agricultural sector grow in order to avoid a drag on industry and on overall economic development? And will accelerated population growth help or make matters worse? To answer these and related questions, we shall develop a **simple two-sector model.**

The modern version of the two-sector labor-surplus model was first developed by W. Arthur Lewis.[3] Lewis, like Ricardo before him, pays particular attention to the implications of surplus labor for the distribution of income, and hence it is the Lewis version of that labor-surplus model that is most relevant to the discussion in Chapter 4. The concern in this chapter, however, is with the relationship between industry and agriculture. The model we use to explore that relationship is one developed by John Fei and Gustav Ranis.[4]

The Production Function

Our starting point is the agricultural sector and the **agricultural production function.** A production function, as indicated earlier, tells us how much output we can get for a given amount of input. In our simple agricultural production function we assume two inputs, labor and land, produce an output, such as grain. The production function of Figure 3–4 differs from that of Figure 3–2, because instead of showing two inputs, labor and capital, on the axes, it shows output and one input, labor. Because increases in labor must be combined with either a fixed amount of land or with land of decreasing quality, the production function indicates diminishing returns. Put differently, the **marginal product of labor** is falling, which means that each additional unit of labor produces less and less output.

The next step in constructing our model is to show how rural wages are determined. The standard assumption in all labor surplus models from Ricardo to the present time is that rural wages will not fall below a minimum level. Thus in its more general form the concept of labor surplus includes not only situations where the marginal product of labor is zero, but also situations where the marginal product of labor is above zero but less than the minimum below which rural wages will not fall. In the Fei-Ranis model and in other labor-surplus theories the usual assumption is that rural wages do not fall below the **average product** of farm labor in households with a labor surplus. The logic behind this view is that a laborer in a farm household will not look for work outside the household unless he

3. W. Arthur Lewis, *The Theory of Economic Growth* (Homewood, Ill.: Richard Irwin, 1955).

4. Gustav Ranis and John C. H. Fei, *Development of the Labor Surplus Economy* (Homewood, Ill.: Richard Irwin, 1964).

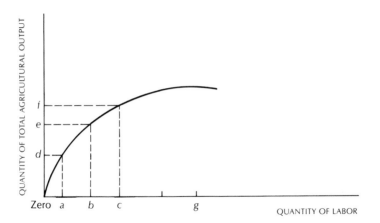

FIGURE 3–4   The Production Function. In this figure, a rise in the labor force from a to b leads to an increase in output of de; an equal increase in labor from b to c leads to a smaller rise in output. At point g further increases in the amount of labor used do not lead to any rise in output at all. Beyond point g the marginal product of labor is zero or negative, so additional Labor causes no increase or a reduction in output.

or she can earn at least as much as he or she would receive by staying at home. These concepts in diagrammatic form are presented in Figure 3–5.

Figure 3–5 can be derived directly from Figure 3–4. The *total* product per unit of labor in Figure 3–4 is converted into the *marginal product* per unit of labor of Figure 3–5. The concept of a minimum wage (represented by the dotted line *hi*) was then added to the diagram. This minimum wage is also sometimes called an **institutionally fixed wage** to contrast it with wages determined by market forces. In a perfectly competitive market,

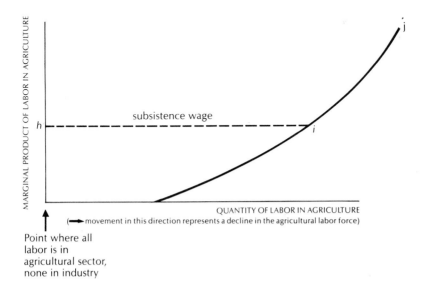

FIGURE 3–5   Marginal Product of Labor in Agriculture. As the quantity of agricultural labor decreases, the marginal product increases.

wages will equal the marginal product of labor for reasons that will be discussed at greater length in Chapter 8. Thus once labor is withdrawn from agriculture to a point where the marginal product rises above the minimum wage (point *h* in Figure 3–5), wages in agriculture will follow the marginal product curve. To hire away from the farm, factories in the city will have to pay at least as much as the workers are earning on the farm. Thus the line *hij* in Figure 3–5 can be thought of as the **supply curve of labor** facing the industrial sector. Actually the usual assumption is that the supply curve of labor in industry is a bit above the line *hij* because factories must pay farmers a bit more than they are receiving in agriculture to get them to move.

The key feature of this supply curve of labor is that unlike more common supply curves, it does not rise steadily as one moves from left to right but has a substantial horizontal portion. Formally this means that the supply curve of labor up to point *i* is **perfectly elastic. Elasticity** is a measure of responsiveness. Technically, it is the percentage change occurring in one variable (in this case, the supply of labor) arising from a given percentage change in another variable (in this case, wages).[5] Perfect elasticity occurs when the ratio of these two percentages equals infinity. From the point of view of the industrial sector this means that that sector can hire as many workers as it wants without having to raise wages until the amount of labor is increased beyond point *i*.

The final steps are to add a demand curve for labor in the industrial sector (Figure 3–6) and then to combine the three figures into a single model.

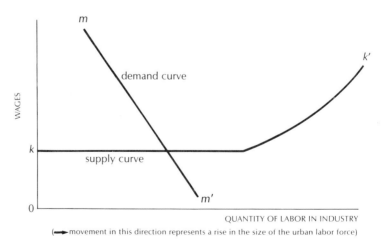

FIGURE 3–6 **The Supply and Demand for Industrial Labor.** The supply curve *kk'* is drawn directly from Figure 3–5. Demand *mm'* is derived from the industrial production function.

5. The term "**elasticity**" refers to the percentage change in one variable that results from a percentage change in another variable and is presented as a ratio. In the case discussed here, the elasticity is the ratio of the percentage change in the supply of labor ($\Delta L/L$) to the percentage change in the wage rate ($\Delta W/W$). Algebraically,

$$\text{Elasticity} = \frac{\Delta L/L}{\Delta W/W} = \frac{\Delta L}{\Delta W} \cdot \frac{W}{L}.$$

In the case of perfect elasticity, this ratio approaches infinity.

As we see in Figure 3–6, this demand curve can be derived from the industrial production function. To simplify our model, we ignore this step and draw in the demand curve mm'. The supply curve in Figure 3–6 is derived from Figure 3–5. Ok in Figure 3–6 is assumed to be slightly higher than the subsistence wage in Figure 3–5. The supply curve of labor to industry turns up when withdrawal of labor from agriculture can no longer be accomplished without a decline in the agricultural output (when the marginal product of labor rises above zero) because at that point the relative price of agricultural produce will rise, and this will necessitate a commensurate rise in urban wages. The demand curve for labor in industry is determined by the marginal product of labor in industry, and hence the demand curve can be derived from the industrial production function.[6]

To combine Figures 3–4, 3–5, and 3–6, one additional piece of information is needed, the size of the nation's labor force. Many models use total population rather than the labor force, and this switch has little effect if the labor force is closely correlated with total population. The size of the labor force in Figure 3–7 is represented by the line zero to p, as labeled in part A. In order to combine the three figures, Figure 3–4's relation to the others is made clearer if it is flipped so that an increase in labor in agriculture is represented by moving from right to left rather than the reverse. Handled this way, a movement from left to right represents both a decline in the agricultural labor force and a rise in the industrial labor force, that is, a transfer of labor from agriculture to industry.

If a surplus-labor economy starts with its entire population in agriculture, it can remove a large part of that population (pg) to industry or other employment without any reduction in farm output. Industry will have to pay that labor a wage a bit above subsistence (the difference between $p''k$ and $p'h$) to get it to move, but as long as there is some way of moving the food consumed by this labor from the rural to the urban areas, industrialization can proceed without putting any demands on agriculture. Even if agriculture is completely stagnant, industry can grow. As industry continues to grow, however, it will eventually exhaust the supply of surplus labor. Further removals of labor from agriculture will lead to a reduction in farm output. A shift in industrial demand to mm will force industry to pay more for the food of its workers; that is, the *terms of trade* between industry and agriculture will turn against industry and in favor of agriculture. It is this shift in terms of trade that accounts for the rise in the supply curve of labor between g'' and i''. Industry must pay more to get the same amount of food to feed its workers.

The Fei-Ranis model can be used to explore the implications of population growth and a rise in agricultural productivity, among other things. To simplify, if one assumes that there is a close relationship between population and the labor force, then an increase in population from, say p to t will not increase output at all. The elastic portion of both the urban and rural labor supply curves will be extended by $p't'$ and $p''t''$ respectively and thus

---

6. A factory owner under competitive conditions is willing to pay up to but no more than what a laborer contributes to increase the volume of output of the factory. The increase in output value contributed by the last laborer hired is by definition the marginal revenue product of that laborer.

FIGURE 3–7   **The Two-Sector Labor-Surplus Model.** The limit imposed by the country's population (zero to p in part A), coupled with the agricultural production function, allows us to analyze the effects of industry wages on the mix between agricultural and industrial labor.

postpone the day when industrialization will cause wages to rise.[7] This point where wages begin to rise is sometimes referred to as the **turning**

---

7. In the industrial labor supply and demand part of Figure 3–7, part C, it is also necessary to move the labor demand curves to the left since the zero point on the horizontal axis has been moved to the left. These new demand curves, $s's'$, $m'm'$, and $n'n'$, therefore, are really the same as ss, mm, and nn. That is, the quantity of labor demanded at any given price is the same for $s's'$ as ss and so on.

point. Most important, if population rises without any increase in food output, the average amount of food available per capita will fall. From the
standpoint of everyone but a few employers who want to keep wages low
and profits high, population growth is an unqualified disaster. Wages may
actually fall in the urban areas, and the welfare of the great mass of farmers
will certainly fall. It is a model such as this, even if only imperfectly understood, that people often have in mind when they speak of population growth
in wholly negative terms.

How fast agricultural production must grow depends on what happens
to a number of different variables. If industry's demand for labor is growing
very rapidly, for example, agricultural productivity must grow rapidly enough
to keep the terms of trade from turning sharply against industry and thereby
cutting into industrial profits and slowing or halting industrial growth.[8] On
the other hand, as long as there is a surplus of labor and no population
growth, it is possible to ignore agricultural productivity growth and concentrate one's resources on industry.

David Ricardo, using similar although not identical reasoning, was concerned with keeping population growth down to avoid using poorer and
poorer land in order to get a sufficient food supply. He also feared the
impact of increasing wages, which he saw as leading to a twofold disaster.
Following Thomas Malthus, he argued higher wages would lead to workers
having more children. Further, they would cut into the profits that initially
had provided the funds for investment in capital and that had allowed the
rural surplus labor to move to cities and be employed in industry. Modern
labor-surplus theorists would not agree with Ricardo's harsh policy pre-
scriptions, but they would see the problems facing today's developing
countries in a similar light.

The Neoclassical Two-Sector Model

By changing many of the assumptions in the labor-surplus model, many of
its implications can be explored. Here we take up the implications of one
assumption, the labor-surplus assumption. Many economists simply do not
agree that a surplus of labor exists in today's developing nations, even in
India or China. These economists have developed an alternative two-sector
model that is sometimes referred to as a **neoclassical model.**

The framework developed in Figure 3–7 can also be used to explore the
implications of the neoclassical assumptions. A simple neoclassical model
is presented in Figure 3–8.

The implications of population or labor force growth in the neoclassical
model are quite different from what they were in the labor-surplus model.
An increase in population and labor in agriculture will raise farm output
(see dotted line t in Figure 3–8A), and any removal of labor from agriculture will cause farm output to fall. That is, the neoclassical model is different from the labor-surplus model; the marginal product of labor is never
zero, and wages instead of being set above the marginal product of labor,

8. Agricultural productivity in the model presented here refers to a shift in the agricultural
production function causing a given amount of labor input in agriculture to produce a larger
amount of agricultural output.

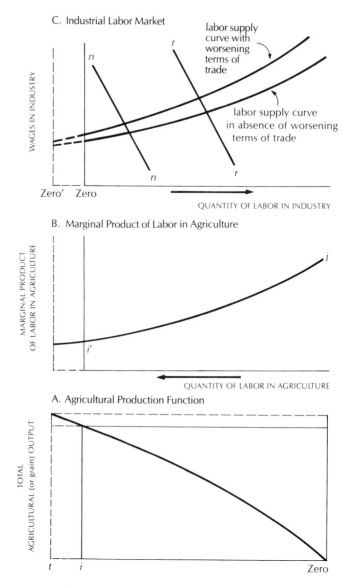

C. Industrial Labor Market

B. Marginal Product of Labor in Agriculture

A. Agricultural Production Function

Figure 3–8 A Neoclassical, Two-Sector Model. The key difference between Figures 3–7 and 3–8 is the agricultural production function (Figure 3–8A). Limited land resources do lead to slightly diminishing returns in the agricultural sector, but the curve never flattens out; that is, the marginal product of labor never falls to a minimum subsistence level, so there is no minimum subsistence or **institutionally fixed** wage in Figure 3–8B. Wages instead are always determined by the marginal product of labor in agriculture. Finally, the supply curve of labor to industry no longer has a horizontal section. Since removal of labor from agriculture increases the marginal product of labor remaining in agriculture, industry must pay an amount equal to that marginal product plus a premium to get labor to migrate to the cities. The supply curve of labor to industry rises for another reason as well. As labor is removed from agriculture, farm output falls; and in order to extract enough food from the agricultural sector to pay its workers, industry must pay higher and higher prices for food. Only if industry is in a position to import food from abroad will it be able to avoid these worsening terms of trade. If imports are not available, rising agricultural prices will lead to a higher value of output and hence higher wages for workers in agriculture. As in the labor-surplus case, industry will have to pay correspondingly higher wages to attract a labor force.

are equal to it. Thus in a neoclassical model population growth is not such a wholly negative phenomenon. The increase in labor is much less of a drain on the food supply since that labor is able to produce much or all of its own requirements, and there is no surplus of labor that can be transferred without a consequent reduction in agricultural output.

If industry is to develop successfully, simultaneous efforts must be made to ensure that agriculture grows fast enough to feed workers in both the rural and urban sectors at ever-higher levels of consumption and to prevent the terms of trade from turning against industry. A stagnant agricultural sector, that is one with little new investment or technological progress, will cause wages of urban workers to rise rapidly and thereby to cut into profits and the funds available for industrial development. Where in the labor-surplus model planners can ignore agriculture until the surplus of labor is exhausted, in the neoclassical model there must be a balance between industry and agriculture from the beginning.

Two-sector models of both the labor-surplus and neoclassical type can become very elaborate, with dozens or even hundreds of equations used to describe different features of the economy. These additional equations and assumptions will also have an influence on the kinds of policy recommendations an economist will derive from the model. But at the core of these more elaborate models are the labor-surplus and neoclassical assumptions about the nature of the agricultural production function.

These same points can be made in a less abstract way by turning to Chinese and African examples of the relationship between industry and agriculture during economic development.

Labor Surplus in China

In China by the 1950s most arable land was already under cultivation, and further increases in population and the labor force contributed little to increases in agricultural output. Urban wages rose in the early 1950s, but then leveled off and remained unchanged for 20 years between 1957 and 1977. If allowed to do so, tens of millions of farm laborers would have happily migrated to the cities despite urban wage stagnation. Only legal restrictions on rural-urban migration, backed up by more than a little force, held this migration to levels well below what would have been required to absorb the surplus. Population growth that averaged 2 percent a year up until the mid-1970s continued to swell the ranks of those interested in leaving the countryside. In short, China over the past three decades was a labor-surplus country.

As pointed out earlier, China did invest in agriculture, but only enough to maintain, not to raise, per-capita food production. The rural-urban migration that did occur was not fast enough to eliminate the rural labor surplus, but it was enough to require farmers to sell more of their production to the cities. Thus the prices paid to farmers for their produce were gradually raised, while the prices paid by farmers for urban products remained constant or fell; that is, the rural-urban *terms of trade* shifted slowly but markedly in favor of agriculture.

To get out of this labor-surplus situation, Chinese planners in the late 1970s had both to accelerate the transfer of workers from rural to urban employment and to take steps to keep the rural pool of surplus labor from constantly replenishing itself. Accelerating the growth of urban employment was accomplished by encouraging labor-intensive consumer goods (textiles, electronics, etc.) and service industries (restaurants, taxis, etc.). To feed this increase in urban population, the government increased food imports, shifted more investment funds to agriculture, and allowed a further improvement in rural-urban terms of trade.

To keep the rural pool of surplus labor from replenishing itself, planners slowed those kinds of farm mechanization that had the effect of reducing the rural demand for labor. Most important, planners attacked the surplus at its source by a massive effort to bring down the birth rate. By 1980 the population growth rate in China had slowed from 2 to 1.2 percent a year, and the rate stayed below 1.5 percent throughout the 1980s. By the mid-1980s rapid industrial and services growth in and around the cities was absorbing nearly 10 million new workers a year. But because of past population growth, the work force in the 1980s and 1990s was still growing by 15 million new entrants each year, so the surplus in the rural area was not yet falling in absolute numbers.

Labor Surplus in Africa

Africa, as already pointed out, had low population densities relative to the availability of arable land. In nations such as Kenya, increases in population could be readily accommodated in the 1950s and 1960s by opening up new land or by converting land to more intensive uses (for example, from pasture to crops). Therefore, increased population was more or less matched by rises in agricultural production. Food output, at least in the richer nations such as Kenya, kept up with the needs of both the expanding rural population and with the even more rapidly growing urban sector. Planners felt little pressure either to improve the rural-urban terms of trade or to increase state investment in agriculture. In short, until recently Kenya fit reasonably well the assumptions of the neoclassical model.

Because Kenya's land resources were not unlimited and because population growth continued at the extraordinarily high rate of close to 4 percent per annum, by the late 1970s Kenya was beginning to acquire some of the characteristics of a labor-surplus economy; and planners were having to adjust to the policy implications (more investment and better prices for agriculture, a greater effort to reduce population growth) of these new conditions. But throughout the 1980s Kenya's population grew at 3.8 percent per year and difficulties in raising crop yields by intensive methods led to an 11 percent decline in per-capita food production during the decade.

This discussion of the relations between the agricultural and industrial sectors during the process of economic development has gone as far as we can productively go at this stage. Analysis of the patterns of development using data on shares of the two sectors of GNP provided an insight into the

patterns that have occurred in the past and might be expected to recur in the future. Two-sector models have made it possible to go a step further and to acquire an understanding of some of the reasons why different patterns of industrial and agricultural development might occur. In later chapters the validity of the labor-surplus versus neoclassical assumptions for today's developing world will be explored at greater length. There will also be extended discussions of the nature and problems of industrial and agricultural development that will include further consideration of the nature of relations between the two sectors.

INDUSTRIAL PATTERNS OF GROWTH

To know precisely which industries would develop at each stage in a nation's growth would be a very valuable piece of information for economists. Plans could be drawn up that could concentrate a nation's energies on particular industries at particular stages. If all industrial development began with textiles, for example, then planners could focus their attention on getting a textile industry started and worry about other sectors later. Similarly, if only nations with high per-capita incomes could support the efficient production of automobiles, planners in countries beginning development would know that they should avoid investing resources in the automobile industry until a later stage.

Empirical Approaches

Chenery and Taylor[9] have used the terms early industries, middle industries, and late industries. **Early industries** are those that supply goods essential to the populations of poor countries and are produced with simple technologies, so that their manufacture can take place within the poor country. In statistical terms the share of these industries in GNP rises at low levels of per-capita income, but that share stops rising when income is still fairly low and stagnates or falls thereafter. Typically included in this group are food processing and textiles. **Late industries** are those whose share in GNP continues to rise even at high levels of per-capita income. This group includes many consumer durables (refrigerators, cars) as well as other metal products. **Middle industries** are those that fall in between the other two categories.

Unfortunately, it is frequently difficult to decide in which category a particular industry belongs. For many industries the nineteenth-century experience of European nations or of the United States is a poor guide because many industries that are important today did not even exist then. The nuclear power industry, for example, did not exist prior to World War II, and even the chemical-fertilizer sector as we think of it today did not really begin until well into the twentieth century.

9. Chenery and Taylor, "Development Patterns."

A way around the problem of changing technologies over time is to use data for countries at different levels of development at a given point in time. Data of this sort are called **cross-section data,** and, while they solve the one problem, they introduce others. In several Arab states petroleum accounts for a large share of GNP because these nations have unusually rich underground resources. In Malaysia soil and climate have been favorable to producing rubber, palm oil, and timber. Singapore and Hong Kong, which have no natural resources to speak of, have taken advantage of their vast experience in foreign trade to develop textiles, electronic equipment, and other manufactures for export. In short, the share of particular industries in the GNP of individual countries is determined by endowments of natural resources, historical heritages of experience with commerce and trade, and many other factors. There is no single pattern of industrial development, or even two or three patterns, that all nations must follow as they progress out of poverty. Some industries where the techniques used are easier to master, such as textiles, are more likely to get started in the early stages of development than others, such as the manufacture of commercial aircraft. And there is some regularity in the patterns of what people consume as they move from lower to higher incomes. Engel's law has already been mentioned as a part of the explanation for the declining share of agriculture in GNP. The same law has much to do with why the share of food processing within industry falls as per-capita income rises. But before planners can decide which industries to push in one country, they must know the particular conditions facing that country as well as these more general patterns.

Theoretical Approaches

Economists' debates on balanced and unbalanced growth predate much of the quantitative work on patterns of development. **Balanced-growth** advocates such as as Ragnar Nurkse or Paul Rosenstein-Rodan[10] argued that countries have to develop a wide range of industries simultaneously if they are ever to succeed in achieving sustained growth. What would happen in the absence of balanced growth has often been illustrated with a story of a hypothetical country that attempted to begin development by building a shoe factory. The factory is built, workers are hired and trained, and the factory begins to turn out shoes. Everything goes well until the factory tries to sell the shoes it is producing. The factory workers themselves use their increased income to buy new factory-made shoes; but of course they are able to produce far more shoes than they need for themselves or their families. The rest of the population is mainly poor farmers whose income has not risen, and hence they cannot afford to buy factory-made shoes. They continue to wear cheap homemade sandals. The factory in turn, unable to sell its product, goes bankrupt and the effort to start development comes to an end.

10. Ragnar Nurkse, *Problems of Capital Formation in Underdeveloped Countries* (New York: Oxford University Press, 1953); and Paul N. Rosenstein-Rodan, "Problems of Industrialization of Eastern and Southeastern Europe," *Economic Journal* (June–September 1943), reprinted in *The Economics of Underdevelopment,* A. N. Agarwala and S. P. Singh, eds. (New York: Oxford University Press, 1963).

The proposed solution to this problem is to build a number of factories simultaneously. If a textile mill, a flour mill, and a bicycle plant, and many other enterprises could be started at the same time, the shoe factory could sell its shoes to the workers in these factories as well. In turn, shoe-factory workers would use their new income to buy bicycles, clothing, and flour and thus keep the other new plants solvent. This kind of development is sometimes referred to as **balanced growth on the demand side** because the industries developed are determined by the demand or expenditure patterns of consumers (and investors). **Balanced growth on the supply side** refers to the need to build a number of industries simultaneously to prevent supply bottlenecks from occurring. Thus, in building a steel mill, planners need to make sure that iron and coal mines and coking facilities are also developed, unless imports of these inputs are readily available. At a more aggregated level, it is also necessary to maintain a balance between the development of industry and agriculture. Otherwise, as pointed out earlier, the terms of trade might turn sharply against industry and thereby bring growth to a stop.

One problem with the balanced-growth argument is that in its pure form it is a counsel of despair. A poor country with little or no industry is told that it must either start up a wide range of industries simultaneously or resign itself to continued stagnation. This across-the-board program has sometimes been referred to as a **big push** or a **critical minimum effort.** By whatever name, it is discouraging advice for a poor nation that is taxing its managerial and financial resources to the limit just to get a few factories started.

In the discussion of patterns of industrial development, however, we pointed out that there is little evidence that all nations have to follow a set pattern. Some nations have emphasized one set of industries while other nations concentrated on different ones. Proponents of **unbalanced growth,** especially Albert Hircshman, recognize these differences and use them to suggest a very different pattern of industrial development.[11] Nations, they say, could and did concentrate their energies on a few sectors during the early stages of development. In most cases there was little danger of producing more shoes than could be sold.

Certain industrial products have ready markets, even among the rural poor and even in the absence of a big push towards development. A worker in a nineteenth-century factory, for example, could produce 40 times as much cotton yarn per day as a peasant with a spinning wheel in a dark rural cottage. From the peasant's point of view, therefore, it made sense to buy factory yarn and to concentrate effort on a more productive activity, such as weaving that yarn into cloth. Initially much of this yarn was imported into places like India and China from factories in Britain, but it was not long before entrepreneurs in China and India discovered that cotton yarn could be produced more cheaply at home than purchased as an import. Thus they substituted domestic production for imports. **Import substitution,** as this process is called, is one way a nation can find a ready market

11. Albert O. Hirschman, *The Strategy of Economic Development* (New Haven, Conn.: Yale University Press, 1958).

for one of its own industries. The market is already there, and all a country's planners have to do is ensure that the domestic industry can compete effectively with the imported product. How this can be done is a subject to which we shall return in Chapter 16. Here the main point is that import substitution is one way of beginning industrialization on a limited and selective basis rather than with a balanced big push. Another way is to rely on exports, as England did during the Industrial Revolution. If it is impossible to sell all a factory's product at home, it is often possible to sell the product abroad, assuming that product could be produced at a cost that is competitive. Some of the most rapidly developing nations from the 1960s through the 1980s have begun exporting manufactures at a very early stage in their development process.

Backward and Forward Linkages

Unbalanced growth advocates such as Hirschman, however, did not content themselves with simply pointing out an escape from the dilemma posed by balanced-growth proponents. Hirschman developed the unbalanced-growth idea into a general interpretation of how development ought to proceed. The central concept in Hirschman's theory is that of **linkages.** Industries are linked to other industries in ways that can be taken into account in deciding on a development strategy. Industries with **backward linkages** make use of inputs from other industries. Automobile manufacturing, for example, uses the products of machinery and metal-processing plants, which in turn make use of large amounts of steel. The building of an automobile manufacturing plant, therefore, will create a demand for machinery, and steel. Initially this demand may be supplied by imports, but eventually local enterpreneurs will see that they have a ready market for domestically made machinery and steel, and this demand stimulates them to set up such plants. Planners interested in accelerating growth, therefore, will emphasize industries with strong backward linkages because it is these industries that will stimulate production in the greatest number of additional sectors.

Forward linkages occur in industries that produce goods that then become inputs into other industries. Rather than start with automobiles, planners might prefer to start at the other end by setting up a steel mill. Seeing that they had a ready domestic supply of steel, entrepreneurs might then be stimulated to set up factories that would make use of this steel. In a similar way successful drilling for oil will encourage a nation to set up its own refineries and petrochemical complexes rather than ship its crude oil to other nations for processing.

Both forward and backward linkages set up pressures that lead to the creation of new industries, which in turn create additional pressures, and so on. These pressures can take the form of new profit opportunities for private entrepreneurs, or pressures can build through the political process and force governments to act. Private investors, for example, might decide to build factories in a given location without at the same time providing adequate housing facilities for the inflow of new workers or roads with which to supply the factories and transport their output. In such cases government planners might be forced to construct public housing and roads.

While on the surface the balanced and unbalanced-growth arguments appear to be fundamentally inconsistent with each other, when stated in less extreme forms they can be seen as opposite sides of the same coin. Almost everyone would agree that there is no single pattern of industrialization that all nations must follow. On the other hand, quantitative analysis suggests that there are patterns that are broadly similar among large groups of nations. While nations with large amounts of foreign trade can follow an unbalanced strategy for some time, a nation cannot pick any industry or group of industries it desires and then concentrate exclusively on those industries throughout the nation's development, cannot follow in effect an extreme form of an unbalanced-growth strategy. The very concept of linkages suggests that extreme imbalances of this sort will set up pressures that will force a nation back toward a more balanced path. Thus the ultimate objective is a degree of balance in the development program. But planners have a choice between attempting to maintain balance throughout the development process or first creating imbalances with the knowledge that linkage pressures will eventually force them back toward the balance. In terms of Figure 3–9, the issue is whether to follow the steady balanced-growth path, represented by a solid line, or the unbalanced-growth path, represented by a dashed line. The solid line is shorter, but under certain conditions a nation might get to any given point faster by following the dashed line.

APPENDIX: DERIVING THE SOURCES OF GROWTH EQUATION

There are six steps to deriving the sources of growth equation from the standard aggregate production function. To simplify the presentation, we shall assume that there are only two factors of production, capital and labor.

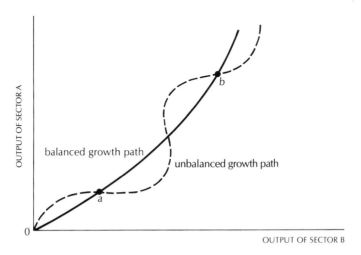

FIGURE 3–9 **Balanced- and Unbalanced-Growth Paths.** The solid line between points a and b is shorter than the dotted line, but because of the impact of linkages, a country traveling along the dotted line may get from point, a to b in less time than a country traveling along the solid line or balanced-growth path.

1. Assume an aggregate production function:

$$Y = F(K, L, t),$$ [3–7]

which is continuous and homogeneous to degree 1, where

> $Y =$ national income or product
> $K =$ capital stock
> $t =$ time (shift in basic production function)
> $L =$ labor force.

2. Differentiate this production function with respect to time.

$$\frac{dY}{dt} = \left(\frac{\delta F}{\delta K} \cdot \frac{dK}{dt}\right) + \left(\frac{\delta F}{\delta L} \cdot \frac{dL}{dt}\right) + \left(\frac{\delta F}{\delta t} \cdot \frac{dt}{dt}\right)$$ [3–8]

where the symbol δ is used to represent the partial derivative.

3. Divide through by Y, and insert L and K in equation.

$$\frac{1}{Y} \cdot \frac{dY}{dt} = \frac{1}{Y}\left(\frac{\delta F}{\delta K} \cdot \frac{dK}{dt} \cdot K \frac{1}{K} + \frac{\delta F}{\delta L} \cdot \frac{dL}{dt} \cdot L \cdot \frac{1}{L} + \frac{\delta F}{\delta t}\right).$$ [3–9]

4. Rearrange terms.

$$\frac{dY/dt}{Y} = \frac{(\delta F/\delta K)\, K}{Y} \cdot \frac{dK/dt}{K} + \frac{(\delta F/\delta L)\, L}{Y} \cdot \frac{dL/dt}{L} + \frac{\delta F/dt}{Y},$$ [3–10]

where

$$G_Y = \frac{dY/dt}{Y} = \text{growth rate of income,}$$

$$G_K = \frac{dK/dt}{K} = \text{growth rate of capital,}$$

$$G_L = \frac{dL/dt}{L} = \text{growth rate of labor force,}$$

and $$W_K = \frac{(\delta F/\delta K)\, K}{Y} = \text{share of product of capital in national income.}$$

5. Assume perfect competition, so that wages and the interest rate equal the marginal product of labor and capital respectively. If

$$\frac{\delta F}{\delta L} = \text{wage rate,}$$

then

$$W_L = \frac{(\delta F/\delta L)\, L}{Y} = \text{share of wages in national income,}$$

and if

$$\frac{\delta F}{\delta K} = i \text{ (rate of interest),}$$

then

$$W_K = \frac{i \cdot K}{Y} = \text{share of income of capital in national income,}$$

and

$$a = \frac{\delta F / \delta t}{Y} = \text{increase in output as share of income not explained by increase in factors.}$$

6. Substitute G_Y, G_L, G_K, W_L, W_K, and a into Equation 3– 10, which then gives one the sources-of-growth equation:

$$G_Y = (W_K \cdot G_K) + (W_L \cdot G_L) + a. \qquad [3\text{--}11]$$

This equation can also be rewritten in the form

$$a = (\text{the residual}) = G_Y - (W_K \cdot G_K) - (W_L \cdot G_L). \qquad [3\text{--}12]$$

Countries with reasonably good statistical systems regularly publish data on the growth rate of national product (G_Y) and the labor force (G_L). Data on the growth rate of the capital stock (G_K) are more difficult to find because estimates of the capital stock are readily available only for industrialized nations. Economists who work with developing-country data, therefore, sometimes rewrite the $W_K \cdot G_K$ component of Equation 3–11. By not inserting K into Equation 3–10, that part of Equation 3–10 becomes

$$\frac{dF}{dK} \cdot \frac{dK/dt}{Y},$$

where

$$\frac{dF}{dK} = \text{the interest rate as previously assumed}$$

and

$$\frac{dK/dt}{Y} = I = \text{the share of gross domestic investment in gross domestic product.}$$

The share of gross domestic investment (I), or capital formation in gross domestic product, is regularly calculated for most countries.

Data on the shares of labor income in national income (W_L) are the total wages and salaries paid to workers plus the imputed wages of farmers. The share of capital income in national income (W_K) is made up of interest income and profits. In a two factor model, W_K would encompass all property income, including the rent on land.

When economists such as Edward Denison calculate the sources of growth, they generally use more than two factors of production. Labor, for example, is usually divided into unskilled and skilled labor of various types. Foreign exchange earnings are sometimes treated as a separate factor of production from capital, and so on. There often is an attempt to break down the residual measure of productivity increases (a) into its various components. Some of these refinements can be used in estimating the sources of growth in developing countries, but others are not possible because of the limited availability of relevant developing-country data.

4

Development and Human Welfare

Even if they suffered a slowdown in the 1980s, most developing countries still have experienced significant economic growth over the past three or four decades. This chapter assesses the impact of this growth on the material well-being of the nearly 4 billion citizens of the developing countries. Logically, economic growth is a necessary, but not sufficient, condition for improving the living standards of large numbers of people. It is *necessary* because if there is no growth, people can be made better off only by taking income and assets from others. In poor countries, even if a small segment of the population is very rich, the potential of this kind of redistribution is severely limited. If GNP per capita is $200, the best a country can do through income redistribution is to give each citizen $200 a year.[1] Economic growth, by contrast, makes it possible for some or even all people to become better off without making anyone worse off.

Economic growth is not a *sufficient* condition for improving mass living standards, however, because it can lead to increased wealth only for the few. For at least three reasons, we cannot assume that higher per-capita GNP necessarily means higher incomes for all, or even most, families.

First, governments promote economic growth not just to improve the welfare of their citizens but also, and sometimes primarily, to augment the

---

1. There is, however, a view which argues that if assets are redistributed first, faster growth will result. This is taken up in the last section of this chapter.

power and glory of the state and its rulers. Much of the wealth of ancient

Egypt was invested in the pyramids. Modern LDCs may buy ballistic missile systems, develop nuclear weapons, or construct elaborate capital city complexes in deserts and jungles. When the gains from growth are channeled to such expensive projects, they provide little immediate benefit to the nation's citizens.

Second, resources may be heavily invested in further growth, with significant consumption gains deferred to a later date. In extreme cases, such as the Soviet collectivization drive of the 1930s, consumption may actually decline dramatically over long periods. Soviet consumers are still waiting, with growing impatience, for the era of mass consumption. Normally, the power to suppress consumption to this extent in the name of economic growth is within the power only of totalitarian governments.

Third, income and consumption may increase, but those who are already relatively well off may get all or most of the benefits. The rich get richer, the old saw says, and the poor get poorer. (In another version, the poor get children.) This is what poor people often think is happening. Sometimes they are right.

The question of who benefits from economic growth is not new. In Victorian England, rising inequalities in income and wealth and persistent poverty among the lower classes were widely perceived and frequently discussed. Social philosophers like Karl Marx and novelists like Charles Dickens made these issues their major themes. Defenders of the status quo responded either by denying that things were as bad as the critics charged or by arguing that the conditions they deplored were a necessary part of a process of change that would ultimately benefit all strata of society.

Despite the efforts of a few nineteenth-century pioneers in "economic arithmetic" and of later economic historians, we cannot precisely measure the dimensions of nineteenth-century inequality and poverty. What is clear is that improvement occurred during the late nineteenth and early twentieth centuries in England and other capitalist countries that we now consider developed. The gains came as real wages rose and governments enacted reforms (antitrust legislation, progressive taxation, unemployment insurance, social security, and, after 1930, stabilizing monetary and fiscal policies) that helped to mitigate the worst inequalities and assure some minimal living standard for all members of society. Contrary to Marx, who had predicted ever-worsening inequality and instability leading to the collapse of the "bourgeois system" itself, workers in the rich capitalist countries ultimately did reach an era of mass consumption that allowed them to share in the gains from economic development.

The issue that concerns us here is the prospects of the poor majorities of Asia, Africa, and Latin America, who remain desperately poor by the standards of the ordinary citizen of a rich Western country, or even by those of an East European worker. As industrialization proceeds and their nations' GNPs rise, what will happen to their individual economic welfare? When can they hope to reach an era of mass consumption?

During the early years of the current period of interest in economic development, roughly 1950 to 1965, development specialists ignored the problems of inequality and poverty and tacitly assumed that when per-capita GNP rises everyone becomes better off. Evidence that certain sections of the population were not benefiting was sometimes shrugged off with the statement that in due course the benefits of economic development would "trickle down" to them. Since there were few statistics on income distribution in developing countries at this time, it was easy to overlook the question of how the benefits of development were distributed.

Doubts about whether development was benefiting the poor arose in India as early as 1960. By the late 1960s enough income distribution statistics had been compiled for Indian and other LDCs to rock the complacent. The new data confirmed what some had already suspected, that income inequality is generally higher in poor countries than in rich countries. Further, they suggested that inequality was rising in many developing countries and the mass of people in some countries were not benefiting at all from development. Finally, and more controversially, some writers claimed that the poor were actually becoming worse off, at least in certain large and very poor countries such as India and Bangladesh.

Interest in problems of inequality and poverty waned in the 1970s and almost disappeared in the 1980s. Sadly, the reason for diminished interest is not that these problems have been solved but that they have been eclipsed by seemingly larger and more immediate problems. With economic growth rates declining sharply and even turning negative for years on end in many African and Latin American countries, the most pressing need has seemed to be to deal with the factors that have brought growth to a halt: the debt crisis in the case of Latin America and a host of troubles, much debated, in the case of sub-Saharan Africa.

While inequality may strike people as more of a problem when per-capita income is growing than when it is stagnant, poverty is likely to be an even greater problem in periods and regions of slow economic growth. In the following pages we consider what has been learned about poverty and inequality in the developing countries. We shall deal first with concepts of economic welfare, then with the recent historical record, next with theories about the causes and effects of inequality and poverty, and finally with policies to help ameliorate inequality.

CONCEPTS AND MEASURES

Income Distribution

The most common way to evaluate the effect of development on economic well-being is through the study of income distribution. Two types of income distribution are generally cited: the functional distribution and the size distribution. The **functional distribution** refers to the division of national income or output among the factors of production, traditionally identified as land, labor, and capital. It can be used to measure the contributions made to production by the different factors. The **size distribution** measures the amount of income of all functional kinds received by individuals or families. It shows the shares of total income received by high-, middle-, and low-income families, and is commonly used as a direct measure of welfare.[2]

The functional and size distributions of income are related measures. Since the size distribution is determined largely by ownership patterns of the productive factors (including "ownership" of one's own labor services) and the role each factor plays in the production process, the functional distribution of income has a major influence on welfare levels. For example, if ownership of land and capital is narrowly distributed, then anything that enhances the returns to these factors will tend to worsen the size distribution of income. Conversely, a higher return to unskilled labor, the most widely distributed factor of production, will make for a more equal size distribution. In the discussion that follows, we will concentrate primarily on the size distribution, but its relationship to the distribution of income across the various factors of production should be kept in mind.

Many practical problems are involved in measuring the size distribution of income. Ideally, average income over several years should be used since earners in developing countries often experience wide income fluctuations as a result of the vagaries of nature, markets, and their own governments. Cumulated lifetime income would be an even better measure, because earnings vary systematically with age. But such refinements are seldom practical, and most studies take income over a particular recent period (a month or year) as their basis. Other practical decisions involve precisely how to define income and how to collect data. Usually a sample survey of households is undertaken. Even when considerable care and ingenuity are exercised, the resulting statistics are likely to be of questionable accuracy. Respondents may not know what their income is, or they may be afraid to disclose it, perhaps thinking that their taxes will go up. Generally, reported incomes are understated. If a household income survey is projected over all households, the total ought to equal the household share of national income implied in the national estimates.[3] In practice a shortfall of "only" 15 or 20 percent of national income is regarded as a good result for a household income survey. In general, the uncertainties of these statistics require the analyst to tread cautiously when trying to interpret them.

Once the data have been collected, the next step is to analyze them. Respondents (either individuals or households) are first ranked by income size. The best ranking criterion is household income per capita, since family members in LDCs usually pool their incomes and welfare is thus affected both by the total income received and by the number of family members to be supported.

2. One could argue that the distribution of consumption or wealth should be measured instead. Consumption measures the volume of goods and services actually consumed, so it could be equated with material welfare. But income represents potential consumption, including a part of the potential which is not realized in the current period because it is saved to yield higher consumption later on. Wealth, finally, defines the potential to earn and to consume, especially when human capital is included in the definition of wealth (see Chapters 9 and 10). But the distribution of wealth is notoriously hard to measure, and statistics on wealth distribution are rare.

3. **National income** equals gross national product less depreciation and indirect taxes; the household share of national income would also exclude profits retained (not distributed as dividends) by corporations.

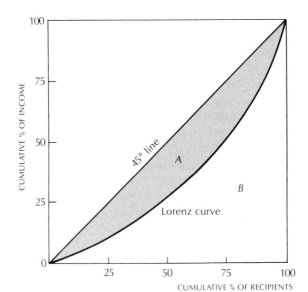

FIGURE 4–1   Lorenz Curve. The further the Lorenz curve bends away from the 45-degree line, the greater is the inequality of income distribution. Dividing the shaded area (*A*) by the total area under the 45-degree line (*A* + *B*) gives one measure of inequality, the Gini concentration ratio.

The data can be arranged in various ways. The most common method is the **Lorenz curve,** shown in Figure 4–1. To draw a Lorenz curve, income recipients are ranked from lowest income to highest along the horizontal axis. The Lorenz curve itself shows the percentage of total income accounted for by any cumulative percentage of recipients. The shape of this curve indicates the degree of inequality in the income distribution. The curve must by definition touch the 45-degree line at the lower left corner (0 percent of recipients must receive 0 percent of income) and again at the upper right corner (100 percent of recipients must receive 100 percent of income). If all recipients had the same income, the Lorenz curve would lie along the 45-degree line (perfect equality). If only one individual or household received income, it would trace the lower and right-hand borders of the diagram (perfect inequality). In all actual cases, of course, it lies somewhere in between. The inequality of the distribution curve is greater the further it bends away from the 45-degree line of perfect equality (the greater the shaded area *A*).

Inequality Measures

Statisticians have long been interested in defining a single number that adequately expresses the degree of overall inequality present in an income distribution. All common statistical measures, such as the range and standard deviation, have serious faults. The most frequently used statistic, the

Gini concentration ratio, is derived from the Lorenz curve. This ratio is most easily understood as the value of area *A* divided by area *A+B* in Figure 4–1. That is, the larger the share of the area between the 45-degree line and the Lorenz curve, the higher the value of the Gini concentration ratio. One can see from Figure 4–1 that the theoretical range of the Gini ratio is from 0 (perfect equality) to 1 (perfect inequality). In practice, values measured in national income distributions have a much narrower range, normally from about 0.25 to 0.60. Some examples are shown in Table 4–1.

Like all other indicators that have been proposed to measure inequality, the Gini concentration ratio has its problems. For one thing Lorenz curves can intersect; this can cause curves with different shapes to generate the same Gini ratio. This happens when one distribution is very unequal in one part of its range, say, from the bottom to around the middle, while another is unequal in a different part, say, in terms of the income shares of the very richest families. Another problem is that the Gini ratio's extreme reference standard, perfect equality, makes the measure generally insensitive to changes in distribution. This insensitivity is greatest for changes in the incomes of low-income groups, which may be small in absolute terms but still important in percentage terms to the poor households themselves, and also perhaps an important form of redistribution in policy terms.[4]

Any measure that tries to encompass the entire Lorenz curve in a single statistic must contain an element of arbitrariness. One way around this is to look only at a particular part of the curve. Thus if we are interested in how the poor are faring, we might examine the absolute and relative incomes of the poorest 30 or 40 percent of the distribution. Conversely if we are interested in the concentration of wealth at the top of the distribution, the top 5, 10, or 20 percent could be studied. This tells us what we want to know for particular purposes, but at the cost of generality; it ignores what is going on in the rest of the distribution.

Some of these points are illustrated in Table 4–2, which compares the income distributions of Tanzania, Egypt, and Indonesia during the years 1970 to 1975. All three countries had fairly unequal income distributions, but which was the most unequal? The Gini concentration ratio says Indonesia, yet the bottom 20 percent of the distribution did better in Indonesia than in either of the other two countries. And Tanzania gave a large share of total income to households in the highest quintile of income recipients. So which distribution is really more unequal? In a borderline case like this, there is no clear answer. Indonesia's distribution was more unequal in some senses, Tanzania's in others. Egypt's distribution was less unequal than the other two in most, but not quite all, respects. The crossing Lorenz curves produced by these distributions are shown in Figure 4–2.

---

4. In the Philippines in 1970–71, the lowest 20 percent of the income distribution received only 5.2 percent of total income while the top 10 percent of households got 38.5 percent of total income. Taking 1 percent of total income from the richest group and giving it to the lowest 20 percent would raise the income of the poor by 19 percent, a meaningful increase. Yet it would lower the Gini concentration ratio only from .461 to .445, assuming that the redistributive gain is shared equally by the lowest two deciles.

TABLE 4–1   Income Distribution in Selected Countries[a]

Country	% of income received by: Lowest 40%	% of income received by: Highest 20%	Gini concentration ratio[b]
Low-income countries			
Bangladesh	17.3	45.3	.375
Zambia	10.8	61.1	.537
India	16.2	49.4	.413
Kenya	9.0	60.4	.542
Sri Lanka	13.3	56.1	.485
Indonesia	14.4	49.4	.430
Middle-income countries			
Philippines	14.1	54.7	.461
Egypt	21.4	47.2	.378
Ivory Coast	8.6	61.4	.556
Colombia	12.7	53.0	.469
Tunisia	11.8	55.0	.488
Peru	12.9	51.9	.458
Costa Rica	11.6	56.5	.485
Mexico	9.9	57.7	.523
Malaysia	13.9	51.2	.445
Brazil	8.1	62.6	.569
Uruguay	14.3	47.4	.423
Argentina	14.1	50.3	.442
South Korea	16.9	45.3	.378
Venezuela	13.9	50.6	.441
High-income countries			
Taiwan	20.0	41.4	.326
Singapore	14.0	48.9	.422
Hong Kong	16.2	47.0	.396
New Zealand	15.9	46.7	.387
Australia	15.5	42.2	.374
United Kingdom	17.3	39.5	.338
France	18.4	40.8	.338
Canada	17.4	39.4	.338
West Germany	19.5	38.7	.315
Sweden	21.2	36.9	.288
United States	15.7	41.9	.369
Japan	21.9	37.5	.285
Switzerland	16.9	44.6	.378
East European countries[c]			
Poland	21.6	40.7	.308
Yugoslavia	17.1	42.8	.363
U.S.S.R.	21.6	40.9	.309
Hungary	25.0	35.6	.244
Czechoslovakia	26.1	34.3	.224
East Germany	23.8	39.4	.278

[a]Dates of the surveys underlying these estimates vary by country; they range from 1965 to 1988. Countries are categorized and ranked by their GNP per capita in 1988.
[b]Approximate Gini concentration ratios calculated from grouped data (that is, from data that have been aggregated by income-size groups).
[c]Estimates for socialist countries include the estimated value of special benefits received by the privileged group (*nomenklatura*); see Morrisson.
Sources: World Bank, *World Development Report 1990* and 1989; Wouter van Ginneken and Jong-goo Park, eds., *Generating Internationally Comparable Income Distribution Measures* (Geneva: International Labour Office, 1984), pp. 5, 176; Jacques Lecaillon et al., *Income Distribution and Economic Development. An Analytical Survey* (Geneva: International Labour Office, 1984), p. 26; Montek S. Ahluwalia, "Inequality, Poverty and Development, *Journal of Development Economics* 3 (1976): 340; Christian Morrisson, "Income Distribution in East European and Western Countries," *Journal of Comparative Economics* 8 (1984): 121–138.

TABLE 4–2   Comparisons of Income Distribution in Tanzania, Egypt, and Indonesia

| Country | Income shares | | | | | | Gini concentration ratio |
	Bottom 20%	Second 20%	Third 20%	Fourth 20%	Top 20%	Top 10%	
Tanzania (1969)	5.8	10.2	13.9	19.7	50.4	35.6	.420
Egypt (1974)	5.8	10.7	14.7	20.8	48.0	33.2	.403
Indonesia (1976)	6.6	7.8	12.6	23.6	49.4	34.0	.430

Source: World Bank, *World Development Report 1985*, pp. 228–229.

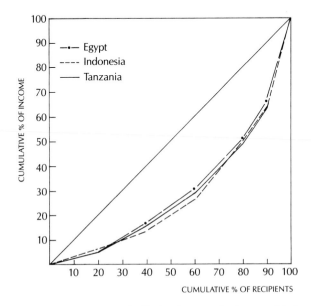

FIGURE 4–2   **Lorenz Curves for Income Distribution in Tanzania, Egypt, and Indonesia, c. 1970–1975.** When Lorenz curves intersect, as do the curves for Tanzania, Egypt, and Indonesia, there is no clear measure of relative inequality.

Poverty Measures

While inequality is clearly a matter of relative incomes, the concept of **poverty** implies that some households are poor in an absolute sense. But an objective definition of poverty is surprisingly hard to formulate. Calculations of the minimum income level necessary for physical survival indicate that one can survive on very little if one chooses.[5] Efforts to link poverty to its specific manifestations—starvation, severe malnutrition, illiteracy, substandard clothing and housing—have not been much more successful.

5. George Stigler calculated that Americans could purchase a physiologically adequate diet for $8 per month per person (in 1950 prices) by limiting themselves to a diet of wheat flour, evaporated milk, cabbage, spinach, and dried navy beans. See Stigler, *The Theory of Price*, rev. ed. (New York: Macmillan, 1952), p. 2. The fact that very few choose to do so indicates the importance of the psychological and social aspects of poverty.

The fact is that poverty is not just a matter of absolute incomes; it also implies something about relative incomes. In social terms, the poor are those who must live below what most people in a particular time and place regard as the minimum acceptable standard. Thus while practically everyone in the United States receives a higher income than almost everyone in, say, Chad, there are still (relatively) poor people in the United States and (relatively) nonpoor people in Chad. Different standards apply in the two places. In psychological terms, the poor are those who feel deprived of what is enjoyed by other people in the society of which they consider themselves to be a part (their *reference group*). Reference groups are probably expanding as education and communication improve. Formerly, peasants might have compared their own status with that of the village elites at most. Now they are becoming increasingly aware of the living standards of urban elites in their own countries, and even of the standards that prevail in the rich countries. The sense of deprivation may well be growing.

Measurement of the amount of poverty existing in a country usually begins with the drawing of a poverty line. Ideally, this line should be defined in terms of household income per capita. Households with per-capita incomes below the poverty line are defined as poor whereas those with incomes above the line are not poor. The simplest measure of the extent of poverty is the percentage of poor households in the total. A better measure, however, would also take account of the extent to which the incomes of the poor fall below the poverty line. Reduction of poverty would then be measured through a fall in the percentage of poor households in the total and also through increases in the absolute incomes of the poor.

Table 4–3 illustrates these points, using as an example one of the most successful cases of poverty and inequality alleviation. Sri Lanka in 1953 had a low per-capita income, relatively great inequality (as measured by the Gini ratio), and a large population of poor people (defined here as receiving a monthly per-capita income below 100 rupees in 1963 prices). Over the succeeding two decades inequality declined and outstanding prog-

TABLE 4–3   Changes in Income Distribution and Poverty in Sri Lanka, 1953–1973

Measure	1953	1963	1973
Income shares of quintiles			
Bottom 20%	5.2	4.5	7.2
Second quintile	9.3	9.2	12.1
Third quintile	13.3	13.8	16.3
Fourth quintile	18.4	20.2	21.6
Top 20%	53.8	52.3	42.9
Gini concentration ratio	.46	.45	.35
Mean monthly income per capita			
(rupees)[a]	117	134	150
Mean monthly income of bottom 40%			
(rupees)[a]	42	46	72
Percent of households below 100			
rupees/month[a]	63	59	41

[a] In 1963 prices.
Source: Gary S. Fields, *Poverty, Inequality and Development* (London: Cambridge University Press, 1980), p. 197.

ress was made in reducing poverty, as can be seen from the rise in the mean income of the bottom 40 percent of the income distribution and from the sharp decline in the percentage of households below the poverty line. Note that this was achieved with only modest growth in average income; according to the statistics, monthly income per capita rose only 28 percent in 20 years, while the average income of households in the lowest four deciles of the distribution rose by 71 percent. Few developing countries have been able to duplicate this achievement.

The poverty analyst can apply similar or different standards across differing times and places. World Bank publications sometimes refer to the quantity and distribution of "absolute poverty" in the world; these calculations are made using a simple global poverty line.[6]

Equality and Equity

Equality is an objective statistical measure used mainly to determine how far any actual distribution diverges from the standard. Equity, on the other hand, is a normative (ethical) concept: what is equitable depends on one's values. Many Americans, for example, believe in equality of opportunity but think that considerable inequality of results may be justified by interpersonal differences in ability, effort, training, willingness to take risks, and stage in the life cycle. Thus, quite apart from the fact that there can be a trade-off between equity and economic growth (greater inequality than one would like may be needed to induce people to save more and work hard), most concepts of equity allow for some degree of inequality in the distribution of income.

Basic Human Needs and Social Indicators

The poverty approach measures purchasing power in the hands of the poor. But some students of development, including many from disciplines other than economics, object to using income as the measure of welfare. Of course, they say, higher incomes help make it possible for people to live better and longer, but why do we not look to see whether these changes actually occur? Efforts to measure a wide variety of **social indicators** go back many years. More recently interest has centered on seeing whether **basic human needs** are being satisfied. Lists of basic human needs vary, but most include minimal levels of nutrition, health, clothing, shelter, and opportunities for individual freedom and advancement. Some of these, at least, can be measured.

The World Bank periodically publishes data on social indicators obtained from various sources. A selection of these data is shown in Table 4–4. Some of the indicators listed—infant deaths, life expectancy, nutritive consumption, and adult literacy—reflect the degree to which basic human needs

6. For a probing discussion of these measurement problems, see Amartya K. Sen, *On Economic Inequality* (New York: W. W. Norton & Company, 1973). A good short discussion is provided by Richard Szal and Sherman Robinson, "Measuring Income Inequality," in *Income Distribution and Growth in the Less-Developed Countries,* Charles R. Frank and Richard C. Webb, eds. (Washington, D.C.: Brookings Institution, 1977), pp. 491–533.

TABLE 4–4   Illustrative Social Indicators for 1988

Indicator	GNP per capita (1988)				
	<$250	$250–$500	$500–$2,200	$2,200–$6,000	>$6,000
Infant deaths/ 1,000 live births	124 (22)	97 (30)	57 (29)	40 (28)	11 (12)
Life expectancy at birth (years)	49 (2)	54 (7)	64 (7)	68 (6)	75 (3)
Physicians/100,000 inhabitants	10 (18)	20 (25)	94 (160)	164 (187)	225 (84)
Hospital beds/100,000 inhabitants	95 (56)	146 (103)	261 (230)	386 (309)	792 (422)
Access to health care (% of population)	52 (14)	58 (21)	82 (21)	93 (9)	99 (2)
Energy consumption per capita (kg of oil equivalent)	40 (23)	166 (180)	591 (595)	2,085 (1,074)	4,342 (2,050)
Passenger cars/ 1,000 inhabitants	2 (1)	6 (4)	31 (25)	102 (57)	296 (154)
Phones/1,000 inhabitants	3 (2)	6 (3)	51 (39)	136 (87)	549 (275)
Daily calorie supply/person	2,088 (250)	2,194 (243)	2,580 (388)	3,083 (408)	3,298 (261)
Daily protein supply (g/person)	55 (13)	56 (13)	65 (14)	86 (17)	99 (8)
Newspaper circulation/ 1,000 inhabitants	4 (3)	18 (25)	53 (46)	114 (68)	312 (145)
Adult literacy rate (%)	39 (22)	49 (19)	68 (20)	82 (15)	95 (6)

Source: World Bank, *Social Indicators of Development 1989* (Baltimore: Johns Hopkins Press, 1989). Figures in parentheses are standard deviations.

are satisfied in countries at different levels of GNP per capita. Others (newsprint consumption, radios, and motor vehicles) indicate consumption of items that might be regarded as less basic. Remaining indicators are less directly related to welfare. Some, such as energy consumption and newspaper circulation, measure the sophistication of the economy and society. Finally, a fourth group of indicators, represented in Table 4–4 by the provision of physicians and hospital beds, indicates levels of services which may contribute to basic needs satisfaction, which is itself measured more directly by other indicators.[7]

Two interesting points come out of an examination of Table 4–4. One is that as a rule improvement in social indicators goes hand in hand with a rise in per-capita GNP. In Table 4–4 it is striking that every time we move to a higher income group, the average value of each social indicator for the countries covered by the World Bank's data increases. But the second point is that, within each income class, variations among countries are large.

7. Besides being an approach to measuring welfare, basic human needs is also a strategy for welfare-oriented development. This aspect is discussed in the last section of the chapter.

This is demonstrated by the high values for standard deviations shown in the table.[8]

Social indicators are hard to combine into an overall measure of a nation's social development. A decade ago, an imaginative move in this direction was made by the Washington-based Overseas Development Council (ODC). The ODC's physical quality of life index (PQLI) was an aggregation of three widely available indicators of the basic human needs variety: life expectancy at age one, the infant mortality rate, and the literacy rate.[9] Each indicator was assigned a scaled value from 0 to 100, with the best and worst known cases setting the limits of the scale. An unweighted average of the three indicators was then taken. The PQLI was interpreted by its promoters to suggest that the richest countries do not always enjoy the highest quality of life, and that at least a few countries (for example, Sri Lanka, Cuba, Guyana, and South Korea) have been able to achieve a comparatively high quality of life at levels of per-capita income well below those of the industrialized nations.

Recently the United Nations Development Program (UNDP) published a human development index, which combines measures of life expectancy, literacy, and GNP per capita in the manner of the PQLI.[10] All these indexes are at least somewhat arbitrary and some appear to have been manipulated to reflect the political views of their compilers. For example, the human development index disregards increases in per-capita GNP above about $5,000 per capita; this suggests that raising per-capita income from the level of, say, Libya to that of Switzerland makes no contribution to human development. In any case, these indexes generally yield country rankings which are highly correlated with per-capita GNP. The largest deviations are caused by obvious cases such as the oil-exporting countries, which have high GNP capita income (at least in years when oil prices are high) and low values on the social development indexes.

Distribution Weights

Several years ago a study group convened by the World Bank proposed a novel and ingenious way to integrate the study of economic growth and welfare, involving the use of **distribution weights**.[11] These are illustrated in

8. The standard deviation is a measurement of the average variation among observations. It can be defined as

$$(d^2/n)^{1/2},$$

where d is the deviation of each observation from the mean and n is the number of observations. A large standard deviation indicates a wide spread among the observations, while a small one suggests that most observations have values close to the mean. In a normal, or bell-shaped, distribution over 60 percent of all observations lie within one standard deviation of the mean.

9. See Morris David Morris, *Measuring the Condition of the World's Poor. The Physical Quality of Life Index* (New York: Pergamon Press for the Overseas Development Council, 1979).

10. United Nations Development Program, *Human Development Report 1990* (New York: Oxford University Press, 1990.)

11. Hollis B. Chenery et al., *Redistribution with Growth* (London: Oxford University Press, 1974).

TABLE 4–5   Illustration of Distribution Weights

| Country | Period | Income growth | | | Growth rate using: | | | Initial Gini coefficient |
		Top 20%	Middle 40%	Lowest 40%	Income weights	Population weights	Poverty weights	
South Korea	1964–70	10.6	7.8	9.3	9.3	9.0	9.0	.34
Brazil	1960–70	8.4	4.8	5.2	6.9	5.7	5.4	.56
Colombia	1964–70	5.6	7.3	7.0	6.2	6.8	7.0	.57
Peru	1961–71	4.7	7.5	3.2	5.4	5.2	4.6	.59
Sri Lanka	1963–70	3.1	6.2	8.3	5.0	6.4	7.2	.45
India	1954–64	5.1	3.9	3.9	4.5	4.1	4.0	.40

Source: Chenery et al., Redistribution with Growth, p. 42.

Table 4–5, which compares six countries for which income distribution estimates separated by several years are available. During the periods concerned these countries had average annual GNP growth rates ranging from 4.5 percent for India to 9.3 percent for South Korea. Their initial income distributions varied from quite egalitarian (Korea), through moderately egalitarian (India and Sri Lanka), to very unequal (Brazil, Colombia, and Peru). The distribution of amounts added to total income during the periods studied also differed among the six countries. In Colombia and Sri Lanka inequality declined; in the other countries it rose.

These varying development experiences can be evaluated using three different weighting schemes:

First, conventional national accounting implicitly uses **base-year income share** as its weighting system. In measuring GNP, statisticians do not disaggregate income into different income groups; they simply measure total income for the entire population. But under this aggregate measure, if the top 20 percent of households received half the income in the base year, their income growth gets a 50 percent weighting in figuring out the growth rate or society's income (GNP). By this criterion Korea grew more than twice as fast as India and the other countries fell in between.

Second, **population weights** give each income group a weight equal to its share in the total population. This is an egalitarian approach that gives everyone's income growth equal weight. Under population weighting Korea remains the country with the best performance, but Colombia and Sri Lanka, in which the income distribution improved during the period, begin to look better relative to the other countries, in which distribution worsened.

Third, **poverty weights** go one step further and assign a greater weight to income growth for the poor. Various weights can be used; the ones employed in Table 4–5 imply a moderately pro-poor bias: whereas population weights are 0.2, 0.4, and 0.4 respectively for the three income groups, the poverty weights selected were 0.1, 0.3, and 0.6. In other words income gains for the poorest group are valued at one and one-half times as much as under the population weights scheme, gains for the middle group at three-quarters as much, and gains for the richest group at half as much. Under this weighting scheme, as the table shows, Colombia's and Sri Lanka's performances look even better, while Brazil slips from its original position of second to fourth place.

These weighting schemes evaluate the change in welfare during the period. They should be read in conjunction with the initial degree of inequality, which is shown in the right-hand column of Table 4–5. Thus while India and Korea showed increases in inequality during the period, evaluation of their performance should be tempered by the fact that they started from relatively equal initial distributions. Brazil and Peru, by contrast, experienced worsenings of distributions that were already highly unequal to begin with.

The flexibility of the distribution-weights approach is appealing, but there are difficulties with it, both in principle and in practice. Who makes the value judgments implicit in the choice of weights? Those economists who have proposed the reweighting schemes are egalitarian-minded, but do their values coincide with those of poor societies and their governments? University of Chicago economist Arnold Harberger has demonstrated that seemingly modest reweighting schemes imply that a society is willing to accept a large loss in efficiency in return for some redistribution, and he has gone on to argue that most governments reveal by their actions that they are not in fact so interested in redistribution as such.[12] Harberger believes that governments instead show commitment to the satisfaction of basic human needs for food, education, health services, and so on. Yet not to reweight also implies a value judgment—namely, in favor of the existing distribution of income.

A practical impediment to the widespread use of reweighting schemes is the weakness of statistics on the distribution of income. For most developing countries the analyst is fortunate to have one reasonably reliable estimate of the distribution of income. In very few instances are there the two or more comparable estimates required to say how the benefits of economic growth have been distributed. Even in a country like Sri Lanka, a pioneer both in the collection of income-distribution statistics and in the redistribution of income, questions have been raised about whether the improvement of income distribution thought to have occurred between the early 1960s and the early 1970s actually took place.

Universally acceptable measures have not been found and never will be. Development brings about many changes, and an evaluation of its effect on welfare inevitably depends on the importance one attaches to each type of change. Varying degrees of emphasis on growth, inequality, and poverty lead to varying assessments. A system of distributive weights can express one evaluator's values, but the values of other observers may well diverge. Agreement is possible only in the loose sense that most people would regard successful development (in welfare terms) as encompassing rising per-capita output, reduced poverty, improved health and longevity, and at least no dramatic worsening of inequality.

---

12. Arnold Harberger, "Basic Needs versus Distributional Weights in Social Cost-Benefit Analysis," *Economic Development and Cultural Change* 32, no. 4 (April 1984): 455–477.

PATTERNS OF INEQUALITY AND POVERTY

In his 1955 presidential address to the American Economic Association, Simon Kuznets suggested that the relationship between per-capita GNP and inequality in the distribution of income may take the form of an inverted U. That is, as per-capita income rises, inequality may initially rise, reach a maximum at an intermediate level of income, and then decline as income levels characteristic of an industrial country are reached. Kuznets based this proposition on the mere fragments of data available at the time for estimating income distributions in a few rich and poor countries and on trends in distribution over time in a few European countries.

Evidence for Kuznets' Inverted U

Although controversial, Kuznets' insight has held up pretty well as much larger bodies of data have been amassed over the years. We now have estimates of income distribution in more than 70 countries, although some of these are of dubious quality. Table 4–6 summarizes the results of estimates made for 69 countries between 1965 and 1988. Inequality can be measured in this table using any of three measurements: the share of total income received by the poorest 40 percent, the share of the top 20 percent, or the Gini concentration ratio. By all three measures, inequality first rises, then peaks, and finally falls, just as Kuznets predicted in 1955. This result has often been obtained in studies of cross-section data.

 Cross-section data (that is, estimates made for a number of different countries at approximately the same time) provide most of the available evidence on the relationship between income levels and inequality. The estimates in Table 4–6 are, in effect, cross-section data, although the country data refer to slightly different years. Time-series data (comparable estimates at different times for particular countries) are rarer. For many countries there is still only one good estimate of income distribution (at most!). Even

TABLE 4–6 Estimates of Inequality and Poverty in Relation to GNP per Capita (unweighted averages within groups)[a]

Country groups	Number of countries included	Percent of income received by: Lowest 40%	Percent of income received by: Highest 20%	Gini concentration ratio	Mean income of lowest 40% (dollars)	GNP per capita (dollars)
Low-income countries	15	14.4	49.4	.430	115	265
Middle-income countries	27	12.7	54.0	.473	1,430	455
High-income countries	21	18.3	40.5	.337	12,485	5,740
East European countries	7	22.6	38.7	.285	*	*

*Estimating GNPs for East European economies is difficult, and estimates vary widely. See "Grossly Deceptive Product," *The Economist* (March 10, 1990): 71.
[a]Unweighted averages within groups.
Sources: Same as Table 4–1.

where two or more surveys have been made, differences in survey design and execution may make it hard to compare results. Nevertheless, there are now a few developing countries for which successive estimates provide a reasonably clear view of how inequality has changed over time. These suggest that while the pattern hypothesized by by Kuznets is plausible, it is not inevitable. One recent survey suggested that while inequality has tended to increase over intervals for which changes can be measured in developing countries, it has been almost equally likely to do so in developed countries.[13] Another study concludes pragmatically that "rapid growth in a mixed economy is consistent with unchanged, or even improved, income distribution, even at early stages of development."[14]

In summary, the inverted-U relationship discerned by Kuznets holds up well in the cross-section data but is less clearly present in the limited amount of time-series data available. Even in the cross-section view shown in Table 4–6, per-capita GDP, using the hypothesized curvilinear relationship, explains only about one-half of the intercountry variation in Gini coefficients. A calculation based on data for 61 countries (excluding the East European socialist countries, which have markedly less inequality than other countries at their income level) yields the following equation:

$$G = -0.116 + 0.183 \log Y - 0.014 \log Y^{2,} \qquad [4-1]$$

where G = the value of the Gini coefficient and log Y = the natural logarithim of GNP per capita. The R^2 (share of variation explained) of this equation is .50.

Exceptional Cases

Many individual countries have substantially more or less inequality than might be expected at their per-capita income level. Sri Lanka has often been cited as an example of relatively equal income distribution in a low-income country, although inequality in that country seems to have increased significantly since the late 1970s (see boxed example). South Korea and Taiwan are both famed for their ability to combine rapid growth with relatively equal income distributions. Latin American countries are known for high inequality, but Argentina and Uruguay have inequality measures far below the normally high levels for the region. Conversely, while socialist countries generally have less inequality than developed capitalist countries, several capitalist nations have more equal income distributions than Yugoslavia, a socialist state. Developing countries with unusually high inequality include Kenya, Ivory Coast, Zambia, Peru, Brazil, and Mexico. Among developed countries, New Zealand, Switzerland, and (increasingly in the 1980s) the United States have above-average levels of inequality (see Table 4–1).

13. Gary S. Fields, "Changes in Poverty and Inequality in Developing Countries," *World Bank Research Observer* 4, no. 2 (July 1989): 176.

14. Gustav F. Papanek and Oldrich Kyn, "The Effect on Income Distribution of Development, The Growth Rate and Economic Strategy," *Journal of Development Economics* 23 (1986): 55–65.

Explanations of Inequality

Analysts have tried to identify factors other than per-capita income that explain the amount of inequality present in a given country. As Table 4–6 indicates, socialist countries generally have less inequality than nonsocialist countries with comparable GNPs per capita.[15] Since socialist countries must maintain significant wage differentials for incentive reasons, their lower inequality is attributable less to differences in the distribution of labor income than to the far smaller flow of property income that results from severe restrictions on private ownership of land and capital.

Efforts to explain variations in inequality among nonsocialist countries have had mixed results. One influential study concluded that higher enrollment rates in primary and secondary schools and a higher GNP growth rate are associated with reduced inequality, given the level of GNP per capita, while a higher growth rate of population goes with greater inequality.[16] However, no study has been able to explain much more than half the intercountry variation in inequality, and some of the results obtained have been contradictory. We still lack a general explanation of income distribution in relation to economic growth that closely conforms with the known facts.

One approach has been to try to identify the types of societies (in social and political as well as economic terms) where inequality is likely to be high or low. Irma Adelman and Cynthia Taft Morris found that income distribution is typically relatively equal in two kinds of countries: very poor nations dominated by small-scale or communal (jointly farmed) agriculture and well-developed nations in which major efforts have been made to improve human resources.[17] This conclusion qualifies the Kuznets hypothesis and suggests some of the factors that may be associated with the inverted-U pattern. Very poor countries may be quite egalitarian, it says, but only if their economies are dominated by small peasant farms and not by large farms or mines. Rich countries can also be egalitarian, but only if their people have been permitted to share in development by upgrading the productivity of the labor resources that they supply to the economy.

By implication, countries with intermediate income levels are likely to have considerable inequality. This same study found the income share of the poorest 60 percent of the income distribution to be smallest where well-entrenched foreign or military elites control the most productive economic sectors and receive most of the benefits of development.

How Growth Reduces Poverty

Logically, if the income share of the poor rises with growth, their absolute income must also rise, since they are getting an increasing share of an

---

15. Note, however, that absolute income is also relatively low in socialist countries. Per-capita income in East Germany, the richest country in this group before it merged with West Germany in 1990, was about half that of capitalist West Germany.

16. See Montek S. Ahluwalia, "Income Inequality: Some Dimensions of the Problem," in *Redistribution with Growth*, Chenery et al., pp. 3–37, and Montek S. Ahluwalia, "Inequality, Poverty and Development," *Journal of Development Economics* 3 (1976): 307–342.

17. See Irma Adelman and Cynthia Taft Morris, *Economic Growth and Social Equity in Developing Countries* (Stanford, Calif.: Stanford University Press, 1973).

increasing total. But what if their share declines, as may occur in the early stages of development? The answer is that even in this case poverty alleviation is still closely associated with per-capita GNP. The mean income of the poor in a given society is very closely associated with GNP per capita ($R^2 = .97$), as the following equation, based on the data in Table 4–6, suggests:

$$log\ Y_p = -1.687 + 1.088\ log\ Y, \qquad [4-2]$$

where log Y_p = the natural logarithim of the mean income of the poorest 40 percent of families and log Y = the natural logarithim of GNP per capita.

The share of the population living in poverty is also closely related to per-capita GNP ($R^2 = .95$), at least if we adopt a global poverty line (in this case $370 per capita, the poverty line used in the *World Development Report 1990*). The equation, again based on the data in Table 4–6, is:

$$P = 477.992 - 103.656\ log\ Y + 5.589\ log\ Y^2, \qquad [4-3]$$

where P = the percentage of households with less than $370 per capita, log Y = the natural logarithm of GNP per capita, and log Y^2 = the square of the natural logarithm of GNP per capita.

In summary, while there are many reason why people may be poor, the most important one is that they live in poor countries.[18] Assuming that what we see in cross-section data will hold up in time series, these calculations lead us to expect that raising per-capita income will almost certainly increase the absolute income of the poor and will probably also reduce the proportion of the population living in poverty, as measured by a global poverty line.

Another indication of the close association between poverty and low national income per capita is the geography of world poverty. In 1985, more than half the world's 1 billion-plus poor (defined as per-capita income below $370 in 1985 purchasing power parity dollars) lived in the low-income countries of South Asia (Table 4–7). Worldwide, more than 80 percent of

TABLE 4–7   Geographic Distribution of World Poverty, 1985

Region	Number of poor (millions)	% of region's population	% of world poor
South Asia	520	51	47
(India)	420	55	38
East Asia	280	20	25
(China)	210	20	19
Sub-Saharan Africa	180	47	16
Latin America and Caribbean	70	19	6
Middle East and North Africa	60	31	5
Eastern Europe	6	0.5	1
All developing countries	1,116	33	100

Source: World Bank, *World Development Report 1990*, p. 29.

18. See also Ahluwalia, "Income Equality" and "Inequality, Poverty, and Development."

the poor in 1985 lived in low-income countries with per-capita GNP of less than $500.[19] There were of course absolutely poor people in other regions, but their numbers were much smaller.

While most poor people continue to be found in the poorest countries, differences in rates of economic growth are causing the incidence of poverty to fall in Asia but rise in sub-Saharan Africa. Although still large, Asia's share in world poverty is declining—East Asia's especially rapidly—while sub-Saharan Africa's share is rising. The World Bank projects that between 1985 and the year 2000 the number of poor people in East Asia will drop from 280 million to fewer than 100 million and the number in South Asia from 520 million to fewer than 400 million. Over the same period, poverty in sub-Saharan Africa is expected to rise from 180 million to more than 250 million. The gradual shift of world poverty from faster-growing Asia to virtually stagnant Africa is further proof that economic growth reduces poverty whereas a lack of economic growth, especially when accompanied by rapid population increases (see Chapter 7), allows poverty to rise.

In all third-world regions and countries, the prevalence of poverty is greater in rural areas than in urban areas. World Bank estimates suggest that in the 1980s 80 percent or more of the poor lived in rural areas in most Asian and African countries. In Latin America, which is more urbanized, the urban poor are a larger share of the total, but the prevalence of poverty (the percentage of the population that is poor) is still greater in the countryside. Although there are urban slums in many countries, urbanization is clearly an important part of the poverty reduction process.

Two qualifications must be attached to the strongly indicated conclusion that poverty is associated with low national per-capita income and tends to be eradicated as per-capita income rises. First, it applies to *absolute* poverty measured using a global poverty line. *Relative* poverty is far more persistent. Few people are living on $370 a year in the United States, but many receive incomes far below a reasonable U.S. standard. Second, some time-series studies for particular countries have shown stagnation or even decline in the incomes of the poor and increases in the number of poor people or both. Many of these findings have been challenged, but they do at least warn us not to assume complacently that economic growth will necessarily or rapidly eliminate poverty.

Income Distribution Models

The most ambitious efforts made to study the determinants of income distribution and the effects of various policies are comprehensive models of income distribution as it is generated by the overall workings of an economy. In one of the best-known studies, quantitative economists Irma Adelman and Sherman Robinson modeled the South Korean economy.[20] Their computable general equilibrium (CGE) model (see further discussion in Chapter 6) includes specifications of price and quantity adjustments in both

19. World Bank, *World Development Report 1990*, p. 29.
20. Irma Adelman and Sherman Robinson, *Income Distribution Policy in Developing Countries. A Case Study of Korea* (Stanford, Calif.: Stanford University Press, 1978).

factor and product markets and allows for substitution possibilities in production and consumption in response to changes in relative prices. A dynamic version of the model projects investment by sector on the basis of profitability, expectations, and government financial policies. The model forecasted that economic growth would continue in Korea, but most of the gains would go to the urban population and the income distribution would steadily worsen. Experimental runs of the model to simulate the effects of various policy packages showed that most policies would have little effect on income distribution. Some supposed antipoverty policies actually gave disproportionate benefits to the rich and the middle-income groups. The most promising policies for bettering income distribution were those that either improved relative prices received by agricultural producers (their internal terms of trade) or encouraged rural-to-urban migration. Foreign trade policies, working largely through these two factors, had significant impacts on inequality and poverty.

Four case studies help to round out the picture of world poverty created by the global statistics and research that we have been discussing. If they achieve nothing else, these case studies show that one should be cautious in generalizing about development, inequality, and poverty. Much depends on the circumstances of the individual country and the type of development pursued.

South Korea

South Korea has enjoyed an extraordinarily high rate of economic growth (per-capita income growth averaged nearly 7 percent a year from 1965 to 1988), which has helped to alleviate poverty and satisfy basic needs. The Korean development pattern has been highly equitable, compared with virtually all other developing countries, for two reasons. First, assets, especially land, were distributed relatively equally before rapid growth began; second, Korea pursued a pattern of development that did not greatly concentrate income or wealth. When Korea emerged from Japanese colonial rule at the end of World War II, the many large production units that had been Japanese-owned were either nationalized or broken up and redistributed. Two land reforms subdivided the larger agricultural holdings and virtually eliminated tenancy (in which land is owned by one person but farmed by another, who pays rent for its use).

The rapid economic growth which began in the early 1960s emphasized the modernization of small- and medium-sized firms (although by the 1970s, large-scale firms were formed). Foreign ownership was held to a minimum. Manufacturing for export boomed and absorbed a larger share of labor-force growth than in almost any other country. The Korean educational system, which accommodated all children at its lower levels and then rigorously selected the few best performers for continuation to its higher levels, supported both equity and growth. All these factors contributed to a rapid decline in poverty. Inequality has risen slightly as the country transformed itself economically and began to emphasize growth in large firms, but it has remained lower than in other third-world countries and comparable to inequality in the most developed western countries. Korea, then, is a clear-cut case of rapid growth with equity.

Brazil

Brazil has grown faster than most other Latin American countries, but the consequences for human welfare have been somewhat equivocal. A large, naturally rich country, Brazil has made impressive strides toward the creation of a modern, diversified economy. Some of its industries and modern cities bear comparison with those in the rich countries. Brazilian agriculture has also made progress in important areas, such as the development of soybeans as a major export crop alongside coffee and other traditional items. But economic growth has been uneven both in time (it has gone through several stop-and-go phases) and space.

Whole sections of the country, such as the poor northeast, have been largely excluded from development. Even the big, modern cities in the south (Rio de Janeiro, Sao Paulo, Belo-Horizonte) have appalling urban slums, sometimes located right beside luxurious, architecturally impressive, new constructions. Many of the factors that have led to equitable growth in Korea are reversed in Brazil: asset ownership is highly concentrated; there has been no land reform; access to education is uneven and heavily influenced by wealth; development, in both manufacturing and agriculture, has emphasized large production units; technologies adopted have tended to be capital-intensive. The results are very high inequality and little progress toward poverty alleviation, despite rapid growth of the economy and some increases in the real incomes of the poor.

Sri Lanka

Sri Lanka has grown at low-to-average rates through most of its history. As a result of the country's open democratic system of government and the articulateness of its well-educated electorate, all Sri Lankan governments since independence in 1948 have had to be populist to survive. A system of social benefits that included cheap staple foods, and free schooling and medical services, helped to produce a healthy, literate populace. Inequality was kept relatively low, and despite low income levels the worst manifestations of poverty (premature deaths, malnutrition, illiteracy) have been avoided to a remarkable degree. The trouble was that economic growth was too slow to provide either adequate financing for the welfare system or employment for the growing labor force, especially the educated youths seeking white-collar jobs. Chronic popular dissatisfaction led to repeated changes in government at the polls and an unsuccessful youth revolt in 1971. In 1977 a new government inaugurated an effort to accelerate growth by emphasizing labor-intensive manufacturing, irrigation, and tourism. This led to accelerated economic growth, but also rising income inequality. Tragically, conflict between the island's majority Sinhalese community and the minority Tamils has severely limited the benefits realized from the post-1977 growth strategy.

India, like Brazil, is a big country with areas of both dynamism and stagnation. Also like Brazil, it has emphasized inward-looking development to build a self-sufficient, subcontinental economy. Like Sri Lanka, India is a poor country, which has generally not grown very rapidly. There has been substantial development in some regions, such as Bombay and the Punjab, through either industrialization or successful adoption of the Green Revolution in food-grain production. Other areas, like Bihar state, remain desperately poor. One southern state, Kerala, has a Sri Lanka-like pattern of high basic-needs satisfaction together with low income and growth. Overall inequality measures for India usually come out rather low because there are so many poor people and only relatively small classes of the comfortable or rich. About 50 percent of the population lives below the officially defined poverty line, and this proportion has changed little over the years. In the 1980s there was some economic liberalization, accelerated economic growth, and a modest rise in distributive inequality.

THEORIES OF INEQUALITY AND POVERTY

During the classical period of economic thinking questions of poverty and inequality and their relationship to economic growth received much emphasis. This is particularly evident in the work of David Ricardo, who wrote in the early 1800s, when England was a developing country.

Ricardo's Two-Sector Model

We saw in Chapter 3 that Ricardo pioneered the two-sector model of development. His analysis suggested that if England did not abolish the corn laws, which protected grain farmers from foreign competition, and allow imports of food to fuel its industrial revolution, income would be redistributed from capitalists to landlords. (Wages, he assumed, would remain at the subsistence level.) Since Ricardo regarded landlords as spendthrifts and thought that economic growth was financed by the savings of the thrifty capitalist class, he concluded that this redistribution would harm economic growth.

Although his theory was innovative and internally consistent, all Ricardo's predictions about income distribution and economic growth turned out to be wrong. Rent (income to landlords) has not taken a growing share of national income in industrializing countries but has remained a rather small share. The profit share (income to capitalists) has not been squeezed out. And wages have not been held to the subsistence level but have risen, at least in the later stages of industrial development; the share of wages in national income, if anything, has tended to rise. There are several reasons why actual trends have not matched those predicted in Ricardo's model. One is that England did adopt free trade, as Ricardo wanted. But even if it had not, diminishing returns would probably have been largely offset by technological change, which would have made it possible to grow increasing amounts of food on land of given quantity and quality. Ricardo also overestimated the strength of the Malthusian population mechanism (see Chapter 7), which he thought would hold wages at the subsistence level.

Marx's View

Karl Marx also believed that capitalist development would create an increasingly unequal distribution of income. Capitalists, he thought, had an incentive to create a "reserve army of the unemployed," whose brooding presence would ensure that the wages of employed laborers stayed at the subsistence level. (Marx hotly rebutted the Malthusian theory that demographic forces created the labor surplus and called this line of thinking an insult to the working class.) In Marxian thought, the owners of capital dominate both the economy and the "bourgeois state." But as capitalism develops, the rate of profit falls and crises occur and cause firms to fail and industrial concentration to rise. Eventually, in a final apocalyptic crisis, capitalism itself collapses, to be replaced by socialism. Only then, according to Karl Marx, can the lot of the workers improve.

Although Marx was enormously influential as a critic of capitalism and revolutionary prophet, his prediction of how income distribution would evolve over time was no more accurate than Ricardo's.

The Neoclassical Theory

The dominant theory used today to explain income distribution in *developed* countries was worked out in the late nineteenth and early twentieth centuries. This is the **neoclassical (marginal productivity) theory,** which postulates that all factors of production (now more numerous than land, labor, and capital, to take account of quality differences) are in scarce supply and that their rates of return are set equal to their marginal products in competitive factor markets. This theory is also relevant to *developing* countries, but its applicability there is more debatable than its relevance to developed countries because the theory's assumption that product and factor markets are perfectly competitive is less valid in an LDC setting.

The Labor-Surplus Model

An alternative to the neoclassical theory for analyzing income distribution in developing countries is provided by the labor-surplus model of W. Arthur Lewis. It was Lewis who first observed that conditions in less-developed countries are in some ways more similar to those which prevailed in the industrialized countries before the Industrial Revolution than they are to conditions in those same countries today. A useful theory to analyze the workings of a low-income economy, therefore, might be built on classical rather than neoclassical assumptions. This insight led Lewis to his celebrated model of "economic development with unlimited supplies of labor," which utilized the Ricardo-Marx assumption that labor is available in unlimited quantity at a fixed real wage, rather than being a scarce factor of production that must be bid away from other uses, as in the neoclassical theory. The implications of the surplus-labor model for the importance of agricultural development and the role played by population growth were discussed in Chapter 3. What remains is to bring out the implications of the model for the distribution of income.

The labor-surplus model suggests that inequality will first increase and later diminish as development takes place. It is thus consistent with Kuznets' generalization about what has actually occurred. Lewis gives two reasons why an initial rise in inequality might be expected. One is that the income share of the capitalists (i.e., those who control capital, including state-owned enterprises) rises as the size of the modern, or capitalist, sector increases. The second reason is that inequality in the distribution of labor income also rises during the early period, when increasing but still relatively small numbers of laborers are moving from the subsistence wage level to the capitalist-sector wage level, which Lewis says tends to run about 30 percent higher in real terms.

If this seems counterintuitive, imagine that there are no wage differentials *within* either sector of the dual economy but a 30 percent differential *between* the two sectors, as Lewis assumes. In this case, inequality in the distribution of labor income would be zero at the beginning of the development process, when all the workers were employed in the low-wage sector, and zero again at the end of the process, when all the workers are employed in the high-wage sector. At all points between these two extremes, there would be some inequality in the distribution of labor income. In our simple model, inequality in the distribution of labor income would rise up to the point at which half the labor force is employed in the high-wage sector and then decline.

The tendency for inequality to rise during the early part of the development process is strongly reversed (as explicitly depicted in the Fei-Ranis extension of the Lewis model; see Chapter 3) when all the surplus labor is finally absorbed into modern-sector employment. At that point, labor becomes a scarce factor of production, and further increases in demand require increases in real wages to bid labor away from marginal uses. The model suggests that the resulting rise in the general wage level brings about not only an eventual downturn in inequality but also the long-awaited abolition of poverty, at least by former standards.

In the Lewis version of the labor-surplus model, inequality is not just a necessary *effect* of economic growth; it is also a *cause* of growth. A distribution of income that favors high-income groups contributes to growth because high-income profit-earners save to obtain funds for expanding their enterprises. The more income they receive, the more they invest. Their saving and investment are essential for increasing productive capacity and thus bringing about output growth. In a famous quotation, Lewis says that "the central problem in the theory of economic development is to understand the process by which a community which was previously saving and investing 4 or 5 percent of its national income converts itself into an economy where voluntary saving is running about 12 to 15 percent of the national income or more."[21] The answer, he argues, lies with the 10 percent of the

21. W. Arthur Lewis, "Economic Development with Unlimited Supplies of Labor," *The Manchester School* 22 (May 1954): 155.

population which receives 40 percent or more of national income in labor-surplus countries. Growth occurs when they save more, not because their marginal propensity to save increases but because their aggregate income and share in total income go up. This happens because the profit share in income increases with the growth of the modern sector while the wage share remains constant.

Not only does inequality contribute to growth, but attempts to redistribute income "prematurely" run the risk of stifling economic growth. As in Ricardo's theory, anything that raises urban wages cuts into profits, and hence into savings, investment, and economic growth. Some of the factors that could have this effect include a rise in the price of food relative to the price of manufactured goods and actions by trade unions or government to bargain for or legislate increased modern-sector wages. This would gain little anyway because, as noted earlier, in poor countries there is not much to redistribute; everyone will benefit in time, the Lewis model suggests, if they wait for the development process to run its course. A temporary increase in inequality is the price that must be paid for these gains.

The implications of the labor-surplus model have been presented at some length because this has been the dominant paradigm for the past 30 years. It is far from universally accepted, however, and is subject to increasing challenge today. Several questions have been raised about the model. Will the capitalists actually save or will they indulge in luxury consumption? If they do save, will they necessarily invest at home or will they seek higher rates of return abroad? How fast will the capitalist (modern) sector absorb labor, particularly since it may be using capital-intensive technology imported from the developed countries and inappropriate to the factor endowment of a poor labor-surplus economy? (See Chapter 8 for discussion of this issue.) Finally, can governments in today's developing countries afford to wait for the accumulation process to work and for the benefits of growth eventually to be distributed throughout the society, or do poverty, population growth, and political instability require interventions to redistribute income sooner?

There are probably no firm, categorical answers to these important questions. Some capitalists will save and invest their savings locally, while others will consume their high income or invest abroad. What they do probably depends on a complex set of factors relating to the characteristics of the upper-income group in a partiuclar country and to the local investment climate. Nor does making the government the capitalist necessarily solve the problem. Although a few governments have been able to follow the Soviet model of rapid accumulation under a system of state capitalism, many others have proved unable to evolve the combination of discipline and incentives needed for publicly owned enterprises to generate surpluses (see Chapter 21).

STRATEGIES FOR GROWTH WITH EQUITY

Countries in Asia, Africa, and Latin America have demonstrated the difficulties of trying to redistribute before growing. "Socialism" has been a

popular slogan in many countries, connoting immediate redistribution through
direct controls on economic activity, elaborate social service networks,
consumer subsidies, reliance on cooperatives, and other populist devices.
Especially when undertaken by "soft states," which find it hard to enforce
their own mandates on the populace, these measures have generally failed
to achieve their redistributive objectives and have often stifled economic
growth. Burma, Ghana, and Jamaica are three examples among many.
Moreover, even when carried out relatively successfully, directly redistributive policies achieve their objective only in a rather limited sense. This
appears to have been the case, for example, in the Peruvian "national revolution" of the 1970s, which redistributed income to the urban working
class but left the poorest elements of society (Andean peasants, mainly of
indigenous origin) comparatively untouched. Many similar cases could be
cited.

Is there then no alternative to the stern trade-off between growth and
equality postulated by Lewis? Contemporary development thinking and
experience have in fact suggested three alternative models. If Lewis's classical model may be characterized as "grow first, then redistribute," the
alternatives could be described as a radical "redistribute first, then grow"
model and two reformist models: "redistribution with growth" and "basic
human needs."

Redistribute First, Then Grow

The radical model is epitomized by the experience of the Asian socialist
economies, especially the People's Republic of China. Socialist development in these countries began with the expropriation of capitalists and
landlords. Their property was then either subdivided among small-scale
producers, or more often, placed under some system of collective ownership. Confiscation has two kinds of effects on income distribution. The
immediate impact is to eliminate the property income of the previous owner
and assign this income either to the state or to the new owners of the subdivided property. This can have a substantial impact on income distribution
if the amount of profit or rent involved is large. In the longer run, however,
the second effect of confiscation can be even more important. This effect
works through the productivity of the confiscated asset (factory, farm, etc.)
under its new ownership and management. If the asset is managed as efficiently, or more efficiently, than under the prior ownership, then the redistributive effect holds up over the long run. If, however, the asset is less
productive under the new arrangement, then some of the redistributive effect
is dissipated. The old owner has lost the property income, but the new
owners have not benefitted proportionately. The management of a confiscated asset is thus an important determinant of its redistributive effect.

Countries that pursue a radical pattern of development are not exempted
from the need to amass a surplus and reinvest it productively if they wish
to grow. Development in the Soviet Union, which followed a basic-indus-
try strategy, involved a continuous effort to hold down consumption and
squeeze a surplus out of the general population, particularly the peasants.
Inequality was limited because most property income accrued to the state,

but the system is currently under fire because it has not succeeded in providing substantial increases in the consumption standards of the Soviet people.

The People's Republic of China tried to follow a more-balanced development pattern. By balancing the emphasis on heavy industry with attention to smaller scale, decentralized, and more labor-intensive production units—by "walking on two legs," as the Chinese say—and by not stinting on basic human services, China was able to achieve a more-equitable pattern of development than was achieved by the Soviet Union, and in a much poorer country.

By the late 1980s dissatisfaction with the radical approach to economic development had become nearly universal. In the Soviet Union, Gorbachev launched *perestroika* (restructuring), an attempt to introduce market principles into the Soviet economy. The Chinese government also experimented with freer markets; it shifted the responsibility for farm production decisions from collectives to families and permitted foreign investors to establish factories in some regions. These reforms dramatically accelerated production growth, but they also widened economic inequalities, which created political strains. The future of economic liberalization in China is currently in doubt after popular demands for democracy were answered by the crackdown which followed the Tienanmin Square crisis of June 1989.

The Chinese Communists contend that their development experience has little to teach other countries that operate under different social systems. It is true that some features of the Chinese approach are probably available only to a strong regime that gained power through a revolution. Yet a modified version of the redistribute-then-develop approach has been used in Taiwan and South Korea, where rural landholdings were redistributed shortly after World War II, and development has proceeded rapidly and comparatively equitably.

Redistribution with Growth

The desire to avoid both the extremes of concentrated industrial development as depicted by the Lewis model and radical restructuring of asset ownership has naturally led to a search for a middle way—**redistribution with growth,** as a study sponsored by the World Bank called it. Is there, in other words, a way in which the gains from economic growth can be redistributed, so that over time the income distribution gradually improves—or at least does not worsen—as growth proceeds?

The basic idea of redistribution with growth (RWG) is that government policies should influence the pattern of development in such a way that low-income producers (in most countries, located primarily in agriculture and small-scale urban enterprises) will see improved earning opportunities and simultaneously receive the resources necessary to take advantage of them. According to the World Bank study group, seven types of policy instruments could be employed to this end: (1) measures to alter the prices of labor and capital, to encourage the employment of unskilled labor; (2) "dynamic redistribution" of assets by directing investment to areas in which the poor may be owners of assets, such as land or small shops; (3) greater education to improve literacy, skills, and access to the modern economy; (4) more progressive taxation; (5) public provision of consumption goods, such as basic foods, to the poor; (6) intervention in commodity markets to aid poor producers and consumers; and (7) development of new technologies that will help make low-income workers more productive. All these policy possibilities are discussed in other chapters of this book.

The way in which these elements could be combined into an effective national policy package will naturally vary with a country's circumstances. A rural-based, equity-oriented development strategy is often proposed for large, predominantly rural countries such as India.[22] For these countries, it is argued, the time required for the modern sector to soak up all the surplus labor existing in the traditional sector would be far too long for any reasonable standard of equity to be achieved, or political stability to be maintained. A strategy emphasizing rural development, it is hoped, will bring about a much more equitable pattern of development than could ever be attained through emphasis on urban and industrial growth. (Rural development is discussed in Chapter 18.)

On the other hand, countries in which the modern sector is large relative to the traditional sector face a less severe trade-off. These countries can hope to have an integrated, modern economy in a much shorter period and in the meantime have a much larger surplus available to redistribute to the traditional sector through social services and rural development projects.

The RWG approach has attracted a lot of interest among those who want to see the welfare of the third-world poor improve but wish to avoid violent social revolution. Indeed the reader may note that many of the ideas included in the RWG package are treated sympathetically in this book. In practice, the RWG approach is the one used by most developing-country governments that regard poverty reduction as a serious policy objective. Yet one must accept that the changes brought about by such a strategy will occur slowly in most countries. Development is usually a gradual business, and even the changes in equality and poverty that were projected by the World Bank's study group, which was intellectually and emotionally committed to the approach, struck many readers as disappointingly small and gradual.

Basic Human Needs

Pessimism about how fast economic development, even if it is poverty-focused, can improve the well-being of the poor in most LDCs is a factor contributing to interest in the **basic human needs** (BHN) approach. Although advocates of RWG and BHN share the same objectives, they differ on the best means of achieving them. While RWG stresses increases in the productivity and purchasing power of the poor, BHN emphasizes the provision of public services, along with entitlements to the poor to make sure they get access to the services provided.

The BHN strategy aims at providing several basic commodities and ser-

---

22. For example, see John Mellor, *The New Economics of Growth. A Strategy for India and the Developing World* (Ithaca, N.Y.: Cornell University Press, 1976).

vices to the poor: staple foods, water and sanitation, health care, primary and nonformal education, and housing. The strategy includes two important elements. First, it requires finance to ensure that these basic needs can be provided at costs that the poor can afford. Second, it includes service networks to distribute these services in forms appropriate for consumption by the poor, especially in areas where the poor live.

The possibility of using fiscal policy to ameliorate poverty is discussed in Chapter 12. Redistribution of income through a combination of progressive taxation and public expenditures on social service programs has been an important part of twentieth-century reform movements in western industrial countries. The potential of this form of redistribution for less-developed countries used to be downplayed because the public sector is smaller in these countries and thus has less revenue-raising power; because the government pursues multiple objectives in its tax and expenditure policies and thus cannot devote itself wholeheartedly to redistribution; and because there are many difficulties of identifying, designing, and implementing public consumption and investment projects that can affect the incomes of the poor. However, there is a more positive side to the picture. Many LDCs now collect 20 percent or more of the GNP in government revenues. While the room for progressive taxation is often limited in developing countries, their tax systems can at least be made less regressive, even when direct (income) taxes are paid by only a small fraction of the population. Indirect taxes, such as customs duties, excises, turnover taxes, and sales taxes with exemptions, can lend a modest element of progressivity. Finally, much can be done on the expenditure side of the budget to improve the distribution of benefits from public services. Some of these possibilities will be discussed in Chapters 9 and 10, which deal with education and health.

For BHN programs to redistribute income, services must be offered on a subsidized basis. Otherwise redistribution will not work because the poor will either spend too much of their meager income on the services offered or be deterred by high user charges and not take advantage of them at all. If the poor do not consume the services offered, the income transfer can be perverse. In many countries, for example, government-run universities admit selectively only the well-qualified secondary school graduates, yet charge low fees, and thus subsidize the well-to-do. For the poor to be reached, appropriate forms of service must be emphasized: primary schools instead of universities, village clinics instead of intensive-care units in urban hospitals. Second, the system must be extended to the poor in their villages and urban slums. There must actually be schools and clinics, teachers and primary health workers, and they must work where the poor live. So far most LDC social service networks have not met this challenge, although there are some honorable exceptions.

Much of the appeal of BHN derives from its link to the notion of investment in human capital. Many kinds of education, health, and other social expenditures can improve the quality of human resources. When such expenditures are directed particularly toward the poor, as for instance in primary education or rural community health programs, they become ways to reduce poverty by increasing the productivity of the poor.

The World Bank's review of the problem of third-world poverty in its
World Development Report 1990 spotlights two basic actions for poverty reduction: policies to increase the productivity of the main resource owned by poor—their labor—and the provision of basic social services to the poor. This supports the importance of satisfying basic needs as a complement to a RWG-influenced strategy, but not as an alternative. Countries that are not achieving economic growth usually find it extremely difficult to satisfy basic human needs.

Structural Adjustment and the Poor

Many of the countries in sub-Saharan Africa, Latin America, and elsewhere that experienced slow economic growth, or none at all, in the 1980s have undertaken programs of "structural adjustment" in cooperation with the IMF and World Bank. As explained in Chapter 5, these countries have agreed to make major policy changes—correcting macroeconomic imbalances and reforming macro and sectoral policies—in exchange for external assistance. The transitional costs of these programs—for example, the loss of consumer and producer subsidies—can be substantial, and critics charge that they fall disproportionately on the poor. The impact of structural adjustment on the children of the poor was documented by a group of analysts assembled by UNICEF, the United Nations Children's Fund. This group called for "adjustment with a human face," a set of policies that would permit growth to resume, raise the productivity of the poor, improve the equity and efficiency of social services, compensate the poor for deficits in nutrition and health services during adjustment periods of limited duration, and improve monitoring of the conditions of effected low-income groups, particularly children.[23] "Adjustment with a human face" can be regarded as an adaptation of the BHN and RWG ideas to fit the circumstances of the 1980s, especially in sub-Saharan Africa.

While macroeconomic adjustment programs can undoubtedly be carried out in ways that give greater attention to the plight of the poor, the analysis of this chapter suggests that a more fundamental solution to the problem of poverty in third-world countries that have not been growing is a resumption of economic growth itself, combined with the provision of basic social services to the poor and policies that seek to increase their participation in the development process.

Growth and Equity: Key Policy Issues

Probably the single most promising way of achieving greater equity during growth under the reformist approach is to give greater emphasis to employment creation. By appropriate price incentives and other measures to absorb more labor in relatively productive forms of employment, the inequality generated by the Lewis-type employment shift can be mitigated and the labor surplus can be eliminated in a shorter time, as discussed in detail in Chapter 8.

23. See Giovanni Andrea Cornia, Richard Jolly, and Frances Stewart, eds, *Adjustment with a Human Face*, 2 vol. (New York: Oxford University Press (Clarendon), 1987).

The other touchstone of equitable growth is the relationship between the prices of rural and urban outputs. If farm prices are held down to depress urban wages and increase the investible surplus, then the majority of the poor who live in the rural areas and depend mainly on agriculture for a living will suffer. (There are also likely to be food supply problems; see Chapter 18.) Of course, if agricultural prices rise too high, growth will be choked off. But an equity-focused strategy rules out the squeeze-the-farmer approach that has often been attempted in the past and remains in effect in some LDCs (for example, many in Africa) today.

Finally, one can ask whether governments of less-developed countries will in fact take advantage of these opportunities to reduce inequality arising during the course of economic growth. This is an important question of political economy. Marxists argue that governments are controlled by particular social classes and act in the best interests of those classes. Certainly, many third-world governments are heavily influenced by civilian or military elites and for this reason are much less prone to egalitarian reform in their actions than in their verbal pronouncements. But political motivations are perhaps more mixed than the Marxists believe. Some governments may be inclined to make limited reforms for essentially conservative reasons: to forestall upheavals or demands for more radical changes. Others may be motivated toward reform by a different kind of political incentive: in countries where ethnic, tribal, or religious distinctions form an important basis for political activity, it may not be the rich but rather a large, less-wealthy social group whose interests are primarily reflected in government policy. In such cases—for example, the Malays of Malaysia—ambitious redistributive programs may be launched even by relatively conservative governments.

5

Guiding Development: Markets Versus Controls

Market forces can propel the processes of development described in the last three chapters. But skillful policies can accelerate these changes and virtually all governments have attempted to push development faster than market forces might have allowed. Two sets of policy tools are available. The first depends on a **capitalist** or **market economy** and its competitive energies, but tries to make the market work more efficiently and comprehensively. The second rejects the autonomous, self-regulating nature of a market economy and substitutes government controls, resulting in a *socialist* or **command economy.** In this chapter we compare these two very different systems for guiding development and then show why and how governments have moved away from controls toward market-based policy tools in the last decade or so.

MANAGING DEVELOPMENT

From World War II until the 1980s, capitalism and socialism competed for adherents throughout the world, nowhere more intensely than in the devel-

102

GUIDING
DEVELOPMENT:
MARKETS
VERSUS
CONTROLS
(Ch. 5)

oping countries. Neither of these systems was ever pure. All market economies were managed by their governments and for that reason were sometimes labeled **mixed economies.** And all command economies were tempered by unregulated and often illegal markets. In the 1980s even the socialist countries began adopting market systems, and by the end of the decade the command economy was rapidly disappearing. Debates about economic management still range over a continuum of market mechanisms versus controls, but largely within the context of a mixed economy. Still, it is useful to keep in mind the capitalist-socialist dichotomy that marked the postwar world.

Market Economies

Most countries depend on market mechanisms, rather than government controls, to allocate most goods, services, and factors of production. Three arguments favor market allocation. First, the market can allocate thousands of different products among consumers, according to their preferences, and thousands of productive inputs among producers and get the maximum output from available inputs.[1] These complex allocative tasks, if handled by the state, are an enormous government responsibility with attendant high costs for decision making and control. Second, markets are frequently more flexible than governments and better able to adapt to changing conditions and automatically provide incentives for growth, innovation, and structural change that governments either cannot manage or are slow to achieve. Third, reliance on markets encourages private economic activity and disperses economic power. Economic pluralism, in turn, is one element tending to encourage democratic government and individual liberties.

Despite these substantial advantages, there are some circumstances in which markets do not perform well on their own. Economists have identified a number of cases, called **market failures,** where the market system, left to itself, may not operate efficiently.

1. Modern economies are marked by growing concentration and **monopoly** or **oligopoly power,** where one or a few sellers gain control of a market. In developing countries, **economies of scale** (the decline of unit costs as output rises) may be so large relative to market size that monopoly is inevitable in some industries, whereas oligopoly is the rule in many others. Truly competitive markets, where no one seller or buyer has any influence over market prices, typically exist in agriculture, fishing, handicraft industries, construction, transportation, retail trade, personal services, and sometimes banking. In much of mining, manufacturing, utilities, airlines, communications, and wholesale trade, monopoly or oligopoly are common. One or a few firms are able to raise their prices, and consequently their profits, by restricting output, so that consumers pay more and obtain less than they would in a competitive market. In large economies, governments can try to limit the exercise of monopoly pricing in some sectors by

---

1. The principles of market economies underlying these allocations are familiar to those who have taken an introductory course in microeconomics.

regulating the size of firms and breaking up the largest ones. In all econo-

mies, competing imports—actual or potential—curtail monopoly power in
manufacturing industries and in some services by forcing domestic firms to
meet competition from abroad. However, this antimonopoly weapon is seldom used in developing countries. Price controls are often employed instead.
If government cannot prevent monopoly pricing, it can capture some of the
benefits from monopolists by taxing the resulting profits at high rates.

2. **External economies** are the benefits of a project, such as a hydroelectric dam, that are enjoyed by people not connected with the project, such
as the downstream farmer whose production rises because the dam prevents floods. External economies are important benefits in many **overhead**
investments, such as dams, roads, railroads, and irrigation schemes. Although
in principle the beneficiaries could be charged for all external benefits, in
practice they cannot be. It may be difficult and costly to control access to
the facilities and difficult even to identify the beneficiaries or the extent to
which they benefit. Hence a private investor would not be able to realize
revenue from this aspect of the project's output. Because private investors
cannot easily charge for externalities and because such projects take large
investments with long repayment periods, private investors are unlikely to
undertake them. Governments do so instead. Another kind of external
economy is central to the balanced-growth strategy discussed in Chapter
3. If several industries are started at the same time, the resulting labor force
may be large enough to create an internal market for the output of all industries and backward linkages may create adequate markets for producer goods
industries. But a single private investor who depended on these newly created markets would not invest without strong assurances that the other
investments would take place simultaneously. Government must intervene
to ensure that these external benefits can be realized.

3. **External diseconomies** are costs not borne by the firm. The pollution of
air and water is a widely recognized problem in the industrial world and
increasingly so in developing countries. Polluters would bear all the costs
of reduced emissions and effluents, but they benefit only as average members of the population of the affected area, so have little incentive to control pollution on their own. The same situation arises with **common resources,**
such as forests, fisheries, or open grazing land, that can be used by many
people who do not own them. For example, the first cattle to graze on open
range land find abundant grass, so costs to the herders are low. But as more
cattle graze, there is less grass for each and herders must go further afield
to find it. Herding costs rise for everyone, so society as a whole faces
higher marginal costs than do individual herders. The *tragedy of the commons* is that overgrazing so degrades the rangeland that fewer and fewer
cattle can be fed there, yet each private herder continues to have an incentive to graze cattle on the open range. Both pollution and common resources
require some kind of intervention by government, preferably a tax but frequently control over access. This forces private producers to bear costs
closer to the social cost and consequently to reduce pollution or common
resource exploitation to levels closer to the social optimum.

4. Markets may not accommodate the changes in economic structure
required for development. The most frequently cited example is the **infant**

104

GUIDING
DEVELOPMENT:
MARKETS
VERSUS
CONTROLS
(Ch. 5)

industry, one brand-new to a society, whose productivity increases and whose costs fall over time because managers and workers are "learning by doing." Although the industry can become profitable over several years, investors may be too short-sighted to finance the new firms. This can justify a **protective tariff** (a tax on competing imports) or **initial subsidy** (where the government bears some start-up costs) to make an infant industry more profitable in the short run. But the long-run gains in productivity may only be realized if the tariff or subsidy is gradually reduced and the new industry is eventually forced to compete with imports (or other domestic firms).

The infant-industry argument has even greater force for the economy as a whole because experience in any industry creates a more skilled and productive labor force and makes economic activity more attractive for investors. This "infant economy" phenomenon is closely akin to the balanced-growth strategy because it also depends on external economies: as trained, experienced workers leave one employer to work for another, the second firm benefits from the training provided by the first. Sectorwide (or even economywide) protective tariffs could be justified by this effect, although a devalued exchange rate combined with offsetting taxes on traditional exports would be a superior intervention, for reasons that will be explored in Part 4.

5. **Underdeveloped institutions** exclude large numbers from the market. In developed economies consumers "vote" with their dollars for the goods the economy should produce. But in developing economies, remoteness, poverty, and illiteracy prevent many subsistence farmers, rural laborers, and their families from "voting" on many goods and in money markets, so these groups have little influence on the types of goods and services supplied. Special efforts are required to bring them into the monetary economy. Even for those in the monetary economy there is **inadequate information** about markets and products, so many consumers remain ignorant about the goods and services being offered, workers know little about job opportunities, and producers cannot easily learn about changing market conditions. Perhaps the best example is in banking, which generally remains urban-based and employs standards of services, modeled on Western banking methods, that exclude most of the rural and much of the poor urban population. Similarly, investors, producers and traders find it difficult to hedge against the **risks** of doing business in changing circumstances, because financial, commodity, and insurance markets are underdeveloped or missing altogether. Government may have to encourage or establish some of these missing institutions to help markets function better.

6. Economywide markets for labor, credit, and foreign exchange do not always adjust rapidly enough to balance supply and demand as conditions change, and **macroeconomic imbalances** characterize every modern economy. Wages that adjust slowly, low short-run elasticities of supply or demand, and misinformed expectations cause shortages and surpluses that can require governmnet interventions such as monetary management, fiscal policy, exchange rate adjustments, and incomes policies. We will hear more about such **macroeconomic management** tools through this book.

7. To a considerable extent market economies require intervention not

only because of inherent market failures but also because societies impose on them **national goals** that even well-functioning markets cannot satisfy. Establishing policies that favor poorer majorities over entrepreneurially accomplished minorities is one example. If ethnic Chinese in Malaysia and Indonesia, or ethnic Indians and Pakistanis ("Asians") in Kenya, already dominate the production and distribution system of those countries, then unguided economic growth is likely to improve their relative position over time. To expand the role of the indigenous majority and allow it to catch up requires government intervention. Markets can be very effective in stimulating rapid growth that automatically generates demands for the output of small farmers and the self-employed, creates jobs to absorb poor workers, and generally helps to relieve poverty. Nevertheless, these market forces are often led by—and hence favor—people and firms that are already successful. Thus market-oriented growth may concentrate incomes initially, as we saw in the discussion of Kuznets' proposition in Chapter 4, even while relieving poverty. It is only after growth has been rapid for some time that the income distribution begins to equalize. But the reduction of inequality is often considered too urgent to await the operation of market forces, and intervention is considered necessary. This may be true for other goals as well, such as greater employment creation or reduced dependence on foreign goods, capital, technology, and skills. Even accelerated growth, typically served well by market economies, may require intervention if savings levels are initially low.

These market failures provide some of the reasons that governments intervene in market economies. The particular interventions chosen are not always ideal. Worse, they often work against the goals they are supposed to achieve. The most egregious examples will be explored in later chapters: legislation on wages, pensions, and job security that concentrate incomes and reduce employment; interest rate ceilings that reduce and bias investment; tariffs and import controls that intensify dependence on imports; and food price controls that discourage farm production. Nevertheless, because markets are imperfect and governments have political goals that markets must serve, intervention is the rule. Usually interventions work best and avoid undesired side effects if they are aimed to improve the functioning of markets and to work indirectly through prices to alter supply and demand, rather than operating directly through controls. A central aim of development policy in a mixed economy is to structure these interventions to achieve their aims with minimal incidental costs.

Socialist Economies

Socialism can be defined as governmnet ownership and control of the means of production. Whether a country is socialist or not is a matter of degree. The clear examples have been the Communist countries—the Soviet Union, the Eastern European countries until 1989, China, North Korea, Vietnam, and Cuba—in which government ownership and control have dominated industry and services and strongly influenced agriculture. Some Western

106

GUIDING
DEVELOPMENT:
MARKETS
VERSUS
CONTROLS
(Ch. 5)

European countries, such as Sweden and Great Britain, have for a time been governed by socialist political parties that nationalized key industries, and many other countries have large state-owned enterprise sectors, but these economies retain the market character of mixed economies.

What distinguishes the Soviet and other command economies is government control over production. Whereas *in mixed economies the market sets prices* as signals for production and consumption, *in Soviet-type economies central planners control the quantities* produced and consumed. Official prices become irrelevant to production and investment decisions. But prices, along with quantity rationing, still regulate demand, because no government is able to give directives to each household about its complete consumption basket. Prices also serve an accounting function; they determine how much income is transferred from household to government-owned producers (and vice versa, through wage payments), among producers, and from producers to the government.

In order to manage a Soviet-style economy, it is necessary to begin with a plan. Typically, governments have operated with one-year plans for controlling current output and five-year plans to guide major investment projects. The ways in which the Soviet Union and, until the 1980s, China drew up plans are not radically different from the procedures followed in mixed developing economies, as described in the next chapter. What separates a centrally planned economy from the others is the way in which plans are carried out. Once broad goals and quantitative targets for individual industries have been decided, planners give direct orders to firms on how much to produce and the quantity of inputs that can be used in production. Firms cannot buy the necessary inputs in a market, but must apply to government organizations for the delivery of needed items. The firm must pay for these items, but willingness to pay does not determine whether it gets them. Only if the plan says it should receive a certain amount of steel, for instance, will that amount actually be delivered.

In reality, the Soviet-type system does not follow the plan quite so rigidly. A variety of both legal and illegal devices, including markets, provide some flexibility. Nevertheless many allocations that are handled by impersonal market forces in mixed economies are decided by the commands of bureaucrats in centrally planned economies. The command system therefore needs large numbers of people trained to manage the complex tasks of deciding which firms ought to get particular inputs. Hundreds and even thousands of different kinds of inputs must be parceled out to tens of thousands of individual enterprises. If the inputs go to the wrong enterprises, those enterprises will have surpluses piling up in their warehouses while other enterprises will operate below capacity. Large inventories are characteristic of this kind of system.

The advantage of the command system is that it gives central planners a high degree of control over the economy and, with that control, the power to restructure key sectors. The system, however, does not put a high premium on the productive use of resources. The problems of inefficiency increase if people with skills adequate to manage such a system are in short supply, as is often the case in developing countries. Even though China had sufficient numbers of such people or was able to train them with Soviet help in the 1950s, by the late 1970s China began to experiment with greater use of market forces in order to reduce inefficiency.

The leaders who designed the Soviet economic system began from the premise that prices determined by the market could not be relied on to guide production. This basic view of the market was reinforced by the pronounced emphasis in the Soviet Union, and later in China, on machinery and steel as leading sectors in their industrialization programs. Since neither economy had much of a steel or machinery industry to begin with, planners were faced with an extreme form of the infant industry problem and with very large external economies, because the main demand for steel was from a machinery sector that did not yet exist. In general the price system is less effective when the change in economic structure being contemplated is rapid and massive. What the Soviet Union desired in the 1930s when it introduced this system, and what China also wanted in the 1950s, was precisely such a rapid and massive restructuring of economies that were fundamentally agricultural into ones that were based on machinery and steel.

Recent history has demonstrated the limitations of the centrally planned economy. It was effective in mobilizing resources in the early days of communism: few nations have ever industrialized as rapidly as the Soviet Union. But the Soviet system has not been efficient in allocating the myriad goods, services, and factors of production among thousands of competing uses. It has been particularly ineffective in producing consumer goods. And, once these economies became more industrialized, the command system was unable to adjust easily to changes in the economic environment. Widespread discontent by workers and consumers in the 1980s began to force Communist countries to reform their economies, a process that was overtaken dramatically by the revolutionary political changes in Eastern Europe in 1989. Most Eastern European economies are now moving toward the greater use of market mechanisms. The 1990s is the stage for a massive, radical historical experiment in economic reform, one without precedent.

Few developing countries other than China have had the administrative and decision-making capacity to control production through central planning. Only North Korea, Vietnam, and Cuba have tried. In the 1970s, Tanzania, avowedly socialist, placed the majority of modern industries under public ownership, nationalized much wholesale and retail trade, and attempted to socialize its agriculture. Nevertheless the government did not try to set output targets and most units, public or private, continued to respond to market-determined prices. Interventions in setting these prices, though substantial, were not markedly greater in socialist Tanzania than in many nonsocialist developing countries such as Bolivia, Kenya, and Indonesia. India based its first development plan on Soviet models that emphasized investment in capital goods and other heavy industries and espoused public ownership of these sectors. Yet even when India's economy was ostensibly socialist, less output was produced in public enterprises that in avowedly capitalist South Korea.

108 THE MARCH TOWARD MARKETS

GUIDING
DEVELOPMENT:
MARKETS
VERSUS
CONTROLS
(Ch. 5)

It is clear from the perspective of the 1990s that all kinds of governments—capitalist and socialist, industrial and developing—have been reducing the scope of controls and adopting market mechanisms instead to guide their economies. What explains the popularity of controls before reforms became common? And what explains this historic march away from controls toward market mechanisms?

The Appeal of Controls

We have already given two reasons that governments might want to resort to controls to hasten development. Controls may be essential if policy makers are impatient for large structural changes, as were the leaders of the Soviet Union before World War II and China after 1949. And within a mixed economy, controls can be used to correct for market failures that might otherwise retard development or yield politically and socially undesirable outcomes. After World War II, a confluence of historical factors pushed many governments of developing countries to employ controls rather than market mechanisms as the means to accelerate economic development.

The Great Depression of the 1930s had destroyed confidence in market capitalism. The antidote to depression offered by John Maynard Keynes—and accepted for decades by most economists and governments—was active intervention to stimulate the economy through fiscal policy. Price controls and quantity rationing helped guide the U.S. economy through the Second World War. After the war, European recovery was substantially aided by the U.S. Marshall Plan. The U.S. government not only provided vast amounts of capital (equivalent to 1.5 percent of its GNP over four years), but also encouraged governments of war-torn economies to plan for public investment in postwar recovery.

In Asia and Africa, economies had been highly regulated by the colonial powers before and after the war. After independence in 1947, India's new leaders followed the interventionist tendencies of Fabian socialism and the British Raj to a planned and regulated economy. As other countries in Asia and Africa emerged from colonialism over the next two decades, many of them emulated India. The Soviet Union's rapid industrialization under communism also impressed the leaders of these newly emerging nations. The older nations of Latin America, especially Argentina, Brazil, and Mexico, had taken advantage of the war to build their own industries to supply goods once imported from the United States. After the war, Argentine dictator Juan Peron and others built on this base a highly protected manufacturing system that spurred industrial growth for a time. Even in capitalist United States, as in Western Europe, government intervention in markets was the norm, from the New Deal of President Franklin Roosevelt during the depressed 1930s to the Great Society of President Lyndon Johnson in the 1960s.

Economic thought encouraged these tendencies. Chapter 3 described Paul

Rosenstein-Rodan's 1943 theory of the big push and Albert Hirschman's
1958 retort, the strategy of unbalanced growth. Both strategies assumed
that markets would not work adequately for rapid development and both
invited some form of government intervention. Latin American economist
Raul Prebisch and European economist Hans Singer were influential in
arguing that world demand could not grow fast enough to accommodate
the rapid growth of food and raw material exports, on which most developing countries depended.[2] This **export pessimism** was taken as strong support for a strategy of **import substitution,** which required government
intervention to protect local manufacturers. Perhaps the most influential
article of all was W. Arthur Lewis's 1954 theory of the labor-surplus economy, also explained in Chapter 3. Though Lewis did not advocate intervention, one implication of his theory was the need to transform a developing
economy rapidly away from traditional, stagnant agriculture towards dynamic
industry. This, as the Soviet Union and China appeared to show, could be
accomplished by a command economy. These treatises and others like them
set the tone for development economics at least until the mid-1960s. Even
if national leaders did not know about these works, their economic advisers
were strongly influenced by them.

These historic and intellectual tendencies influenced many governments
to try a range of interventions in search of economic development. By the
early 1970s, the vast majority of third-world countries could be characterized as mixed economies with a strong dose of controls. A development
adviser, flying into almost any developing country picked at random, could
expect to find high protective tariffs and quantitative restrictions over
imports, strict controls over foreign exchange dealings, ceilings on interest
rates and floors under wages, government-set prices of vital commodities
from food grains to fuel, restrictions on private investment, many government-owned firms displacing private companies, harassment of people
operating in the informal sector, and many other interventions.

Resurgence of the Market

Most of these interventions are still visible in the developing world, but
they are no longer so ubiquitous and many countries have begun to shed
many of these controls. The pronounced trend of the 1980s was toward
economic reform that substituted market mechanisms for controls in many
aspects of economic policy. No corner of the world has been immune.
Deregulation was a byword of economic policy in the United States under
President Jimmy Carter in the 1970s, although the approach was later associated with President Ronald Reagan. Western Europe moved toward open,
integrated markets throughout the 1980s and headed for full economic integration in 1992. The roll call of developing countries undertaking market

2. United Nations (by Raul Prebisch), *The Economic Development of Latin America and
its Principal Problems* (Lake Success, N.Y.: United Nations, 1950) and; Hans W. Singer,
"The Distribution of Trade between Investing and Borrowing Countries," *American Economic Review* 40 (1950): 470–485. See also Ragnar Nurkse, *Equilibrium Growth and the World
Economy* (Cambridge, Mass.: Harvard University Press, 1961).

110

GUIDING
DEVELOPMENT:
MARKETS
VERSUS
CONTROLS
(Ch. 5)

reforms, including Mexico, Chile, Bolivia, Ghana, Kenya, Tanzania, Bangladesh, and Indonesia, grew throughout the decade. In the communist world, China led the way after the death of Mao Zedong in 1976 and the return to power of Deng Xiaoping in 1978, though it has slowed the pace of reform since the events of Tiananmen Square in 1989. The explosions in Eastern Europe at the end of 1989 were fueled by a reform process, both economic and and political, that had been building pressure for several years, starting in Poland and Hungary and spreading, for a time, to the Soviet Union under President Mikhail Gorbachev.

Many factors combined to stimulate market reforms in the developing world. First was a series of negative causes: controls and other market interventions just did not work very well. Protection and import substitution spurred industrial growth at first, but then industrial development sputtered in country after country. Price interventions generally had unintended consequences: high protective barriers bred inefficient manufacturing; interest rate ceilings suppressed the evolution of financial systems, depressed monetary savings, and encouraged unproductive investment; minimum wages, if they had any impact at all, stifled employment growth and exacerbated inequalities; and ceilings on food prices and taxes on agricultural exports discouraged farmers and retarded productivity growth in agriculture.

Controls by government engendered political and bureaucratic reactions by private entrepreneurs and managers, instead of the innovative and competitive behavior needed for sustained development. Regulations created higher-than-necessary profits, which economists call **rents,** for those able to gain favorable treatment from bureaucrats or to evade the rules. Widespread corruption and other forms of **rent-seeking** diverted the energies of entrepreneurs, investors, managers, and traders from productive activities, wasted scarce resources, and reduced economic growth.[3] The almost universal proliferation of public enterprises extended ineffectual bureaucratic behavior into activities that private enterprises could have handled more effectively and more efficiently.

The consequences of these interventions became apparent toward the end of the 1960s. In 1970, influential studies by economists at Williams College and Oxford University chronicled the failures of import substitution and all the interventions that generally accompanied it.[4] The explosive rise of oil prices in the 1970s, then their precipitate fall in the 1980s, and the accompanying accumulations of unserviceable debt, exposed the failures of some interventionist development strategies. These swings in economic fortune required flexible, creative responses from all economies. But regimes mired in controls were too rigid to cope with the unstable economic environment.

The near stagnation of many developing economies in the 1970s and 1980s

---

3. Anne O. Krueger, "The Political Economy of Rent-Seeking," *American Economic Review* 64, no. 3 (1974).

4. Henry J. Bruton, "The Import Substitution Strategy of Economic Development," *The Pakistan Development Review* 10 (1970): 123–146, and Ian Little, Tibor Scitovsky, and Maurice Scott, *Industry and Trade in Some Developing Countries* (London: Oxford University Press, 1970).

stood in stark contrast to the rapid and sustained growth of four East Asian

newly industrialized countries during the same period. South Korea, Taiwan, Hong Kong, and Singapore, all of which grew by 8 to 10% a year for 20 years or more, provided the positive reasons for the conversion to economic reforms. Hong Kong and Singapore had economies governed largely by market forces. In South Korea and to a lesser degree Taiwan, however, government intervened forcefully. What these four had in common was a strategy of depending heavily on export growth to lead development. This outward-looking strategy is explored in Chapter 17. In essence, by inducing private firms to seek markets overseas, these countries took advantage of the large world market and simultaneously exposed their manufacturing firms to the discipline of competition on international markets. It was this competitive industrial base that permitted the four East Asian countries to sail through the economic crises of the 1970s and 1980s with relative ease.

Development economists of the **neoclassical school** began to promote the virtues of market-oriented, outward-looking development even before the oil and debt crises. Chicago economist Theodore Schultz won his Nobel Prize partly for this work in the early 1960s showing that so-called traditional farmers were rational decision makers whose techniques were well-adapted to the conditions and constraints they faced. One implication was that market incentives, accompanied by new technologies, would induce farmers to change their methods and raise productivity.[5] The promise of a dynamic agriculture was realized with the coming of the Green Revolution in Asia. The 1970 studies of import substitution, mentioned above, suggested the obvious alternative strategy of more open, market-oriented economies. By the late 1970s, a series of country studies by trade economists Bela Balassa, Jagdish Bhagwati, and Anne Krueger had established a strong empirical case that outward-looking strategies work better than import substitution.[6] We will further explore the reasons for this in Chapters 16 and 17.

At the core of the argument for market-guided development is the proposition of neoclassical economics that markets create competition and competition stimulates the growth of productivity. The discussion of growth accounting in Chapter 3 showed how the growth of income per capita can be attributed to two sources: growing supplies of the productive factors, especially capital available to each worker, and increases in the productivity of all factors used in production. Rapid capital accumulation—high investment rates—have been achieved for sustained periods by both well-functioning market economies (Japan and the four newly industrialized countries of Asia) and command economies (the Soviet Union and China). But when it comes to raising the productivity of capital, labor, land, and

5. Theodore W. Schultz, *Transforming Traditional Agriculture* (New Haven, Conn.: Yale University Press, 1964).

6. Bela Balassa, "Exports and Economic Growth: Further Evidence," *Journal of Development Economics* 5, no. 2 (1978): 181–189; Jagdish Bhagwati, *Foreign Exchange Regimes and Economic Development: Anatomy and Consequences of Exchange Control Regimes* (Cambridge, Mass.: Ballinger Press, 1978); and Anne O. Krueger, *Foreign Exchange Regimes and Economic Development: Liberalization Attempts and Consequences* (Cambridge, Mass.: Ballinger Press, 1978).

112

GUIDING
DEVELOPMENT:
MARKETS
VERSUS
CONTROLS
(Ch. 5)

other resources **(factor productivity),** some market economies do quite well whereas command economies have a notoriously poor record. Among mixed economies, greater market orientation—less government intervention and more openness to world markets—appears to promote gains in factor productivity.

There are several reasons why this should be so. In market economies, competition and the profit motive force producers—farmers, industrial firms, service industries, and individual workers—to operate as efficiently as possible and to reduce costs (raise productivity) whenever they can. Those who cannot use their resources efficiently or cannot find profitable markets for their output earn less than others who can, and their businesses may fail. These individual attempts to operate more efficiently, compelled by market forces, translate into a more productive economy so long as any market failures are compensated. When market forces do not guide production decisions, the incentive for productivity gains is weaker. Price distortions draw labor, capital, and other factors into less-productive employment, for example from efficient export industries into protected import-substituting ones. Government regulations establish incentives for rent-seeking and bribery; entrepreneurs and managers then spend more time dealing with and influencing government officials and less time making their plants run more efficiently. Protection behind high tariffs, other import barriers, and investment restrictions insulates firms from competition, both foreign and domestic, and permits them to earn profits even when they use resources inefficiently. When governments themselves enter into production through state-owned enterprises, the profit motive of their managers is diluted by political and bureaucratic concerns: noneconomic goals are imposed by government; bureaucratic rules and procedures govern key decisions on investment, finance, and wages; and managers' careers often depend more on their ties to government leaders than on their firms' performances.

There is some empirical support for the proposition that markets, particularly the exposure of firms to competition in foreign markets, contribute to factor productivity growth. A recent cross-country comparison by economists Moshe Syrquin and Hollis Chenery suggests that outward orientation has some impact on the growth of both gross domestic product and total factor productivity.[7] The results for 106 countries are summarized in Table 5-1. For Syrquin and Chenery, outward orientation means that a country has a higher-than-average ratio of exports to GDP given its per capita income and population. They also distinguish between **primary-oriented** countries, which have higher-than-average shares of primary goods (agricultural and raw materials) exports to total exports, and **manufacturing-oriented** countries. Regardless of this classification, outward-oriented countries had significantly higher GDP growth rates than inward-oriented ones from 1950 to 1983 (column 1).

The impact on factor productivity is not so clear-cut, however. For primary-oriented countries, openness did lead to substantially higher produc-

7. Moshe Syrquin and Hollis B. Chenery, "Three Decades of Industrialization," *The World Bank Economic Review* 3, no. 2 (1989): 145–181.

TABLE 5–1 Impact of Outward Orientation on Growth[a]

	Countries	GDP growth 1950–83	Total factor productivity growth	
			1960–70	1970–82
Primary-oriented	55			
Inward-oriented	37	3.9	1.1	0.4
Outward-oriented	28	5.0	2.0	−0.2
Manufacturing-oriented	41			
Inward-oriented	23	4.7	2.2	0.2
Outward-oriented	18	5.5	2.4	0.9

[a] Growth rates in percent per year.
Source: Syrquin and Chenery, "Three Decades of Industrialization," *The World Bank Economic Review* 3, No. 2, 1989.

tivity growth during the relatively stable decade of the 1960s. During the 1970s, however, when oil prices forced major readjustments and other commodity prices first rose and then fell, all countries' productivity growth was much lower. The outward-oriented primary exporters then had lower productivity growth than their inward-oriented counterparts, perhaps because they had more severe adjustments to make. In contrast, there was little difference in productivity growth among manufacturing-oriented countries during the 1960s, but the outward-oriented economies did better when major adjustments were required in the 1970s. In manufacturing-oriented countries, where resource endowments matter less and trade strategies matter more, there seems a clear if moderate margin in favor of outward orientation.

The results are not dramatic, but this is not surprising. Openness is not the only factor contributing to productivity growth; entrepreneurial talent, educated workers, and cultural values are also important. Several countries that are open in the sense of having high ratios of exports to gross national income may lack other requirements for growth, whereas some inward-looking countries may have them in abundance. Under the circumstances, the apparently narrow differences in productivity growth in the Syrquin-Chenery data support the proposition that openness contributes to productivity growth. Economists believe that openness works because it introduces competition (as well as wider markets and the ability to attain economies from larger-scale production). Then, by extension, we conclude that markets, which create competition, also work to raise productivity.

IMPLEMENTING MARKET REFORMS

Over the past several decades, therefore, a strong case has been built favoring a greater role for market forces in the management of the economy. But how does a nation used to widespread government intervention wean itself from overuse of bureaucratic commands in favor of more market influence? Is it simply a matter of dismantling the government's role in the economy

114

GUIDING
DEVELOPMENT:
MARKETS
VERSUS
CONTROLS
(Ch. 5)

and allowing market forces to take over? Or do market-oriented reforms require a different role for government, not necessarily a lesser role?

To make the transition from a regulated economy to a well-functioning market economy, five conditions need to be met, each of which will be explored in greater depth in subsequent sections:

1. *Prices must become reasonably stable* and the macroeconomy should be close to equilibrium. Macroeconomic instability—large budget deficits, rampant inflation, and a severe drain on the balance of foreign payments—discourages productive activity and invites widespread government interference with market forces.

2. *Most goods and services must be bought and sold through market mechanisms,* and not allocated through administered arrangements such as import licensing, output quotas, ration shops, government agencies, and public enterprises. Most developing countries and all socialist countries allocate a significant share of goods and services through nonmarket mechanisms.

3. *There must be competition,* either within the domestic market or from abroad, if productivity gains are to be achieved. In some cases the economy is too small to sustain more than one firm in an industry and government restrictions on imports eliminate competition from foreign firms. In other instances there are several firms in the industry but their own collusion or government allocation of quotas for critical inputs effectively removes competitive pressure. Centrally planned economies favor monopolies in more industries in part because it makes planning easier.

4. *Relative prices should reflect relative scarcities* in the economy. It is possible to have a market system with highly distorted prices, but it is not possible to have an efficient market system under such circumstances. Price distortions in many developing economies are pervasive and "getting prices right" is a major objective of most market-oriented reforms.

5. *Firm managers, farmers, and other decision makers must be able and willing to respond to market signals.* Firms must maximize profits by increasing their sales or cutting their costs, or they must follow some rule that is a close approximation of profit maximization. Economists tend to assume that firms will maximize profits because it is in their own interest to do so. But in a world riddled with government interventions, profits are obtained by extracting greater subsidies, price supports, and the like from the government, not by increasing the economic efficiency of the firm.

These five transitional requirements incorporate two market failures discussed earlier: macroeconomic stability is in both lists and competition is the antidote to monopoly power. Other market failures are also relevant to reform. Prices that reflect relative scarcities suggest taxation or other corrections for external costs and benefits. And economies in transition from controls to market mechanisms are deficient in the market institutions, especially those for diversifying risk and conveying information, that are necessary to make markets work efficiently. Though essential to long-term development, corrections for these market failures are usually not addressed in transitional reforms and are mentioned only incidentally in the next sections.

Stabilization of the Macroeconomy

In theory a market can work while prices are rising rapidly. In practice price increases above a certain level will trigger government interventions in the form of general price freezes or specific price controls. If price controls are put in place without first curing the underlying causes of inflation, the result will be excess demand for the goods whose prices were frozen. To deal with this excess demand, the government either must introduce rationing or stand by while long lines form at shops selling the goods in short supply—an informal kind of rationing. Either way the goods end up being distributed by some nonmarket mechanism, through ration coupons or to those who are first in line and most willing to wait. In the Soviet Union it is normal for citizens to carry shopping bags with them at all times on the chance that some shop has just gotten a new supply of some scarce item. Under rationing, those who first obtain scarce goods frequently turn around and sell them in the **parallel or black market,** where prices are higher than in the official market and can exceed the prices that would prevail in an uncontrolled market.

What is the level of inflation that triggers this kind of intervention? The answer is in part political. Some societies such as those in South America are accustomed to very rapid inflation and rates of 20 or 30 percent a year are considered relatively stable. Other societies, China for example, consider any rate above 10 percent intolerable, whereas West Germany feels uncomfortable with inflation approaching 5 percent a year.

Inflation leads to distortions in relative prices and the decisions based on them. Groups that are organized to wield political power, such as unionized labor, large firms, the military, and civil servants, compete intensely to protect their shares of national income. The result is a distortion of relative prices away from scarcity values to reflect instead the outcome of these political struggles. Relative prices themselves become volatile, and this reduces the information they convey to participants in the economy. For example, **real interest rates** (interest rates corrected for inflation) often become negative and thus reduce the supply of long-term funds for investment. Exchange rates usually become **overvalued;** the central bank offers, for instance, too few pesos (the local currency) to people with dollars to sell; this discourages exports and encourages imports.

These distortions and the uncertainty about future rates of inflation cause people to acquire land, gold, and other assets whose prices will rise with inflation, rather than productive assets, or to transfer their financial wealth overseas. With rapid inflation, entrepreneurs and managers spend more time trying to profit from inflation and devote correspondingly less energy to producing more efficiently. After all, large and sustained productivity gains might reduce costs by 3 to 5 percent a year, not much compared with rates of inflation from 10s to 100s of percents a year.

Stabilization programs are designed to stem inflation and correct the other imbalances associated with it, notably deficits in the government budget and in the balance of foreign payments. Often the International Monetary Fund (IMF) works with the country to introduce a package of stabilization policies. At the core of the package is the notion that inflation is caused

116

GUIDING
DEVELOPMENT:
MARKETS
VERSUS
CONTROLS
(Ch. 5)

when the supply of money increases faster than the demand for it. To correct this and other imbalances, a typical program will contain some or all of the following remedies. (1) A reduction in the government's budget deficit, through higher taxes and reduced expenditure, is needed because deficits are financed either by money creation or by borrowing from private savers, which crowds out private investment. (2) To control growth of the money supply, restrictive targets are set for central bank credit to the government and the commercial banks. (3) The exchange rate may be devalued and thus raise the price of foreign exchange in domestic currency. This helps to correct a balance-of-payments deficit by stimulating exports and restraining the demand for imports. (4) Price controls may be removed, so that markets can reduce the distortions in relative prices; administered prices may be adjusted for the same reason. Interest rates, food prices, utility rates, and transport fares are often affected. (5) Targets are set for restraining wage increases. If wages increase faster than productivity, they push up the cost of production and thus contribute to inflation.[8]

When deficits in the budget or balance of payments occur, they must either be reduced through economic adjustment or be financed from overseas. To assist in financing deficits, the IMF may help the government to reschedule its foreign debt payments, especially those due to commercial banks. The IMF itself offers loans—called **standby credits**—for three to five years at moderate interest rates to help close the balance-of-payments gap. This is intended to ease the pains of stabilization by permitting the corrective measures to be less drastic than they would otherwise have to be. However, disbursement of the loan (as well as debt relief) is contingent on successful implementation of the measures designed to stabilize the economy. This *quid pro quo*—loans and debt relief in return for policy reform—is known as **conditionality.**

The IMF stabilization package is controversial. Most economists accept that imbalances, particularly budget deficits, have to be corrected and inflation curbed if growth and development are to be sustained. One issue, however, is the speed of adjustment. Stabilization is likely to require some rise in unemployment and a decline in income for some groups, although the imbalances themselves might have caused similar problems. The more abruptly these measures are enforced, the greater will be the dislocations. Yet a gradual implementation may undermine the government's credibility and make it more difficult to complete the stabilization.

A second issue is the effectiveness of reducing inflation by reducing budget deficits and growth in the money supply. Orthodox economists believe that inflation is partly or substantially caused by excess money growth. But a school of heterodox economists, led by Lance Taylor of the Massachusetts Institute of Technology, believe that many wages and other prices are set by predetermined, nonmarket rules. For example, in inflation-prone countries in Latin America, labor agreements sometimes adjust wage rates to compensate for inflation, a practice called **indexing.** And many firms set their prices by calculating a fixed percentage, or margin, over the costs of

---

8. In the appendix we further explore stabilization programs, using analytical tools developed in later chapters.

production, a practice called **markup pricing.** To the extent that these practices prevail, a reduction in the growth of the money supply will not reduce inflation for some time, as unions and firms continue their habit of raising wages and prices to make up for past losses to inflation and to protect against future inflation. Instead, with prices rising faster than the money supply, the result is layoffs and bankruptcies. Eventually, perhaps, the unions and firms will adjust their expectations and inflation will abate, but it can take years and may require more than the economic measures contained in stabilization packages. Fundamental agreements among employers, workers, and government may be needed to change the entrenched habits of indexing and markup pricing; sometimes these agreements are forced by coercive measures, often by military governments.[9]

Ultimately this is an empirical matter: are prices **flexible,** moving up and down with demand, or **fixed,** insensitive to reductions in demand? Most economies have a mixture of both kinds. Prices for most agriculture, many services, and some manufactured goods are flexible. But in some industries, especially those with a few large-scale firms, fixed pricing may prevail. In countries with entrenched and politicized labor unions and concentrated industries, prices are more likely to be inflexible. When, in addition, the income distribution is very unequal, a government is often unable to win a broad consensus on stabilization measures. These conditions seem characteristic of some Latin American countries, where the experience with stabilization programs has been mixed, with many notable failures, such as Brazil and Argentina in the 1980s, and some successes, notably Bolivia in 1985 (see box). In Asia, governments have been better able to use stabilization packages to correct budget and payments imbalances and control inflation.

Stabilization that Worked: Bolivia, 1985–1986[10]

From August 1984 to August 1985, prices in Bolivia rose by 20,000 percent, the most rapid inflation in Latin American history. During September 1985, inflation was stopped cold and prices actually began to fall. How did this happen?

The hyperinflation of 1984–85 was the culmination of events under the regime of President Siles Zuazo, which in 1982 became Bolivia's first elected government in 18 years. Declining foreign aid and commercial bank lending, combined with rising international interest rates and debt payments, led to a growing payments deficit: net resource flows into Bolivia declined

9. For a review of these controversies, see Tony Killick, ed., *The Quest for Stabilization: The IMF and the Third World* (London: Heinemann Education Books, 1984); Lance J. Taylor, *Varieties of Stabilization Experience: Toward Sensible Macroeconomics in the Third World* (Oxford: Oxford University Press, (Clarendon), 1988); and John Williamson, ed., *IMF Conditionality* (Washington, D.C.: Institute for International Economics, 1983). The Taylor books is for advanced students.

10. This account is drawn from Juan Antonio Morales and Jeffrey D. Sachs, "Bolivia's Economic Crisis," in *Developing Country Debt and the World Economy*, J. D. Sachs, ed. (Chicago: University of Chicago Press, 1989), pp. 57–79, and Jeffrey D. Sachs, "The Bolivian Hyperinflation and Stabilization," *American Economic Review* 77 no. 2 (May 1987): 279–283.

118

GUIDING
DEVELOPMENT:
MARKETS
VERSUS
CONTROLS
(Ch. 5)

by 10 percent of GDP over three years to a net outflow of $190 million in 1983. To compensate for this loss of revenue, the government resorted to central bank credit and thus increased the money supply. This, combined with wage increases granted to organized labor, caused accelerating inflation. Rising prices caused a precipitate decline in tax revenues, from 9 percent of GDP in 1981 to only 1.3 percent in 1985, and led to rapid depreciation of the exchange rate, both of which fed back into higher inflation. By 1985 the public had lost all confidence in the *boliviano* and most transactions were denominated in dollars.

In August 1985 the newly elected government of President Victor Paz Estenssoro took power and instituted a radical stabilization program along orthodox lines. The *boliviano* was devalued and made fully convertible into dollars; a sharp rise in the prices of goods and services sold by government corporations, together with a freeze on public sector wages, immediately cut the budget deficit; a tax reform was proposed and later enacted to increase revenues and avoid future deficits; and the treasury went on a cash flow basis and spent no more than its incoming cash revenues. The elimination of the deficit reduced the need to obtain central bank credit and restricted the money supply; this in turn curbed price increases and stabilized the new exchange rate. In contrast to other Latin American stabilizations, no price controls were employed and some existing controls were eliminated. The stabilization was aided by a standby agreement with the IMF and the subsequent resumption of lending by the aid donors, including the World Bank. But the moratorium on debt payments to commercial banks, begun under the Siles government, was maintained.

The abrupt elimination of the government's deficit and its ability to stabilize the exchange rate made its program credible to the public. The Paz government's task was easier because the previous government's policies had been completely discredited and the economy was in a shambles. The government was even able to carry out the kind of unpopular measures that might have toppled other regimes, notably the layoff of 21,000 workers employed by the inefficient government tin mining company, COMIBOL, and the sharp curtailment of government expenditures. After the first few months of dramatic reform, inflation did resume, but at levels of 10 to 15 percent, one of the lowest rates in Latin America.

Dismantling Controls

Once stabilization has been achieved, or even while it is being achieved, the other four elements of a well-functioning market system must be put in place. Many of the measures designed to accomplish this task come under the heading of what the World Bank calls **structural adjustment.**

A critical step at the outset is to make as many goods as possible available for purchase on the market rather than through some allocation mechanism of the government bureaucracy. Thus an important element in trade reform is to remove government quotas on imports. Import licensing is a way of transferring allocations from the market to the government. In many developing countries firms starting up a new factory must get licenses to purchase land, to get foreign exchange for imports of capital equipment and intermediate inputs, and even to buy electricity. Negotiations to acquire these licenses can drag on for years. In the agricultural sector, fertilizer and pesticides are sometimes distributed through a state commercial network in amounts determined by government, rather than by farmers' willingness to purchase and use these inputs. Most of these interventions were justified at their origin by the market failure and distributional arguments outlined at the beginning of this chapter. Others, restrictions on foreign investment for example, are justified on political or security grounds. When restriction is piled on restriction, however, the cumulative effect is to remove large parts of the economy from participation in the market.

Dismantling such controls over production, marketing, and consumption is a central feature of structural adjustment packages. Reforms that end controls are called **liberalization** or **deregulation.**

Ensuring Competition

In many developing countries competition is seen as something to be avoided. Foreign competition in particular is considered unfair because foreign firms have years more experience than the country's new domestic firms. The solution is often to prohibit entry into the domestic market by foreign firms. Competition between domestic firms is also seen to waste resources. Why have three firms when one or two can produce all that is required? Fewer firms can achieve economies of scale and produce at lower average cost. Competition is disorderly, so the argument goes, and some firms will fail and put people out of work.

Waste caused by the bankruptcy of a company is visible to all, but waste caused because the company felt no pressure to produce more efficiently is not so apparent. Hardly anyone noticed that the U.S. automobile companies had largely ignored the demand for smaller cars until the Japanese came along with their compacts and subcompacts. Competition is the force that pressures everyone to do better. The desire to produce goods that were competitive in international markets was one reason for the rapid growth of the four East Asian tigers. State-owned enterprises are often inefficient in part because the state frequently awards monopoly control of their market to these enterprises. With monopoly control they can set prices high enough to cover their high costs and can sell goods of inferior quality. Under the circumstances, why bother working hard to lower costs? Industries built behind a wall of protection from foreign imports may never be able to compete in foreign markets. Managers in these industries, as already pointed out, will put most of their energy into lobbying to maintain that protection, rather than learning how to meet the competition.

Centrally managed economies, such as those of the Soviet Union and China before the recent reforms, allow little real competition among enterprises. The government allocates inputs and tells firms how much to produce. Pressure to surpass the targets set by the state provides some impetus to produce more efficiently, but this kind of pressure is a poor substitute for competition between firms, in which the loser will have a smaller mar-

120

GUIDING
DEVELOPMENT:
MARKETS
VERSUS
CONTROLS
(Ch. 5)

ket share, lower profits, and fewer employees, and may go out of business. Command economies are notorious for their profligate waste of resources.

Reform programs attempt to introduce competition into markets where it has been limited or absent. In larger nations, or in industries with few economies of scale, there can be several firms in any industry. Competition between these domestic firms can be fostered simply by dismantling import or investment licensing, quotas over output, controls over prices, and other government interventions that give some firms advantages over others.

If the domestic market is small and one or a few firms dominate the industry, or if domestic firms fail to compete vigorously, the only viable competition comes from abroad, in the form of competing imports. Thus deregulation of import controls and reduction of tariffs provide the competitive stimulus for improved productivity and higher quality. Another way to infuse domestic industry with competitive urges is to bias the entire structure of incentives toward exports, away from domestic sales. Import liberalization should be part of this strategy, but it also encompasses exchange rate devaluation, direct and indirect subsidies, preferential credit, investment in ports and other infrastructure, and many other measures to support exporters. In order to take advantage of more profitable sales in foreign markets, domestic firms must improve both their quality and their productivity, and learn to market aggressively. This is the outward-looking approach used by the four East Asian "tigers."[11]

Moving toward Scarcity Prices

Although competition creates the stimulus for firms to maximize profits and improve productivity, **relative prices** are the signals that tell firms how to manage their resources to earn the highest rewards. If the relative prices reflect the real scarcities in the economy, firms that maximize profits and consumers who maximize their utility will automatically act to make the most out of all resources on behalf of the economy as a whole. This is called **static efficiency**. Scarce resources, such as capital or energy, should have relatively high prices to conserve their use; abundant resources, such as unskilled labor in poor economies and educated workers in rich ones, should receive relatively low wages so they will be used more intensively in production. When market prices dictate these allocations of scarce and abundant resources, a greater value of output can be achieved for any given expenditure on inputs.

Despite these advantages of market-determined prices, governments have regularly intervened to set prices and shield them from market influences. In principle these price controls were designed to correct for market failures and thus to bring prices in line with real scarcities. In reality, price setting was generally a political process based on political and not economic objectives. More often than not, government intervention led prices further away from real economic scarcities.

---

11. Not all the measures listed are always advocated for outward-looking strategies. Subsidies and preferential credit, though they do promote exports, also distort the economy away from scarcity prices.

A major objective of structural adjustment reforms, therefore, is to reduce or remove these distortions generated by government intervention. In the majority of developing countries, the list of distorted prices is a long one. (1) Tariffs raise the price of imports and competing domestic goods. If tariffs were at a uniform rate on all imports, the distortions would not be so great. But tariffs typically vary from 0 to 50 percent and rates of 200 percent are not uncommon. (2) Interest rates on loans are frequently held well below market rates in a misguided attempt to promote investment by reducing the cost of finance. Low rates discourage saving, however, and this reduces the availability of finance. Cheap loans meant for the poor are usually syphoned off by the well-connected rich, while the poor pay very high rates on the loans available through informal credit markets. (3) Small numbers of well-organized urban workers can sometimes pressure governments to support demands for high wages and nonwage benefits or to restrict layoffs. Poorer, unorganized workers in both the urban and rural areas continue to receive lower, market-set wages. The larger factories, faced with higher labor costs, cut back on employment and substitute machines where they can. (4) Gasoline and other fuels are often sold at prices below those of the world market; this encourages the wasteful use of energy and generally favors well-off consumers. (5) Food prices are frequently kept low for urban workers even though this can mean that the poorer rural population gets paid less for their crops.

The political nature of price-setting is readily apparent. For every government-determined price, there are winners, who receive more for their output or pay less for their inputs, and losers. Price distortions most often occur when the beneficiaries of a price change are few and concentrated, while the losers are large in number and dispersed. A tariff on bicycles, for example, will raise the profits to the owners of a nation's handful of bicycle factories. A small increase in prices may mean very large increases in profits. Those paying the higher price will number in the millions in a large country, but they will be scattered unevenly across the country and are unlikely to organize to protest the increase. Since the tariff is built into the price of the bicycle, these consumers may not even be aware that government intervention caused the higher prices. The producers will know, however, and will be in a position with their increased profits to help those who helped them. Where the beneficiaries of price distortions are large in number, as in the case of food price subsidies, other kinds of political pressures can arise. Removal of food subsidy frequently triggers rioting that can topple governments.

Structural adjustment reforms designed to correct price distortions, therefore, frequently run into stiff resistance. There is no question that most of these distortions lower the welfare of the nation as a whole even as they benefit selected groups and individuals. Removing the distortions will raise the general welfare. But by how much? There is no easy answer to this question. Some economists argue that ''getting prices right'' is the very essence of reform to spur development. Others point out that models simulating the effect of price reforms taken alone produce relatively modest benefits in many cases, although the benefits are positive. In the real world of structural adjustment reform, it is usually not possible to separate

122

GUIDING
DEVELOPMENT:
MARKETS
VERSUS
CONTROLS
(Ch. 5)

out reform efforts to correct price distortions from those that contribute to the four other elements that make markets work. Most successful reform packages, therefore, involve a combination of reforms of which removing price distortions is one.

Responding to Market Signals

Perhaps the least understood of the reforms needed to make markets work are those that induce producers to act in accordance with market signals. The rule is simple enough: producers should maximize profits by cutting their costs or increasing their sales. Economists typically assume that producers automatically maximize profits.[12] A firm's owners seek to earn high incomes for themselves. But what happens when the firm is run by managers who are hired by the owners? What happens if the firm is owned by the state and managers are appointed to their posts by the government?

Some of the early socialist theorists, the Polish economist Oscar Lange for example, thought this problem could be solved by simply ordering managers of state-owned enterprises to maximize profits. These orders would be necessary because, with the state receiving the profits, higher profits no longer necessarily meant higher incomes for the managers. It is to the credit of these early theorists that they recognized that the issue had to be solved. If firms did not maximize profits, getting prices right would not necessarily lead to the better allocation of resources. Prices work by raising profits to producers of goods in short supply. The prospect of earning higher profits stimulates producers to increase production of scarce items. But if the producers are not rewarded by higher profits, they may not respond to higher prices. The early theorists had correctly diagnosed the problem, but their solution—ordering managers to maximize profits—was insufficient.

Increasing the role of the market often works most easily in agriculture. As Theodore Schultz emphasized, farmers, like owners of small businesses, are profit maximizers.[13] If prices are raised on a particular crop, say coffee in Kenya, farmers will plant more land in coffee but less in maize, because by doing so they will raise their income. Reform can therefore be effective simply by freeing up prices of agricultural products so that prices reflect society's demand for those products and by making inputs such as fertilizer available through the market rather than through state trading companies. Family farmers respond to deregulated prices and supplies because it is profitable for them to do so.

Small-scale industrial and commercial enterprises behave much like family farmers. Managers and owners are the same people and increased profits go directly to the managers. In developing countries, this direct link between ownership and management holds even for moderately large firms, which are often owned by one or a few families. But as firms increase in size and complexity, the direct link is broken. Owners hire professional

---

12. But recall the structuralists, led by Lance Taylor, who assume firms mark up their prices to cover costs plus a percentage profit; this is not the same as maximizing profits.

13. Schultz, *Transforming Traditional Agriculture*.

managers, whose ownership stake in the firm is limited. Incentive bonuses based on profits can help motivate managers, but are not a perfect substitute for direct ownership. Single or family owners give way to many stockholders whose control over managers is diffuse and often ineffective. In the United States, boards of directors seldom restrain managers and many large shareholders, especially pension funds and other institutions, are not even represented on the boards.

In the case of **state-owned enterprises,** even the owner has goals other than profit maximization. Government-appointed managers are often directed to keep their prices low to help consumers, to employ more people than needed, to invest and locate in less-developed (and less-profitable) regions, to contribute to the political campaigns of the ruling party, and to do many other things. Profits and efficiency may not even be a specified goal.

One solution to this problem of multiple goals is to **privatize** the enterprise. If it is private, the argument goes, the connection between management goals and profits will be restored. In nations such as Poland and Hungary, for example, reformers gave up trying to change the incentives of larger state enterprises so that they would behave more in accordance with the rules of a socialist market system. The government bureaucracy could not be stopped from constantly intervening in the decisions of firm managers in ways inconsistent with profitability. Hungarian and Polish reformers, as a result, came to the conclusion that only complete privatization would solve the problem.

But privatization is not always the solution that it appears to be. In developing countries the pervasiveness of government interventions in the market often means that even private firms are closely tied to the government. Profitability depends on government providing licenses to import key inputs at low duties and a favorable exchange rate or on credit from government banks at low interest rates. If state subsidies are pervasive, cutting costs and increasing sales become almost incidental to the firm's profitability.

For a reformer attempting to introduce profit maximization, it is essential to cut the ties that bind the enterprise to the government bureaucracy. The enterprise, whether public or private, must stand on its own or be permitted to fail. Privatization can help. But privatization will not work unless the government disengages from setting the firm's prices, determining its outputs, and otherwise preempting the key decisions that determine profitability.

The task, however, is not simply one of eliminating government. Some government functions, taxation for example, are essential. One cannot eliminate taxes. But one can change the way taxes are paid in a manner that achieves the objective of breaking the ties between government officials and enterprise managers. The key is to reduce the discretionary authority in the hands of these officials. Tax rates should be few and clear and exemptions minimal and automatically applied. There should be as little room as possible for negotiation between the tax authority and the enterprise over what the latter's tax obligation should be. The more tax rates are set automatically rather than negotiated, the less is the temptation

124

GUIDING
DEVELOPMENT:
MARKETS
VERSUS
CONTROLS
(Ch. 5)

on the part of the government to use these negotiations to pressure the enterprise to do what government wants, not necessarily what the market dictates. What is true for taxes holds for import regulations, investment approvals, and any other necessary or residual interventions left to government after deregulation is complete.

The Transition to a Market System

Stabilization and structural adjustment present a formidable array of issues for a reforming government: the credibility of the whole reform package, the timing of measures, and the magnitude of change.

Success in reforming an economy depends crucially on the **credibility** of the entire package.[14] If budget deficits remain high, or for any other reason money creation is not slowed, the public will anticipate continued or higher inflation. If the real exchange rate is allowed to appreciate because inflation outruns nominal devaluations, as happened in Chile and elsewhere, export industries become unattractive to investors. If import liberalization is undertaken tentatively, or if past attempts have been reversed, investors will put their money into the old protected industries. To establish credibility, governments need to manage their reform program decisively, despite its complexity.

Credibility also depends on the public's perceptions about stabilization and liberalization, which often differ from reality. In judging the effects of policies, the public is most likely to compare situations before and after, when the proper comparison is with and without. A stabilized economy may look worse than the observed precrisis economy, but could well be an improvement over the situation that might have developed without stabilization, which of course cannot be observed. Leaders and officials in many countries have a deep-seated statist bias towards controls and often maintain an illusion that government controls are effective when they are not. These perceptions by government and the public make it more difficult to plan and implement reforms. Disappointing results with past stabilization and reform efforts make it more difficult to convince the public to support new initiatives.

The influence of foreign aid institutions on credibility is two-edged. The International Monetary Fund and the World Bank provide additional resources that can ease the transition to an open economy and help to protect incomes during the transition. Foreign aid can enhance the position of reforming elements within a government and can be used by government to sell stabilization programs to the public. However, additional resources also make the crisis seem less intense and reforms less necessary. Moreover, IMF presence has increasingly become a focal point for opposition to economic change. Although governments of countries such as Egypt and

14. Political scientist Joan Nelson has explored issues of credibility, timing, and magnitude as director of a multicountry study of stabilization programs. See "The Political Economy of Stabilization: Commitment, Capacity and Public Response," *World Development* 12, no. 10 (1984): 983–1006.

Zambia have deflected public ire by ceasing to negotiate with the IMF, the result has only been to delay necessary stabilization, quite possibly to a more difficult time.

Public debt plays a similarly dual role. To a point, the need to pay off foreign creditors can be used to steel the public to a degree of austerity. But at some point debt becomes a liability, as the public begins to wonder why their standard of living should decline so that foreign bankers' profits can be maintained. In the long run, it probably requires convincing arguments about the population's own well-being to sustain either stabilization or reform efforts.

Implicit in the discussion of credibility are the questions of **timing** and **magnitude**. Should reforms be pushed through quickly or phased in gradually? There are times in a country's history when economic and political forces provide a brief opportunity for dramatic reforms. Probably the single most convincing observation on timing, by political scientist Joan Nelson, is that the beginning of a new regime is the time to act.[15] Recently elected regimes have the momentum of popular support, used to good effect by President Jayawardana in Sri Lanka in the late 1970s and dramatically by President Victor Paz Estenssoro in Bolivia in 1985 (see boxed example, p. 117). New regimes of any kind have a brief initial period when they can blame problems on the previous government. Early success obviously has political benefits for the regime. But as time goes on, growing ties between government and its supporters *(clients)* in the private sector make policy change increasingly dangerous for any regime.

In these circumstances, credibility is probably served by rapid, decisive, comprehensive action. The big-bang approach to reform tried by Poland in the 1980s is one example.[16] Such **shock treatment** is also consistent with the economics of reform.[17] The move from an inward-looking, distorted economy to an outward-looking, liberal one requires policy action on many different fronts. However, shock treatment across the board is unrealistic. Few governments have the decision-making or managerial capacity to implement such draconian programs. Fundamental organizational and behavioral changes, both inside and outside of government, are often essential; yet they take months or years to implement. Such reforms may involve not only the operation of government agencies, but also the functioning of labor and capital markets. For example, when capital markets are deregulated both central and commercial bankers have to learn to operate with new credit instruments in more competitive markets.

These considerations suggest **gradualism**.[18] A slower pace for reform, however, means that the benefits of reform take longer to materialize, and

15. Nelson, "The Political Economy of Stabilization."

16. Using a different metaphor, one Polish official was reported to have said, "You can only take one leap over a chasm."

17. Sebastian Edwards and Sweder van Wijnbergen, "Disequilibrium and Structural Adjustment," in *Handbook of Development Economics*, Vol. 2 Chenery and Srinivasan, pp. 1481–1533.

18. Michael Michaely, "The Timing and Sequencing of Trade Liberalization Policy," in *Economic Liberalization in Developing Countries*, Armeane M. Choksi and Demetrius Papageorgiou, eds. (London: Basil Blackwell, 1986).

126

GUIDING
DEVELOPMENT:
MARKETS
VERSUS
CONTROLS
(Ch. 5)

this makes it more difficult to mobilize support. Gradualism also gives opposition forces a better chance to mobilize and throws a shadow over government's credibility. Asian governments have been more adept at implementing reform over long periods than have governments in Latin America, with the exception of Chile.

How large are the necessary changes? To the extent that some prices will remain controlled—especially the exchange rate, interest rates, and food prices—government must decide how fast and how much to change them. The technical answer depends on the economy's ability to respond quickly to price change, represented by the relevant **supply and demand elasticities.** The lower these elasticities, the greater the needed changes in prices to accomplish a given balance or shift of resources. Yet if elasticities are low, then large and rapid changes in prices will cause greater disruptions, more unemployment and more idle capacity, and thus more opposition to reform. If stabilization is part of the reform package, then rapid and decisive action can mean severe contraction of the economy, exacerbating the disruptions and encouraging political challenges to reform.

Latin American structuralists have long maintained that economic change is tightly inhibited by economic, social, and political obstacles, so reform is likely to be ineffective or to cause severe disruptions and hardship. Neo-classical economists argue that economies are flexible enough over the medium term to base reforms on market rules. This same debate takes place on many levels and in most of the sectors of the economy. It will reappear often in the chapters that follow.

For all of the complexity involved in meeting these conditions for efficient markets, an increasing number of countries are making the effort to do so. Some of the most successful efforts have been in Asia. Hong Kong and Singapore were relatively free market economies from the beginning. South Korea used government controls extensively in the 1970s but systematically dismantled many of the controls in the 1980s. Taiwan has based its remarkable growth on small firms guided by market forces. China was one of the first avowedly socialist developing economies to introduce market reforms, first into agriculture and, after 1984, with less complete success, into industry. Indonesia moved from a government-regulated industrial and financial system in the 1970s to a more market-oriented economy in the 1980s (see boxed example).

In Latin America, many market reforms have stumbled over failed stabilization programs, including those in Argentina and Brazil during the 1980s. Among the exceptions, Bolivia's successful stabilization and reform has already been described. In its almost two decades of stabilization and structural adjustment, Chile took many wrong turns but seems to have found a workable formula during the 1980s. Mexico has been deregulating its trade and industry in recent years while meeting large debt payments. In Africa, the most notable reforms have been attempted in countries such as Ghana, Uganda, and Tanzania, which had fallen into stagnation or even economic anarchy before righting themselves, and in The Gambia, whose government had to rationalize its economic management to avoid being swallowed up by Senegal. The Ivory Coast and Kenya, never in such dire straights, have flirted with mild reforms that produced marginal results.

Indonesia is an oil-producing country that suffered major losses when, from 1984 to 1986, world oil prices fell by half. Indonesia's annual export earnings were cut by $6 billion, about a quarter of total export revenues. At the same time, with export revenues denominated in dollars and much of its debt denominated in Japanese yen, the falling dollar added nearly 40 percent to Indonesia's annual debt service payments. These two external shocks forced the Indonesian government first to stabilize its economy and then to make it less dependent on oil exports for both foreign exchange earnings and government revenues. The government of President Soeharto had been in office for two decades when the crisis struck and had already laid the groundwork for stabilization and reform. Indonesia's currency, the rupiah, had been fully convertible into foreign currencies since 1970. Devaluations in 1978 and 1983 had kept the rupiah in reasonable alignment with the dollar. Government was prevented by law from financing budget deficits from domestic sources, though it could, and did, borrow overseas. A tax reform enacted in 1983, which introduced a 10 percent value-added tax, had already begun to shift the burden of government revenues from oil exports to domestic taxes. When the oil market collapsed in 1985–86, the government acted quickly to correct imbalances: civil service salaries were frozen for four years, overall government spending net of debt service fell by 6 percent of GDP, and a 33 percent devaluation of the rupiah in September 1986 enhanced the competitiveness of nonoil exports, upon which export growth now depended. Because budget deficits were kept small and not financed by bank credit, money creation and hence inflation could be kept under control. Despite the devaluation, prices rose by only 9 percent a year in 1986 and 1987 and then by around 6 percent in the next two years.

With the economy stabilized, policymakers instituted a strong but gradual five-year reform, called a *deregulation,* of Indonesia's international trade regime and its financial markets. In 1985 the President responded to corruption and costly delays in the customs service by bringing in a foreign private firm to manage customs, a bold and unprecedented reform. In 1986 exporters were exempted from paying duties on imported inputs and allowed to buy them without regard to existing import restrictions. From 1986 to 1988, a series of deregulation packages eased the nontariff barriers to many imports. Financial reform packages in 1988 and 1990 allowed banks to determine their own deposit and lending rates, phased out subsidized credit, and otherwise deregulated financial markets. In some respects the banks have been slow to respond to market signals, but they have competed vigorously for savers' deposits and have vied to open new branches to serve customers all over the country, in both urban and rural areas. Restrictions on domestic and foreign investment were reduced substantially in 1989, and the Jakarta stock exchange, now encouraged by government, experienced a boom in 1989 and 1990.

These reforms showed results almost immediately. The dollar value of nonoil exports rose by 22 percent a year from 1985 to 1989 and from 32 to 61 percent of total export earnings. As money flowed into the bank

128

GUIDING
DEVELOPMENT:
MARKETS
VERSUS
CONTROLS
(Ch. 5)

deposits, domestic credit expanded from 15 percent of GDP in 1985 to 32 percent in 1989. Government revenues rebounded, and GDP growth resumed and reached 6 percent in 1989. A long-serving government, with shrewd policy leadership and a history of cautious reform, acted quickly to adjust to a major external shock and then took deliberate steps to transform its economy into one of the more dynamic export-led developers in Asia.

6

Planning Models

Although economic planning and controls are giving way to market forces as the primary vehicle of development, governments still devote considerable effort to national planning and economists still work on mathematical planning models. There are a number of reasons for this. First, economic models can be useful, and sometimes essential, to the policymakers concerned with macroeconomic management and stability. Second, models of economic structure can give a rough picture of an economy's potential to achieve long-run development goals such as income growth, employment creation, and poverty alleviation. Such models can also evaluate the outcomes to be expected from alternative strategies under consideration. Third, cost-benefit models have been developed to guide government toward public investments that maximize the economic returns for a given expenditure or that minimize the economic costs of achieving social and economic goals. Fourth, if markets are to guide private activities toward development goals, governments need to correct or compensate for inherent market imperfections; this requires some coordination and planning. Finally, comprehensive models force economists to marshal all extant data on an economy, test the internal consistency of the data, and establish a research agenda to gather additional information on crucial but poorly understood mechanisms in the economy.

Six planning models are covered in this chapter: a simple Keynesian macroeconomic growth model, interindustry (input-output) analysis and its extension, the social accounting matrix, linear programming, computable general equilibrium models, and cost-benefit analysis.[1]

1. Readers who are shy of mathematics should be able to comprehend the basic concepts of this chapter without mastering the mathematical treatments.

Models can yield outcomes that are **consistent** or **optimal.** The distinction can be illustrated with a simple example. A traveler who has a two-week vacation and a budget of $4,000 to spend wants to travel to Kenya to see as much big game as possible. The tourist is offered three itineraries by the travel agent. The consistency problem is, simply, which of these itineraries is *feasible* within the constraints of $4,000 and two weeks? The consistency problem becomes an optimality problem if asked another way: Which of the feasible itineraries will enable the traveler to *maximize* satisfaction by seeing the most species of game?

A consistent plan can be illustrated in terms of the **production possibility frontier** of Figure 6–1. The production possibility frontier shows the maximum feasible output of two goods, X (say, necessities) and Y (say, luxuries), in an economy with a given endowment of productive resources or a given period such as 1, 5, or 20 years. The more of good Y the economy wants to produce, the less of X it can produce, because resources (land, labor, and capital) must be taken from the production of necessities (X) to be used in production of more luxuries (Y). Consistency models ensure that any plan resulting from them would place the economy *within* its frontier, at a point like A, or at best *on* the frontier, at a point like B. Any point, like C, beyond the frontier is unobtainable.

To illustrate an optimal plan it is necessary to review the concept of **indifference curves,** illustrated in Figure 6–2. The individual's indifference curve assumes that a single consumer may purchase two goods, X (necessities) and Y (luxuries), in various combinations. If the consumer were to purchase quantities X_a and Y_a, he or she would achieve a certain level of

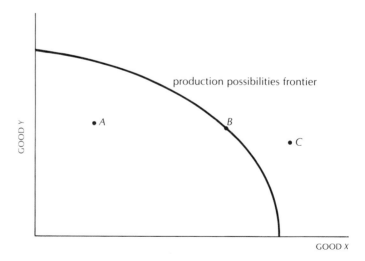

FIGURE 6–1   **Consistency.** Consistency as shown by the production possibilities frontier. Points such as A or B, below or on the frontier, are consistent with this economy's endowment. Point C, beyond the frontier, is not.

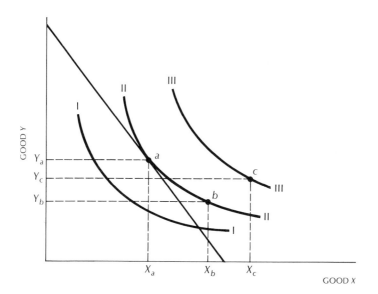

FIGURE 6–2 Indifference Curves and the Budget Constraint. Each indifference curve traces out a series of points that yield an individual the same level of satisfaction. The budget line shows the possible purchases of both goods for a given income and relative price. A consumer's highest possible level of satisfaction occurs at the tangency of the budget line and an indifference curve.

satisfaction. Other combinations of purchases, such as X_b and Y_b, may yield the same level of satisfaction to the consumer. If so, then points a and b lie on the same indifference curve, labeled II in the diagram. Indifference curve II is the locus of all combinations of the two goods that give the same satisfaction to the consumer as does the combination X_a and Y_a. Any indifference curve to the northeast of II, such as curve III, contains combinations of the two goods that yield greater satifaction to the consumer than does any point on curve II. That is, the combination X_c and Y_c is preferred by the consumer to X_a and Y_a (or to X_b and Y_b). Similarly, combinations along curve I, to the southwest of curve II, are inferior to those along curve II.

Introduction of the **budget line** (or **constraint**) completes the picture. The budget line gives the combination of goods X and Y that can be purchased by the consumer within the limits of the person's income. The slope of the budget line gives the relative price of one good Y in terms of the other X; the intercepts are the points where the consumer's entire income is spent on either good X or good Y. The consumer can maximize his or her level of satisfaction by consuming at point a, where the budget line is tangent to indifference curve II. The consumer cannot reach any other point on curve II, such as b, and still satisfy the budget constraint. (Nor would the consumer want to, since he or she is indifferent between combinations a and b.) Any combination of purchases on higher indifference curves, such as point c on curve III, would require more income than the consumer has. And there is no need to accept less satisfaction on a curve such as I, even

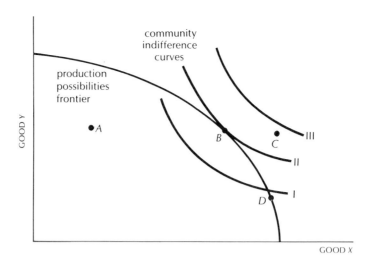

FIGURE 6–3 **Optimality as Shown by the Production Possibilities Frontier.** Indifference curves I, II, and III represent the consumption preferences for an entire community, analogous to those for an individual. The production frontier is analogous to the individual's budget constraint. The optimal combination of the two goods, *X* and *Y*, is given by point *B*, where indifference curve II is tangent to the production frontier. The country cannot achieve a higher level of satisfaction, such as indifference curve III, given its resource and production constraints.

though it lies partly within the budget constraint, since greater satisfaction is achievable at point *a*.

It takes very restrictive assumptions to use indifference curves, which are valid for individuals, to represent the consumption choices for an entire community or country. However, the concept of **community indifference curves** is useful—and often used—to demonstrate many theories in economics. Figure 6–3 shows a set of community indifference curves superimposed on the production frontier of Figure 6–1. In planning models, society's welfare is represented by an **objective** or **welfare function** that measures the nation's development goals in a way that will be explained later in this chapter. The community indifference curves of Figure 6–3 can also represent increasing values of this objective function. The production frontier is to society what the budget constraint is to the individual: society's resources and technologies permit it to consume only the quantities of *X* and *Y* on or to the southwest of the frontier. An optimal planning model seeks solutions like point *B* in Figure 6–3, for which the value of the objective function is at its maximum given the resource (and hence the production) constraints on an economy.

KEYNESIAN MODELS

The simplest and best-known consistency model for planning is the Harrod-Domar model, introduced in Chapter 3:

$$g = s/k,$$

[6–1]

in which g is the annual growth rate of gross domestic (or national) product,

s is the saving rate, and k is the incremental capital-output ratio. If k is
known, then planners can decide on a target rate of growth (g) and calculate the consistent rate of saving (s) needed to obtain that growth. Alternatively, they can determine a feasible rate of saving and calculate the
growth rate consistent with it.

The Harrod-Domar equation is the basis of many macroeconomic growth
models, some of which can be quite elaborate. To illustrate these models,
a still quite simple version would begin by turning the Harrod-Domar
investment relationship, Equation 6–1 into a more realistic form, such as

$$\Delta Y_t = Y_t - Y_{t-1} = (1/k)\Delta K_{t-1} = (1/k)(I_{t-1} - \delta K_{t-1}), \qquad [6\text{--}2]$$

which can be written as

$$Y_t = Y_{t-1} + (1/k)(I_{t-1} - \delta K_{t-1}). \qquad [6\text{--}3]$$

In Equation 6–2, Y is gross domestic (or national) product, K is the capital
stock, I is gross investment (i.e., it includes an allowance to replace depreciated capital), k is the ICOR of Equation 6–1, and δ is the rate of depreciation of existing capital stock. The subscripts refer to the current year t
and the previous year $t-1$. Note that here we simplify by assuming it takes
investment just a year before it can produce output. This is the entire supply side of our elementary model and indicates how much the economy can
produce.

The demand side of the model, showing how output is used, can be contained in five equations, all in the spirit of Keynesian macroeconomic (multiplier) analysis:

$$S_t = sY_t \qquad [6\text{--}4]$$
$$I_t = S_t + F_t \qquad [6\text{--}5]$$
$$M_t = mY_t \qquad [6\text{--}6]$$
$$M_t = E_t + F_t \qquad [6\text{--}7]$$
$$C_t = Y_t - I_t + F_t. \qquad [6\text{--}8]$$

The new variables are S = gross domestic savings, F = foreign saving (the
same as foreign aid plus foreign investment), M = imports of goods and
services, E = exports of goods and services, and C = consumption. The
parameters are s, the domestic saving rate, and m, the import rate, known
as the propensity to import. They, like k, are assumed to be known values.
Equation 6–4 is a Keynesian saving function, in which saving is a constant
proportion s of income. Equation 6–5 says that gross investment must be
financed by domestic saving and foreign saving. Equation 6–6 determines
imports as a constant fraction m of income, whereas Equation 6–7 says
that imports must be financed by export earnings and foreign capital (saving). Equation 6–8 determines consumption as a residual between income
and saving, but puts it in terms of domestic investment and foreign saving,
using Equation 6–5.

Any system of independent, linear equations, such as the six of our model
(Equations 6–3 though 6–8), can be solved if the number of equations equals
the number of unknowns. In this model, however, there are ten variables
(Y_t, Y_{t-1}, K_{t-1}, I_t, I_{t-1}, S_t, F_t, M_t, E_t, and C_t), four too many. Three

them, the so-called lagged variables, Y_{t-1}, K_{t-1}, and I_{t-1}, are considered to be known, because they represent values from an earlier year for which we presumably have data. A fourth E_t is usually estimated separately, because exports depend on factors outside the model, mainly domestic supply capacity for export goods and the state of world markets. That leaves just six unknowns to be found from the six equations, and the model can be solved for all variables.

Suppose, however, that another variable F_t, the flow of foreign saving (aid plus foreign investment), was also estimated independently of the model. This is quite realistic since foreign aid is a matter for negotiation and private foreign investment in LDCs is not always closely related to domestic economic variables. Then we have a model with only five unknowns (Y_t, I_t, S_t, M_t, and C_t), but six equations, so the model is **overdetermined:** one of the six equations cannot be satisfied, except by chance. Put another way, one of the equations—and we are not sure yet which one—is not necessary for the model; it is **redundant.** This kind of redundancy is characteristic of planning models.

To see which equations might be redundant, let us trace through the working of the model. Potential national income (measured, let us say, as GNP) is already known from the first equation, since it depends only on lagged variables, those determined in the previous year. Thus both saving (Equation 6–4) and imports (Equation 6–6) can be found directly. However, each of these variables also appears in another equation. Saving helps determine investment from Equation 6–5. But what if government has a target income growth rate? Then to make income grow at the target rate in the following year $t+1$, investment must be

$$I_t = k(Y_{t+1} - Y_t) + K_t. \qquad [6-9]$$

This is merely a rearrangement of Equation 6–3, with a change of subscripts to the next period, which says that gross investment must be adequate to increase income from Y_t to Y_{t+1} and to cover depreciation of the existing capital stock K_t. With foreign capital fixed, the target level of investment from Equation 6–9 might require national saving more or less than that forthcoming from Equation 6–4. If more, then the economy will not grow at the target rate, because Equation 6–4 sets a limit to the level of saving, a level inconsistent with the growth target. Saving becomes a **binding constraint** on investment growth. If Equation 6–9 requires less saving than available, the growth target is consistent with saving behavior and the saving equation (Equation 6–4) is redundant.

Imports might present another problem. Imports include both consumer and producer goods, the requirements of which are determined by national income (Equation 6–6). But what if the separately estimated level of exports and foreign capital give a different level of financeable imports from Equation 6–7? If more can be financed, then Equation 6–7 is redundant and the model is consistent. If, however, the sum of exports plus foreign capital is less than necessary imports, then income cannot reach the target level of Y_t; it would have to be lower to get along with fewer imports. In this case the foreign exchange equation (Equation 6–7) becomes a binding constraint on production. Moreover, since most capital goods are imported (an important feature left out of this simple model), the shortage of imports would prevent investment from being high enough to attain the growth target.

This fairly primitive macroeconomic planning model—Equations 6–3 to 6–8—is one version of the **two-gap model** developed by Stanford University economist Ronald McKinnon, Harvard University economist Hollis Chenery, and others.[2] The two gaps refer to Equation 6–5, which balances investment against domestic and foreign saving, and Equation 6–7, which balances imports against export earnings and foreign saving. Under the model's rigid assumptions, only one of these equations will be in balance on the basis of previously determined values of the variables. This becomes the binding constraint; the other is redundant. After the fact, both equations will be in balance, but the redundant one will balance because of subsequent adjustments in the variables, as, for example, a drop in exports or in investments. Targets are consistent with resource constraints (the two balance equations, Equations 6–5 and 6–7) only if one is just balanced and the other redundant, in which case no greater growth can be achieved without some structural change in the economy or a greater influx of foreign resources, or if both are redundant, in which case higher targets can be achieved.

Models like this one can be made much more complicated by **disaggregating** some of the relationships, breaking them into component variables and relationships; by separating the economy and model into sectors, such as agriculture, industry, and services; and by adding factors of production, such as various categories of labor, natural resources, kinds of imports, and so forth. Each new factor of production adds a resource balance or constraint equation, so that these become multigap models. But the basic principles of solution and of planning remain the same.

INTERINDUSTRY MODELS

Macroeconomic models, such as the Keynesian models, lack detailed information on the many agricultural, industrial, and service industries that make up an economy. The interactions—or **linkages**—between these sectors are of crucial significance for planners, who simultaneously need to keep overall macroeconomic balances in view to ensure consistency. The tool designed to accomplish these tasks is the **input-output** or **interindustry table.** Its two inventors suggest its flexibility and usefulness. The Russian-born economist Wassily Leontief developed input-output tables at Harvard during the 1930s to help understand the workings of a modern economy and later to help with postwar planning in the United States. About the same time, though working independently, the Russian economist Leonid Kantorovich developed the same tool, allowing both for final demands and for the use of intermediate products within industry, to help planners in his country set quantity targets for Soviet production. The two economists eventually won Nobel Prizes for their efforts.

2. Ronald McKinnon, "Foreign Exchange Constraints in Economic Development," *Economic Journal* 74 (1964): 388–409, and Hollis B. Chenery and Alan Strout, "Foreign Assistance and Economic Development," *American Economic Review* 56 (1966): 679–733.

The essence of an input-output table is to display the flow of output from one industry to another and from industries to final users (consumers, investors, and exporters). A highly simplified example is shown in Table 6–1, which contains only four sectors: primary products, manufactured consumer goods, manufactured producer goods, and services. Sectors shown in rows are producing industries, whereas those shown in columns are users. For example, row 1, "Primary industry," indicates that agriculture, forestry, and mining produced $20 (million, billion, or whatever unit is convenient) worth of products used within the sector (for example, feed for livestock); it produced $65 worth sold to consumer goods manufacturers (such as wheat for bakeries or cotton for textiles), $50 worth sold to producer goods industries (for instance, wood for pulp or iron ore for steel), and $10 worth sold to services (perhaps meat for restaurants). These intermediate uses totaled $145 (column 5). Final products, such as corn for consumption or cocoa for export, were valued at $245, so that total output was $390. Similarly, producer goods manufacturers sold $60 worth of output, such as chemicals, to consumer goods manufacturers (row 3, column 2), and so on.

Each producer is also a user of intermediate goods, and its purchases are shown in the columns of the input-output table. For example, consumer goods manufacturers (column 2) bought $65 worth of primary products, which we know from inspecting row 1, and also $30 from within the sector (for example, textiles used in clothing), $60 from producer goods industries (such as chemicals or paper used in printing), and $15 from services (for instance, banking services, transportation of goods). Total purchases for this sector, given in row 5, were $170. These industries added value of $120, including wages, rents, depreciation, interest, and profits, so that total output was valued at $290. This must be equal to the total output shown in row 2 for manufactured consumer goods. Each row shows output allocated according to uses (including final demand), whereas each column shows the costs and profit of producing the output. Rules of accounting tell

TABLE 6–1   Simplified Input-Output Table (Flow Matrix), Value in Dollars

As Producers	1. Primary industry	2. Manufactured consumer goods	3. Manufactured producer goods	4. Services	5. Total intermediate uses	6. Final use	7. Total use
1. Primary industry	20	65	50	10	145	245	390
2. Manufactured consumer goods	0	30	0	0	30	260	290
3. Manufactured producer goods	50	60	70	15	195	50	245
4. Services	40	15	50	70	175	200	375
5. Total purchases	110	170	170	95	545		
6. Value-added	280	120	75	280		755	
7. Total output	390	290	245	375			1,300

(As Users)

us that these must give the same total. This applies to the total columns (5, 6, and 7) and rows as well. Column 6, "Final use," gives the sum of consumption plus investment plus exports less imports by sector. Add these and the result must be the gross national product, $755. Row 6 gives value-added by sector, and the sum of its entries must also yield the GNP.

National input-output tables are much larger than the example shown here. Small ones may have 15 to 20 sectors, while those developed for the United States economy have close to 500 sectors. Moreover, the columns giving final uses and the rows giving value-added may be broken down into their components and considerably refined. Quantities of capital, labor, and essential imports (goods not produced in the country) can be added as rows to the bottom of the table and show the investment, labor, and foreign exchange requirements of expanded output. In this form, the input-output table is also called a **flow matrix.**

To turn the input-output table into a usable tool for planning or analysis, a crucial assumption is required. Interindustry tables are based on observations of a single year's activity for each sector, merely a snapshot of the economy. If it is assumed that the ratio of purchases and value added to total production is fixed for every industry and will prevail in the future, then this accountant's snapshot of costs becomes an economist's production function with fixed coefficients. It says that for any industry, inputs and costs must expand proportionately with output. Table 6–1 can be converted into a matrix of ratios, called **input-output coefficients,** which is done in Table 6–2. Each column in Table 6–1 has been divided through by its total, so that the second column, for example, now gives the ratios of inputs to output for consumer goods industries: each unit requires 0.23 of primary goods, 0.10 of consumer goods, 0.21 of producer goods, 0.05 of services, and 0.41 of value-added.

The resulting table of coefficients, known as the **A-matrix,** can be seen as a set of production functions for each sector shown in the columns. These fixed-coefficient production functions are often called **Leontief production functions.** The **elements** (coefficients) of input-output tables are usually designated a_{ij}; the subscripts refer to the row (i, for input) and column (i) in that order. Thus, a_{12} is the output of primary products needed per unit of consumer goods, a value of 0.23, whereas a_{43} is the 0.20 units of services needed to produce one unit of manufactured producer goods.

The Leontief matrix is particularly suited to solving the following kind

TABLE 6–2   Coefficients Matrix

	1. X_1	2. X_2	3. X_3	4. X_4
1. Primary goods (X_1)	0.05	0.23	0.20	0.03
2. Consumer goods (X_2)	0.00	0.10	0.00	0.00
3. Producer goods (X_3)	0.13	0.21	0.29	0.04
4. Services (X_4)	0.10	0.05	0.20	0.18
5. Total purchases	0.28	0.59	0.69	0.25
6. Value-added	0.72	0.41	0.31	0.75
7. Total output	1.00	1.00	1.00	1.00

of problem: starting with a target growth rate for an economy over five years, planners can estimate a bill of final goods—those commodities and services purchased by private consumers, investors, government, and foreign importers—that will be demanded at the higher income level. Approximately how much output will be required from each branch of industry to produce that set of final goods? If we can estimate the required output, then it should be possible to determine roughly the amount and kinds of investment needed to produce it.

The answer to the central question, how much of each good, is not immediately obvious. Let us say that 100 units of manufactured consumer goods will be needed. We know from Table 6–2 that this will require, for example, 21 units of producer goods (coefficient $a_{32} \times 100$). But the story does not end there, because to manufacture those inputs, producer goods industries will in turn purchase, for example, 4.2 units of primary goods (20 units needed for consumer goods times a_{13}, or 20×0.21). To produce this 4.2 units, primary industries require 0.5 units (4×0.12) of producer goods, and so on, through an endless chain of outputs and inputs. How can we solve the problem?

Start by asking a simple question: for any level of output of the four products, which we now label X_1 through X_4, how much of one product, primary goods X_1, will be required? The answer is

$$X_1 = a_{11}X_1 + a_{12}X_2 + a_{13}X_3 + a_{14}X_4 + F_1. \qquad [6\text{--}9]$$

This says that enough X_1 must be produced to cover the input needs of each of the producing sectors, given by the input-output coefficient times the level of output, or $a_{ij}X_j$, plus the amount of X_1 needed for final demand F_1. The same is true for each of the other products:

$$X_1 = a_{11}X_1 + a_{12}X_2 + a_{13}X_3 + a_{14}X_4 + F_1 \qquad [6\text{--}10]$$
$$X_2 = a_{21}X_1 + a_{22}X_2 + a_{23}X_3 + a_{24}X_4 + F_2 \qquad [6\text{--}11]$$
$$X_3 = a_{31}X_1 + a_{32}X_2 + a_{33}X_3 + a_{34}X_4 + F_3 \qquad [6\text{--}12]$$
$$X_4 = a_{41}X_1 + a_{42}X_2 + a_{43}X_3 + a_{44}X_4 + F_4. \qquad [6\text{--}13]$$

We already know the values for F_1 through F_4, because these are the final goods required by our growth targets. Since we have four equations (Equations 6–10 through 6–13) and four unknowns (the values of total output, X_1 through X_4, we can solve this set of linear simultaneous equations for each of the outputs and get our answer that way. This is a mechanical process that any student of intermediate algebra (or a computer) can easily complete.[3]

This basic calculation, yielding the total production needed for any bill of final goods, has been at the heart of planning in the Soviet Union, where it is called the method of **materials balances,** and in other command economies. When the requirements of total production are checked against the capacity in each sector, it becomes a test of consistency: Is present capac-

3. For those who know matrix algebra, this set of equations can be solved by inverting I-A, where I is the identity matrix and A is the Leontief matrix of Table 6–2. The result is a matrix of **direct plus indirect** input coefficients, usually labeled r_{ij}. The matrix is called the **Leontief inverse.**

ity adequate for projected final uses, industry by industry? If not, as is **139**
likely in any growing economy, plans must provide enough investment in INTERINDUSTRY
MODELS
additional capacity so that each sector can produce the required output.
The resulting requirement for investment can then be checked against
available savings and foreign investment, one of the constraints of the macroeconomic model. Similarly, requirements for labor of varying skills, for
imports (foreign exchange), and for other scarce factors of production can
be measured against anticipated supplies. One of these constraints, **manpower requirements,** has received considerable attention from education
planners who utilize input-output techniques to project the demands for
education implied by growth targets.

Thus the input-output table can provide a comprehensive but detailed
model of the economy, one capable of tracing through the implications for
all resources of any output or growth target. This is the most complete form
of consistency planning that has been done, although only a minority of
developing countries including South Korea, Malaysia, India, and Mexico
have used it in this way. Despite its power, the input-output model has
some serious drawbacks. First, the assumption of fixed coefficients rules
out the real possibility that targets may be met not by proportional growth
of all factors of production but through the substitution of abundant factors, like unskilled labor, for scarce ones, like capital. This possibility was
suggested in Chapter 3 when the Harrod-Domar model was contrasted with
a neoclassical production function. The concept of substitution is central
not only to neoclassical economic theory, but also to much real-world economics. The fuel crisis of the 1970s, for example, was solved partly by
substitution of more abundant fuels, like coal, for oil. Solutions to the
greenhouse effect and other environmental problems will also require substitution of cleaner-burning fuels, or of solar energy, for coal and oil.

The fuel crisis and environmental concerns also suggest the need for
technological innovations, or improvements, another possibility not handled
easily by interindustry methods. Any time new technologies appear, new
coefficients are required in the Leontief table. If planners anticipate such
changes, they can make approximate allowances by adjusting the initial
coefficients, for example, by reducing petroleum inputs relative to outputs
as oil prices rise. Nor can tables of fixed coefficients handle economies of
scale and learning by doing, both of which increase factor productivity with
growth.[4]

Social Accounting Matrix

As complex as an input-output table can become, it describes only a portion of an economy and leaves many essential policy concerns untouched.
An innovation of the 1970s, the **social accounting matrix** or SAM, amplifies
the Leontief model to accommodate far more economic data. Table 6–3
shows a simplified schematic diagram of a typical social accounting matrix.
The SAM is laid out as an input-output table. Rows represent amounts

4. For an introductory text on input-output analysis, see Hollis B. Chenery and Paul Clark,
Interindustry Economics (New York: Wiley, 1959).

TABLE 6–3 Simplified Social Accounting Matrix

	Expenditures								
Receipts	1. Activities	2. Commodities	3. Factors	4. Enterprises	5. Households	6. Government	7. Capital	8. Rest of world	9. Total
1. Activities		domestic sales						exports	total sales
2. Commodities	intermediate demand				household consumption	export subsidies government consumption	investment		total demand
3. Factors	factor payments								value-added
4. Enterprises			gross profits			transfers			enterprise income
5. Households			wages	distributed profits		transfers		foreign remittances	household income
6. Government	indirect taxes	tariffs	factor taxes	enterprise taxes	direct taxes				government receipts
7. Capital				retained earnings	household savings	government savings		net capital inflow	total saving
8. Rest of world		imports							imports
9. Total	total payments	total absorpiton	value-added	enterprise expenditure	household expenditure	government expenditure	total investment	foreign exchange	

Source: Sherman Robinson, "Multisectoral Models," in Handbook of Development Economics, Vol. 2, Chenery and Srinivasan, p. 897. [Reprinted with permission.]

received by suppliers of goods, services, and factors of production; these are the producers of the interindustry matrix, Table 6–1. Columns represent expenditures, amounts paid out by users of goods and services, the users in Table 6–1. Each row and column taken together can be seen as an account for each entity, covering receipts and expenditures, so that each row and column must balance.

To see how the matrix works, follow down column 1, "Activities," which are productive units such as the steel industry or the restaurant industry. In row 2 we find that the activities account purchased intermediate inputs from the commodities account, such as coke and iron ore for the steel industry or food for the restaurant industry; this is the interindustry core of the input-output matrix of Table 6–1, subsumed into one cell of our simplified SAM. Row 3 shows the payments by activities to factors of production—land, labor, and capital. Add indirect taxes (sales and excise taxes) paid to government (row 6), and the total represents payments to all suppliers or total cost of production. Follow across row 1, representing receipts (sales) by these same activities, and we find that they receive payments from domestic sales (under column 2, "Commodities"); from exports (column 8, the "rest of world"); and from "Government" (column 6) if export subsidies are paid. The sums of column 1 and row 1 must be equal, because total payments must equal total receipts; profits are implicitly included under factor payments.

The information contained in rows and columns 1 to 3 can be found in most input-output tables. The major innovation of the social accounting matrix is the addition of a row and a column representing each of the institutions that make up the economy: enterprises, households, and government. In addition, the matrix adds an account for capital and one for the rest of the world. Now we find that commodities (row 2) are sold to activities (intermediate demand, column 1), for household consumption (column 5), for government consumption (column 6), and for investment (column 7); the total represents domestic demand. Reading down column 5, we learn that households pay for (consume) commodities (row 2), pay direct or income taxes (row 6), and save (row 7).

The SAM is a comprehensive account for the entire economy. Each of the national accounting aggregates can be found in the table. Gross domestic product at factor cost can be found as the sum of either row 3 or column 3. Gross domestic expenditure (consumption plus investment plus exports minus imports) can be read from elements of the commodities and rest-of-world accounts. Account 6 presents the government budget; the row gives revenues and the column shows expenditures. Row 7 shows the sources of savings, which must be matched by column 7, its uses as investment. Account 8 provides the balance of payments and shows the sources of foreign exchange (column 8) used to purchase imports (row 8).

Table 6–3 is a highly simplified SAM. These accounts can be subdivided in many ways. You already know that accounts 1 and 2 can be broken into many industrial sectors, covering all producers of goods and services in an economy. By dividing households into different income categories and firms into different types and sizes (publicly owned versus private firms, large versus small firms, corporations versus partnerships or family-owned businesses), we could obtain a detailed picture of who owns and supplies the different factors of production, who receives various kinds of income and how much, in what kinds of industries and organizations workers of various skills are employed, and so forth. This detail gives a comprehensive picture of how production in an economy results in the observed income distribution among households (or, in the jargon of mathematically minded economists, how production relationships **map** into income distribution).

Social accounting matrices serve four purposes in economic planning. At the most basic level, SAMs provide a comprehensive and consistent framework to organize masses of economic data, including the national accounts, balance of payments, household budget surveys, government accounts, income tax information, financial market accounts, and other sources. Once organized into a SAM and added up in the relevant rows and columns, this data can be checked to ensure internal consistency. Second, when this has been done, the SAM provides a detailed and comprehensive picture of the economy. Third, the SAM highlights areas where data are missing and thus defines an agenda for research. Fourth, when this economic picture has been completed, the SAM can be converted into a dynamic model of the economy and used to determine how various interventions might affect the economy in detail.[5]

Linear Programming

Input-output analysis is useful for answering the question: Do we have adequate resources to achieve our targets? Planners often ask a different question: Given our resources, how can we use them to achieve our goals to the greatest extent possible? That is, instead of planning a merely consistent use of resources, we would like to plan an optimal allocation of resources. Linear programming is a technique used to answer the second question. At the core of a linear programming model is the same input-output table used in consistency planning. It also includes a set of resource constraints, as in consistency models. The major difference is in the treatment of goals. Consistency models start with specific values for one or more goals, which we called targets. Linear programming uses a **welfare** or **objective function** instead.

An objective function is simply an algebraic expression that contains one variable for each of the goals that must be taken into account. To combine these into one formula, each goal must have a **priority** or **welfare weight,** which expresses its importance relative to other goals. Such weights are arbitrary because economics provides no scientific guidance to selecting values for priority weights. Thus, for example, a government may hold three quantifiable economic goals important: (1) increase in national income (G_1), (2) employment creation (G_2), and (3) additional income for the poorest 40 percent of society (G_3). Say the first goal is arbitrarily given a weight of 1. If employment creation—which would have to be measured in terms

5. Social accounting matrices were introduced by Graham Pyatt and Erik Thorbecke in *Planning Techniques for a Better Future* (Geneva: International Labour Office, 1976).

of wages paid to new jobholders—is considered half as important, then its weight w_2 would be 0.5; and if redistribution, expressed as increases in income to the poorest 40 percent, is considered 75 percent more valuable than income increases on average, then its weight w_3 would be 0.75. (Weight w_3 is not 1.75, because increases in income to an average recipient are already counted with a weight of 1 in G_1. Here we only want to count the added weight if the recipient is poor.) Thus the objective function would be

$$W = w_1G_1 + w_2G_2 + w_3G_3 = G_1 + 0.5G_2 + 0.75G_3. \qquad [6-14]$$

A linear program would choose the activities or quantities of output that would maximize the value of the objective function, subject to two sets of constraints. First, production of each good must satisfy the input-output relationships of the Leontief inverse matrix. In order to obtain high values for Equation 6–14, the model will emphasize production in those activities that give rapid growth, high employment, and income for the poor. But whatever activities it selects, it must provide for enough output of each commodity and service to ensure that the required intermediate inputs are produced. Second, the production of these goods and services must satisfy the resource constraints and not use more factors of production than the economy has available. In practice, and because this is a model of linear equations, only one of the resources will be used fully and its supply exhausted. Other resources will generally not be fully employed; these are redundant.

The model works, in effect, by trying out a first solution, consisting of outputs and resource inputs that are consistent. This set of values results in trial value for the objective function. The model (or more correctly, the computer program that simulates the model) then searches for a set of variables which, while still consistent, will improve the value of the objective function. Eventually the program will find a value of the objective function upon which it cannot improve. This is the solution, the set of outputs and resource inputs that maximizes the welfare function. The process can be viewed in terms of Figure 6–3 as a search from within the production frontier (a point as A) to find the point of tangency of the objective function with the production frontier (point B).

Linear programming is a step forward in sophistication from input-output analysis. It depends on the same assumptions, however, and is therefore limited in the same ways. Programming has been widely and effectively used in certain microeconomic applications in agriculture and industry, such as combining nutrients to feed livestock for maximum biological growth or planning industrial processes to minimize costs. Its use as a sectoral or national planning tool has been limited to experiments, principally by academic economists, to apply the technique and draw general lessons about economies such as Brazil, Chile, India, Israel, Mexico, and South Korea.

These experiments have shown that linear programming is useful not so much for its detailed portrayal of optimal resource allocations, but, perhaps paradoxically, for the macroeconomic picture it provides, based on detailed analysis. Its particular strength is in measuring the trade-offs among different development strategies. It major weakness lies in its linear equations, which tend to give unstable and extreme results. To avoid these, it is necessary to insert artificial limiting conditions that have no counterparts in real economies and thus make it difficult to interpret the results.[6]

Computable General Equilibrium Models

Linear programming models have severe limitations as representations of mixed economies where markets determine outcomes and substitution is important. To represent the complex market-based interactions of mixed economies and the kinds of policy interventions that are feasible, economists have developed the **computable general equilibrium model** or CGE. CGEs come in many forms, from relatively simple models of a few equations to models as comprehensive as the social accounting matrix, on which they can be based.

The key technical innovation of CGEs is that they escape the constraints of linearity. The Leontief and linear programming models would represent production of a commodity X_1 as

$$X_j \leq a_{ij}X_i, \qquad X_j \leq b_jK_j, \qquad X_j \leq c_jL_j, \qquad [6\text{--}15]$$

where X_i is one or more commodity inputs in the production of X_j; K_j is the capital used in the X_j industry and L_j is its labor force; and the coefficients a, b, and c are the required inputs of the commodity, capital, and labor, respectively, used in producing X_j. This is the **fixed proportions production function** pictured as an L-shaped production isoquant in Figure 3–1; it comes directly from the a coefficients matrix of an input-output table, such as that shown in Table 6–2. We have already discussed the shortcomings of a model employing these linear relationships.

A CGE model, in contrast, uses the **neoclassical (or variable proportions) production function,** depicted in Figure 3–2, to represent some input-output relationships. With this innovation, not only can the interindustry format be represented, but the possibilities of factor substitution, productivity increases, and economies of scale can also be included. A fairly simple neoclassical function would be

$$X_j \leq a_{ij}X_i; \qquad X_j \leq L_j^{\alpha_j}K_j^{\beta_j}. \qquad [6\text{--}16]$$

The input-output relation is unchanged from the linear production function, but the contributions of labor and capital to value-added can be variable. Moreover, economies of scale can be accommodated by having the sum of the coefficients, $\alpha_j + \beta_j$, exceed 1. Productivity increases could be represented by inserting a time trend into Equation 6–16. Similarly, a CGE would contain consumption functions that permit substitutability among consumer goods, such as

$$p_jX_j = \eta_jY_d, \qquad [6\text{--}17]$$

6. The standard text on the economic theory of linear programming is Robert Dorfman, Paul Samuelson, and Robert Solow, *Linear Programming and Economic Analysis* (New York: McGraw-Hill, 1958).

which says that consumers spend a constant proportion η_j of their disposable income Y_d on good X_j; if p_j, the price of the good, rises, consumers will buy a proportionately smaller quantity of X_j. This very simple demand equation yields a map of indifference curves like that of Figure 6–2.

CGEs can become quite complex and represent each cell of a disaggregated SAM model as a nonlinear expression such as Equation 6–16 or 6–17. These are **behavioral relationships,** the supply and demand functions that describe in mathematical terms the ways in which producers utilize factors and consumers respond to market prices. In addition, the model must contain equations representing constraints on the availability of each of the factors used in production, and **balance equations** representing each of the accounting relationships of the rows and columns in the SAM. Because a CGE can incorporate substitution, productivity increases, and economies of scale, it can be a much better representation of real economies than its linear predecessors, without resort to the artificial constraints that are needed to make a linear programming model behave.

This major improvement in economic modeling has a cost: a sophisticated computer program is required to solve these complex models. However, such programs exist and can now be handled routinely by an experienced operator with a modern desk-top computer. Once a CGE model has been built, it can be tested and run repeatedly at low cost: as a consistency model; as a simulation model, tracing out many different solutions with varying specifications of the model; or as an optimizing model. With the development of the CGE, it has become feasible to test hypotheses about economic development and to try out policy recommendations within a general equilibrium framework, accommodating the many interactions that mark a real economy.[7]

PROJECT APPRAISAL

The models discussed so far have ranged from the macroeconomic treatments such as the Harrod-Domar model to disaggregated treatments of sectors (agriculture, industry) or of industries (rice farming, plastics manufacturing). One of the most commonly used tools of planning, **cost benefit analysis** or **project appraisal,** refers to a still more disaggregated activity, the investment project, such as an irrigation system, a single plastics factory, a hydroelectric dam, or a road. This technique has its genesis in the kind of analysis done by private firms on their alternative investment prospects. When a firm lays out its investment plans (called capital budgets), it tries to select investments that will yield the highest profit for a given amount of finance. The firm's calculation involves three steps, as explained in the next section.

7. Advanced students should consult Kemal Dervis, Jaime de Melo, and Sherman Robinson, *General Equilibrium Models for Developing Countries* (London: Cambridge University Press, 1982), and Robinson, "Multisectoral Models," in Chenery and Srinivasan, *Handbook of Development Economics,* volume 2.

The first step in the firm's investment decision is to forecast the **net cash flow** of an investment. Net cash flow measures the difference between the cash revenues from the sale of the product and the cash outlays on investment, material inputs, salaries and wages, purchased services, and so forth. Costs that do not deplete the cash resources of the firm, of which depreciation is the most prominent example, are not counted.

The second element involves the observation that cash received in the future is less valuable than cash received immediately, because in the interim the firm could earn interest (or profits) on these funds by investing them in bonds or savings accounts (or in additional, revenue-earning production facilities). For example, a firm or individual, asked to choose between $1,000 today or $1,000 next year, would take the money now and place it in a savings account earning, say, 8 percent a year. Then after one year the interest payment would boost the savings account balance to $1,080. So the prospect of $1,000 a year from now should be envaluated as equivalent to only $1,000 ÷ 1.08 = $926. This process, reducing the value of future flows because funds earn interest over time, is called **discounting.** Because interest is also earned on previous interest, discounting must allow for **compound interest.** In the second year another 8 percent would be earned on the balance of $1,080 and increase it to $1,166. The payment of $1,000 two years from now would then be discounted to yield a **present value** of only $1,000 ÷ 1.166 = $858. A general expression for the present value P is

$$P = F/(1+i)^n \qquad\qquad [6-18]$$

where F is the value to be realized in the future ($1,000 in our example), i is the interest rate (8 percent), and n is the number of years. As the interest rate or the delay in payment increases, the present value decreases.

An investment project will result in a series of net cash flows over time: they flow out in the early years as investments are made; then they become positive, perhaps gradually, as the new facilities begin to generate revenue in excess of recurrent costs. Such a **time profile** of net cash flow is depicted in Figure 6–4; it is the most common of several possible profiles. To summarize the value of this net cash flow in a single number, each year's net cash flow is multiplied by the respective discount factor and the resulting present values are added to give the **net present value** (NPV). Thus,

$$\text{NPV} = \sum_{t=0}^{n} (B_t - C_t)/(1+i)^t, \qquad\qquad [6-19]$$

where B_t and C_t are the benefits (revenues) and costs, including investment, in each year t; i is the discount rate; and n is the life of the project. For a firm, the correct discount rate is the average cost at which additional funds may be obtained from all sources, the firm's cost of capital.

If the net present value of a project, discounted at the firm's average cost of capital, happens to equal zero, this implies that the project will yield a net cash flow just large enough to repay the principal of all funds invested in the project and to pay the interest and dividends required by lenders and

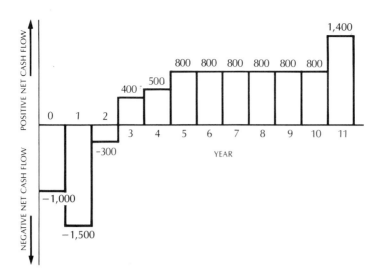

FIGURE 6–4 **Time Profile for Investment: Net Cash Flow.** The cash flow of a project can be represented by a bar diagram. Cash outflows are shown by bars below the horizontal axis; inflows by bars above the axis. Years 0 and 1 show investment in construction and equipment and hence negative cash flows; year 2 is the start-up period; years 3 and 4 show gradually increasing output and cash inflows; years 5 through 10 show steady output and cash inflows; and the project is assumed to end in year 11, when the salvage value of equipment swells the cash inflow.

shareholders. In that case, when NPV = 0, the discount rate has a special name, the **internal rate of return** (IRR). If the net present value is positive, then the project can cover all its financial costs with some profit left over for the firm. If negative, the project cannot cover its financial costs and should not be undertaken. Clearly the higher the net present value, the better the project.

Another measure of project desirability is the **benefit-cost ratio,**

$$\text{BCR} = \sum_{t=0}^{n} B_t(1+i)^{-t} \bigg/ \sum_{t=0}^{n} C_t(1+i)^{-t}. \qquad [6\text{--}20]$$

When NPV = 0, BCR = 1, so that desirable projects have an NPV greater than zero or a BCR greater than one. Although the BCR can be useful, it has the disadvantage that its precise value depends on sometimes arbitrary decisions about which cash flows to include in the numerator and which in the denominator. Neither the NPV nor the IRR calculation suffers from this ambiguity. However, the IRR has a different problem: there will be more than one IRR for a cash flow if at any time after the initial investment the cash flow again turns negative.

The cash flow of Figure 6–4 is discounted at a rate of 12 percent in Table 6–4, using Equation 6–19. The net present value is a positive $518; this indicates that the investment project will earn enough to repay the total investment ($2,500 over years 0 and 1) with a surplus of $518.

We come now to the final step in project appraisal, comparison among

TABLE 6–4   Net Present Value

Year	Cash flow[a] from Figure 6–4 (dollars)	Discount factor[b] at 12%	Present value[c] (dollars)
0	−1,000	1.000	−1,000
1	−1,500	0.893	−1,340
2	− 300	0.797	− 239
3	400	0.712	285
4	500	0.636	318
5	800	0.567	454
6	800	0.507	406
7	800	0.452	362
8	800	0.404	323
9	800	0.361	289
10	800	0.322	258
11	1,400	0.287	402
Net Present Value[d]			+518

[a] Cash flow = $(B_t - C_t)$ from Equation 6–16.
[b] Discount factor = $1/(1 + i)^t$ from Equation 6–19. In this example, i = 12 percent; t takes the value of each year, 0 to 11. Discount factors for a range of discount rates are readily available in discount tables. [See, for example, the appendix table in Michael Roemer and Joseph J. Stern, *The Appraisal of Development Projects* (New York: Praeger, 1975)].
[c] Present value = cash flow × discount factor.
[d] Net present value = algebraic sum of the present values.

projects. We already know that a project should be considered for investment only if its net present value is positive. But how to choose among
many projects, all with positive NPVs? The answer is to select that set of
projects which will yield the highest total net present value for the entire
investment budget. This assumes that the firm has a set of alternative projects to consider at any one time and an investment budget that can accommodate several but not all of these.

Opportunity Costs

A country wishing to derive the greatest possible future income (or consumption) from the resources available for investment faces the same problem as the investing firm. The only difference is that the country is interested
in resource flows and their **opportunity costs,** rather than cash flows. When
any project in the public or private sector uses goods and services, it denies
these to other possible projects. For example, investment in a dam requires
utilization of savings that could otherwise be invested in a rural road or a
textile factory; cotton used in that factory could otherwise have been
exported to earn foreign exchange; or the labor used to build the road might
have otherwise been used to build the dam or to grow cotton. To society
the cost of undertaking a project is the value of the resources—goods and
services—used to invest in and operate the new facilities. The value of
these resources is measured in terms of the net benefits they would have
provided if used in some alternative project, the opportunity cost.

A simple illustration should capture this point. A textile factory is built
and hires labor away from the rural areas. To the textile firm, the cost of
labor is the wages paid. To society, however, the cost is the reduction in
the value of production, net of costs, in the rural areas. If 10 laborers migrate

to take jobs in the new factory, their opportunity cost would be the reduction in agricultural output due to their leaving the farm, net of the nonlabor
recurrent costs of producing that output. This reduction in net output is the
value of the marginal product of price theory and is the opportunity cost of
labor in this situation.[8] Similarly, if the investment in the textile mill means
that savings will be drawn away from other projects that would on average
have earned a return of 12 percent, then the opportunity cost of capital is
12 percent, and this should be used as the discount rate in evaluating the
textile mill. Because project appraisals are most conveniently done at **constant prices,** netting out inflation, the discount rate is a **real rate of interest,**
net of inflation. If, in this example, inflation were 10 percent a year, the
corresponding nominal interest rate, the rate observed in the market, would
be 23 percent.[9]

Foreign exchange plays a special role in cost-benefit analysis. Most
developing countries face a shortage of foreign exchange, in the sense that
export revenues and foreign investment are not adequate to finance the
imports needed to achieve growth and other development targets. When a
project requires imports, such as capital equipment or raw materials, it
reduces the foreign exchange available to other projects. If it yields additional foreign exchange, by exporting its output or by substituting domestic
production for imports, it benefits other projects by providing more foreign
purchasing power. Thus, the opportunity cost or benefit of any good that
could be imported or exported should be measured as the net amount of
foreign exchange the good represents. For example, the cotton used in the
textile mill might have been exported otherwise; if so, its opportunity cost
would be the foreign currency it would have earned as an export. If the
cloth produced by the mill would have been imported in the absence of the
project, its opportunity cost (a benefit in this case) would be the foreign
exchange that would otherwise have been spent on cloth imports.

Shadow Prices

The opportunity costs of goods and services are estimated for the economy
as a whole and are called **shadow prices** or **social opportunity costs.** The first
approximation of a shadow price—for land, labor, capital, foreign exchange—
is the price paid by private participants in the market. Many interferences
in the market distort market prices from their social opportunity cost: taxes
and subsidies of all kinds, monopoly power, minimum wages, interest rate
controls, tariffs and import quotas, price controls, and so forth. Prices that
are observed in the market need to be adjusted for these effects before a

8. The value of the marginal product of a factor of production can be defined as the price
of a commodity multiplied by the additional physical output that results when one unit of the
factor is added to the production process with all other factors held constant.

9. The formula relating these is: $1 + i_n = (1 + i_r)(1 + p)$, where i_n is the nominal rate of interest, i_r is the real rate, and p is the rate of inflation. Normally we know the nominal rate and
need to calculate the real rate:

$$i_r = \frac{1 + i_n}{1 + p} - 1 = \frac{i_n - p}{1 + p}.$$

For small values of p, i_r can be approximately by $i_r = i_n - p$.

good approximation of shadow prices can be found. A simple example is the wage of textile workers. If the government imposes minimum-wage regulations, the factory will probably have to pay a wage above the opportunity costs of rural migrants and urban workers who are outside the formal, protected urban wage sector.

Estimation of shadow prices is a research task that requires intimate knowledge of the workings of an economy, both its macroeconomic relationships and the microeconomic behavior of its factor markets. It is a task to be undertaken by a central planning agency, which then instructs other planning units—ministries, public enterprises, regional and local governments—in the application of these economy-wide shadow prices to the appraisal of development projects. Not only does shadow price estimation help improve the selection of development projects, but the estimation of these opportunity costs teaches the researchers a great deal about the working of the economy, an important by-product for a central planning agency.

Although there remains much controversy among economists on the precise estimation of shadow prices, some general results have emerged for a wide range of developing countries. First, and most significant, the shadow foreign exchange rate tends to be higher than the official rate in terms of local currency per dollar, perhaps 10 to 50 percent higher. This reflects the widespread use of import duties and quotas, as well as the reluctance of many countries to devalue their exchange rate despite the inflation of domestic prices. Part IV explores these problems. As a consequence, any export project that earns more foreign exchange than it uses, or any import-substituting project that saves more than it uses, gets a boost from the shadow exchange rate. In terms of the net cash flow profile of Figure 6–4, application of the shadow rate to such projects will raise the positive net cash flows of years 3 through 11 proportionately more than it raises the negative flows of years 0 through 2, giving the project a higher net present value at the same discount rate.

Although salaries and wages of skilled employees probably require no adjustment from market to shadow prices, it is frequently true that the opportunity cost of unskilled workers is lower than the wage in formal, urban labor markets. Thus any project using unskilled labor, especially if it is located in a rural area, gets a boost because the shadow wage reduces costs without changing benefits.

The social discount rate can represent either the opportunity cost of investment and saving in the private sector, or the rate at which policy-makers wish to discount future benefits. The first method yields discount rates of 10 to 15 percent for the LDCs. The second approach usually employs a lower discount rate, but entails a shadow price of investment that raises the effective cost of capital. In either case discounting at social rates treats capital as a very scarce factor and so discourages any project with high initial investment costs, long gestation periods, and low net cash flows in the productive years. This system favors projects that generate their net benefits early, because these can be reinvested in other productive projects for continued growth, and projects that use abundant resources, especially labor, instead of scarce ones like capital.

Project appraisal using social opportunity costs is a simple and powerful device to further certain national goals. Its underlying tenet is that saving should be allocated to investments yielding the greatest future income or consumption and thus automatically accommodate the goal of efficient resource use to promote maximum growth. This further implies that scarce resources, like foreign exchange, are more highly valued than the market would indicate. The subsidiary goals of improving foreign exchange earnings or reducing dependence on imports are also built in, because any project that efficiently increases exports or reduces imports is given a correspondingly higher net present value by the shadow exchange rate. Once the central planners establish a system of appraisal with shadow prices, then every agency that designs, evaluates, and proposes investment projects is automatically incorporating these national goals in their work.

An illustration of the power of shadow pricing is contained in Table 6–5. It depicts two projects with identical cash flows. However, one project (the textile mill) earns more foreign exchange than the other (a telecommunications system), net of foreign exchange expenditures, and also uses more labor. Because the shadow wage rate is below the market rate, the economic net present value of both projects is raised, but the more labor-intensive textile project benefits more (part 2). When the shadow exchange rate is applied, the net present value of the exchange-earning textile mill is raised considerably, but that of the telecommunications system, which is a net user of foreign exchange, falls and becomes negative (part 3).

TABLE 6–5 Effects of Shadow Pricing on Cost-Benefit Analysis

---

1. Take two projects with identical cash flows, but project A earns more net foreign exchange and uses more labor than project B:

Project	Investment (first year)	Net annual cash flow (next 5 years)	Net present value at 10%
A. Textile mill of which:	− 1,000	+ 300	+ 137
Net foreign exchange earned	− 500	+ 400	
Wages paid	− 350	− 100	
B. Telecommunications system of which:	− 1,000	+ 300	
Net foreign exchange earned	− 800	0	
Wages paid	− 100	− 50	+ 137

2. *Shadow wage* is 75% of market wage, so all wage costs reduced by 25%. This results in the following net cash flows:

	Investment	Net annual flow	NPV (10%)
A. Textile mill	− 913	+ 325	+ 319
B. Telecommunications system	− 975	+ 313	+ 212

3. *Shadow exchange rate* is 20% above official rate, so net foreign exchange flow is raised by 20%. This results in the following net cash flows:

	Investment	Net annual flow	NPV (10%)
A. Textile mill	− 1,100	+ 380	+ 340
B. Telecommunication system	− 1,160	+ 300	− 23

Not all national goals can be conveniently incorporated into project appraisal, however. Two are of particular concern. The use of low shadow wages for unskilled workers will encourage employment creation but only insofar as this is efficient, in the sense that workers' opportunity cost is below the net benefit they would produce in the project. Government may, however, want to encourage employment beyond this point, because a job is the most significant way that people can participate in development and employed workers may be deemed politically more stable than the unemployed. If projects such as rural public works employ people inefficiently for the sake of employment, then the role of cost-benefit analysis is to estimate the cost of the employment in terms of the greater net benefits that might be earned if investment and labor were allocated to other projects that employ fewer people.

A second class of goals, income redistribution or poverty alleviation, can also be served by project appraisal, because low shadow wages encourage the employment of low-income labor. The impact may be weak, however, because distributional goals are still subordinate to efficient growth in the cost-benefit framework. Situations requiring structural change and large investments to alleviate poverty may not measure up to the high efficiency standard of project analysis in the short run. For this reason some economists have suggested, and some governments have considered, using welfare weights in a project analysis. These would place a higher value on net additional income to certain target groups, such as families in the lower 40 percent of the income distribution. (We have already seen such a welfare weight: w_3 of the linear programming objective function, Equation 6–14, gave an additional value of 75 percent to any income going to the poorest 40 percent of society.) Then projects generating such incomes would have higher NPVs than otherwise and would tend to be selected more frequently.

The method is potentially powerful, but has its dangers as well. The welfare premiums are arbitrary weights, subject to planners' or politicians' judgments. This in itself is not bad, but these weights can so overwhelm the other, economically based shadow prices that project selection comes down to a choice based almost entirely on arbitrary weights. This gives a false sense of precision.

Shadow prices based on existing economic conditions are not value free, either. They imply a welfare weighting scheme that accepts the existing income distribution and the resulting pattern of demand. A compromise is to keep the two goals separate, make measurements of net present values using only the economic variables, then identify separately the redistributional benefits of projects. The two can then be compared, giving decision makers a trade-off to consider and the opportunity to make clear choices of goal priorities.

We have skirted an issue of terminology. When a firm undertakes investment analysis, it can be called **commercial project appraisal,** which uses *market prices.* Traditionally, once *shadow prices* are introduced to reflect the goal of efficient growth and the real scarcities of productive factors, it has been called **social project appraisal.** The implication may be too large,

however, because only economic, and not other social, goals are incorporated. The World Bank, which undertakes a large fraction of the project
analysis done in the world, has shifted to a more accurate terminology. It
calls the second form **economic project appraisal.** The term "social appraisal"
is reserved for a third stage, in which welfare weights are applied to reflect
distributional goals. But readers should be wary, because this distinction
has not been universally accepted.

Transforming Market Prices into Shadow Prices

If governments undertake projects on the basis of economic appraisals,
using shadow prices, an implementation problem arises. A firm, whether a
public or private enterprise, can only be financially sound if it covers costs
and earns a profit at market prices. The shadow prices of planners exist
only on paper; no one pays them or receives them in the marketplace. For
example, consider a public enterprise producing paper; its investment is
encouraged by the planning ministry because it employs many workers
whose opportunity cost is low. However, the enterprise must pay its workers not the low shadow wage, but the higher minimum wage set by the
government. If this causes the firm to lose money, it could go bankrupt, in
which case the economic benefits to the country would be lost. (A private
firm, of course, would never undertake such an investment.) Hence if the
government wants the project implemented, it would have to compensate
the enterprise. The most effective compensation would be a direct subsidy
to wages, up to the difference between the shadow and minimum wages.
Not only would this improve the firm's cash flow, but it would also give
the firm an incentive to use more labor because its wage costs would be
lower. This is precisely what government wants: to employ more workers,
an abundant resource with low opportunity costs, and less of other, relatively scarce factors of production, like capital and foreign exchange.

The same holds for any productive factor that is shadow-priced: labor,
capital, foreign exchange, and specific commodities. Whenever shadow prices
push projects that are commercially unprofitable into the realm of the economically profitable, a subsidy may have to be paid to induce a firm to
undertake the project. And, conversely, if economically undesirable projects are nevertheless profitable at market prices, government should consider imposing taxes to discourage firms from undertaking such projects.

This leads to a more general point about shadow prices. They represent
the opportunity costs that ideally functioning markets should be generating
to give the right price signals to private producers and consumers. If any
of the market imperfections, discussed in Chapter 5, intervene to distort
market prices from this ideal, then one object of government policy might
be to move all market prices toward shadow prices, either by removing
imperfections or by imposing compensatory taxes and subsidies. If government can accomplish this, then resources would be used efficiently, that is,
according to their relative scarcities. Generally, this would promote economic growth, although some interventions might still be necessary to
accommodate externalities, infant industries, and institutional deficiencies.

HUMAN
RESOURCES

7

Population

The chapters in Part 2 deal with the human factor in economic development. People play a dual role in the development process: on the one hand they are its ultimate beneficiaries; on the other they provide the most important input into the process of production growth and transformation that is called economic development.

In view of this dual role, what attitude should one take toward the growth of population at the family, national, and global level? Should population growth be limited on the ground that it creates more mouths to feed and bodies to clothe, frequently in households and societies that are having trouble feeding the mouths and clothing the bodies that they already have? World population projections and estimates of natural resource availability can make frightening reading. Yet each new individual can also bring additional labor power, and even more important, additional human spark and creativity to help solve the many problems that society faces. The argument for some form of population limitation is strong, but agreement is not universal, and there are important social, political, and moral issues to be weighed.

The decision of how many children to have is an intimately personal one. Traditionally, it has been left to the choice of the couple involved, but all societies condition these individual decisions in many ways. Arguments for conscious policy intervention to limit population growth must depend either on the rationale that couples do not know how to achieve their desired family size or find it too expensive to do so, and thus must be helped to achieve it, or else on the belief that individual reproductive choices impose excessive social costs at the national or international levels. A few governments have intervened to *promote* reproduction; they have argued that the national interest requires that more children be born than people would have if left on their own. Arguments *against* intervention in reproductive decision making may appeal either to the value of freedom for the individual or to the supposed advantages of a larger population for a nation or social group.

The view of humans as an economic resource has quantitative and qualitative dimensions. Often in economic theory the quantitative aspect is emphasized while the qualitative aspect is downplayed or ignored. Many economic models assume that labor is homogeneous (undifferentiated) and thus can be measured satisfactorily by counting bodies, or hours or days of work. Other models make only a broad distinction between skilled and unskilled labor. Few take any account of the importance of gender. Such models, although useful for revealing particular truths, are extreme simplifications, since the study of economic development clearly demonstrates that the qualitative aspects of the human contribution to production are at least as important as the quantitative aspects.

Development specialists often talk about "developing human resources" or "investing in human capital." The analogy to natural resources and physical capital is appropriate in many ways. But it can be misleading if it is taken to imply that the nature of "human resources" and their contribution to production are understood as fully as the contributions of a lathe, a road, or a ton of bauxite. The role of human resources is far more complex and mysterious than any of these. To what extent, and in what ways, human resources can be created through an investment-like process are questions to be addressed in Chapters 8 to 10. This chapter lays a foundation for the later discussion by reviewing some of what is known about population and development.

DEMOGRAPHIC MEASURES

Demography, the study of population, has its own specialized vocabulary. The **birth rate,** also called the **crude birth rate,** is births per thousand of population. Likewise, the (crude) **death rate** is deaths per thousand of population. The **rate of natural increase** is the difference between the birth rate and the death rate, but it is conventionally measured in percentage terms or per hundred rather than per thousand. Say an LDC has a population of 10 million at the start of a given year. During that year it experiences 400,000 births and 150,000 deaths. If net international migration is zero (that is, if the number of immigrants equals the number of emigrants), its population at the end of the year will be 10,250,000. The midyear or average population is used in calculating the birth rate, death rate, and rate of natural increase, which in this case turn out to be 39.5, 14.8, and 2.47 respectively.

One way of expressing the growth potential of a population is through its **doubling time.** For a population growing at a constant rate, doubling time is approximately 70 divided by the growth rate. Thus a population growing at 1 percent a year doubles in about 70 years, whereas one growing at a steady 2 percent per annum will be twice as large in just 35 years, and a population growing at 3 percent a year will double in 23 years and a few months.[1]

Crude birth and death rates reflect the interaction between the *age structure* of a population and its *age-specific fertility and death rates.* Comparisons of crude birth and death rates across populations with different **age structures** (different shares of various age groups in the total population) can be misleading. For example, some LDCs have crude death rates as low as those in the developed countries, even though more people die each year in any particular age group in the LDC. The explanation is that the populations of the LDCs are much younger and young people are less likely to die than older people in all countries. In other words, LDC populations are concentrated in age ranges (older children and youth) where death rates are low.

Thus for some purposes it is important to use age-specific demographic rates. The **infant death rate** is a measure which differs sharply between rich and poor countries. It is defined as deaths in the first year of life per thousand live births. Thus if 40,000 of the 400,000 babies born in our hypothetical country die before reaching their first birthdays, the infant death rate is 100. Similar age-specific death rates can be calculated for other age groups, using mean population in the age group as a base.

Life expectancy is the number of additional years that the average person of a given age will live if age-specific death rates remain constant. It is a purer measure of mortality than the crude death rate because it is unaffected by the age distribution of the population. **Life expectancy at birth** is the most frequently used version of this measure. The **fertility** of a population refers to its propensity to have children. An **age-specific fertility rate** is the average number of children born each year to women in a particular age group. The **total fertility rate** is the sum of the age-specific fertility rates applying to a particular group (cohort) of women as they move through their reproductive years. In other words, it is the number of children the average woman will have in her lifetime if age-specific fertility rates remain constant.

A BRIEF HISTORY OF HUMAN POPULATION

We hear many expressions of concern about high rates of population growth and rising population densities in places such as Egypt, Mexico, and Bangladesh. But rising population densities are a very old story. For years peo-

---

1. The formula for exponential growth is

$$P_t = P_0 e^{rt}$$

where P_0 = population in the base year, P_t = population t years later, e = the base of the natural logarithm (2.7183), and r = the annual growth rate. If $P_t = 2P_0$, then

$$2P_0 = P_0 e^{rt}$$
$$2 = e^{rt}.$$

It turns out that $2 = e^{.7}$ (approximately). This means that rt, the product of the growth rate (expressed as a decimal) and the number of years, must equal 0.7. At 2% annual growth, for example, $0.02 \times 35 = 0.7$.

ple have been saying, "This cannot continue"; yet it does. How do current demographic trends fit into the history of human experience?

World population has been growing more or less continuously since the appearance of life on earth, but the rate of growth has been unprecedentedly high in the past 200 years. Four demographic eras in the history of humanity can be distinguished.[2]

The Preagricultural Era For perhaps half a million years, humans lived a precarious existence as hunters, gatherers, and, at least occasionally, cannibals. Population density, the number of people per square kilometer, was very low. It had to be, since a given population required a vast extent of land to sustain itself. The birth rate was probably high, but the death rate was nearly as high, and the rate of natural increase was very low. When this unimaginably long era ended with the introduction of settled agriculture about 12,000 years ago, the world's population was perhaps no more than 100 million.

From Settled Agriculture to the Industrial Revolution The development of settled agriculture revolutionized the capacity of the earth to sustain human life. During the years leading up to the Industrial Revolution of the late eighteenth and early nineteenth centuries, the food supply grew and became more reliable. The death rate fell, life expectancy increased, and population growth gradually accelerated to around 0.5 percent a year. This growth, however, was set back at intervals by plagues, famines, and wars—any of which could wipe out as much as half the population in a given area. As late as the fourteenth century, the Black Death, or bubonic plague, killed one-third of the population of Europe. Nevertheless, by 1800 the world's population was about 1.7 billion.

From the Industrial Revolution to World War II The Industrial Revolution, which marked the start of modern economic growth, further expanded the population-carrying capacity of the earth. Innovations in industry were matched by innovations in agriculture, permitting the transfer of labor to industry while raising the productivity of the remaining agricultural laborers enough to feed the growing urban population. Improved transportation, especially transcontinental railroads and fast, reliable ocean shipping, further boosted world food output in the late nineteenth century and made it possible to grow more basic foodstuffs in the areas best suited for this activity and to get supplies to food-deficit areas quickly in emergencies. Famines declined in frequency and severity. Food prices fell in many parts of the world. Meanwhile, modern medicine, sanitation, and pharmaceutical production began to develop. All these factors helped to reduce the death rate. Population growth accelerated, reaching about 1 percent per annum by World War II. This third demographic era lasted until 1945, when the population of the world was slightly less than 2.5 billion.

A feature of the third demographic era was major change in the location of world population. Between 1846 and 1930, more than 50 million people

2. Based on Lester R. Brown, *In the Human Interest* (New York: W. W. Norton & Company, 1974), pp. 20–21; for an informative and enjoyable longer presentation, see Carlo Cipolla, *The Economic History of World Population,* 7th ed. New York: Barnes & Noble, 1978).

left Europe to settle in other parts of the world. The United States received
the bulk of them, whereas smaller numbers went to Canada, Brazil, Argentina, Chile, South Africa, Australia, and New Zealand. It is estimated that the proportion of world population that was of European stock grew from 22 percent in 1846 to 35 percent in 1930, when the Great Depression put an end to mass international migration.[3] During this same period millions of laborers and merchants from densely populated India and China moved to more sparsely settled areas in Southeast Asia, Africa, the South Pacific, and elsewhere. The existence of colonial empires facilitated this movement.

The Post-World War II Period The latest demographic era has seen further dramatic improvements in food supply and disease control. Techniques introduced in the developed countries during the preceding era spread throughout the globe. People became more aware of famines and epidemics in "remote" parts of the world and less willing to tolerate them. The result was a veritable revolution in death rates and life expectancy. Plummeting death rates in many areas caused rates of natural increase to rise to 2 or even 3 percent. As its doubling time shortened drastically, world population passed 5 billion in 1987.

Despite the dramatic acceleration of change and foreshortening of the demographic eras, population growth has slowed in some parts of the world.

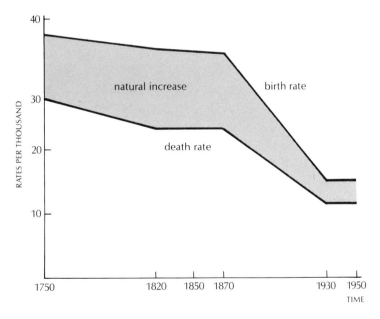

FIGURE 7–1 **The Demographic Transition in England and Wales, 1750–1950.** The decline in the death rate preceded the decline in the birth rate; this created a period of fairly rapid (about 1 percent per annum) natural increase in the late eighteenth and early nineteenth centuries. After 1870 the birth rate fell more rapidly; this sharply reduced the rate of natural increase. *Source:* Carlo Cipolla, *The Economic History of World Population.*

3. For discussion, see Cipolla, *Economic History.*

The industrial countries have experienced a **demographic transition.** Initially, these countries had birth and death rates that were both high, a pattern followed by a decrease in the death rate. This, in turn, raised the rate of natural increase. Some years later, this was followed by a drop in the death rate, which cut natural increase to around 1 percent. The demographic transition as it occurred in England and Wales is depicted in Figure 7–1.

During the present demographic era, the developing countries have apparently begun to experience a demographic transition of their own. Shortly after World War II death rates began to fall almost everywhere. The causes of this drop in mortality are discussed in Chapter 10. Death rates in the LDCs began to decline at much lower levels of per-capita income and fell much faster than these rates had previously fallen in the developed countries. An example is given in Figure 7–2 (drawn to the same scale as Figure 7–1), which depicts the demographic experience of Ceylon (now Sri Lanka) during the twentieth century. These early and sharp death rate declines, which by now have been achieved for practically the entire population of the world, have not always been followed by the lagged decline in the birth rate evident in Sri Lanka since 1955. In some countries the birth rate has fallen little, if at all. Just how the "new demographic transition" will work in the third world is a question to which we will return.

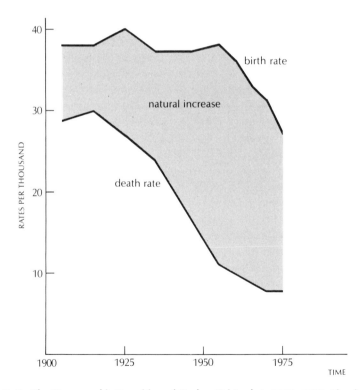

FIGURE 7–2   **The Demographic Transition of Ceylon (Sri Lanka), 1900–1975.** The death rate fell very sharply after 1920. There was no decline in the birth rate until about 1960. Very high rates of natural increase (over 2 percent per annum) were experienced in the 1950s and 1960s.

The world today exhibits a demographic dualism. The developed countries of Europe and North America have passed through the demographic transition and now have crude birth rates below 20 and rates of natural increase well under 1 percent. Since their populations are aging, their growth rates are likely to remain low.[4] In some developed countries current fertility is no longer sufficient to replace the existing population. Zero population growth (ZPG), promoted by some as a desirable target in view of limitations on natural resources, seems near in the industrialized countries.

The less-developed countries are at a much earlier stage of the demographic transition—if indeed they are entering a comparable transition process. Many low-income countries have crude birth rates of 40 or more. Yet their crude death rates are below 20, sometimes less than 10. This combination produces rates of natural increase of 2 to 3 percent, or even more. Since three-fourths of the world's population live in developing countries, the average growth rate of world population is nearly 2 percent, as shown in Table 7–1.

Table 7–2 shows some demographic and population-structure characteristics of countries at different levels of GNP per capita. Part A of this table reflects the demographic transition pattern. With only a few aberrations, such as those caused by the atypically low birth rates of India and China, birth rates decline steadily as one moves up the income scale from countries with per-capita incomes below $250 to countries with annual incomes

TABLE 7–1 **World Population by Region and Development Category, 1988[a]**

| | Total population | | Population density (per sq km) | Annual growth rate 1980–88 (%) |
	Number (in millions)	% of total		
Region				
Africa	609	12	20	3.0
Asia and Pacific	3,007	59	83	1.9
Europe	784	15	28	0.4
U.S. and Canada	272	5	14	1.0
Latin America and Caribbean	429	8	21	2.2
Development Category				
Developing countries	4,318	85	43	1.9
Low-income	2,881	56	78	2.0
Middle-income	1,437	28	23	1.8
High-income	783	15	23	0.7
World total	5,101	100	38	1.8

[a] Includes rough population estimates for Afghanistan, Kampuchea, Lebanon, and Taiwan.
Source: World Bank, *World Development Report 1990.*

---

4. But demographic behavior does sometimes surprise the experts. They were confounded, for example, by the post-World War II "baby boom" in the United States.

TABLE 7–2 Demographic and Population Characteristics of Countries by Level of GNP per Capita, 1988[a]

A. Demographic Characteristics

Income group	Crude birth rate (per 1,000)	Crude death rate (per 1,000)	Rate of natural increase (%)	Infant death rate (per 1,000 live births)
Below $250	44	16	2.8	120
$250–500	29 (38)	9 (13)	2.0 (2.5)	65 (84)
$500–2,200	30	8	2.2	55
$2,200–6,000	22	10	1.2	34
Above $6,000	14	9	0.5	10

B. Population Characteristics

Income group	Population below 15 years (% of total)	Growth rate of urban population 1980–88 (%)	Urban population (% of total)
Below $250	45	6.3	18
$250–$500	34 (42)	na (4.9)	36 (25)
$500–$2,200	36	3.6	55
$2,200–$6,000	29	1.9	64
Above $6,000	20	0.8	77

[a]Figures in parentheses exclude India and China.

Sources: World Bank, World Development Report 1990, and United Nations, Department of International Economic and Social Affairs, Demographic Yearbook 1987 (New York).

of $6,000 or more. Death rates decline sharply at about $250 per capita, then change little. The highest rates of natural increase are now in the low-income countries. (Formerly, they were in the middle-income countries, but death-rate decline has outpaced birth-rate decline in many low-income countries.) The infant death rate is a particularly sensitive measure of death rate decline; it falls by 92 percent from the poorest group of countries in Table 7–2 to the richest group. Table 7–3 gives the same information as Table 7–2 for selected countries and thus provides some idea of the range of intercountry variation.

Because of their high birth rates, developing countries have populations in which children make up large shares of the total—45 percent on average in the poorest countries, versus only 20 percent in high-income countries (see Table 7–2B). A country with a young population is said to have a high **dependency ratio,** or ratio of nonworking-age population (conventionally defined as 0 to 14, and 65 and over) to working-age population. A high dependency ratio depresses per-capita income by requiring that the output of a given number of producers by shared among a larger number of consumers.

The spatial distribution of the population is another concern in many low-income countries. **Urbanization** is an inevitable concomitant of development (Table 7–2B). Many have feared that the growth of urban areas through migration from the countryside is proceeding too fast and causing serious social problems. Yet when third-world governments have tried to staunch the flow, they have enjoyed little success. The reason is that peo-

TABLE 7–3 **Demographic and Population Characteristics of Selected Countries, 1988**

A. Demographic Characteristics

Country	Crude birth rate (per 1,000)	Crude death rate (per 1,000)	Rate of natural increase (%)	Infant death rate (per 1,000 live births)
Latin America				
Bolivia	42	14	2.8	108
Brazil	28	8	2.0	61
Chile	23	6	1.7	20
Colombia	26	6	2.0	39
Peru	31	9	2.2	86
Africa				
Ghana	45	13	3.2	88
Kenya	47	11	3.6	70
Tanzania	48	13	3.5	104
Asia				
China	21	7	1.4	31
India	32	11	2.1	97
Indonesia	28	9	1.9	68
South Korea	16	6	1.0	24
Malaysia	30	5	2.5	23
Pakistan	46	13	3.3	107
Sri Lanka	22	6	1.6	21

B. Population Characteristics

Country	Population below 15 years (% of total)	Average growth rate of urban population, 1980–88 (%)	Density (per sq km)	Urban population (% of total)
Latin America				
Bolivia	44	4.3	6	50
Brazil	36	3.6	17	75
Chile	31	2.3	17	85
Colombia	36	3.0	28	69
Peru	39	3.1	16	69
Africa				
Ghana	47	4.2	59	33
Kenya	51	8.2	39	22
Tanzania	49	11.6	26	30
Asia				
China	28	na	114	50
India	37	4.0	248	27
Indonesia	37	4.8	92	27
South Korea	27	3.7	424	69
Malaysia	37	4.9	51	41
Sri Lanka	33	1.3	252	21

Source: World Bank, *World Development Report 1990.*

ple have found they can better themselves in several ways by moving to the cities. Not only do they earn higher incomes than they could have obtained in the rural areas, but they gain better access to schooling for their children and social services of other kinds. This is what people seek in rural-urban migration, and studies have shown that by and large they find it.

This raises an important question: if rural-urban migration is good for the people who move, can it really be bad for society? It is true that there are external social costs associated with the migration process: congestion may make it harder to provide adequate urban infrastructure (housing, roads, sewers, etc.) and social services. This can be seen as a problem of **common property.** We all benefit from having fresh air to breathe, and we all lose when the air becomes polluted, but as individuals we have little incentive to avoid polluting because doing so has little effect on the air that we ourselves breathe. Is not some form of social intervention therefore needed to limit pollution so that we all may have fresher air to breathe?

Probably, but many of the social costs of urbanization arise because governments feel obliged to provide facilities to urban populations that they do not provide to rural populations. If they choose to provide better facilities in the cities than in the villages, they can hardly complain when people avail themselves of the opportunity to get improved educational, health, and recreational services. The common perception of urbanization as a problem contains an element of class bias. Ruling elites sometimes feel threatened by rapid growth in the number of poor people who live, so to speak, within marching distance of the palace.

Some third-world governments have tried to accelerate the development of secondary towns or backward regions of the country. To the extent that these policies attempt to counteract the existing pattern of incentives affecting the location of population and economic activity, they frequently fail. To make them succeed, governments have to commit large amounts of their own resources to the backward areas in the form of infrastructure and public facilities. It may be that nothing less than a radical shift in development strategy to a genuine emphasis on the intensification and diversification of the rural economy will do the job.

THE DEMOGRAPHIC FUTURE

When extrapolated into the future, even modest-seeming population growth rates soon generate projected total populations that may seem unthinkable. For example, continued growth at 1.8 percent (the average growth rate from 1980 to 1988) would bring world population to 6.3 billion by the year 2000 and 15.4 billion by 2050.

This type of projection, beloved by popular writers, is frightening to many. It is hard to imagine life in a world with two or three times as many people as there are today. How will this expanded population live? How will the globe's finite supplies of space and natural resources be affected? Should population growth be slowed down? Can it be slowed down? These are obviously vital questions that concern everyone.

Linear extrapolations of current trends are not valid because after accelerating for more than two centuries, would population growth is now starting to slow down. Many developing countries, like the industrial countries before them, are undergoing a demographic transition. But differences in the experiences of the two groups of countries are already evident. Although the decline in death rates in the developing countries is occurring at much

TABLE 7–4   Crude Birth Rate Decline in 92 Developing Countries, 1960–1988[a]

Region	Crude birth rate		% decline, 1960–1988	1988 Population of included countries (millions)
	1960	1988		
Africa	50	47	6	571.5
Asia				
China	39	21	46	1,088.4
Others	48	34	29	1,508.1
Latin America	42	28	33	422.3
Total	45	31	31	3,590.3

[a]Includes countries with population of 1 million or more; all group averages are weighted by population.
Sources: World Bank, *World Development Report 1984* and 1990.

lower levels of per-capita income than previously, it is not yet known how fast birth rates will fall. In the last two decades or so the beginnings of birth rate decline have become visible in many, but not yet all, developing countries. As Table 7–4 shows, the crude birth rate in the third world fell by nearly one-third between 1960 and 1988. China, which cut its birth rate by almost one-half, was a major contributor to this reduction. A few smaller countries (such as Singapore, Hong Kong, Malaysia, and Cuba) experienced comparable birth rate declines. Most countries in Asia and Latin America had some birth rate decline, but many in Africa have not. No one can be sure how far or fast the global trend toward lower birth rates will move. Demographic projections are adjusted up or down as each new census or survey result comes in.

There is no doubt, however, that world population will be much bigger in the future than it is now. This is assured by the phenomenon of **demographic momentum.** Fertility reduction takes time to bring population growth to a halt because populations that have been growing rapidly have large numbers of people in, or about to enter, the most fertile age brackets. Even if all the world's couples were to start today having only enough children to replace themselves in the population—what is called the **replacement level of fertility**—growth would continue into the early part of the twenty-first century. Demographers now believe that the replacement level of fertility may be reached around the year 2025. This would cause world population to stabilize at about 10 billion near the end of the twenty-first century.[5]

THE CAUSES OF POPULATION GROWTH

So world population growth will continue for at least another 100 years. The bulk of this growth will occur in the third world, with an increasing share in Africa. Viewpoints on this prospect vary widely, and discussions of world population can turn acrimonious. Questions of whose population is to be limited, and by what means, are clearly sensitive. Before we can

5. See Thomas W. Merrick, "World Population in Transition," *Population Bulletin* 41, no. 2 (January 1988): 8–16.

confront such issues intelligently, we must consider what is known about both the causes and the effects of rapid population growth. In particular, a course on economic development must concern itself with the two-way relationship between the growth of population and the rise in average income levels and structural change that we term economic development. We deal first with economic development as a cause of population growth.

Malthus and His World

The most famous and influential demographic theorist of all time was Thomas R. Malthus (1766–1834). His pessimistic view of the principles underlying human reproduction and the prospects of economic development is well known. Malthus believed that "the passion between the sexes" would cause population to expand as long as food supplies permitted. People would generally not limit procreation below the biological maximum. Should wages somehow rise above the subsistence level, they would marry younger and bear more children. But this situation could only be temporary. In time, the rise in population growth would create an increase in labor supply, which would press against fixed land resources and eventually, through diminishing returns, cause wages to fall back to the subsistence level. If this process went too far, famines and rising deaths would result. Malthus did not think that the growth of food supply could stay ahead of population growth in the long run. In a famous example he argued that food supplies grow according to an arithmetic (additive) progression while population follows an explosive geometric (multiplicative) progression.

We can see that in the grim Malthusian world population growth is limited primarily by factors working through the death rate, which he called "positive checks." In this deceptively mild phrase Malthus included all the disasters that exterminate people in large numbers: famines, wars, and epidemics. It was these phenomena, he believed, that generally constituted the operative limitation on population. Only in later editions of his famous *Essay on the Principle of Population* did he concede the possibility of a second, less drastic, category of limiting factors: "preventive checks" working through the birth rate. What Malthus had in mind here were primarily measures of "restraint," such as a later age of marriage. Unlike latter-day "Malthusians" he was not an advocate of birth control, which as a minister he considered immoral. Even while grudgingly recognizing that humankind might voluntarily control its own numerical growth, however, Malthus invested little hope in the possibility.

The gloominess of the Malthusian theory is not surprising considering that its author lived during the early years of the Industrial Revolution. In all prior history (that is, through the first two demographic eras outlined above) population had tended to expand in response to economic gains. Now with unprecedented economic growth underway in the world he knew, what could Malthus expect except an acceleration of natural increase as death rates fell? That indeed was happening during his lifetime.

Malthus did not live to witness the rest of the European demographic transition. As we saw in Figure 7–1, the early decline in death rates was followed, with a lag, by a fall in fertility; beginning in the middle of the nineteenth century, dramatic increases in wages were recorded. Why did all this happen? Wages rose, despite accelerating population growth, because capital accumulation and technical change offset any tendency for the marginal product of labor to decline. It appears that the death rate fell through a combination of the indirect effects of higher incomes (better nutrition and living conditions) and the direct effects of better preventive and curative health measures. The fall in the birth rate is harder to understand. There are both biological and economic reasons to expect, as Malthus did, that fertility would rise, not fall, as income went up. Healthier, better fed women have a greater biological capacity to conceive, carry a child full term, and give birth to a healthy infant. Also, people marry earlier when times are good, and better-off families have the financial capacity to support more children. Why then do increases in income seem to lead to declines in fertility? An answer to this question must be sought in post-Malthusian demographic theory.

Mechanisms for Reducing Birth Rates

The first stage of the demographic transition is marked by a decline in the death rate, particularly a reduction in deaths among infants and young children. This in itself is a very good thing and no humane person or government would wish to reverse the trend. The question of how to reduce the rate of population growth therefore narrows down to a matter of cutting the birth rate.

Three kinds of demographic change affect the crude birth rate. The first is change in the population shares of different age groups and sexes. A rise in the share of people of reproductive age (roughly 15 to 45) increases the birth rate, as we saw earlier in the discussion of demographic momentum. Conversely, if the proportion of older people in the population goes up, as is happening in many industrial countries today, the birth rate drops. Similarly, unbalancing the sex ratio (for example, through migration of males) reduces the birth rate, whereas correcting a previously unbalanced ration increases it. However, these structural effects are quantitatively important only in rather special circumstances.

The second demographic mechanism that influences the birth rate is change in the share of people of reproductive age who are married. This is affected by the proportion who marry at some time in their lives, by the average age of first marriage, and by the divorce rate.

The third factor is marital fertility, the rate at which married couples reproduce. Historical birth rate declines have come about mainly because of declines in marital fertility. Later age of marriage has also been important in some cases, for example in the drop of the Irish birth rate after the potato famine of the 1840s.

It has been suggested that there are three basic preconditions for a significant decline in marital fertility. (1) Fertility must be subject to conscious choice; it must be socially acceptable for a couple to decide how many children they want to have. (2) Reduced fertility must be seen as advantageous; there must be perceived social and economic benefits to having fewer children. (3) Effective techniques of fertility reduction must be available;

couples must know about them and agree to employ them.[6] Some theorists believe the first and third preconditions are only facilitating influences. The active force working for lower birth rates, they argue, is perceived incentives for individuals to have fewer children.

Modern Theories of Fertility

Modern theories of fertility try to explain how people use the available mechanisms for determining the number of births. Many of these theories employ a supply and demand framework. Looked at this way, family planning programs work mainly on the supply side. They can reduce the birth rate by making it easier and cheaper for people to regulate the number of births and come closer to their desired family size. They may also affect the demand side of this equation—the number of children people want to have—but probably not much. The social motivations that led the government to undertake a family planning program—perceived crowding and strain on national resources, perhaps some pressure from foreign aid organizations—are likely to be very different from the private considerations that influence individuals. Couples are unmoved by general, remote-sounding arguments.

Why, then, do people have children? Is is because they are moved by Malthus's "passion between the sexes" and do not know how to prevent the resulting births? Or do they have many children because they are tradition-bound, custom-ridden? Or is it perhaps rational in some social settings? All three positions have some merit. The case for the first one was stated by a Latin American doctor at an international conference a few years ago. "People don't really want children," he said. "They want sex and don't know how to avoid the births that result." This viewpoint captures the element of spontaneity that is inevitably present in the reproductive process. Yet the evidence suggests that all societies consciously control human fertility. In no known case does the number of children that the average woman has over her childbearing years even approach her biological capacity to bear children. All societies practice methods of inhibiting conception, aborting pregnancies, and disposing of unwanted infants, even societies that have had no contact with modern birth control methods.

It has been said that many children are the social norm in traditional societies, that society looks askance at couples who have no or few children, that a man who lacks wealth can at least have children, that a woman's principal socially recognized function in a traditional society is to bear and rear children. Such norms and attitudes are important, but they are probably not the decisive factors in human fertility. Fertility is evidently determined by a complex combination of forces, but social scientists in recent years have given increasing credence to the elements of individual rationality in the process. Simply stated, they believe that most families in traditional societies have many children because it is rational for them to do so. By the same token people in modern societies have fewer children

---

6. Michael S. Teitelbaum, "Relevance of Demigraphic Transition Theory for Developing Countries," *Science* 188 (May 2, 1977): 420–425.

because that is rational behavior in the circumstances in which they live.

It follows that to reduce fertility in developing countries, it is necessary to
alter the incentives.

Although some would regard it as a cold, inhumane way of looking at the
matter, it is nevertheless true that children impose certain costs on their
parents and confer certain benefits. To the extent that couples are influenced by these benefits and costs, are able to calculate them, and are capable of carrying out their reproductive plans, it follows that to reduce the
birth rate it will be necessary to increase the ratio of costs to benefits.

The benefits of having children can be classified as economic and psychic.
Within a few years of their birth, children may supplement family earnings
by working. On family farms and in other household enterprises there is
usually something that even a very young child can do to increase production. And in many poor societies large numbers of children work for wages
outside the home. In the longer run children provide a form of social security in societies lacking institutional programs to assist the elderly. In some
cultures it is considered especially important to have a son who survives to
adulthood; in view of high infant and child mortality, this can motivate
couples to keep having children until two or three sons have been born.
Besides these economic benefits, which are probably more important in a
low-income society than in a more-affluent one, children can also yield
psychic benefits, as all parents know.

The costs of children can also be categorized as economic and psychic.
Economic costs can be further divided into explicit (monetary) and implicit
(opportunity) costs. Children entail cash outlays for food, clothing, shelter,
and sometimes for hired childcare services and education. Implicit costs
arise when childcare by a member of the family (usually, but not always,
the mother) involves a loss of earning time. Psychic costs include anxiety
and loss of leisure-time activities. Some of the costs felt by parents parallel
costs of population growth experienced at the national level. For example,
more children in a family may mean smaller inheritances of agricultural
land, an example of a natural resource constraint operating at the family
level. Similarly, it may be harder to send all the children in a larger family
to school; this reflects the pressures on social investment which are felt
when population growth is rapid.

Viewing childbearing as an economic decision has several important
implications. (1) Fertility should be higher when children can earn incomes
or contribute to household enterprises at a young age than when they can
not. (2) Reducing infant deaths should lower fertility because fewer births
will then be needed to produce a given desired number of surviving children. (3) The introduction of an institutionalized social security system should
lower fertility because then the need for parents to depend on their children
for support in their old age is reduced. (4) Fertility should fall when there
is an increase in opportunities for women to work in jobs that are relatively
incompatible with childbearing, essentially work outside the home. (5) Fertility should be higher when income is higher because the explicit costs are
more easily borne.

The first four theoretical predictions have been pretty well verified in
empirical studies. The fifth, however, is in glaring conflict with observed

reality. In the real world fertility is usually negatively related to income, not positively related as simple theory predicts. The negative relationship shows up both in time-series date—fertility usually declines through time as income rises—and in cross-section date—fertility is generally higher in poor countries than in rich countries; also,in most societies middle- and upper-income families have fewer children than poor families.

Several theorists have tried to explain this anomaly. Gary Becker of the University of Chicago, a pioneer of "the new household economics," views children as a kind of consumer durable that yields benefits over time. Couples maximize a joint (expected) utility function in which the "goods" they can "buy" are (1) number of living children, (2) "child quality" (a vector of characteristics including education and health), and (3) conventional goods and services. The constraints faced by parents in Becker's model are (1) their time and (2) the cost of purchased goods and services. Becker explains the fall in fertility as income rises over time by saying that the cost of children tends to rise, especially because the opportunity cost of the parents' time goes up. He believes that the spread of contraceptive knowledge also plays a part. Given the rising cost of child *quantity*, Becker argues that many parents opt to invest in child *quality*, and spend more money on a decreasing number of children.[7]

Whereas Malthus erred in basing his theory of population on an assertion that human nature is immutable, Becker has been criticized for going too far in the opposite direction and exaggerating the extent to which couples consciously select their family sizes using a benefit-cost calculus. Although others argue that socially conditioned changes in tastes and values are an important part of the demographic transition, Becker regards tastes as given.

Rivaling Becker's purely economic model of fertility is the more eclectic framework of University of Pennsylvania demographer Richard Easterlin, who directly addresses people's motivation to use the available means of fertility control. He says this is determined by two factors. One is the demand for children, defined as the number of surviving children a couple would have if fertility regulation were costless; this is essentially a matter of tastes, which Easterlin, unlike Becker, believes do change over time. The second factor influencing people's interest in fertility control is natural fertility, which Easterlin defines as their potential number of children if fertility were not deliberately limited; this is determined partly by biology and partly by culture. Besides motivation to limit fertility, Easterlin believes the cost of controlling fertility is another important influence on the actual use of means to limit births. To Easterlin, cost includes not only market costs, such as the cost of contraceptives, but also psychic costs deriving, for example, from social disapproval of particular fertility limitation practices. Easterlin thus explains declining fertility in the real world as the combined effect of changing tastes and the declining cost of fertility control.

For the population policymaker, Becker's theory emphasizes the importance of changing incentives to have children if one wishes to reduce fertil-

---

7. See Gary Becker, *A Treatise on the Family* (Cambridge, Mass.: Harvard University Press, 1981).

ity, whereas Easterlin's approach points to the need to change tastes and reduce the market and psychic costs of practicing birth control.[8]

173
ANALYZING THE
EFFECTS OF
RAPID
POPULATION
GROWTH

The demographer John Caldwell explains the demographic transition in somewhat different terms that are still consistent with the general idea of rational choice. He argues that the main reason why large families are rational in traditional societies is that extended family relationships cause net inter-generational wealth transfers to flow from younger to older generations. According to Caldwell, as nuclear families become more common and the emotional and economic ties between generations weaken in the course of modernization, the direction of the intergenerational flow of wealth reverses. Since parents must now transfer net wealth to their children, rather than receiving net wealth from them, they opt to have fewer children.[9]

ANALYZING THE EFFECTS OF RAPID POPULATION GROWTH

Two questions are important for population policy. What are the effects of population growth on development and human welfare? And if population growth is thought to have harmful effects, how can these harmful effects best be reduced or eliminated?

Optimum Population

The theory reviewed in the preceding section implies that at the family level population tends toward an optimum, in the sense that people have the number of children they consider beneficial to their overall welfare. Yet when asked, many parents in LDCs say that they would rather have fewer children than they have. Also, several studies show that rates of sickness and death are higher among children in large families, especially those born later in the family. So perhaps parents' judgments about an optimal family size change after they have become parents and have formed a more realistic appraisal of the costs and benefits of children.

When we consider the relationship between population and welfare at the national level, the question that arises is whether individual preferences should be allowed to determine how large a population a country has. What are the effects of population growth on development and human welfare? Is there a case for the state to intervene to curb, or in some instances perhaps to encourage, human reproduction?

We can begin to attack this issue by considering the relationship between per-capita income and the size of the population in a given country. Would per-capita income be higher or lower if the population were larger than it is? In dynamic terms, which are more relevant for policy, the question is whether the future growth of per-capita income would be faster or slower if the rate of population growth were increased or reduced.

8. See Richard Easterlin, "Modernization and Fertility: A Critical Essay," in *Determinants of Fertility in Developing Countries*, Vol. 2, R. Bulatao and R. Lee, eds. (New York: Academic Press, 1983), pp. 562–586.
9. See John C. Caldwell, "Toward a Restatement of Demographic Transition Theory," *Population and Development Review* 2, nos. 3–4 (September–December 1976): 321–366.

An answer to this question can be reached through successive approximations. The oldest and simplest answer is that with every mouth comes a pair of hands. This implies that economic activity is scale-neutral, that per-capita income is unaffected by the size or growth rate of the population. But this ancient piece of folk wisdom is all too obviously an oversimplification. It ignores the role of nonlabor resources and the possibility (which so concerned Ricardo and Malthus) that diminishing returns will be encountered as population expands.

A somewhat more sophisticated approach that meets this objection is the optimum population theory: for any given country at any particular time with a fixed supply of nonlabor resources, there is a unique population size at which per-capita income is maximized. The idea is that at suboptimal levels of population, per-capita income is lower than it could be because there is not enough labor to utilize the available nonlabor resources efficiently, whereas at levels above the optimum, per-capita income is also lower because there is too much labor and diminishing returns set in. This relationship is graphed in Figure 7–3.

Optimum population theory is consistent with the intuition that there can be underpopulated countries and overpopulated countries. It is not hard to believe that immigration into the United States, Canada, and Australia during the nineteenth century raised per-capita income in those countries. (It is harder to think of underpopulated countries in today's world, although some in East and Southern Africa might qualify.) Nor is it implausible to think that Bangladesh's per-capita income would rise if some millions of its population could somehow be made to disappear. The trouble with the

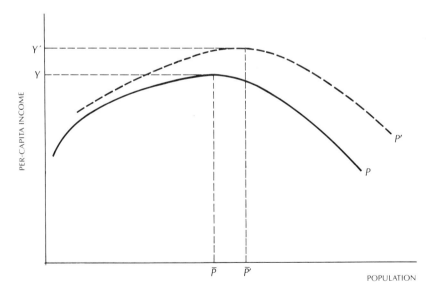

FIGURE 7–3 **The Theory of Optimum Population.** Curve P shows that, at levels of population below $\bar{P}$, an increase in population leads to an increase in income per capita, but beyond $\bar{P}$, more population reduces average income. $\bar{P}$ is the optimum level of population. Discoveries of new resources, capital accumulation, or technological change can shift the curve upward to P', with a new, higher optimum population $\bar{P}'$.

approach is that it is a static framework and can take only limited account for dynamic factors. Capital accumulation, technical change, and natural-resource discoveries make it possible simultaneously to raise per-capita income and to increase the optimum population over time.

175
ANALYZING THE
EFFECTS OF
RAPID
POPULATION
GROWTH

Dynamic Models of Population Growth

Figure 7–3 depicts what economists call comparative statics. The optimum population theory shows how income per capita is determined at a point in time, given population, stocks of other resources, and technology. It also indicates how income per capita is affected by, say, a one-time improvement in technology, but it does not show what would happen through time as population and capital stocks grow, as resource supplies stabilize or decline, and as technology changes. A dynamic model would try to do that.

The pioneering work in dynamic modeling of population's effect on material welfare was published in 1958 by Princeton University demographer Ansley Coale and Duke University economist Edgar Hoover, who created a macroeconomic model of population growth and development in India.[10] According to the analysis of Coale and Hoover, a reduction in the Indian birth rate would help growth in per-capita income in two important ways. First, slower population growth would lower the dependency ratio, reducing consumption and increasing saving at any given level of income. Second, as labor force growth slowed about 15 years later, the amount of investment needed to provide a constant amount of capital per worker for a growing number of workers (called *capital widening*) would go down and permit more investment to be used to increase capital per worker (*capital deepening*). These two kinds of benefit from slower population growth would be felt both at the household level and at the national level.

Concern about the Effects of Population Growth on Development

Later model builders have generally supported the findings of Coale and Hoover. Their analyses are thus consistent with the long-standing view that rapid population growth impedes development. During the 1970s the U.S. Agency for International Development, the World Bank, and other international aid agencies gave heavy emphasis to population policy as a criterion for judging the seriousness of the development effort of a potential aid recipient. A comprehensive review of population change and development conducted by the World Bank in 1984 found that rapid population growth depresses private savings, necessitates more capital widening, and discourages capital deepening that would raise productivity and per-capita income.[11] In addition, many writers called attention to the deleterious effects of population growth on the environment. They noted that rising population densities have caused deforestation in many parts of the third world as

10. Ansley J. Coale and Edgar M. Hoover, *Population Growth and Economic Development in Low-Income Countries: A Case Study of India's Prospects* (Princeton, N.J.: Princeton University Press, 1958).
11. See World Bank, *World Development Report 1984*, pp. 51–206.

rural people move up the hillsides in search of more agricultural land and firewood. Indeed, depletion of all nonrenewable resources is accelerated by rapid population growth. Maintaining a stable or rising per-capita food supply has not been so great a problem as Malthus anticipated, but it has proven difficult in wide areas of sub-Saharan Africa. The World Bank, among many others, has also pointed to the impact of growing total population on urbanization, which brings with it extra costs that society must bear.

The proposition that population growth retards increases in per-capita income has obvious appeal in developing countries (including many in Asia, Egypt, and most Caribbean islands) where population density is already so high in relation to land and other natural resources that diminishing returns have probably set in. Even in areas where population density is lower, however—certain land-rich areas in sub-Saharan Africa and South America—rapid population growth can press on scarce capital resources and inhibit capital deepening and efforts to improve public services. It thus can be argued that it reduces the growth of per-capita income in both types of LDCs.

Recall from the earlier discussion of fertility determinants that although some of the pressures created by high population growth and density are felt by individuals, others are not. For example, excessive growth in the number of school-age children makes it difficult for society to provide schooling of adequate quality for everyone. Although a reduction in the average number of children per family would contribute to a solution of this problem, particular couples would not find publicly financed educational facilities any better if they had fewer children (although they *would* be better able to meet the private costs of schooling). One argument for policy intervention to bring about a more-moderate rate of population growth is that such social diseconomies can be avoided.

It is also argued that rapid population control in particular countries produces external diseconomies at the international level. There are nationalistic reasons, related to prestige and sometimes also to military power, why particular states may want to have larger populations. But this can disrupt international relations and injure other countries. Policies to expand national populations may increase the likelihood of war by making larger armies possible and by heightening competition for land and other resources. They may create pressures for migration from densely populated countries to other countries whose population growth is under control. For all these reasons there is a case for an international effort to limit world population. The main problem is to decide whose population is to be limited. Possibilities for doing much about population at the global level are limited by the linkage of the population problem to other issues of international politics and by the locus of population policy, which is at the national level.

Doubters and Dissenters

Despite the arguments for limiting population growth in developing countries, the results of population modelers, and the views of powerful aid organizations, there have always been dissenters from the majority opinion that rapid population growth is harmful to economic development in the **177**

ANALYZING THE
EFFECTS OF
RAPID
POPULATION
GROWTH
third world. These contrary views have received some support recently
from empirical researchers, who have found it difficult to identify or mea-
sure population growth's deleterious effects.

Here are some examples of analysts who have doubted that faster population growth retards growth in per-capita income or even claimed that it
is beneficial.

(1) The Australian economist Colin Clark was one of the first to comment
on the lack of empirical support for the proposition that population growth
impedes economic growth. He claimed that the empirical relationship
between the growth rate of population and that of per-capita income was
in fact positive.[12]

(2) The Danish economist Ester Boserup concluded from her historical
studies of agricultural development that population growth serves as a
stimulus to agricultural intensification and technological improvement.[13]

(3) Julian Simon of the University of Illinois has mustered a variety of
arguments in favor of population growth, notably that a larger population
is likely to contain more entrepreneurs and other creators, who can make
major contributions to solving the problems of humanity. He calls human
ingenuity the "ultimate resource" that can overcome any depletion of other
resources.[14]

(4) Rati Ram of the University of Illinois and Theodore W. Schultz of the
University of Chicago have pointed out that the longer life spans that
accompany falling death rates and faster population growth in the LDCs
increase the incentives for investment in human capital and make labor
more productive.[15]

(5) A recent review of population and development sponsored by the
National Academy of Sciences addressed a series of assertions about the
negative effects of population growth and generally found that empirical
evidence to support them is weak.[16]

Conclusion: A New Consensus?

Despite these doubts and dissents, most analysts still believe that in the
circumstances of nearly all LDCs slower population growth would permit
per-capita income to rise more rapidly. But the issues are complex, and
evidence for the notion that slower population growth by itself would create large benefits is not strong. The authors of the National Academy of

12. See Colin Clark, "The 'Population Explosion' Myth," *Bulletin of the Institute of Development Studies,* Sussex, England (May 1969), and Colin Clark, "The Economics of Population Growth and Control: A Comment," *Review of Social Economy* 28, no. 1 (March 1970):
449–466.
13. See Ester Boserup, *The Conditions of Agricultural Growth* (Chicago: Aldine, 1965).
14. See Julian L. Simon, *The Ultimate Resource* (Princeton, N.J.: Princeton University
Press, 1981), and Julian L. Simon, *Theory of Population and Economic Growth* (Oxford: Basil
Blackwell, 1986).
15. Rati Ram and Theodore W. Schultz, "Life Span, Savings, and Productivity," *Economic Development and Cultural Change* 27, no. 3 (April 1979): 394–421.
16. See National Academy of Sciences, *Population Growth and Economic Development:
Policy Questions* (Washington, D.C.: National Academy Press, 1986).

Sciences report put it this way: "On balance, we reach the qualitative conclusion that slower population growth would be beneficial for most developing countries. A rigorous quantitative assessment of these benefits is difficult and context-dependent." [17]

As emphasis on the role of population growth in retarding economic developments lessens, it has been suggested that a "new consensus" on the relationship between population growth and economic development may be forming. [18] Analysts may now be slower to blame population growth for development problems and more cautious about assertions that individuals' reproductive decisions create heavy social costs. Political and institutional factors intermediate the relationship between population growth and development. A high rate of population growth does not necessarily slow down economic growth, and a lower population growth rate will not necessarily accelerate it. The new consensus would reject casting population growth as the "villain" in the story of third-world development, although it may be the "accomplice."

POPULATION POLICY

Most LDC governments today are on record as favoring slower population growth and have also formulated policies, usually family planning programs, for attempting to achieve it. Most of the strongest commitments have come from Asian governments. Latin American governments, when they provide family planning services officially or permit private organizations to do so, usually justify their actions mainly or entirely as efforts to promote the welfare of mothers and children. Some African governments are committed to population growth limitation, whereas others are indifferent or openly pronatalist (see boxed example of Kenya). The population policies of Communist regimes have varied among countries and from time to time. China has achieved what is probably the most effective control over population ever attained by any government through its "planned births" campaign (see boxed example).

Population and Family Planning in Kenya

Kenya is an African country with low population density at present but a high growth rate and explosive demographic potential. With a crude birth rate of 47 per thousand and a crude death rate of 11 (see Table 7–3), Kenya has one of the highest rates of natural increase observed anywhere. And this growth shows no signs of slowing down anytime soon. A survey taken in the late 1970s found that Kenyans regarded eight children as an ideal family size, up from six in the 1960s. The total fertility rate in 1988 was 6.9. At its present rate of growth, Kenya's population will double in less than 20 years.

17. Ibid. p. 90.
18. The title is borrowed from Merrick, "World Population in Transition."

Why Kenyans are so very fertile is not clear. Although Nairobi, the capital, is a prosperous, modern city, the country is still 78 percent rural. The per-capita GNP of $370 (1988) is very unequally distributed. Water shortages severely restrict the cultivatability of much of Kenya's land, and in some of the fertile areas there are large farms. Many Kenyans, therefore, must make a living from holdings that are either too small or too poorly watered to ensure an adequate income.

Surprisingly, the Kenyan government adopted a policy of population limitation as early as 1966. Despite substantial international aid, however, the national family planning program has been unable to make much headway. It is said that the late President Jomo Kenyatta, who issued the 1966 statement, subsequently refused to lend public support to family planning. Part of the problem was Kenya's keen tribal rivalries, which made each group fear that if it adopted birth limitation it would only be boosting the power of its competitors. In recent years, however, as the dangers of continued rapid population growth have become both evident and imminent, President Daniel Arap Moi's government has actively supported a revived family planning effort.

Population and Family Planning in China

Since 1971, China has made unique progress toward gaining control over the growth of its massive population. By doing so, it has not only made a large numerical impact on the total population of the globe but has also provided important lessons to other low-income countries interested in fertility reduction. But some of the techniques used to reduce the number of births in China may not be transferable to other political and cultural settings, and others would not be widely acceptable because of the loss of personal freedom they involve.

Population policy in China has been anything but constant. After the Communist takeover in 1949 Chairman Mao Zedong repeatedly asserted that "revolution plus production" would solve all problems, with no need to limit population growth. China's first census, conducted in 1953, revealed such a large population (nearly 600 million) that it shook this complacency. But birth control campaigns from 1956–1958 and from 1962–1966 had only limited results and were interrupted by Mao's famous policy reversals, the Great Leap Forward of 1960 and the Cultural Revolution of the late 1960s. Only in 1971 was a serious and sustained effort launched. At that time the crude birth rate, already reduced by the disruptions of the Cultural Revolution, stood at 30. By 1983 it had been cut to 19.

The "planned births" campaign of 1971 was reportedly launched at the personal initiative of Premier Zhou Enlai. It established three reproductive norms *(wan xi shao)*: later marriage, longer spacing between births, and fewer children. To implement these norms, the highly committed post-Mao leadership set birth targets for administrative units at all levels throughout China. Responsibility for achieving these targets was placed in the hands of officials heading units ranging from provinces of 2 to 90 million people down to production teams of 250 to 800. The national government held information and motivation campaigns to persuade people to have fewer children, but it was left to local officials to fill out many details of the program and finance much of its cost. A wide range of contraceptives was offered and family planning was closely linked to efforts to improve child and maternal health care.

While national spokesmen maintained that participation in the program was voluntary, local officials with targets to fulfill often applied pressure. At the production-team level, birth planning became intensely personal, as couples were required to seek approval to have a child in a particular year. (The application could be accepted, or they might be asked to wait a year or two.) Such extreme methods seem to have worked and been reasonably well-accepted in China, presumably because of its cohesive social structure and strong government authority from the national down to the neighborhood level.

The most popular form of birth limitation in China has been the intrauterine device (IUD). Two other major forms have been abortion and sterilization of both women and men.

The *wan xi shao* campaign lowered fertility, but population projections continued to be a matter for concern and in 1979 the "one child" campaign was promulgated. Couples were now told that "only children are better children" and urged to take a pledge to stop at one. Those who do so often receive special incentives, such as an income supplement, extra maternity leave, and preferential treatment when applying for public housing. The "one child" campaign flies in the face of traditional son-preference by asking half of China's couples to stop reproducing before they have had a male child and appears to have been associated with some resurgence of female infanticide or neglect of girl babies, but it did succeed in reducing fertility to the replacement level by the mid-1980s. The target now is to stabilize the population at about 1.2 billion early in the twenty-first century.

Although some aspects of China's population program will doubtless remain unique, countries interested in strengthening their own programs could learn from China's strong information activities, its use of a wide range of contraceptive methods, and its decentralization of many aspects of planning and implementation to local authorities.

Political, moral, and religious problems have arisen in connection with population policy in a number of countries. Some countries are pronatalist for nationalistic reasons, perhaps because they want to have enough people to hold areas of low population density against external challenges. Others (Guyana, Lebanon, Nigeria, Malaysia, and Singapore, to name a few) have internal racial, tribal, religious, or ethnic divisions that make population policy a sensitive matter, since it involves the balance of power among the various groups. Still other countries have provoked adverse political reactions by adopting methods of population control regarded as excessively zealous, offensive to local belief, or callous in their disregard of individual rights. Indira Gandhi's surprising defeat in India's 1977 general election was attributed in part to the population policy of her emergency government. Despairing of controlling population growth by conventional means, the government added male sterilization to its list of promoted family planning methods. Incentives were offered to those who agreed to be sterilized, and quotas were assigned to officials charged with carrying out the program in different parts of the country. Problems arose when force was allegedly used against low-status individuals by officials anxious to fill their quotas. The result was a setback not only for Indira Gandhi's government but also for Indian family planning.

The thinking about population and development reviewed here casts light on both the rationale for population policy in the LDCs and the proper design of programs to reduce fertility. Population policy must be grounded in consideration of the effects of rapid population growth in a low-income country. Its design should pay attention to the modern theories of fertility determination.

There are two main arguments for the promotion of family planning in an LDC. One is that, through information dissemination and access to contraceptives, couples can be helped to realize their reproductive plans. The second argument is that high fertility has social costs that are not taken into account by individuals but should be offset by government on behalf of society by subsidizing family planning, penalizing couples who have many children, or both. The first argument enjoys wide support, but the second is more controversial. The World Bank's 1984 *World Development Report* supported both arguments,[19] but the National Academy of Science's recent review called into question the magnitude of population growth's social costs.

Policy Alternatives

The alternatives facing a policymaker who wishes to reduce population growth include family planning, population redistribution, more drastic measures like abortion or sterilization, and policies that alter reproductive incentives.

In essence, **family planning programs** do two things: they make one or more forms of contraception more widely or cheaply available, or both; and they undertake information and propaganda activities to urge people to use them. These programs have achieved good results in some cases but had little or no discernible effect in others. They appear to work best where there is a pre-existing desire for smaller families, at least in some parts of the population. Most of the family planning programs that have been relatively successful in reaching a large number of acceptors and retaining a large stock of current users over time are to be found in countries that are rapidly attaining higher literacy, reduced infant death rates, and more widespread female employment outside the home.[20] In countries where these factors are absent, family planning tends to catch on among the relatively well-off, the urbanized, and the educated, but it spreads very slowly among the rest of the population.

19. See World Bank, *World Development Report 1984*, pp. 51–206.
20. This list of factors is based on empirical research. Some of the reasons why these factors should be influential were suggested earlier.

The record, however, is not clear-cut. In some parts of rural Indonesia, family planning has had a measurable effect on the birth rate, despite comparatively low levels of income, education, and health services (see the following boxed example). Integrating contraceptive services with other services, especially maternal and child health services, seems to help. Even if population growth is not reduced, enabling women to improve the spacing of births has health and welfare benefits that women recognize and that contribute to acceptance of the program.

Population and Family Planning in Indonesia

Indonesia is the fifth most populous country in the world. Its 175 million people (1988) inhabit a chain of islands stretching some 3,000 miles along the equator. Two-thirds of all Indonesians live on Java and Bali, small islands that make up only 7 percent of the land area. In the rural areas of Java and Bali, population densities are among the highest in the world, land holdings are small and shrinking, and decent jobs are hard to find.

For many years transmigration to the less fertile but relatively uncrowded outer islands of Sumatra, Kalimantan, and Sulawesi has been promoted as a way of easing population pressure in Java and Bali. But this has never made a dent in population growth in these core islands, nor has it lowered existing densities. Indeed, although some migrants move toward available agricultural land in the outer islands, many others flock to Java's cities, where the best income-earning opportunities are concentrated.

Indonesia's population policy reversed gears in the late 1960s. Sukarno, the ardent nationalist who was president from 1945 to 1966, often proclaimed his belief that Indonesia had too few people, not too many. "We have rich natural resources," he said. "We need more people to exploit them." Yet Sukarno's government failed to develop the country's resources, and by the mid-1960s Indonesia's masses were desperately short of food, clothing, and medical care.

Suharto, the second president, tried to rebuild the economy. He also declared approval of population limitation, and in 1970 an official family planning program was launched. Although most people in Indonesia are still poor and ill-educated, this program has succeeded beyond anyone's expectation. Greatest attention was paid to, and greatest success achieved in, the rural parts of Java and Bali. The program was imaginatively conceived, well-managed, and implemented largely through existing village institutions. Pills were used as the main method of contraception. By 1980 fertility in key areas had fallen by 15 to 20 percent. In other areas fertility remained high; in still others it was low, but only because of low female fecundity resulting from ill-health and malnutrition.

During the 1980s fertility reduction in Indonesia has been further spurred by rapid expansion of educational opportunities. Parents now see greater possibilities for sending their children to high school and college and are limiting the number of children they have as a way to save more and thus realize these dreams. Indonesia's official goal is to cut fertility in half by the year 2000. Although this ambitious target may not be realized, a deter-

mined government will still have succeeded in improving a critical demo- **183**
graphic situation under circumstances that experts considered quite POPULATION
unfavorable for family planning. POLICY

A second broad approach to population policy would be to try to move people from one part of the country to another to improve the fit between population and the availability of land and other resources. This *population redistribution* may help to accommodate a growing total population in limited circumstances, but the magnitude of the effect is not likely to be great. First, there must be empty but habitable space into which people can be moved. Then, particularly if the government is going to organize the movement, a considerable investment of capital and formidable organizational capacity will be required. It is hard to move enough people to make a real difference, as experience in Brazil, Indonesia, and elsewhere shows. We have already noted that the kind of mass international population redistribution that was a major factor in the nineteenth century is unlikely to occur in today's world, although smaller movements of people (motivated by political as well as economic considerations) are still taking place.

Methods of population control more drastic than contraception, such as abortion and sterilization, have played an important part in the slowdown of population growth in several European, South American, and East Asian countries. These methods are often regarded as objectionable on moral grounds. When forced on resisting populations, as in India during the emergency of the mid-1970s, they can backfire. Yet when acceptable to local mores, they may help to bring about a rapid decline in fertility.

Besides family planning, many other government policies indirectly influence fertility levels by *altering incentives to have children*. Some governments have used these policies to complement the effects of their family planning efforts. The policies include increased education for girls, especially the attainment of basic literacy for all women in countries that have not yet reached this target; increased job opportunities for women outside the home; formal social security systems—a realistic option only for middle-income countries; a ban on child labor; compulsory schooling up to a certain age; and a rise in the status of women, which will give them greater control over their own lives. The use of monetary incentives and disincentives geared to the number of children per family has also been advocated. The trouble with these measures is that although they may discourage parents from having an additional child, they frequently penalize those children already born. For example, levying higher charges for the medical care and schooling of third and subsequent children may indeed cause parents to have fewer children, but it may also result in lower quality care for children who, through no fault of their own, are born late into large families.

Reduction of infant mortality can be also be considered an indirect population policy. According to the child replacement thesis, the number of children that a couple has is geared to the number it expects to survive; accordingly, if survival prospects improve, then the birth rate—if not necessarily the rate of natural increase—will fall.

A country that once emphasized policies to provide disincentives for large families, albeit in rather special circumstances, is Singapore. There 60 percent of the population lives in public housing, and nearly everyone is heavily dependent on the government for a variety of social services. In a campaign to limit population growth, the government of Singapore discriminated among users of public services on the basis of how many children they have. People with large families paid higher maternity fees, got lower priority in school election, and received no extra income tax deductions or housing space. Abortion and sterilization (male and female) were made available on demand at nominal fees. All this was backed up by a determined information campaign. Singapore's tough policy contributed to a dramatic fall in population growth, although rapid economic and social change in the Southeast Asian city-state has probably had an even greater impact. In fact, the campaign was so successful in reducing fertility that recently the Prime Minister has reversed himself and urged educated women in particular to have more children so that the quality of the population can be maintained!

A final idea for indirectly influencing fertility is that *improvement in the distribution of income* will cut the birth rate. (The complementary proposition, that unequal income distribution leads to higher fertility, has also been put forward.) This makes sense, since poor households have perhaps three-quarters of the babies born in a developing society and it is their income that must rise if an increase in income is to bring about a decline in fertility. A related idea is that a generally equitable pattern of development, including improving social services for the poor, will convince people that their lives are improving and they are gaining increasing control over their own destinies, and lead to an especially rapid decline in fertility. These are attractive hypotheses and there is some evidence to support them, but it is not conclusive.

Family Planning versus Development?

Some people, with diverse perspectives, argue that governments should worry less about population policy, concentrate more on *economic development*, and leave it to the demographic transition to bring about a decline in fertility. At the first United Nations World Population Conference, held in Bucharest in 1974, a popular slogan was, "Take care of the people and the population will take care of itself." There and elsewhere, verbal wars have been waged between family planners and developmentalists. Ideology often becomes entwined in the debate. Marxist spokesmen routinely contend that population pressure in capitalist countries is merely one more manifestation of class conflict. In a socialist society the problem will disappear because it will be possible to organize society "scientifically," and thus provide full employment and satisfaction of everyone's basic needs. In the meantime, capitalist efforts to promote family planning are seen as just one more futile attempt to stave off the coming revolution. Interestingly, the United States delegation to the second World Population Conference, held in Mexico City in 1984, provided a mirror image of this argument by contending that population would be less of a problem if LDC governments gave freer rein to private enterprise.

The earlier review of facts and theories suggests that family planning versus development is a false dichotomy. The fertility decline that completes the demographic transition can be hastened *both* by family planning *and* by economic development. Family planning alone is unlikely to reduce the birth rate; we have seen that it seldom works well in settings where there has been little development. Moreover its effects on marital fertility need support from a trend toward a higher age of marriage, and this is also more likely to come about in a more rapidly developing society.

Yet family planning has made its own independent contribution to LDC fertility decline in recent years, as studies have shown.[21] Both in Latin America and the Caribbean and in Asia, more than 50 percent of married couples now practice family planning.[22] The use of contraceptive methods has clearly reduced fertility in these areas. By the same token, in sub-Saharan Africa, the least-developed region and also the one with the highest levels of fertility and rates of natural increase, fewer than 10 percent of couples practice family planning. In reality family planning and development are more complements than substitutes.

21. W. Parker Mauldin and Bernard Berelson, "Conditions of Fertility Decline in Developing Countries, 1965–75," *Studies in Family Planning* 9, no. 5 (1978). See also "Fertility and Family Planning Surveys: An Update," *Population Reports* Series M, no. 8, Baltimore,/ Johns Hopkins University, September–October 1985).

22. Based on "most recent estimates" reported in World Bank, *Social Indicators of Development 1989* (Baltimore: Johns Hopkins Press, 1989).

8

Labor's Role

The dual role of people as both the beneficiaries of economic development and a major productive resource is particularly evident in discussing labor and employment. Labor employed in economic activity is likely to be costly (that is, have an alternative use, as discussed below) in the same way that the use of other scarce resources is costly. But employing the available labor supply offers two important benefits. First, because of market imperfections, it may be possible to increase production through policies that encourage better use of available labor and the adoption of technologies more appropriate to the factor endowments of less-developed countries. Second, even if total output does not rise, increased employment of poor people can be an effective and relatively low-cost way to increase their share of total income, and thus diminish poverty and distributive inequality.

A perplexing problem is how best to measure the quality of labor used in production. Given the supplies of capital and natural resources available, as well as a range of applicable technologies, the level of GNP attainable depends on the amount of labor available. But what is the "amount of labor available?" We could simply count the number of people potentially available for work—the number of people who are not underage, overage, or infirm—but this could be misleading. Labor productivity, or quality, varies widely in the real world, depending on several factors.

One of these is people's attitudes and values. How highly do they value the goods and services that can be earned by working? Are people willing to abandon traditional social settings and take up jobs in unfamiliar environments, such as factories, mines, and plantations? Do they come to work on time? Do they exert themselves on the job? Can they tolerate routinized operations? Is saving for the future important to them or do they live for the moment? Although economic theories usually abstract from the effects of values and attitudes on productivity, in the real world they are significant. Values and attitudes are acquired, not inborn. The work of sociologists and psychologists indicates that they are shaped by experiences in the home, in school, and on the job. In a sense they are thus a consequence of economic development, but they are also one of its causes. The subject is not yet well-enough understood for values and attitudes to be readily manipulated as a means of promoting development, although many governments try to do so.

A second set of influences on labor productivity is the skills possessed by the population. If values and attitudes refer to the way people look at the world, skills are what they know how to do. Some skills are widely usable; others are specific to particular environments. One needs to know different things to work effectively in an Asian rice field, a Detroit auto factory, or an Arctic fishing community; skills that are vital in one of these settings may be useless in another. Compared with attitudes and values, skills are acquired in a more straightforward and easily understood manner. The process can be called education, although the term is used here in a broader sense than is usual.

Finally, labor productivity is affected by the health and nutrition of the working population. People must possess the physical and mental stamina necessary, first to learn economically useful skills and then to apply them in the workplace. Education and health merit extended treatment and are taken up in Chapters 9 and 10. Here we concentrate on quantitative aspects of the human factor in development.

ANALYZING EMPLOYMENT ISSUES

Quantitative aspects of labor's role include growth in the number of laborers, patterns of employment, structure of labor markets, and methods of measuring labor supply and its utilization. We take up these issues in turn.

Growth of Labor Supply

A major difference between the development challenge faced by LDCs today and the one overcome by the industrial countries in the early phase of their own development is that the growth rate of labor supply is faster in the LDCs. In most developing countries the number of people who want to work is currently increasing at more than 2 percent a year. Since nearly all adult males and many adult females seek work outside the home, the rise in the number of potential workers is closely related to the increase in total population. Labor force growth lags population growth by 15 to 20 years, depending mainly on how long children stay in school. When health improves and more children survive from infancy to adulthood, population growth accelerates; this leads to faster labor force growth after 15 to 20 years.

TABLE 8–1   Growth of Labor Force, 1965–2000[a]

	Annual percent growth rate		
	Actual		Projected 1985–2000
	1965–1980	1980–1985	
Low- and middle-income Asia	2.1	2.3	1.7
Latin America and Caribbean	3.0	2.6	2.4
Middle East and North Africa	2.5	3.1	2.9
Sub-Saharan Africa	2.5	2.3	2.6
All developing countries	2.3	2.4	2.0
High-income countries	1.4	1.1	0.6
East European countries	1.1	0.8	0.5

[a]Weighted averages based on 1986 population.
Source: World Bank, World Development Report 1988, pp. 282–283.

Similarly, a fall in the birth rate leads to reduced labor force growth, but only after 15 years or so. Growth in the LDC labor force speeded up in the 1960s and 1970s, and is expected to remain rapid through the remainder of this century, as Table 8–1 shows.

Patterns of Employment

One of the best-known characteristics of labor in developing countries is that most people work in agriculture. Agriculture's share of the labor force is highest in the poorest countries and declines systematically as GNP per capita rises. The shares of both industrial and service workers rise to offset this decline (Table 8–2). Individual countries generally follow this pattern with case-to-case variations, as depicted in Table 8–3.

TABLE 8–2   Employment Shares in a Typical Developing Country

	Level of per-capita GNP in 1988 dollars					
% of employment in:	$250	$420	$700	$1,400	$2,800	$5,600
Primary production	81	75	65	52	38	24
Industry	7	9	13	19	26	33
Services	12	16	22	29	36	43

Source: Moshe Syrquin and Hollis B. Chenery, "Patterns of Development, 1950 to 1983," World Bank Discussion Papers, Washington, D.C., 1989, p. 20.

Another well-known fact about LDC labor is that wages are generally low by the standards of industrial countries. In developing countries labor is generally plentiful relative to the supply of complementary resources that could raise labor productivity and permit higher wages to be paid. Nearly all complementary resources are scarce: capital equipment, arable land, and foreign exchange, as well as those less tangible but important resources, entrepreneurship and managerial capacity. Thus, low wages are easily understood from the perspective of an elementary supply-demand analysis.

TABLE 8–3 Employment Shares in Some Representative Countries, 1980

	Agriculture	Industry	Services
Low-Income Countries			
Tanzania	86	5	10
India	70	13	17
China	74	14	12
Ghana	56	18	26
Sri Lanka	53	14	33
Kenya	81	7	12
Pakistan	55	16	30
Middle-Income Countries			
Bolivia	46	20	34
Indonesia	57	13	30
Peru	40	18	42
Colombia	34	24	42
Malaysia	42	19	39
South Korea	36	27	37
Chile	17	25	58
High-Income Countries			
United Kingdom	3	38	59
Japan	11	34	55
West Germany	6	44	50
Australia	7	32	61
United States	4	31	66
East European Economies			
Czechoslovakia	13	49	37
Poland	29	39	33
U.S.S.R.	20	39	41

Source: World Bank, *World Development Report 1988,* pp. 282–283.

It is not demeaning to LDC workers, however, to note that another cause of low productivity and pay is the characteristics of the workers themselves. Through no fault of their own, few of them have the education and work experience required for high productivity. Indonesia's 1980 population census revealed that only 32 percent of adults had completed primary school, a mere 10 percent had gone on to secondary education, and a microscopic 0.5 percent had been to a university. Few indeed had ever worked in a factory or had other good opportunities for on-the-job training. In many LDCs these proportions are even lower. Often LDC workers lack even the capacity to do sustained physical labor because their health and nutritional status is low.

Yet LDCs also have in their work forces persons of consummate learning and outstanding abilities. Another characteristic of LDC labor is that differentials among the wages received by different skills and education levels are wider than in developed countries. Skilled manual workers in developed countries may earn 20 to 40 percent more than their unskilled counterparts. In Asia, they are likely to earn 40 to 80 percent more, in Latin America 70 to 100 percent, and in Africa the skill differential can be 100 percent or more. Earnings differentials attributable to higher levels of education are also much larger in developing countries. In part these large earnings differentials exist because the rarity of skills and schooling attracts a larger market premium. Another factor may be segmented LDC labor markets and "efficiency wage" considerations, discussed in the following section.

A final characteristic is widespread underutilization of the available labor supply. For reasons discussed below, much of this underutilization takes the form of **disguised unemployment**, rather than the visible unemployment familiar in industrial countries. That is, people do have some kind of a job, and may even work long hours, but their contribution to output is small. With some reallocation of resources and improvement of institutions, their labor could be made more productive. This is a major challenge for development policy.

To recapitulate, low wages and productivity, large wage differentials, rapid growth of labor supply, and underutilization of the existing supply of labor all characterize developing countries. There are, however, many intercountry variations. While most Asian countries are now entering a period of declining labor-force growth, countries in sub-Saharan Africa and elsewhere are still in a period of accelerating growth (see Table 8–1). The degree of labor underutilization also varies greatly, depending mainly on the supply of arable land and other complementary resources in relation to the working-age population.

The Structure of Labor Markets

It is useful to think of labor services as being bought and sold in markets like other goods and services. In the economist's "perfect market," given certain assumptions, prices are set to cause goods to be allocated efficiently. But labor markets are notoriously imperfect, and none are more so than those of the LDCs. Wages (the "price" of labor) are not entirely determined by competitive forces. This section describes a pattern of segmented labor markets, which may help to explain wage and employment determination in the LDCs.

A "typical" LDC could be represented by a three-tiered employment structure, consisting of an urban formal sector, an urban informal sector, and rural employment. Figure 8–1 is a schematic representation of these three markets.

The **urban formal sector** is where almost everyone would like to work if they could. It consists of the government and large-scale enterprises such as banks, insurance companies, factories, and trading houses. People welcome the opportunity to work in a modern facility and be associated with a prestigious name, but the main attractions of formal-sector employers are that they pay the highest wages and offer the steadiest employment. One reason they pay more is that they hire virtually all the university- and secondary-school-educated labor in the country. But they also tend to pay more for given types of labor than the smaller firms pay—more, indeed, than they would have to pay just to attract the number of workers they need.

Why do formal-sector firms pay as much as they do, when there are many unemployed people who would work for less? Sometimes formal-sector firms pay more because the government presses them to do so (for example, through minimum wage laws or pressures to be model employ-

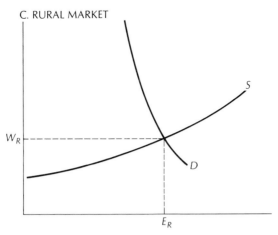

Figure 8–1. **The Three-Tiered Employment Structure.** A. Wage (W_F) is above market-clearing level; there is a queue $(L_F - E_F)$ of job applicants. B. Wage (W_I) clears the market but is lower than the formal-sector wage (W_F) in part A. C. Wage (W_R) clears the market but is lower than the urban informal-sector wage (W_R) clears the market but is lower than the urban informal-sector wage $(W_I$ in part B); supply of labor is highly elastic.

ers), but often they do so quite voluntarily. The efficiency wage theory postulates that worker productivity is a positive function of the wage paid.[1] For several reasons, better-paid workers may be more productive. First, they may be better nourished, and therefore physically better able to work. Second, they be inherently better workers, since firms that pay higher wages can be more selective about whom they hire. Next, they may stay where they are longer, learn by doing, and reduce the firm's labor turnover. Finally, higher wages may make them work harder because they fear to lose such a good job. With wages held above market-clearing levels by some or all of these factors, there is always a queue of workers ($E_F - L_F$ in Figure 8–1A) waiting for jobs with urban formal-sector employers. A routine job-opening announcement may attract hundreds, or even thousands, of applicants.

Alongside the large urban formal-sector establishments—or, more likely, in the alleys behind them—are the smaller enterprises of the **urban informal sector.** These shops and curbside establishments produce and trade a wide range of goods and services; sometimes they compete with the larger enterprises, and sometimes they fill gaps that the formal-sector firms do not find it profitable to enter. Often this sector provides jobs for migrants who have come to town from the rural areas to seek work in the urban formal sector but have been unable to find it. However, studies in several third-world cities indicate that many of the people who earn their income in this way are long-time urban residents and veterans at their particular lines of work.

The urban informal sector can be easy to enter; one can set up as a street hawker or in dozens of other lines of work with only a tiny amount of capital. For those who lack even the 10 to 100 dollars of capital needed to be self-employed, there is always the opportunity to work for others, although the wages may be lower than those offered by the urban formal sector. Domestic servants form one such group, a large and important one in every developing country. The urban informal sector can provide incredible amounts of low-wage employment and a useful array of goods and services (see box).

The Urban Informal Sector in Indonesia

Although the informal sector is hard to define, there is no denying its importance as a source of jobs, income, and a wide array of goods and services in many developing countries. In-depth studies carried out in Jakarta by the Center for Policy and Implementation Studies under the direction of Harvard anthropologist Marguerite S. Robinson focused on three specific activities that are important in the Indonesian capital: *becak*-driving (a *becak* is a three-wheeled peddle rickshaw); scavenging of waste materials such as metal, rags, and glass; and curbside retailing (hawking).

---

1. On efficiency wage theory, see Joseph E. Stiglitz, "Economic Organization, Information, and Development," in *Handbook of Development Economics*, Vol. 1, Chenery and Srinivasan, pp. 93–160; George A. Akerlof and Janet L. Yellen, eds., *Efficiency Wage Models of the Labor Market*, (Cambridge University Press, 1986), Introduction pp. 1–21; and Lawrence F. Katz, "Efficiency Wage Theories: A Partial Evaluation," *NBER Macroeconomics Annual 1986* (Cambridge, Mass.: National Bureau of Economic Research, 1986), pp. 235–276.

The studies showed that these activities provide jobs for hundreds of thousands of workers at earnings levels that compare favorably, on average, with what the same workers could earn in the formal sector. Informal-sector workers are often migrants from rural areas who regularly remit substantial sums to relatives left behind in the villages. They produce low-priced goods and services (e.g., short-distance transportation, inputs for small-scale industries, and small-lot retailing) that lower the cost of living for working-class households and, ironically, permit formal-sector employers to pay lower wages. Jakarta's scavengers recycle a variety of waste materials with an efficiency that modern industrial societies, which lack an equally efficient technology (at their high wage rates) for separating materials so that they can be reprocessed, should envy.

Although informal-sector entrepreneurs provide many benefits to their families, their numerous employees, and their customers, they are often viewed negatively by the municipal authorities. Their activities are frequently suppressed, and efforts to help them are often misguided (for example, new markets may be developed at sites less favorably located than those habitually used by traders; the authorities then wonder why many of the new sites remain empty whereas traders who do move to them may fail to repay their government loans!). More-enlightened policy must be based, not only on empathy for people who are struggling to survive, but also on an understanding of how their enterprises really contribute to development.

Because it is easily entered, the urban informal-sector labor market tends to be in equilibrium (Figure 8–1B). New entrants can generally find something to do, even if their presence tends to drive down wages slightly for all participants.

Although in visualizing the urban informal sector one tends to think first of massive urban agglomerations such as Mexico City, Lagos, and Calcutta, smaller cities and towns also provide significant amounts of urban informal-sector employment. Market towns often draw rural workers to participate in activities linked to the farm economy: marketing and processing of local agricultural produce, distribution of basic consumer goods and farm inputs, transportation, and repair services.

Even the urban informal sector is likely to pay higher wages than the **rural labor market**, employment outside the cities. In part this wage differential is illusory because urbanites have to pay higher prices for food and housing than rural residents, and they are often forced to buy things (water, fuel, building materials) that are obtainable free (that is, without monetary cost although large expenditures of time and effort are often required) in rural areas. But even after allowance has been made for differences in living costs, surveys indicate that most urban residents, even recent rural-urban migrants, are better off than all but the wealthiest rural residents.

As assumed by dual-economy models of development (presented in Chapter 3), rural employment in low-income countries commonly means work by family members, not for wages but for a share in the output of a family enterprise. Yet there is almost always a market for hired labor, particularly in some seasons. Depending on the amount of population pressure and the prevailing pattern of land tenure, there will be a large or small number of people who must depend on wage employment because they have no land to farm or not enough to support their families. These agricultural laborers typically make up the very lowest income stratum in a poor country. Even when their number is small, however, rural households commonly trade labor back and forth at different times of the year, sometimes on a cooperative or barter basis but more often for wages in cash or kind. While rural people work primarily in agriculture, small-scale nonagricultural activities (trade, services, crafts) provide important supplements to agricultural income in many developing countries.

Measuring Labor Supply and Utilization

The structural complexity of LDC labor markets makes it hard to apply concepts that are relatively straightforward in developed countries. In both types of country, policymakers want to measure the supply of labor available to the economy and determine how fully the available labor supply is being utilized.

In developed countries labor supply is measured through the **labor force** concept. The labor force includes everyone who has a job or is actively looking for one. Its size is determined by three factors: (1) the size of the population; (2) its composition in terms of age groups and sexes; (3) and the labor force participation rates of these groups, which reflect social factors such as educational patterns and the willingness of women to work outside the home. The short-term responsiveness (elasticity) of the supply of labor can be large under unusual circumstances, as when women in many countries went to work in factories for the first time during World War II. But normally it is low. Developed countries experiencing full employment, as many European nations did during the 1950s, can easily have their economic growth constrained by the available supply of labor.

In LDC conditions, the available labor force is generally not a constraint on development, although skilled labor and management can be very scarce. Typically, more people would like to work than are working, and many who are working are underutilized. Moreover, the meaning of "having a job" or "actively looking for work" is harder to pin down in the LDC context, where multiple job holding, part-time work, and work for one's own family all tend to be more common than in a developed country. The number of "discouraged workers" (those who have stopped looking for work because they believe none is available) is also likely to be greater in less-developed than in developed countries. Using the conventional definitions, women participate increasingly in the labor force as development proceeds and the number of jobs outside the home rises. This suggests that at low levels of development there is a large reserve of female labor not apparent in the statistics, but ready to come forth when reasonably attractive work opportunities open up. In fact, of course, these women are already working hard in the home, where by convention they are not counted as part of the labor force.

In developed countries, labor underutilization is measured primarily through the concept of **unemployment.** The unemployed are defined as those who do not have a job but are actively looking for one. The familiar **rate of unemployment** is total unemployment as a percentage of the labor force. In industrial countries this rate is a closely watched indicator of economic performance.

In developing countries the rate of unemployment understates labor underutilization, often by a large factor. Surveys have indicated that India has a lower rate of unemployment than the United States. Yet most observers would agree that underutilization of labor supply is much greater in India than in the United States. Semideveloped countries with per-capita income levels much higher than India's (for example, Malaysia, the Philippines, or almost any Latin American country) have also been measured in surveys as having far higher rates of unemployment. One reason for these anomalies is suggested by analyzing the types of people who are reported as unemployed when labor force surveys are carried out in developing countries. Many of them are young and live in urban areas; they are far better educated than the population in general, and many have never worked before. The inference is clear. The unemployed, as measured in these surveys, tend to be those who can afford to remain unemployed while they search for the type of job, undoubtedly in the urban formal sector, that they want and for which they believe their educational attainment qualifies them. They are in fact likely to come from the better-off families in society and to be supported by their parents through an extended period of search for the ''right'' job.

The very poor may appear less often in the unemployment statistics of developing countries, and when they do appear, they do not remain unemployed for so long. Because they lack resources, they cannot be without work for more than a brief period or they and their families may starve. Therefore, the poor must accept almost any job that becomes available. It has been ironically observed that in a poor country unemployment is a luxury. Unemployment is usually part of a job search that can be long and costly. Those best situated to make this search are the relatively privileged. Because LDCs lack unemployment insurance and other forms of social support common in the developed countries, job seekers must be supported either by their families (which sometimes make large sacrifices for the purpose) or by such casual work as they can find.

If the standard concept of unemployment is an inadequate measure of labor underutilization in developing countries, what better measure might be devised? This is a complex matter because there are, in fact, several different kinds of underutilization common in LDCs (Table 8–4), and it is hard to encompass them all in any single measure.

It has been argued that disguised unemployment (the lower right-hand quadrant of Table 8–4) is the major form of labor underutilization in poor countries. Workers in this category are fully, but unproductively, employed in the rural sector or urban informal sector. Standard examples include the street vendor who sits for hours just to make one or two low-value sales, the shoeshine boy, and the goatherd. These people, it is argued, contribute

TABLE 8–4   Types of Labor Underutilization in Developing Countries

Type	Unemployment	Underemployment
Visible	Mostly urban new entrants	Rural labor; seasonal
Invisible	Mostly women ("discouraged workers")	Rural labor + urban informal sector ("disguised unemployment")

little or nothing to production. Like those classified as unemployed, they could be put to work somewhere else in the economy at little or no opportunity cost. We will discuss the merits of this argument as a guide to development policy later on. The important point here is that although this category of labor underutilization may be large and important, it is exceedingly difficult to define and measure precisely.

One country profile of labor underutilization, based on a framework similar to Table 8–4, was provided by the 1970 International Labor Office (ILO) employment mission to Colombia.[2] Visible unemployment in urban areas was running at 14 percent of the labor force, but the mission estimated that when discouraged workers and the underemployed (those involuntarily working short hours) were taken into account, urban labor underutilization rose to at least 25 percent. Adding disguised unemployment, as indicated by extremely low income, raised it to one-third of the labor force. In rural areas everyone was apparently employed at the peak season, but at least one-sixth of the labor force earned incomes low enough to be characterized as disguised unemployment.

The many difficulties of defining and measuring labor utilization make it uncertain just how the overall degree of labor utilization varies with the level of economic development. The highest rates of visible unemployment, often reaching 10 to 20 percent of the labor force, have been measured in the urban areas of low- and middle-income countries. According to broader definitions of underutilization, still larger shares of the labor force are underutilized and overall underutilization is probably greatest in the poorest countries. Disguised forms of underutilization are relatively more important in the poorest countries than in the somewhat richer ones. In the semideveloped countries covered by labor utilization surveys, disguised unemployment was significant but quantitatively somewhat less than open unemployment.

Nor is it easy for trends to be established with certainty. In the 1960s it was widely feared that accelerated population growth would lead to massive unemployment in the developing countries. During the decade of the 1970s, many observers thought that the degree of labor underutilization in most LDCs was increasing. However, a careful review of the data showed that this was probably not the case.[3] The point is that nearly everyone in developing countries must work to live. The main issue, therefore, is not

2. International Labor Office, *Towards Full Employment* (Geneva: ILO, 1970), pp. 13–28.
3. Peter Gregory, "An Assessment of Changes in Employment Conditions in Less Developed Countries," *Economic Development and Cultural Change* 28, no. 4 (July 1980): 673–700.

how many job seekers find employment, but rather what *kind* of work they **197**
find to do—how productive they are and how good an income they earn.   LABOR
                                                                                     REALLOCATIOI

LABOR REALLOCATION

We cannot talk about employment policy in developing countries without broaching an issue that has been debated extensively by development theorists: how can underutilized labor be used in a development strategy? In theoretical writings of the 1950s it was frequently asserted that large numbers of people engage in work which adds nothing to national output. Two well-known writers who emphasized this idea and made it a cornerstone of their analyses of how development proceeds were the Finnish economist Ragnar Nurkse and Nobel laureate W. Arthur Lewis.[4] Nurkse saw the reallocation of surplus labor to more productive uses, especially labor-intensive construction projects, as a major source of capital formation and economic growth. Lewis envisaged a similar reallocation process, but he pictured the "capitalist sector," essentially industry, as the principal employer of the surplus labor. (Chapters 3 and 4 discuss Lewis's theory in detail.) Both theorists regarded the labor reallocation process as nearly costless, but they worried about how to capture from the agricultural sector the food necessary to feed the reallocated laborers.

This approach to development theory opened up a debate on two issues: what extra laborers actually contribute to LDC agricultural production and how readily any excess labor can be mobilized in industry or in construction projects. Three conclusions emerged from this debate. First, extra laborers do increase agricultural production, contrary to Nurkse's and Lewis's assumption. The marginal product of labor is almost always positive, not zero, but it may be very low in densely populated countries. At least this is true on a year-round basis. If there is really such a thing as zero-marginal product labor, the condition is likely to be seasonal. Second, even if forgone output were zero or negligible, there would be other costs associated with the physical movement of labor from agricultural pursuits to industry or construction. These will be discussed shortly. Third, although long-term growth consists of reallocating labor to more productive uses, there are no free, or even very easy, gains to be had in the short run.

In more positive terms, it can be said that in almost all countries and times there are opportunities to work at some positive wage and marginal product, although these may be very low. If some remain unemployed despite such opportunities, the probable reason is that they reject the wage offered as too low to compensate for their loss of leisure or the chance to search for a better-paid job.

Costs and Benefits of Reallocating Labor

Given these findings, how should an LDC government look at an employment-creating development project? In Chapter 6 we saw that any devel-

---

4. Ragnar Nurkse, *Problems of Capital Formation in Underdeveloped Countries* (Oxford: Basil Blackwell, 1957, first published in 1953), and W. Arthur Lewis, "Economic Development with Unlimited Supplies of Labour," *The Manchester School* 22 (May 1954): 139–91.

opment project can be evaluated using social cost-benefit analysis. An important part of the social cost of any input is its **opportunity cost**, its value in its next best alternative use. Labor hired for an urban formal-sector project might well be drawn from the urban informal sector. The worker who moves out of the urban informal sector may in turn be replaced by someone from the rural sector. In this example, the output lost is that of the worker who was formerly in the rural sector—the worker at the end of the employment chain. For this reason, some analysts believe that the wage paid to casual agricultural laborers provides a good measure of the social cost of unskilled labor.

However, this measure, although a good indicator of output forgone through labor reallocation, probably understates the true social cost of employing labor, which has other components that are likely to be significant.

One such component is **induced migration.** An influential model of rural-urban migration, developed by John R. Harris and Michael P. Todaro and described more fully in the following section, implies that migrating workers are essentially participants in a lottery of relatively high-paid jobs in the towns.[5] When new urban jobs are created, the lottery becomes more attractive to potential migrants. Depending on their responsiveness to this improved opportunity, it is possible that more than one worker will migrate for each job created. If so, the output forgone may be that of two or more agricultural workers, not just one. Family ties may multiply this effect. If a male worker migrates and brings his family with him, additional output may be lost because the wife and children find fewer employment opportunities in the town that in the rural areas; for example, they do not have land on which to grow food.

In addition to forgone output, certain **costs of urbanization** should be included in computing the social cost of urban job creation. Some of these costs are internalized by the worker, and presumably taken into account in the migration decision: the higher cost of food, housing, and other items in the town. Other costs are external and must be borne by society as a whole: social services that are provided only to the urban population or that are more expensive in the town, pollution, congestion, and additional security requirements. It is these costs that make many third-world governments frown on urbanization, however much they may desire industrialization.

Finally, there is the possibility of a reduction in national savings, which has worried development theorists and Soviet-style economic planners alike. If labor that has been adding little to agricultural output but has been consuming a larger share of that product is withdrawn from the sector, who controls the food thus freed up? The employment may want to transfer the food that the rural worker was consuming to feed the same worker in the city. Its fear is that the remaining rural population will simply increase its per-capita consumption. Since the urban labor force must be fed—from imports, if not from domestic production—the planners' concern is that aggregate national consumption will rise and national savings will fall and

5. John R. Harris and Michael P. Todaro, "Migration, Unemployment and Development: A Two-Sector Analysis," *American Economic Review* 60, (March 1970): 126–42.

reduce the growth of GNP. The problem is exacerbated when the new urban
workers get higher wages and thus want to consume more food than they were consuming in the rural areas.

During the 1930s this concern moved Soviet planners to drastic measures to extract a surplus from a resistant rural population. Governments of developing countries generally have neither the means nor the desire to suppress food consumption, so they may indeed experience some decline in savings. This is far from pure loss, however, because the added consumption is a gain to some members of society. In any case there are better ways to increase saving than through coercive controls on food consumption.

The primary benefit of urban employment is added output. A highly productive project can easily repay all the costs discussed above, but low-productivity make-work projects in urban areas may incur costs with few offsetting benefits. Labor-intensive projects in rural areas, especially those employing seasonally underutilized labor, may also waste resources but are likely to be more beneficial because they do not require workers to migrate. These projects are discussed toward the end of this chapter.

A secondary benefit of urban job creation is the training it may provide. In LDCs opportunities to learn skills useful in the modern economy are concentrated in urban areas. For example, the ability to operate and repair machinery of all kinds is typically rare. A worker who comes to town can acquire these skills. In doing so, the worker may benefit and obtain higher wages if employment as a skilled worker can be found. But the worker also confers an "external benefit" on society because everyone benefits when bus drivers, auto mechanics, appliance repairpeople, and others who work with machinery learn to do their jobs better. This applies both to employers, who can hire labor from a more skilled pool, and to consumers, who get better service at lower prices.

It is evident that developing through the reallocation of low-productivity labor is a more complex business than Nurkse and Lewis imagined in the 1950s. Nevertheless, employment expansion remains an important means of both expanding output and redistributing income. A government that can create projects in which the marginal product of labor exceeds its social cost, taking into account all the elements discussed here, can achieve both of these objectives simultaneously. Output rises and more income goes to poor, unskilled workers. Less-productive forms of employment creation, in which the social cost of labor exceeds its marginal product, can be acceptable as redistributive measures if income redistribution is desired and other ways of achieving it are unavailable. But they would achieve more equity only by sacrificing growth.

Internal Migration

Most of the internal migration that takes place in the course of economic development is from rural to urban areas. Theorists have long argued that economic factors dominate the decision to migrate. Some early writers distinguished between pull and push factors, saying that rural-urban migration can result either from favorable economic developments in the town or from adverse developments in the countryside. The Harris-Todaro model of rural-urban migration, introduced above, integrates these two sets of factors by focusing on the wage differential which pulls rural workers to the city. Yet there is something to the older notion. Just as eighteenth-century English cottagers were pushed into the town by the Enclosure Movement, so peasants in eastern India move to Calcutta primarily because of wretched conditions in the surrounding countryside, rather than out-standing income or employment opportunities in Calcutta itself. By con-trast, the growth of dynamic third-world cities such as Sao Paulo and Nairobi could be attributed at least partly to pull factors.

The Harris-Todaro model is an important formulation of the role of eco-nomic incentives in the migration decision. The model assumes that migra-tion depends primarily on a comparison of wages in the rural and urban labor markets. That is,

$$M_t = f(W_u - W_r), \qquad [8-1]$$

where M_t is the number of rural to urban migrants in time period t, f is a response function, W_u is the urban wage, and W_r is the rural wage. Since there is unemployment in the town (assume that there is none in the coun-tryside) and every migrant cannot expect to find a job there, the model postulates that the *expected* urban wage is compared with the rural wage. The expected urban wage is the actual wage times the probability of finding a job, or

$$W_u^* = pW_u, \qquad [8-2]$$

where W_u^* = expected urban wage and p = probability of finding a job.
    A simple way of defining p is

$$p = \frac{E_u}{E_u + U_u} \qquad [8-3]$$

where E_u = urban employment and U_u = urban unemployment. In this for-mulation all members of the urban labor force are assumed to have equal chances of obtaining the jobs available, so W_u^* becomes simply the urban wage times the urban unemployment rate. Migration in any given time period then depends on three factors: the rural-urban wage gap, the urban unem-ployment rate, and the responsiveness of potential migrants to the resulting opportunities.

$$M_t = h(pW_u - W_r), \qquad [8-4]$$

where M_t = the migration in period t and h = the response rate of potential migrants.

As long as W_u^* exceeds W_r, the model predicts that rural-urban migration will continue. It will only stop when migration has forced down the urban wage or forced up urban unemployment sufficiently that $W_u^* = W_r$. It is also possible that W_r is greater that W_u^*, in which case there will be a flow of disappointed urban job seekers back to the countryside.

An interesting feature of this model is that an increase in the urban wage (W_u) requires an increase in unemployment to restore equilibrium. In other

words, an increase in the demand for labor or anything that raises wages in
the cities is likely to induce more migration and thereby worsen urban unemployment.

Critics of the Harris-Todaro model point out that the equilibrium condition specified by the model is seldom attained. It is common for urban wages to be, say, 50 to 100 percent higher than rural wages and for urban unemployment to run at 10 to 20 percent of the labor force. If the figures stay in this range, the expected urban wage (W_u^*) remains above the rural wage (W_r). Migration in practice does not seem to close the gap between W_u^* and W_r as the model predicts. The model can be rescued, however, by assuming (realistically) that not all urban jobs turn over, that is, are available in the "lottery." In this case, the probability of a migrant not finding a job is higher than the unemployment rate. For example, if the unemployment rate is 20 percent, the probability of a migrant's finding a job might actually be 50 percent or less, not 80 percent as implied by the simplest version of the model.

Reverse migration from town to country is significant in many countries. Although Harris and Todaro interpret such movement as disappointed urban job seekers returning home in despair, much of this two-way or *circular* migration is clearly intentional. Young, unattached males are particularly likely to migrate temporarily to towns, mines, or plantations, work for a while, and amass savings, which they then take back to the rural areas to invest in land, farm improvements, or marriage. This pattern of migration has been especially common in parts of Africa, perhaps because in many African cultures women normally tend the crops after the men have planted them. The opportunity cost of absent males outside the planting season is thus low.

Economic factors are not the only important influences on migration decisions. Studies show that distance and social ties are also significant. Migrants to expanding urban areas tend to come from nearby rural regions, and peasants pushed out of their native districts by a calamity are likely to go to the nearest large town. People often move to areas where members of their family, village, or ethnic group have settled.

Although most internal migration in developing countries is from rural to urban areas, interregional differences in economic opportunity can bring about substantial rural-to-rural movement as well. Countries fortunate enough to possess lightly settled yet cultivable regions may try to bring about such movement as a matter of public policy, as we saw in Chapter 7. Unless there are massive physical or legal barriers to the settlement of relatively empty areas, however, such interregional movements tend to occur spontaneously. This happened in Nepal, for instance, where farmers moved from the densely packed Kathmandu Valley into the southern *terai* region, and in many parts of Africa and South America. Unforced movements of population from one region of a country to another are likely to be socially beneficial. People make these moves to benefit themselves and their families. Even in the most congested slums of such major LDC cities as Sao Paulo, Lagos, and Jakarta, migrants report that they are better off than they were in the rural areas and generally they do not want to go back.

Society is likely to benefit as well from an improved spatial allocation of labor relative to other resources. But two factors could make social costs greater than benefits. First, distorted incentives, such as artificially high wages and subsidized urban services, can inflate private benefits. Second, external costs such as congestion, pollution, and crime are borne equally by migrants, who benefit from migration, and by their predecessors, who do not. If these distortions and externalities are large, social costs may exceed benefits.

International Migration

International migration, which has continued at a high level in recent years,[6] is frequently regarded as a different matter altogether. To bring a degree of cool rationality to this often-heated subject, it is helpful to distinguish between unskilled labor and skilled or educated labor. This distinction may not matter when we look at the problem from the global point of view: it has been argued that world GNP is maximized when everyone works where the salary, and therefore presumably the productivity, is greatest. But it is important from the viewpoint of the LDCs because skilled and unskilled labor have different opportunity costs.

There are two reasons why the migration of educated, highly skilled labor is abhorrent to most developing countries and has been stigmatized as the "brain drain." One is that such people represent one of the LDCs' scarcest resources. The other is that in most cases their education has been time-consuming, expensive, and heavily subsidized by the state. If they depart for foreign lands, not only are their services lost but a high cost must be incurred to train a replacement. Yet if they are so productive, why are they not paid enough to keep them at home? The answer may be nonmarket influences on the salary structure. For example, if most doctors and engineers work for the government and their salaries are held down to avoid politically embarrassing salary differentials, it is not surprising that many of them seek an opportunity to emigrate. International agencies, which recruit in a worldwide labor market, typically pay far more for the same skills than national governments. This is why one finds Pakistani experts working in Egypt, for example, even as Egyptian experts are employed in Pakistan, although both groups could probably work more effectively in their own countries.

Although it surely does raise world GNP, international migration of the educated worsens the distribution of income between rich and poor countries. To offset this effect, Jagdish Bhagwati of Columbia University has proposed a tax on the brain drain, to be collected by the governments of developed countries to which professional and technical personnel from

---

6. From 1985 to 1990 eight developing countries each supplied 200,000 or more net emigrants: Mexico, the Philippines, China, Lebanon, Pakistan, India, El Salvador, and Colombia. The United States was by far the largest receiving country with nearly 3 million net immigrants, including an estimate of illegal entrants. Australia, Canada, and Saudi Arabia each admitted more than 300,000 in this period. See Fred Arnold, "International Migration: Who Goes Where?" *Finance and Development* 27, no. 2 (June 1990): 46–47.

underdeveloped countries have migrated.[7] The proceeds of the tax would

be transferred to the poor countries of origin as compensation for their loss
of talent.

In contrast, international migration of unskilled labor can be beneficial
to the country of emigration. Unskilled workers are more plentiful, so their
loss is likely to be felt less keenly by the sending economy. There are even
significant offsetting benefits. One is remittances: unskilled migrants are
less likely to take their families along and are thus more likely to send
money back. This makes labor a kind of national export. Countries such as
Turkey, Algeria, and Egypt have long relied on worker remittances as a
significant source of foreign-exchange earnings. A second potential benefit
is training. Unskilled workers who go abroad generally return to their native
lands after a few years and bring back usable skills acquired abroad.

Some LDC governments have begun to look more favorably on worker
emigration. Despairing of generating enough employment at home, they
have begun to encourage their people to go abroad, at least for a while.
South Asian countries, for example, took advantage of lucrative employment opportunities in the Middle East in the 1970s and 1980s. When education is particularly cheap, even the emigration of trained personnel may
be encouraged. The Philippines has been exporting doctors and nurses in
quantity for years.

EMPLOYMENT POLICY

The origin of the employment problem in the developing countries is the
rapid growth of the population and labor force, which has caused the supply of labor to increase sharply relative to the natural resource base. But
there are also problems on the demand side of the labor market. Although
capital stock has typically risen even faster than labor force, capital has
been deployed in ways that have kept labor absorption well below its
potential. It was once thought that industrialization would readily solve the
employment problem in most LDCs. This was the premise, for example,
of India's first two 5-year plans. But experience has shown that although
industrial sector employment has grown rapidly in many cases, it has been
unable to absorb the expanding labor force. A simple example will help to
explain why this is so.

Labor Absorption through Industrialization

Industrial sectors in developing countries typically grow rapidly from a low
base. In low-income countries between 1965 and 1983, value-added in
industry (defined to include manufacturing, utilities, and construction) grew
at an average rate of 7.1 percent a year. Yet employment growth in the
sector was only 60 percent as fast, or 4.3 percent a year. The amount of
industrial employment growth expected from a given rate of output growth

7. Jagdish Bhagwati and Martin Partington, *Taxing the Brain Drain: A Proposal* (Amsterdam: North-Holland, 1976).

can be expressed by the following formula:

$$\Delta E_i = \eta g(V_i)S_i, \qquad\qquad [8-5]$$

where ΔE_i = annual employment growth in industry, expressed in percentage points of labor force growth; η = an elasticity relating the growth of employment to the growth of value-added; $g(V_i)$ = growth in industrial value-added, expressed in percentage points; S_i = industrial employment as a fraction of total employment. Industry absorbed 9 percent of the labor force in low-income countries in 1965, so

$$\Delta E_i = 0.6 \times 7.1 \times 0.09 = 0.4. \qquad\qquad [8-6]$$

This means that only four-tenths of 1 percent of the labor force was absorbed by industrial expansion each year. Yet the labor force grew at 2.1 percent a year from 1965 to 1983. Thus, fewer than one-fifth of the workers entering the labor force found jobs in industry. The rest had to do the best they could in primary production or in the service sector.

Is this too pessimistic a depiction of the problem? On the brighter side it can be noted that only direct employment creation in industry has been taken into account. Some additional **indirect job creation** can be expected in sectors with either forward or backward linkages to the industrial sector, such as service activities that distribute its products and agricultural and mining activities that supply its inputs (linkages within the industrial sector are already accounted for in the calculation). Indirect job creation can be significant in some circumstances, as when the capacity to process domestically produced primary commodities is expanded, but it is frequently limited for industrialization of the import-substituting type, which has few forward or backward linkages. Chapter 16 will discuss this in detail. **Secondary job creation** also occurs as workers employed in high-paying industrial jobs spend their incomes. Businesses supplying them with consumer goods of various kinds prosper, and this creates additional employment.

Since industrial jobs are often among the most productive and best paid in the economy, it is important to ask what can be done to improve industrial-employment creation. In the formula given above, raising ΔE_i requires increasing η, $g(V_i)$, S_i, or some combination of them. Industry's share in employment (S_i) will rise only gradually through time. In the medium term, industrial labor absorption can be increased by raising either the growth rate of sectoral value-added $g(V_i)$ or the employment elasticity η.

A few countries have been able to expand industrial employment much faster than average. These are the nations that have achieved the greatest success in exporting labor-intensive manufactured products. Outstanding among them are South Korea, Taiwan, Hong Kong, and Singapore, known collectively as the *four tigers*. There are two separate aspects to their achievement. First, by breaking into the export market, they have been able to reach higher growth rates of industrial output $g(V_i)$, because they have freed themselves from dependence on growth of the domestic market for manufactured goods. Second, they have achieved high values of η because the goods they chose to export, at least at the start of their export drives, were those which used large amounts of their most plentiful resource, labor.

These countries have experienced values of η of around 0.8 instead of the more typical 0.4 to 0.6. Thus South Korea after 1963 was able to absorb as much as half of its total labor force growth in manufactured exports alone, at a time when most LDCs were absorbing less than 5 percent of their labor force growth in this activity.[8] Can other LDCs take lessons in employment policy from South Korea and the other tigers? We take up this question in the next section.

The employment performance of industry is particularly distressing when we remember that this sector should not only be soaking up a good share of labor force growth, but also gradually drawing labor away from less productive forms of employment in peasant agriculture, petty services, and cottage industry. When industry fails to achieve either of these ends, employment in these less-productive sectors must rise rather than fall. This can lead to stagnant, or even declining, levels of worker productivity and income. There is evidence that this is in fact happening, especially in some of the poorest and least rapidly growing countries.

Although the above discussion was couched in terms of industry, it can be applied to the entire urban formal sector. Large trading companies, financial organizations, transport and communication facilities, public utilities, and the like may collectively be even more important for intersectoral labor transfer than industry. And they, too, often fail to increase their employment fast enough to employ the growing labor force.

Elements of a Solution

In principle the problem of labor underutilization could be attacked on either the supply or the demand side. In practice, however, little can be done to bring about a supply-side adjustment. Labor supply grows steadily from year to year. It is hard to discourage people from seeking work. Nor would most policymakers wish to do so, given the advantages of employment creation as a means of income redistribution, and the psychological and political advantages of enabling everyone to participate in the economy. The only real supply-side potential is to reduce the growth of labor supply in the long run by limiting population growth.

Some years ago it was widely believed that increasing the supply of certain types of skilled labor would produce a strong expansionary effect on employment generally through the increased absorption of complementary unskilled labor. Thus India in its early postindependence years tried to eliminate a perceived labor bottleneck by expanding the supply of engineers, on the supposition that employment in construction and other activities could be increased in this way. The number of Indian engineers increased rapidly. The effect on general employment is hard to determine, but the effect on the engineers was clear-cut: there were soon far too many of them, and many were unemployed. The moral is that although skill shortages can constrain employment and output growth, they can sometimes be

8. Susumu Watanabe, "Exports and Employment: The Case of the Republic of Korea," *International Labour Review* 106, no. 6 (December 1972): 495–526.

eliminated relatively quickly and easily through the expansion of education and training programs or through migration. In other countries, where education is less-developed, skill formation may be much more difficult and time-consuming.

Since the potential for correcting the labor-market disequilibrium by working on the supply side is quite limited, policy must concentrate on the demand side of the equation. Many different kinds of policy affect the economy's ability to create jobs for a growing labor force. Wage, industrial promotion, fiscal, foreign trade, and education policies—all have important implications for employment.

Earlier we identified two different approaches to employment creation. One is to stimulate output, especially in relatively high-productivity and high-wage sectors of the economy. The other is to try to increase the amount of labor used to produce a given amount of output. The first approach will be discussed in Chapters 17, 18, and 20, which deal with the growth of exports, agriculture and industry. The second is examined here.

Production can be made more labor-intensive in two general ways. One is to alter relative prices and thus create incentives for businesses to substitute labor for capital. The other is to develop technologies more appropriate to the factor proportions prevailing in developing countries.

Factor Pricing Distortions

The prices of labor and capital faced by modern-sector firms in less-developed countries are frequently distorted in ways that make capital artificially cheap relative to labor. This distortion can inhibit labor absorption at several levels. At the sectoral level it can promote the growth of sectors that are technologically better-suited to capital-intensive production (for example, basic metals) and hinder the growth of sectors that tend to be more labor-intensive (for example, textiles). At the level of interfirm competition, it can promote the appearance and growth of plants using relatively capital-intensive technologies (these may be large, foreign-owned, or both) and accelerate the decline and disappearance of more labor-intensive units. At the plant level it can promote the use of machines in place of people.

These factor price distortions usually result from some form of government action. Artificially high wages may be imposed on modern-sector firms by minimum-wage laws intended to protect workers' incomes, by government support of trade union demands, or by pressure (especially on foreign and state-owned enterprises) to be model employers. Some governments levy payroll or social security taxes on modern-sector payrolls and thus raise the cost of labor to the employer. In Latin America, restrictions on firing workers are frequently so severe that employers think twice before hiring them in the first place. When jobs once done by foreigners are taken over by citizens, nationalist pressure can cause salaries to be kept at their previously high, internationally competitive levels.

All these policies promote the welfare of relatively small groups at the expense of much larger ones. Minimum-wage laws and similar measures, if effectively enforced (and often they are not), can improve wages and

working conditions for those workers fortunate enough to get jobs in modern-sector firms. But by raising the cost of labor, these measures limit the
ability of existing firms to absorb more workers and inhibit the creation of
more enterprises like them. In this way, they harm the much larger group
of workers who either are unemployed or work in the informal and rural
sectors.

Why do governments of countries with serious employment problems
enact such measures as minimum-wage laws? The answer is that relatively
small but well-organized, vocal, and visible groups of modern-sector workers, nearly always located in urban areas, use their political power to press
for enactment of these laws, or for increases in the statutory minimum
wage once a system of minimum wages is established. In some Latin American countries, minimum wages are indexed to inflation; this ensures that
they remain high in real terms. Under a minimum-wage system the government accepts direct responsibility for the earnings of workers in the protected sectors. If it resists a strongly backed demand for a rise in the minimum
wage, it is inviting political trouble. Of course the government is also
responsible for the welfare of those who lose from the wage increase because
their chances of ever getting a job in the protected high-wage sector are
reduced. But their loss is less easily perceived than the wage gain of the
protected workers, and the government is less likely to be held accountable
for it.

Artificially cheap capital reinforces the effect of artificially expensive labor.
In many LDCs, interest rate ceilings make capital equipment cheaper for
those preferred customers who can obtain the credit necessary to buy it.
(For the rest, of course, capital may become more expensive, or even
unobtainable, as banks and other financial institutions direct the available
funds to their preferred customers.) Overvaluation of the domestic currency in terms of foreign exchange can have a similar effect. It forces the
imposition of a licensing system for foreign exchange, imports, or both,
and this in turn makes artificially cheapened capital goods available to those
who can obtain the necessary licenses.

Like minimum wages, interest ceilings, foreign-exchange control, and
import licensing all serve the interests of influential minorities. New York
University economist Lawrence White has shown how preferred access to
imports and credit in Pakistan led to the increasing concentration of industry and commerce in the hands of an elite group known as the *twenty families*.[9] Licensing systems also receive strong support from officials of the
license-granting authorities, who can earn substantial illicit income from
the bestowal of their favors.

Another way governments make capital artificially cheap is by gearing
investment incentives to the amount of capital invested. Often a firm that
invests $50 million is given a longer tax holiday or a shorter write-off period
than one that invests only $5 million. This creates incentives for capital-
intensive industries to set up in the country and for firms facing a range of
possible technologies to select more capital-intensive modes of production.

9. Lawrence White, *Industrial Concentration and Economic Power in Pakistan* (Princeton,
N.J.: Princeton University Press, 1974).

What can be done to correct these factor price distortions? The most straightforward approach is for governments to avoid the kinds of price-distorting policies mentioned above, or if they have already instituted them, to deregulate as soon as possible. Often, however, they are reluctant to do so, out of either concern for the welfare of workers already holding modern-sector jobs or fear of the political power of those who benefit from artificially high wages or artificially cheap capital and foreign exchange.

Price distortions that cannot be removed can in theory be offset by taxes or subsidies. Economists have argued that the artificially high labor costs faced by modern-sector employers should be countered by a wage subsidy. This advice has been followed rarely, if at all. However, a few countries have adopted investment incentives that depend in part on the number of jobs an investor creates.

An important question about all proposals for correcting factor price distortions is how great their employment-creating effect is likely to be. Technically speaking, this depends on the **elasticity of substitution,** which can be defined as

$$\sigma = \frac{\Delta(K/L)}{\Delta(w/r)} \quad \frac{w/r}{K/L},$$

where K is the amount of capital, L the amount of labor, W the wage rate, r the cost of capital, and Δ signifies a change. The elasticity of substitution is thus the percentage change in the capital/labor ratio, $\Delta(K/L)/(K/L)$, that results from a given percentage change in the ratio of the price of labor to that of capital, $\Delta(w/r)/(w/r)$. (The expression w/r is also called the **wage-rental ratio.**) Thus, if a 10 percent decline in the wage-rental ratio leads to a 5 percent fall in the capital-labor ratio, then the elasticity of substitution is 0.5. In these circumstances a 10 percent decline in the wage-rental ratio would mean that in the future it would take 5 percent less investment (capital) to employ a given amount of labor; alternatively, a given amount of investment would employ 5 percent more workers.

Debates over the efficiency of employment creation through the correction of factor price distortions range elasticity optimists against elasticity pessimists. The optimists argue that the employment effects are likely to be large because investors tend to be rational profit maximizers who have a range of possible outputs and technologies open to them. When faced with cheaper labor relative to capital, they will therefore adjust by: (1) concentrating on goods that can be produced relatively efficiently using a lot of labor relative to capital and (2) using more labor-intensive technologies in some or all of their operations. (The optimists assume that investors have a "shelf" of appropriate technologies available to them, an issue to be explored in the following section.)

The pessimists, on the other hand, contend that the response to a change in the wage-rental ratio may be small or nonexistent. They note that in some modern industries technology permits little substitution of labor for capital. Examples include **process industries** such as petrochemicals and wood pulp. In such industries, highly capital-intensive technologies may be

absolutely more efficient than any less-capital-intensive alternatives. That is, they may use less capital per unit of output as well as less labor. In many cases these technical characteristics are linked to economies of scale: a plant must be very large, as well as highly capital-intensive, to be efficient. An LDC government might well think twice before establishing such an industry, but it would be ill-advised to try to make it small-scale or labor-intensive.

Elasticity pessimists also point out that many firms sell in protected markets and therefore do not necessarily have to maximize profits; that they may prefer the most modern (capital-intensive) technologies for their own sake; and that they may produce goods mainly for middle-class consumption, to which capital-intensive technologies are better suited than labor-intensive technologies. For all these reasons the pessimists argue against the policies advocated by the optimists. They would expect, for example, that a wage subsidy would do more to increase business profits than to expand employment.

Figures 8–2 and 8–3 show the differences between what the pessimists and the optimists have in mind. Which is the better depiction of the real world? It might seem simple to calculate the elasticity of substitution in developing countries and settle the argument once and for all. Indeed, many econometric estimates have been made. Quite a number of these studies have found the value of σ to range from 0.5, not a dramatically high value but high enough to encourage the elasticity optimists, up toward 1.0. But

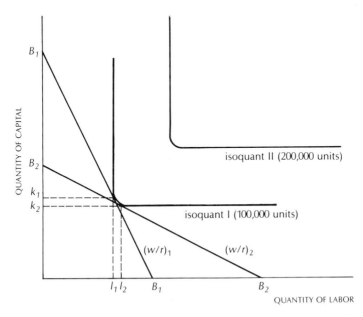

FIGURE 8–2 **Factor Substitution with Relatively Fixed Factor Proportions (Low Elasticity of Substitution).** Possibilities for producing given levels of output with different factor combinations are severely limited. When the wage-rental ratio falls from $(w/r)_1$ to $(w/r)_2$, there is little effect on the amounts of labor and capital used to produce 100,000 units of output.

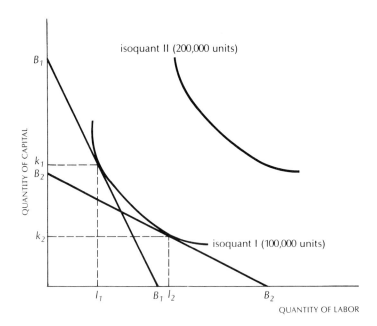

FIGURE 8–3 **Factor Substitution with Relatively Variable Factor Proportions (High Elasticity of Substitution).** Possibilities for producing given levels of output with different factor combinations are much greater than in Figure 8–2. When the wage-rental ratio falls, the amount of capital used is sharply reduced while employment expands significantly.

other writers have criticized these estimates on various grounds: they assume labor and capital to be **homogeneous,** that is, of uniform quality, when in fact they are not; they ignore the roles of other factors of production, such as management; they often deal with industries that are defined so broadly as to encompass a variety of outputs; and so on. Modest changes in assumptions, the critics note, can lead to large differences in conclusions.

Thus the debate between the optimists and the pessimists is not so easily resolved. However, there remain good reasons for believing that the relative prices of labor and capital can make a significant difference for employment creation. First, whatever the range of technologies available for producing a particular item, factor prices can have an important influence on employment by affecting the choice of goods to be produced. Recall the example of the successful exporters of labor-intensive manufacturers mentioned earlier. Second, even if the technology of a core production process is fixed and capital-intensive, opportunities exist for using large amounts of labor in subsidiary operations such as materials handling. Similarly, in construction some operations are best done by machines at almost any wage-rental ratio, but others lend themselves to labor-intensive methods if labor costs are low enough.

Third, employers are much more responsive to relative factor prices if they are forced to sell their products in competitive markets than if they can sell in protected markets. An important study conducted in Indonesia by Harvard Business School professor Louis Wells showed that while the nonmaximizing behaviors cited by the elasticity pessimists are real enough, business executives indulge them much more freely in protected markets.[10]

When competition forces them to seek the most-profitable technologies and factor proportions, both domestic and foreign business executives find ways to economize on capital and substitute more labor in labor-rich, capital-scarce countries.

A broad conclusion that emerges from these three points is that open competition promotes appropriate factor choices. Increasing the degree of competition, both within a given economy and among economies (as we will see in Chapters 16 and 17), can go far toward validating the assumptions of the elasticity optimists and making it possible to promote employment by reducing factor price distortions.

The Role of Technology

For the employment problem to be solved, or even significantly ameliorated, technology appropriate to the factor endowments of the low- and middle-income countries is clearly needed. How can such technology be acquired?

The LDCs face a paradoxical situation: they must depend on the developed countries to provide the great bulk of their modern technology, yet most of what these countries have to offer is inappropriate for use in countries with plentiful labor and scarce capital and skills. Since the beginning of their industrialization processes, the United States and Europe have had a scarcity of labor relative to other factors of production. Nearly all their innovations accordingly aimed at saving labor. The result in almost every productive sector has been a sequence of increasingly mechanized and automatically controlled technologies, each more appropriate than the last for a country with scarce labor and plentiful capital, but less and less appropriate for a country with the opposite factor endowments.

Excessive capital intensity is only one dimension of the inappropriateness of developed-country technology for the LDCs. Since the economies of even the smaller industrial countries are generally much larger than those of even the most populous developing countries, technologies are frequently designed to be efficient at a much larger scale of operation than the developing countries can hope to attain in the foreseeable future. In addition borrowed technology may necessitate the use of skills that are unavailable in poor countries, and thus may require the importation of foreign technicians. Finally, it may be designed to produce the wrong type or grade of product: for example, no-iron synthetic fabrics in countries where cotton is cheaper and there is plenty of labor to wash and press cotton garments.

Despite all these dimensions of inappropriateness, rich countries remain the main source of technology for poor countries. Well over 90 percent of the world's expenditure on technology research and development takes place in rich countries. Third-world countries invite multinational corpora-

10. Louis T. Wells, "Economic Man and Engineering Man: Choice of Technology in a Low-Wage Country," in *The Choice of Technology in Developing Countries: Some Cautionary Tales,* C. Peter Timmer et al., eds. (Cambridge, Mass.: Harvard University Center for International Affairs, 1975), pp. 69–93.

tions to invest in their leading sectors. They obtain equipment through official aid programs. The investors and aid givers, East or West, can only provide what they know and have available. In the absence of appropriate policies in the developing country, the result is often the transfer of inappropriate technology.

Technology Policies

How can technology available from developed countries be adapted to LDC needs? Four possible methods have been suggested.[11] First, LDCs can use developed-country technologies but make peripheral modifications, for example, in materials handling. Second, they can borrow old technologies from the industrial countries. American technology of 20, 30, or even 50 years ago may be more appropriate to the setting of, say, India, than the methods and machines used in the United States today. A third possible source of appropriate technology is selective borrowing from the industrial countries. Former British, French, American, and Dutch colonies in Southeast Asia gradually learned after independence that Japanese equipment was often better-suited to their needs than the machines they had formerly imported from the metropolitan country. Now machines from Korea, Taiwan, and mainland China are replacing Japanese equipment. Fourth, LDCs can do their own research and development to evolve technologies specifically designed to fit local conditions. Sometimes indigenous technologies developed over the years by local farmers, craftsmen, and fishermen provide a promising basis for this work.

Making these types of appropriate selections and adaptations is neither simple nor straightforward. The American economist Larry E. Westphal has suggested that what is needed is a broad-based "acquisition of technological capacity," which can only be developed through "learning by doing."[12] The Republic of Korea purposively set out to acquire technological capability in several industries in which it thought it could develop a comparative advantage. Making the ability to export increasing amounts, initially with the aid of government subsidies, its criterion for continued support, Korea succeeded in developing industries that could hold their own in international competition without further subsidization. Some economists have argued that this result can also be achieved through judicious import substitution.[13] Either way, the key point is that productivity must

11. See Frances Stewart, "Technology and Employment in LDCs," in *Employment in Developing Nations,* Edgar O. Edwards, ed. (New York: Columbia University Press, 1974), pp. 83–132, and Henry Bruton, "Technology Choice and Factor Proportions Problems in LDCs," in *Surveys in Development Economics,* Norman Gemmell, ed. (Oxford: Basil Blackwell, 1987), pp. 236–265.

12. See Larry E. Westphal, Linsu Kim, and Carl J. Dahlman, "Reflections on the Republic of Korea's Acquisition of Technological Capability," in *International Technology Transfer: Concepts, Measures, and Comparisons,* Nathan Rosenberg and Claudio Frischtak, eds. (New York: Preger, 1985), pp. 167–221 and Howard Pack and Larry E. Westphal, "Industrial Strategy and Technological Change. Theory versus Reality," *Journal of Development Economics* 22 (1986): 87–128.

13. See Larry E. Westphal, "Fostering Technological Mastery by Means of Selective Infant-Industry Protection," in *Trade, Stability, Technology and Equity in Latin America,* Simon

be raised through learning by doing; this will permit the industry in question to stand on its own after a few years.

Despite this potential, few countries have succeeded in making the development of appropriate technology a dynamic force in their economic development. One important reason has already been suggested: when competitive pressures are absent, incentives to adapt technology to local conditions are weak. Barriers to communication are also significant. It is hard for someone sitting in Surabaya or Sao Paulo to know just what technologies—new and modern, or older vintages—are available in New York or Nagasaki. Finally, it must be said that most third-world governments have not yet fully awakened to the need to promote local research and development. Their universities are usually preoccupied with teaching, and official research institutes in various field are often slow to be set up or experience severe staffing difficulties once they open their doors. Sometimes in these circumstances the most useful research and development work is done by foreign firms with a long history of operations in the country.

The British economist Frances Stewart has identified three broad schools of thought on technology policies for third-world countries. The first group, which she calls the **price incentive school,** stresses "getting the prices right," because it believes that factor prices that reflect social costs will not only lead to the selection of the most efficient techniques out of the currently available range but will also create incentives for more appropriate technologies to be developed. The opposing **technologist school** believes that this mechanism of induced innovation cannot be relied upon to do the job and urges that a conscious decision to invest more in technological development be taken. Finally, a **radical reform school** takes a broader view of the matter. It argues that both the array of goods produced and the methods used to produce them are inherent features of social systems. How can one expect anything but capital-intensive methods and products targeted for middle-class consumption from the multinational corporations? The creation of appropriate technologies and use of appropriate factor proportions, this last group argues, require that production be reoriented toward a multitude of cheap items for mass consumption. This in turn requires massive redistribution of income, which cannot be achieved without a social revolution. Hence the problem of inappropriate technology and inadequate job creation can only be solved in the context of a radical reform of society.

As Stewart sensibly concludes, there is a degree of truth in each school of thought. Evidence for the efficacy of radical reform comes from China, which has apparently found social and technological solutions to permit that state's vast labor force to be employed more fully and productively than ever before. Chinese industry "walks on two legs," combining large-scale, relatively capital-intensive production units with smaller, more labor-intensive and decentralized plants. Large-scale public works projects, such as dams and irrigation channels, have been another important form of labor

---

Teitel, ed. (New York: Academic Press, 1982), pp. 255–279, and Bruton, "Technology Choice and Factor Proportions Problems in LDCs."

absorption. Finally, intensified agricultural technologies using much larger amounts of fertilizer and other modern inputs have made it possible to increase agricultural employment productively. Appropriate technology is combined with strong production organization at the local level. The rural commune contrives to provide full employment for all its members in a combination of agricultural and nonagricultural activities.

Other socialist developing countries have trouble deciding just which way they want to go. Different conceptions of African socialism prevalent in Tanzania in the early 1970s stressed decentralized small-scale industry, increased processing of domestic raw materials, and creation of a modern, self-sufficient, state-run economy, but did not show how these ideas could be reconciled.

Other Employment Policies

Some theorists have argued that *improving income distribution* would accelerate job creation. According to this argument, goods consumed by poor people tend to be more labor-intensive than items consumed by those who are better-off, so redistribution of income in favor of the poor would make the pattern of demand more favorable to employment creation. Unfortunately, most of the studies undertaken to evaluate this proposal have concluded that the amount of employment generated by such a shift in demand would not be very great. A major stumbling block seems to be that although the goods consumed by the middle- and upper-income groups are indeed more capital-intensive than those consumed by the lower-income group, the better-off groups also consume more services, many of which are almost pure labor, such as household services. Moreover, goods consumed by the rich and poor often use the same intermediate inputs, for example, steel. Thus a shift in the pattern of final demand may have only a limited impact on the structure of production.

One useful approach to employment creation is to seek out *investments that complement labor* rather than substitute for it. Such investment opportunities probably exist in every sector of the economy. In agriculture, for example, mechanization of the planting and harvest functions may displace massive quantities of labor, but investments in irrigation actually create employment by making it possible to cultivate the same land more intensively and through a greater proportion of the year. A different kind of complementary investment, discussed earlier, is training to fill skill bottlenecks.

Even though capital is scarce in low-income countries, paradoxically their stocks of capital equipment are often underutilized. In many countries factories produce at only 30 to 60 percent of capacity, shift work is rare, tractors sit idle in fields, bulldozers rest by roadsides. If a way could be found to *increase capacity utilization* and put this idle capital to work, there would be a sharp upswing in the demand for labor, achievable in the short run, without having to wait for new investments to be made and mature. Unfortunately, this appealing prospect is hard to realize. There are many reasons for unused capacity, including fluctuations in demand and inadequate supplies of materials. Despite the scarcity of capital, distorted prices in some developing countries may make it cheaper for firms to let equipment stand idle part of the time than to use it more intensively.

Generally speaking, *small informal-sector establishments* use less capital and more labor to produce a given type of output than larger formal-sector firms. One reason may be that small firms face prices for labor and capital that are closer to their social opportunity costs. Minimum-wage laws, unions, and payroll taxes all have little or no application to informal-sector firms. And not being preferred customers of the banks—indeed, often not dealing with banks at all—they have no access to rationed credit at artificially low interest rates. This situation has led many governments and international agencies to pay special attention to small-scale industry, as further discussed in Chapter 20.

Small firms often provide much-needed jobs to workers who cannot find work in larger firms. This valuable social function is sometimes impeded by government policies that discriminate against small firms. Such policies range from overvalued exchange rates and investment incentives available only to large firms to regulatory harassment and disruptively selective enforcement of tax and licensing requirements. Although discrimination against small-scale industry is obviously inappropriate, the long-term potential of small-scale industry is more debatable. Normally the relative importance of small firms declines in the course of economic development (see Table 8–5). Small firms that survive the transition to industrialization are progressive enterprises that have adapted to changing economic conditions and found ways to use resources just as productively as large firms. In some countries, such as Japan historically and Taiwan in recent decades, small-scale industry has continued to play a major role in industrial employment and value-added up to high levels of per-capita income. These small firms have been able to flourish in a competitive environment, unlike the subsidized and protected small-scale industry of India, which has stagnated and remained a drain on the exchequer.

TABLE 8–5   **Share of Small Establishments in Total Manufacturing Employment, 1980s (percent)**

GNP per capita ($)	Distribution of employment by size class (%)			
	1–4 workers	5–19	20–99	100+
$100–$500	64	7	4	25
$500–$1,000	41	12	10	37
$1,000–$2,000	11	13	14	61
$2,000–$5,000	8	11	17	64
Over $5,000	4	6	20	70

Source: Tyler S. Biggs, "Firm Transformation in the Tropics," forthcoming.

When all else fails, governments may institute **food-for-work programs** to provide at least part-time or temporary employment to groups that are particularly distressed or well-placed to give the government trouble if their needs are not looked after. Many of these programs have been financed by foreign food aid, either by paying the participants with food or by selling the food and using the counterpart funds thus earned to help pay the cost of the program.

Food-for-work programs promise to combine construction of a socially useful facility with income redistribution to some of the poorest elements in society. It has been discovered, however, that the promise has been fulfilled only occasionally in the dozens of such programs that have been undertaken.[14] Many food-for-work programs have been plagued by bad management, and in some countries local elites have found ways to capture most of the benefits; sometimes they have even forced peasants to labor at low wages to provide a road or irrigation ditch that only increases the value of the landlord's property. Implementing an effective food-for-work program is a challenging task, best undertaken by governments (such as China's) that possess both a strong commitment to economic and social equity and the capacity to enforce that commitment.

GOVERNMENT STRATEGIES

The desirability of accelerating the creation of productive employment, especially in countries hoping to combine a reasonable measure of equity with economic growth, is evident. Its feasibility is much less straightforward. Many different types of public policy impinge on employment creation. It is not really possible to draw up an employment plan for a developing country, only a general development plan stressing employment as one in a set of interrelated objectives.[15] The importance of employment as an objective of development policy and planning has received full recognition only in the last two decades. Policymakers and scholars alike are still learning what is involved in increasing productive employment in developing countries.

What is clear is that the context of the particular developing country—its size and economic structure—makes a difference for the kind of employment creation strategy to be pursued. South Korea and Singapore have been able to solve their employment problems by emulating the Japanese pattern of whirlwind industrialization based largely on the export market. Medium-sized, semi-industrialized countries like Malaysia and the Philippines may be able to follow a similar path, with modifications permitted by their richer natural-resource endowments. Larger, more agricultural countries must take a more-balanced approach. At best they may be able to develop rapidly following a continental model, as Brazil seems to be doing. At worst, as in Bangladesh and the other very poor countries, a long period of reliance on job creation in agriculture and other rural activities will be required.

14. J. W. Thomas, et al., "Public Works Programs in Developing Countries: A Comparative Analysis," World Bank Staff Working Paper No. 224, February 1976.

15. This did not prevent the ILO, under its World Employment Programme, from preparing a series of such plans through the use of visiting missions—for Colombia, Sri Lanka, Iran, Kenya, the Philippines, and the Sudan. While useful as a means of publicizing the goal of employment creation and as illustrations of how employment-oriented development planning can be carried out, these plans have not in any literal sense been implemented by the governments concerned.

9

Education

The previous chapter discussed labor as a homogenous resource in economic development, a quantity of human power available to produce goods and services. But numbers of workers cannot tell the whole story. Attempts to attribute economic growth to growth in the factors of production always leave an unexplained residual, as we saw in Chapter 3. One important explanation for that residual is the improvement in the quality of human resources that leads workers to be more productive. Labor quality may be enhanced by education of either children or adults, as well as by improved health and nutrition for children and working adults, by migration of workers to places with better job opportunities, and by fertility reduction.

Some of these activities are discussed in other chapters. At this point we want to stress their common characteristics. In each case someone—either the community as a whole, employers, the individuals concerned, or their parents—makes a decision to use scarce resources to improve the productivity, present or future, of human beings. In an influential presidential speech to the American Economic Association in 1960, Nobel laureate Theodore Schultz suggested that such activities could be considered a process of accumulating capital, which could later be drawn upon to increase a worker's productivity and income. He called this investment in **human capital**. This form of investment, said Schultz, is every bit as important as investment in physical capital, but until his speech it had largely been neglected by academics and policymakers alike.[1] Subsequent work by Schultz and

---

1. See Theodore W. Schultz, "Investment in Human Capital," *American Economic Review* 51 (January 1961): 17.

others elaborated the idea of investment in human capital, applying it to all the human resource development activities mentioned above. A fuller idea of what the concept implies should emerge from the discussion of it in the context of education later in this chapter.

Studies sponsored by the World Bank lend further support to the idea that human resource development has an important bearing on economic growth.[2] There is reason to believe that the relationship is two-way and mutually supporting. On the one hand growing economies can and do devote increasing resources to improvement of educational, health, and nutritional standards. But it is also apparent that investment in human resources helps to accelerate economic growth. It does this by increasing labor productivity, encouraging greater physical investment, and reducing the dependency burden of the population. These contributions to growth are especially evident in the case of education.

TRENDS AND PATTERNS

Education can be defined broadly as all forms of human learning or more narrowly as the process that occurs in specialized institutions called schools. It is unquestionably the most important form of human resource development, in several senses.

First, there is tremendous popular demand for education, particularly for schooling, in virtually all countries, developing and developed alike. Often in developing countries the number of people seeking admittance to schools far exceeds the number of places available. In Indonesia (see boxed example) there was a tremendous popular response when the government made primary schooling widely available. Obviously, people everywhere believe that education is beneficial for themselves and their children.

Education in Indonesia

In 1973, as he was working on his country's second five-year plan, the chairman of Indonesia's National Development Planning Board registered displeasure at statistics received from the Ministry of Education. The data showed that only 54 percent of 7 to 12 year olds were enrolled in primary school. Worse, the ministry projected no rise in the percentage of children enrolled over the next five years. The major reasons were: too few of Indonesia's 60,000 villages had primary schools, trained teachers were in short supply, textbooks were scarce and expensive, and many poor rural households were unable to pay even the modest fees charged to attend school. The chairman decided that something drastic had to be done.

The solution was a special program to improve rural children's access to schools by cutting red tape and building primary schools in villages that did not yet have them. These new schools were then staffed with newly

2. See World Bank, *World Development Report 1980* and the working papers cited therein, and George Psacharopoulos and Maureen Woodhall, *Education for Development. An Analysis of Investment Choices* (New York: Oxford University Press, 1985).

trained teachers and provided with millions of just-printed library and text-books. Meanwhile, school fees were abolished at the primary level. The program was funded through loans from the World Bank and the high oil revenues that Indonesia fortunately received during the 1970s. Would rural parents respond to the improved opportunity by sending their sons and daughters to school? They did. By 1983, after more than 60,000 new schools had been built and over 100,000 existing schools rehabilitated, about 95 percent of 7 to 12 year olds had signed up for school. The program was a great success.

But every development success brings new problems in its wake. In the 1980s the Indonesian government struggled to cope with the rising tide of primary school graduates who wanted to go on to secondary school and eventually university. Oil prices had fallen, and the government could not afford to build enough public high schools to accommodate all who wanted to attend them. Many parents could not afford to send their children to private schools. To this day, therefore, enrollment in secondary and higher education remains restricted largely to the minority of students from better-off families who can afford to pay. Nor is it clear where the farmers of the future will come from, since virtually everyone who has completed primary school wants to leave farming and seek a living elsewhere.

A second reason for believing that education is important is that education and income are highly correlated at both the individual and the societal level. Figure 9–1 shows typical patterns relating age, educational attainment, and earnings in two developing countries. Although not all high school graduates, for example, earn more than all who completed only primary school, the majority do, and on average their earnings are much higher. People the world over intuitively recognize this correlation and consequently try to obtain the largest possible amount of schooling for themselves and their children.

The correlation between national income levels and educational attainments is also strong. As we saw in Chapter 1, illiteracy is rife in the very poorest countries and diminishes steadily as one goes up the income scale (see also Table 9–1). Mass education is still a relatively recent phenomenon in the poorer countries. When most adults now living were children, schooling was far less prevalent than it is today. Yet all but the very poorest countries currently educate large fractions of their school-age populations (middle columns of Table 9–1), so the educational attainment of the adult population is rising fast.

The relationships shown in Figure 9–1 and the top part of Table 9–1 are averages. There are many contrary cases: of rich individuals and societies that have received little schooling, and of well-educated individuals and highly schooled societies whose incomes are relatively low. Some of the intercountry variations are shown in the bottom part of Table 9–1. On average, however, the correlation between education and income is a strong one. But does this mean that education *causes* a person's, or a nation's, income to rise? Could causation not flow in the opposite direction, indicating merely that richer countries and families spend more on education, as

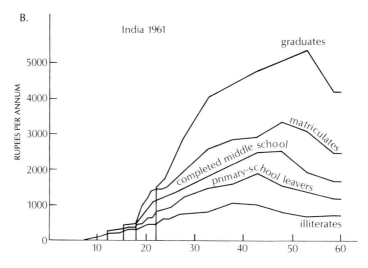

FIGURE 9–1   **Age-Earnings Profiles in Mexico and India.** The lines on the graph represent mean earnings at different ages of people with varying amounts of formal education. On average, people who stay in school longer earn higher incomes.
Sources: Martin Carnoy, ''Rates of Return to Schooling in Latin America,'' *Journal of Human Resources* (Summer 1967): 359–374, and M. Balug, R. Layard, and M. Woodhall, *Causes of Graduate Unemployment in India* (Harmondsworth, England: Allen Lane, Penguin Press, 1969), p. 21.

they do on other goods and services? Or, finally, are higher income and education the common results of some unidentified third factor? These questions are explored later in the chapter.

A third reason why education is important is that large sums are spent to acquire it. Education is a major item in both household and national budgets. Because their people want it, and to some extent also because they think it will stimulate development, LDC governments devote a substantial fraction of their resources to the creation and operation of school systems.

TABLE 9–1 Educational Statistics in Relation to GNP per Capita and for Selected Countries (1980s)[a]

Income group	% of illiterate adults	Enrollment ratios[b] Primary school Gross	Enrollment ratios[b] Primary school Net	Secondary school gross	Higher school gross	Approximate public expenditure dollars per pupil % of GNP	Approximate public expenditure dollars per pupil Primary	Approximate public expenditure dollars per pupil Secondary	Approximate public expenditure dollars per pupil Higher
	A. By income group
Below $250	61	60	41	12	1.9	2.8	22	105	1,202
$250–$500	51	75	67	23	2.6	3.7	37	209	1,584
$500–$2,200	32	102	85	48	13.8	4.4	184	386	1,696
$2,200–$6,000	18	104	92	69	17.7	5.3	321	491	2,509
Above $6,000	5[c]	101	93	86	27.9	5.6	2,554	2,751	5,856
	B. For selected countries
Tanzania	na	66	50	4	0.2	4.1	19	204	2,895
China	31	132	98	43	2	2.7	13	36	586
India	57	98	na	39	9	3.4	30	65	na
Pakistan	70	52	na	19	5	2.1	25	38	1,155
Kenya	41	96	91	23	1	7.0	62	159	2,888
Ghana	47	71	na	40	2	3.4	28	59	1,226
Sri Lanka	13	104	100	66	4	3.8	na	na	169
Indonesia	26	118	98	46	7	2.0	na	na	na
Bolivia	26	91	83	37	17	0.4	1,375	2,960	na
Colombia	12	114	73	56	14	2.7	40	80	400
Peru	15	122	97	65	25	3.3	117	237	77
Chile	6	103	90	70	18	3.6	156	149	581
Brazil	22	103	84	39	11	4.5	236	524	2,825
South Korea	na	104	100	89	37	4.2	400	400	300
Hungary	2	97	95	70	15	5.6	337	548	2,043
U.K.	2	106	100	83	22	5.0	1,700	2,900	5,400
U.S.	2	100	95	98	60	6.7	1,700	4,200	7,900
Japan	2	102	99	96	28	5.0	2,900	3,100	10,000

[a] Year of most recent estimate available varies by country.
[b] Enrollment ratios express enrollment as a percentage of the school-age population. Gross enrollment ratios relate total enrollment of students of all ages to the size of the age group that normally attends that level of schooling; they can exceed 100%. Net enrollment ratios show the percentage of the pertinent age group that is enrolled.
[c] Rough estimate; many industrial countries with very high literacy rates no longer publish statistics on illiteracy.
Sources: UNESCO Statistical Yearbook 1989 (Paris: UNESCO, 1989), and World Bank, *World Development Report 1990*.

Table 9–1 indicates that the expenditure of 3 to 5 percent of GNP in public funds was typical even in the 1980s, a difficult decade for many developing countries. Private expenditures on education, which are harder to measure, are left out. Some 15 to 20 percent of the government budget commonly goes for education. If we regard education in less-conventional terms as an industry, we see that it is one of the largest in all economies, ranked in terms of either value-added or employment.

Types of Learning

We have been treating the terms "education" and "schooling" as if they were synonymous, as one does in everyday parlance. Modern usage by specialists, however, applies the term "education" to a broader concept, akin to the notion of learning. This emphasizes that there are different forms of learning that are important and can be seen as substitutes for each other in some circumstances. Usually three principal types of learning—education in the broad sense—are identified.

Formal education takes place in institutions called schools. It usually involves young people who have not yet begun their working lives.

Nonformal education can be thought of as organized programs of learning that take place outside schools. Often the participants are adults. Programs of nonformal education are usually shorter, more narrowly focused, and more applied than programs of formal education. They may teach occupational skills or other subjects such as literacy, family life, or citizenship.

Informal education is learning that takes place outside any institutional framework or organized program. People learn many important things at home, on the job, and in the community.

Although other definitions of the three terms can easily be found, these indicate the basic differences among them. In the rest of this chapter we will use them in the above senses.

Characteristics of LDC Education

School systems in most third-world countries have expanded tremendously over the last four decades. Countries that emerged from colonialism after World War II usually inherited narrow-based systems designed to educate only the local elite and a small cadre of literate clerks. Most colonial regimes distrusted the educated "native" and feared the consequences of mass education. Even in Latin American, where most countries became independent early in the nineteenth century, a rigid class structure confined schooling essentially to the rural elite and better-off urbanites.

After independence, the political imperatives changed radically. Pledged to change so much in so short a time, newly independent governments found that one of the most popular things they could do relatively quickly was to build schools. While a modern economy might be decades away, a modern-looking school system could be built in just a few years. Now the incentive was to expand schooling rapidly.

As Table 9–2 shows, school enrollments at all levels in developing countries grew from about 100 million in 1950 to 700 million by 1987. During the 1950s the number of students enrolled more than doubled. In the 1960s and 1970s the growth rate of enrollment declined gradually, but the absolute number of students added each decade continued to rise. In the 1980s, with primary school enrollments nearly 100 percent in many countries and financial problems constraining expansion at higher levels, overall enrollment growth slowed further to less than 2 percent a year.

Enrollment growth came in waves; it hit the primary schools first; then, as more children finished primary schooling, high schools; and finally the universities, technical colleges, and other institutions of higher education. The spread of the system differed from country to country. A relatively westernized Asian country like Sri Lanka, which adopted a free schooling policy at independence in 1948, was able to achieve practically universal primary schooling by the 1950s and then to press on rapidly with expansion of the higher levels until financial difficulties forced a slowdown of enroll-

TABLE 9–2 School Enrollment in Developing Countries,[a] 1950–1987 (millions)

	1950	1960	1970	1980	1987
Primary					
Africa	7	17	30	59	68
Asia	71	164	234	319	335
Latin America	15	27	44	65	72
Total	93	208	307	443	475
Secondary					
Africa	—	2	4	14	21
Asia	6	12	66	124	154
Latin America	2	4	11	18	23
Total	8	18	80	156	198
Higher					
Africa	—	—	—	1	2
Asia	1	1	5	12	19
Latin America	—	1	2	5	7
Total	1	2	7	18	28
All Levels					
Total	102	228	395	617	701

[a]North Korea is excluded from these statistics. South Africa and Japan are regarded as developed countries and are also excluded. Continents may not add to the total because of rounding error and the exclusion of a few small countries (— indicates less than 500,000).

Sources: UNESCO Yearbook of Educational Statistics 1972 (Paris: UNESCO, 1973), and *UNESCO Statistical Yearbook 1989.*

ment expansion in the 1960s. Other countries, in Latin America and elsewhere, began rapid enrollment expansion at the higher levels of schooling long before universal primary schooling was attained. Often this pattern resulted from a concentration of political power that gave more weight to elite interests than to those of the general population. Elsewhere, as in the more conservative Muslim countries, it was a consequence of the low priority attached to education for girls.

Rapid expansion often created *teacher shortages* that led to increasing class sizes and the use of less highly trained teachers. Sometimes it proved possible to expand teacher training and overcome the worst of the shortages after a few years. In many countries, however, teacher shortages persist to this day, particularly in remote regions where teachers, like other public servants, are reluctant to go.

The expansion of schooling began to cause fiscal strains as early as the 1960s. Few developing countries have been able to satisfy the social demand for education from public funds. African and Latin American nations that experienced slow economic growth, stagnation, or even declines in GNP per capita during the 1980s found it difficult even to maintain past educational standards. Nevertheless, as Table 9–3 indicates, enrollment ratios generally continued to rise during the 1980s. The exception was sub-Saharan Africa, where gross enrollment ratios in primary schools fell between 1980 and 1987 in 15 of the 29 countries for which data are available. For LDCs as a whole, government expenditures on education grew little during the 1980s, however (see the incomplete data cited in Table 9–3), so the quality of schooling probably declined in some of the more hard-pressed countries. It is also likely that private funding paid a larger share of the bill as private

TABLE 9–3   Changes in Enrollment Ratios and Central Government Expenditure on Education during the 1980s

| | Gross enrollment ratios | | | | | | Central government expenditure as a % of: | | | |
| | Primary | | Secondary | | Tertiary | | Government budget | | GNP | |
	1980	1987	1980	1987	1980	1987	1981	1988	1981	1988
Low income countries:	93	104	29	37	4	5	na	na	na	na
China	117	132	34	43	1	2	na	na	na	na
India	76	98	28	39	9	10	2	3	1	1
Other	70	79	19	26	2	3	12	9	2	2
Middle income countries	100	104	41	54	11	17	14	13	4	2
Developing countries in:										
Sub-Saharan Africa	77	68	15	17	1	2	16	14	4	3
East Asia	114	125	36	45	3	6	na	na	na	na
South Asia	74	89	26	35	7	8	3	4	*	1
Europe, Middle East, N. Africa	92	97	50	57	11	13	na	12	na	4
Latin America & Caribbean	105	108	39	49	15	17	11	11	2	1
Severely indebted countries[a]	104	104	45	53	16	19	12	11	2	2
All developing countries	95	104	32	41	6	8	na	na	na	na

[a] As classified by the World Bank. Includes Argentina, Bolivia, Brazil, Chile, Congo, Costa Rica, Cote d'Ivoire, Ecuador, Honduras, Hungary, Mexico, Nicaragua, Peru, Philippines, Poland, Senegal, Uruguay, and Venezuela.
*Less than 0.5 percent.
Sources: Based on data given in World Bank, *World Development Report 1983, 1984,* and *1990.*

schools and colleges sprang up to offer places to disappointed applicants to the public institutions.

Major reasons for the inefficiency of educational expenditures have been the high frequencies of **dropouts,** those who withdraw from schooling before completing an academically meaningful course of study, and **repeaters,** those who require more than the prescribed number of years to complete the program. Most educators believe that a child who does not complete at least five or six years of school gains little from attendance; yet millions fail to do so. In large measure these problems result from poverty. The various costs of keeping a child in school become too heavy an imposition on the poor household after a while.

In view of such problems, it is not surprising that learning achievements in developing country schools are often low. The World Bank reports that scores on standardized arithmetic and science achievement tests administered to fourth to eighth graders during the 1970s and early 1980s averaged 35 to 40 percent in low- and lower-middle-income countries, compared with 50 to 60 percent in high-income countries. In reading tests the difference was 49 percent versus 70 percent.[3] There is even evidence that those who master specific skills in school sometimes lose them in later life through

3. *Primary Education, A World Bank Policy Paper* (Washington, D.C.: World Bank, 1990), p. 13.

lack of use. Functional literacy is likely to be retained only by those who

have access to written materials and some incentive to read and write daily.
Many third-world people have neither.

Severe inequalities among regions and social classes characterize most developing-country school systems. In many countries a child who lives in a major city or comes from a favored socioeconomic background is much more likely to receive schooling—and vastly more likely to get high-quality schooling—than a student from a rural area or a more ordinary socioeconomic setting. Since education tends to lead to a better job and a higher income, this pattern of educational provision worsens the distribution of opportunity and income. Some economists believe that an improved distribution of schooling could be a major force for achieving a more-equal distribution of income. Governments in developing countries have only begun to address these problems and potentials.

Another reason why limited learning seems to take place in third-world school systems is what British scholar Ronald Dore calls the "diploma disease."[4] According to Dore and others, these systems are not primarily in the business of conveying knowledge and skills at all, but are more concerned with certification or credentialing. Dore argues that in late-developing countries an individual's fitness is often judged by the academic credentials that he or she possesses. And of course successful completion of a given level of schooling is the main qualification for admittance to the next highest level. In most developing countries, nationwide examinations are given at certain stages in the schooling process to determine the student's fitness for educational advancement or employment. These exams take on tremendous importance, and this causes teachers to bend their classroom efforts to the task of preparing students for them, and student to put in long hours outside school cramming for them. Dore contends that this perverts the true purpose of education and escalates the cost of a selection process that might be carried out more cheaply in other ways.

Some countries where enrollment expanded rapidly in the 1950s and 1960s experienced severe **educated unemployment** after a few years. India and the Philippines, two Asian pioneers in the expansion of secondary and higher education, acquired large pools of job-seeking graduates unable to find "suitable" employment. Sri Lanka, with its long-standing commitment to free schooling, found half its recent university graduates unemployed by the 1970s. A few lucky countries experienced a subsequent upswing in economic growth, which soaked up this pool of unemployed labor. One was South Korea, which had many frustrated out-of-work graduates in the late 1950s but was experiencing a shortage of educated workers by the 1970s. However, in many countries educated unemployment seems to have become a permanent feature of society.

Poor fit between school curricula and the needs of the job market seems to aggravate the problem. Harvard University education expert Russell Davis reported that in the 1970s the employment exchange in Calcutta was daily thronged with college graduates (some of them "firsts," recipients of top

---

4. See Ronald Dore, *The Diploma Disease. Education, Qualification and Development* (Berkeley: University of California Press, 1976).

academic honors) in mathematics, English, and physics. Yet employers who approached the same office seeking workers skilled in air conditioning, silk-screen printing, or plumbing came away disappointed.[5] In such circumstances, graduates must eventually take jobs irrelevant to their education. College-graduate taxi drivers are said to be common in Manila. Employers then have to use on-the-job training to convey the skills that workers will need.

Nonformal education played little part in the inherited educational system. Significantly, however, many government departments that required technical skills conducted specialized training programs for their own staffs. This shows that needed skills were not being supplied by the formal education system. Nor were they available through informal education, since the limited experience with modern economic activities meant that accumulated on-the-job learning was necessarily low.

EDUCATION'S ROLE IN DEVELOPMENT

Education is many things to many people. Besides the economic benefits already mentioned, education up to a certain level is often seen as an inherent right. Education has also been promoted because it can socialize people. Through a common schooling experience. it has often been thought, people from different national, social, ethnic, religious, and linguistic backgrounds can be encouraged to adopt a common outlook on the world. Since many developing countries have diverse populations and must place a high premium on the attainment of greater national unity, this is often an important objective for them. Education is also thought to confer civic benefits. Some political scientists believe that at least a minimal level of schooling is a prerequisite for political democracy.[6]

Thinking about how education can be used to promote economic development has changed considerably over the years. During the 1950s much of the discussion centered on the need for trained manpower. Manpower planning, outlined below, became a popular way to analyze a developing country's manpower needs. Its emphasis on middle- and high-level trained manpower implies that secondary and higher education are most in need of expansion. Yet as we have seen the 1950s was also a period of rapid growth in primary school enrollments. In 1959 a number of Asian governments subscribed to the **Karachi Plan,** which pledged them to provide at least seven years of compulsory, universal, and free schooling by 1980.

Disillusionment with this approach followed in the 1960s. Many governments found their budgets strained by the attempt to expand all levels of

5. Russell Davis, "Planning Education for Employment," Harvard Institute for International Development, Development Discussion Paper no. 60, June 1979.

6. Yet education does not guarantee the existence of democracy, as many examples of countries with educated populations but undemocratic governments attest. (The role of education in the recent upsurge of democracy in Latin America and Eastern Europe could be debated.) And there are examples of democratic systems in countries with relatively little education: India, Jamaica, Guyana, and Colombia. So the relationship of education to democracy is not clear-cut.

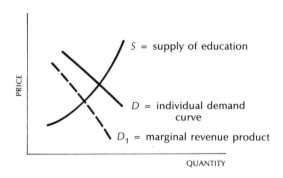

FIGURE 9–2 Apparent and Real Demand for Schooling. Basing their expectations on current earnings differentials, people demand large amounts of schooling, as indicated by demand curve D. Since rapidly growing numbers are now obtaining education, however, the marginal return on schooling will actually be lower (demand curve D^1). As discussed below, the higher individual demand curve D could also be explained by a pure preference for education as a consumption good.

schooling simultaneously. Demand seemed unquenchable; expansion of capacity at one level of schooling only increased the demand for places at the next-higher level. Paradoxically, the continuing boom demand for schooling was accompanied by an apparent decline in its benefits to the individual. The rise of unemployment among the educated caused officials to wonder whether more and more resources should be devoted to expanding the school system, just so people could be unemployed. As shown in Figure 9–2, excess demand resulted from a market failure: because individuals lacked information about educational trends, they expected higher returns to investments in schooling than they were able to realize.

This cost-consciousness fit well with a new method of analyzing educational investments, introduced during the 1960s. Cost-benefit analysis, based on human capital theory, compared the costs and the benefits of education, as we shall see below; manpower analysis, in contrast, considered only the benefits. By the 1970s, however, disillusionment had spread to the human capital approach. A search for alternative concepts of education's role began, and is still underway.

Education remains tremendously important in developing countries. Indeed, larger numbers of people and sums of money are involved than ever before. Current concerns include how to finance the amounts of education that people want, how to improve quality, and how to provide basic education to those who are still excluded. In March, 1990 four United Nations agencies sponsored the **World Conference on Education for All,** which focused on problems in basic education: more than 100 million children, including at least 60 million girls, with no access to primary schooling; more than 960 million adults, two-thirds women, who are functionally illiterate; more than one-third of all adults who have no access to printed knowledge; more than 100 million children who fail to complete basic education programs; and millions who satisfy the attendance requirements but do not require essential knowledge and skills. The conference tried to raise consciousness and mobilize resources to solve these problems.

Manpower Planning

In any economy there is a tendency for people with given levels of educa-tion to hold certain types of jobs. In developing countries, for example, nearly all employed university graduates work at professional, technical, or managerial jobs, usually either in government or as independent profes-sionals. People whose schooling ended at the secondary level tend to hold middle-level jobs in the clerical, sales, and service occupations. Half or more of the labor force in the typical developing country is made up of farmers and agricultural laborers who received little or no formal educa-tion.

It is tempting to jump from these observable facts to the assumption that a certain level of education is *required* if a person is to fill a particular occupational role. If this were the case, it would follow that a growing economy, which is expected to undergo a shift in occupational structure toward more professional, technical, and industrial workers, must follow a defined pattern of educational development to obtain the kinds of trained people it will need.

Manpower planning is based on this assumption. It presumes that the economy's need for educated labor can be predicted and the growth of the educational system planned to avoid both manpower shortages, which may retard economic growth, and manpower surpluses, which waste educa-tional resources and may lead to educated unemployment or "brain drain."

Manpower planning starts with a prediction of manpower needs. This can be based on employer projections or extrapolation of past trends, although both are highly unreliable. A more sophisticated method, devel-oped by Dutch Nobel laureate Jan Tinbergen and American economist Herbert Parnes, tries to deduce the future employment pattern from a pro-jection of GNP growth. It starts from a target growth rate of GNP during the planning period, which must be at least several years long, since the training of middle- and high-level manpower takes time. Next, it estimates the structural changes in output by sector of origin needed to achieve that overall growth rate. Third, employment by sector is estimated, using assumptions about labor productivity growth, or about the elasticity of employment growth relative to output growth, which is its inverse. Fourth, employment by industry is divided into occupational categories using assumptions about the "required" structure in each industry; these are then summed across industries to get the economy's required occupation mix. Finally, occupational requirements are translated into educational terms via assumptions about what sorts of education are appropriate for each occupational group.

These five steps lead to an estimate of manpower requirements in some future year. To project manpower supply in the same year, one first adjusts the current stock of manpower for expected losses through retirement, death, emigration, and withdrawal from the labor force. Next, one projects increases to manpower supply resulting from outputs of the school system, immigra-tion, and labor force entry by nonworking adults. The projected manpower supply is then compared with projected requirements. If a gap results, it is usually assumed that it must be closed through accelerated school enrollments. Occasionally other ways of increasing manpower supply, such as upgrading less-skilled workers or bringing in foreign workers, are considered.

A major weakness of the manpower planning approach is that the relationships it assumes fixed are often unstable and unpredictable in the real world. Labor productivity is affected by many factors, and often changes unexpectedly. The occupational mix also changes, for both exogenous (external) and endogenous (internal) reasons. For example, new technologies may be introduced and bring a new set of occupational requirements into being. Or a change in relative wages may induce employers to hire a different mix of workers; such price adjustments are assumed away in the model. In the long run, changes in the occupational mix occur as a direct result of changes in the supply of educated labor. People with more schooling increasingly do jobs that previously were done by less-educated persons. This can be called **educational deepening**.

Further undercutting the logic of manpower planning is the absence of a unique education-occupation linkage. The knowledge required to do virtually any job can be acquired through formal, nonformal, or informal education. Similarly, only a small fraction of what is learned in most educational programs is unique to a specific occupation; much more of it is applicable to a range of jobs.

Manpower planning also fails to account for the cost of education. Manpower "requirements" are assumed to be absolute, and the conclusion always seems to be that a projected gap should be filled through educational expansion, generally of secondary and higher formal education. Yet these types of schooling are relatively expensive in many LDCs (right-hand columns of Table 9–1). Alternative, possibly cheaper, ways of dealing with the problem, such as nonformal education or on-the-job training, are seldom considered.

These objections, plus the emergence of the competing cost-benefit approach, have doomed manpower planning to limbo as far as most academic specialists are concerned. However, the approach is still used by practical planners to gain at least a rough idea of what a developing country's possible manpower problems are. It often appeals to politicians, who like its apparent precision. They like to be told, say, that the country needs to train 125 architects by the year 2000. As a matter of political economy, manpower planning is more likely to be influential when it projects deficits than when it projects surpluses. Deficits offer an apparently strong rationale for expanding a particular type of education. In many developing countries, however, schooling has expanded so much that few manpower deficits can be legitimately projected. In these circumstances, society's demand for education and the political pressures that go with it generally ensure that the school system continues to expand at a faster rate than would be indicated by manpower planning, which tends to be ignored.

Cost-Benefit Analysis

The hypothesis underlying human capital theory is that individuals, or their governments on their behalf, spend money on education, health, and other human services primarily for the purpose of raising their incomes and pro-ductivity. The added output and income that result in future years, then, become a return on the investment made. Application of this idea to formal education begins with a set of **lifetime earnings curves,** such as those in Figure 9–1. These curves, which show average earnings at various ages for people with particular amounts of schooling, have been calculated for many populations. Nearly all of them have three characteristics. First, given the amount of schooling, defined in terms of either years of school or the high-est level attained, earnings increase up to a maximum level that is reached around age 40 or later, and then level off or decline. Second, for those with larger amounts of schooling, the curve is higher, and steeper in its rising phase; although people with more schooling start work a bit later in life, they usually begin at a higher earnings level than those with less schooling who are already working. Third, more schooling leads to later attainment of maximum earnings and to higher earnings in retirement. All three fea-tures can be seen in the curves for Mexico and India shown in Figure 9–1.

Cost-benefit analysis, introduced in Chapter 6 as a planning tool and used in Chapter 8 to analyze employment, can be used to make both private and social calculations of the value of education. To understand the *private rate of return,* begin by imagining a set of parents faced with a decision on how much schooling to provide a child. They have a rough idea of what the lifetime earnings curves look like and regard them as a prediction of what the child would earn at different levels of educational attainment. Although it may strain one's credulity, it is necessary to think of these parents as calculating the discounted present value of the future earnings stream attached to each level of schooling and comparing it with the cost of attain-ing that level of school.

The present value of prospective earnings in any future year can be defined as

$$V_0^t = \frac{E_t}{(1+i)^{t'}} \qquad [9\text{--}1]$$

where V_0^t = the present value of earnings in year t, E_t = the earnings in year t, and i = the rate of interest (opportunity cost of the parents' capital). The earnings are discounted to the present, using the rate of interest i.

The discounted present value of the entire stream of earnings until year n is therefore

$$V = \sum_{t=1}^{n} \frac{E_t}{(1+i)^{t'}} \qquad [9\text{--}2]$$

This is the benefit side of the cost-benefit calculation. The private costs of schooling—those borne by private households—are of two types, explicit and implicit. **Explicit costs** involve actual outlays of cash. The most obvious example is tuition fees, but it is important to recognize that even "free"— that is, tuition-free—schooling entails costs, explicit as well as implicit. Some cash outlays are almost always required for books, uniforms, trans-portation, and other purposes. Even such modest explicit costs can serve as a significant barrier to school attendance for children from poor families.

Implicit costs take the form of the forgone earnings of students who would be working as wage-earners or as unpaid but productive workers on family farms and in family enterprises if they were not in school. In general these opportunity costs are highest for older students and higher levels of schooling, but in settings in which young children can work productively, they may be a factor even at the primary level, particularly for the poorer households.

The costs of schooling are incurred before its benefits are received. Whether a particular educational investment is worthwhile can be determined by comparing the discounted present values of the benefit and cost streams, as explained in Chapter 6. If discounted benefits exceed discounted costs, using a relevant rate of interest to discount both streams, then the investment should be made. If discounted costs exceed discounted benefits, the investment is not worth making. More commonly in educational analysis, however, the **internal rate of return** on the investment is calculated. This, as we saw in Chapter 6, is the discount rate that equates the discounted present values of the benefit and cost streams. We can solve for the internal rate of return using the following equations.

$$\sum_{t=1}^{n} \frac{E_t}{(1+r)^t} = \sum_{t=1}^{n} \frac{C_t}{(1+r)^{t'}} \qquad [9\text{--}3]$$

or

$$\sum_{t=1}^{n} \frac{E_t - C_t}{(1+r)^t} = 0, \qquad [9\text{--}4]$$

where C_t = the private costs (explicit and implicit) incurred in last year t and r = the internal rate of return. Using this approach, the family's rate of return on an investment in education would then be compared with the returns on other investments they might make. The family would invest in education if it offered the highest return.

There is also a **social** or **economic rate of return,** which is calculated using a more comprehensive measure of cost: all costs of education, public as well as private, are now included on the cost side of the calculation. In other words, public-sector outlays that are not reimbursed by tuition are added in here. Because income taxes are a cost to the individual but not to society as a whole, income should be measured after payment of income taxes when the private rate of return is estimated and before payment of income taxes when the social (economic) rate of return is estimated. This would make both benefits and costs higher in the social rate-of-return calculation than in the private rate-of-return calculation. Depending on the relative magnitude of the cost borne directly by the government and the income tax collected, the social (economic) rate of return to education could be either higher or lower than the private rate of return.

In practice, however, calculations done for developing countries generally measure income before taxes in estimating both the private and the social rate of return. This is done partly because personal income taxes are

TABLE 9–4   Some Estimates of Rates of Return to Education

Country	Year	Social			Private[a]		
		Primary	Secondary	Higher	Primary	Secondary	Higher
Latin America							
Brazil	1970	na	24	13	na	25	14
Chile	1959	24	17	12	na	na	na
Colombia	1973	na	na	na	15	15	21
Africa							
Ethiopia	1972	20	19	10	35	23	27
Ghana	1967	18	13	17	25	17	37
Kenya	1971	22	19	9	28	33	31
Asia							
India	1978	29	14	11	33	20	13
Indonesia	1978[b]	22	16	15	26	16	na
Pakistan	1975	13	9	8	20	11	27
South Korea	1971	na	15	9	na	16	16
Developed Countries							
Japan	1976	10	9	7	13	10	9
United Kingdom	1978	na	9	7	na	11	23
United States	1969[c]	na	11	11	na	19	15

[a]Income measured before payment of income taxes.
[b]Social rates refer to 1978, private rates to 1977.
[c]Private rates for secondary and higher education have declined since 1969; 1976 estimates are 11 and 5 percent, respectively. For social rates, no later estimates are available.
    Source: George Psacharopoulos, "Returns to Education: A Further International Update and Implications," *Journal of Human Resources* 20, no. 4 (April 1985): 583–604.

less important in developing countries than in developed countries and partly because tax data are difficult to obtain. If the same measure of benefits (income before taxes) is used in calculating both the private rate of return and the social rate of return, while a wider range of costs is included in the social rate-of-return calculation, it follows that the private rate of return must be higher than the social rate of return when this less satisfactory method of calculation is used (as in Table 9–4).

The usual form of social cost-benefit analysis of education is more comprehensive than private cost-benefit analysis only on the cost side. The various social benefits of education, all those which are not reflected in higher earnings, are excluded from the calculation, even in social cost-benefit analysis. It would be better to include them, but benefits such as greater social cohesion and enhanced ability to participate in politics are hard to quantify.[7]

Many private and social rates of return to investment in education have been estimated for both developed and developing countries. Representative results are displayed in Table 9–4. All the rates shown in the table are marginal rates. That is, they indicate the return on the additional investment needed to move from one level of educational attainment to the next-higher level.

7. One bold attempt to list and value some nonmarket benefits of education suggested that their total value may be roughly equal to that of the benefits reflected in higher earnings in the labor market. See Robert H. Haveman and Barbara L. Wolfe, "Schooling and Economic Well-Being: The Role of Nonmarket Effects," *Journal of Human Resources* 19, no. 3 (Summer 1984): 377–407.

Three principal conclusions emerge from Table 9–4 and similar calculations. First, rates of return to education in developing countries are generally high; often they are higher than the rates of return earned on investments in physical capital. Education looks like a good investment in most LDCs. Second, the highest social rates of return are usually earned on primary schooling, particularly in countries where primary schooling is still far from universal. In countries where almost everyone has completed primary schooling, like the United Kingdom and the United States, the rate of return at the primary level becomes indeterminate because there is no lower level with which to compare it. Third, the spread between private rates of return (where income is measured before taxes) and social rates of return can be large because the government sometimes bears most of the costs. Examples from Table 9–4 are secondary education in the United States and higher education in the three African countries. In other cases most of the costs of schooling are privately financed and the spread between the two rates of return is small.

Cost-benefit analysis can also be used to value the human capital created by the educational process. The value of human (or any) capital is derived from the stream of income that it will earn in the future. This income stream is capitalized by discounting it to the present. The formula for discounting the earnings created by a person's schooling—from primary school through the highest level attained—is given in Equation 9–5. E_t in the formula represents the *additional* sum earned each year, compared with someone who received no schooling. Conceptually, the value of human capital created by other forms of investment besides education could also be measured by discounting additional future earnings, but actually measuring the amount of human capital created would be more difficult in these cases because the added earnings are harder to measure.

$$\text{NPV} = \sum_{t=1}^{n} \frac{E_t}{(1+r)^{t}} \qquad [9\text{--}5]$$

Cost-Benefit Analysis in Educational Planning

Of what practical value are cost-benefit calculations of education? The idea is that private rates of return can serve as guides to individual educational choices whereas social rates can inform public investment and policy decisions. But doubts surround the validity of both claims.

From the private point of view, the main problem is predicting what the structure of earnings will be in the future. The procedure outlined above implicitly assumes that the current earnings structure provides an accurate guide to the future, but in fact relative earnings can change considerably for reasons originating on either the demand or the supply side of the labor market. In many developing countries in recent years the numbers of people possessing all kinds of academic credentials have increased much faster than the numbers of jobs traditionally held by people with these credentials. The result, discussed in Chapter 8, is that school leavers tend to be unemployed for a long period of time, following which they may accept lower salaries than their predecessors obtained. When such educational deepening is taking place, the incomes earned by previous school leavers become a poor guide to the future, since the rate of return to a particular level of schooling is likely to decline.

Despite this tendency, applicants continue to besiege the secondary schools and universities of most developing countries. How is this to be explained? Some observers interpret it as evidence that applicants for schooling are not motivated exclusively, or even primarily, by a desire for economic gains, but want more schooling mainly for social or psychological reasons (an economist would say that they value education as a consumption good). An alternative explanation is that when schooling is heavily subsidized by the government, the private rate of return remains reasonably high even when the social rate dips in response to educated unemployment and the continuing devaluation of academic credentials. This latter thesis has been used to explain the continuing strong demand for secondary and higher education in countries such as India and Sri Lanka. It suggests that education can be simultaneously a good investment for the individual and a bad investment for society.

In applying the cost-benefit approach to educational planning, the starting point is again data on lifetime earnings by level and type of education, along with information on the costs—explicit and implicit, private and public—of providing each level and type of education. The social rates of return on the various levels of education (primary, secondary, higher) and types of education (academic, vocational, nonformal, on-the-job) can then be calculated and compared. A rational government would expand those forms of education showing high social rates of return and cut back on those showing low rates of return.[8]

There are, however, a number of questions that can be raised about this procedure. As with manpower planning or any other planning methodology, its results are only as good as its assumptions, and some of these are questionable. Like the hypothetical parents discussed earlier, cost-benefit analysts must worry about how the structure of earnings may change in the future. In addition, they must weigh factors that are of no concern to the private decision maker.

If education is to be treated as an investment comparable to a road or steel mill, it must be justified in terms of its contribution to national output. From the social point of view, higher earnings are not sufficient justification unless they are caused by higher productivity. The usual way of linking earnings to productivity is to assume that wages are equated to the marginal product of labor through the workings of a perfectly competitive labor market. But if wages and salaries are more influenced by other factors (for example, the salaries paid to expatriates in colonial days, see Chapter 8), then wages or earnings are not necessarily equal to marginal product and become imperfect indicators of social benefits. In theory this problem could be dealt with by using shadow wages or opportunity costs (estimates of

---

8. More precisely, activities showing a rate of return higher than the opportunity cost of capital (the return thought to be obtainable if the funds were invested outside the education sector) would be expanded and those with lower rates would be contracted.

what wages would be under competitive conditions) instead of actual wages, but this is difficult in practice.

A second and closely related issue is whether the relationship between education and earnings is truly causal. Up to now we have in effect assumed that differences in average earnings are both associated with differences in education and also caused by these differences. This is not strictly the case, since both education and earnings are also partly the results of other factors, such as individual ability and socioeconomic origin. People who are more able or who come from favored backgrounds may do better both in school and in the workplace. According to the screening hypothesis, the main role of education is not so much to train people as to select those individuals who will do best in the job market.

Even if we agree that education raises earnings, there is a question of how this works. Do schools teach skills that turn out to have economic value, or do they only socialize people to work better—to be punctual in their attendance and conscientious in completing their assignments? These issues have been much debated, but recent research lends strong support to the view that underlies cost-benefit analysis of education: skills learned in school, especially literacy and numeracy, account for most of the differential in earnings associated with higher levels of schooling.[9]

The cost-benefit approach implicitly assumes that educational categories adequately specify the types of labor relevant to the labor market. In other words, it assumes that there is perfect substitutability within each educational category. If categories are specified only by level (primary, secondary, higher), this assumption is obviously crude. Surely there are significant differences between graduates of academic and vocational high schools, or between graduates of medical and legal faculties. Separate calculations should be made for these major different types of education, but even this leaves out the quality dimension. In the real world, graduates of the "best" schools, which may be best solely or mainly in terms of popular perceptions, earn far more than graduates of the "inferior" institutions. Finally, alternatives to schooling—nonformal education and on-the-job training—tend to get left out of the comparison altogether. If the Ministry of Education is responsible for educational planning but these programs are provided by other ministries, the tendency is to downplay them.

Like any planning tool, cost-benefit analysis can provide information, but it cannot be used mechanically to dictate solutions. It does provide a useful measure of the productivity of the existing pattern of investment in education. If, for example, the social rate of return to primary schooling is high, this suggests that investment at this level is likely to be socially remunerative. Similarly, large differences between private and social returns may help explain patterns of educated unemployment, as we have seen. But the value of these calculations is always limited by the assumptions on which they are based. It is particularly hard to determine how fast the

9. See M. Boissiere, J. B. Knight, and R. H. Sabot, "Earnings, Schooling, Ability, and Cognitive Skills," *American Economic Review* 75, no. 5 (December 1985): 1016–1030, and John B. Knight and Richard H. Sabot, *Education, Productivity, and Inequality. The East African Natural Experiment* (New York: Oxford University Press for the World Bank, 1990).

social rate of return will decline as a particular variety of education is expanded. To know this, we would have to calculate the elasticities relating earnings differentials to the relative supplies of different kinds of labor.

In spite of the attractiveness of its base in human capital theory—at least for those who admire neoclassical economic theory—the cost-benefit approach is of only limited use in practical educational planning. This brings us to the question of what alternatives might exist.

Educational Policy in Kenya and Tanzania and Its Results

Kenya and Tanzania are neighboring East African countries that are similar in size, colonial heritage, resource endowment, economic structure, and level of development. After gaining independence in the early 1960s, each country tried to provide all its children with seven years of primary schooling. When growth in the numbers of primary school graduates pushed the demand for secondary schooling beyond the governments' limited financial capacity to provide places in government secondary schools, however, policy in the two countries diverged. Influenced by manpower forecasts that projected limited need for secondary school graduates, Tanzania severely restricted its provision of secondary school places and rationed admissions on the basis of performance on a national examination. As in Kenya, government secondary schools were highly subsidized. Kenya also limited the creation of government schools (although less severely than Tanzania), but it permitted the establishment of private *harambee* (self-help) schools that met much of the excess demand that could not be satisfied by the government schools. As a result, by the 1980s Kenya had far more secondary school graduates than Tanzania.

The results of this policy divergence in otherwise similar circumstances have been intensively analyzed by researchers funded by the World Bank.* Their studies indicate that Kenya's educational policy performed much better than Tanzania's, both in raising labor productivity and in spreading education more equitably among the population. Although earnings differentials related to education narrowed as the supply of educated people increased and some of Kenya's secondary school graduates had to accept jobs beneath their expectations, Kenya's heavier investment in human capital paid off handsomely in productivity gains. Kenya's more permissive policy was also more equitable, particularly in permitting greater intergenerational mobility as students from farm or working class families had better opportunities to obtain secondary-level education. This was true even though access to Kenya's private secondary schools depended on ability to pay. By limiting access as it did, Tanzania created larger rents for those who were able to obtain secondary schooling. Those from favored backgrounds were able to perform better, on average, on the qualifying exam, and they received large subsidies once admitted.

---

*Knight and Sabor, *Education, Productivity, and Inequality;* see also Arthur Hazlewood et. al., *Education, Work, and Pay in East Africa* [Oxford: Oxford University Press (Clarendon), 1990].

Methodologically, the Kenya-Tanzania comparison supports the cost-benefit approach to analyzing educational decisions and casts doubt on the manpower planning approach. Although the Tanzanian planners were correct that their economy would not "need" the additional high school graduates that faster expansion of secondary schooling would have provided, the productivity benefits of an additional investment in secondary schooling would have more than repaid its cost. Given the Tanzanian government's well-known commitment to socialism, it is particularly ironic that the equity consequences of its educational policy were also less-favorable than those of the policy followed by the capitalist-minded government of Kenya.

Alternative Viewpoints

Most educational policy decisions are made pragmatically, in response to those political pressures that bear most strongly on the decision makers at any particular moment. Manpower projections and cost-benefit analyses are undertaken from time to time, but they seldom have more than a small impact on what actually happens. Because of the intellectual limitations of the two analytical approaches outlined above, more elaborate *formal modeling* has sometimes been attempted, but has had even less influence. This was the case with several linear programming models of education and its relationship to the economy that were constructed in the 1960s and 1970s, as well as with efforts to synthesize the manpower and cost-benefit approaches.

Some economists and sociologists—*radical critics*—altogether reject the idea that education raises productivity. An element in their critique, mentioned earlier, is that education acts as a screen or sieve to select the fortunate few who are then "credentialed" to hold elite positions in society. To this the more radical critics add that those who pass through the sieve and receive the prized credentials tend strongly to be the ones who started from privileged positions in life. The school system, they say, essentially reproduces the class structure from generation to generation. Those not destined for elite positions receive a form of education intended to make them more amenable to a subservient role in society. They are taught diligence, punctuality, and respect for authority. The solution to all this lies not in any conceivable reform of the school system within the framework of capitalist society, but in the radical reform of the social structure and economic system. Less-conventional radical critics argue that efforts should be made to revamp schooling as we know it to permit true learning to take place or to use mass education as a means of raising the consciousness of the poor regarding their oppressed condition.[10]

In view of these criticisms and proposals, it is interesting to see how Communist regimes manage their school systems. They strongly empha-

10. Iconoclastic analyses of education in developing countries include Ivan Illich, *Deschooling Society* (New York: Harper & Row, 1970); Paolo Freire, *Pedagogy of the Oppressed*, translated from the Portuguese by Myra Bergman Ramos (New York: Seabury Press, 1970); and Ronald Dore, *The Diploma Disease* (Berkeley: University of California Press, 1976).

size universal attainment of basic literacy and numeracy, and then restrict secondary and higher education rather severely (or just higher education in the richer Communist states), while heavily emphasizing the attainment of specific vocational skills. In the Soviet Union and other East European countries, as in the West, opportunities to obtain the more restricted types of schooling seem to go disproportionately to those from favored social positions. The Communist regime most noted for radical reform efforts has been that of China, especially during the Cultural Revolution of the 1960s, but Chinese educational policy subsequently returned to something much closer to the Soviet or Western model.

A very different critique and reform proposal argues for **market-based reforms.** Educational planning has failed, say these critics: all proposed methodologies are inadequate and choices about what kinds of schooling to provide and whom to educate should therefore be left to market forces. An obvious objection to this proposal is that if the market gives the wrong price signal, it will only encourage people to respond in the wrong ways. As long as education is subsidized, people will tend to purchase too much of it relative to other goods and services. This bias could be corrected by reducing the degree of subsidization and charging people something much closer to the actual cost of providing schooling. But that would only serve to strengthen another objection to the market solution: that it takes no account of equity considerations. Proposed means of making a market system more equitable include liberal use of scholarships for the poor but deserving and—more far-reaching—creation of educational vouchers, a special currency that could be distributed according to any criteria deemed equitable and used to purchase any kind of schooling.

Like the radical reform proposals, those coming from the right have been more discussed than implemented. Most governments prefer to retain a much tighter grip on educational activities than this type of reform would permit. The main role of the market in third-world education, as noted earlier, is to provide places for those who are unable to gain admittance to public institutions, and even this is permitted only in certain countries.

An older reform proposal is that school curricula should be made more practical, for example by replacing academically-oriented schools with agricultural, technical, and **vocational schools** emphasizing the teaching of useful skills. Some vocational schools have succeeded and made valuable contributions to development, but many others have failed. In a well-known article, University of Chicago educationist Philip Foster traced a series of unsuccessful experiments in Ghana going all the way back to the mid-nineteenth century. He attributed the persistent failure to "the vocational school fallacy," the idea that certain manual skills regarded as necessary for economic development should be stressed, when in fact the structure of incentives favors "impractical" academic training that opens the door to employment in the urban formal sector.[11] A major problem with government-run vocational schools is that they often fail to provide the skills actually

11. Philip J. Foster, "The Vocational School Fallacy in Development Planning," in *Education and Economic Development,* C. A. Anderson and M. J. Bowman, eds. (Chicago: Aldine, 1966), pp. 142–63.

required by private employers. Yet when adequately funded and run in
close coordination with potential employers, vocational schools can make a real contribution to development.

A final reform proposal is to give much greater emphasis to **nonformal education.** [12] Proponents of nonformal education argue that it is more practical, cheaper, more flexible, and better able to reach lower-income groups than formal education. Although there have indeed been many successful nonformal education projects—in basic education (literacy and numeracy), family education (health, nutrition, child care, family planning), community education (cooperatives, community projects), and occupational training—it seems more realistic to regard nonformal education as a complement to formal education than as a rival. It generally teaches different skills and reaches a different audience (mainly adults) from the schools. One criticism of nonformal education is that, like vocational schools, it perpetuates a two-tiered social system. The favored class gets into the schools whereas the less-favored have to make do with programs of nonformal education.

12. Philip H. Coombs with Manzoor Ahmed, *Attacking Rural Poverty: How Nonformal Education Can Help* (Baltimore: Johns Hopkins Press, 1974).

Health and Nutrition

The goal of improving health conditions in developing countries has often been accorded a low priority, both by the LDC governments and by development specialists. In nearly every developing country the Ministry of Health has little bureaucratic clout and receives one of the smallest budget allocations. Development specialists have followed suit; as far as we know ours is the first development economics textbook to include a chapter on health and nutrition.

Neglect of the subject has been partially reversed in the past two decades. Interest in health and development was boosted by the attention given to equity-oriented development strategies in the 1970s and later by concern about the effect that slower economic growth in the 1980s was having on the health of children, especially in Africa. Throughout the period, expenditures on health, like those on education, have increasingly been regarded as investments in human capital.

The health-development relationship is a reciprocal one. Economic development tends to improve health status, whereas better health contributes to economic development. But proponents of health-sector programs frequently warn that development alone cannot be relied on to cut morbidity and mortality, that special programs in nutrition, health care, and environmental sanitation are also needed. Occasionally they cite examples of how development can worsen health or argue that the provision of appropriate health programs can do the job by itself, even in the absence of significant overall development. Critics of this view stress the relationship

of health status to income level and observe that the benefits of specific
health measures are sharply reduced when the surrounding socioeconomic
and physical environments remain unfavorable to health. We will return to
this debate later in the chapter, as well as to the reciprocal issue of how
health contributes to economic development.

HEALTH IN THE THIRD WORLD

What is health? How can one tell whether an individual, or a society, is
healthy or sick? The definition of health is surprisingly elusive. The World
Health Organization (WHO), which is the United Nations agency responsible for programs to improve health standards, defines it as "a state of
complete physical, mental and social well-being," but this goes far beyond
what is normally meant by health. For most people, health is simply the
absence of disease and infirmity. But this can be a highly subjective definition. Conditions such as infection with intestinal parasites or first-degree
(mild) malnutrition, which are seen as disease in countries with high health
standards, may be so common in countries with lower standards that they
are not even recognized as abnormal.

The health status of an individual can be determined through clinical
examination by a qualified health professional. But this would be an expensive way to measure the health status of an entire population, so for that
we usually rely on statistics. Health statistics measure **morbidity** (sickness)
and **mortality** (deaths). Morbidity statistics are seldom adequate. Not only
is a clear-cut definition of sickness lacking, but many sick people in poor
countries never consult a doctor or enter a hospital, so they fail to come
into contact with the statistical system. Mortality data are considerably
better: death seldom goes unnoticed, and most countries now have reasonably complete official systems of death registration, although significant
gaps remain in some cases. Death statistics are most useful for assessing
the health status of a population when they include detailed information on
the person who has died (age, sex, place of residence, and so on) and on
the cause of death. However, data on the cause of death are usually weak
in low-income countries.

Patterns and Trends

Despite what one hears about famine and many other major challenges to
health in developing countries, the fact is that health conditions in these
countries are improving gradually. Life expectancy rose everywhere as
mortality declined in the 1950s and 1960s. Life expectancy is the average
number of years members of a given population are expected to live. We
cannot, of course, know how long any particular individual will actually
live. But we can predict the average longevity of a class of people (for
example, males age three), using the recent mortality experience of the
relevant group (in this case, all males) as a guide. Life expectancy at birth
is the form of the statistic most often cited, as in Table 10–1, but the con-

TABLE 10–1 Life Expectancy at Birth by Income Group and for Selected Countries, 1960 and 1988

| | Life expectancy | |
	1960	1988
By income group		
Below $250		50
$250–$500		63[a]
$500–$2,200		65
$2,200–$6,000		68
Above $6,000		75
In selected countries		
Latin America		
Bolivia	43	53
Brazil	55	65
Chile	57	72
Colombia	53	68
Africa		
Ghana	40	54
Kenya	41	59
Tanzania	42	53
Asia		
China	na	70
India	43	58
Indonesia	41	61
South Korea	54	70
Malaysia	53	70
Pakistan	43	55
Sri Lanka	62	71

[a]Heavily influenced by the inclusion of China's life expectancy of 70; without China, life expectancy in the $250–$500 income group would be 58.
  Sources: World Bank, *World Development Report 1985 and 1990.*

cept really refers to expected years of *remaining* life and can thus be applied to people of various ages, as in Table 10–2.

The average crude death rate (CDR) for low-income countries is now 10 deaths per thousand population, the same as for socialist countries. However, this average is heavily influenced by the successful experience of China, where the CDR was seven in 1988. In low-income countries other than China and India, where the CDR was 11, the crude death rate averaged 13 per thousand in 1988. In middle-income countries, the rate was 8, even lower than in high-income countries, where the CDR was 9.

TABLE 10–2 Comparison of Male Life Expectancy in Bangladesh and Sweden

| | Additional years a male is expected to live if he is now: | | | | |
	Newborn	Age 1	Age 5	Age 15	Age 65
Sweden (1976)	72.1	71.8	67.9	58.1	13.9
Bangladesh (1974)	45.8	53.5	54.4	46.3	11.6
Difference	26.3	18.3	13.5	11.8	2.3

Source: United Nations, *Demographic Yearbook, Historical Supplement* (New York: United Nations, 1979), pp. 553, 558.

Recall from Chapter 7, however, that the crude death rate is strongly influenced by the structure of the population. There are still big differences between rich and poor countries in life expectancy (see Table 10–1) and infant death rates (look back at Table 7–2, where we saw that the infant death rate falls from 120 per thousand in countries with GNP per capita of $250 or less to 10 per thousand in countries with $6,000 or more). The average male in a high-income economy lives 14 years longer than his counterpart in a low-income economy—22 years longer if we compare the industrialized economies with low-income economies other than China and India. Women live longer than men in developed countries and also in some developing countries, but in large parts of the developing world—China, South Asia, the Middle East, and North Africa—their life expectancy is lower than that of males.[1]

The correlation between income level and mortality is high but by no means perfect. The lower part of Table 10–1 shows life expectancy statistics for selected LDCs in 1960 and 1988. A few of the countries listed in this table have life expectancies far above the average for their income levels. China and Sri Lanka are particularly notable (see boxed example on pages 246–47), but the populations of Chile and Kenya also stand out as more long-lived than the other countries in their regions and income classes. Almost every country listed in Table 10–1 raised life expectancy by 10 years or more between 1960 and 1988. Life expectancy in Indonesia rose by 20 years, nearly a 50 percent increase.

The biggest impact on life expectancy comes through the reduction in mortality among the very young. This is dramatically illustrated in Table 10–2, which compares male life expectancy at various ages in Sweden and India. These two countries differ enormously in life expectancy at birth. Yet for males who survive the early years of life, differences in remaining life expectancy fall sharply. Whereas in Sweden and other countries with high health standards expected years of further life decline steadily as a person ages, in Bangladesh a surviving five-year-old can actually expect to live eight more additional years than a newborn. As Table 10–2 shows, in 1974 the average newborn male in Bangladesh would not reach his 46th birthday, whereas a five-year-old could expect to live to age 59. This is testimony to the terrible extent of infant and child mortality in the poorest countries.

The cross-section data in the upper part of Table 10–1 are consistent with the history of mortality in the industrial countries. Figure 10–1 shows how life expectancy has risen over the long run in different groups of countries. The early-developing countries experienced a slow, steady rise in life expectancy after 1850. Japan, a later developer, was able to extend life more rapidly and reach a level close to that of the early developers by about 1960. Less-developed countries have also been able to achieve rapid increases

---

1. A comparison of sex rations in various national populations has led Harvard economist and philosopher Amartya Sen to conclude that "More than 100 Million Women are Missing." See his article of that title in *The New York Review of Books* (December 20, 1990): 61–66. Females in these countries receive inferior nutrition and health care for a combination of cultural and economic reasons, and this adversely affects their longevity.

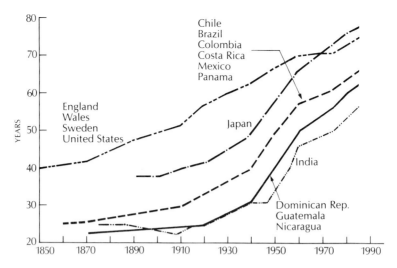

FIGURE 10–1 **Trends in Life Expectancy in Selected Countries.** Life expectancy rose gradually in Europe and the United States and more rapidly in Japan. It is rising rapidly in the LDCs, too, but they are still far behind the developed countries.
Sources: World Bank, *Health Sector Policy Paper,* 2d ed. (Washington, D.C.: 1980), p. 10; updated using data from World Bank, *World Tables,* 1989–90 ed.

in life expectancy, particularly over the past 50 years. But these increases still leave their life expectancy far below that in the rich countries (Table 10–1), and the countries no better off in many cases than the developed countries were in the early twentieth century (see Figure 10–1).

A reader who has heard concern expressed about serious and worsening child health problems, especially in sub-Saharan Africa, during the slow-growth decade of the 1980s might well ask whether the picture drawn here of improving global health status is not too rosy. Granting that there certainly are serious health problems in Africa—and elsewhere—and also that African health statistics leave much to be desired, the impression given by the basic statistics published by the World Bank[2] is that health measures in most of the nations of sub-Saharan Africa continued to improve, albeit slowly in many cases, during the 1980s. Food supply was often perilous; average daily calorie intake declined between 1980 and 1988 in 6 of the 32 countries for which data are given in the *World Development Reports.* Yet life expectancy continued to lengthen and the infant death rate is reported to have fallen in all these countries.

Although large gaps remain between the health status of populations in rich and poor countries, the general picture is that these gaps have narrowed in recent decades and continue to narrow. This contrasts with gaps in GNP per capita, which have widened and continue to do so. Next we need to consider why.

---

2. World Bank, *World Tables,* 1989–90 ed., and *World Development Report,* various years.

Interesting research by University of Pennsylvania demographer Samuel Preston shows that the cross-section relationship between income and life expectancy is parabolic in form and has been shifting upward during the twentieth century (Figure 10–2).[3] That is, at any given level of real income per capita, people are tending to live longer as time goes by. However, the relationship between income and life expectancy has become looser in recent decades. Preston found that rising income accounted for only 10 to 25 percent of the rise in life expectancy between the 1930s and 1960s. Other factors accounted for 75 to 90 percent of the increase.

What could explain this loosening of the relationship between income and life expectancy? Increasing literacy may have contributed. Preston stresses the international spread of health technology and a growing similarity of values regarding its application.

Although the international spread of health technology has been a major factor in the worldwide decline in death rates and rise in life expectancy that has occurred since World War II, its impact has sometimes been exaggerated. A debated case is that of Sri Lanka (then still called Ceylon), where a fall in the crude death rate of 43 percent between 1945 and 1949 was originally attributed almost entirely to the control of malaria through the use of DDT. Later it was established that DDT was only part of the story

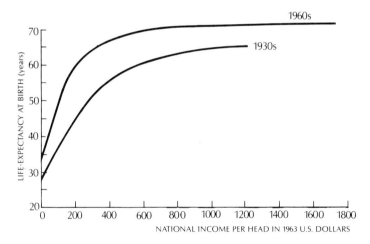

FIGURE 10–2 **Relationship between Life Expectancy at Birth and National Income per Head.** In both decades, people in richer countries could expect to live longer. Between the 1930s and the 1960s, the curve shifted up; citizens of countries with given real income levels lived longer on average. Note also that the curve for the 1960s is flatter than the curve for the 1930s; except for very poor countries (below $500), per-capita income was no longer so important a determinant of mortality as it had been in the 1930s.
Source: Preston, "The Changing Relationship Between Mortality and Level of Economic Development," pp. 231–248, adapted from p. 235.

3. Samuel H. Preston, "The Changing Relationship between Mortality and Level of Development," *Population Studies* 29, no. 2 (July 1975): 231–248. Continuing subsequent rises have been charted by the World Bank. See *World Development Report 1984*, p. 70, but note that the labels on the curves for 1972 and 1982 shown there are reversed.

and that longer-run and more general factors such as rising income, wide-spread literacy, and availability of low-priced foodstuffs were also influential.

Health in Sri Lanka

The small Asian country of Sri Lanka enjoys unusually good health and life expectancy compared with other low-income countries. This favorable experience is attributable to a combination of good fortune and the policies followed in the period since independence in 1948.

A small island located on the trade routes between Europe and East Asia, Sri Lanka had early contact with Western colonialism. The British, who controlled the island after earlier periods of Portuguese and Dutch domination, began to introduce modern medicine in the early nineteenth century. Campaigns to eradicate smallpox and yaws began in 1802. A civil medical department was started in 1858, a Contagious Diseases Ordinance enacted in 1866, and a medical school opened in Colombo, the capital, in 1870. In the early twentieth century Ceylon's tea, rubber, and coconut plantations were required to provide medical care for their workers and their families, and a school health program was started. In the 1940s a network of rural hospitals was built. The compact, self-contained nature of the island supported these efforts, and when it gained its independence in 1948, Ceylon already had unusually high health standards compared with other Asian countries.

Credit for continued improvement since 1948 belongs primarily to the government of Sri Lanka, which has consistently accorded a high priority to improving the health of its people. From the start medical care was free to all. More important, efforts were made to extend the service network to all parts of the island. These efforts were continuously hampered by shortages of funds. Sri Lankan hospitals have always been crowded, and the provision of additional beds ran only marginally ahead of population growth between 1950 and 1980. Efforts to train more doctors were partially offset by the emigration of physicians to countries where much higher incomes could be earned. The only dramatic change was in the supply of nurses and paramedics, which nearly tripled in relation to population between 1950 and 1980. This increase provided essential support for the extension of primary care to the rural areas.

Measures of mortality and morbidity show striking improvement in the past four decades. Epidemics have been eliminated and diseases such as typhoid, tuberculosis, and malaria have declined sharply as causes of death. Crude and infant death rates have fallen, and life expectancy has climbed to 71 years. Sri Lanka has become, with China, one of the rare examples of a country with a poor but healthy population.

Not all this improvement is attributable to medical services. Sri Lanka is also unusually advanced in education. Near-universal literacy is thought to have promoted better health conditions. Another positive factor is the comparative rarity of malnutrition, which results from a relatively equal distribution of income and the policy of subsidizing basic foods. Although the average calorie intake is only average for countries at Sri Lanka's income level (see Table 10–4), the calories are probably better distributed among the population than in most other countries.

Medical services in Sri Lanka form a colorful mosaic. The indigenous *ayurvedic* system coexists with Western medicine and receives some official support. Psychological disorders are treated by trance dancers or exorcists in some cases and by Western-trained psychiatrists in others.

National statistics on causes of death, although weak, do permit comparison between rich and poor countries, and illuminate the historical pattern of death rate decline by cause. Important causes of death in poor countries, mainly affecting the young and accounting for more than half of all deaths, have included infectious, parasitic, and respiratory disease such as diarrhea, pneumonia, malaria, whooping cough, polio, tetanus, and diptheria. All these diseases—many of which have come to be known as tropical diseases in the twentieth century although they were major killers in temperate countries in earlier centuries—are now well-controlled in rich countries, where diseases of the circulatory system and cancer have replaced them as major causes of death. Now infectious, parasitic, and respiratory disease are coming under control in developing countries as well. As people in these countries live longer, they too are succumbing in increasing numbers to heart disease and cancer, since they have been spared an earlier death from another cause.

Despite these improvements, a number of endemic and epidemic diseases continue to affect large populations in the third world. Some of these diseases—tuberculosis, malaria, cholera—are prominent causes of death. Others do not kill large numbers but limit people's lives and may contribute to a premature death, which is officially ascribed to some other cause. One such kind of disease is parasitic conditions, which are almost universal in some areas. It has been estimated that perhaps one-fourth of the world's population has roundworms. Another is malnutrition, which is rare in its easily recognized clinical form but common at a subclinical level, where its effects, although destructive, are more subtle and difficult to detect.

EFFECTS OF HEALTH ON DEVELOPMENT

Having considered the effect of development on health, it is now time to ask what better health can contribute to development. Can health expenditures legitimately be regarded as a form of investment in human capital? Before addressing this question, it is important to recognize that the validity of health services as a developmental activity does not rest entirely on our ability to prove that health expenditures increase national output. Better health is an important goal in its own right. Health increases human potentialities of all kinds and is rightly regarded as a basic human need. Everyone can benefit from better health in the present, and improved health for the young will lead to a healthier population in the future.

Like education, health services improve the quality of human resources, both now and in the future.[4] Better health for workers can provide immediate benefits by increasing the workers' strength, stamina, and ability to concentrate while on the job. Better child health and nutrition promote future productivity by helping children develop into stronger, healthier adults. In addition they supplement the acquisition of productive skills and attitudes through schooling. It has been shown that healthy, well-fed children have higher attendance rates and are able to concentrate better while they are in school.

Unlike education expenditures, which increase only the quality of human resources, health expenditures also increase their quantity in the future by lengthening expected working life. This complements educational investments, since other things being equal, returns to education will be higher if people can work and earn for longer periods.

Returns to investment in health, however, are even harder to quantify and verify empirically than returns to investment in education. For one thing there is no simple measure, analogous to years of schooling, for the amount invested in the health of any particular individual. The economic effects of better health are also hard to measure. The quantitative effects (extended working life) can be gauged in additional years worked, but what value should be put on them? In a private cost-benefit analysis expected additional earnings can be used, but in a social cost-benefit analysis the social marginal product of labor should be estimated to determine the value to society of extended working life. This opens up the complex question, already addressed in Chapter 8, of what the productivity of the marginal worker really is. In an economy in which marginal productivity is very low, the production benefits of extended working life are necessarily small. The qualitative effects of health expenditure (increased worker productivity and earnings) are also hard to measure because increases in productivity or earnings attributable to improvement in health may be difficult to identify.

Research to measure the effects of better health on labor productivity has yielded varying results. Several attempts have been made to measure the effects of improved health and nutrition on workers whose productivity can easily be measured (for example, plantation and road construction workers). In general, these studies reveal smaller productivity effects than expected.[5] It may be that people find ways to adapt to wide ranges of ill-health and malnutrition without greatly reducing their productivity: they may not feel well, but they can still work. If so, improving health would not necessarily increase productivity. But it still would be desirable from a humanitarian point of view.

Besides increasing the quantity and quality of human resources, health expenditures can also increase the availability or productivity of nonhuman

---

4. For a comprehensive statement of the case for regarding health expenditures as investment in human capital, along with some U.S. examples, see Selma Mushkin, "Health as an Investment," *Journal of Political Economy* 70, no. 5, part 2 (Supplement, October 1962): 129–157.

5. For a summary, see Jere R. Behrman and Anil B. Deolalikar, "Health and Nutrition," in *Handbook of Development Economics,* Vol 1, Chenery and Srinivasan, pp. 631–711, especially pp. 683–692.

resources. The clearest example is the large tracts of land rendered uninhabitable or unusable by endemic diseases. Malaria and yellow fever blocked access to many parts of Latin America, Africa, and Asia before these diseases were brought under relatively effective control in the twentieth century. Even today schistosomiasis makes it unsafe for people to enter lakes and streams in sections in Africa, and trypanosomiasis (African sleeping sickness) restricts the range of the livestock industry. So far no chemical means of control has been discovered for either of these diseases. China, however, has made progress against schistosomiasis through mass campaigns aimed at ridding lakes and streams of the snails that transmit the parasite. Improved control of ankylostomiasis (hookworm) and other parasitic conditions would increase resource availabilities in a different way. The effective productivity of resources devoted to food production would be increased.

We have seen that the productive benefits of health expenditures, although easy to hypothesize, have proven difficult to verify empirically. But even the effects on health status are sometimes hard to measure. The main reason is the multiplicity of factors that go together to determine health status. For example, a study of the health effects of projects to provide safe water supplies to a number of villages in Lesotho found, surprisingly, that provision of a clean water source failed in many cases to lead to a significant reduction in the prevalence of water-borne and water-related diseases. One explanation was that water-borne diseases are also transmitted by other means, such as contaminated food, and the provision of a safe water source alone does not protect villagers from infection through other sources.[6]

Health improvement has one effect that could be considered a social cost: by reducing the death rate, it increases population growth. Admittedly, the decline in the death rate may in turn encourage a drop in fertility, which would reduce the overall positive impact on population growth; but studies indicate that the magnitude of this replacement effect, if it exists at all, is likely to be small. At this point, however, we confront a question of ethical values. Even if population growth is acknowledged to be injuriously high, universally espoused values make it unacceptable to reduce that growth by allowing persons already born to die when the means to save them are at hand. It follows that this "cost" should not be used as an argument against health improvements and that other means should be found to limit population growth if this is considered to be an important social objective.

ENVIRONMENTAL HEALTH

The health planner, like the physician, should carefully diagnose before he or she prescribes. Health planning must address the real health problems found in the less-developed countries. Some of the causes of sickness and premature death in the LDCs that deserve more careful examination are

---

6. Richard Feuchem et al., *Water, Health and Development: An Interdisciplinary Evaluation* (London: Tri-Med Books, 1974), Chap. 9.

TABLE 10–3   Access to Drinking Water and Sanitation in Developing Countries, 1980[a]
(percent of population)

Region	Drinking water			Sanitation		
	By house connection	By public standpoint	None	By sewer connection	Other	None
Urban population						
Africa	29	37	34	11	43	46
Asia	— 64 —		36	— 30 —		70
Latin America	71	7	22	42	14	44
Rural population						
Africa	— 22 —		78	— 20 —		80
Asia	— 31 —		69	— 6 —		94
Latin America	— 20 —		80	— 20 —		80

[a]Covers 51 countries.
Source: World Health Organization, *The International Drinking Water Supply and Sanitation Decade. Review of National Baseline Data, as at 31 December 1980* (Geneva: United Nations, 1984): 21.

environmental health problems, malnutrition, and lack of medical care of adequate quantity, quality, and type.

The principal problem of **environmental sanitation** in low-income countries is the contamination of the water supply, and sometimes also of food and soil, with human waste. This occurs in villages and cities alike. Although most urban residents have access to piped drinking water, the public water supply is often rendered unsafe by contamination in the distribution process as a result of a faulty or nonexistent sewage system. Few rural residents enjoy either piped water or decent sanitation. Table 10–3, although based on fragmentary data, gives some idea of the dimensions of the problem.

Many of the infectious, parasitic, and respiratory diseases that cause so much sickness and death in poor countries are water-borne. Typhoid, dysentery, and cholera are leading examples. Their prevalence results in much sickness among adults and frequent deaths among infants and malnourished children. A second type of environmental sanitation problem arises from housing with insufficient space, ventilation, and access to sunlight. This situation, which is more likely to occur in urban than in rural areas, promotes the spread of air-borne diseases such as tuberculosis.

Sanitation improvement programs primarily involve the problems of waste disposal and water supply, particularly the need to keep the one system from contaminating the other. In villages this means safe wells and properly constructed privies or latrines. Simple technologies are available for such improvements. In urban areas matters become more expensive and complex. It will be a long time before all developing-country cities have decent sewage disposal and water supply systems, let alone adequate housing for their growing populations.

Historically, improvements in sanitation seem to be closely associated with reduction in diseases and become effective long before successful treatments have been discovered. So far in the contemporary third world the experience has been mixed. Some projects to improve water supply and waste disposal methods have led to dramatic reductions in disease. Others, as noted earlier, have had no discernible effect.

MALNUTRITION

Malnutrition is a major source of ill health and premature death in the LDCs. Table 10–4 gives the most commonly cited nutritional statistic, average daily caloric intake. These figures are derived from **national food balance sheets,** accounts which estimate human food consumption by taking the total supply of food (production plus imports) and subtracting other uses (exports; processing, spoilage, and rodent-infestation losses; livestock feed; and industrial uses). What remains must have been consumed by human beings. The resulting quantities of the various foodstuffs are then converted into nutrient values using standard equivalencies for the items concerned. These estimates of nutritional intake can be compared with recommended daily consumption figures, which attempt to say how many calories and other nutrients a person would have to consume to maintain

TABLE 10–4 Daily Per-Capita Calorie Supply for Income Classes, Regions, and Selected Countries, 1965 and 1986

	Total 1965	Total 1986	Percent change
Income groups			
Below $250	1,989	1,980	−0.5
$250–$500	1,935	2,423	25.0
$500–$2,200	2,353	2,748	16.8
$2,200–$6,000	2,861	3,246	13.5
Above $6,000	3,038	3,348	10.2
Regions and selected countries			
Africa	2,197	2,392	8.9
Ghana	1,950	1,759	−9.8
Kenya	2,289	2,060	−10.0
Tanzania	1,832	2,192	19.7
Asia	1,991	2,484	24.8
West Asia	2,152	3,058	42.1
South Asia	2,062	2,282	10.7
India	2,111	2,238	6.0
Pakistan	1,761	2,315	31.5
Sri Lanka	2,153	2,400	11.5
East Asia	1,906	2,636	38.3
China	1,926	2,630	36.6
South Korea	2,256	2,907	28.9
Malaysia	2,247	2,730	21.5
Oceania and Indonesia	1,936	2,649	36.8
Indonesia	1,800	2,579	43.3
Europe	3,097	3,359	8.5
North and Central America	2,959	3,374	14.0
South America	2,442	2,630	7.7
Bolivia	1,869	2,143	14.7
Brazil	2,402	2,656	10.6
Chile	2,592	2,579	−0.5
Colombia	2,174	2,542	16.9
Peru	2,325	2,246	−3.4

Source: World Bank, *World Development Report 1990.*

good health, given a certain body weight and at least a minimum level of daily activity.

The statistics in Table 10–4 indicate that average daily caloric intake rose between 1965 and 1986 in all major regions, in most (but not all) individual countries, and at all levels grouped by GNP per capita except the lowest (those countries which had not yet managed to climb above $250 per capita by 1986). Moreover, actual intake in 1986 exceeded estimated requirements (approximately 2,300 calories per day) in all but the poorest countries and in all regions except South Asia. While this is a generally favorable situation, one has to be aware of some snares in interpreting these figures. They could be used to underestimate the seriousness of the nutrition problem, for two reasons.

First, the definition of the minimum daily requirement is arbitrary. If people do not receive the nutrition needed to maintain a given body weight and activity level, they adapt by weighing, and doing, less. For example, lower requirements are sometimes defined for Asian countries than for other regions because Asians tend to be small. But their smallness is at least partially attributable to inadequate nutrition in the past. When Asians regularly get enough to eat, as the Japanese have since World War II, and the Chinese and Koreans more recently, their average weight and height, and thus their caloric requirements, increase rapidly from one generation to the next.

The second reason these averages can mislead is that available food is unequally distributed. Even in a country where the average daily intake is 2,000 calories or less, there are at least a few people who eat as well as people in the developed countries. Meanwhile, as discussed below, large parts of the population are likely to experience significant caloric deprivation. The problem is that while the ample—even excessive—intake of the well-fed few raises the national average, it in no way diminishes the deficit suffered by those who cannot obtain the recommended minimum. Averages computed for large and diverse populations are particularly likely to understate the nutritional problem by offsetting surpluses against deficits in this way.

Because of this problem, it may be more revealing to count malnourished people than to count calories. According to an estimate covering 87 countries but excluding China, 34 percent of the third world's population received insufficient calories for an active working life in 1980. Sixteen percent were so poorly nourished that their bodily growth was likely to be stunted and their health seriously endangered.[7] By far the largest number of malnourished people in 1980, 470 million, were found to be in South Asia, where 50 percent of the population received insufficient calories. In sub-Saharan Africa 44 percent of the population was malnourished, and in Latin America 13 percent.

The prevalence of malnutrition and its injurious effects is greatest among children. In the early 1970s WHO estimated that 3 percent of third-world children were afflicted by severe (third-degree) malnutrition, which gives rise to clinical conditions such as kwashiorkor, a protein-deficiency disease

7. World Bank, *Poverty and Hunger: Issues and Options for Food Security in Developing Countries* (Washington, D.C.: World Bank, 1986).

marked by bloated bellies and glassy stares, and marasmus, a condition brought on by shortage of both calories and protein. Another 25 percent suffered from moderate (second-degree) malnutrition and a further 40 to 45 percent from mild (first-degree) malnutrition.[8] These conditions are indicated by substandard rates of physical development. Malnutrition was said to be present as a primary or contributing factor in more than half of all deaths among children under five in low-income countries. It can turn otherwise mild childhood diseases, such as respiratory problems, gastrointestinal difficulties, and measles, into killers.

Most of the malnutrition in the world today is of the type known as protein-calorie malnutrition (PCM). Conditions caused by deficiencies of specific nutrients—such as rickets, scurvy, and beri-beri—have generally diminished in importance. Among the remaining deficiency diseases the most important are vitamin A deficiency, which can cause blindness, and iron-deficiency anemia. At one time it was thought that shortage of protein was the principal nutritional problem of the third world, since protein is necessary for physical and mental development. Subsequently, however, it was discovered that most of the children whose diets are protein-deficient also suffer from a deficiency of calories, and if protein is added to the diet while calories remain insufficient, development is little affected because the added protein is used up as energy. Accordingly, calories are now regarded as the limiting factor in nutrition, and most programs attempt to supplement calories first and protein, vitamins, and minerals only secondarily.

The rising average calorie intakes shown in Table 10–4 have probably been accompanied by a fall in the extent of PCM. This should be measured directly, however, because of the tendency of these averages to mislead. Just as the upper half of Table 10–4 shows that national average nutritional levels are closely related to GNP per capita, different income groups within countries may also have very different consumption levels. If income distribution worsens, it is possible for the number of malnourished people to increase at the same time as the average caloric intake goes up.

Food Consumption

What causes malnutrition, and how could nutritional improvement contribute to economic development? The determinants of human nutritional levels can be analyzed using microeconomic consumption theory. The consumption of food, like that of other goods and services, can be thought of as determined by three elements: income, relative prices, and tastes. Engel's Law, as we saw in Chapter 3, says that households spend an increasing amount, but a decreasing proportion, of income on food as their incomes rise. Very poor households devote more than half their incomes to food and have relatively high income elasticities of demand for food; that is, a significant proportion of any additional income will be used to buy food. At higher income levels, the share of income devoted to food pur-

---

8. See Alan Berg, *The Nutrition Factor: Its Role in National Development* (Washington, D.C.: Brookings Institution, 1973), p. 5.

chases falls to one-quarter or less, and the income elasticity of demand for food becomes quite low. Thus, income is an important determinant of food consumption levels, particularly at lower levels of household income. However, recent research has indicated that increases in income are less likely to raise calorie intake in the population as a whole than we previously thought, because people evidently spend a large share of increased income on better quality or greater variety of food, rather than on more calories.[9]

Prices are also important, because of both income effects and substitution effects. A change in the price of a basic foodstuff like rice, wheat, or corn can have a significant effect on the purchasing power of a poor household. If the household spends, say, 30 percent of its income on rice and the retail price of rice increases by 20 percent, this amount to a 6 percent cut ($0.3 \times 0.2 = 0.06 = 6$ percent) in the household's already-low purchasing power. For this reason staple food grain prices are a basic indicator of welfare levels among the poor—and also of political stability—in many low-income countries.

Substitution effects can also be significant. Even if people strongly prefer particular foods, large price differences can cause them to shift to cheaper substitutes for the more expensive foods that they prefer. This is especially true for the very poor. Hence it was possible to induce large numbers of people in East Pakistan (now Bangladesh) to consume U.S. surplus wheat instead of rice, the favored food grain, when there was a rice shortage during the 1960s. Similarly, desperately poor families are sometimes forced to "trade down" from the preferred food grain to a cheaper source of calories, usually either a hard grain like sorghum or a starchy root crop such as manioc (cassava).

A powerful argument for the influence of income on food consumption and nutritional status has appeared in recent discussions of famine. Most people associate famine with a precipitous drop in the overall food supply, usually as a result of crop failure, but Harvard economist Amartya Sen has shown that in several historical famines the total availability of food did not decline. The real problem, Sen argues, is likely to be people's **food entitlements:** their ability to obtain food, whether through purchase, rationing, or other forms of distribution.[10] Contemporary food policy analysts define their goal as **food security,** a situation in which all people, at all times, have access to enough food to permit them to lead active, healthy lives.

Both income and price influence the consumption of *food,* not necessarily or directly the consumption of nutrients derived from food. When people spend more on food, they may or may not obtain better nutrition. Some of their additional expenditure goes for a larger *quantity* of food, but much of it, especially above minimal income levels, goes for higher *quality*. Quality is defined in terms of subjective tastes. Foods regarded as higher in quality need not be more nutritious than less-favored competitors, and they may even be nutritionally inferior. Every nutritionist can tell horror stories about the deterioration in nutritional standards as development proceeds:

---

9. Behrman and Deolalikar, "Health and Nutrition."
10. Amartya Sen, "Ingredients of Famine Analysis: Availability and Entitlements," *Quarterly Journal of Economics* 96, no. 3 (August 1981): 433–464.

FIGURE 10–3 Various Measures of Food Consumption Relative to Household Income Level.
Food expenditure rises with income, but at a declining rate. Some of the rise goes for improved quality, whereas consumption of starchy staples declines.
Source: C. Peter Timmer, Walter P. Falcon and Scott R. Pearson, *Food Policy Analysis* (Baltimore: Johns Hopkins Press, 1983), p. 57.

carbonated beverages replace natural drinks, commercial infant foods replace mother's breast milk, and various junk foods are increasingly consumed by children and adults. Statistics make it clear, however, that these cases run against the general pattern of improved nutrition in relation to increasing income depicted in Figure 10–3. In general, people with higher incomes have at least a somewhat higher caloric intake and a more varied diet, which is superior in terms of nutrients other than calories.

Food beliefs and tastes can impede nutritional improvement. Every culture has beliefs about the health effects of various foods that are not supported by modern nutritional science. Traditional feeding taboos for infants and new mothers are particularly injurious in many developing countries. In most human environments one can point to nutritional potentials that remain underexploited for reasons of taste and habit. For example, soybean products provide a much cheaper source of protein than animal products, yet they are eaten in quantity only in East Asian countries where they are standard protein sources. Nutritionists can counter the economist's assertion that income is the main influence on nutritional status by demonstrating that even very poor households could eat more nutritiously if they had the necessary information and chose to do so.

Thus all three of the factors we have examined—income, prices, and tastes—are significant contributors to the determination of nutritional status. Emphasis on the role of each factor leads to a different approach to nutritional policy, as will be seen.

The distribution of food within a family is another important aspect of individual nutritional status. When food is scarce, children and older adults tend to find their rations disproportionately reduced.[11] It is understandable that in dire circumstances families channel scarce food to the working adults on whose continued health and strength the survival of all family members ultimately depends. This makes it hard to devise programs to improve the nutritional status of the more vulnerable family members, such as infants and new mothers, since feeding programs aimed at them may create consumption shifts within the family that cause the breadwinner, rather than the intended recipient, to receive the extra food.

Nutritional Interventions

The first problem to be solved when designing a nutrition improvement program is to select a target group.

Infants and children face the greatest nutritional problem in the third world. Infants are usually adequately fed through the breastfeeding stage, but they may suffer a nutritional decline after weaning. If not corrected, this decline will reduce their energy levels and physical growth. This in turn may decrease their resistance to disease and impair their ability to learn in school. It has also been argued that malnutrition causes severe, even irreversible, retardation of mental development, but this assertion is now regarded as controversial at best. Even so, nutritional deficiencies among third-world children must be regarded as important because they are so widespread and have such serious consequences.

Pregnant and lactating women also merit special attention because of their relationship to the child nutrition problem. While carrying or nursing a child, a woman has especially heavy nutrition requirements because she is "eating for two,"as the saying goes.

Whether working adults should be specially targeted for nutrition intervention is more debatable. Conceivably, improved nutrition for this group could have the most direct and immediate effect on economic growth if its productivity were thereby increased. But we have seen that there is mixed evidence on whether their productivity is reduced by the degrees of malnutrition prevailing in most LDCs and whether it would be improved by nutrition intervention. In any case, since working adults tend to get favored access to whatever food is available, it is not clear to what extent their food supply is reduced when the family as a whole is short of food.

Several different types of nutrition intervention are possible. In the 1950s attention focused on the severely malnourished, who required hospital treatment. Later the emphasis shifted to treatment of milder cases outside hospitals. Supplementary feeding programs were instituted in a number of countries. Their greatest difficulty turned out to be reaching the intended beneficiary group at reasonable cost. School lunch programs can be helpful, but the worst nutritional deficiencies are likely to be among preschool

---

11. Children with *high parity*—those born into families where there are several older siblings—are particularly likely to suffer. Studies have shown that such children have higher mortality rates, presumably because large families strain supplies of income, food, and parental attention.

children. Even when the intended beneficiaries are reached and fed, eval-
uators of feeding programs suspect that substitution frequently takes place
in the home: children are fed less to compensate for the school lunch, and
the net increase in the family's food supply thus goes to the adults rather
than the children.

The best way to get supplementary food to infants and small children is
to integrate food distribution with **maternal and child health** (MCH) programs. These programs aim to provide health services to mothers and infants
through local clinics while also providing nutritional surveillance. The food
offered can serve as an inducement for mothers to bring their children into
an MCH center regularly for weighing, examination, and treatment if necessary. Persuasion and linkage with other services that may be desired,
such as family planning, also promote these programs. Without such efforts,
very few third-world mothers bring their babies in for examination by a
health professional unless they are obviously sick.

Other conventional nutrition improvement programs include the promotion of **backyard gardens** to provide dietary supplementation and **nutritional
education** conducted in schools, adult education courses, and the like. Since
these programs are inherently limited in scope, there have been attempts
to develop broader, more general types of programs. **Food supplementation**
(fortification) has sometimes had dramatic success in overcoming specific
nutritional deficiencies, such as through the addition of iodine to the salt
supply in goiter-prone areas. Fortification of bread and other basic foodstuffs to increase their protein content has been attempted in several areas,
with mixed results. Still less successful have been efforts, some of them
widely heralded for a time, to develop commercially compounded **new foods**
whose exceptional nutritional values would overcome the problem of malnutrition. The high cost of new foods usually puts them beyond the reach
of those low-income consumers who are likely to be malnourished.

Growing interest in malnutrition and the limited success of conventional
approaches have led to increasing attention to still broader programs, such
as **campaigns to increase national food production** and **food price subsidization** for low-income urbana consumers. There is no doubt that food-grow-
ing peasants, such as small-scale rice or corn producers, eat better when
their farms become more productive. Similarly, a price cut for staple food
items—made possible by higher farm production and greater supplies—can
provide a substantial boost in both purchasing power and nutritional status
for the urban poor, as we have seen.

The main problems with staple-food subsidization programs are how to
limit them to the intended beneficiaries and how to finance them. Recipients of subsidized foodstuffs (or food stamps, as in the U.S. program) may
sell them to buy other goods which they prefer. While this practice is consistent with the idea of consumer sovereignty, it may defeat the purpose of
nutritional improvement. Subsidy programs can be expensive, especially
when their scope is broad. Egypt and Sri Lanka are two countries that have
had food subsidy programs extending to nearly the entire population. In
both cases subsidization of basic foodstuffs (wheat, beans, lentils, vegetable oil, meat, fish, and tea in Egypt; rice, wheat, and sugar in Sri Lanka)

probably increased the real income of the poor and improved their nutritional and health status. But the cost of the program grew to around 15 percent of government expenditure in both countries and became a threat to fiscal stability. In both cases efforts to cut back on the subsidy bill led to political instability: riots in both countries, and in Sri Lanka the defeat at the polls of more than one government.

The cost-effectiveness of different approaches to nutritional improvement has been debated.[12] Targeted programs that deliver nutritional services to specific groups of beneficiaries—for instance, school lunch programs or baby-weighing programs—can involve high logistical and supervision costs per beneficiary served. More general programs, such as fortification or food subsidies, may achieve a lower cost per recipient but entail a different kind of cost problem: leakage of program benefits to people other than the intended beneficiaries. Providing nutritional services, especially food subsidies, to large segments of the population can be costly, as the experiences of Egypt and Sri Lanka illustrate. Experience with World Bank–sponsored projects in Brazil, Colombia, Indonesia, and the Indian state of Tamil Nadu suggests that well-designed targeted programs can be more cost-effective than general programs.[13]

MEDICAL SERVICES

Most LDCs have too few health services, too poorly distributed. Public expenditures on health services are much smaller in developing than in developed countries, even as a percentage of GNP, as seen in Table 10–5.

TABLE 10–5 Health Personnel, Facilities, and Expenditures (late 1980s)

Country's GNP per capita	Per 100,000 population[a]			Public expenditures[b]	
	Hospital beds	Physicians	Nursing persons	Percent of GFNP	Dollars per capita
Below $250	30	8	27	0.7	1
$250–$500	134 (94)	62 (25)	65 (85)	0.4 (1.0)	1.4 (4)
$500–$2,200	71	80	123	1.3	20
$2,200–$6,000	109	240	86	1.1	35
Above $6,000	247	222	878	4.0	524

[a]Figures in parentheses exclude India and China.
[b]Figures in parentheses exclude India; no data on health expenditures are available for China.
Sources: World Bank, *World Development Report 1990*, and International Monetary Fund, *Government Finance Statistics Yearbook 1989* (Washington, D.C.: International Monetary Fund, 1989).

12. Cost-effectiveness is a concept akin to the benefit-cost ratio, which was discussed in Chapter 6 (see footnote 8, page 149). But whereas in the benefit-cost ratio both benefits and costs are measured in money terms, cost-effectiveness uses a nonmonetary measure of benefits. In the case of a nutrition intervention, for example, greater cost-effectiveness would consist of achieving a larger amount of nutritional benefit for a given program expenditure. Alternatively, it could be defined as achievement of a given amount of nutritional benefit for less program expenditure.

13. Alan Berg, *Malnutrition. What Can Be Done? Lessons from World Bank Experience* (Baltimore: Johns Hopkins Press for the World Bank, 1987).

In terms of dollars per capita, these outlays are woefully inadequate. Governments in the poorer countries typically spend only 1 to 2 dollars per capita.[14] The inadequacy becomes clearer when we consider that in developing countries, in contrast to the United States, the public sector finances the bulk of the modern, Western-style medical and health services. Private doctors and hospitals are typically few and are patronized mainly by well-to-do urban residents. In most countries there are also indigenous practitioners of various kinds: herbalists, exorcists, and acupuncturists. Typically the masses of people consult both modern and indigenous healers upon occasion, depending on the nature of the ailment and on their access to the various systems of medicine.

Low medical expenditures in the past have led to inadequate stocks of health facilities and personnel in most developing countries, as Table 10–5 indicates. Medical training in many of the poorest countries may not benefit society because doctors are highly mobile, and once trained, many emigrate to seek higher income elsewhere (see boxed example on Cuba). In many cases, increasing the supply of nurses and other health auxiliaries may be a better way to improve services.

Health in Cuba

When Castro's forces took over in January 1959, Cuba was a middle-income country with reasonably plentiful but poorly distributed health care personnel and facilities. Average income was higher than in most other Latin America countries, life expectancy at birth was over 60 years, and the population was more than 50 percent urban. But inequalities were marked. Havana, with only 22 percent of the population, had 55 percent of the hospital beds in the country, whereas Oriente province, one of Cuba's poorest regions, had 35 percent of the population but only 15 percent of the hospital beds. There were 6,300 doctors to care for a population of 8 million.

In the first three years after the revolution, 3,000 physicians left the country; most emigrated to the United States. This is probably the first time in history when a country lost such a high percentage of its doctors in so short a time. Massive training efforts were inaugurated to make up this deficit. By 1971, 30 percent of all university students were studying medicine. By 1979, after more than 20 years of massive training efforts, the ratio of doctors to population was finally restored to about what it had been in 1958.

Despite having to cope with this massive problem of medical personnel, Cuba made major strides toward the achievement of high health standards for its entire population. To do so, it reorganized its health services and improved their distribution among social classes and regions of the country. A new system of hospitals and clinics was set up; it stretched from

14. These figures are distorted by the extreme disparity in the pay of medical personnel, especially doctors, between rich and poor countries. A purchasing-power parity adjustment of the sort discussed in Chapter 3 would roughly triple the per-capita expenditure figures for the poorest countries and double those of the somewhat less poor. By any measure, however, the figures would remain abysmally low. See Frederick Golladay, "Health Problems and Policies in Developing Countries," World Bank Staff Working Paper No. 412, August 1980.

provincial hospitals serving areas of about 1 million people down to health centers serving communities of 25,000. Given the initial disparities, new facilities were constructed primarily in the rural areas. Thus while the number of hospital beds available in Havana increased by only 8 percent in the decade after the revolution, the increases in Camaguey and Oriente provinces were 184 and 147 percent respectively. Over half the new health centers built were allocated to rural areas which previously had no such facilities. Services in the new system were provided virtually free; this encouraged greater use by the public.

Medical personnel participated in the planning and management of health services, but the broad guidelines were laid down by the political leadership, dominated by the Communist Party. After the introduction of local elections in 1976, community participation in health care planning increased.

Social and economic change have supported these improvements in medical services. Economic growth has generally been slow. Public policy has emphasized equitable distribution of basic necessities. Primary foodstuffs are rationed and price-controlled. Literacy is now estimated at 96 percent and elementary school attendance is universal (uniquely among Latin American countries). Housing problems have been chronic among Cuba's urban population, now 65 percent of the total, but are gradually being remedied by the construction of apartment houses.

Mortality indicators for Cuba have improved from good to excellent. The infant death rate was only 12 per thousand in 1988, and the crude death rate was a minuscule 7 per thousand. Life expectancy at birth was 76 years. The birth rate was 18 per thousand, so the rate of natural increase was a low 1.1 percent. Family planning is not officially promoted because the country is perceived as suffering from a labor shortage, but contraceptives are freely available to those who want them.

In addition to being inadequately supplied, health services in poor countries are very unevenly distributed among the population. Capital cities and other major urban areas usually have several times as many doctors in relation to population as rural areas. Similar if slightly smaller disparities exist for hospital beds and primary health workers.

The usual public health service is organized on a referral basis, so in theory patients from rural areas with acute medical problems are sent to better facilities in the towns and, if necessary, in the major cities, for care. Generally, however, this referral system works poorly. The lower reaches of the system seldom provide easily accessible services to the whole country. For large parts of the population in most low-income countries, even the most rudimentary public health facility is so far away that, given the prevailing poor transportation systems, it is in practice inaccessible. When patients do go to a government clinic or hospital, they often find that they have to wait many hours and possibly pay unauthorized fees before receiving any attention at all. Even then the care they obtain may be slipshod and half-hearted. As a result, rather than using the systems for routine services and referrals as intended, people tend to ignore it except in acute emergencies, and then go directly to a hospital.

Managerial and logistical problems overwhelm some third-world health systems. Many of the vaccines administered, for example, have been rendered ineffective by age and exposure to heat, and sterile conditions for medical procedures are all but impossible to maintain. Reuse of needles without proper sterilization and other unsanitary procedures, always a means of spreading diseases such as hepatitis, now threaten to accelerate the spread of AIDS (acquired immune deficiency syndrome), which has appeared in many developing countries and already affects large parts of the population in some of them, particularly in Africa.

Medical resources are often distributed ineffectually among different types of ailments and forms of treatment. In many countries large fractions of tight health budgets have been devoted to acquiring state-of-the-art medical technologies for hospitals in the capital city or at the local medical school. Does it make sense for a country that is not providing even rudimentary medical care to sick infants to acquire the capacity to do open-heart surgery? For the cost of a single complicated medical procedure, basic attention could be provided to hundreds of rural patients. Why then do so many countries opt for what appears to be a severe maldistribution of their scant health resources? One reason appears to be urban bias, the general tendency in developing countries for urban populations to benefit disproportionately from government expenditures and policies.[15] Urban bias in the provision of medical services has many causes; one is that the powerful national elites centered in urban areas, especially the capital city, want good medical care for themselves and their families. A second reason is nationalism: "Our doctors are just as good as doctors in the advanced countries; they can do open-heart surgery, too." Yet a third reason is the technology-mindedness that many doctors share with engineers and other professionals. Medicine is often regarded as an outstanding example of the transfer of inappropriate technology from developed to developing countries. These three factors can interact, as when the self-interest of the elites prompts them to indulge the technology-mindedness of the doctors.

Still another shortcoming of public health services in most LDCs relates to the balance between preventive and curative services. Since, as we have seen, curing all the sick is beyond the means of many poor countries, the possibility that sickness and death can be reduced more cheaply through preventive measures deserves careful examination. Measures such as inoculation campaigns, mosquito spraying, and rat killing have produced dramatic improvements in health conditions in some low-income countries, most notably in China. Many LDCs still spend too much on curative services relative to preventive activities.

It is thus evident that inadequate, maldistributed, and inappropriate medical services in poor countries are themselves contributors to sickness and premature death. What can be done about it?

Improved medical services depend on the extension of coverage to the entire population and on the development of service patterns more appropriate to the health needs and resource availabilities of a developing coun-

---

15. Urban bias has been defined and analyzed by Michael Lipton, *Why Poor People Stay Poor: Urban Bias in World Development* (Cambridge, Mass.: Harvard University Press, 1977).

try. Many experts believe that a reformed health system would include the following elements: (1) active and continuous promotion of community health, instead of intermittent treatment of specific conditions in individuals; (2) management of the system by nonphysicians; (3) training health-care auxiliaries recruited from the community to diagnose and treat simple ailments; and (4) limited referral of difficult cases.

The health care systems evolved by socialist developing countries such as China and Cuba are sometimes taken as models by those interested in similar reforms. In 1976 China reported spending over 60 percent of its health care budget in rural areas and sending half its medical school graduates to assignments in the countryside. Like other developing countries it has experienced difficulty in getting health professionals to live in rural areas. China has countered this tendency, however, and through its well-known system of health auxiliaries, it is providing—for the first time—decent health care to its enormous peasant population. As of 1976 official sources reported that there were 1.5 million "barefoot doctors" working in the country, doing preventive work, treating patients at home and in the fields, assisting with mass health and sanitation campaigns, and disseminating information on family planning and maternal and child health care. In addition there were reported to be some 3 million part-time health auxiliaries assisting in the same activities. These efforts have contributed to levels of health and life expectancy unusual for a country with China's still low income level.

The development and dissemination of simple cures for widespread health problems must accompany the spread of medical services into the rural areas. For example, at present about 10 percent of all children born in the developing countries die of diarrhea before reaching the age of 10. Yet there is a simple inexpensive technology that can prevent most of these deaths: oral rehydration therapy (ORT), which is nothing more than a solution of sugar and mineral salts in water. ORT counteracts dehydration, which is the direct cause of diarrhea deaths. A scientifically designed and tested ORT formula is being disseminated by organizations such as the United Nations Children's Fund (UNICEF), but even folk versions of the remedy, such as rice water and simple mixtures of sugar and table salt, may be effective. Sickness and early death among children in poor countries could be sharply curtailed by spreading knowledge and availability of this remedy throughout the third world, and developing others like it.

HEALTH SERVICES AND THE MARKET

We saw in this chapter that public health services in developing countries are severely underfinanced. A recent World Bank publication notes that prices have generally played only a minor role, either in generating resources to finance health services or in determining who should have access to them.[16] According to the World Bank, only 7 percent of the cost of publicly

16. Emmanuel Jimenez, *Pricing Policy in the Social Sectors. Cost Recovery for Education and Health in Developing Countries* (Baltimore: Johns Hopkins Press for the World Bank, 1987).

provided services is currently recovered through user fees. These observations have led to proposals to increase fees charged for health services and institute charges for services currently provided free. The revenue thus generated would be used to expand health services. Since this is a textbook on the *economics* of development, it behooves us to conclude this chapter on health and development by considering the merits of this proposal to increase the role of prices in the provision of health care in developing countries.

In his analysis of the possibility of charging higher prices for educational and health services, World Bank economist Emmanuel Jimenez proposes that we distinguish between services that yield personal benefits enjoyed only by the individual recipient and those that have substantial external benefits for the broader society. When external benefits are large, the price charged for the service must be set below its cost, or else society will be deprived of valuable benefits. Broadly speaking, one would probably not want to charge for most preventive health services, but one might be more willing to place a reasonably high fee on many curative services. If there is excess demand for these services, fees could probably be raised without reducing the quantity of services provided. Additional revenues would be generated; if these were then reinvested in service provision, services could then be expanded, perhaps by enough to meet the previously unfulfilled demand. If there is no excess demand for services, the effect of a fee increase on revenues and the level of service would depend on the elasticity of demand for health services. Available evidence suggests that this demand is highly inelastic, since people regard at least some kinds of health services—particularly, one suspects, curative services in health emergencies—as necessities. Jimenez notes, however, that user fees for the highest-cost services can be raised close to the cost of providing them only if medical insurance is widely available, since few of the people unfortunate enough to require such services are likely to be able to afford them.

One should approach the possibility of financing expanded health services in developing countries through higher user fees with a critical frame of mind. There is little doubt that increasing expenditure on health services would benefit both economic growth and human welfare in the short run in most LDCs. Yet this kind of earmarked tax is neither necessarily the best way to raise the funding for such an expansion, nor a sure way of garnering additional resources for this purpose (in a society that places a low priority on health, the funds might be diverted to other programs in any case). Serious objections can also be raised to fee charging, not only because of the external benefits mentioned by Jimenez but also on equity grounds.

As discussed above, the kinds of services the LDC governments *should* be spending the bulk of their health budgets on are those that yield major benefits to society in general and particularly to poor people in rural and urban areas. One wishes to expand these services substantially in most countries, not to discourage their use through the imposition of substantial fees. Government expenditure on health and other social services cannot fulfill its potential for improving income distribution and lessening the grinding effects of poverty if it is accompanied by fees that discourage the use of these services by the very people we want to reach.

Health services may thus be one area where potentials for using the price system, so frequently advocated in this textbook, are limited. It should be noted, however, that this skepticism about the desirability of charging for health services is only warranted *if* the emphasis in health services is on primary and preventive services aimed at the masses of people, as advocated in this chapter. If, on the contrary, the services offered are primarily those which benefit the rich, then of course high fees should be charged. But this, as we hope to have made clear by now, is no way to run a public health service in a developing country.

PART 3

CAPITAL
RESOURCES

Capital and Saving

Of all the approaches to development mentioned in Chapters 2 and 3, the emphasis on capital formation was perhaps the most influential and durable, for a number of reasons. First, it had respectable theoretical underpinnings—the simple but elegant Harrod-Domar model, discussed in Chapter 3. Properly viewed, the Harrod-Domar model provides insights into vital aspects of the development process, because it focuses on the difficulties involved in meeting the investment requirements for assuring substantial and steady growth without high rates of inflation or unemployment. However, more mechanistic interpretations of the Harrod-Domar model postulated a lockstep relationship between growth in investment and national income. The view that capital formation was the key to growth, called **capital fundamentalism,** was reflected in the development strategies and plans of many countries. The development problem was viewed essentially as one of securing investment resources sufficient to generate some chosen target rate of national income growth. The implications of target rates of income growth for employment and income distribution were rarely examined, as it was widely assumed that faster growth rates would in and of themselves ameliorate both unemployment and extreme income inequality.

Second, capital fundamentalism resonated with the aims and approaches of foreign aid donors of the 1950s and 1960s, by furnishing a readily explicable, apparently clear-cut basis for the justifying aid "needs." Capital shortage was then widely judged to be the single most important barrier to accelerated economic development, and a heavy premium tended to be placed on framing development plans that reflected this point of view. The best-crafted of such plans, such as Pakistan's third 5-year plan in the early 1960s, were able to show heavy initial capital requirements and a need for large early injections of foreign capital, especially foreign aid. Large initial contributions of aid, it was thought, would generate new flows of domestic savings and reduce aid requirements in the long run.

Third, capital fundamentalism was durable because its framework was flexible enough to incorporate new economic ideas of the 1960s, especially the concept of human capital discussed in Part 2 of this book. The selective embedding of human capital considerations into the framework further strengthened the argument that capital formation was the linchpin of development. The incorporation of human capital into the framework was no minor embellishment, for the size of the human capital stock relative to the physical stock can be quite large. Estimates place the value of the human capital stock in the United States in the mid-1970s as roughly equal to that of the stock of physical capital.

High levels of capital formation made possible by the initial abundance of savings matter little for income growth—much less for employment creation and improving income distribution—when capital is deployed in projects of low productivity. These include the much-ridiculed, large-scale showcase steel mills and thousands of inefficiently small hydroelectric plants; expensive higher education systems; and ultramodern cardiac care centers serving small elites in capital cities. Further, massive investment projects financed by foreign savings, however productive, may have little impact on income growth when host country policies are poorly suited for capturing an equitable share of the returns from such projects. Particularly before the mid-1960s, there were several instances in which host countries, especially those with sizable natural resource endowments, have ultimately had little to show from major foreign investment projects other than the scrap content of equipment left behind at the end. We return to this problem in Chapters 14 and 19.

INVESTMENT REQUIREMENTS FOR GROWTH

The critical role of savings and capital in creating income growth has been well-established in industrial societies. For example, the sources-of-growth analysis introduced in Chapter 3 has been employed to show that expansion of physical capital inputs alone has been responsible for about half the growth in aggregate income of nine developed countries from 1960 to 1975.

Analyses of the relative contribution of capital to growth in developing countries are neither as numerous nor, owing to data limitations, as conclusive as those for the United States and other OECD members. However, the available sources-of-growth calculations suggest that the impact of capital formation on growth is considerable in those countries as well, particularly for the early stages of development; at higher levels of income, productivity growth appears much more important. Studies in middle-income nations such as Korea, the Philippines, and Mexico indicate that in the sixties and seventies, growth in the physical capital stock, quite apart from growth in the stock of human capital, may have contributed from one-fourth to one-third of income growth, with estimates' clustering toward the higher figure; the contribution is as much as one-half in poorer countries. None of these studies incorporates the contribution of human capital to income growth, so the results understate the role of capital formation, and therefore savings, in income growth.

In any case, although capital accumulation is no longer viewed as a panacea for poor countries, it is nevertheless clear that even mildly robust growth rates in incomes can be sustained over long periods only when societies are able to maintain investment at a sizable proportion of GDP. This proportion can rarely be much less than 15 percent and in some cases it must be as high as 25 percent, depending on the environment in which capital accumulation takes place and on what rate of income growth is deemed essential to allow progress toward basic societal goals. Growth aspirations probably do not vary as widely as did recorded growth performance between low- and middle-income countries from 1980 through 1988, in which average growth in real per-capita income was only 1.5 percent in the former (excluding China and India) and 2.6 percent in the latter. (Refer to Table 11–2). In general, if LDCs seek growth in real per-capita income that at least matches that for the middle-income countries from 1980 onward, then—given rates of population growth in low income economies of about 2.6 percent in the past decade (excluding China)—the requisite rate of aggregate income growth would have to be at least 6 percent per annum.

Effective Use of Capital

Given a goal of 6 percent growth in real aggregate income, annual investment requirements would then depend on both the volume of available savings and on the environment in which capital formation occurs. In developing countries where basic macro (economywide) prices (exchange rates, interest rates, wage rates) are approximately equal to scarcity values for factors of production, scarce capital is likely to be deployed where it can be applied most effectively with more abundant labor. In such circumstances a given addition to the capital stock can generate increments to output that exceed those in countries where production is more capital-intensive (see Chapter 3). Depending on the structure of basic macro prices such as interest rates and exchange rates and the orientation of public sector decision makers, the ICOR can vary from under 3:1 to 7:1 and even higher, as shown in Table 3–4. Consider the investment implications of an ICOR of 2.5 compared with an ICOR half again as high, or 3.75. For countries with an ICOR of 2.5, a necessary, but not sufficient, condition for achieving sustained aggregate growth in output of 6.0 percent per year is securing capital resources equivalent to 15 percent of GNP. However, countries with an ICOR of 3.75 will need to invest 22.5 percent of GNP to attain the same rate of output growth. Thus more efficient deployment of capital can substantially reduce the savings effort required for sustained growth.

Capital- or Labor-Intensive Investment: A Hypothetical Case

In the presence of immobilities of productive factors of the type discussed at the end of this chapter, a pervasive pattern of capital-intensive production in capital-short countries leads to lower rates of income growth, strong suppression of consumption, or both. To illustrate, consider two small low-income countries that are initially identical in all important respects: per-capita income of $400 in 1990, population of 2.5 million, an investment ratio in 1990 of 15 percent, and similar patterns of exports, imports, agriculture, and industry. From 1980 to 1990, both followed essentially the same development strategy, which produced an historic incremental capital-output ratio of 3.5 each. And each experienced real GDP a growth rate of about 5 percent over the 10-year period.

In 1990 new governments in both countries altered past development policies. For the next decade country A's government chose a strategy involving heavy outlays on large-scale, capital-intensive investments, such as oil refining, paper mills, and steel mills. As a result of this change, and supported by other government policies, the ICOR was expected to rise from 3.5 to 4. Country B, on the other hand, decided in 1990 to shift to a strategy emphasizing more labor-intensive investments in agriculture and industry, including textile mills, commercial firewood forests, coastal fisheries, and shoe manufactures. Decision makers in country B expect the ICOR to decline from 3.5 to 3 as a result. These two capital-output ratios are within the high range for developing countries given in Table 3–2. In this example we overlook contributions of other factors to growth.

We assume that both countries faced similar constraints on investment finance during the period 1985 to 1990. For both, resources available for investment (from both domestic and foreign sources) are most likely to expand by no less than 5 percent per year ("low") and by no more than 10 percent per year ("high"). The implications of these alternative investment availabilities for GDP growth are presented in Table 11–1.

A striking implication can be drawn from Table 11–1. The table shows that the efficiency with which capital is used can be much more important for GDP growth than for raising the volume of investment. For the entire five-year period, the ICOR of country A is only 25 percent higher than that of country B. But after five years country B has a higher GDP than country A, even when investment resources grow at twice the rate in country A, as in country B. At 5 percent growth in investment in country B, average annual GDP growth is also 5 percent, whereas in country A even 10 percent growth in investment leads to only a 4.2 percent average annual GDP growth. To accomplish this, by the fifth year country A must find investment resources equal to 19.7 percent of GDP. With an investment ratio of only 15 percent in 1995, country B can still grow faster than the maximum that is possible for country A.

On the other hand, if investment resources available to both countries were to grow at 10 percent per annum, aggregate income in B would be 6 percent higher than in A by 1995, even though they began at the same level. Although a 6 percent difference in total income after five years may not seem large, when placed in proper perspective it can be quite significant.

TABLE 11–1   GDP and Investment under Two Different Strategies (millions of U.S. dollars)

	1990	Invest-ment growth rate (%)	1991	1992	1993	1994	1995	Average annual growth (%)	1995 % of invest-ment to GDP
Investment availability									
I. Low	150.0	5.0	157.5	165.4	173.6	182.3	191.4	5.0	—
II. High	150.0	10.0	165.0	181.5	199.6	219.6	241.6	10.0	—
GDP Country A: Capital-intensive strategy (ICOR = 4)[a]									
I. Low	1,000	5.0	1,037.5	1,076.9	1,118.3	1,161.7	1,207.3	3.8	15.9
II. High	1,000	5.0	1,037.5	1,078.8	1,124.2	1,174.1	1,229.0	4.2	19.7
GDP Country B Labor-intensive strategy (ICOR = 3)[a]									
I. Low	1,000	5.0	1,050.0	1,102.5	1,157.6	1,215.5	1,276.3	5.0	15.0
II. High	1,000	10.0	1,050.0	1,105.0	1,165.5	1,232.0	1,305.2	5.5	18.5

[a]To simplify presentation, the example assumes that all investment resources in any given year are available by the beginning of that year and that there is only a one-year lag between the time investment resources are available and the time they begin to yield output.

There are few developing countries in the world that spend as much as 6 percent of GDP on education (Jordan and Costa Rica were exceptions in 1987), and except for Panama and Costa Rica no LDC spends as much as 3 percent on public health. Merely because it uses capital more efficiently than country A, country B would, in the extreme, possess the capacity to more than double real outlays for education or triple expenditures on public health programs. Alternatively, if both countries place a high premium on national autonomy and are therefore apprehensive over foreign participation in their economies, it is much more likely that country B will satisfy this goal since it will have less need to resort to foreign capital to finance a substantial share of its development effort. An investment ratio of 15 percent is clearly much easier to support from domestic resources than the 20 percent required for country A to attain the same level of GDP growth.

Investment Ratios in LDCs

The heavy emphasis on capital-intensive investment often found in developing countries is to some extent the unintended result of government policies. But it may also be attributed to a pervasive belief that only capital-intensive technology is efficient, and the choice of technology is not sensitive to relative prices of labor and capital. The discussion in Chapter 8 casts significant doubt on the notion that the choice of technique of production in LDCs is largely unaffected by price signals. Policies that result in underpricing capital and overpricing labor do seem to cause firms and government agencies to adjust by adopting techniques involving more capital and less labor than would be the case in the absence of such policies. However, Chapter 8 also reminds us that wherever found, bias toward capital intensity in investment cannot always, or even usually, be fully explained in terms of distorted price signals. Nor is it legitimate to assume that capital intensity always represents vice and that labor-using investment always denotes virtue. For example, those who would advocate a conscious, reverse bias in favor of labor-intensive methods of underground coal or tin mining have either never visited the hazardous labor-intensive facilities for these activities (for example, in Bolivia and Indonesia) or are unaware of the large surpluses available from capital-intensive mining that can be deployed for labor-intensive investments in other fields. Even in agriculture there are sound arguments, advanced in Chapter 18, for mechanization to increase both productivity and employment.

In the typical labor-surplus situation, 6 percent annual growth in real income cannot be sustained over extended periods in the absence of investment ratios of at least 20 percent (in the economies emphasizing more labor-intensive approaches) and 25 percent (in the capital-intensive strategies). Securing investment ratios of 20 or more percent has proven a difficult task for many LDCs, and in particular for some of the 40 nations (other than India and China) falling into the World Bank's category of low-income countries (see Table 11–2, first two columns).

Nevertheless, about half the countries in this group did manage to increase the share of gross domestic investment to gross domestic product over the period 1965 to 1988. For this set of countries as a whole, investment's share rose from 19 percent in 1965 to 28 percent in 1988 (but only from 14 to 18 percent with China and India excluded). The 36 lower-middle-income countries did manage to expand investment shares by 21 percent over the period, while the investment share in upper middle-income nations increased but slightly. Investment shares in 1988 ranged from 10 percent of GDP in Niger, Haiti, and Sudan to over 30 percent in Mozambique, Somalia, China, and Lesotho. Among the upper-middle-income countries, only Algeria and Yugoslavia managed to reach or surpass 30 percent levels. Table 11–2 shows that both low- and middle-income countries had achieved, on the average, higher investment ratios in 1988 than even the advanced industrialized countries.

Sources of Saving

Developing countries, particularly the poorest 40 nations, were able to finance their higher investment-to-GDP ratios by intensified saving mobilization efforts directed at savings from various sources, both domestic and foreign, public and private. Before turning to an examination of recent patterns of investment finance, it will be useful to consider a simplified taxonomy of saving.

TABLE 11–2   Gross Domestic Investment and Gross Domestic Savings Rates, 1965 and 1988

Category[d]	Gross domestic investment[a] (as % of GDP)		Gross domestic savings[b] (as % of GDP)		Resources gap[c]	
	1965	1988	1965	1988	1965	1988
Low-income[e]	19 (14)	28 (18)	18 (12)	26 (14)	−1 (−2)	−10 (−6)
Middle-income	21	25	21	27	0	2
Lower-middle-income	19	23	18	24	−1	1
Upper-middle-income	24	25[f]	25	27[f]	1	2
Oil exports	20	25	24	24	4	−1
OECD members	17	22	17	22	0	

[a]Gross Domestic Investment is defined as all public and private-sector expenditures for additions to the stock of fixed assets plus the net value of inventory changes.
[b]Gross Domestic Savings is calculated by deducting total consumption from Gross Domestic Product.
[c]Gross Domestic Investment minus Gross Domestic Savings.
[d]Groups defined as in Table 1–1.
[e]Figures in parentheses exclude China and India.
[f]Figure for 1987.
Source: World Bank, World Development Report 1990, Table 9.

Taxonomy of Saving

The allocation of resources between present and future consumption (saving) is one of the most fundamental economic choices facing any economy. This choice affects not only the rate of economic growth a country can enjoy, but also the standards of living for future generations yet unborn.

For a country, the total supply of available savings S is simply the sum of domestic savings (S_d) and foreign savings (S_f). Domestic saving may be broken down into two components: government, or public-sector, saving (S_g) and private domestic saving (S_p). Government saving consists primarily of budgetary saving (S_{gb}) that arises from any excess of government revenues over government consumption, where public consumption is defined as all current government expenditure plus all capital outlays for military hardware. Examples of public-sector consumption include expenditures for food subsidies; for meeting recurring costs such as salaries for civil servants and police; for purchasing stationery, fuel, and arms; and for maintaining roads and bridges, plus interest on the national debt. In focusing on this savings component, it is important to note that a country could still have positive public savings even when the overall government budget is in deficit, because budget expenditures include capital outlays, or investment, that represent uses of public savings. In a very few countries savings of government-owned enterprises (S_{ge}) have also contributed to public sector savings (see Chapter 12). Private domestic savings also arise from two sources: corporate saving (S_{pc}) and household saving (S_{ph}). **Corporate saving** is defined as the retained earnings of corporate enterprises (corporate income after taxes minus dividends paid to shareholders). **Household saving** (S_{ph}) is simply that part of household income not consumed. Household saving includes saving from unincorporated enterprises (single proprietorships, partnerships, and other noncorporate forms of business enterprise).

In most LDCs unincorporated business enterprise is by far the dominant form of business organization.

Foreign saving also comes in two basic forms: **official foreign saving** (S_{fo}) or foreign aid, and **private foreign saving** (S_{fp}), which may be broken down into two separate components. The first is **external commercial borrowing,** or *debt* finance, symbolized (S_{fpd}). LDC borrowers, including governments, agree to repay the amount of the loan (the principal) as well as interest on the loan, in accordance with prearranged schedules. The second major component of private foreign savings, **direct investment,** represents *equity* finance, symbolized by (S_{fpe}). Returns to equity are called dividends and are paid only when profits are made.

To recapitulate, total available saving may be viewed in the first instance as

$$S = S_d + S_f = (S_g + S_p) + (S_{fo} + S_{fp}). \tag{11-1}$$

For purposes of understanding saving patterns and policies, saving may be disaggregated further to

$$S = [(S_{gb} + S_{ge}) + (S_{pc} + S_{ph})] + (S_{fo} + S_{fpd} + S_{fpe}). \tag{11-2}$$

Reliance on different sources of saving differs greatly among developing nations, depending not only on factors such as the level of per-capital income, natural resource endowments, and sectoral composition of GDP, but also on the nature of saving mobilization policies adopted by particular governments. The balance of this chapter identifies the determinants of domestic saving and its various components. Chapter 14 will examine foreign saving, its patterns, and the controversies surrounding it.

Domestic Savings

Relative to 1965, LDCs as a group had by 1988 greatly intensified their efforts to mobilize domestic savings. Although many relied heavily on foreign savings as a source of investment finance, the rise in investment ratios depicted in Table 11–2 was accompanied by a roughly commensurate increase in the share of gross domestic savings in GDP. Although these averages mask some major differences in the savings performances for countries within each category, the general picture is one of some success in mobilizing additional domestic savings since 1965. Table 11–3 depicts the evolution of savings and investment ratios for a group of 24 LDCs in Asia, Africa, and Latin America, chosen to represent a wide range in per-capita income, natural resource endowments, and ideological orientation. Among countries in this table, domestic saving rates in 1988 ranged from a negative 5 percent to a positive 38 percent. Table 11–3 underscores the significance of income levels for savings mobilization efforts. Among the low-income countries only China, India, Kenya and OPEC member Indonesia had savings rates of 20 percent or more in 1988, while among the middle-income group 8 of the 12 in the table have saving rates of over 20 percent. We would ordinarily expect a lower ratio of saving in poor countries relative to middle-income countries simply because there is less available for saving after subsistence needs are met.

TABLE 11–3   Domestic Savings of Selected Developing Countries, 1965 and 1988

Country	Gross domestic saving as % of GDP		Gross domestic investment as % of GDP		Domestic saving as % of domestic investment	
	1965	1988	1965	1988	1965	1988
Low-income countries[a,b]	18 (12)	26 (14)	19 (14)	28 (18)	95 (80)	93 (78)
Ethiopia	12	4	13	16	92	25
Tanzania	16	−5	15	21	107	−24
Bangladesh	8	3	11	12	73	25
Mali	5	−4	18	15	28	27
Nigeria	12	15	14	13	86	115
China	25	37	24	38	104	97
India	15	21	17	24	88	87
Pakistan	13	13	21	18	62	72
Kenya	15	22	14	26	107	85
Ghana	8	6	18	12	44	50
Sri Lanka	13	13	12	23	108	56
Indonesia	8	25	8	22	100	114
Middle-income countries[b]	21	27	21	25	100	108
Lower-middle-income countries	18	24	19	23	95	104
Bolivia	17	6	22	11	77	54
Philippines	21	18	21	17	100	106
Senegal	8	9	12	15	67	60
Egypt	14	8	18	20	78	40
Guatemala	10	8	13	14	77	57
Colombia	17	22	16	21	106	105
Mexico	19	23	20	20	95	115
Malaysia	24	36	20	26	120	138
Brazil	22	28	20	23	110	122
Upper-middle-income countries	25	27[c]	24	25[c]	104	108[c]
Algeria	19	31	22	31	86	100
Uruguay	18	14	11	10	164	140
South Korea	8	38	15	30	53	127

[a]Figures in parentheses exclude China and India.
[b]Countries ranked in ascending order of per-capita income in 1988 (see Table 1–1).
[c]Figure for 1987.
Source: World Bank, World Development Report 1990, Appendix Table 9.

It is also evident from Table 11–3 that the more prosperous LDCs tend to cover a larger share of their investment needs with local savings. Whereas six of the poorer LDCs relied on foreign savings for more than one-third of investment finance by 1988, only four of the middle-income countries in the sample exhibited that much dependence on foreign savings. Indeed, in eight of the middle-income nations, domestic saving rates equaled or exceeded domestic investment rates in 1988. On average, the table also shows that although domestic saving rates increased appreciably from 1965 to 1988 in many low- and middle-income countries, the share of domestic saving in total investment finance rose little in middle-income nations, and actually declined in two-thirds of the poorer countries—sharply in four cases.

Moreover, the continuing strong savings performance of China and India in the group of low-income countries masks a serious decline in both saving rates and the share of investment financed locally in the other low-income nations included in Table 11–3.

Table 11–3 does not begin, however, to portray adequately the diversity of savings performances across more than 100 developing countries. In 1988, 8 LDCs had negative rates of domestic savings; in Mozambique, Chad, and Lesotho negative saving amounted to more than 10 percent of GDP. But in that same year, 16 LDCs, including the 7 depicted in Table 11–3, had positive savings rates of 25 percent or more per year.

Government policies have had a major impact on the ability of developing countries to mobilize domestic savings. We will see in the next three chapters that some nations have actively sought to deploy policies to encourage savings growth and have utilized instruments well-suited for that purpose. In still more nations, governments have been no less concerned with the promotion of domestic savings but have relied on policy tools ill-suited for savings mobilization. Finally, in a small group of countries, government policies appear to have been designed with little or no regard for their implications for domestic savings. As might be expected, savings have generally responded positively to policy initiatives in the first group of countries, less so in the second group, and have tended to stagnate or decline in the third.

Government Savings

Where present, government savings have arisen almost wholly from an excess of total tax revenues over public consumption expenditures (S_{gb}). Chapter 12 shows that in very few cases do savings by government enterprises (S_{ge}) ever materially contribute to aggregate government savings. Given the very minor role of S_{ge}, the discussion of government saving in this chapter is confined to budgetary savings.

During the 1950s and 1960s, one of the basic tenets of typical development strategies was that the investment expansion required for sustained income growth could not proceed in the absence of major efforts to increase the share of government savings in GDP. It was commonly held that growth in private savings was inherently constrained by such factors as low per-capita incomes and high private consumption propensities among wealthy families with the greatest capacity for savings. Limited availabilities of foreign savings also led planners, as well as aid donors, to stress the necessity of programs for mobilizing government savings. In almost all cases, the preferred means for achieving this goal was to raise the ratio of tax collections to GNP (the tax ratio), through significant reform of the tax structure if possible or through increases in existing tax rates if necessary. Underlying this view was a belief that the propensity to consume out of an additional dollar of income was substantially less in the public sector than in the private sector. In this view diversion of income to the government should increase national saving rates. This engendered a prevailing view among many LDC planners that rising tax ratios were associated with successful development strategies, a view reinforced by policies of foreign aid donors. In the 1950s and 1960s many donors, including the United States, utilized tax ratios and tax-effort indices as prime indicators of national commitment to belt-tightening in recipient countries. Countries willing to suffer higher domestic taxes were seen as more deserving of aid, other things equal.

It is not easy to increase tax collections in LDCs. Except for those countries blessed with valuable natural resource endowments, developing countries would not be expected to have tax ratios nearly as high as is common in the industrial countries, if for no other reason than their much lower per-capita incomes, which allow a much smaller margin for taxation after subsistence needs are met. Whereas typical tax ratios for developing countries in 1988 ranged between 14 and 16 percent, the ratio of central government taxes to GNP in 1988 in the 21 wealthy member countries of the OECD averaged about 25 percent.[1]

Despite the difficulties involved, many LDCs have been able to raise their shares of taxes in GNPs since the 1960s. One study showed small advances in the average tax ratio for a group of 47 developing countries from 1950. For these nations as a group, the typical share of tax in GNP hovered at about 11 percent in the 1950s. By 1972 to 1976 the average tax ratio had risen to 16 percent.[2]

The average tax ratio has fluctuated about that level ever since; it increased to nearly 18 percent in the early eighties, when sharply higher world oil prices resulted in pronounced increases in tax collections in several oil-exporting LDCs such as Mexico, Indonesia, and Venezuela, and then slipped to about 15 percent during the subsequent period of depressed world oil prices (1982 to 1987). Table 11–4 suggests that although the tax ratio tends to be much lower in very poor countries (below $500 per-capita income), tax ratios do not vary much with income beyond that level.

Particularly during the fifties and sixties, the conventional fiscal wisdom held that vigorously applied policies of savings mobilization through higher taxes would yield substantial improvement in the overall national savings rate. But higher taxes lead to higher savings only if the government's **marginal propensity to consume** (MPC) out of increased taxes is less than the private sector's propensity to consume out of the marginal income from which it pays increased taxes.[3] Government saving made possible through budget surpluses unquestionably played a major role in the early stages of Japan's economic development. But other success stories for saving mobilization through budget policy are difficult to find. Unfortunately, there is evidence that for most LDCs, the government's MPC out of taxes has been sufficiently high that increased taxation may easily have resulted in less,

---

1. The range for central government tax ratios in 1988 in the OECD countries was from a little over 19 percent in the United States to nearly 50 percent in the Netherlands. World Bank, *World Development Report 1990*, Table 12, Appendix.

2. Alfred Tait, Wilfred Gratz, and Barry Eichengreen, "International Comparisons of Taxation for Selected Developing Countries," *International Monetary Fund Staff Papers* 26, no. 1, (March 1979): 123–156.

3. The marginal propensity to consume (MPC) refers to the amount of consumption out of each incremental (marginal) unit of income. Thus, if government spends $80 out of each additional $100 in tax revenue on consumption, the government's MPC is 0.80.

TABLE 11–4 Tax Ratios in 120 Countries: Overall and by Type of Tax, 1988

Per-capita income	Total taxes as % of GNP[d] (tax ratio)	Particular taxes as % of GNP (central government only)				
		Taxes on foreign trade	Income taxes	Internal indirect taxes (sales, excise)	Social Security taxes[a]	Other taxes[a]
Low-income (below $545)[b,c]	14.4	3.7	5.2	5.7	0.1	0.6
Lower-middle-income ($545–$2,199)	12.5	2.5[c]	3.31	4.9	0.7	0.5
Upper-middle-income ($2,200–$5,999)[c]	15.9	1.7	4.1	5.0	3.0	1.2
High-income (above $6,000)	24.4	0.3[c]	9.31	5.7	8.9	0.7
Average, all countries	20.9	2.0[c]	6.2[c]	5.6[c]	2.4[c]	0.8

[a] Average of all countries for which data were available.
[b] Excludes China and India.
[c] Figures for 1987.
Source: Derived from World Bank, *World Development Report 1990*, Table 12.

not more, total domestic savings. This phenomenon has become known as the Please effect, after Stanley Please of the World Bank, who first brought it to widespread attention.[4] Whether or not the Please effect is widespread, we will see in Chapter 12 that higher taxes can and do displace some household and business savings in the private sector.[5] And experience over most of the past three decades does show rather strong consumption propensities on the part of governments.

While tax ratios in LDCs typically rose marginally over the 1960s and 1970s, before leveling off in the mid-eighties, the share of public-sector consumption expenditures expanded at rapid rates over the same period, generally in excess of GDP growth. In low-income countries (exclusive of India and China), the share of public-sector consumption expenditures in GNP rose from 8 percent in 1960 to 12 percent in 1983, where it remained in 1988. In middle-income nations, the share of public-sector consumption in GDP has risen even more sharply over the past three decades: from 11 percent in 1960, to 13 percent in 1983, and to 15 percent in 1988.[6]

This experience was widespread. It is worth emphasizing that in many countries much of the growth in public-sector consumption has been intended to promote development. Some governmental salary adjustments have been

4. Stanley Please, "Savings Through Taxation: Reality or Mirage?" *Finance and Development* 4, no. 1 (March 1967): 24–32.

5. Some analysts find a high degree of substitutability between government and private savings; others do not. See, for example, the exhaustive survey in Raymond F. Mikesell and James E. Zinser, "The Nature of the Savings Function in Developing Countries: A Survey of the Theoretical and Empirical Literature," *Journal of Economic Literature* 11, no. 1 (March 1973): 1–26. One article surveyed in this contribution indicated that an additional one dollar of government savings is associated with a 57-cent decline in private savings. Another article indicates a positive relationship between public and private savings.

6. World Bank, *World Development Report 1990*, and *1985*, Appendix Table 5.

meant to keep and attract qualified civil servants, and many governments

have strengthened their efforts to maintain roads, schools, health facilities, communication networks, and the like. But when higher government consumption has been traceable to rapid buildup of military purchases (which we will look at in the next chapter), excessive procurement of materials, or upkeep of a large government vehicle fleet dominated by Mercedes or Bentleys, the effects have been unhelpful to national development.

Nevertheless, rapid growth in public-sector consumption over the past three decades, coupled with modest increases in tax ratios, has meant that the growth in government savings has not been a major source of investment finance in most LDCs. And it will be evident from Chapter 14 that although foreign saving has been a growing share of investment finance in many low-income countries since 1960, this was not so for LDCs as a group, particularly the middle-income nations. We may wonder, then: What was the source of the additional saving required to cover significantly higher investment ratios (see Table 11–2) over that period? To answer that question we now look at the private sector.

Private Domestic Savings

Until quite recently, economists, aid donors, and many LDC decision makers tended to view private domestic savings as decidedly secondary to government savings and foreign aid as a source of investment finance. There is, however, some evidence that in many LDCs private savings have come to play a major role in supporting capital formation. Data compiled by the World Bank, summarized in Table 11–5, indicate that many LDCs have been able to restrain growth in private consumption over long periods and thereby expand the pool of private savings. Among low-income nations, this was particularly true for India and China, where the share of private consumption in GDP declined from three-quarters to about two-thirds between 1965 and 1988. This ratio also declined in other low-income nations and in middle-income nations as well. But, here again, aggregate figures mask important differences between countries. Among 31 low-income countries for which data is available, the share of private consumption fell in 14 and rose in 17. And among middle-income countries, the share of private consumption in GDP fell by more than 5 percentage points in 13 of the 54 nations. Although data on consumption growth are subject to large errors, the available evidence suggests that, except for a relatively small group of the poorest nations, growth in private consumption was held in check in most LDCs after 1965.

We have seen that the share of taxes in GDP rose only slightly in most LDCs over the past three decades. If higher taxes do not account for the drop in the share of private consumption in GDP, then the share of private saving must have increased. In any case, the most plausible source of a large share of finance for the rising investment ratios reported in Table 11–2 was private domestic savings. For LDCs in general, at least one of the components of private domestic savings must have risen at a fairly robust rate. But if so, it is difficult to determine which of the components played the more important role—household saving or business saving. To begin to

TABLE 11–5   Rates of GDP and Private Consumption, Shares of Private Consumption in Total GDP (95 countries, 1965–1988)

	Annual rate of growth (% per year)					
	Real GDP[a]		Real private consumption[a]		% share of private consumption in GDP[a]	
Category	1965–1980	1980–1988	1965–1980	1980–1988	1965–1980	1980–1988
Low-income countries (excluding China and India)	5.5	2.0	4.4	2.8	78	74
All low-income countries	5.4	6.4	4.1	5.2	70	65
Lower-middle-income countries	6.5	2.6	6.2	2.2	71	64
Upper-middle-income countries	5.6	3.3	7.1	2.9	63	60[b]
All middle-income countries	6.1	2.9	6.6	2.5	67	59

[a] Weighted average.
[b] Figure for 1987.
Sources: World Bank, *World Development Report, 1990,* Tables 2, 8, 9.

answer this question, and to gain further insights into fundamental relationships in the development process, it is useful to consider the economic theory of private-sector savings behavior.

DETERMINANTS OF PRIVATE SAVINGS

Theories of household saving behavior were initially developed as part of the postwar Keynesian revolution in economic thought to explain saving patterns in industrial countries. The applicability of these theories to the study of saving behavior in LDCs has been frequently called into question in recent years.[7] Nevertheless, current controversies over the determinants of saving behavior in LDCs are almost impossible to understand without reference to earlier studies developed for the analysis of private saving in industrial nations.

Household Saving Behavior

All theories of household saving behavior seek to explain the following three observed patterns: (1) within a particular country at a given time, higher-income households tend to save larger fractions of their income than

7. See especially Angus Deaton, "Saving in Developing Countries: Theory and Review," *Proceedings of the World Bank Annual Conference on Development Economics,* Washington, D.C., World Bank, 1989.

lower-income households; (2) within a particular country over time, household saving ratios tend to be roughly constant, more so in industrial than
in developing nations; and (3) across countries, household saving ratios
vary with no clear relation to income. To help reconcile these "stylized
facts," we will consider four alternative explanations of household saving
behavior: the Keynesian absolute-income hypothesis, the relative-income
hypothesis, the Friedman permanent-income hypothesis, and the Kaldor
class-savings hypothesis.

Economists once widely believed in the general applicability of a simple
income-saving relationship. Household saving was viewed as directly
dependent on current disposable income (household income after direct
taxes). The propensity to save out of current disposable income was thought
to rise with income. This was known as the **Keynesian absolute-income
hypothesis,** after the famed British economist John Maynard Keynes, who
propounded the idea in the 1930s. In this view the saving-income relationship would be expressed as

$$S = a + sY^d, \qquad [11\text{--}3]$$

where S = saving, Y^d = current disposable income, a = a constant ($a < 0$),
and s = the marginal propensity to save ($0 < s < 1$). The constant a is generally taken to be negative to signify that at low levels of income, saving
will be negative. Under this formulation saving ratios (saving as a fraction
of GDP) should be expected to rise over time in all countries where income
is growing. But the historical record in both developed and developing
countries provides very weak support for the Keynesian hypothesis.

At best the Keynesian formulation may depict saving behavior over the
very short term, but it breaks down as a long-run proposition. The Keynesian formulation explains only the first household saving pattern, but not the
second or third. An alternative view of the income-consumption relationship, the **relative-income hypothesis,** focuses on the longer term. In its simplest form this hypothesis holds that consumption (and therefore saving)
depends not only on current income but also on previous levels of income
and past consumption habits. One form of the relative-income hypothesis,
called the **Duesenberry hypothesis** after Harvard economist James Duesenberry, who originated the concept in the late 1940s, may be expressed as

$$C_1 - a + (l - s)Y^d_1 + bC_h, \qquad [11\text{--}4]$$

where C_1 = consumption in period 1, Y^d_1 = income in period 1, C_h =
previous high level of consumption, $0 < s < 1$, and $0 < b < 1$. Thus, under
the relative-income hypothesis, the short-run consumption (saving) function in an economy tends to ratchet upward over time. As income grows
over the long term, consumers adjust their spending habits to higher levels
of consumption. But in the short run they are reluctant to reduce, and slow
to raise consumption levels should income fall (or rise) temporarily. The
relationship between the Keynesian absolute-income hypothesis and the
Duesenberry relative-income hypothesis is depicted in Figure 11–1.

The Duesenberry hypothesis was formulated as an explanation of consumption and saving behavior for the United States. Later researchers argued

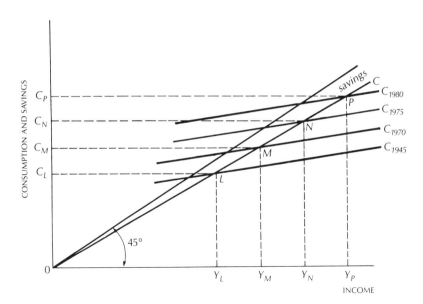

FIGURE 11–1 Consumption and Saving in the Short and Long Term with Rising Income over Time. The 45-degree line shows all points at which consumption is equal to income. Four short-run consumption functions are shown for each of the years 1960, 1970, 1975, and 1980 representing what people would have spent at various levels of income in those years. Consumption lines for each year plot Equation 11–3, with

$$C = Y_d - S = -a(1-S)Y_d;$$

because $a < 0$, $-a > 0$. The flatness of these curves reflects consumers' reluctance to change consumption habits in the short run. In each of these years, actual (current) income was Y_L, Y_M, Y_N, and Y_P respectively. Thus actual consumption in each of those years was C_L, C_M, C_N, and C_P. The points L through P trace out a long-term consumption function. Consumption, and thus savings, tend to be a constant proportion of income over time.

that it may also be applicable to LDCs. Some have suggested that a *demonstration effect* operates to cause consumption in LDCs to ratchet upward as incomes grow. Internationally mobile and worldly wise upper-income groups in LDCs are thought to emulate the high-consumption patterns of the wealthiest income groups in developed countries; successively lower income groups in LDCs tend to emulate the patterns of higher-income groups, so that consumption in the society as a whole tends to be a high and stable function of income. Indeed, the British economist Nicholas Kaldor once estimated that if the richest families in Chile had the same consumption propensities as families at the same *relative* income position in developed nations (but at higher absolute levels of income), the Chilean savings rate in the 1950s could have been doubled.[8] The relative-income hypothesis explains all three of the observed savings patterns cited earlier.[9]

8. Nicholas Kaldor, "Problemas Economicas de Chile," *El Trimestre Economico* 26, no. 102 (April–June 1959): 193, 211–212.

9. More recent studies of factors affecting saving behavior among high-income elites in LDCs include Robert H. Frank, "The Demand for Unobservable and other Non-positional Goods," *American Economic Review* 75 (March 1985): 101–116, and Philip Musgrove, "Income Distribution and Aggregate Consumption Function," *Journal of Political Economy* 2, no. 88 (June 1980): 504–525.

Other approaches developed to explain consumption and saving behavior in developed countries have been applied to LDCs. The most influential of these has been the **permanent-income hypothesis,** first formulated by Milton Friedman at the University of Chicago in the 1950s. In the Friedman view income consists of two components: permanent income and transitory income. The basic idea is simply that because individuals expect to live for many years, they make consumption decisions over a horizon that includes the entire life cycle. The permanent-income component is not to be regarded as expected lifetime earning. Rather it should be viewed as the mean income at any age regarded as permanent by the household, which in turn depends on both its time horizon and foresight. **Permanent income** is the yield from wealth, including both physical and human capital assets (education and so on) at the disposal of the household. Friedman held that individuals can predict with a reasonable degree of assurance the magnitude of these flows over their lifetimes and that they gear their consumption to what they perceive to be their normal, or permanent, income, which tends to be stable over time. Furthermore, in the most-restrictive variant of the permanent-income hypothesis, consumption tends to be a constant proportion of permanent income and to approach 100 percent of permanent income. Thus any saving that occurs will primarily be out of **transitory income:** unexpected, nonrecurring income such as that arising from changes in asset values, changes in relative prices, lottery winnings, and other unpredictable windfalls. In the most extreme version of the permanent-income hypothesis, individuals are held to save 100 percent of any transitory income. But econometric research since 1970 has called into question this assumption; some studies show a fairly high propensity to consume out of transitory income.

The permanent-income hypothesis may be expressed

$$S = a + b_1 Y_p + b_2 Y_t \qquad [11-5]$$

where S = saving, a = a constant, Y_p = permanent income, and Y_t = transitory income. As noted, in the most extreme version $b_1 = 0$ and $b_2 = 1$, so all savings arise from the transitory component of income and all of this component is saved. Modified versions of the permanent-income hypothesis hold only that saving out of permanent income is constant over a person's lifetime, but can be positive, and that although the propensity to save out of transitory income is high, all transitory income may not be saved. Equation 11–5 can represent this version with $0 < b_1 < b_2 < 1$.

Several studies have sought to test the applicability of the permanent-income hypothesis to a variety of developing countries in Asia and Latin America. The results are far from conclusive, but in toto they do lend some support to the modified versions of the hypothesis: people do tend to save a higher proportion of transitory, as opposed to permanent, income.

A particularly interesting study by Angus Deaton in 1989, based on the framework of life-cycle permanent-income models, stresses the importance of precautionary motives in household saving behavior, particularly among poor rural families in LDCs. Deaton argues that for these groups saving is not so much a matter of accumulation as it is a method of smoothing consumption in the face of volatile income. Essentially, Deaton is saying that poor rural households dissave as often as they save and behave as if their primary motive for saving is to protect their living standards against disasters.[10] In general the permanent-income hypothesis has proven helpful in understanding all three observed savings patterns. Chapter 15 assesses the implications of modified versions of the permanent-income hypothesis in understanding the effects of fluctuating export income on growth.

One further model of household savings behavior merits attention: the **class theory** of the British economist Nicholas Kaldor. This approach views consumption (saving) habits to be sharply differentiated by economic class. Workers, who receive mainly labor income, are thought to have far weaker savings propensities than do capitalists, who receive primarily property income (profits, interests, rents). The class-saving hypothesis is represented as

$$S = S_w L + S_c P, \qquad [11–6]$$

where s_w = workers' saving propensities out of labor income, s_c = capitalists' savings propensities out of property income, L = labor income, P = property income, and $0 < s_w < s_c < 1$.

The class-savings hypothesis explains the first pattern and also explains the third pattern if factor shares (relative shares of labor and capital income) differ across countries. But the difference between the class-saving hypothesis and the permanent-income hypothesis may be more apparent than real. It is difficult to see why households, in their spending-saving decisions, treat labor income any differently than property income: a peso is a peso, a rupee of property income is no different from a rupee of labor income. However, property income of households, particularly that from unincorporated enterprises, tends to fluctuate more than labor income. The permanent-income hypothesis suggests that propensities to save out of variable income streams are higher than out of more stable streams. In addition property income is more concentrated in higher-income groups. Thus studies of saving behavior based on the class model that show markedly higher saving out of property income may really be recording the effects of higher propensities to save out of higher fluctuating income.

All of the hypotheses discussed above view income, whether current, relative, or permanent, as the principal determinant of savings behavior. But income is by no means the only determinant of aggregate private-sector savings behavior, particularly in LDCs. As we will see in Chapter 13, the permanent income hypothesis concedes a role for interest rates in affecting savings behavior. Beyond that, many economists have stressed the effects of such explanatory variables as the age structure of a nation's population and location (rural versus urban families).

Changes in the age structure of a nation's population are found to have significant effects on private savings in several countries. In general, the proportion of any increases in income saved tends to be less in younger

10. Deaton, "Saving in Developing Countries," pp. 61–81.

households than in older ones. Younger families are rearing children and accumulating belongings, but they earn lower incomes. To illustrate, the average ratio of savings to income for older households in Chile in 1964 was found to be twice that of younger households.

There is a strong tendency around the world for rural households to save higher fractions of their incomes than urban households with comparable levels of income—a phenomenon observed in a number of countries, including both Korea and Yugoslavia in the early 1970s. This behavior is also consistent with the permanent-income hypothesis, because farmers' incomes are more variable than those of urban wage earners.

The relative-income hypothesis and the permanent-income hypothesis provide a basis for understanding the lack of strong correlation across LDCs between per-capita income and the ratio of private savings to GDP. Non-income factors such as the age structure of the population and rural-urban differences help explain why private saving ratios do vary across countries, even at comparable levels of per-capita income.

Corporate Saving Behavior

We have seen that there is no shortage of hypotheses purporting to explain the determinants of household saving. There is, however, little consensus among economists about the determinants of corporate saving, particularly in developing countries. Indeed there is little general agreement on the determinants of corporate savings even in developed countries. For example, in the United States a major question on research in business finance has been to explain why U.S. corporations pay out such a high proportion of their after-tax income in dividends, despite strong tax and other incentives to retain earnings (save) within the firm.

In developed countries the share of corporate savings in total income is typically less than 5 percent, and the share of corporate savings in total net private saving is typically less than 25 percent. For example, over the period 1981 to 1985, corporate saving was 16% of the total in Japan, 10 percent in Belgium, about 21 percent in Canada and the United States, and close to 30 percent in West Germany and Britain. However, in Scandinavian nations, the corporate saving share tends to be much higher, 60 percent in Finland and 80 percent in Sweden, for example.[11] Such data are not available for large numbers of LDCs, but it is known that in only a few countries (Colombia, Pakistan, and Panama in the 1960s) have corporate savings represented a sizable share of total savings over any significant period.

Corporate saving in LDCs is relatively small primarily because the corporate sector in most LDCs is relatively small. For a variety of reasons there are fewer pressures and incentives in LDCs for doing business in the corporate form. The principal reasons for organizing as a corporation in the private sector are to limit the liability of enterprise owners to amounts

11. Roger S. Smith, "Factors Affecting Saving, Policy Tools and Tax Reform: A Review," *International Monetary Fund Working Paper No. 89 / 47*, May 23, 1989, Table 2.

invested in a business and to facilitate enterprise finance through the issue of equity shares (stocks). Although these advantages are substantial in developed countries with well-developed commercial codes, civil court systems, and capital markets, they are smaller in most LDCs, where collection of commercial claims (e.g. company debts) through courts is relatively difficult and where, as shown in Chapter 13, capital markets are poorly developed when they exist at all.

As usual, however, there are important exceptions to these generalizations. In some developing countries corporations are both numerous and quite large. Each year since 1980, *Fortune Magazine*'s annual list of the 500 largest corporations outside the United States includes several dozen from developing nations.[12] Examples include conglomerates such as Bavaria (beverages and food processing) in Colombia and Hyundai (automobiles) in Korea, and enterprises such as Alpargatas (textiles and shoes) in Argentina, the diversified firm Tata in India, and Villares (steel products) in Brazil. But, except in Korea and Brazil, even in middle-income LDCs such corporations are not numerous, do not ordinarily account for a large share of private-sector business activity, and clearly do not provide a high proportion of domestic savings.

In all but a few of the highest-income LDCs, the great bulk of private-sector farming and commercial and manufacturing activity is conducted by unincorporated, typically family-owned enterprises, which will be discussed in Chapter 20. Some of these fall into the category of medium-scale establishments (from 20 to 99 workers). Very few are large-scale enterprises. The great majority are small-scale operations (fewer than 20 employees), which, in spite of their abundance, do not account for a sizable share of either value-added or savings.[13] Nevertheless the noncorporate sector manages to generate more than 50 percent of domestic saving in LDCs as a group, and this sector is the only consistent source of surplus in the sense that its saving exceeds its investment. Even for a high-income country like the United States, with a large corporate sector, income from unincorporated enterprise in 1976 was about double the value of corporate profits (after taxes). For those closely held, largely family-owned and -managed firms, enterprise profits become an important part not of corporate savings, but of gross household income. The available evidence indicates, and economic theory suggests, that household savings account for the overwhelming share of private savings in LDCs and that the chief source of household savings is probably household income from unincorporated enterprises.

---

12. *Fortune Magazine,* "World Business Directory," various issues 1980–1990.

13. One study for 21 LDCs in the 1960s shows that small-scale enterprises, although constituting 80 percent of industrial establishments, are responsible for an average of only 13 percent of industrial value-added. See Randev Banerji, "Small-Scale Production Units in Manufacturing: an International Cross Section Overview," *Weltwirtschafliches Archiv* 114, no. 1 (1978). See also Donald Snodgrass, "Small-Scale Manufacturing Industries [in Indonesia]: Patterns, Trends and Possible Policies," Harvard Institute for International Development Discussion Paper no. 54, March 1979.

INTERNATIONAL MOBILITY OF CAPITAL
AND DOMESTIC SAVING MOBILIZATION

287

INTERNATIONAL
MOBILITY OF
CAPITAL AND
DOMESTIC
SAVING
MOBILIZATION

This chapter has focused primarily on patterns and determinants of domestic savings mobilization. The next two chapters examine policy options for mobilizing domestic savings, while Chapter 14 is concerned with issues in foreign savings. In practice, however, the distinction between domestic and foreign saving is rather more blurred than implied up to this point, to the extent that capital is mobile across national borders, particularly in the long run. The issue of the international mobility—or lack of mobility—of capital is one of the most important questions in economic policy; it is also one about which empirical evidence has been, at least until very recently, most scanty.

Short- and Long-Run Mobility

''In the long run we are all dead.'' With this pithy remark, the British economist John Maynard Keynes closed his landmark volume, *The General Theory of Employment, Interest and Money*. In doing so, Keynes sought to jolt governments into undertaking demand-side policy measures that would have the desired short-term effects of pulling the world economy out of the deep depression of the thirties. The statement was appropriate at the time, but ever since the long run has had a bad press: Keynes' remark has been frequently employed as a verbal talisman against proponents of a longer-run focus on the effects of government policies on the economy. This has been particularly unfortunate in developing countries, inasmuch as it is the long-term effects of policies that are the most significant for growth and development. Furthermore, although it is indeed true that we are ''all dead in the long run,'' when the long run is defined as sufficiently long, the long run in economic analysis is not always defined in terms of decades, or even years. The long run in some industries, such as mining of hard minerals, may be as long as 10 years; in commercial chicken farming in the United States, the long run may be defined in terms of *months*, for that is how long it takes for new firms to enter and exit the business in responses to changes in poultry prices.

In any case, the distinction between short and long run is among the most fundamental in economic analysis. Not a small share of the unintended, and usually perverse, effects of economic policies are traceable to failure to recognize that the short-term results of policies may be very different from the long-term results. The **short run** is defined as a period of time in which both capital and labor resources are locked into their present uses. The **long run** is defined as a period of time sufficiently long to allow economic agents (including resource owners) to adjust to changed circumstances, including economic policy changes that affect the returns to capital and labor. In the long run, resources may enter (or leave) an activity in response to higher (or lower) returns. Both capital and labor, then, tend to be much more *mobile* in the long run.

It is generally recognized that capital is particularly mobile across sectors of a given economy in the long run, even when highly immobile in the short run. For example, the enactment of price controls on wheat in 1991 ordinarily will not lead to a movement of capital from wheat farming in 1991 (the short run) even if low, controlled prices result in negative profits in 1991. But if the controls are extended through 1993, we would then expect some proportion of capital invested in wheat farming to have left. The longer such a policy remains in place, the more capital will tend to flow to other domestic activities not subject to price controls.

But what of the mobility of capital across national boundaries? The degree to which capital is **internationally mobile** is a topic of considerable debate and has a profound bearing on possibilities for success in all economic policies in any given country, particularly so for these geared toward mobilization of savings. This is most apparent in the case of private foreign savings. Private capital abroad, whether it arrives in the form of direct foreign investment or borrowings from foreign banks, is obviously *inwardly* mobile, from the LDC perspective. Foreign-source capital is also clearly outwardly mobile in the long run: foreign debts are eventually repaid by most countries, on the basis of prearranged schedules, and dividends on foreign equity investment return capital to overseas investors when direct investments turn out to be profitable.

International capital mobility, however, is a two-way street. Domestic saving in LDCs, like domestic saving in wealthy countries, may be highly mobile internationally as well, both in the short and in the long run. The degree of short-run outward mobility is exemplified by such episodes of massive capital flight as plagued Mexico in 1981 to 1982, and Indonesia in 1983 and early 1986, just prior to expected major currency devaluations in each country. In Indonesia in 1986, short-term capital flight reached nearly $100 million per *week* in a two-month period. Longer-term outward mobility is illustrated by the sizable outward migration of capital in Hong Kong in 1983 through 1985 and in the Philippines in 1985 and 1986. In the former, capital departed in response to uncertainties surrounding the 1982 announcement by the British of their plans to return the colony to Chinese sovereignty in 1997. In the latter, wealthy Filipinos sent capital abroad in large amounts as a hedge against the possibility of the assumption of political power by opponents of the Marcos government.

A high degree of international capital mobility, then, can be both a blessing and a curse for LDCs. Inward mobility expands opportunities for finance of domestic investment by foreign savings. But high *outward* mobility constrains the effectiveness of several policies intended to expand domestic savings mobilization. For example, in the short run, enactment of higher income taxes on corporations may allow a higher government savings. But if capital is internationally mobile, the long-run result may well be to encourage domestic, as well as foreign, capital owners to dispatch their funds to other countries to restore the rate of return prevailing before the taxes were increased.

Evidence of International Capital Mobility

289

INTERNATIONAL
MOBILITY OF
CAPITAL AND
DOMESTIC
SAVING
MOBILIZATION

In the distant as well as the more recent past, policymakers and economists have tended to overlook the **domestic** policy implications of international capital mobility. One reason for this oversight has been the widespread existence of domestic controls on international capital movements and an equally widespread view that these controls were effective. It is true that official controls (both explicit and implicit) on capital flows abound in the world economy, particularly among LDCs. For example, in the five-year period 1978 to 1982, explicit controls on the international movement of capital existed in 72 percent of the 149 countries that are members of the International Monetary Fund (IMF).[14] Furthermore, even in those countries that employ no explicit capital controls, *implicit* controls may hinder the international mobility of capital. These include institutional restrictions that act as barriers to investments outside the domestic economy. In the United States, examples include laws that prevent savings institutions from investing in real estate abroad, and state government rules on pension funds that preclude such institutions from investing in overseas assets. Most developing countries have adopted similar regulations for the portfolios of their financial institutions.

The pervasiveness of controls on international capital movements would seem to indicate that international capital mobility may be quite limited in both the short and the long run. There are, however, considerations that suggest otherwise. First, the number of nations having explicit controls on capital movements has been diminishing. Indonesia, for example, abandoned all official foreign exchange controls in 1970. Britain followed suit in 1979, as did France in 1986. With the implosion of communism in 1989 to 1990, several Eastern and Central European countries began to move to relax exchange restrictions. Second, controls may be evaded in whole or in part. There is no empirical evidence that capital controls are administered with anything close to 100 percent effectiveness, in either developed or developing countries, particularly in the latter.[15]

Third, there is a significant body of empirical evidence that suggests a fairly high degree of long-run international mobility of capital is sufficient to cause capital's real after-tax return to converge toward about 7.5 percent

14. Jeremy Grenwood and Kent Kimbrough, "Capital Controls and The World Economy," *Canadian Journal of Economics* 19, no. 2 (1986): 111–116.

15. Capital controls in such countries as Ghana (1963 to 1986) have been notoriously porous. Tight restrictions on the amount of dollars that could be removed from Ghana were easily evaded by several devices, including overinvoicing imports: the importer merely requests the exporter abroad to place a higher value on the goods than the true price. The exporter, on receipt of payment, merely deposits the excess in the importer's bank account in the exporter's country. Long-standing controls in Colombia before 1968, Argentina before 1979, India, and numerous other countries did not prevent the buildup of large resident-owned foreign currency holdings outside these countries in the past. Presumed stringency of capital controls did not prevent Indian multinational firms from exporting substantial capital while becoming significant foreign investors in Southeast Asia before 1975.

in both rich and poor countries.[16] The significance of this finding is that in the *absence* of moderate mobility, rates of return would be far higher in low-income countries, where capital is relatively scarce, than in high-income countries, where capital is relatively more abundant. Another 1985 study covered 115 countries, both developed and developing, and found significant evidence of a high degree of international capital mobility.[17]

In sum, although it is clear that capital is not perfectly mobile in or out of developing countries even in the long run, it is also clear that neither the design nor implementation of economic policies in LDCs may be based on the assumption that, given time, capital will not emigrate in response to policies that affect its return.[18]

16. Arnold Harberger, "Vignettes on the World Capital Market," *American Economic Review* 70, no. 2 (May 1980): 331–337.

17. Larry Summers, "Issues in National Savings Policy," National Bureau of Economic Research Working Paper No. 1710, Cambridge, Mass., September 1985.

18. For further discussion of the implications of the openness of economies and the growing international mobility of capital, see Joel Slemrod, "Tax Principles in an International Economy," in Michael Boskin and Charles E. McLure Jr., *World Tax Reform: Case Studies of Developed and Developing Economies* (San Francisco: ISC Press, 1990) Chap. 2.

Fiscal Policy

The next two chapters focus on two sets of government policy instruments that operate across all sectors of an economy: fiscal policy and financial policy. Both sets of instruments can play critical roles, for good and ill, in the mobilization of domestic saving. Moreover, both types of policies have far-reaching effects on income distribution, employment, efficiency and economic stability. In this chapter we focus on **fiscal policy,** which encompasses all measures pertaining to the level and structure of government revenues and expenditures. **Financial policy,** the subject of Chapter 13, includes not only monetary policy, but a wide variety of policy measures affecting the growth and allocation of financial assets in an economy.

As the terms are used in this book, **government revenues** consist of all tax and nontax revenues flowing to the government treasury, including surpluses of public enterprises owned by governments and domestic borrowing by the treasury. **Government expenditures** are defined as all outlays from the government budget, including those for current expenditures such as civil service salaries, maintenance, military costs, interest payments, and subsidies to cover losses by public enterprise, as well as capital expenditures such as outlays for the construction of irrigation canals, roads, and schools and for the purchase of nonmilitary equipment owned by government.

Fiscal policy operates through both the tax and expenditure sides of the government budget. The locus of decision making on fiscal policy in LDCs is typically split between two agencies: the Ministry of Finance (the Treasury Department) and the Ministry (or Board) of Planning. In most countries the Ministry of Finance is assigned primary responsibility for the design and implementation of tax policy and for decisions concerning current government consumption expenditures. The Ministry of Planning typically holds sway on decisions concerning government capital expenditures. This separation of responsibilities over budget policy is so common, and of such long standing, that many economists and policymakers tend to reserve the term "fiscal policy" for that which is done by the Ministry of Finance, and use the term "development policy" for that which is under the ultimate control of the Ministry of Planning. This book accepts this convention, with reservations. The present chapter focuses primarily on those aspects of fiscal policy which deal with government consumption expenditures and taxation. Criteria for decision making on public capital expenditures were considered in Chapter 6. But the distinction between public capital and consumption spending is essentially an arbitrary one, both in theory and in practice.

THE GOVERNMENT BUDGET: GENERAL CONSIDERATIONS

Much of economic policy operates through the tax and expenditure sides of the government budget. To be sure, many government activities have an importance all out of proportion to their relative significance in the overall government budget. This is particularly true for the conduct of financial policy (discussed in the next chapter); government regulation of competition, trade, and investment; and operations of public enterprises (except in countries where public enterprises receive heavy subsidies from the government budget). In any case, in this chapter, the term "public sector" refers only to that part of government operations reflected in the expenditure side of the budget.

All societies, from those organized under *laissez faire* principles to those under socialism, require a public sector, simply because even under the best of conditions, the market mechanism cannot perform all economic functions desired by households. Because of *public goods* and other types of *market failures* discussed at the beginning of Chapter 5, the market alone cannot satisfy all consumer wants, even when societies have a strong preference for decentralized decision making. For private goods, such as trousers or frankfurters, the signals provided by unfettered competitive market mechanisms guide producers to satisfy consumer demand efficiently. For pure public goods, the market fails entirely. There are a few examples of pure public goods; national defense and lighthouses are generally cited as illustrations. The term "public good" refers to a good or service that exhibits two traits: *nonrival* consumption and *nonexcludability*.

In nonrival consumption, one person's use of a good does not reduce the benefits available to others. That being the case, no one has any incentive to offer to pay for the good: if it is available to one, it is available to all. Nonexcludability means that it is either impossible, or prohibitively expensive, to exclude anyone from the benefits once the good is available. In either case, the private market cannot provide the good; market failure is total. For other public goods the characteristics of nonrival consumption and nonexcludability are present but less-pronounced and the market can function only in an inefficient way. Examples include vaccination against contagious diseases, primary education, police protection, and mosquito abatement. Therefore, it is evident that the appropriate role of the public sector is, to a significant degree, a technical issue. Extension of the public sector beyond that required to provide public goods and to correct for other market failures is an ideological issue, to be settled through a political process. Most countries—industrial and developing—have extended the size of the public sector well beyond that required for technical reasons, to include income redistribution and the public ownership and operation of airlines, shipping, utilities, manufacturing enterprises, and banks.

GOVERNMENT EXPENDITURES

In the late 1800s, the German political theorist Adolph Wagner propounded his famous *law of expanding state activity*. The thrust of Wagner's law was that the relative size of the public sector in the economy has an inherent tendency to grow as per-capita income increases. Although few fiscal economists accept Wagner's law without several qualifications, it is nevertheless true that poor countries do have smaller public sectors than rich ones, when size of the public sector is measured as the ratio of government expenditure to GDP. As may be noted from the sample of countries listed in Table 12–1, the overall proportion rises steadily with per-capita income, from about 24 percent in the lowest income LDCs to 40 percent in the high-income industrial market economies.

TABLE 12–1 Government Expenditures as Percent of GNP, by Function,[a] 1988 (central government only)

Spending category	Low-income countries[b]	Lower-middle-income countries[c]	Upper-middle-income countries[d]	OECD countries[e]
Military spending	1.16[f]	3.90	7.06	2.63
Education	2.01	4.20	2.65	3.48
Health	0.97	1.95	1.38	3.80
Housing and social security	1.28	3.64[g]	6.98	15.31
Economic services	6.55[h]	5.03	5.55	4.75
Other	11.03	9.80	9.13	10.66
Total spending	24.31	28.35	30.40	40.19

[a] The figures are simple averages of the data for countries listed in footnotes b to e.
[b] Includes Ethiopia, Malawi, Nepal, Burikina faso, Mali, Uganda, Nigeria, Zambia, India, Pakistan, Kenya, Togo, Ghana, Sri Lanka, Indonesia, and Myanmar.
[c] Includes Bolivia, Philippines, Yemen Arab Republic, Zimbabwe, Papua New Guinea, Morocco, El Salvador, Thailand, Botswana, Tunisia, Turkey, Peru, Jordan, Chile, Syria, Costa Rica, Mexico, Mauritius, Panama, and Brazil.
[d] Includes Hungary, Uruguay, Argentina, Yugoslavia, Venezuela, South Korea, Portugal, and Oman.
[e] Includes Ireland, New Zealand, Australia, United Kingdom, Italy, Belgium, Netherlands, Austria, Canada, Denmark, West Germany, Finland, Sweden, United States, and Norway.
[f] Does not include Ethiopia.
[g] Does not include Peru.
[h] Does not include Indonesia.
Source: World Bank, *World Development Indicators 1990*, Table 11.

All categories of central government spending except economic services tend to rise with per-capita income, but those for health, housing, and social security grow at the most rapid rates, as may be seen in Table 12–1. Much of the differential between high-income OECD nations and middle-income countries is due to much higher levels of government spending on housing and social security in the former. Excluding these outlays, the share of central government spending in GDP for all countries is about 25 percent. Defense spending as a percentage of GDP is only marginally higher in the richest nations than in the poorest, and central governments in the wealthiest countries appear to spend a lower proportion of GDP on education than in lower-middle-income LDCs. Note, however, that in nations with a federal structure such as the United States and Canada, most government spending on education is done by subnational levels of government (states and localities) and therefore is not included in the figures in Table 12–1.

Hundreds of books and articles have been written on the reasons for differences in government expenditure across nations and through time. The results of the studies often conflict. Although associated with income growth, these differences do not seem to be related in any systematic way to population growth, but may be strongly influenced by other demographic factors such as urbanization.

Expenditure Policies and Public Saving

The effects of government capital spending on growth were long viewed as unambiguously positive. Critics of capital fundamentalism have succeeded in demonstrating than not all public investment has contributed to growth, much less to development. But there is still a pervasive belief that public investment should have a higher priority than recurrent outlays, which are still widely considered to be unproductive. Recurrent costs of development programs are by convention labeled as government consumption; this implies that outlays for such purposes do not increase productive capacity. Yet although most governments focus their attention on new investments, they often do not make adequate provision for the recurrent operational and maintenance costs of previous investments. This gives rise to wasteful underutilization of public-sector capital, and in some cases to its rapid decay.

These observations notwithstanding, it is also true that in many countries there may be some scope for expanding public savings by curbing growth of several types of recurrent expenditure: the Please effect, discussed in the last chapter, does have empirical support. We will examine the main categories of recurrent, or "consumption," expenditures of government to determine how wide this scope may be.

For many countries, the five most significant categories of recurrent expenditure are: (1) outlays for wages and salaries of civil servants and the military; (2) outlays on nondurable goods and services, including those for public-sector employees, maintenance, and all spending on military equipment; (3) interest payments on the government debt; (4) transfers to subnational government; and (5) subsidies and other transfers to individuals.

Services and Nondurable Goods

In poor LDCs, services and nondurable goods typically account for between half and three-quarters of total recurrent expenditure, as illustrated in Table 12–2. The three principal items are: (1) salaries and benefits for civil servants and the military, (2) outlays on maintenance and repair, and (3) other military spending. In most developing countries, salaries and benefits account for more than half of total expenditures for goods and services.

The stereotypical image of public-sector bureaucracies in LDCs is one of bloated **payrolls** and inefficient, corrupt, even indolent performance. The evidence for this view is essentially anecdotal, not systematic; reliable

TABLE 12–2 Government Consumption (Recurrent) Expenditure by Type as a Percentage of Total Current Spending in Selected Developing Countries, 1982–89[a]

	Wages and salaries	Other purchases of goods and services	Interest payments on public debt	Transfers to subnational government	Subsidies and other transfers
Low-income countries					
Ethiopia 1987[b]	42	42	8	na	8
Ghana 1988	48	29	13	na	11
India 1988[b]	14	18	22	28	19
Indonesia 1988	20	11	22	15	32
Nigeria 1987[b]	8	5	72	0	11
Pakistan 1986	5	59	18	13	4
Sri Lanka 1988	22	23	27	2	26
Sudan 1982	13	35	9	na	43
Tanzania 1985	20	40	13	na	27
Zaire 1983	31	40	16	8	5
Zambia 1982	38	30	8	0	19
Lower-middle- income countries					
Bolivia 1986	40	24	6	0	30
Brazil 1987	9	10	38	16	27
Chile 1988[b]	17	11	11	na	61
Colombia 1984	64	16	2	1	12
Egypt 1987[b]	25	31	13	na	31
Malaysia 1987[b]	36	20	28	5	11
Morocco 1987	46	18	21	na	15
Peru 1987[b]	——— 62 ———		14	0	23
Syria 1981	37	38	——— 25 ———		
Thailand 1988	38	33	20	2	7
Turkey 1988	31	13	19	na	38
Upper-middle- income countries					
Argentina 1987	19	8	9	24	40
South Korea 1989[b]	16	31	6	30	17

[a] Rows may not add up to 100 due to rounding.
[b] Figures are all or in part provisional.
na indicates that figures for "transfers to subnational government" are not available; in such cases, the figures listed under "Subsidies and other transfers" include all transfers.
Source: International Monetary Fund, *Government Financial Statistics Yearbook 1988* and *1989,* country tables.

international comparisons of civil service performance are almost non-existent. It is easy to accumulate anecdotes involving bureaucratic snafus, stupidities, corruption, and shortsightedness in both developing and developed societies. No firm judgments can be made on the extent of overstaffing of public agencies or overremuneration of officials or bureaucratic extravagance in LDCs relative to industrial countries: civil service payrolls in Massachusetts and New Jersey may be as bloated as in many developing countries. And although there are examples of gross venality and blatant use of political patronage in public-sector hiring in segments of the civil service systems of some developing countries (and many U.S. cities), there are also examples of first-rate professionalism and codes of conduct that may rival those found in industrial countries, as in the Indian and Malaysian civil service systems.

There may be some countries in which the salary bill for civil servants could be compressed sufficiently to augment government savings. But in others, like Bolivia, Peru, and Kenya, civil service salaries remain so low relative to those available in the private sector that it has been difficult to attract and hold the type of qualified public-sector managers, secretaries, and technicians essential for efficient government operation.

About the only safe generalization that can be made about civil service systems in LDCs is that they appear no more, or less, responsive to the socioeconomic changes that accompany development than any other group in society. In the 1950s it was almost impossible to discuss Latin American development without hearing repeated mention of the ''antidevelopmental'' effects of the famous *mordida* (bite) then commonly demanded by civil servants for doing what they should—or should not—be doing. It was commonly believed then that such behavior was the result of both low civil service salaries and unalterable cultural habits. In the early 1960s many Western and Korean social scientists felt that widespread corruption and inefficiency in the Korean government were immutable, owing both to practices that became acceptable under decades of Japanese occupation and to the influence of the Confucian ethic. One hears much less of such claims today, whether for Latin America or Korea. Although civil service reformers may not wish to use the Colombian or South Korean experience as models for other countries, there can be no mistaking the palpable verve and professionalism displayed by substantial numbers of civil servants in those countries by the 1980s, cultural habits notwithstanding.

If there is waste in government procurement in some areas, there are other areas where, for lack of funds, governments have been too miserly in appropriating funds, particularly with regard to **maintenance costs** for upkeep of the public-sector capital stock and for many vital operating expenses. The phenomenon is aptly characterized by Peter Heller:

In Colombia, new tarmac roads have suffered rapid and premature deterioration for lack of maintenance. Throughout West Africa, many new schools have opened without qualified teachers, educational materials, or equipment. Agricultural projects are often starved for extension workers, fertilizer, or seeds. In the Sahel, pastoral wells constructed for livestock projects have fallen into disrepair. In

Underfinancing of recurrent costs is pervasive across countries, including the United States, where items such as bridge maintenance have been long-postponed in many states. In LDCs, however, this pattern is exacerbated by the policies of aid donors, who strongly support capital projects, and as a matter of policy have been reluctant to support the recurrent costs of these projects. As a result, painfully accumulated public-sector capital stock tends to deteriorate rapidly until eventually requiring not incremental maintenance outlays but expensive new public works. Few countries are in a position to expand public savings by further compressing this category of recurrent expenditures.

The share of **military spending** in GDP differs by region, from a low of about 1.5 percent in Latin America to 7 percent in East Asia and 14 percent in the Middle East and North Africa.[2] For the countries included in Table 12–1, military spending rises from about 1 percent of GDP in the poorer nations to 7 percent in upper-middle-income countries. Except for the United States (5.6 percent), military spending in OECD countries tends to be lower than in middle-income LDCs.

Military spending is directed toward noneconomic goals, such as defense against external threats and internal instability. What is known about the impact of military spending on economic growth? Clearly, LDCs as well as OECD nations could expand public savings significantly by reducing military spending. Beyond that, the topic is controversial. Nevertheless, recent research[3] suggests that high military spending has many more negative effects on growth than positive ones, including the large contributions made in some nations by military spending to the debt crises (Chapter 14), the diversion of scarce resources from more productive civilian uses, and the effects of highly import-intensive military outlays on balance-of-payments problems.

Interest Payments

A major budgetary cost for many LDCs is interest on government debt: in countries included in Table 12–2 this item has recently ranged from an anomalous low of 2 percent in Columbia to 72 percent in Nigeria, with a central tendency of about 22 percent. With recurrent costs running about 80 percent of total government expenditures in most developing countries, interest costs are typically about 17 percent of the budget.

Interest obligations arise from past government budget deficits that were financed by internal or external borrowing or both. Interest payments on foreign borrowing grew rapidly in several LDCs from 1970 until 1984 when net capital inflows into many countries came to a halt (see Chapter 14). Because interest on government debt reflects past decisions about deficit

---

1. Peter Heller, "Underfinancing of Recurrent Development Costs," *Finance and Development* 16, no. 1 (March 1979): 38–41.
2. World Bank, *World Development Report 1988,* p. 106.
3. Anita Bhatia, "Military Expenditure and Economic Growth," Washington, D.C., World Bank, 1987.

finance and external borrowing, interest outlays are difficult to reduce, even if budgets are balanced and borrowing ceases. Interest payments can only be radically reduced in countries that default on their international debt liabilities, as in the case of Peru in the mid-eighties.

Subsidies

A variety of subsidies and other transfers account for substantial shares of recurrent expenditures in LDCs. In Table 12–2, the proportion is rarely less than 5 percent, more commonly about 20 percent, and in some cases as high as 40 percent and more. These figures include subsidies paid to offset deficits of state-owned enterprises.

Other than payments to cover state enterprise losses, recurrent budget subsidies take a variety of forms. The most common are those for consumption of food. Like Indonesia, Sri Lanka provided heavy subsidies on rice consumption from 1960 to 1979; Colombia has at various times given substantial subsidies to consumers of food, as have Egypt and India. The usual mechanism is to distribute price-controlled foods through state-owned entities and then to absorb losses in food distribution through budgetary transfers to these enterprises. During the 1970s most oil-producing countries generously subsidized the domestic use of refined oil products. Budgetary subsidies have also been common for rural electrification (Malaysia and Philippines), contraceptive devices (Indonesia), fertilizer (Indonesia and Sri Lanka), air travel (Pakistan, for travel between East and West Pakistan before 1971), bank interest payments on saving deposits (Indonesia), and urban bus services (Colombia, Indonesia, and others.)

In virtually all countries employing budgetary subsidies, the stated purpose has been income redistribution. For foods, especially grains, the argument appears plausible, even if the ultimate effect is not always what was intended. Heavy subsidies on fertilizer use in Indonesia had a high payoff in higher rice production and rural incomes. The role of many other subsidies in securing goals of income redistribution is less clear, however, as we shall see. Whatever the ultimate impact of budget subsidies on income distribution, it is clear that in many countries substantial sums are involved and that efforts to remove or reduce them meet with strong resistance virtually everywhere. Riots following the reduction of food subsidies have occurred in Sri Lanka, Egypt, Turkey, Zambia, and other countries, and social disturbance followed the reduction of gasoline subsidies in Indonesia, Colombia, and Thailand when these were coupled with increases in urban bus fares. It is clear why governments often view proposals to reduce subsidies with even more reservations than proposals for tax increases.

State-Owned Enterprises

A substantial portion of governmental outlays for subsidies and other transfers (Table 12–2) has been devoted to covering large deficits in state-owned enterprises (SOEs). Four decades ago, SOEs were not numerous in developing countries and were, with notable exceptions such as Turkey and Mexico, typically confined to a few sectors of their economies. Commonly, SOEs were limited to the so-called natural monopolies (decreasing-cost public utilities), monopoly production of sumptuary products such as liquor, beer and, tobacco and so-called basic necessities such as salt and matches.[4]

With independence after World War II, there was a rapid expansion in the number and relative importance of state enterprises in developing economies. This was particularly so in Africa, where more than half the SOEs were established between 1967 and 1980; in Tanzania alone, the number of state enterprises increased 10-fold from 1965 through 1985.[5] By 1980, SOEs were common, and often dominant, in manufacturing, construction, banking services, natural resource industries, and agriculture. Although SOEs were typically small-scale undertakings in most LDCs prior to 1950, many are now among the largest firms in their countries, and some are among the largest enterprises in their fields anywhere in the world.

The relative economic importance of state firms in developing countries is apparent from Table 12–3, which shows the percentage share of such firms in GDP for a number of non-oil-exporting LDCs. Major oil-exporting nations are excluded from the table (but not the discussion in subsequent sections) as outliers, given the extraordinarily high share of state oil companies in GDP and gross investment, especially in periods of high oil prices, such as 1974 to 1983 and 1989 to 1990. Although the share of the enterprises in GDP is, on the average, slightly lower than in industrial nations (9.6 percent), the average share in developing countries almost doubled during the 1970s, while that for industrial countries showed little change.[6] The average share of SOEs in total investment in developing countries however, was nearly $2\frac{1}{2}$ times that in industrial countries at the end of the 1980s. And although the share of state firms in GDP is markedly higher in Africa

TABLE 12–3 Output Shares of State-Owned Enterprises in Selected LDCs (latest year available)[a]

% share of SOEs in GDP	Country
0–3%	Nepal, Philippines, Guatemala
3.1–6%	Colombia, Thailand, Argentina, Paraguay, Bangladesh
6.1–10.0%	Benin, Botswana, Kenya, Liberia, Mali, Sierra Leone, Korea, Sri Lanka
10.1–15%	Ivory Coast, Tanzania, India, Taiwan, Bolivia, Chile
15.1–20%	Senegal
20.1–30%	Guinea, Tunisia
Above 30.1%	Zambia, Guyana

Average for Africa:	17.5%
Average for Asia:	8.0%
Average for Latin America:	6.6%

[a] Most observations are for the years 1978 through 1980. Others are primarily for 1976 and 1977.
Source: Adapted from R. P. Short, "The Role of Public Enterprises."

4. For a good discussion of some of the reasons for the development of large public enterprise sectors in developing nations see R. P. Short, "The Rule of Public Enterprises: An International Statistical Comparison," IMF, Dept. Memo 83 / 34, Washington, D.C., 1983.
5. World Bank, *World Development Report 1988.*
6. Short, "The Role of Public Enterprises," p. 1.

than Asia or Latin America, the relative share of developing country SOEs in gross investment approaches or exceeds one-quarter of GDP in virtually all regions.[7]

Deficits in the state enterprises averaged 4 percent of GDP across all developing countries in the mid-1970s. The problem worsened in the period 1981 to 1984, particularly in such countries as Brazil, Costa Rica, the Dominican Republic, Ecuador, Egypt, Philippines, Turkey, and Venezuela, where SOE deficits have been between 3 and 12 percent of GDP. In all of these nations, the rest of the public sector would have generated a fiscal surplus, excluding the net transfers to the state enterprises.[8]

Intergovernmental Transfers

Transfers from central to subnational governments are conventionally treated as recurrent expenditures, even though subnational governments (provinces, departments, counties, municipalities) may use the proceeds for capital formation such as construction of schools and hospitals. However, some countries, such as Indonesia, classify some transfers as capital spending and others as consumption, so international comparisons are difficult. Table 12–2 shows that transfers to subnational governments (including revenue sharing) constitute a sizable proportion of recurrent spending in a few countries (India, Indonesia, Korea) and a very small share in others (Bolivia, Sri Lanka, Thailand, Zaire). In a few cases subnational governments with small transfers have access to rich sources of revenue. This is true for Bolivia, where oil-producing provinces receive large oil royalties, and for Malaysia, where the state governments of Sabah and Sarawak earned substantial tax revenues from the export of tropical timber. In most unitary states, such as Chile, virtually all government affairs at all levels are run from the capital, and subnational units of government have few responsibilities to go with their limited sources of local revenue.

Elsewhere, including many federal countries, transfers of funds from the central government to subnational units is essential because the center has monopolized the most productive sources of tax revenue. In most cases, national governments impose income taxes because subnational governments lack the resources and skills required to administer such a complex tax, and could not do so effectively anyway because the income tax base can easily migrate within a country. Similarly, the major source of tax revenue for some developing countries—import duties—must necessarily remain a central government resource, since most countries have only a few serviceable ports.

We have just seen that there are few easy ways to reduce government recurrent expenditure to achieve higher public savings. The scope for doing so is often greatest in the areas of military spending and subsidies to cover deficits of state-owned enterprises. Together, these two categories of recurrent spending often account for 7 to 10 percent of GDP. Indeed, by

---

7. Malcolm Gillis, ''Tacit Taxes and Sub-Rosa Subsidies,'' *More Taxing Than Taxes,* Richard Bird, ed., forthcoming.

8. World Bank, *World Development Report 1988,* p. 171.

1990, many low- and middle-income nations, including Mexico and Poland, **301**
and many Francophone African countries have moved to "privatize" many TAX POLICY
AND PUBLIC
of their biggest money losers.[9] Interest payments, wages and salaries of SAVING
civil servants, and transfers to subnational governments are not easily
compressed in any country, particularly in very low income ones.

Despite the difficulty, LDC governments have in recent years increasingly squeezed expenditures and raised public saving, often as part of comprehensive adjustment programs to deal with inflation and fiscal crises. One
detailed study of 15 low- and middle-income nations revealed that real
reductions in recurrent spending, averaging 5 to 6 percent, were achieved
in the 1980s.[10] Such measures expand the scope for public saving, which is
primarily intended to finance public investment. However, in this sample
of 15 nations, public investment spending suffered even more from cutbacks: capital spending by government fell by more than 30 percent in real
terms.

TAX POLICY AND PUBLIC SAVING

For much of the postwar period, extending well into the 1970s, the most
widely prescribed measures to boost public saving were policies to raise
tax collections, especially increased tax rates and new taxes. This tendency
was reinforced by policies of aid donors and the advice of foreign experts,
who encouraged countries to generate high tax ratios, by making full use
of their taxable capacity. **Taxable capacity** was defined in terms of an index
comprised of per-capita income, mineral and oil exports, and the share of
foreign trade in GDP. High values for these variables suggested higher taxable capacity, either because of a higher margin of income over subsistence
(high per-capita income) or because of the accessibility of the tax base in
oil- and mineral-exporting economies and highly open economies. Exports
and imports are easily taxed because they pass through bottlenecks (ports),
where they are more easily tracked than are items in domestic trade.

By the mid-1980s, however, there was a wide consensus shared by
development specialists and government officials, that high tax ratios were
not necessarily a virtue, nor low tax ratios a vice, in mobilizing domestic
savings. Tax ratios reflect both opportunity and ideology. Sub-Saharan
African countries in particular tend to tax themselves more heavily relative
to their taxable capacities than do countries in Asia.[11] Ideology may be a
factor, but a high tax ratio may also reflect the fact that opportunities for
mobilizing other types of savings, especially private savings, are limited

9. Alfred H. Saulniers, "Improvement in Public Enterprises in Francophone Africa," in
Public Enterprises at the Crossroads, John Heath, ed. forthcoming.

10. Norman L. Hicks, "Expenditure Reductions in Developing Countries," Washington,
D.C., World Bank, 1988.

11. For the late 1970s, the average tax ratio for sub-Saharan African countries was 18.0
percent; that for Asia was but 15.0 percent. By 1985, tax revenues as a percent of GDP were
about 23 percent in Africa, 16 percent in East Asia, and only 12 percent in South Asia. (See
Vito Tanzi, "Quantitative Aspects of Tax Systems in Developing Countries," in David Newberry and Nicholas Stern, eds. *The Theory of Taxation for Developing Countries,* (London:
Oxford University Press, 1987), and World Bank, *World Development Report* 1988, p. 82.

because of poorly developed and organized financial systems. Latin American countries tend to dominate any list of countries with low tax effort. This may merely reflect the relatively greater ease with which private savings can be mobilized through the financial system in Latin America (see Chapter 13). Since 1945, there have been extended periods of robust growth of organized financial markets in many Latin American countries, particularly in Mexico, Brazil, Argentina, and Chile, and more recently in Colombia and Venezuela.

Tax measures can be used to expand public saving, or to shrink a destabilizing government deficit, only if the Please effect, discussed in Chapter 11, is weak or absent. And even when the government's marginal propensity to consume is significantly less than 1, there is no guarantee that the higher public saving made possible by higher tax revenues will result in an appreciable expansion of *overall* national saving; as shown later in this chapter, some part of any higher taxes will come out of private saving.

Where the Please effect is not a concern, then a number of tax measures are available for increasing public saving or reducing destabilizing deficits. These include: (1) periodic increases in rates imposed under existing taxes; (2) enactment of new taxes to tap previously unutilized sources of revenue; (3) improvements in tax administration that allow greater collection under existing taxes at present tax rates, by reducing tax avoidance and evasion; and (4) major reform of the entire tax structure, involving elements of options 1, 2, and 3. For many countries options 1 and 2 offer only slight hopes for increased collections. Options 3 and 4 are perhaps the most difficult to implement, but if feasible, are much more likely to achieve the desired results.

Recall from Table 11–5 that the share of taxes in GNP in high-income nations (per capita income above $6,000), at nearly 25 percent, tends to be about two-thirds more than in developing countries. Table 12–4 gives the share of each broad type of tax in overall government tax revenue for 1975 and 1985. There, it may be seen that the major differences in the composition of tax collections between industrial and developing countries lie in two categories of taxation. The share of foreign-trade taxes, primarily import duties, was roughly 9 to 20 times greater in the developing countries than in industrial countries in 1985. On the other hand, the share of social security and property taxes is much higher in industrial countries: more than 10 times greater than in low-income countries and $2\frac{1}{2}$ times greater than in middle-income countries. Domestic income taxes furnish a somewhat higher share of total revenues in industrial nations, whereas the relative share of commodity (sales and excise) taxes is not appreciably different. Reasons for these similarities and differences are provided in the following sections.

Taxes on International Trade

Trade taxes furnish less than 1 percent of tax revenues in the United States. Although reliance on taxes on foreign trade has diminished in recent years, particularly in middle-income countries, tax revenue structures in developing countries have historically depended heavily on import duties. Many

TABLE 12–4   Composition of Tax Systems by Major Type of Tax: Developing and Industrial Nations, 1975 and 1985

Type of tax[a]	Tax category as % of total tax collection[g]	
	1975	1985
Taxes on international trade[b]		
Low-income nations[c]	36.6	36.5
Middle-income nations[d]	24.2	18.3
Industrial nations[e]	4.0	1.6
Domestic income taxes (Personal and Corporate)		
Low-income nations	28.3	25.7
Middle-income nations	30.4	32.3
Industrial nations	34.9	35.3
Social security and property taxes		
Low-income nations	3.1	2.7
Middle-income nations	14.6	13.8
Industrial nations[f]	31.5	32.4
Domestic commodity taxes (Sales and Excises)		
Low-income nations	28.0	32.1
Middle-income nations	26.6	31.0
Industrial nations	28.5	29.4

[a] Central government only.
[b] "Taxes on International Trade" include import and export taxes.
[c] For low-income LDCs, import taxes are roughly 5 times more important than export taxes.
[d] For middle-income LDCs, import taxes are about 12 times more important than export taxes.
[e] Export taxes are virtually nonexistent in industrial countries.
[f] This category of tax is, for industrial nations, dominated heavily by social security taxes.
[g] Totals for each group of nations do not add to 100% owing to the omission of several minor types of tax not widely used across countries, e.g., stamp taxes, travel taxes, etc.
    Source: Adapted from J. F. Linn and D. L. Wetzel, "Public Finance, Trade and Development," WPS #181, Washington, D.C., World Bank, 1989.

low-income nations remain markedly dependent upon import duties. This is particularly so for countries like Afghanistan, Sierra Leone, Gambia, Uganda, Rwanda, Sudan, Togo, and Yemen, where at least half of total government revenue has long come from taxes on imports. Dependence on import duties is much less marked in middle-income countries, which have developed alternative sources of tax revenue.

For most countries attempts to raise further revenues through higher duties is infeasible and undesirable on economic grounds. Higher import duties intensify the incentive for smuggling or evading tariffs. Various studies have shown that for countries with already high duty rates, the incentive to smuggle increases disproportionately with further increases, so that a 10 percent rise in duty rates can result in an increase in smuggling activity by more than 10 percent, as illustrated by the boxed example of Colombia. And in mountainous countries such as Afghanistan and Bolivia or archipelago nations such as Indonesia and the Philippines borders are especially porous to smuggled imports.

Tax Rates and Smuggling: Colombia

In Colombia before 1969, when the import duty rate on cigarettes was over 100 percent, it was virtually impossible to purchase duty-paid cigarettes.

At such high rates import duty collections on cigarettes were nil and the market was flooded with smuggled foreign brands. In 1969 the duty rate was reduced to 30 percent. Cigarette smuggling on the poorly policed Caribbean coast of that country continued, but duty-paid packages began to appear in the mountainous interior, and duty collections on this product soared. Smuggling profits possible under a 30 percent duty were no longer high enough to compensate smugglers for the risks of arrest. Similar phenomena have been observed in Indonesia, Bolivia, and elsewhere.

Reliance on import duties for additional revenues may be infeasible for another reason. Except in open economies such as South Korea, Singapore, and Malaysia, the typical structure of import duties in developing countries is, as explained in greater detail in Chapter 16, heavily cascaded: the highest rates of duty in virtually all countries are imposed on consumer durable goods, particularly luxury goods (appliances, cameras, and so on), lower rates are applied on such intermediate goods as cement and leather, and the lowest duty rates are put on capital goods and imported items viewed as basic necessities (food, grains, fish, kerosene). When countries have sought additional revenues from tariffs, consumer goods already subject to high tariffs have been taxed even higher. Higher rates on necessities were considered inadvisable for equity reasons, and higher rates on capital goods and intermediate goods were deemed unacceptable because it was believed that this would retard industrialization programs. But the enactment of higher duties on consumer goods, particularly luxury consumer goods, generally did not produce higher revenue. The reason is simple: the price elasticity of demand is not zero for any consumer good, and for many already subject to very high duties, price elasticity is relatively high, in some cases -2.0 or more. For an import already subject to a 150 percent duty, such as stereos, and with a demand price elasticity of -2.0, a 10 percent increase in duty rates would actually decrease tax revenue on this item by about 2 percent.[12]

Export taxes are constitutionally prohibited in the United States and are extremely rare in other industrial countries. But export taxes are not uncommon in LDCs, particularly in tropical Africa and Southeast Asia. Taxes are ordinarily imposed on exports of raw materials such as timber (Ivory Coast and Liberia), tin (Malaysia), jute (Pakistan), and diamonds (Botswana) and on foodstuffs such as coffee (Colombia), peanuts (the Gambia and Senegal), cocoa (Ghana), and tea (Sri Lanka).

Twenty developing countries relied on export taxes for more than 10 percent of total tax revenue in the early 1980s, but in only seven countries,

---

12. This result comes from applying the formula

$$\frac{dR/R}{dt/t} = 1 + E\left(\frac{t}{1+t}\right),$$

where R = total duty collections on stereos
t = rate of duty
E = price elasticity of demand.

than 20 percent of revenue. Export taxes are often imposed in the belief
that they are paid by foreign consumers. That is, the taxes themselves are
thought to be exported to consumers abroad, along with the materials.
Chapter 19 shows, however, that the conditions necessary for exporting
taxes on exports to foreign consumers are rarely present.

Export taxes are also employed to promote nonrevenue goals, including
increased processing of raw materials within natural-resource-exporting
LDCs. This is done by imposing high rates of export tax on unprocessed
exports (cocoa beans or logs) and lower or zero rates of tax on processed
items fabricated from raw materials (plywood and tin ingot). In principle,
this use of export taxes should increase local value-added on natural-resource
exports and thereby generate greater employment and capital income for
the local economy. Unfortunately, in many cases the result has been that
a government gives up more in export-tax revenues than its country gains
in additional local value-added, particularly when processed raw materials
are exported tax free. One study documents several instances in Southeast
Asia and Africa where the additional value-added gained in heavily protected local processing of logs into plywood was typically less than half the
amount of export tax revenue that would have been collected had timber
been exported in the form of logs.[13]

Personal and Corporate Income Taxes

Harried ministers of finance, perceiving slack in personal and corporate
income taxes, often resort to rate increases in these taxes, with no change
in the tax base. The results are usually disappointing, particularly for the
personal income tax. Even in middle-income LDCs, only a very small proportion of the population is covered by the personal income tax: only 2
percent in the 1970s in Ghana, Peru, and almost all other developing countries, though higher in Burma, Kenya, and Turkey. In contrast, about half
the population in the United States filed income-tax returns in 1980. Thus,
few developing countries can rely heavily on the personal income tax for
revenues. Whereas the personal income tax accounts for just over two-
thirds of all federal tax in the United States, rarely does the personal income
tax account for as much as 10 percent of total central government revenues
in LDCs.

In Colombia, for instance, the personal income tax is as well developed
as in any LDC. Yet even though this tax is typically responsible for as
much as 15 to 18 percent of national government revenues, a large share of
it is paid by a small number of people: in the early 1970s the top 4 percent
of households paid two-thirds of the total tax.[14] In general, personal income
taxes are paid largely by urban elites. Not only are these groups usually

13. Robert Repetto and Malcolm Gillis, eds., *Public Policies and the Misuse of Forest
Resources* (New York: Cambridge University Press, 1988), "Conclusions," Chap. 10.

14. Malcolm Gillis and Charles E. McLure, Jr., "Taxation and Income Distribution: The
Colombia Tax Reform of 1974," *Journal of Development Economics* 5, no. 3 (September
1978): 237.

the most vocal politically, but over the years they have developed such a variety of devices for tax evasion and avoidance that rate increases stand little chance of raising additional revenues.

Rate increases for corporate taxes are not usually productive either. In only 16 of 82 developing countries did the corporation income tax account for more than 20 percent of total taxes in recent years. And in most of these countries, corporate tax collections usually originated with foreign natural-resource firms. Except for several middle-income countries such as Argentina, Korea, Taiwan, and Mexico, the corporate form of doing business covers but a small portion of the private sector. To be sure, most state-owned firms are corporations, but few such firms outside the natural-resources sector earn sizable taxable profits. Even fewer pay substantial income taxes.

Sales and Excise Taxes

A much more promising source of additional government revenue is indirect taxes on domestic transactions such as sales and excise taxes. **Sales taxes,** including **value-added taxes,** are broad-based consumption taxes imposed on all products except those specifically exempted, such as food, farm inputs, and medicine. **Excise taxes** are also taxes on consumption, but these levies are imposed only on specifically enumerated items—typically tobacco, alcoholic beverages, gambling, and motor fuel. Thirteen LDCs in the early 1980s relied on general sales taxes for more than 20 percent of revenues, while in fourteen, excises accounted for more than one-fifth of revenues.[15]

Virtually every developing country imposes some form of sales tax. In most the tax is not applied to retail sales because of the burdensome administrative requirements of collecting taxes from thousands of small retailers. In the past, as in Chile before 1970 and in some Indian states, the tax was imposed as a gross turnover tax collected at all levels of production and distribution, with harmful implications for efficiency, income distribution, and virtually every objective of tax policy. In developing countries, administrative problems are more tractable when the sales tax is confined to the manufacturing level: a much smaller number of firms is involved and the output of manufacturers is far more homogenous than sales of retailers or wholesalers. For these reasons many low-income countries have utilized either the single-stage or the value-added form of manufacturers' tax, usually exempting very small producers. This kind of sales tax, however, involves more economic distortions than either a wholesale or a retail tax, and for that reason, as well as for revenue motives, more and more middle-income LDCs have turned to taxes at the retail level.[16]

Increasingly, these taxes have taken the form of one or another variant of the value-added tax (VAT), widely seen as the most effective method of

15. Tanzi, "Quantitative Aspects of Tax Systems."
16. For a full discussion of the distortions involved in different forms of sales tax, see John Due and Raymond Mikesell, *Sales Taxation: State and Local Structure and Administration* (Baltimore: Johns Hopkins Press, 1983).

TABLE 12–5   Two Decades of Value-Added Taxation in Selected Developing Countries
1968–1988

Country	Year VAT first introduced	VAT revenues as % of GDP[c]	VAT revenues as % total tax revenue[c]	Basic VAT rate (%)	Other VAT rates (%)
1. Colombia	1966[a]	2.1	27.0	10	04, 6, 20, 35
2. Brazil	1967	6.5	28.7	17	
3. Uruguay	1968	4.6	23.5	20	12
4. Ecuador	1970	1.3	12.4	6	
5. Bolivia	1973[a]	na	na	10	
6. Chile	1975	8.1	37.4	20	0, 0.5, 33, 35, 50, 90
7. Costa Rica	1975	3.7	17.4	10	
8. Argentina	1875	1.9	14.9	18	5, 23
9. Nicaragua	1975	2.8	10.4	10	25
10. Honduras	1976	1.5	12.2	5	6
11. Panama	1977	1.9	9.1	5	
12. Korea	1977	4.0	25.1	10	0, 2, 3.5
13. Mexico	1978	3.2	19.7	15	0, 6, 20
14. Haiti	1982	1.1	11.5	10	
15. Peru	1982	4.3	31.2	6	
16. Guatemala	1983	1.6	24.8	7	
17. Dominican Republic	1984	0.9	9.9	6	
18. Madagascar	1984	3.2	26.4	15	
19. Turkey	1985	3.1	21.9	10	
20. Indonesia	1985[b]	2.9	16.7	10	
21. Niger	1986	na	na	25	15, 35
22. Portugal	1986	na	na	16	0, 8, 30
23. Taiwan	1986	na	na	5	
24. India	1986[b]	na	na	na	
25. Malawi	1988[b]	na	na	na	

[a] Introduced initially as a manufacturer-level VAT; later converted to a retail VAT.
[b] Manufacturers-level VAT.
[c] 1983 data, except Indonesia (1987).
na = not available.
Source: Adapted from Milka Casanegra-Janchter, "Problems of Administering a Value-Added Tax in Developing Countries," in *Value-Added Taxes in Developing Countries,* Malcolm Gillis, Gerry Sicat, and Carol Shoup, eds., forthcoming.

taxing consumption yet developed. Nearly 60 countries, including all members of the European Community (EC), have adapted the VAT since it was first adopted in its comprehensive retail form in Brazil in 1967.[17] Nearly 40 LDCs had adopted the tax by 1989, either to replace older, outdated forms of sales tax or to allow them to reduce reliance on harder-to-collect income and property taxes. Table 12–5 provides a chronology of adoption for the VAT in 25 selected LDCs, as well as the share of the VAT in GDP and in overall tax revenues.

Virtually all developing and industrial countries using the VAT have chosen to extend the tax through the retail level. A VAT extended through the retail level, particularly the types used in the overwhelming majority of nations, has a tax base that is virtually identical to a single stage of retail sales tax and, when imposed at the same rate as the latter tax, will generate

17. Carl Shoup, "Choosing Among Types of VAT," in *Value-Added Taxation in Developing Countries,* Malcolm Gillis, Carl Shoup, and Gerry Sicat, eds. (Washington: World Bank, 1990).

almost identical revenues. Both are indirect taxes on consumption.[18] A subsequent section discusses why the VAT has become the tax of choice in such a wide variety of nations.

Excise taxes might appear to represent an ideal source of additional tax revenue. They are typically imposed on sumptuary items having relatively inelastic demand. When the price elasticity of demand for such products is very low, (as for tobacco products) or is relatively low (as for alcoholic beverages) an increase in excise tax rates will induce little reduction in consumption of the taxed good. If price elasticity is as low s -0.2, as is not uncommon for cigarettes, then an additional 10 percent excise tax on this product would yield an 8 percent increase in tax revenues. Moreover, it is a hallowed theorem in optimal tax theory that taxes levied on items with inelastic demand and supply involve the smallest losses in economic efficiency or, what is the same thing, the least excess burden. **Excess burden** is defined as a loss in private welfare over and above the amount of government revenue collected from a tax.[19] Further, many agree—with much justification—that consumption of both tobacco and alcohol should be discouraged on health grounds.

All three considerations would seem to argue for heavy reliance on excise taxes in developing countries. However, it is unfortunately true that in addition to low price elasticity, items such as tobacco and alcoholic beverages have low income elasticity and thus tend to be more important in the budgets of low-income than high-income households. It follows that excise taxes on sumptuary items are decidedly regressive: poor people pay a higher proportion of their income in excise tax than do rich people—a serious matter when the sumptuary items constitute a substantial portion of spending by poor people, as in most developing countries. In Indonesia, for example, the poorest 20 percent of Javanese households spent about 5 percent of total income on heavily taxed cigarettes in 1976, as opposed to 3.5 percent of income for persons with income more than 5 times as high.

New Sources of Tax Revenues

If higher rates on existing taxes are unlikely to raise revenues much, a second option for increasing public savings is to tap entirely new sources of tax revenues. In many LDCs, whether by accident, design, or simply inertia, many sources of tax revenue may have been overlooked entirely. Many countries do not collect taxes on motor vehicle registrations; some do not utilize urban property taxes as a significant source of revenue; many do not apply corporation income taxes to the income of state-owned enterprises. Kenya, for example, does not seriously tax farm land, and a few

18. As used in virtually all LDCs and all industrial countries, the VAT is properly seen as an indirect tax on consumption: the base of the tax includes only consumption goods and services. A VAT can be structured such that the tax base is all income, but this tax is more difficult to administer and has been used in few nations (Argentina, Turkey). See Shoup, ''Choosing Among Types of VAT.''

19. For a further discussion of optimal taxation and excess burden, see Figure 12–1 and also Joseph Stiglitz, *Economics of the Public Sector* (New York: W. W. Norton & Company, 1985).

countries such as Indonesia until 1984 do not collect personal income taxes on salaries of civil servants.

The service sector furnishes other examples. Telephone service exists in all but the very poorest countries and is widespread in many, but is often untaxed. Some service establishments, such as restaurants and cabarets, are commonly taxed, but services of beauty shops, parking lots, tire-recap businesses, photofinishing firms, modern laundries, and foreign-travel agencies are among the more common items excluded from the tax base. Not only is taxation of this category of spending attractive from a revenue standpoint, but in LDCs such services typically face relatively income-elastic demand: because families with higher incomes purchase proportionately more of these items, they would tend to bear the greater burden of taxation, consistent with the equity objectives of fiscal policy. However, these services constitute a small fraction of consumption, even for upper-income groups, so their revenue potential is limited.

Changes in Tax Administration

A far more significant option for increasing tax revenues is to implement changes in tax administration that permit more taxes to be collected from existing tax sources, even at unchanged tax rates. The potential for increased revenues from such action is very large, and seldom realized, in virtually all developing countries. Shortages of well-trained tax administrators, excessively complex tax laws, light penalties for tax evasion, corruption, and outdated techniques of tax administration all combine to make tax evasion one of the most intractable problems of economic policy in LDCs.

Studies in Colombia indicate that in 1975 as many as 50 percent of small establishments did not file income tax returns and that underreporting of income among professionals (lawyers, doctors) was as high as 70 percent. Evasion of sales taxes during the same period was between 40 and 50 percent. Still other studies suggest that widespread corruption remained in the Colombian Tax Service in the mid-1970s even after a decade of intensive effort to curtail such practices: for every peso of bribes paid to tax assessors, the state lost about 20 pesos in tax revenue.[20] Similar, if not worse, patterns have been reported in other countries. For Bolivia in the period from 1964 to 1966, it has been estimated that about 60 percent of property income was not reported to the tax administration, while in Argentina in the same period taxpayers succeeded in hiding over 50 percent of total income.[21] In Jamaica the actual tax base in 1983 was less than two-thirds of the potential tax base.[22] For comparison, underreporting of total income

20. Jaime Vasquez and Caro and Gabriel Palomeques, "Reforma Tributaria: Brechas Entre Propositos, Normas y Realidades," Bogota, Tercer Seminaro de Economia Colombiana, Mayo de 1976.

21. Oliver Oldman and Daniel M. Holland, "Measuring Tax Evasion," paper presented at the Fifth Annual General Assembly of the Inter-American Center of Tax Administration, Rio de Janeiro, May 17, 1971, pp. 33–37.

22. J. Alm, R. Bahl, and M. Murray, "Tax Base Erosion in Developing Countries," *Natural Tax Journal* (forthcoming).

amounted to about 13 to 15 percent in the United States and Canada in the 1960s.

Such figures suggest that even modest efforts to collect a greater share of the taxes legally due might increase revenues by as much as 50 percent in some countries, without increasing tax rates. Nevertheless, there are few examples of even mild success in such undertakings, but many examples of unfulfilled expectations. Korea has been among the more successful. In 1966 it sought to increase tax collections by 40 percent through more effective enforcement alone. This ambitious target was not met, but in five years the Korean revenue service was able to reduce underreporting of nonagricultural personal income from 75 percent to slightly less than 50 percent. Virtually every serious study of the problem indicates that measures to curtail tax evasion in LDCs promise no quick fixes to the revenue problem. Rather, the capacity for limiting tax evasion, like many other socioeconomic phenomena observable in LDCs, tends to follow a pattern of secular improvement associated with economic development.

Fundamental Tax Reform

The final policy option available for increasing tax revenues is the most difficult to implement, but the most effective when it can be done. Fundamental tax reform requires junking old tax systems and replacing them with completely new tax laws and regulations. Implementing tax reform engenders enormous technical and informational, not to mention political, difficulties in all countries. In general, governments resist genuine efforts to reform the tax structure until fiscal crisis—in the form of massive budgetary deficits—threatens. Even during a fiscal crisis, it is difficult to mobilize a political consensus to allow unpopular tax measures to pass. Tax policies that protect favored groups and distort the allocation of resources did not just happen; more likely they were enacted at the behest of someone, ordinarily the privileged and the powerful.

It is probably true that tax reform is a topic about which more has been said, to less effect, than almost any topic in economic policy. This is no less true for the United States than for 50-odd LDCs where major tax reform efforts have been mounted since 1950. That the process is painful and slow is evident from the experience of several countries: in the United States the time lag between the birth of tax innovations (tax credit for child-care expenses, inflation proofing of the tax system) and their implementation is usually at least 15 years. If anything, the lag may be slightly shorter in developing countries.

In spite of the difficulties involved, some LDCs were able to carry through fundamental reforms in tax structure and administration before 1980. The classic example is that of Japan in the 1880s, when that society began its transformation to a modern industrial power. Korea implemented a major tax reform program in the early 1960s, as did Colombia (see following boxed example) and Chile in the 1970s. But also during the 1970s major tax reform efforts went for naught in many more countries: Bolivia, Ghana, Liberia, and Peru, among others.

In 1974 Colombia implemented one of the most ambitious tax reform programs undertaken. The Colombian experience illustrates both the potential payoffs and the difficulties involved in any serious tax reform effort.

In the last quarter of 1974 the new government of Alfonso Lopez Michelsen, in the midst of a national crisis, enacted a tax reform of very large magnitude. The reform, nearly a decade in the making, was engineered by an extraordinary group of officials as well-versed in fiscal economics as any treasury department in the world. The reform package was comprehensive: it involved nearly all tax sources. It was geared to all four fiscal policy objectives: growth, equity, stability, and efficiency. The instruments employed were well-suited to the objectives sought. The reform contained measures to increase progressivity that are still absent in tax systems of the United States and Canada. Numerous anomalies in the tax system that encouraged waste and inefficiency in the private sectors were introduced and were allowed to stand for a short time before they were struck down by the Colombian Supreme Court.

The reform's most striking initial achievements were its effects on tax-revenue growth and income distribution. In the first year following the reform, tax revenues grew by 45 percent, or more than twice the growth rate in revenues in the years prior to the reform. The early impact on income distribution was just as striking: in its first year the reform served to shift as much as 1.5 percent of GDP away from the top 20 percent of the income earners—a rare feat.

Many of the achievements of the reform effort proved short-lived, however. The reform initially caught most powerful economic interests with their defenses down. But by 1976 groups injured by the reform were able to have many key measures watered down or repealed, and taxpayers began to develop defense mechanisms against the new law and to exploit loopholes uncovered by the best legal minds in the country. Also, the reform effort paid far too little attention to the practical problems of implementation and to the strengthening of tax-collection procedures. Nevertheless many of the innovations introduced in 1974 survived relatively intact through 1980, and many revenue-hungry and equity-oriented tax officials in other Latin American countries viewed much of the 1974 reform package as a model worth detailed study.

Since 1980, however, the pace of tax reform has quickened notably, not only in developing and industrial nations, with many similarities in the various reform programs. Throughout much of the postwar period, tax systems were commonly fine-tuned in order to achieve a wide variety of nonrevenue objectives. In particular, governments in developed and developing nations alike commonly sought substantial income redistribution through the use of steeply progressive tax rates. Also, complex and largely inadministrable systems of tax incentives were widely used in attempts to redirect resources to priority economic sectors, to promote foreign investment, regional development, and even stock exchanges.

While fine-tuning tax systems may someday yield the desired results, this requires, at a minimum, strong machinery for tax administration and traditions of taxpayer compliance. Within developing countries, at least, there has been growing recognition that these conditions seldom prevail. Consequently, governments increasingly have turned away from reliance upon steeply progressive tax rates and complicated, costly tax incentive programs.

The 1980s saw a worldwide movement toward an entirely different type of tax system, with a shift toward vastly simplified taxes imposed at much flatter rates and with much broader bases[23], and with increasingly greater reliance upon consumption rather than income taxation. Recent tax reform programs in Bolivia, Chile, Colombia, India, Indonesia, Jamaica, and Malawi exemplify most of these trends.[24]

Two aspects of this worldwide movement in tax reform are especially salient. First, top marginal income tax rates of 60 to 70 percent were not uncommon among developed and developing nations from 1945 to 1979. But in the past decade, and particularly from 1985 through 1989, nation after nation has slashed the top marginal rate, often substantially. Table 12–6 shows that in just the five years after 1985, 35 developing nations reduced the top marginal rate of income tax, sometimes sharply, as in Bolivia, Brazil, Colombia, Costa Rica, Indonesia, Jamaica, Mexico, the Philip-

TABLE 12–6   Developing Countries Reducing Their Highest Rates of Income Tax 1985–1989[a]

	1985	1989		1985	1989
1. Argentina	45	35	18. Nigeria	70	55
2. Bangladesh	60	50	19. Pakistan	60	45
3. Barbados	60	50	20. Papua New Guinea	50	45
4. Bolivia	30	10	21. Peru	50	45
5. Botswana	60	50	22. Philippines	60	35
6. Brazil	60	25	23. Senegal	65	60
7. Chile	56	50	24. Singapore	40	33
8. Colombia	49	30	25. South Korea	70.1	63.7
9. Costa Rica	50	25	26. Sri Lanka	55	40
10. Dominica	55	45	27. Sudan	70	40
11. Ghana	60	55	28. Swaziland	50	45
12. Guatemala	48	34	29. Tanzania	95	55
13. India	61.9	50	30. Thailand	65	55
14. Indonesia (1984)	50	35	31. Trinidad and Tobago	70	45
15. Jamaica	57.5	33.3	32. Turkey	55	50
16. Kenya	65	50	33. Uganda	70	60
17. Mexico	55	40	34. Zambia	80	75
			35. Zimbabwe	61.1	60

Note: Among developing nations, only Lebanon raised the top rate of income tax between 1985 and 1989.
Source: Adapted from Bruce Barlett, Deputy Assistant Secretary, U.S. Treasury, "The Worldwide Tax Revolution."

23. Joseph A. Pechman, ed. *World Tax Reform: A Progress Report* (Washington, D.C.: Brookings Institute, 1988), Introduction, p. 13.

24. A number of these cases are discussed in Malcolm Gillis, ed. *Tax Reform in Developing Countries* (Durham, N.C.: Duke University Press, 1989).

pines, Sudan, and Tanzania. During the same period, 20 industrial nations ranging from Australia and Austria through the United Kingdom and the United States also cut the top rate sharply.[25]

In many of these cases, sharp cutbacks in the highest tax rates were accompanied by reforms involving a very substantial broadening of the income tax base, through the reduction of special tax incentives, abolition of tax shelters, and the like. This pattern was especially notable in Bolivia, Colombia, Indonesia, Jamaica, and Sri Lanka, so that even with a rate reduction, higher-income groups often ended up paying a higher proportion of total taxes than before.

Reasons for the worldwide shift toward lower tax rates on broader income tax bases are not difficult to find. First, income taxes imposed at high marginal rates have not been administrable, even in wealthy countries such as the United States. With high marginal tax rates, the incentive to evade taxes (through concealment of income) or avoid taxes (through hiring expensive legal talent to devise tax shelters) is very high. Second, the growing mobility of capital across international boundaries[26] has meant that the risk of capital flight from a particular country increases when that country's top rates of income tax exceed those prevailing in industrial nations, where tax rates have been falling. Finally, the operation of the income tax systems of such developed nations as the United States and Japan has placed downward pressure on the tax rates everywhere. This is because of the *foreign income tax credit,* wherein a country like the United States allows foreign income taxes to be credited (subtracted) from U.S. taxes due on income repatriated from abroad, but only up to the amount of tax payable at U.S. rates, which reduced from 50 to 28 percent in 1986. Finally, high marginal rates of income tax did not prove to be particularly efficacious in correcting severe inequalities in income distribution whether in rich or poor countries.

The second striking feature of recent tax reforms worldwide has been the steadily growing number of countries adopting the value-added tax. Several reasons account for the popularity of the VAT; the two most important are its reputation as a "money machine" and its administrative advantages, relative to other forms of sales taxes and to income taxes.[27]

The record of the VAT in generating large amounts of revenue quickly, and in a comparatively painless fashion, has given it a reputation as a money machine. Although this reputation stems largely from the experience in European countries, the record in LDCs does lend some support to the alleged revenue advantages of the VAT. In Indonesia, the 4 percent share of value-added tax in GDP in 1987 was nearly 3 times the share garnered in

25. Other than the four industrial nations listed above, these included Belgium, Canada, Denmark, Finland, France, Greece, Iceland, Ireland, Italy, Japan, New Zealand, Norway, Spain, Sweden, and Taiwan. Bruce Barlett, "The Worldwide Tax Revolution," *Wall Street Journal,* August 29, 1989.

26. For a cogent discussion of the implications for taxation of growing international mobility of financial and physical capital, see Dwight R. Lee and Richard B. McKenzie, "The International Political Economy of Declining Tax Rates," *Natural Tax Journal* 42, no. 2 (March 1989): 79–87.

27. For a full statement of these reasons, see Alan A. Tait, *Value-Added Tax* (Washington, D.C.: International Monetary Fund, 1988), Chap. 1.

1983 by the taxes it replaced. And for half of the 20 LDCs in Table 12–5, the share of VAT in GDP was higher than 3 percent; in all but one of these cases, the VAT constituted at least 20 percent of total tax revenue. Still, in four of the countries listed in Table 12–5, VAT revenues were less than 1½ percent of GDP. Notwithstanding the marked revenue success of the VAT in nations such as Brazil, Chile, and Indonesia, its reputation as a money machine appears to have been at least slightly overstated.

Twenty years ago, it was common to hear the claim that the VAT was largely self-administering. This is not so, but it is nevertheless true that the tax-credit type of VAT has three principal advantages over single-stage retail and nonretail sales taxes in limiting the scope for evasion. First, the VAT is self-policing to some extent because underpayment of the tax by a seller (except, of course, a retail firm) reduces the tax credits available to the buying firm. Even so, firms that are also subject to income taxes have incentives to suppress information on purchases and sales in order to avoid both the value added and income taxes. Also, this possible advantage of the VAT is diminished when evasion at the final (retail) stage of distribution is endemic. Second, cross-checking of invoices enables the tax administration to match invoices received by purchasers against those retained by sellers. The cross-check feature is a valuable aid in audit activities, but is no substitute for a true, systematic audit. Third, the fact that a large share of the VAT is collected prior to the retail level is an advantage particularly because in most LDCs an abundance of small-scale retail firms do not keep adequate records. In sum, the administrative advantages of the VAT are very real, if sometimes exaggerated by enthusiastic proponents of the VAT.[28]

TAXES AND PRIVATE INVESTMENT

Fiscal policy influences capital information in the private sector by affecting both the capacity and the incentive to save and by affecting incentives to invest in private projects. Taxes impinge more directly, but not necessarily more importantly, on both sets of incentives than do government expenditures, and will be our prime focus here.

Taxes and Private Saving

An increase in taxes on households will come partly out of consumption and partly out of savings, but the effects of taxes in reducing consumption and saving, respectively, is a matter of some dispute. Some cross-country studies of saving behavior suggest that increases in taxes in LDCs merely reduce private-sector consumption with little or no effect on saving. Other studies cited in Chapter 11 conclude that there is a high degree of substitutability between private savings and taxes. The truth probably lies slightly closer to the latter observation.

28. For a succinct summary of some of these issues, see John F. Due, "Some Unresolved Issues in Design and Implementation of Value-Added Taxes," *National Tax Journal*, 42, no. 4 (December 1990): 383–398.

Different taxes will have different impacts on the **capacity to save.** Although heavy sales taxes on highly price-elastic items of luxury consumption will curtail rates of growth of consumption for such items, heavy taxes on corporate income may come in large part at the expense of business savings that might have been plowed back into company investment. Where upper-income groups have a high propensity to consume, as has been often argued to hold for elites in many Latin American countries, increased taxes on them may have little impact on private savings. But where the same groups display strong savings propensities, as many argue is true for some ethnic minorities in Africa and Southeast Asia, higher taxes will have a relatively greater impact on saving. Further, heavier taxes on foreign natural resource firms will ordinarily have minimal negative impact on the availability of private domestic saving unless such firms have local joint-venture partners and cut their dividends to them in response to reduced profitability.

There is less uncertainty concerning the effects of different **forms** of taxes on **incentives to save,** but even here offsetting considerations are present. Taxes on consumption probably impinge less severely on private savings than do taxes on income in most developing societies. Perhaps the only exception to this statement arises when households save primarily for the later purchase of items subject to heavy consumption taxes. Some observers have argued that this motivation for saving is common in many low-income LDCs, where the nature of extended-family relationships makes household saving difficult. In some societies households with incomes above subsistence share resources with poorer households within the family group to help them meet subsistence needs. This pattern is characteristic of many African countries and of many parts of rural Asia. Under such circumstances household saving is largely devoted to the purchase of prized durable goods, such as transistor radios, bicycles, and sewing machines. In developed countries and middle-income LDCs these are typically viewed as consumer goods that are strong candidates for taxation. But it may well be that in some countries heavy taxation of such items also reduces incentives to save. It is even questionable whether products such as bicycles, sewing machines, and even small outboard motors should be viewed as consumer goods in low-income societies. Purchasing a bicycle or a small outboard may allow a rural family to market garden produce and fish more easily, whereas sewing machines are ordinarily bought to generate extra income for the household.

On balance, consumption-based taxes are probably more favorable for growth in private saving than are income-based taxes. Virtually all LDCs tax consumption through such indirect means as sales and excise taxes. These levies, although not inherently regressive, are often perceived to be so. This perception has led many tax reformers to argue for direct taxes on consumption. Under a direct consumption tax, taxpayers would annually report total consumption as well as income. Consumption below the level thought minimally necessary for an adequate living standard would be exempt, and any consumption above that level would be taxed at rates that rise progressively with total consumption. If such a levy could be administered, it would stimulate savings, since a household could reduce its tax liability by not spending. Direct consumption taxes have been seriously proposed for the United States (1977), Britain (1978), Sweden (1976), and Australia (1976). Among LDCs they have been proposed for India, Guyana, and Sri Lanka and actually enacted in India in the 1950s. The Indian experiment was short-lived, however, as the tax required information beyond the capacities of the tax administration at the time; it proved impossible to administer. But in the 1990s the administrative problems, both real and imaginary, of direct consumption taxes are not so great as to preclude their consideration in many developing and industrial countries.

Taxes can affect incentives to save in other ways. To the extent that national savings rates are responsive to the after-tax rate of return on savings (a question examined in the next chapter), heavy taxes on income from capital (dividends and interest) reduce the volume of private savings available for investment. Likewise, to the extent that people save mainly to finance retirement, social security taxes can also reduce private and aggregate national saving if the social security system is financed on a pay-as-you-go basis (that is, from current revenues), as in the United States, Colombia, the Philippines, and India. Under a social security system financed in this manner, it is argued that individuals covered by the system will reduce their saving in anticipation of receiving future social security benefits. But there will be no corresponding increase in public saving because the social security taxes paid by those covered now are not set aside and invested, but rather are used to pay benefits to those already retired.

This is an important point, because many proposals have been made—and some enacted—for social security systems in Asia and Latin America intended to help increase the national saving rate. The argument that social security systems can foster domestic savings is correct only under two circumstances, both relatively uncommon in LDCs. First, social security systems that operate as true retirement funds can clearly help mobilize capital resources—provided the funds are invested in projects with an adequate social marginal rate of return. Under such systems, called the **provident-fund approach,** the taxes collected from those covered are invested by the government in assets that earn returns; payments are made to retirees out of these returns rather than from taxes collected by those still working, as under the pay-as-you-go system. Under this approach, used in Chile, Singapore, and for some workers in Malaysia and a few other countries, any decline in the private savings of those paying social security taxes is largely offset by a concomitant rise in public savings. But the provident-fund approach is not widespread.

Even the pay-as-you-go system can increase national saving rates in its early years of operation if benefits are denied to those who retired before the system was implemented, and if social security tax rates are set high enough to cover benefit payments for the first decade or so. In the early years the number of workers covered is large relative to the number of retirees, so that the disbursement of benefits is small compared with the inflow of revenues. Therefore a government seeking new temporary sources of public saving could enact a pay-as-you-go system for social security that would serve this purpose for a few years. Sooner or later, however, such a system would tend to reduce overall domestic savings, though not neces-

sarily by as much as the social security taxes paid by covered workers.

Taxes and Capital Mobility

If a country's tax system operates to reduce private savings, it will tend to curtail private domestic investment. Beyond that effect, taxes can affect both the amount and allocation of private domestic investment undertaken out of any given volume of private capital available for investment.

We saw in Chapter 11 that in spite of exchange controls and similar restrictions, capital tends to be fairly mobile across international boundaries. If there are opportunities for earning returns abroad that promise higher after-tax returns than those available in a particular developing country, domestic capital will tend to flow to these opportunities. Of course, a critical factor determining after-tax returns in a given country is the nature of taxes on capital there. Suppose, for example, that capital owners in the Philippines can secure, on the average, before-tax returns equal to 15 percent of their investments and that capital income in that country is subject to a 50 percent tax. After-tax returns are then 7.5 percent. The same funds invested in well-developed capital markets in Hong Kong, where capital is less scarce, might obtain only a 12 percent return before taxes, but are taxed at only, say, 15 percent. The after-tax return in Hong Kong is therefore 10.2 percent. The difference of 2.7 percent in after-tax returns may be large enough to induce movement of Philippine savings to Hong Kong. In general, countries that attempt to impose substantially heavier taxes on capital income often experience outflows of domestic saving to countries employing lower tax rates on capital. This movement is quite distinct from the type of *capital flight* from developing to developed countries often observed in countries experiencing severe domestic political turmoil or exchange-rate uncertainties.

There is no shortage of low-tax foreign opportunities facing domestic savers in LDCs. *Tax havens* such as Panama and the Bahamas have been attractive to Latin American investors since the 1960s. Likewise, Hong Kong and Singapore financial markets draw substantial inflows of savings from other Asian countries. Increasingly, enterprises from countries such as India, with relatively high taxes on capital income, have become major investors in other developing countries where after-tax returns are higher than at home.

Most countries have recognized that capital is fairly mobile across national boundaries and have sought to keep taxes on capital income from reaching levels much above those prevailing worldwide. This is evident from an inspection of corporate income tax rates prevailing in most LDCs. In Latin America corporate tax rates are typically found in a band of from 25 to 40 percent, compared with 34 percent in the United States in 1990. In Southeast Asia corporate tax rates—other than those of Hong Kong—cluster in a narrow range of from 30 to 40 percent; the rate in Hong Kong is less than 20 percent.

Countries have sought to impede the outward mobility of capital through such devices as controls on movement of foreign exchange, imposition of domestic taxes on worldwide income of residents, and other devices. Flourishing business in tax-haven countries, coupled with very large investment holdings by LDC citizens in the United States, Switzerland, Hong Kong, and Singapore, are ample testament to the limited effectiveness of such controls.

Partly in order to stem capital outflow, and also to direct private investment into priority areas, such as basic industry, exports, or backward regions, many LDC governments selectively offer substantial tax incentives to domestic investors. The two main types of incentives are income tax holidays, wherein approved investments are exempted from income tax obligation for specified periods ranging from 3 to 10 years, and tax credits for investment, wherein a government allows an investor to subtract some portion of initial investment (usually 20 to 25 percent) from his income tax liabilities. On rare occasions these types of incentives for domestic investment have produced the desired results, but these devices suffer from a number of administrative and efficiency limitations. Because of these limitations, Indonesia in 1984 abolished all tax incentives and replaced them with the most effective tax incentive ever offered: lower tax rates for **all** firms.

INCOME DISTRIBUTION

As indicated in Chapter 4, a basic thrust of economic policy in many developing countries has been the mitigation of extreme income inequality. For decades developed and developing countries alike have sought to use the fiscal system, particularly taxation, to redress income inequalities generated by the operation of the private market. Social philosophers from John Stuart Mill and the eminent nineteenth-century Chilean historian Francisco Encina to John Rawls in the 1970s have sought to establish a philosophical basis for income redistribution, primarily through progressive taxes. Karl Marx also favored steeply progressive taxes in bourgeois societies, but for reasons other than income redistribution. Rather, in Marx's view, heavy taxes on capitalists were essential for speeding the decline of the capitalist state and its replacement by a socialist order.

There is no scientific basis for determining the optimal degree of income redistribution in any society. And across developing countries different views prevail as to the ideal distribution of income. But in virtually all countries the notion of *fiscal equity* permeates discussions of budgetary operations. In the overwhelming majority of countries fiscal equity is typically defined in terms of the impact of tax and expenditure policy on the distribution of economic well-being. Progressive taxes, those that bear more heavily on better-off citizens than on poor households, and expenditures whose benefits are concentrated on the least advantaged are viewed as more equitable than regressive taxes and expenditures.

On the tax side of the budget, the materialistic conception of equity requires that most taxes be based on **ability to pay.** Ability to pay can be measured by income, consumption, wealth, or some combination of all three. Clearly, individuals with higher incomes over their life span have a greater ability to pay taxes, quite apart from the moral question of whether they should do so. Indeed the redistributive impact of taxation is almost always expressed in terms of its effects on income. However, philosophers from the time of Hobbes have argued that consumption furnishes a better index of ability to pay than income; in this view tax obligations are best geared to what people take out of society (consume) rather than what they put into society (as measured by income).

In practice developing countries have relied heavily on these two measures of ability in fashioning tax systems. Personal and corporate income taxes employ income as the indicator; sales taxes and customs duties are indirect assessments of taxes on consumption. But the ability to pay is not the exclusive guide to the assessment of taxes in all countries. Religious and cultural values often provide other bases for establishing tax liability. Nevertheless most societies do largely define equity in taxation as requiring taxation on the basis of ability to pay, and this is commonly interpreted to mean progressivity. At a minimum, equity is usually assumed to require the avoidance of regressive taxes whenever possible. There are a number of tax instruments that have been employed to secure greater progressivity in principle, if not in practice; all suffer from limitations to one degree or another.

Personal Income Taxes

The most widely used device for securing greater progressivity has been steeply progressive rates under the personal income tax. In some countries in some periods, nominal or legal marginal income tax rates have reached very high levels, even for relatively low incomes. thus, for example, tax rates applicable to any income in excess of $1,000 in Indonesia in 1967 reached 75 percent, largely because tax rates were not indexed to rapid inflation; in Algeria in the 1960s all income in excess of $10,000 was subject to marginal tax rates of nearly 100 percent; Tanzania imposed top marginal rates of 95 percent as late as 1981.

Although in most LDCs marginal income tax rates are considerably lower than the examples above and, as apparent from Table 12–6, have been falling, some LDCs still attempt to impose rates in excess of 50 percent.[29] Countries such as Brazil, Colombia, Costa Rica, Mexico, Singapore, and Sri Lanka generally hold maximum marginal rates to 40 percent or slightly less, and the maximum income tax rate in Indonesia has been 35 percent since that country implemented tax reform in 1984.

29. Ten of the sixteen countries imposing income tax rates in excess of 50 percent in 1989 were in Africa, two were in Latin America, and the remainder were in Asia. Barlett, ''The Worldwide Tax Revolution.''

If the tax administration machinery functioned well, and if capital were immobile among countries, the pattern of actual tax payments of high-income taxpayers would resemble the legal, or theoretical, patterns described above. In fact taxes actually collected as a percent of income (**effective tax rates**) in most countries fall well short of theoretical liabilities for several reasons.

Faced with high income tax rates, taxpayers everywhere tend to react in three ways: (1) they evade taxes by concealing income, particularly capital income not subject to withholding arrangements; (2) they avoid taxes by altering economic behavior to reduce tax liability, whether by supplying fewer labor services, shipping capital to tax havens abroad, or hiring lawyers to find loopholes in the tax law; and (3) they bribe tax assessors to accept false returns.

For all of these reasons, the achievement of substantial income redistribution through progressive income taxes has proven difficult in all countries, including the United States and also the three Scandinavian nations where tax rates were long among the world's most progressive. Tax avoidance is the favored avenue for reducing tax liability in the United States, where use of the other methods can result in imprisonment. Indeed, heads of governments in both the United States (1971) and Sweden (1985) were found by the tax administration to have overstepped the bounds of propriety in avoiding taxes. But where tax enforcement is relatively weak, particularly where, as in virtually all LDCs, criminal penalties for evasion are absent and tax officials are deeply underpaid, tax evasion and bribery are more commonly utilized. The scope for substantial redistribution through the income tax is thus even more limited than in the United States or Sweden.

Notwithstanding these problems, a significant share of the income of the wealthiest members of society is caught in the income tax net in many developing countries. Revenues from personal income tax collections in countries such as Colombia, South Korea, and Chile have been as high as 15 percent of total taxes and in a few other countries have run between 5 and 10 percent of the total. In virtually all developing countries the entirety of such taxes is collected from the top 20 percent of the income distribution. This means, of course, that the very presence of an income tax, even one imposed at proportional rather than progressive rates, tends to reduce income inequality. Income taxes, together with taxes on luxury consumption, constitute about the only feasible means of approaching income redistribution goals through the tax side of the budget.

Taxes on Luxury Consumption

In view of the difficulties of securing a significant redistribution through income taxes, many countries have sought to employ heavy indirect taxes on luxury consumption as a means of enhancing the progressivity of the tax system. Efforts to achieve this goal usually center on internal indirect taxes, such as sales taxes, and on customs duties on imports, but not excises on tobacco and alcohol.

Several developing countries have found that, provided tax rates are kept to enforceable levels, high rates of internal indirect taxes on luxury goods and services, coupled with lower taxes on less income-elastic items, can contribute to greater progressivity in the tax system. For revenue purposes countries typically impose basic rates of sales tax on nonluxuries at between 4 and 8 percent of manufacturer's value. This is equivalent to retail taxes of between 2 and 4 percent because taxes imposed at this level exclude wholesale and retail margins. Food, except that consumed in restaurants, is almost always exempted from any sales tax intended to promote redistributive goals. In LDCs the exemption of food by itself renders most sales taxes at least faintly progressive, given the high proportion (up to 40 percent in many middle-income developing countries) of income of poor households spent on food. Sales taxes involving a limited number of luxury rates of between 20 and 30 percent at the manufacturer's level have been found to be workable in many LDCs, including Colombia, Chile, Taiwan, and Korea.

The redistributive potential of sales tax rates differentiated in this way is, however, limited by the same administrative and compliance constraints standing in the way of the heavier use of income taxation in LDCs. While sales taxes are not as difficult to administer as income taxes, they do not collect themselves. A manufacturers' sales tax system employing three or even four rates may be administratively feasible in most countries, even when the highest rate approaches 40 percent. Rates much higher than that, or reliance on a profusion of rates in an attempt to fine-tune the tax, lead to substantial incentives and opportunities for tax evasion. Jamaica had over 15 rates prior to 1986, and Chile had over 20 from 1960 to 1970. In recognition of these types of problems, Indonesia adopted a flat-rate manufacturers' tax in 1985: the tax applies at a rate of 10 percent on *all* manufactured items and all imports. The tax is nevertheless slightly progressive since it does not apply to items that do not go through a manufacturing process, including most foodstuffs consumed by low-income families.

Although the use of internal indirect taxes, such as sales taxes, can contribute to income redistribution goals without causing serious misallocation of resources, the same cannot be said for the use of customs duties. Sales taxes are imposed on all taxable goods without regard to national origin, including goods produced domestically as well as abroad. Tariffs apply only to imported goods. Virtually all countries, developed and developing, utilize customs duties to protect existing domestic industry. Developing countries in particular employ customs duties as the principal means of encouraging domestic industry to produce goods that were formerly imported. This strategy, called **import substitution,** is examined at length in Chapter 16.

Deliberate policies to encourage import substitution through the use of high protective tariffs might, under certain conditions, lead to results sought by policymakers. But accidental import substitution arises when tariffs are used for purposes other than protection, and this is unlikely to have positive results, except in rare instances. Many countries use high tariffs to achieve heavier taxation of luxury consumption. Often heavy tariffs are imposed on imported luxury items for which there is no intention of encouraging domestic production. Thus many Latin American and some Asian countries have levied customs tariffs of 100 to 150 percent of value on such appliances as electric knives, hair dryers, sporting goods, video-cassette recorders, and mechanical toys. For most countries these items are clearly highly income-elastic and are apt candidates for luxury taxation.

But efforts to tax luxuries through high customs duties leads to unin-tended—and almost irresistible—incentives for domestic production or assembly of such products. In virtually all countries save the very poorest, alert domestic and foreign entrepreneurs have been quick to seize on such opportunities. By the time local assembly operations are established, they can usually make a politically convincing case that the duties should be retained to enable local production to continue, even when value-added domestically is as low as 10 percent of the value of the product. Such oper-ations, if subject to any local sales taxes, usually succeed in being taxed at the basic tax rate, usually 5 to 10 percent. By relying on tariffs for luxury taxation, the government ultimately forgoes the revenues it previously col-lected from duties on luxury goods, as well as severely undermining the very aims of luxury taxation.

If, instead, higher luxury rates on imports are imposed under a sales tax collected on both imports and any domestic production that may develop, unintended import substitution can be avoided. The use of import tariffs for luxury taxation—indeed for any purpose other than providing protec-tion to domestic industry—is one illustration of the general problem of using one economic policy instrument (tariffs) to achieve more than one purpose (protection, luxury taxation, and revenues). Reliance on import duties for revenue purposes is subject to the same pitfalls just discussed: if it is desired to increase government revenues from imports, a 10 percent sales tax applied both to imports and any future domestic production will yield just as much revenue as a 10 percent import duty, without leading to accidental protec-tion.

Corporate Income and Property Taxes: The Incidence Problem

Income taxes on domestic corporations and property taxes are often men-tioned as possible methods for securing income redistribution through the budget. It is true that corporate income is ultimately received, through div-idends and capital gains, almost exclusively by the upper 5 to 10 percent of the income distribution. It is also true that ownership of wealth, which in many LDCs largely takes the form of land, tends to be even more concen-trated than income. But to a greater extent in developing than developed countries, efforts to secure significant fiscal redistribution through heavier taxes on domestic corporations and property are limited both by adminis-trative and economic realities.

Administrative problems bedevil efforts to collect income taxes from domestic firms to at least as great an extent as for income taxes on individ-uals. Hence, in many countries such as China and Pakistan, where corpo-rate taxes on local firms have been important, as much as two-thirds to three-fourths of nonoil corporate taxes flow from state-owned firms, not from private firms owned by high-income individuals. Taxes on land should be subject to less-severe administrative problems, since it is an asset that cannot be easily hidden. However, land valuation for tax purposes has proven difficult even in Canada and the United States; it is more difficult in developing countries. Other than Colombia, few LDCs have been able to assess property at anything approaching its true value.

Economic realities hinder efforts to achieve greater progressivity in the tax system through heavier use of corporate and land taxes, because of the tendency for taxation to unintentionally burden groups other than those directly taxed. This is the **incidence** problem. The incidence of a tax refers to its ultimate impact: it is not who actually pays the tax to the government, but those whose incomes are finally affected by the tax when all economic agents have adjusted in response to the tax. The point of incidence is not always the point of initial impact. Taxes on domestic corporations may reduce the incomes of capitalists, who in turn might shift their investment patterns to reduce taxation. The incomes of workers they employ and the prices charged to consumers may be affected as well. In the end taxes on land and improvement may not much reduce the incomes of landholders, but they may be reflected in higher prices charged to consumers. Ultimately, all taxes are paid by people, not by things such as corporations and property parcels.

The implications of incidence issues may be illuminated by a simple application of incidence analysis to the corporation income tax. Consider a profit-maximizing company that has no significant monopoly power in the domestic market. If taxes on the company's income are increased in 1992 then after-tax returns to its shareholders in 1992 will be reduced by the full amount of the tax. In the short term, incidence of the tax is clearly on shareholders. Since shareholders everywhere are concentrated in higher income groups, the tax will be progressive in the short run. If capital were immobile, unable to leave the corporate sector, the long-term incidence of the tax would also rest on shareholders and the tax would be progressive in the long run as well.

But in the long run capital can move out of the corporate sector. To the extent that capital is mobile domestically, but not internationally, the corporate tax will also be progressive in the long run. Returns on capital remaining in the corporate sector will be reduced by the tax. Untaxed capital owners employed outside the corporate sector will also suffer a reduction in returns, because movements of capital from the taxed corporate sector will drive down the rate of return in the nontaxed sector. Because the corporate tax reduces returns to capital throughout the economy, all capital owners suffer, including owners of housing assets, and, in a closed economy, the long-run incidence is again progressive.

However, no LDC is a completely closed economy; indeed, we saw in Chapter 11 that capital has in recent years become much more mobile internationally. To the extent that capital is mobile across national borders, and to the extent that higher returns are available in other countries, domestic capital will migrate to escape higher corporate taxes. But as capital leaves an economy, both new and replacement investment and, ultimately, output, will be curtailed, and the marginal productivity of workers will fall. Prices of items produced with domestic capital will therefore rise. In this way an increase in corporate taxes may be borne by domestic consumers, who pay higher prices for the reduced supply of corporate-sector goods. Similarly, domestic workers, whose incomes are reduced when production is curtailed, may bear a part of the burden of corporate tax.

Hence the corporate tax may be regressive (worsen the income distribution) in the long run. The degree of regressivity will depend on whether consumption by low-income groups is more or less capital-intensive, and on the relative position in the income distribution of workers losing their jobs or suffering declining real wages. In the end capital owners may suffer no significant decline in their incomes. Although there are other plausible conditions under which an increase in the corporation income tax may not result in greater relative burdens on capitalists, the scenario outlined above is sufficient to illustrate that often the intentions of redistributive tax policy may be thwarted by all the workings of the economy. Clearly, defending a **priori** assumptions that all taxes imposed on wealthy capital owners will ultimately be paid by them is difficult.

Limited Effects of Redistribution Policy

The foregoing discussion suggests that whereas some tax instruments may achieve income redistribution in LDCs, the opportunities for doing so are limited in most countries—a conclusion supported by a large number of empirical studies. With few exceptions these show that the inability to administer personal income taxes effectively, failure to utilize the limited opportunities for heavier taxes on luxury consumption, overreliance on revenue-productive but regressive excise taxes, and inclusion of food in sales taxes, all combine to reduce significantly the redistributive impact of LDC tax systems. By and large, LDC tax systems tend to produce a tax burden that is roughly proportional across income groups, with some tendency for progressivity at the very top of the income scale. As a result the very wealthy do pay a somewhat greater proportion of their income in taxes than the poor, but the poor still pay substantial taxes: at least 10 percent of their income in many cases studied (Argentina, urban Brazil, Colombia, Jamaica, and six others).[30] This is the predominant pattern even in countries, such as Colombia, Jamaica, Tanzania, and Chile before 1970, that have placed strong policy emphasis on the use of tax tools to reduce income inequality. One can only conclude that in the absence of such efforts, the after-tax distribution of income may have been even more unequal. This suggests that although difficult to implement and often disappointing in results, tax reforms intended to reduce income inequality are not futile exercises in LDCs, and they may serve the purpose of preventing taxes from making the poor worse off.

30. These Latin American studies have been summarized in Richard M. Bird and Luc Henry DeWulf, "Taxation and Income Distribution in Latin America:" A Critical View of Empirical Studies" *International Monetary Fund Staff Papers* 20, (November 1975):639–62. Results of studies on Indonesia and Jamaica may be found in Gillis, *Tax Reform*, Chaps. 4 and 5.

The limits of tax policy suggest that if the budget is to serve redistributive purposes, the primary emphasis must be on expenditure policy. Indeed where redistribution through expenditures has been a high priority of governments, the results have been generally encouraging. The effects of government expenditure on income distribution are even more difficult to measure than those of taxes. But both the qualitative and quantitative evidence available strongly indicate that in developing countries budget expenditures may transfer very substantial resources to lower-income households, in some cases as much as 50 percent of their income. And the pattern of benefits tends to be progressive: a much higher fraction of income goes to the poor households than to those in the upper reaches of the income distribution.

One study found that in Malaysia in the late 1960s the combined effect of taxes and recurrent government consumption expenditures was to transfer 5 percent of GNP from the two highest income classes to the two lowest income groups, with more than three-quarters of the transfer going to the poor. This figure understates the actual extent of the redistributive impact of expenditures since it does not include the effects of public investment, which was perhaps the most important tool of fiscal redistribution in Malaysia in 1968.[31] Another study found that in Indonesia in 1980 the tax system was only slightly progressive.[32] But the expenditure side of the budget, with its emphasis on food subsidies and primary education, markedly helped the poor; benefits from government expenditure were slightly more than 50 percent of the income of the poorest income group. Similarly, an exhaustive study of the net incidence of the Chilean budget for 1969 shows that although the tax system had virtually no effect on income distribution, government expenditures favored the poor: the lowest income groups received only about 7.5 percent of national income, but about 15 to 18 percent of the benefits from government expenditure.[33]

Obviously not all government expenditures are effective in reducing income inequality. Some, like interest payments on government debt, have the opposite effect because interest income is concentrated in upper-income groups. But it is not difficult to identify those categories of budget outlays that tend to have the most marked effects on the incomes of the poor. Public expenditures on primary, but not university, education tend strongly to reduce income inequality (Chapter 9). Government spending for public health programs, particularly water supply, sanitation, nutritional programs, and rural health clinics, also can have a clearly progressive impact (Chapter 10). Although many poor people live in huge cities such as Jakarta, Sao Paulo, Mexico City, Lagos, and Calcutta, in most developing countries most of the poorest people tend to live in rural areas and wealthy

31. Donald R. Snodgrass, "The Fiscal System of Malaysia as an Income Redistributor in West Malaysia," *Public Finance* 29, no. 1 (January 1972): 56–76.
32. Malcolm Gillis, "Micro and Macroeconomics of Tax Reform: Indonesia," *Journal of Development Economics* 19, no. 2 (1986): 42–46.
33. Alejandro Foxley, Eduardo Aninat, and J. P. Arellano, *Redistributive Efforts of Government Programs* (Elmsford, N.Y.: Pergamon Press, 1980), Chap. 6.

people tend to live in urban areas. Hence programs that reallocate government spending to rural areas (irrigation programs, secondary roads, erosion control) may tend to reduce income inequality overall, particularly in the case of irrigation.

Irrigation and Equity

Many economists have long believed that government investments in irrigation in LDCs were bound to result in significant benefits for poor rural households, primarily by the effects of increased irrigation on agricultural productivity. However, this view was widely questioned by many analysts in the seventies. They claimed that irrigation tends to be adopted faster and more completely by large farmers at the expense of small farmers and landless laborers, because the large farmers are then more able to buy out the small ones and because the technology associated with irrigation is labor-saving.

Recent studies sponsored by the International Food Policy Research Institute (IFPRI)* tend to confirm the older view: government investments in irrigation have not benefitted the larger farmers more than small farmers and landless laborers. Rather, these studies find that the latter groups have made major increases in their income as a result of irrigation. This research was focused on 10 project sites in Indonesia, Thailand, and the Philippines. It found no tendency to merge farms after the introduction of irrigation, and particularly in Indonesia, that the gains to landowners accrued primarily to small farmers. Further, gains to landless labor were substantial, however these are measured. This is primarily because of greater use of labor in the irrigated areas. The income of hired laborers was higher in all areas with irrigation.

Subsidies for consumption of basic foodstuffs also can result in substantial redistribution, provided food subsidy programs are not accompanied by oppressive price controls on production of food by poor farmers. Subsidies to subnational governments are often used to finance the provision of basic human needs, such as water, sewerage, education, and health services, all of which have benefits concentrated in lower-income classes. Housing subsidies favor the poor less frequently, since many programs for housing subsidies (Indonesia, Ghana, Pakistan) are in reality largely confined to government employees, a group that in most countries is relatively well-off.

Not all subsidy programs contribute to income redistribution even when redistribution is the announced goal. The most striking example has been that of subsidies for the consumption of petroleum products, particularly kerosene, in Bolivia, Colombia, Indonesia, Pakistan, and several other oil-producing countries. In all four cases mentioned, a principal justification offered for such subsidies was to assist low-income groups. In Bolivia through

---

*IFPRI Report 8, no. 1, January 1986.

1980, and in Colombia through 1974, this argument was extended to cover gasoline consumption, even though in both countries automobile ownership was largely confined to the upper 5 percent of the income distribution, and in both, urban bus transport was already heavily subsidized. In Indonesia gasoline has been only lightly subsidized, but budget subsidies held prices of kerosene and diesel fuel at less than half the costs of production and distribution. Although it seems plausible that kerosene subsidies strongly favor the poor, this is not the case. The poorest 40 percent of families consume only 20 percent of the kerosene sold. Therefore for every 1 dollar of subsidy to the poor, relatively high-income families received 4 dollars of benefit. And since kerosene can be substituted for diesel fuel, the subsidy program included it as well to prevent diesel users from switching. The result was that subsidies to kerosene and diesel fuel averaged about 5 percent of total tax revenues in Indonesia from 1979 to 1981, a figure exceeding total capital expenditures for education during the same period.

Fiscal policy to redistribute income must be viewed in perspective. It is not the only, and not always the most effective, instrument for redistribution in LDCs. Other chapters, especially Chapter 4, have drawn attention to the pivotal importance for income distribution of land tenure, the terms of trade between rural and urban areas, growth of employment, the relative prices of labor and capital, the openness and market orientation of the economy, and other factors. Taxation and government expenditures can affect most of those factors to some extent, but other, more direct policy instruments may have greater impacts on income distribution. Each of these instruments, some of which force radical changes in the economy, has its economic and political dangers. But a government determined on a more equitable income distribution probably needs to employ all those measures—including progressive taxation and expenditure policies—to some degree.

ECONOMIC EFFICIENCY AND THE BUDGET

Sources of Inefficiency

On the expenditure side of the budget, the tool we earlier called social cost-benefit analysis (Chapter 6) can be deployed to enhance efficiency (reduce waste) in government spending. On the tax side, promotion of economic efficiency is more problematic.

All taxes, save lump-sum levies (poll taxes), lead to inefficiencies to one degree or another. Lump-sum taxes are not realistic options for raising government revenues given their high degree of regressivity. The objective is therefore one of minimizing tax-induced inefficiencies consistent with other goals of tax policy. In most developing societies this objective largely reduces to the necessity of identifying examples of waste engendered by taxes and purging them from the system. If a particular feature of a tax system involves large efficiency losses, called *excess burden* in fiscal economics, and at the same time contributes little or nothing to such other policy goals as income redistribution, then that feature is an obvious can didate for abolition. A full discussion of those elements of tax systems that qualify for such treatment is properly the subject of an extended public finance monograph. We can do little more here than indicate some of the principal examples.

Quite apart from excess burden, discussed below, a major source of inefficiency in taxation not counterbalanced by positive gains in revenues, income redistribution, or other objectives of tax policy is excessive costs of tax administration. In some countries and for some taxes these costs have been so high that they call into question the desirability of using certain taxes for any purposes. This is true for certain kinds of narrow-based stamp taxes widely used in Latin America to collect government revenues on the documentation of transfer of assets, rental agreements, checks, and ordinary business transactions. Like a federal tax on playing cards used in the United States until 1964, many stamp taxes cost more to administer than they collect in revenues.

In some countries even broad-based taxes have had inordinately high costs of collection. For example, sales taxes in Chile and Ecuador in the 1960s cost 1 dollar in administration for each 4 dollars collected, as opposed to about 1 dollar per 100 dollars for most state sales taxes in the United States. And because taxes on capital gains are so difficult to administer everywhere—including North America—costs of collecting this component of income taxes often exceed revenues in many LDCs.

Many LDCs, from Ghana to Colombia to Indonesia, have offered substantial tax incentives to encourage investment in particular activities and regions. Many of these, particularly income tax holidays for approved firms, have proven very difficult to administer, and few have led to the desired result.[34] Given persistently pressing revenue requirements in most countries, granting liberal tax incentives may have no other effect than requiring higher rates of tax on taxpayers who do not qualify for incentives. It is a dictum of fiscal theory that any economic wastes (inefficiencies) arising from taxation increase by the square of the tax rate employed, not proportionately. It is therefore not difficult to see that unsuccessful tax-incentive programs involve inefficiencies for the economy as a whole that are not compensated by any significant benefits. Largely for this reason, Indonesia abolished all forms of tax incentives in a sweeping tax reform in 1984.

Finally, some features of major tax sources as utilized in many LDCs involve needless waste. From our earlier discussion of the use of import duties for luxury tax purposes, it is clear that this is often a major source of inefficiency. The use of progressive tax rates in a corporation income tax (as in Colombia until 1974, Venezuela, Mexico, Brazil, Ghana, and a score of other countries) is another example. Progressive rates of corporate tax, where they cannot be enforced, do little to contribute to income redistribution, and where they can be enforced, they lead to a variety of wastes. Two of the most important are fragmentation of business firms and ineffi-

---

34. See, for example, Arnold C. Harberger, "Principles of Taxation Applied to Developing Countries: What Have We Learned?" in Michael Boskin and Charles E. McLure, Jr., *World Tax Reform: Case Studies of Developed and Developing Countries* (San Francisco: ICS Press, 1990).

ciency in business operation. The incentive for fragmentation is evident: rather than be subjected to high marginal rates of taxes, firms tend to split up into smaller units and lose any cost advantages of size. Where high progressive rates are employed for company income, the tax will take a high proportion (say, 70 percent) of each additional dollar of earnings, so the incentive to control costs within the firm will be reduced. For example, for a firm facing a marginal tax rate of 70 percent, an additional outlay of $1,000 for materials will involve net costs to the firm of only $300, while taxes are reduced by $700.

Neutrality and Efficiency: Lessons from Experience

Experience around the world, both in developed and developing countries, seems to indicate that in societies where efficiency in taxation matters, that objective is best pursued by reliance on taxes that are as neutral as possible. A **neutral tax** is defined as one that does not lead to material change in the structure of private incentives that would prevail in the absence of the tax. A neutral tax system then, is one that relies, to the extent possible, on uniform rates: a tax on all income at a flat rate or a sales tax with the same rate applied to all food and services. A neutral tax system cannot be an efficient tax system.

An **efficient tax system** is one that involves a minimum amount of **excess burden** for raising a required amount of revenue, where excess burden of a tax is defined as the loss in total welfare, over and above the amount of tax revenues collected by the government. Figure 12–1 demonstrates how the excess burden of, say, a commodity tax is the greater the more elastic is

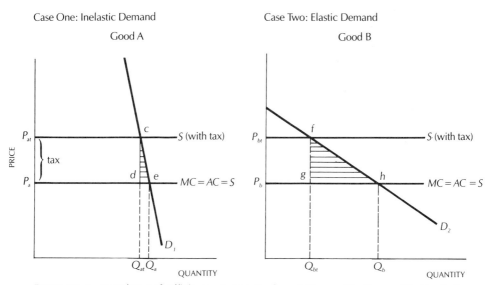

FIGURE 12–1 Taxation and Efficiency: Excess Burden of Commodity Taxes with Constant Marginal and Average Costs, under Competition. The shaded area in each case represents the excess burden of equal tax rates imposed on different goods. The greater the elasticity, the greater the excess burden.

the demand or the supply of the taxes item. The left-hand diagram depicts the inelastic case, good A, while the right-hand diagram shows the elastic case, good B. Constant marginal costs *(MC)* are assumed in both cases, and at the same level for both goods, in order to portray more starkly the contrasting results achieved in those cases. Before the tax is imposed on either good, equilibrium price and quantity are P_a and Q_a for good A and P_b and Q_b for good B. Now impose a tax rate *(t)* on both goods. The new equilibrium (posttax) magnitudes are P_{at} and Q_{at} for good A and P_{bt} and Q_{bt} for good B. For good A, the total amount of government revenue is the rectangle $P_aP_{at}cd$. The total loss in consumer surplus arising from the tax is the trapezoid $P_aP_{at}ce$. The excess of the loss in consumer surplus over the amount of government revenue is the conventional measure of efficiency loss from a tax, or excess burden. For good A, excess burden is the small triangle *cde*. By similar reasoning, excess burden in the case of good B is the larger triangle *fgh*. We may see that taxes of equivalent rates involve more excess burden when imposed on goods in elastic demand.

We can now see that efficient taxation requires neither uniformity nor neutrality, but many different tax rates on different goods, with tax rates lower for goods in elastic demand and higher for goods in inelastic demand. This is known as the **Ramsey rule** or the **inverse elasticity rule.** The problem is that a tax system on this rule would be decidedly regressive: the highest taxes would be required on foodstuffs, drinking water, and sumptuary items. Taxes would be lower on items such as clothing, services, and foreign travel, which tend to be both price- and income-elastic.

The principal of neutrality in taxation is not nearly as intellectually satisfying as a guide to tax policy as is efficient taxation. Nevertheless, neutral taxation is to be preferred as one of the underlying principles of taxation, along with equity, until such time as analysts are able to identify optimal departures from neutrality—and uniformity in tax rates—in real-world settings and until such time as administrative capacities are equal to the task of operating necessarily complicated structures of efficient or optimal taxes.

There is a paradox here. Neutral, uniform-rate taxes are less suited for efficiency goals than perfectly administered efficient taxes. Yet neutral tax systems are more likely to enhance efficiency in the economy than are efficient or optimal systems, since neutral systems with uniform rates can be administered most easily and are much less vulnerable to evasion. This is not to say that neutrality has ever been or should be the overriding goal of tax policy. Governments often undertake very deliberate departures from neutral tax treatment of certain sectors or groups of society in order to achieve other policy goals. But in real-world settings, these departures involve costs, not only in terms of tax administration, but often in both equity and efficiency terms as well. It is important that these costs be made as transparent as possible, so that policymakers may weigh them against expected gains from nonneutrality, including efficiency gains. Under present technology, major departures from neutrality in taxation are not likely to yield benefits commensurate with the costs. Neutrality in taxation may be the most advisable guide to efficiency in taxation for some time to come.

13

FINANCIAL
POLICY

A country's **financial system** consists of a variety of interconnected financial institutions, both formal and informal. Except in a handful of countries (including Liberia and several Francophone African countries), a central bank lies at the core of the organized financial system and is responsible for the control of the money supply and the general supervision of organized financial activity. Virtually everywhere, and particularly in developing countries, the commercial banking system is the most visible and vital component of the formal financial system, as acceptor of deposits and grantor of shorter-term credit. Other elements of the formal financial system include savings banks, insurance companies, and in a few higher-income LDCs, pension funds and investment banks specializing in long-term credit, as well as nascent securities markets. Coexisting with these modern financial institutions are the formal and largely unregulated systems of finance, including pawnshops, local moneylenders, trade credit, and other informal arrangements involving the borrowing and lending of money, such as intrafamily transfers and cooperative credit. In very low income nations, or even in higher-income LDCs with long inflationary histories, the informal financial sector may rival the formal system in size.

Financial policy embraces all measures intended to affect the growth, utilization, efficiency, and diversification of the financial system. In North America and Western Europe the term "financial policy" is ordinarily used as a synonym for monetary policy: the use of monetary instruments to reduce instability caused by fluctuations in either internal or external markets. In the United States these instruments include open-market operations, changes in legal reserve requirements of commercial banks and in shifts in central bank (Federal Reserve) lending (rediscount) rates to commercial banks; these terms are explained later in this chapter. In developing countries the term **financial policy** typically has a much-broader meaning. Monetary policy is part of financial policy, but so are measures intended to encourage the growth of savings in the form of financial assets, to develop money and capital markets, and to allocate credit between different economic sectors.

THE ROLE OF FINANCE IN DEVELOPMENT

For the first two decades after World War II, financial policy was not generally viewed as a significant instrument for promoting economic stability or for encouraging growth and development in LDCs. Until after the Second World War there was a prevailing tradition in economics that monetary changes affected only prices and wages and had little impact on production and employment over the business cycle. Among other things, the Great Depression served to demonstrate that monetary factors could in fact have significant effects on both output and employment. Nevertheless the tradition died hard; many economists in the 1940s and 1950s remained convinced that monetary factors had little influence on the business cycle and consequently downplayed the importance of monetary policy.

Skepticism over the efficacy of monetary policy was perhaps more pronounced in developing countries, particularly those where a substantial portion of economic activity was conducted through barter and related informal transactions outside the money economy. The **monetization ratio**—the proportion of the total goods and services in an economy that are purchased with money—was relatively low in many LDCs, particularly low-income nations in Africa. Even in the 1970s it is likely that only three-quarters of all economic activity in Africa took place within the monetized sector, versus 90 to 95 percent in Asia, the Middle East, and Latin America.[1] The effective use of monetary policy instruments for combating cyclical fluctuations is difficult enough in highly monetized countries such as the United States. In countries where as much as 15 to 25 percent of activity is outside the money economy, it was thought that monetary policy would be even less effective in achieving stabilization goals.

Finally, postwar economic history to 1972 was a period in which fixed exchange rates prevailed virtually everywhere, including LDCs. It is well-established in the literature on money and international trade that, given perfect capital mobility and fixed exchange rates, small countries will find monetary policy ineffective. Over the course of the 1970s policy commitments to fixed exchange rates were relaxed in a few countries. Also, by the

---

1. Anand G. Chandavarkar, "Monetization of Developing Economies," *International Monetary Fund Staff Papers* 24, no. 3 (November 1977): 678–679.

end of the decade there were few countries outside the 12 to 15 poorest where the monetization ratio stood at less than 85 percent. And as we have noted in Chapters 11 and 12, the international mobility of capital is far from perfect. In light of these considerations there was by the early 1980s a growing number of adherents to the view that financial policy, when deftly applied, can contribute something to the maintenance of short-term economic stability.

Less widely accepted, however, is the contention that financial policy can have an important influence over the long-term course of economic development. Earlier views of the role of finance in development held that the effect of financial policies on growth was benign at best. In any case, financial policies were not thought to make much difference for higher living standards. But beginning in the late 1960s, this view began to be strongly countered, most notably by Stanford economists Edward Shaw and Ronald McKinnon.[2] Over the past two decades it has become increasingly clear that financial policies have important implications both for the accessibility of domestic savings to domestic investors and for the efficiency with which these savings are allocated to competing investment purposes. We will explore these implications throughout this chapter.

THE FUNCTIONS OF A FINANCIAL SYSTEM

The financial system provides four basic services essential for the smooth functioning of an economy. First, it provides a medium of exchange and a store of value, called *money,* which also serves as a unit of account to measure the value of the transactions. Second, it provides channels for mobilizing savings from numerous sources and channeling them to investors, a process called **financial intermediation.** Third, it provides a means of transferring and distributing risk across the economy. Fourth, it provides a set of policy instruments for the stabilization of economic activity.

Money and the Money Supply

An economy without money as a **medium of exchange** is a primitive economy. Trade between individuals must take the form of high-cost, inefficient, barter transactions. In a barter economy goods have prices, but they are expressed in relative prices of physical commodities: so many kilos of rice for so many liters of kerosene, so many meters of rope for so many pairs of sandals, and so on. Trading under such circumstances involves onerous information costs.

Few societies have ever relied heavily on barter precisely because of the high costs implicit in this means of exchange. At some point prices of goods and services begin to be expressed in terms of one or more universally

---

2. Edward Shaw, *Financial Deepening and Economic Development* (New York: Oxford University Press, 1973), and Ronald I. McKinnon, *Money and Capital in Economic Development* (Washington, D.C.: Brookings Institution, 1973).

accepted and durable commodities, like gold and silver, or even beads and cowrie shells. The rise of commodity money diminishes the transaction and storage costs of trade, but still involves problems of making exchanges across space and time. Gold and silver prices do fluctuate, and the commodities are thus not fully reliable as **units of account.** As specialization within an economy increases, financial instruments backed by commodities appear. In the last century, with the rise of central banking all over the world, currency has evolved into **fiat** money: debt issued by central banks that is legal tender. It is backed not by commodities of equivalent value, but only by the full faith and credit of the central bank.

As markets widen and specialization proceeds apace, a need arises for still another financial instrument, **transferable deposits.** In the normal course of development, **checking** or **demand deposits**—deposits that may be transferred to any economic agent at the demand of the depositor—appear first and ordinarily bear little or no interest. With further monetization still another financial instrument begins to grow in importance: **time deposits,** which are not legally transferable on demand, but only after stated periods. Time deposits do involve contractual interest payments; higher interest rates induce people to hold greater amounts of deposits in this form. Rising levels of economic activity, however, create increasing needs for transaction balances; individuals will always maintain some balances in demand deposits to meet these needs, but will tend to economize on the levels of such deposits if no interest is paid on them.

While checking (demand) and time deposits are **liabilities** (or debts) of commercial banks, they are **financial assets** for the persons who hold them. Both demand and time deposits are known as **liquid financial assets.** Unlike **nonfinancial assets** that can also be held by households and businesses (inventories, gold, land), demand and time deposits can be quickly and conveniently converted into their currency equivalents. Currency is, by definition, the most liquid of all assets. The concept of liquid financial assets is an important one in any discussion of financial policy in developing countries. For most LDCs, the movement of savers in and out of liquid financial assets may be the prime factor behind the success or failure of a financial policy. We will see that long-term shifts from tangible, or nonfinancial, physical assets to financial assets, particularly liquid assets, bodes well not only for economic growth but also for economic stability.

A country's **money supply** may be defined as the sum of all liquid assets in the financial system. While not all economists agree about what constitutes a liquid financial asset, most vastly prefer this money-supply concept to those commonly employed in early postwar monetary analysis. Formerly the money supply was conventionally defined as the sum of only two liquid financial assets: currency in circulation outside banks (C) plus demand deposits (D), which together are known as M_1 (narrow money). However, it later became clear that because depositors tend to view time and savings deposits (T) as almost as liquid as demand deposits, the former should also be included in any workable concept of money supply, called M_2 (broad money). Finally, for high-income countries, specialized deposit-taking financial institutions have arisen and offer an array of options to savers other than those available in commercial and savings banks. The liabilities of these specialized institutions (O) are included in M_3, total liquid liabilities, the broadest measure of money. Thus,

$$M_1 = C + D \qquad\qquad [13\text{--}1]$$
$$M_2 = M_1 + T \qquad\qquad [13\text{--}2]$$
$$M_3 = M_2 + O. \qquad\qquad [13\text{--}3]$$

For most low-income countries and many middle-income countries, liquid financial assets constitute by far the greatest share of outstanding financial assets. But as income growth continues and the financial system matures, less liquid financial assets assume progressively greater importance. These include primary securities such as stocks, bonds (issued both by government and firms), and other financial claims on tangible (physical) assets that are convertible into currency equivalents with only some risk of loss to the asset holder and are hence less liquid than demand or time deposits.

The evolution of financial activity follows no set patterns across countries. Differing economic conditions and policy emphases may result in widely divergent patterns of financial growth. Nevertheless, the level of financial activity tends to increase relative to economic activity as per-capita income rises over time. M_1, the narrowly defined money supply, may be as low as 10 percent of GDP in very low income countries, and tends to rise more or less steadily to between 20 to 30 percent of GDP in high-income LDCs and industrial countries. As income rises from very low levels, much of the growth in liquid assets tends to take the form first of growth in demand deposits, then in time deposits, and finally in deposits of specialized financial institutions. The ratio of M_3 to GDP can be taken as a measure of the real size (inflation adjusted) of the banking system, a rough gauge of the flow of loanable funds in LDCs.[3] In recent years this ratio has ranged typically from 12 to 15 percent in very poor countries, to an average of about 30 to 50 percent in middle-income nations, to between 70 and 100 percent of GDP in such industrial countries as the United States, Canada, and Italy, and to almost 200 percent in Japan (see Table 13–1). But diversity in financial development is well-exemplified by the fact that in some relatively high-income LDCs (Taiwan and Malaysia), the share of liquid assets in GDP is higher than in many industrial countries.

Liquid assets are not, however, the only source of financial growth. As financial markets widen with the spread of the money economy, they also tend to deepen as a greater variety of financial assets begins to appear. With rising incomes, a growing proportion of financial growth tends to come in the form of nonliquid financial assets, such as primary securities, suitable as a basis for the type of longer-term finance that commercial banking systems cannot easily provide. The **financial ratio** (the ratio of net financial assets to GNP) tends to rise steadily from less than 20 percent of GNP in very poor countries, such as Haiti or Chad, to between 60 and 80 percent in higher-income countries, such as Brazil, South Korea, and Venezuela, and as high as 200 percent in Malaysia by 1985. In very high income coun-

---

3. For all but a few LDCs, M_3 exceeds M_2 only by small amounts.

TABLE 13–1   Liquid Assets (M_3) as a Percentage of Gross Domestic Product in Selected
Countries, 1970–1989[a]

	1970	1980	1989
I. Developed countries	52.2	69.9	72.8
France	62.6	73.9	48.3
Italy	86.8	74.9	80.6
Japan	92.8	145.0	191.3[c]
United Kingdom	55.1	32.4	94.8
United States	70.0	61.4	68.1
II. Developing countries			
Latin America[b]			
Argentina	30.6	31.8	24.5[e]
Brazil	23.1	22.9	35.4[f]
Chile	17.5	21.5	47.1[f]
Colombia	19.8	28.3	33.4
Mexico	33.1	19.5	30.3[d]
Peru	22.8	25.3	23.8[c]
Uruguay	21.5	38.6	54.6
Asia			
India	27.3	38.9	47.5[e]
Indonesia	10.0	17.0	30.5[c]
Malaysia	39.8	80.6	123.0[c]
Philippines	23.4	25.6	25.8[c]
South Korea	37.1	35.8	58.0
Sri Lanka	29.3	39.5	39.3
Taiwan	44.9	98.2 (1978)	———
Thailand	30.7	37.3	69.9[c]
Africa			
Ghana	19.3	18.5	14.7[c]
Kenya	31.4	40.4	40.8[c]
Nigeria	17.5	29.5	31.6[c]
Tanzania	24.8	42.1	28.2[c]

[a] Liquid assets = money + quasimoney + all deposits outside commercial banks (lines 35 + 35 + 44 + 45 of IMF tables).
[b] For almost all the developing countries included in this table M_2 is either equal to or slightly less than M_3.
[c] 1988.
[d] 1987.
[e] 1986.
[f] 1985.
Source: International Monetary Fund, *International Financial Statistics*, (Washington, D.C.: International Monetary Fund, various issues 1970–1990).

tries, including Canada and the United States, total financial assets are
nearly twice as large as GNP, and 3 times GNP in Japan.[4] Here again,
however, there is no evidence of immutable laws of financial development.
Many very high-income industrial countries, including France and Holland, have financialization ratios that are a third of that of Japan. And many
higher-income countries, particularly those with long traditions of inflationary history (Uruguay, Brazil, Argentina), display a lower ratio of financial
assets to GNP than poorer countries such as India and Thailand (89 and 65
percent, respectively).

4. World Bank, *World Development Report 1989*, p. 39.

Financial Intermediation

As financial structures become increasingly rich and diversified in terms of financial assets, institutions, and markets, the function of money as a medium of exchange, store of value, and unit of account tends to be taken for granted except in the context of situations of runaway inflation, discussed later in the chapter. As financial development proceeds, the ability of the financial system to perform its second major function—financial intermediation—grows as well. The process of financial intermediation involves gathering savings from multitudinous savers and channeling them to a much smaller but still sizable number of investors. Generally, households are the only net savers in LDCs.[5] At early stages of economic development a preponderant share of intermediation activities tends to be concentrated in one type of institution: commercial banks. As development proceeds, new forms of financial intermediaries begin to appear and gradually assume a growing share of the intermediation function. These include investment banks, insurance companies, and, ultimately, securities markets. Plentiful intermediaries, however, do not always guarantee successful intermediation.

Financial intermediation activities are best measured through use of **flow-of-funds accounts,** which display the uses of finance by different economic sectors together with the sources of savings by sectors. These are akin to the flow matrix of input-output tables and social accounting matricies (see Chapter 6). Unfortunately, reliable flow-of-funds tables are available for only a few LDCs at present; therefore cross-country generalization about intermediation based on such tables is not yet possible. In the absence of flow-of-funds accounts, we will employ the liquid asset-GDP ratio as an approximate measure of financial intermediation.

Financial intermediation is best seen as one of several alternative technologies for mobilizing and allocating savings. The fiscal system discussed in Chapter 12 furnishes another alternative, and we will see in the next chapter that reliance on foreign savings constitutes still another. Further, we will observe in this chapter that inflation has also been employed as a means of mobilizing resources for the public sector. Indeed a decision to rely more heavily on financial intermediation as a means of investment finance is tantamount to a decision to rely less heavily on the government budget, foreign aid and foreign investment, and inflation to achieve the same purpose.

Transformation and Distribution of Risk

Another major service provided by a well-functioning financial system is the transformation and distribution of risk. All economic activities involve risk taking, but some undertakings involve more risk than others. Individual savers and investors tend to be risk averse; the marginal loss of a dollar

---

5. In our example of 14 LDCs for the seventies and eighties, households saved 12.9 percent of GNP and reinvested 6.0 percent in the household sector. Households supplied the remaining 6.9 percent to the financial sector, whereas the business and government sector drew nearly 9 percent of GNP from the financial sector. Ibid., p. 29.

appears more important to them than the marginal gain of a dollar. But the degree of risk aversion differs among individuals. When risk cannot be diversified, or pooled, across a large number of individuals, savers and investors will demand greater returns, or premiums, for bearing risk, and activities involving high risk will tend not to be undertaken. But high-risk activities may well offer the greatest returns to the economy as a whole. A well-functioning financial system furnishes a means for diversifying, or pooling, risks among a large number of savers and investors. The system may offer assets with differing degrees of risks. Financial institutions that specialize in assessing and managing risks can assign them to individuals having different attitudes toward, and perceptions of, risk. Indeed a per-fectly functioning financial system can reduce all risk premiums to zero, except for those **systematic risks** that can never be diversified away from the domestic economy, such as those arising from national disasters like the 1985 earthquake in Mexico and recessions in the world economy.

Stabilization

Finally, the financial system provides instruments for the stabilization of economic activity in addition to those available under fiscal policy and direct controls. All economies experience cyclical changes in production, employment, and prices. Governments often attempt to compensate for these fluctuations through policies affecting the money supply. Because unemployment in LDCs is rarely of the type that can be readily cured by monetary expansion, the use of financial policy for stabilization purposes generally focuses on efforts to control inflation.

INFLATION AND SAVINGS MOBILIZATION

By the 1980s, **price inflation,** defined as a sustained increase in the overall price level, was generally regarded as a malady, which in its milder forms was annoying but tolerable, and in its moderate form corrosive but not fatal. Runaway inflation, also known as hyperinflation, however, has always been recognized as severely destructive of economic processes, with few offsetting benefits. Whereas a number of influential thinkers in the 1950s and 1960s advocated some degree of moderate inflation (e.g., inflation rates of between 8 and 12 percent) as a tool for promoting growth, few adherents of this view remain, for reasons discussed below. Many others did not actively advocate inflation, but tended to have a higher threshold of toler-ance for a steadily rising general price level than is now common. They believed that development inevitably involved trade-offs between inflation and unemployment and that the wise course was to resolve the trade-off in favor of less unemployment and more inflation. Today few economists still believe in a fixed, long-term relation between inflation and unemployment, and there is a growing body of evidence that restraining inflation may enhance, rather than retard, prospects for long-run growth.

Generalizations about inflation in developing countries are difficult to make. Inflationary experiences across countries are as diverse as their experiences in the fields of literacy, nutrition, and tax collection. Nevertheless, postwar economic history offers some interesting national and regional contrasts in both susceptibilities to, and tolerances for, different levels of inflation. The period prior to the early 1970s was one of relative price stability in developing countries. In the southern cone of Latin America, however, particularly in Argentina, Brazil, and Chile, **chronic inflation**—prices rising 25 to 50 percent per year for three years or more—has been an enduring fact of economic life for much of the past four decades. The experience of these countries indicates that long periods of double-digit inflation does not necessarily lead to national economic calamity in all societies. Seven other countries also experienced chronic inflation from 1950 to 1989, as shown in Table 13–2.

However, a tolerable rate of inflation in one country may constitute economic trauma in another. This may be seen more readily by considering

TABLE 13–2 Inflation Outliers: Episodes of Chronic,[a] Acute,[b] and Runaway[c] Inflation among Developing Countries, 1948–1990

	Average Annual Rates (%)					
	Chronic inflation		Acute inflation		Runaway inflation	
	Years	Rate	Years	Rate	Years	Rate
Argentina	1950–74	27	1977–82	147	1976	443
			1986–87	111	1983–85	547
					1988–89	1,711
Bolivia	1973–83	35	1952–59	117	1983–86	3,394
Brazil	1957–76	35	1979–84	113	1985	227
			1986	145	1987–89	733
Chile	1952–71	29			1973–76	361
	1978–80	36				
	1983–85	26				
Ghana			1973–83	52		
Indonesia					1965–68	306
Mexico			1982–88	88		
Paraguay			1951–53	81		
Peru	1975–77	32	1950–55	102	1988–90	2,033
			1978–87	87		
South Korea			1950–55	95		
Turkey	1973–87	46	1988–89	73		
Uganda			1973–83	62	1985	274
			1988–89	137	1987	238
Uruguay	1948–65	26	1965–68	83		
	1981–83	34	1972–80	68		
			1984–89	68		
Zaire	1981–82	36	1976–80	70		
			1983–89	68		

[a] Annual average inflation rates between 25 and 50 percent for three or more consecutive years.
[b] Annual average inflation rates of greater than 50 percent for three or more consecutive years.
[c] Annual inflation in excess of 200 percent for one or more years.
Source: International Monetary Fund, *International Financial Statistics Yearbook 1990.*

the next phase of the often progressive inflationary disease called **acute inflation.** Acute inflation, defined here as inflation in excess of 50 percent for three or more consecutive years, was experienced by 12 countries over the postwar period, in some cases more than once per country. For Brazil, the progression from chronic to acute inflation did not result in any noticeable slowing of that country's relatively robust economic growth, whatever it may have meant for income distribution. In Ghana, on the other hand, a decade of acute inflation coincided with a decade of decline in GDP per capita. Although it may be tempting to attribute economic retrogression in Ghana to acute inflation, it is more likely that the same policies that led to sustained inflation were responsible for declines in living standards there.[6]

Although acute inflation has proven toxic to economic development in some settings and only bothersome in others, **runaway (hyper-) inflation** has almost always had devastating effects. Inflation rates in excess of 200 percent per year represent an inflationary process that is clearly out of control; seven nations have undergone this traumatic experience since 1950. The nadir of recent inflationary experience occurred in three Latin American countries: Bolivia and Argentina in 1985, Argentina again in 1988–89, and Peru in 1988–89. In Bolivia the annual rate of inflation over a period of several months in 1985 accelerated to a rate of nearly 4,000 percent. In Argentina the monthly rate of price increase was 30.5 percent in June 1985 alone; on an annual basis that would have been an inflation rate of 2,340 percent. In both Bolivia and Argentina for much of 1985, workers had little choice but to spend their paychecks within minutes of receipt, for fear that prices would double or triple over the next week. In Peru, hyperinflation in 1989 gave birth to publications devoted only to the tracking of inflation (see box below).

Hyperinflation in Peru: 1988–1990

The economic and social havoc wrought by hyperinflation is difficult to comprehend for those who have not lived through the experience. The Peruvian hyperinflation which began in 1988 and continued until 1991 provides some rueful examples.

The inflationary process was triggered by large budgetary deficits and sustained by subsequent ongoing deficits, virtual economic collapse, and steadily rising inflationary expectations. Peru had already experienced two serious bouts with acute inflation since 1950 (see Table 13–2), but the pace of inflation in 1989 was the highest in the nation's history: 28 percent per *month,* or about 2,000 percent per year. Moreover, inflation accelerated in the first six weeks of 1990, as prices rose by 6 percent per week, or about 1 percent per day. From January 1989 to December 1990, the value

---

6. For a diagnosis of the causes of the Ghanian economic decline after 1962, see Michael Roemer, "Ghana, 1950 to 1980: Missed Opportunities," and Yaw Ansu, "Comments," both in *World Economic Growth,* Arnold C. Harberger, ed., (San Francisco: Institute of Contemporary Studies, 1984), pp. 201–230.

of the Peruvian currency (the intis) on the free market fell from 1,200 intis per dollar to 436,000 intis per dollar.

This hyperinflation may turn out to be one of the best documented in history: in 1988 Dr. Richard Webb, an internationally respected Peruvian economist, began to publish a magazine devoted essentially to helping producers and consumers cope with the chaos associated with runaway inflation. The magazine, called *Cuanto?* (How Much?) appears monthly. It not only provides details on price developments for a large number of commodities and services, but it manages to extract what little humor there is in a situation where the price of a movie ticket rises while people are waiting in line to buy it or where a taxi driver must carry his fare money in a burlap bag because the domestic currency collected in fares each evening is too bulky to fit in his trousers.

But there is precious little that is funny about hyperinflation. In Peru, it was a story of government employees going without pay for weeks at a time, of indices of poverty nearly doubling from 1987 to 1989, further impoverishing the poorest 40 percent of the population. It was a story of precipitous decline in Gross Domestic Product, and of the rise of pervasive black markets in everything from dollars to gasoline to cement. It was a time when, on each payday, laborers rushed to the market to buy their weekly food supplies before they were marked up overnight. It was a tale of wide variations in price rises, where prices for such items as pencils and chicken increased by more than 25 times from February 1989 to February 1990, but prices of light bulbs and telephone services increased by "only" 10-fold.

Imagine life in Lima, the capital city, in the first few weeks of 1990, for a middle-income family trying to survive. For the first 40 days of the year, increases in the price of dying outpaced the price of living: the cost of funerals rose 79 percent, while house rent rose by 56 percent, and the price of restaurant meals and haircuts increased by 44 percent.

By mid-1990, the economic paralysis of Peru was virtually complete. Peru's hyperinflation will end only when the government is successful in dealing with the principal cause of the catastrophe: large budgetary deficits. Bolivia had already shown how to stop the process in 1985. Mired in 25,000 percent inflation, the government announced that, come what may, it would not spend a peso more than it collected in taxes. Within a half year, runaway inflation ended, and in 1989 inflation was only slightly above 7 percent.

The group of 14 other countries in Table 13–2 is best viewed as falling into two special cases. In one group a succession of very large government deficits, relative to GDP, was financed by borrowing from the banking system (Chile, Indonesia, Peru, Argentina, Ghana). In another group of nations, inflation was caused by a massive expansion of credit to the private sector (Paraguay in the early 1950s and Brazil and Uruguay before 1974). Causes of inflation in these countries are not difficult to identify for the periods in question.

But this group of 14 countries constitutes only a small fraction of LDCs.

Through most of the postwar era most countries have restrained budgetary deficits to more manageable proportions, and few have allowed rates of credit expansion to the private sector to reach uncontrollable levels. Aside from the countries listed in Table 13–2, during 1952 to 1972 there were more years when inflation was marginally greater in developed than in developing countries. Only after the first oil-price shock in 1973 did inflation rates in LDCs tend to exceed those in developed countries. This pattern emerges from Table 13–3, which compares the inflationary history of 23 developing countries and the 21 industrial countries of the Organization for Economic Cooperation and Development (OECD).[7]

TABLE 13–3 Annual Average Rates of Inflation in Selected Developing Countries, 1952–1989

Country		1952–66	1967–72	1973–81	1982–89
A. *South and Central America*					
Costa Rica		1.8	3.8	15.6	27.0
Dominican Republic		1.2	3.2	11.1	21.0[a]
Panama		0.3	2.7	7.9	1.5[a]
Paraguay		12.8	3.0	14.9	21.0
Venezuela		2.3	1.3	10.6	24.1
B. *Africa*					
Cameroon	(1963–66)	5.2	3.1	11.7	9.3[a]
Ivory Coast	(1960–66)	3.1	3.6	14.7	4.3
Kenya	(1960–66)	2.3	2.4	13.7	10.4
Nigeria	(1954–66)	4.0	8.3	17.7	21.4
Senegal		—	3.4	11.1	6.8
C. *South Asia*					
Bangladesh	(1955–66)	4.3	4.8	19.7	10.4
India		4.8	3.7	9.5	8.4
Pakistan		3.8	4.0	14.0	6.1
Sri Lanka		0.8	5.6	10.9	10.5
D. *East Asia*					
Malaysia		−0.2	3.2	7.2	2.5
Philippines		2.7	8.5	14.7	14.7
Singapore	(1960–66)	1.1	1.0	7.9	1.4
Thailand	(1954–66)	2.7	2.2	11.9	3.2
E. *Middle East and North Africa*					
Egypt		1.4	3.3	11.1	17.8
Morocco		2.7	2.5	10.1	6.7
Syria		0.9	2.7	14.5	23.6
Tunisia		2.2	3.0	6.9	8.2
F. Range encompassing 80% of observations		0.9–10.5	2.2–8.3	7.9–14.9	2.5–23.6
G. OECD Inflation[b]		2.2	4.5	9.7	4.7

[a]Figures are for 1982 to 1988.
[b]OECD inflation is the weighted average annual inflation rate for OECD members, which feel steadily from 7.5 percent in 1982 to 2.9 percent in 1987. Figures in the last column are for 1980 to 1989.
Sources: Developing Countries: International Monetary Fund, *International Financial Statistics,* various issues. OECD Nations for 1952 to 1981: OECD, *Economic Outlooks* (Paris: OECD, various issues 1980–88). World Bank, *World Development Indicators* 1990.

7. The format for Table 13–3 was first used in Arnold C. Harberger, "A Primer on Inflation."

Another interesting observation can be drawn from Table 13–3. It is clear from the last row that world inflationary history from 1952 through 1984 was characterized by four distinct periods. For convenience we will take the weighted inflation rates in OECD countries as our measure of world inflation. In the first period, from 1952 to 1966, annual inflation in both industrial countries and most LDCs was held to little more than 2 percent. In the second period (1967 to 1972) inflation almost everywhere surged to nearly 6 percent. In the third period (1973 to 1981) the pace of world inflation accelerated strongly and rose to almost 10 percent by 1979. Finally, in the fourth period, world inflation decelerated to 4.7 percent in 1982 to 1989, still above the rates prevailing in the two decades after 1952. Inflation tended to be somewhat less in LDCs relative to industrial nations in the first two periods and somewhat more in the last two periods. However, what is more striking is the similarity of inflation rates within each period between the more typical LDCs and the industrial countries, as well as the significant change in the rhythm of inflation among the four periods. It seems reasonable to conclude from these patterns that all countries participated in a common process of world inflation, made possible until 1982 by a significant acceleration in the growth of the world money supply (a weighted average of the growth rates of money supply in different nations)[8] in a world of largely fixed exchange rates, or at best intermittent "dirty" floating rates.[9]

Virtually all LDC economies are **open economies;** that is, they depend significantly on international trade. Given the acceleration of inflation in the industrial countries from 1973 to 1981, we shall see that it is reasonable to conclude that both imported inflation, as well as the homegrown variety, are responsible for accelerated inflation in LDCs as a group since 1973.

Forced Mobilization of Savings

Chapter 12 identified a number of problems involved in the use of conventional taxes, such as income and sales taxes, for mobilizing public-sector savings. Another form of taxation is inflation. Governments from the time of the Roman Empire have recognized inflation as an alternative means of securing resources for the state. All that is required is that the stock of money be expanded at a sufficiently rapid rate to result in increases in the

8. The International Monetary Fund now computes and publishes figures on the world money supply, with weights assigned to different countries on the basis of the relative size of economies. The annual growth in the world money stock rose from less than 3 percent in the 15 years before 1967, when world inflation was but 2 percent, to 12.5 percent in the period 1972 to 1976, when world inflation accelerated to nearly 10 percent.

9. Countries employing floating exchange rates allow the value of their currency to fluctuate according to relative supply and demand for that currency in world markets. Countries employing a fixed exchange rate system establish a set value for their currency in terms of one of the major currencies used in world trade, usually the U.S. dollar. Thus, Mexico's currency was defined as 22 pesos to 1 U.S. dollar at the beginning of 1982. A fixed exchange rate will usually be maintained for as long as a country can defend the rate. When that is no longer possible, a new exchange rate is chosen and fixed to some higher (or lower) value. For example, the Mexican peso was devalued to a new fixed rate of 29 pesos to 1 U.S. dollar in February 1982, and later (September 1982) to 60 pesos to 1 U.S. dollar.

general price level, and that people be willing to hold some money balances even as the value of these holdings decline. Inflation then acts as a tax on money holdings. At 15 percent inflation the annual tax on currency is 13 percent, and at 40 percent inflation the tax is 29 percent.[10] These are higher annual tax rates than any country has ever managed to impose successfully on any physical asset, such as housing, automobiles, or equipment. Under extremely high rates of inflation, as in the German hyperinflation of 1922 to 1923 or the Peruvian inflation of 1988 to 1990, households attempt to reduce holdings of money balances to virtually nothing. However, except during runaway inflation, because money is so convenient as a means of exchange and unit of accounts, people will always hold some money balances even if they must pay fairly heavy inflation taxes for the convenience.

Difficulties in collecting conventional taxes, the apparent ease of collecting inflation taxes, the convenience properties of money balances, and the view that inflation taxes are progressive (richer people hold higher money balances) have led many policymakers and economists to view inflation as a desirable means of development finance. During the 1950s and 1960s the influential United Nations Economic Commission for Latin America saw moderate inflation as a means of "greasing the wheels" of development, forcing savings from holders of money balances and transferring such savings to governments that were strapped for investment resources. Accordingly, much effort was expended in the search for what was viewed as an "optimal" rate of inflation for developing societies: the rate that maximizes tax collections, including both conventional taxes and inflation rates.

Implementation of such a forced-savings strategy will tend to curtail private investment, since some of the inflation tax will come out of money balances that would have been used for investment in the private sector. However, proponents of tax maximization through inflation assumed that the government's marginal propensity to invest out of inflation taxes exceeded that of the private sector, and that the government would invest in real assets as productive as the private investment it displaced. Therefore, it was thought, forced-savings strategies would never reduce total investment.

Two implicit assumptions lay behind the argument that the forced-savings strategy would improve economic welfare in LDCs. Collections of conventional taxes were believed to be highly responsive to inflationary growth, i.e., the revenue elasticity[11] of the conventional tax system with

---

10. Say the nominal value of money balances at the beginning of a year is M_n, equal to the real value M_r. Now if price inflation proceeds at a rate p per year, then after one year the real value of money balances M'_r would be

$$M'_r = M_r/(1+p).$$

The tax on these balances is $T = M_r - M'_r$, and the tax rate is $t = M_r$, So

$$t = \frac{M_r - M'_r}{M_r} = \frac{1}{1+p} - 1 = \frac{p}{1+p}.$$

If $p = 40$ percent, $T = p/(1+p) = 29$ percent.

11. The revenue elasticity (E_R) measures the responsiveness of the tax system to growth in GDP. It is defined as the percent change in tax collections divided by the percent change in

respect to nominal income growth is greater than 1. And efficiency losses

from inflation taxes were thought to be less than efficiency losses from the
use of conventional taxes to increase government revenues. Indeed, it can
be shown that under circumstances where (1) a government's marginal propensity to invest out of inflation taxes is unity or greater, (2) the revenue
elasticity of the tax system is also unity or greater, and (3) the marginal
efficiency costs of inflation taxes are less than those for explicit taxes, the
growth-maximizing rate of inflation may be as high as 30 percent. However, these assumptions are so far divorced from economic realities in LDCs
as to undermine severely, if not demolish, the case for forced savings through
inflation.

First, there is little evidence that governments anywhere have a marginal
propensity to invest out of inflation taxes that is near unity; recall Chapter
12's discussion of the Please effect. In order for tax maximization through
inflation to stimulate growth, governments' marginal propensity to invest
would have to rise with inflation. Research by George von Furstenberg of
the IMF and others finds no support at all for even the weakest form of this
hypothesis. Second, the net result of even moderate inflation on a government's total revenues (conventional taxes plus inflation taxes) may actually
be to decrease the government's ability to expand total investment. This
may easily occur if the revenue elasticity of the tax structure is less than
unity, as is the case in many, but not all, LDCs. In such cases the growth
in collections from conventional taxes lags well behind nominal GNP growth.
Particularly in the early stages of an inflationary process, part of the higher
inflation tax collections will be offset by a decline in the real value of conventional tax collections. Third, available evidence suggests that once
inflation exceeds 2 percent per annum, the incremental efficiency losses
from inflation taxes tend strongly to outweigh those from conventional
taxes.[12] And it is well to note that since 1973, typical inflation rates in LDCs
have been far above 2 percent (Table 13–3).

At best then, government mobilization of resources through inflation is a
knife-edge strategy. Inflation rates must be kept high enough to yield substantial inflation taxes, but not so high as to cause holders of liquid assets
to undertake wholesale shifts into real assets in order to escape the tax.
Inflation rates must be kept low enough so that collections from conventional taxes do not lag far behind growth in nominal income and so that
efficiency losses from inflation do not greatly exceed efficiency losses from
higher conventional tax revenues. Paradoxically, then, the inflation tax device
can work best where it is needed the least: in those countries having tax

---

GDP, where $Y =$ GDP, or

$$E_R = \frac{\Delta T / T}{\Delta Y / Y}.$$

If $E_R > 1$, then the tax system is revenue-elastic and taxes rise proportionally more than national
income. For example, if $E_R = 1.2$, then for every 10 percent increase in GDP, tax collections
rise by 12 percent. If $E_R < 1$, the tax system is revenue-inelastic; if $E_R = 0.8$, then with a 10
percent increase in GDP, tax collections rise by 8 percent.

12. George M. von Furstenberg, "Inflation, Taxes and Welfare in LDCs," *Public Finance*
35, #2 (1980): 700–701.

systems that are most responsive to growth in overall GDP and involve low efficiency costs. Countries with revenue-elastic tax systems do not need to resort to inflation in an attempt to finance expanded government investment. In this sense tax reform can be seen as a substitute for inflationary finance, but not the other way around.

Inflation as a Stimulus to Investment

The forced-savings doctrine was not the only argument employed in favor of purposeful inflation. For more than 50 years some economists argued that, even in industrial countries, rising prices can act as a stimulus to private business enterprise, as inflation was thought to be helpful in drawing labor and capital out of declining sectors of the economy and into dynamic ones. If true for industrial societies, then, it was reasoned, the argument might apply with special force in developing countries, where rigidities, bottlenecks, and immobilities were such that resources were particularly likely to be trapped in low-productivity uses. Inflation, it was argued, would help to speed up the reallocation of labor and capital out of traditional of subsistence sectors into the modern sectors with the greatest development potential. Thus moderate inflation was not only seen as inevitable, but desirable: a progressive government would actively seek some target rate of inflation, perhaps as high as 10 percent, in order to spur development.

Experience with development since 1950 strongly suggests that some inflation is indeed inevitable in developing societies seeking rapid growth in per-capita income: factors of production are relatively immobile in the short run, and imbalances and bottlenecks in supply do develop in spite of the most careful planning. However, the deliberate use of sustained inflation to spur development is likely to achieve the desired results only under a limited set of circumstances.

First, if inflation is the result of deliberate policy or can otherwise be anticipated, then in a sustained inflationary process the approaching rise in prices will cause individuals and firms to adjust their expectations of inflation. To the extent that the inflation is anticipated, the supposed beneficial effects will never occur; people will have already taken them into account in their decision making.[13] For industrial societies, it would be difficult, at least for an economist, to accept the idea that behavior does not ultimately adjust to expectations of inflation. In developing countries, where all markets, including that for information, tend to be more imperfect than in developed countries, it might be argued that firms and individuals are less efficient in collecting and using information, including that pertinent to the formation of price expectations. Thus inflation may not be fully foreseen throughout the economy, and consequently rising prices may result in some stimulus to development in the short term. But it should be recognized that over the longer run a successful policy of deliberate inflations depends on people's not understanding the policy.

---

13. This observation dates at least as far back as the early 1930s, to the Swedish economist Knut Wicksell. It contains the germ of the idea behind the rational-expectations school of thought of the 1970s and 1980s.

Second, the argument that deliberate inflation enhances private-sector performance overlooks the effects of inflation on risk taking. Inflation increases the riskiness of all investment decisions. Suppose that businesses can anticipate inflation with a margin of error of plus or minus 20 percent of the actual rate. (If the margin of error is wider, the effects about to be described will be more pronounced.) If inflation has been running at 5 percent per year, there may be a general expectation that it will settle within the range 4 to 6 percent in the near future. But if inflation has been running at substantially higher rates, say, 30 percent, then expectations of future inflation may rationally be in the much broader range of 24 to 36 percent. The entrepreneur therefore faces far-higher levels of uncertainty in planning investments and production. The more uncertain the future and future returns are, the more likely is the entrepreneur to reduce his risks. Investments with long lives (long gestation periods) tend to be more risky than those with short lives. Thus inflation tends to reduce private-sector investment in projects with a long-term horizon; the inhibiting effects rise with the rate of inflation. Unfortunately these are often precisely the types of investments most likely to involve high payoffs in terms of income growth for society as a whole.

Finally, inflation may severely curtail private-sector investment by constricting the flow of funds to the organized financial system if nominal interest rates are not allowed to rise as rapidly as the expected rate of inflation. As we shall see in the next sections, such situations are typical under strategies of shallow financial development.

In any case, many of the arguments developed in favor of deliberate inflation may have been little more than efforts to rationalize failure of many governments (particularly in Latin America from 1950 to 1975) to bring inflation under control. In most cases inflation in developed and developing countries has been more a consequence of policy miscalculation or economic dislocation (oil-price shocks, agricultural disasters, and so on) than a consciously chosen instrument of economic growth. Some reflective observers of inflationary dynamics, such as Albert Hirschman, have maintained that inflation, in Latin America at least, is not usually the outcome of a systematic set of choices designed to promote growth and other policy objectives. Rather, inflation usually represents the consequences of government temporizing, of postponing difficult decisions that might shatter fragile consensus in governments with sharply divided constituencies.[14] Measures to increase collections from conventional taxes, or to reduce government spending on programs enacted at the behest of powerful vested interests, are examples of such difficult decisions. Avoiding such stabilizing changes is tantamount to choosing inflation, in the hopes that at some point in the future a more enduring coalition of constituencies can be assembled to directly confront difficult issues. Seen this way, inflation results not by design but by default.

---

14. Albert O. Hirschman, *Journeys Toward Progress: Studies of Economic Policy-Making in Latin America* (New York: Twentieth Century Fund, 1963), pp. 208–209.

Inflation and Interest Rates

The concept of real interest rates is central to the understanding of the implications of financial policy for growth and development. Interest rates may be viewed as prices of financial assets. The **nominal interest rate** on loans is the stated rate agreed between lender and borrower at the time of contracting a loan. The nominal rate of interest on deposits is the rate offered to savers at the time the deposit is made. The nominal rate is defined as an obligation to pay (on loans) or a right to receive (on deposits) interest at a fixed rate regardless of the rate of inflation. Currency, which is debt of the central bank but a financial asset for currency holders, bears a *nominal* interest rate of zero. In some countries, such as Indonesia, Turkey, and South Korea, interest is paid on demand deposits, but typically this asset receives a nominal return of zero. Time deposits (including savings accounts) always bear positive nominal interest rates, ranging from as high as 30 percent in Indonesia in 1974 (for deposits committed for a two-year term) to as low as 4 percent in Ghana in the early 1970s. When an enterprise borrows from a commercial bank, the interest rate it agrees to pay is quoted in nominal terms, that is, independent of any changes in the general level of prices. Because costs are incurred in intermediating between savers and investors, the nominal lending rates must exceed nominal deposit rates or financial intermediaries will operate at a loss. However, in some countries, governments have, as a part of broader anti-inflationary programs, deliberately set lending rates below deposit rates and have subsidized banks to cover their losses, as in Korea (1960s) and Indonesia (1968 to 1980).

Nominal interest-rate levels—those quoted by banks on loans and deposits—are often subjected to maximum ceilings imposed by governments. For example, usury laws and conventions throughout much of the history of the United States limited nominal interest rates that could be charged on loans both to private citizens and the government. Similar laws have operated in developing countries. Also, several organized religions support limitations on nominal rates to limit usury; this adds moral force to conventions to limit usury.

Nominal interest rates are significant for financial development because the nominal rate governs the height of the *real* interest rate. The **real interest rate** is the nominal interest rate adjusted for inflation, or more precisely, the inflation rate expected by the public. Consider two depositors in different countries in otherwise identical circumstances, except that in one country the inflation rate is expected to be 5 percent and in the other 10 percent. If both receive nominal interest rates of 6 percent, then the real rate of interest in the first case is a positive 1 percent and in the second case a negative 4 percent. The prospective value of the deposit will rise in the first and fall in the second.

Borrowers as well as depositors respond ultimately to real, not nominal, rates of interest. At sustained high rates of inflation, say, 30 percent per year, borrowers will be quite willing, indeed eager, to pay nominal interest rates of 30 percent per year, for loans then are costless: they can be repaid in money with purchasing power well below that at the time of borrowing. Where legal ceilings do not apply on nominal interest rates, they will tend to adjust as expected inflation rises and falls. However, because ceilings on nominal interest rates are widespread and infrequently changed to reflect inflation, the inflation rate in many countries exceeds the nominal interest rate, and a negative real interest rate results.

When expected inflation rates are relatively low, the real interest rate can be calculated by merely subtracting the expected rise in prices from the nominal interest rate. Thus for annual inflation (p) below, say, 10 percent

$$r = i - p, \qquad [13-4]$$

where r = real interest rate, i = nominal interest rate, and p = expected inflation. (For all calculations of the real interest rate, we measure interest rates as decimal fractions, not percents—that is, 0.12 instead of 12 percent.)

Reference to the real interest rate on deposits or other financial instruments can be misleading. At any given time there will be a number of different nominal deposit rates in force in any economy. Nominal interest rates on short-term (say, three-month) deposits will generally be lower than those on longer-term (say, one- or two-year) deposits. Of course the real rate can be computed for any class of deposit. In this chapter it will be convenient to speak of "the" real rate, meaning the one rate that has been selected as an indicator of the structure of deposit rates. And because of difficulties in quantifying the expected inflation rate, the typical surrogate for the expected rate is a weighted average of inflation rates over the recent past (two to four years). "The" real rate of interest on loans is determined in similar fashion: a representative nominal rate on loans is chosen from the multitude of loan rates, and expected inflation is deducted to determine the real rate.

In economies experiencing high inflation and expectations of continued high price-increase rates, Equation 13–4 does not provide a reliable measure of real rates of interest. It then becomes necessary to employ a formula that more accurately recognizes that the corrosive power of inflation on nominal asset values works not instantaneously, but throughout a year:

$$r = (1+i)/(1+p) - 1. \qquad [13-5]$$

For example, inflation in Brazil in 1980 was near 100 percent but the nominal interest rate on one-year time deposits through most of the year was held to no more than 50 percent. Use of Equation 13–3 would indicate a real interest rate on deposits of minus 50 percent, assuming inflation was expected to continue at near 100 percent rates. However, correctly measured to reflect the steady, not precipitous action of inflation on nominal values, the real rate was minus 25 percent, as calculated below:

$$r = (1+0.50)/(1+1.00) - 1$$
$$r = -25 \text{ percent.}$$

This means that depositors who placed their money in a time deposit on January 1, 1980 would by the end of the year have suffered a decline in asset value of 25 percent, even though the nominal rate was a positive 50 percent. Put another way, depositors paid a tax of 25 percent on their inter-est-bearing money balances even if they paid no conventional taxes on their nominal interest income on bank deposits.

In cases where conventional income taxes are collected on interest income, the tax (at rate t) must also be deducted from the nominal rate in order to arrive at the real deposit rate net of taxes r_n:

$$r_n = \frac{1 + i(1 - t)}{1 + p} - 1. \qquad [13\text{--}6]$$

Thus with only a 20 percent income tax on interest, Equation 13–6 shows that the real rate of deposit interest in Brazil would be minus 30 percent.[15] Most countries impose taxes on interest income. A few countries, for example, Indonesia and Chile (for some types of interest), do not impose taxes on such income. But most others do, including Colombia, Thailand, Philippines, and Korea.

The discussion of inflation and real interest rates bring us to the point where we may evaluate the role of financial policy in a systematic fashion. We shall see that the real interest rate is critical in determining the extent to which the financial system will be able to *mobilize and allocate* savings for development finance. It is important to note that this is not the same thing as saying that higher real interest rates will induce households to save higher proportions of their income than would be the case at lower real interest rates. This would imply that the interest elasticity of savings is greater than zero. But if savings and consumption decisions are responsive to the real rate of interest, the effects of financial policy on income growth will be magnified.

INTEREST RATES AND SAVING DECISIONS

In evaluating the impact of financial policy on economic growth, it is important to distinguish between the implications of real interest rates for consumption-saving decisions on the one hand and for decisions about the uses of savings—including the channels through which savings flow—on the other. Debate over the first question revolves around estimates of the interest elasticity of savings (ϵ_{sr}); debate over the second is couched in terms of the elasticity of demand for liquid assets with respect to the real interest rate(ϵ_{lr}).

Where both elasticities are zero, financial policy can only have a minimal role in the development process. Where both elasticities are high and pos-itive, the scope for growth-oriented financial policy can be substantial. Where ϵ_{sr} is small or zero but ϵ_{lr} is positive and large, financial policy may still have significant impacts on savings mobilization through the financial sys-tem. Virtually all economists can agree that the real interest rate has a significant impact on the demand for liquid assets; that is, with higher real rates, a higher proportion of savings will be channeled through the financial

15. Equation 13–6 may also be expressed as follows: $r_n = \dfrac{i(1 - t) - p}{1 + p}$.

system. But as of the mid-1980s, there was no real consensus on the responsiveness of total domestic savings to real interest rates, that is, on the extent to which higher real rates may stimulate an increase in the ratio of savings to GNP, although there is a growing body of evidence, based on empirical studies in both the United States and Canada, that the interest elasticity of saving is not zero.

Research on consumption and saving in both industrial and developing countries has, as noted in Chapter 12, increasingly relied on variants of the permanent-income and life-cycle hypotheses. The results of these studies have conditioned many economists in both developing and developed countries to accept the notion of at least some positive interest elasticity of savings. Studies in the mid-seventies by Michael Boskin and Colin Wright using U.S. data indicate sizable elasticities of savings with respect to real interest rates, between 0.2 and 0.4.[16] Later research by Larry Summers at Harvard and by Canadian scholars suggests that the interest elasticity of saving may be as great as 1.0 or even higher.[17] However, even if these estimates ultimately gain wide acceptance for the United States and Canada, confirmation of similar relationships in the LDC context must awaits results of further econometric research.

We are left with the conclusion that positive real interest rates may be expected to have some useful effect on national savings ratios, but credible empirical estimates have yet to be made for developing countries.[18] What we can say at present is that positive real interest rates result in somewhat higher savings ratios than negative ones, perhaps by a substantial amount, perhaps by very little.

Interest Rates and Liquid Assets

Whereas the role of the real interest rate in savings-consumption decisions is a matter of some dispute, the role of real interest rates in influencing the demand for liquid assets is rarely questioned, whether in developed or developing countries. Indeed there is evidence that the real interest rate paid on deposits plays an even greater role in liquid asset demand in LDCs than in industrial countries. Furthermore, experience with marked adjust-

16. Wright's work in 1975 concluded that the interest elasticity of saving was about 0.2; this suggests that a 50 percent increase in real interest rates (say, from 6 to 9 percent) would provoke an increase in savings of about 10 percent. Boskin's results, strongly challenged by some economists, suggest an interest elasticity of saving twice as high, 0.4. See Colin Wright, "Savings and the Rate of Interest," in *The Taxation of Income from Capital,* Arnold C. Harberger and Martin Bailey, eds., (Washington, D.C.: Brookings Institution, 1969), and Michael J. Boskin, "Taxation, Savings and the Rate of Interest," *Journal of Political Economy* 8b, no. 2, part 2 (April 1978): 3–27.

17. Summers calculated that the long-run interest elasticity of saving may be as high as 2.0. This result was based on simulation using a growth model. More recently, Charles Beach, Robin Boadway, and Neil Bruce found an interest elasticity of saving for Canada of 1.2. See Larry Summers, "Capital Taxation and Capital Accumulation in a Life-Cycle Growth Model," *American Economic Review* 71 (September 1981): 533–544, and Charles Beach, Robin Boadway, and Neil Bruce, "Taxation and Savings: Some Life-Cycle Estimates for Canada," Ontario, Queens University Working Paper Series, August 1985.

18. For a critical discussion on the relationship between savings and interest rates in LDCs, however, see Alberto Giovanni, "The Interest Elasticity of Savings in Developing Countries," *World Development* 11 (July 1983): 601–608.

ments in real interest rates in Korea (1965), Indonesia (1968 to 1969, 1974, and 1983), Taiwan (1962), and a host of Latin American countries, strongly indicates the significance of real interest rates for growth in money holdings and demand and time deposits (M_2).

Liquid assets, or financial assets in general, represent one form in which savings out of past or current income can be held. The demand for liquid assets in economies where nominal interest rates are not allowed to adjust fully to expected rates of inflation, as is true for most LDCs, is typically represented as a function of income, the real interest rate, and the real rate of return available on nonfinancial assets:

$$L/P = d + d_1 Y + d_2 e + d_3 r, \qquad [13-7]$$

where L = liquid asset holdings; Y = real income, that is, money income deflated by the price level; P = price level; e = real return on nonfinancial assets; and r = the real interest rate on deposits; and d is a constant; d_1 and d_3 are expected to be positive, and d_2 negative.

The values for the parameters in Equation 13–7 are readily understandable. As real income (Y) grows, the public will desire to hold more purchasing power in the form of cash, demand, and time deposits, the principal forms of financial assets available in LDCs. In particular, d_1 is positive because at higher levels of real income there will be a greater need for higher real levels of liquid balances to carry out transactions and meet contingencies. Clearly, liquid asset balances furnish a convenience service to asset holders. In industrial societies with highly developed financial systems and securities markets, it might be reasonable to expect something like a proportional relationship between growth in income and growth in demand for liquid assets. However, in developing countries the demand for liquid assets may, given relative price stability, rise at a faster rate than income because of the paucity of other financial assets in which to hold savings. That is, in developing countries the income elasticity of demand for liquid assets may be expected to exceed unity. Indeed, even for fairly wealthy countries such as Malaysia in the 1970s, the demand for liquid assets grew 1.6 times as fast as did real income. For many Latin American countries the long-run income elasticity of money demand is also often above unity. In such circumstances the rate of increase in the supply of liquid assets (M_2) can exceed the rate of income growth by a substantial margin and price stability can still be maintained.

The sign for d_2, the coefficient of the return on nonfinancial assets, is negative since liquid assets are not the only repository for domestic savings. A range of assets, including nonfinancial assets and, in higher income LDCs, nonliquid financial assets such as securities, is available to savers. Higher returns on these nonliquid assets relative to liquid assets will induce a shift of savings out of the latter.

The coefficient of the real deposit rate d_3 has a positive sign, for at higher levels of real interest rates the public will be willing to hold larger liquid balances. Where r is negative, holders of all liquid assets pay hidden inflation taxes on their balances. Because higher rates of inflation tax are imposed

on non-interest-bearing assets (cash and demand deposits) than on interest-   **353**
bearing time deposits, savers will be less willing to hold liquid assets.

INTEREST RATES
AND SAVING
DECISIONS

There have been numerous studies of the demand for liquid assets in a variety of LDCs over the past two decades. In these studies estimates of the elasticity of demand for liquid assets with respect to real interest rates vary according to differing economic conditions across countries. However, in country after country the real interest rate has been found to be a powerful factor in affecting liquid asset demand. In Asia, where controls over interest rates have been most widely liberalized for the longest time, sharp increases in the real interest rate on time deposits (from negative to positive levels) have resulted in dramatic growth in the volume of such deposits. Marked increases in real interest rates were engineered through increases in nominal rates and the slowing down of inflation in the mid-1960s in South Korea, Taiwan, and Malaysia and in the late 1960s and again in 1974 and 1983 in Indonesia. In all cases the share of liquid assets in GNP rose strikingly. On the other hand, many Latin American and West African countries have allowed real interest rates to remain negative over long periods (see Tables 13–4 and 13–5). Consequently growth in the demand for liquid

TABLE 13–4 **Nominal and Real Deposit Interest Rates[a] in Selected Asian and Latin American Countries, 1970–89 (%) (real interest rates in parentheses)**

	1970	1976	1982	1989
Asia				
Bangladesh	—	6.7	12.0	12.0
		(7.8)	(2.3)	(1.8)
Malaysia	3.5	5.5	9.7	3.0 (1987)
	(1.6)	(2.7)	(3.7)	(2.1)
Pakistan	4.2	9.0	10.0	10.0
	(−1.7)	(1.8)	(3.9)	(2.8)
South Korea	22.8	16.2	8.0	10.0
	(12.6)	(0.8)	(0.7)	(4.2)
Thailand	6.0	8.0[b]	8.0	9.5
	(6.1)	(3.8)	(2.6)	(3.9)
Latin America				
Argentina	8.0	242.4	166.2	433.0 (1988)
	(−4.8)	(40.0)	(−25.4)	(20.1)
Brazil	26.4	28.0	49.0	3,554.0
	(3.0)	(−10.1)	(−25.0)	(163.5)
Chile	3.0	93.8	47.9	26.6 (1987)
	(−22.7)	(−38.7)	(34.3)	(5.7)
Colombia	4.1	20.0	29.5	27.7
	(−2.5)	(−0.2)	(3.8)	(1.5)
Peru	5.0	14.5	10.0[c]	8.3 (1984)
	(−0.7)	(14.5)	(−45.0)	(14.5)
Uruguay	6.0	30.2	50.1	84.7
	(−9.9)	(−11.4)	(26.2)	(2.3)

[a] Deposit rates on savings deposits or, where rates on savings deposits are unavailable, rates on shortest time deposits.
[b] Figures are for 1977.
[c] Figures are for 1983.

Sources: Korea 1970, David Cole and Yun Chul Park, *Financial Development in Korea 1945–1978* (Cambridge, Mass.: Harvard University Press, 1983; Thailand 1970, World Bank, *Thailand: Industrial Development Strategy* (Washington, D.C.: 1980), p. 57; Latin American countries 1970, Vicente Gablis, "Inflation and Interest Rate Policies in Latin America," *International Monetary Fund Staff Papers* 26, no. 2 (June 1977); and all countries after 1970: International Monetary Fund, *International Financial Statistics*, various issues.

TABLE 13–5 **Real Deposit Insurance Rates**[a] **in Six West African Countries, 1983–1989**
(in %, for end of period)

Country	1983	1984	1985	1986	1987	1988	1989
Gambia	−1.8	−10.6	−7.2	−25.8	−6.3	2.7	4.2
Ghana	−50.0	−17.8	5.2	−5.6	−16.0	−8.7	—
Ivory Coast	1.4	3.1	5.3	−1.1	4.8	−1.6	8.4
Liberia	7.0	8.5	10.0	3.5	0.8	−3.8	—
Senegal	2.9	0.0	0.1	0.1	0.1	0.1	—
Sierra Leone	−33.9	−32.5	−32.9	−36.9	−59.6	−11.4	−26.3

Sources: International Monetary Fund, *International Financial Statistics Yearbook 1989*, and World Bank, *World Development Indicators 1990*.

assets was minimal in these countries and in most, the share of liquid assets in GDP either declined or remained constant (see Table 13–1) until after financial reforms were implemented in the early eighties.

FINANCIAL DEVELOPMENT

Shallow Finance and Deep Finance

Policies for financial deepening seek to promote growth in the real size of the financial system: the growth of financial assets at a pace faster than income growth. In all but the highest-income LDCs private-sector financial savings predominantly take the form of currency and deposits in commercial banks, savings and loan associations, postal savings accounts, and, in some countries, mortgage banks. Thus for most LDCs growth in the real size of the financial system is primarily reflected in growth in the share of liquid assets in GDP. By contrast, under **shallow finance** the ratio of liquid assets to GDP grows slowly or not at all over time and typically will fall: the real size of the financial system shrinks. Countries able to mobilize large volumes of government savings or foreign savings an sustain high growth rates even under shallow finance policies, although even these countries may find financial deepening attractive for reasons of employment and income distribution. But for countries where mobilization of government savings is difficult and foreign savings scarce or unwanted, deep finance may be essential for sustained income growth. This is because growth in the share of liquid assets in GDP provides an approximate indication of the banking system's ability to increase its lending for investment purposes. We will see that the hallmark of deep financial strategy is the avoidance of negative real interest rates; shallow finance, on the other hand, typically involves sharply negative real interest rates.

Growth in the real size of the financial system enhances its capacity for intermediation: the gathering of savings from diverse private sources and the channeling of these savings into productive investment. The need for financial intermediation arises because savings endowments do not necessarily correspond to investment opportunity. Those individuals with the greatest capacity to save are not usually those with the entrepreneurial talents required for mounting new investment projects. Except in very simple, rudimentary economies, mechanisms are required to channel savings efficiently from savers to entrepreneurs. In rudimentary economies, production in farming, industry, and other activities is small scale and involves traditional technologies. Producers can ordinarily finance most of their modest investment requirements from their current savings, or those of their families (self-finance). Small-scale enterprises employing traditional technologies have an important role to play in development (see Chapter 20). Yet at some stage improvement in productivity (and therefore living standards) in any economy requires the adoption of newer technologies. These typically involve lumpy investments that are ordinarily well beyond the financial capacity of all but the wealthiest families. Where enterprise finance is restricted to current family savings, only very wealthy groups can adopt such innovations. Thus a heavy reliance on self-finance tends to be associated with both low productivity and, usually, persistent income inequality.

Restriction to self-finance also guarantees that many productive opportunities involving high private and social payoffs will never be seized, because even the resources of the small number of very wealthy are not unlimited. Innovative, smaller-scale investors are not the only groups that fare poorly where financial intermediation is poorly developed; savers are penalized as well. Let us first examine the case where even the most basic financial intermediaries—commercial banks—are absent. Under these circumstances the domestic options open to savers are limited to forms of savings such as the acquisition of gold and jewelry, purchase of land and consumer durable goods, or other relatively sterile forms of investment in physical assets. Alternatively, wealthier savers may ship their savings abroad. The common feature of all such investments is that the resources devoted to them are inaccessible to those domestic entrepreneurs who would adopt new technology, begin new firms, or expand production in existing enterprises. Savings in the form of physical assets like gold may be plentiful, as in France or India, but this type of savings is effectively locked away from investors or at a minimum may be trapped in declining sectors of the economy, unable to flow to sectors with the brightest investment prospects.

However, even where financial intermediation is poorly developed, individuals have the option of holding some of their savings in the form of currency. Additions to cash hoards are superior to investment in unproductive physical assets from an economy wide point of view, since at least this serves to curtail the demand for physical assets, reduce upward pressures on their prices, and thus moderate domestic inflation. Nevertheless, savings held in this form are still relatively inaccessible to investors.

There are now virtually no societies where financial systems are as rudimentary as those sketched above. All LDCs have financial institutions, however embryonic, to serve as intermediaries between savers and investors, even where these intermediaries are limited to commercial banks that accept checking (demand) and time (savings) deposits from savers, for purposes of relending to prospective investors at short term. Intermediation flourishes under deep finance, but under strategies of shallow finance intermediation is constricted and the financial system can contribute little to further the goals of economic growth. Later we will see that shallow finance may have unintended effects on employment and income distribution as well.

Shallow Financial Strategy

Shallow financial policies have a number of earmarks: high legal reserve requirements on commercial banks, pervasive nonprice rationing of credit, and most of all, sharply negative real interest rates. Countries rarely, if ever, have consciously and deliberately adopted strategies of shallow finance. Rather, the repression of the financial system flows logically from certain policies intended to encourage, not hinder, investment.

In developed and developing countries alike, policymakers have often viewed low nominal rates of interest as essential for expansion of investment and have controlled interest rate levels tightly. Indeed, so long as the supply of investible funds is unlimited, low interest rates will foster all types of investment activities, as even projects with low returns will appear more attractive to investors. In accordance with that observation, and in the belief that low interest rates are particularly essential to assist small enterprises and small farmers, governments have often placed low ceilings on nominal interest rates charged on all types of loans, quite apart from special credit programs involving subsidized credit for special classes of borrowers. Because financial institutions must ultimately cover costs (or else be subsidized by governments), low legal ceilings on nominal loan rates mean low nominal interest rates on deposits as well.

As long as inflation is held in check, low ceilings on nominal loan and deposit interest rates may not retard growth, even when these ceilings are set below the opportunity cost of capital. Indeed the United States over the period 1800 to 1979 managed rather respectable rates of income growth even in the presence of a set of archaic usury laws and other interest rate controls that (particularly before 1970) often involved artificially low, administered ceilings on interest rates. Even so, throughout most of the period before 1979 real interest rates in the United States remained positive; periods in which real interest rates were sharply negative were intermittent and confined to wartime (1812, 1861, 1917–1918, and 1940–1946).[19]

Usury laws and other forms of interest rate ceilings have been common in developing countries as well, for all the reasons given above plus one more: financial officials in many LDCs, observing gross imperfections in financial markets, have concluded that the market should not be permitted to determine interest rates. Monopoly (or oligopoly) power in financial markets—particularly in commerical banking—does in fact provide ample scope for the banks and other lenders to exercise market power in setting interest rates on loans at levels higher than the opportunity cost of capital.

There are ample observations of gross imperfections in financial systems in LDCs. Barriers to entry into banking and finance often allow a few large banks and other financial institutions to possess an inordinate degree of

---

19. Steven C. Leuthold, "Interest Rates, Inflation and Deflation," *Financial Analysis Journal* (January–February 1981): 28–51.

control over financial markets and thus to exercise monopoly power in setting interest rates. Often these barriers are a direct result of government policies, as governments may have prohibited new entrants into the field, adopted such stringent financial requirements for entry that only the very wealthy could amass the needed capital, or reserved permission for entry to political favorites who were attracted to banking and finance largely by the monopoly returns available when entry was restricted.

In this way one set of government policies—entry restrictions—helps give rise to the need for extensive controls on price charged by financial institutions. Typically these controls take the form of interest rate ceilings imposed to limit the scope of monopoly power in the financial system. Controls by themselves do not necessarily lead to shallow finance. It is the combination of rigid ceilings on nominal interest rates and inflation that impedes financial development and ultimately retards income growth.

Few economists believe that steeply positive real interest rates are essential for healthy growth in the real size of the financial system. In fact, the Chilean experience with very high real interest rates in 1981 to 1983 strongly suggests the opposite. Indeed there is no widely accepted answer to the question: What level of real interest rates is required for steady development of the financial system? Clearly the required real rate will differ across countries in different circumstances. In some, financial growth may continue even at zero or mildly negative real interest rates; for others, moderately high positive real rates of between 3 and 5 percent may be essential.

In an earlier section we saw that apart from a few Latin American countries and Indonesia, most LDCs were able to keep rates of inflation at or below 5 to 6 percent prior to 1973. Inasmuch as nominal deposit rates were typically between 3 and 5 percent, real interest rates tended to be slightly positive or only mildly negative. After 1973 inflation accelerated in many developing countries, including those accustomed to relative price stability; typical rates (again except for several Latin American countries experiencing acute economic instability) varied from 8 to 16 percent. Because few countries made more than marginal adjustments in nominal deposit rates, real interest rates after the early 1970s turned significantly negative in many Asian and Latin American nations (see Table 13–3) and sharply negative in those with inflation rates exceeding 25 percent. Negative interest rates were even more common and enduring in some African countries in the period 1983 to 1989. Table 13–4 displays real interest rates for six countries in West Africa. Of this group, only Senegal consistently recorded positive real rates of interest over the period. And in Sierra Leone the real rate was never positive in any year.

When real interest rates turn significantly negative—much more than minus 3 to 6 percent—then the maintenance of low nominal rates for the purposes of promoting investment and income growth becomes counterproductive. Inflation taxes on liquid financial assets will bring real growth in the financial system to a halt. Sharply negative real rates lead to a shrinkage in the system, as the demand for liquid assets will contract. This tendency is evident from a comparison of Tables 13–1 and 13–3. Countries where real interest rates were only mildly negative, or sharply negative only for short periods of time, experienced little or no growth in the real size of their financial systems as measured by the ratio of liquid assets to GDP. These include the Philippines, Tanzania, and Mexico. But where real interest rates have been sharply negative over extended periods of time, as in Argentina, Peru, Brazil in the 1970s, and Ghana, the real size of the financial system has shrunk. Contraction in the real size of the financial system results in a reduction in the real supply of credit and thus constricts investment in productive assets.

Under such circumstances nonprice rationing of investible resources must occur, and can take many forms. In most LDCs only those borrowers with either the highest quality collateral or the "soundest" social and political connections, or those willing to pay the largest under-the-table inducements to bank officers, will be successful in securing finance from the organized financial system. These criteria do not yield allocations of credit to the most productive investment opportunities.

Negative real interest rates make marginal, low-yielding, traditional types of investment appear attractive to investors. Banks and financial institutions find such projects attractive as well, since they may be the safest and the simplest to finance and involve the most credit-worthy borrowers. Thus such undertakings tend to move to the head of the queue of borrowers. Satisfying the financial requirements of such investors constricts the pool of resources available to firms with riskier projects offering greater possibilities for high yields. Additionally, in the presence of substantial inflation, interest rate ceilings discourage risk taking by the financial institutions themselves, since under such circumstances they cannot charge higher interest rates (risk premia) on promising by risky projects. Also, negative real interest rates are inimical to employment growth, as they make projects with relatively high capital-output ratios appear more attractive than if real interest rates were positive. This implicit subsidy to capital-intensive methods of production reduces the jobs created for each dollar of investment, even as the ability of the financial system to finance investment is shrinking.

Negative real rates of interest tend to lower the marginal efficiency of investment in all of the ways described. In terms of the Harrod-Domar model described in Chapter 3, shallow financial strategies cause higher capital-output ratios. Consequently growth in national income, and therefore, growth in savings, tends to be lower than when real rates are positive. Therefore shallow finance retards income and employment growth even if the interest elasticity of savings is zero. And if savings decisions are responsive to real interest rates, then shallow finance will have even more serious implications for income growth, as the ratio of private savings to GDP will also contract.

Deep Financial Strategies

Deep finance as a strategy has several objectives: (1) mobilizing a larger volume of savings from the domestic economy, that is, increasing the ratio of national savings to GDP (where the interest elasticity of savings is thought to be positive and significant); (2) enhancing the accessibility of savings for all types of domestic investors; (3) securing a more efficient allocation of investment throughout the economy; and (4) permitting the financial process to mobilize and allocate savings to reduce reliance on the fiscal process, foreign aid, and inflation.

A permanent move toward policies involving positive real interest rates, or at a minimum avoidance of sharply negative real rates, is the essence of deep finance. In turn this requires financial liberalization that allows higher nominal rates on deposits and loans, curbing the rate of inflation, or some combination of both.

Given the difficulties involved in securing quick results in reducing inflation to levels consistent with positive real rates of interest, the first step involved in a shift from shallow to deep financial strategies is ordinarily that of raising ceilings on nominal rates for both deposits and loans. In some cases this has required nominal interest rates as high as 30 percent on time deposits (Korea in 1966, Indonesia in 1968 and 1974).[20] In extreme cases of acute inflation the initial step has involved raising ceilings on nominal deposit rates to as much as 50 percent in Argentina and Uruguay in 1976 and to nearly 200 percent in Chile in 1974 (where real interest rates nevertheless remained negative until 1976). As the real rate moves toward positive levels, savers strongly tend to increase their holdings of liquid assets; this allows a real expansion in the supply of credit to investors. Marked increases in flows of savings to financial institutions have been observed when nominal rates were increased substantially, as in Uruguay in 1976, Indonesia in 1968–1969 and 1983, and Taiwan and South Korea in 1965 (see Tables 13–1 and 13–3). Notable responses have also occurred in countries where mildly negative real rates were moved closer to positive levels through increases in nominal rates: these include India and Sri Lanka after 1977 and Turkey after 1980.

Available evidence suggests that countries that attempt to maintain modestly positive real interest rates over long periods tend to be among those with the highest rates of financial growth. Indonesia, Malaysia, and Thailand experienced large increases in the real sizes of their financial systems over the period 1960 to 1989. For virtually the entire period real interest rates were positive in both countries, save for 1973 and 1974 when world inflation unexpectedly surged to double-digit numbers. Real rates have been positive in Taiwan almost every year since 1965, and over that span the ratio of liquid asset to GDP rose to levels characteristic of industrial countries. Nevertheless, one can have too much of a good thing. This is as true for real interest rates as for smoked salmon. One factor contributing to sharply negative real GDP growth rates in Chile in 1982 and 1983 was the emergence of very high real interest rates in 1981 and 1982. The nominal interest rate on loans increased sharply, while at the same time there was

---

20. Ceilings need rarely be increased to the point where they match the *current* rate of inflation. For example, in Indonesia in 1974 the nominal ceiling on two-year time deposits was raised to only 30 percent, even though inflation over the previous 12 months was 42 percent. The increase in nominal rates, coupled with a battery of other measures, convinced depositors that real rates would soon be positive. All that is required is that the inflation expected by savers be reduced to levels closer to the nominal deposit rate.

a very large and unexpected drop in inflation: the real interest rate soared above 30 percent.[21]

Where finance is deep, inflation tends to be moderate; therefore savers are not subject to persistently high inflation taxes on liquid asset holdings. That being the case, they will be less inclined to shift their savings into much more lightly taxed domestic assets such as gold, land, or durable goods, and foreign assets such as currencies or land and securities. Rather, financial resources that otherwise may have been utilized for these purposes flow to the financial system, where they are more accessible to prospective investors. Nonprice rationing of credit, inevitable under shallow finance, will diminish as well. As a result of the capacity of the financial system to identify and support socially profitable investment opportunities expands: higher-risk, higher-yielding investment projects stand a far-better chance of securing finance under deep than shallow finance. Growth prospects are accordingly enhanced.

The preceding discussion represents but a sketch of policies designed to promote financial deepening. The focus has been on the real interest rate on deposits and loans when in fact a variety of other policies may be involved. These include central bank payment of interest on commercial bank reserves, and avoidance of high legal reserve requirements to commercial banks. That positive real interest rates tend to lead to growth in the real size of banking systems is now rarely questioned. Such a development substantially enlarges the real flow of short-term credit, the stock-in-trade of commercial banks. However, investment finance problems do not end with provision of a growing real flow of short-term credit. As economies move to higher levels of per-capita income, the pattern of investment shifts toward longer horizons. Longer-term investment requires longer-term finance. Commercial banks everywhere are ill-suited for providing substantial amounts of long-term finance, given that their deposits are primarily of a short-term nature.

Therefore, as financial and economic development proceeds, the need for institutions specializing in longer-term finance rises accordingly: insurance companies, investment banks, and ultimately equity markets (stock exchanges) become important elements in financial intermediation. Nevertheless the type of well-functioning commercial bank system that tends to develop under deep finance is almost always a necessary condition for the successful emergence and long-term vitality of institutions specializing in longer-term investment finance. Where entry into financial activities is only lightly restricted, longer-term financial institutions may appear spontaneously.

But earlier we observed that entry into the financial field is rarely easy, and other factors also often lead to gross imperfections in financial markets. In such circumstances many LDC governments have found intervention essential in order to develop financial institutions specializing in

---

21. Chilean real GDP growth was minus 13.2 percent in 1982 and minus 2.3 percent in 1983. For a comprehensive discussion of the Chilean economic debacle of 1982–1983, see Sebastian Edwards "Stabilization with Liberalization: An Evaluation of Chile's Experiment with Free-Market Policies 1973–1983," *Economic Development and Cultural Change* 27 (September 1985): 224–253.

longer-term finance. Intervention may take the form of the establishment

361

FINANCIAL
DEVELOPMENT
of government-owned development banks and other specialized institutions to act as distributors of government funds intended as a source of longer-term finance, as in Indonesia and Pakistan. In other cases, as in Mexico, Colombia, and Venezuela, governments have provided strong incentives for private-sector establishment of long-term financial institutions. Finally, in other countries governments have sought to create conditions favorable for the emergence of primary securities (stocks and bonds) markets, the source par excellence for long-term finance. In cases where these measures have been undertaken in the context of financial markets with strong commercial banking systems (South Korea, Thailand, Brazil, Mexico), efforts to encourage long-term finance have met with some success. In cases where commercial banking has been poorly developed as a consequence of shallow finance (Ghana, Uruguay before 1976), or where government has sought to "force-feed" embryonic securities markets through tax incentives and other subsidies (Indonesia, Kenya, Turkey), the promotional policies have been less-effective.

Real Interest Rates and Economic Growth

We have seen that positive real interest rates tend to foster growth in the real size of the financial system. But, must real interest rates be positive for real income growth to occur? Although this remains something of an unsettled question, available evidence does seem to suggest that a higher rate of growth in the financial system has been positively correlated with successful real income growth, at least over the period 1971 to 1980. Certainly this was the case for the 21 countries listed in Table 13–6. The clearest lesson to be drawn from that table is not, however, that positive real interest rates are required for growth, but that avoidance of severely negative real interest rates is good growth strategy. The record of income growth from 1971 to 1980 for countries with only moderately negative real interest rates was not materially lower than those with positive real interest rates.

Informal Credit Markets

The discussion of financial development has dealt with modern credit institutions, the formal market. But in many developing countries an **informal credit market** coexists with modern financial institutions. These markets arise in many forms. In rural India, village moneylenders make loans to local farmers who have no access to commercial banks. In Bangladesh, the 20-year-old Grameen Bank, founded by Muhammad Yunus, provides credit to people in 18,000 of the country's 68,000 villages. The average loan is $60, the maximum $200. Sixty-five percent of the Bangladeshi borrowers are landless women; all loan recipients are poor. But the recovery rate exceeds 97% percent. Interest rates on the loans are not heavily subsidized.[22] In Ghana and other West African countries, market women give

---

22. Information from a public lecture by M. Yunus, Asheville, N. C., October 30, 1990. See also World Bank, *World Development Report 1989*, p. 117.

TABLE 13–6 Selected Developing Countries Grouped According to Interest Rate
Policies: Growth of Real Financial Assets and Real GDP, 1971–1980
(compound growth rates)

	Financial assets[a] (percent growth)	GDP (percent growth)
1. Countries with positive real interest rates		
Malaysia	13.8	8.0
Korea	11.1	8.6
Sri Lanka	10.1	4.7
Nepal	9.6	2.0
Singapore	7.6	9.1
Philippines	5.6	6.2
2. Countries with moderately negative real interest rates		
Pakistan[b]	9.9	5.4
Thailand	8.5	6.9
Morocco	8.2	5.5
Colombia	5.5	5.8
Greece	5.4	4.7
South Africa	4.3	3.7
Kenya	3.6	5.7
Burma	3.5	4.3
Portugal	1.8	4.7
Zambia	−1.1	0.8
3. Countries with severely negative real interest rates		
Peru	3.2	3.4
Turkey	2.2	5.1
Jamaica	−1.9	−0.7
Zaire	−6.8	0.1
Ghana	−7.6	−0.1

[a] Measured as the sum of monetary and quasi-monetary deposits with the banking sector, corrected for changes in the consumer price index.
[b] The period covered is 1974 to 1980.
Source: Ronald I. McKinnon, "Financial Liberalization and Economic Development: A Reassessment of Interest Rate Policies in Asia and Latin America," International Center for Economic Growth, Occasional Paper No. 6, San Francisco, 1988.

credit to farmers by paying for crops in advance of harvest, and they assist their customers by selling finished goods on credit. In South Korea, established lenders literally make loans on the street outside modern banks; this justifies their designation as the "curb" market. In much of rural Africa, wealthy family members make loans to less fortunate kin, and all over the developing world there are cooperative arrangements to raise funds and share credit among members. Even in modern economies, pawnbrokers and others give credit outside the formal credit system.

Informal credit is generally financed by the savings of relatively wealthy individuals, such as local landowners, traders, family members who have moved into lucrative jobs or businesses, and the pooled efforts of cooperative societies. But informal lenders may also have access to the formal banking system and borrow there, to relend to customers with no access to banks. How can they do this if the banks cannot? First, because they know their borrowers so well and may have familial, social, or other ties to them, informal lenders face lower risks than distant, large banks that might loan to the same borrowers. Loan recovery rates are higher (usually much higher than found in large banks in LDCs) because those who borrow in informal markets know that the availability of loans in the future is dependent on repaying current loans. Second, they also face lower administrative costs in making loans. Of course, moneylenders do charge very high interest rates, and this is the second reason they coexist with banks, which are often prevented by law from charging rates high enough to cover the risks and costs of loans in small amounts to very small firms and low-income borrowers.

As modern credit institutions evolve, especially under deep financial policies, they draw customers and resources from the informal market. First, some of the largest and most creditworthy borrowers from informal lenders eventually qualify as borrowers in the formal market. Second, some moneylenders may themselves establish credit institutions within the informal system. Third, banks begin to attract savings from a wider group of households, some of which had previously directed their savings into informal channels. On all counts, the informal market is likely to shrink in size and coverage, though it is likely to exist in tandem for some time. The process may leave behind several kinds of borrowers, such as small farmers, traders, artisans, and manufacturers, who will still depend on the shrinking informal market for their credit. Competitive, efficient, and varied financial institutions—the kind encouraged by deep financial policies—will have incentives to integrate borrowers into the modern market, and thus reduce the adverse impacts of financial development on those who once depended on informal credit markets.

MONETARY POLICY AND PRICE STABILITY

We have seen that apart from a limited number of cases in Asia, prior to the 1970s double-digit inflation was largely confined to a few developing countries in Latin America. By the last decade of this century, inflation had become a serious problem in a number of African and Middle Eastern nations and much of Central America.

Monetary Policy and Exchange Rate Regimes

Appropriate use of monetary policy in controlling inflation depends critically on the type of exchange-rate regime used by a country. Exchange-rate regimes form a continuum with **fixed-exchange rate** systems at one end and systems with **freely floating exchange rates** (also known as **fully flexible exchange rates**) at the other. Under a fixed-exchange-rate (also known as a **pegged-exchange-rate**) system, a country attempts to maintain the value of its currency in a fixed relation to another currency, say the U.S. dollar: the value of the local currency is **pegged** to the dollar. This is done through intervention by the country's monetary authorities in the market for foreign exchange and requires the maintenance of substantial **international reserves** (reserves of foreign currencies), usually equivalent to the value of six or more months' worth of imports.

For example, consider a country such as the Philippines. In December

1990 the Philippine currency, the peso, was fixed at an exchange rate of 27 pesos to 1 U.S. dollar. Because the exchange rate, if left to its own devices, would change from day to day to reflect changes in both the demand and supply of Philippine exports and imports and in capital flows, the government must be prepared to use the nation's international reserves to buy or sell dollars at an exchange rate of 27:1 in order to keep the exchange rate from moving. If, for example, a poor domestic harvest caused the nation to increase its food imports in January 1990, the peso / dollar exchange rate would tend to rise, in the absence of any net sales of dollars from the Philippine's international reserves.

Under freely floating rates, the authorities simply allow the value of local currency vis-a-vis foreign ones to be determined by market forces. Between the two ends of this continuum (see Figure 13–1) lie a number of intermediate options.[23] Closest to the floating exchange rate option is the **wider band** system, wherein the exchange rate of a country is allowed to float or fluctuate within a predefined band of values, say between 12 and 10 pesos to 1 U.S. dollar. But when conditions threaten to push the value of the currency beyond the band, the authorities intervene by buying or selling local currency as appropriate to stay within the band. Further along the continuum away from floating rates is the **managed float,** where there is no particular exchange rate that the authorities are committed to defend, but where they nevertheless intervene continuously at their discretion. A country with steadily shrinking international reserves might, for example, allow the value of its currency to drift downward against the value of other currencies, i.e., allow the exchange rate against other currencies to rise.

FIGURE 13–1   **Continuum of Prototypes of Exchange Rate Regimes.** As one moves from point A on the left to point B on the right, both the frequency of intervention by domestic monetary authorities and the required level of international reserves tends to be lower. Under a pure fixed-exchange-rate regime (point A) authorities intervene so that the value of the currency vis-a-vis another, say the U.S. dollar, is maintained at a constant rate. Under a freely floating exchange rate regime, authorities do not intervene in the market for foreign exchange, and there is minimal need for international reserves; indeed, there can be no balance-of-payments deficit.

Two other systems are closely related hybrids of fixed and floating rules. The **crawling peg,** used over a long period by Brazil and Colombia, involves pegging the local currency against some other currency, but changing this in gradual, periodic steps to adjust for any differential between the country's inflation rate and the world inflation rate. Closest to a fixed-exchange-rate system is the **adjustable peg,** involving a commitment by the monetary

23. For a full discussion of these and other types of exchange-rate regimes, see John Williamson, *The Open Economy and the World Economy* (New York: Basic Books, 1983), pp. 238–241, or Anne O. Krueger, *Exchange Rate Determination* (New York: Cambridge University Press, 1983), pp. 123–136.

authorities to defend the local exchange rate at a fixed parity (peg), while **365**
reserving the right to change that rate when circumstances require. MONETARY
POLICY AND
PRICE STABILITY

The currencies of the major industrial countries have all floated vis-a-vis one another, with occasional intervention by national monetary authorities to prevent very sharp swings in rates. Most LDCs adhere to either the adjustable-peg or the crawling peg system. Since in practice both systems are fixed-rate regimes, for our analysis we will focus most of our attention on monetary policy issues arising under fixed exchange rates in small open economies.

Sources of Inflation

In open LDC economies with fixed exchange rates, the rate of monetary expansion is no longer under the complete control of domestic monetary authorities. Rather, countries with fixed exchange rates may be viewed as sharing essentially the same money supply, because the money of each can be converted into that of the others at a fixed parity.[24] Under such circumstances, the stock of money (M) is by definition the sum of two components: the amount of domestic credit of the banking system that is outstanding (DC), and the stock of international reserves of that country (IR), measured in terms of domestic currency. There is therefore a domestic and an international component of the money supply. Thus we have

$$M = DC + IR. \qquad [13-18]$$

Changes in the domestic money stock can occur either through expansion of domestic credit or by monetary movements that lead to changes in international reserves. That is,

$$\Delta M = \Delta DC + \Delta IR. \qquad [13-19]$$

Under fixed exchange rates a central bank of any small country can control DC, the domestic component, but it has only very limited control over IR, the international component. Under such circumstances LDCs that attempt to keep the rate of domestic inflation below the world inflation rate (through restrictive policies on domestic credit) will be unable to realize this goal. If, fueled by monetary expansion abroad (growth in the world money supply), world inflation initially is running in excess of domestic inflation, the prices of internationally traded goods will rise relative to those of domestic nontraded goods.[25] Imports will fall, exports will rise, and the balance of payments of the LDC will move toward surplus and cause a rise in international reserves. Thus the foreign components of the money stock will rise. This is tantamount to "importation of money" and will eventually

---

24. This section draws substantially on syntheses of monetary and international economics by Arnold C. Harberger. See his "A Primer on Inflation," and "The Inflation Syndrome," paper presented in the Political Economy Lecture Series, Harvard University, March 19, 1981.

25. The above is but one of several mechanisms that led to changes in international reserves sufficient to thwart efforts by LDCs to insulate themselves from world inflation. See Harberger, "A Primer on Inflation" and "The Inflation Syndrome."

undo the effort to prevent the importation of world inflation. Again, a small country on fixed exchange rates can do little to maintain its inflation rate below that of the rest of the world. For very open LDCs with few restrictions on the movement of goods and capital into and out of the country, the adjustment to world inflation can be vary rapid (less than a year). For less-open countries with substantial restrictions on international trade and payments, the process takes longer, but the outcome is inevitable under fixed exchange rates.

The fact that financial policy for stabilization in LDCs with fixed exchange rates is heavily constrained by international developments is sometimes taken to mean that changes in the domestic component of the money stock have no impact on prices in LDCs adhering to fixed exchange rates. On the contrary, excessive expansion in money and credit will surely result in domestically generated inflation that, depending on the rate of expansion, can for a time be well in excess of world inflation rates. However, such a situation cannot continue for long, as excess money creation will spill over into the balance of payments via increased imports and lead to a drain on international reserves and, ultimately, an inability to maintain the fixed exchange rate. As reserves dwindle, the country can no longer defend its exchange rate and devaluation becomes inevitable.[26] Inflation can therefore be transmitted to LDCs through the working of the world economy or can be generated by domestic developments.

Very few developing countries have ever employed floating exchange rates (point B on the continuum in Figure 13–1). A floating-exchange-rate regime would allow countries to insulate themselves from world inflation. Under such a system, the rise in world prices attendant upon world inflation would initially favor exports from the country and discourage imports. As a consequence, the current account of the country's balance of payments would improve (see Chapter 15), international reserves would rise, and the exchange rate would soon appreciate (fewer pesos would be required to buy dollars, for instance). The appreciation in the country's exchange rate would cancel out external price increases and prevent the importation of world inflation.

Under any exchange-rate regime, domestically generated inflation may result from excessive increases in domestic credit from the banking system to either the public or the private sector. Budgetary deficits of the central government must be financed by borrowing. The embryonic nature of money and capital markets in most LDCs generally means that governments facing deficits must ordinarily resort to borrowing from the central bank, a process equivalent to direct money creation via the printing press. The result is a direct addition to the reserve base of the monetary system, an increase in so-called high-powered money. It is important, however, to recognize that not all budgetary deficits are necessarily inflationary. We have seen that a growing economy will be characterized by a growing demand for liquid assets, including money. Moderate budgetary deficits year after year,

---

26. Import controls are frequently used to stem the drain of reserves and avoid devaluation for a time. But import controls engender another set of distortions and inefficiencies—explored in Chapter 16—that eventually require more drastic measures, including devaluation.

financed by the central bank, can help to satisfy this requirement without leading to inflation. In general the money stock may expand at least as fast as the growth in real income, with little or no inflationary consequences.[27]

For a country like Peru, where liquid assets were, prior to the recent hyperinflation, about 25 percent of GDP (see Table 13–1), even a small deficit can result in substantial inflation. For a country such as Malaysia, where the money stock is about 125 percent of GDP, a much larger deficit would be consistent with price stability. In Peru a noninflationary deficit might have to be as low as 0.5 percent of GDP; for Malaysia a budgetary deficit financed by bank credit might be as high as 2.5 percent of GDP with little inflationary consequences.[28] In general, deficits of around 1 percent of GDP or less are not inconsistent with price level stability in typical LDCs. But given a stable demand for liquid assets, much larger deficits will clearly be inflationary.

Use of bank credit to finance government deficits has not been the only source of inflationary monetary expansion in LDCs. Sometimes excessive growth of credit to the private sector has played the most significant role in domestically generated inflationary processes. Nevertheless, as a general rule, inflation rates for a particular LDC that are much in excess of world inflation have usually been traceable to budgetary deficits.

It is evident, then, that for LDCs attempting to maintain fixed exchange rates, efforts to avoid inflation rates in excess of world inflation must primarily be a matter of fiscal policy, not monetary policy. If budget deficits are not held to levels consistent with world inflation, even very deft deployment of monetary policy instruments will be unable to prevent rapid inflation, devaluation, or both. There is still a role for monetary policy in LDCs, but that role must be largely passive. Resourceful use of monetary policy can help by not making things worse, and also by moderating strong inflationary pressures until the budget can be brought under control, provided the latter is done fairly quickly.

We have seen that monetary factors are causes of inflation in both fixed- and floating-exchange-rate countries. In the case of fixed exchange rates, both world monetary expansion and domestic monetary expansion generate inflation; in flexible-exchange-rate countries, inflation arises from domestic monetary sources. But thus far, no mention has been made of so-called nonmonetary causes of inflation. It seems plausible that internal and

27. Earlier we saw that liquid assets are normally between 35 and 50 percent of GDP in most LDCs, or equivalent to roughly four to six months of income. Thus the public is generally willing to hold this much in money balances. A deficit of 2 percent of GDP financed by money creation would add only marginally to the money supply, and may easily be accepted by the public. But a deficit of 8 percent of GDP would increase the stock of money by an amount equal to one more month of income, or by an amount more than the public would be willing to hold (unless nominal interest rates on deposits are greatly increased). The excess would spill over into the higher prices.

28. A deficit of 0.5 percent of GDP in Peru would, if financed by the central bank, cause the stock of money to grow by 1.8 percent, a rate well below the rate of real income growth in that country from 1960 to 1980. A deficit of that size could be financed, while still allowing substantial growth (5 to 6 percent) in credit to the private sector. A deficit of 2.5 percent of GDP in Malaysia, financed also by credit to the government, would also lead to growth in the money stock of only 1.5 percent, clearly well below expansion required to fuel inflation.

external shocks, such as those arising from widespread crop failure in the domestic economy or a drastic increase in prices of imported energy, could have an important effect on inflation in countries suffering such shocks. This is true, but the mechanism whereby nonmonetary factors may initiate or worsen inflation needs to be clearly portrayed.

Nonmonetary disturbances may indeed precipitate policy reactions that lead to domestic monetary expansion large enough to accommodate higher relative prices of food or oil, and large enough to cause inflation. In the absence of accommodating monetary expansion in the face of such shocks, inflation can be contained, but at some cost. In practice failure to allow the money supply to expand to accommodate higher relative prices of important goods leads to increases in unemployment that most governments find unacceptable. Therefore, as a matter of course, governments in such cases usually do attempt to allow monetary expansion sufficient to avoid unwanted consequences for employment. But it is important to remember that however advisable monetary accommodation may be on social and employment grounds, expansion in the money stock is required to fuel inflation, whatever the external or internal factors may be that precipitated the expansion. But this truth, known for centuries, is often incorrectly interpreted to mean that nonmonetary factors cannot "cause" inflation. They can, but only through an expansion of the national or international stock of money or both.

Controlling Inflation through Monetary Policy

The array of available instruments of anti-inflationary monetary policy in developed countries include: (1) open-market operations,[29] wherein the central bank can directly contract bank reserves by sales of government securities; (2) increases in legal reserve requirements of banks, so that a given volume of reserves will support a lower stock of money (and reduce the credit expansion multiplier as well); (3) increases in rediscount rates, so that commercial bank borrowing from the central bank becomes less attractive; and (4) moral suasion, wherein the exhortations of monetary authorities are expected to lead to restraint in bank lending policies.

For virtually all developing countries the first instrument—open-market operations—is not available for inflation control. Securities markets are typically absent or not sufficiently well-developed to allow the exercise of this powerful and flexible instrument, although some countries, including the Philippines and Brazil, have utilized this tool to a limited degree. The other three monetary policy instruments are employed, with varying degrees of success, in developing countries. In addition developing countries often

---

29. Open-market operations are used as an instrument of monetary policy in countries with well-developed financial markets. When the Federal Reserve System in the United States or a central bank in Europe wants to curtail the growth of the money supply, it sells government securities (bonds, bills) in the open market. When a buyer pays for the securities, the effect is to reduce directly the reserves of the banking system, since the funds are transferred from commercial bank deposits or household cash holdings to the account of the Federal Reserve. When the Federal Reserve wants to expand the money supply, it buys securities on the open market and thus directly adds to bank reserves.

resort to two other tools employed only infrequently in developed countries: (5) credit ceilings imposed by the central bank upon the banking system and (6) adjustments in allowable nominal rates of interest on deposits and loans. Governments attempting to control inflation usually resort to all these instruments, often together but sometimes separately, occasionally experiencing temporary success, as in Agentina in 1985, and ocassionally enjoying transitory success, as in Indonesia in 1967 and 1968 and as in Bolivia in 1985–86.

Reserve Requirements

All central banks require commercial banks to immobilize a portion of their deposits in the form of legal reserves that may not be lent to prospective customers. For example, legal reserve requirements for Indonesian and Malaysian banks in the late 1970s were expressed as 30 percent of deposits in domestic currency in the former and 20 percent of all deposits in the latter. Thus in Malaysia, for example, banks were required to add 20 units of currency to reserves for every 100 units of deposits. These figures are not too far out of line with legal reserve requirements in many industrial nations, where reserve ratios of 15 percent for demand deposits and 5 percent for time deposits are common.

Increases in reserve requirements can be used to help moderate inflation. An upward adjustment in reserve requirements works in two ways: it reduces the stock of money that can be supported by a given amount of reserves, and it reduces the money multiplier. The first effect induces banks to contract credit outstanding; the second reduces the growth in the money stock possible from any future increment to reserves.[30] Changes in legal reserve requirements are usually employed only as a last-ditch measure. Even small changes in the required ratio of reserves to deposits can have a very disruptive impact on commercial bank operations unless banks are given sufficient time to adjust.

Credit Ceilings

In some countries, particularly Indonesia from 1947 to 1983 and at various times Malaysia, Sri Lanka, and Chile, credit ceilings have been used as supplementary instruments of inflation control. Indeed the International Monetary Fund often requires countries seeking balance-of-payments support to adopt credit ceilings as a prerequisite for IMF assistance. General ceilings of domestic credit expansion represent a useful method of controlling growth in domestic components of the money supply. Credit ceilings, however, do not allow full control of money supply growth in the overwhelming majority of LDCs operating under fixed-exchange-rate regimes, since the monetary authorities have no control over foreign components of

30. In its simplest form the money multiplier (m) can be expressed as:

$$m = c + 1/c + k,$$

where $c =$ the ratio of currency outside banks to deposits and $k =$ the ratio of reserves to deposits. If k is raised, then m falls.

the money supply. Nevertheless general credit ceilings can sometimes be usefully deployed in combating inflation in countries not experiencing major imbalances in external payments. Unfortunately, ceilings work best where they are needed the least, since countries attempting to deal with chronic inflation are usually the same countries that are experiencing the most destabilizing changes in their international reserve positions. Finally, general credit ceilings are unlikely to have much effect on inflation unless the government simultaneously takes steps to reduce the budgetary deficits that—except in major oil exporting LDCs—are typically the root causes of chronic, acute, and especially runaway inflation.

For example, consider the case of a country with a money supply to GDP ratio of 25 percent, in which inflation has recently surged to 30 percent per annum. In such a country the monetary authorities may have calculated that a restriction of domestic credit expansion to 15 percent may be required to push the inflation rate down to 12 percent (the exact limit will depend on the income and interest elasticity of the demand for liquid assets, the projected growth in real income, and other factors). But suppose that for the coming year the budget deficit is projected at 3 percent of GDP, a level typical in developing countries experiencing chronic inflation. In order to finance this deficit, credit from the banking system to the government would have to increase by 3 percent of GDP. But an increase of credit to the government of 3 percent of GDP would, with a money to GNP ratio of 25 percent, translate into credit growth of 12 percent. Thus of the 15 percent limit on credit expansion, the government would take 80 percent of allowable credit expansion and leave little for the private sector. In such instances government deficits are said to "crowd out" the private sector from credit sources. Initially the monetary authorities may be able to resist private-sector demands to increase the ceiling, but 3 percent growth in private credit in the face of even 12 percent inflation translates into a decline of nearly 9 percent in the level of real credit available. The consequence of adhering to a 15 percent ceiling would therefore be severe disruption in the private sector, including rising unemployment and low real income growth. Few governments anywhere are able to withstand such pressures for long, and inevitably the ceiling is raised to accommodate some or all private-sector credit requirements. Therefore the successful use of ceilings on credit expansion depends primarily on fiscal, not monetary, policy.

Countries often supplement general credit ceilings with specific ceilings on lending to particular sectors of the economy. Indonesia attempted to fine-tune credit controls in this way from 1974 to 1983, with poor results. The system of ceilings was so detailed and cumbersome that domestic banks were unable to come close to exhausting the ceilings. Excess reserves arose. The banks had little choice but to place their excess reserves in deposits overseas, primarily in banks in Singapore. As a result, many domestic firms in Jakarta were forced to seek credit from Singapore banks, which held well over a billion dollars of deposits from Jakarta banks that might have lent to domestic firms at a lower rate, in the absence of credit ceilings.

In most industrial countries the central bank can influence interest rates by variations in the interest rate (the rediscount rate) charged on central bank lending to commercial banks. Otherwise interest rates on deposits and loans are largely left to market forces. Among developing countries very few, including Singapore and Chile (both since 1975), have left interest rate determination to market forces, although in 1981 both Brazil and Turkey experimented with freeing most interest rates from government controls and Indonesia allowed most interest rates to be market-determined from mid-1983. However, for reasons discussed earlier few LDCs are willing to allow interest rates to be determined in the market, largely because money markets are not competitive.

In the large majority of LDCs where loan and deposit rates are regulated, the monetary authorities have sometimes enacted upward adjustments in regulated interest rates as part of an overall anti-inflationary package. Since 1973 the use of such interest rate adjustments has been common in Latin America, and increases in deposit rates and loan rates were major elements in stabilization programs in South Korea and Taiwan in the mid-1960s, and in Indonesia in both 1968 and 1974. The objective in each case is twofold: to stimulate the demand for liquid assets and to discourage loan demand for marginal investment projects on the part of private-sector borrowers. The extent to which such measures can be successful depends on the interest elasticity of the demand for liquid assets and the interest elasticity of the demand for loans. In most of the cases cited above, and particularly in the three Asian countries, both sets of elasticities were evidently sufficiently high, as the stabilization packages did succeed to a large degree.

Moral suasion by the monetary authorities, sometimes called "open-mouth operations" or "jawbone control," is practiced no less extensively in LDCs than in developed countries. Warnings and exhortations to commercial banks to restrict lending or to encourage them to focus lending on particular activities have been quite common in Ghana and were used at various times in Malaysia, Singapore, Brazil, and elsewhere, sometimes prior to imposition of credit ceilings and often to reinforce pressures on banks to adhere to ceilings. In both developed and developing countries, however, moral suasion has proven credible only when accompanied by forceful use of more tangible instruments of monetary control.

14

Foreign Aid, Investment, and Debt

Countries that are unable to generate sufficient domestic saving to fuel their aspirations for economic growth have historically sought finance from other countries. The United States relied heavily on foreign saving, particularly during the antebellum period from 1835 to 1860. Likewise, Russia needed foreign saving to propel its development in the three decades before World War I and the communist revolution. Yet Japan, which has actively discouraged inflows of foreign saving and investment throughout its history, nevertheless became a modern state during the period after the Meiji Restoration of 1868. Foreign saving can help development but is not essential for it.

It is useful to keep these examples in mind at a time when, although a majority of developing countries consider foreign saving to be an important ingredient in their development efforts, controversy surrounds foreign aid, foreign investment, and the debt that has accrued from foreign borrowing. This chapter examines the roles of foreign saving in development and explores some of these controversies.

The concept of foreign saving can be approached from two different directions. Foreign saving can finance the amount by which investment exceeds domestic saving, $S_f = I - S_d$. Alternatively, foreigners can finance the trade deficit, which is the amount by which imports exceed exports, $S_f = M - E$. Because of the way gross domestic or gross national product is measured, foreign saving must be the same whichever definition we use.[1]

Table 14–1 places foreign saving in the context of the balance of payments, consistent with the second definition above. Receipts represent payments of foreign exchange to people or institutions inside the home country; expenditures are payments by the country to the outside world. By far the largest source of receipts for most countries is exports, whereas the largest expenditure is for imports; these two flows are the subject of Part 4 of this book. If we consider only trade in goods and services, excluding interest and dividend payments to and from foreign sources, then the trade balance represents the **net resource transfer** (line 4 of the table). This is the contribution that foreign saving makes to development in terms of goods and services that cannot be financed by exports. In Table 14–1, the net transfer is a small outflow from developing to developed countries; this

---

TABLE 14–1   **Foreign Saving and the Balance of Payments (approximate 1988 magnitudes for non-oil-exporting developing countries in billion U.S. dollars)**

	Receipts (+)	Expenditures (−)
1. Merchandise trade	Exports = 560	Imports = 590
2. Services, except interest and profits	Exports = 80	Imports = 40
3. Trade in goods and services[a] (1 + 2)	Exports = 640	Imports = 630
4. Net resource transfer		Outflow = 10
5. Interest and profits payments	Earned = 20	Paid = 80
6. Trade in goods and all services (3 + 5)	Exports = 660	Imports = 710
7. Net resource flow (net foreign savings)	Inflow = 50	
8. Repayments of principal on debt		Repaid = 70
9. Total payments (6 + 8)	Received = 660	Paid = 780
10. Gross resource flow (gross foreign saving)	Inflow = 120	

[a] Except interest and profits payments.
   Sources: International Monetary Fund, *Balance of Payments Yearbook 1990*, Vol. 2 (Washington, D.C.: International Monetary Fund, 1990), p. 34, and World Bank, *World Debt Tables 1989–90* (Baltimore: Johns Hopkins Press for the World Bank, 1990), p. 79 (line 8).

---

1. This equivalence was discussed in Chapter 6, where for convenience we used the symbol S to stand for S_d and F to stand for S_f; see Equations 6–5 and 6–7.

means that in 1988 the developing countries were not able to turn foreign saving into additional imports for development. This abnormal situation is due to the debt crisis of the 1980s, in which developing countries were faced with large requirements to service previously contracted loans.

If instead we include interest and dividend receipts and payments as part of exports and imports, the trade balance is the **net resource flow** (line 7), and it, unlike the net transfer of line 4, was positive in 1988. This concept of net foreign saving suggests that foreign resources finance goods and services for development (net transfers) as well as the payments of interest and dividends on earlier flows of foreign capital. Net resource flow can also be measured as the inflow of capital net of repayments of principal on loan obligations incurred by the home country. Adding debt principal repayments to the net flows would yield **gross resource transfer** (gross foreign saving, line 10).

Foreign saving includes both official saving and private saving. Most **official saving** is on **concessional terms,** made available either as **grants** (outright gifts) or as **"soft" loans** bearing lower interest rates and longer repayment periods than would be available in private international capital markets. Governments also make some loans on commercial terms, including export credits, equity investments, and **"hard" loans** from the World Bank and regional development banks.[2] Concessional flows are technically called **official development assistance** (ODA), but are popularly called **foreign aid.** Aid can be further divided into **bilateral aid**, given directly by one government to another, and **multilateral aid**, in which the funds flow to an international agency like the United Nations, the World Bank, and the regional development banks (described below), which in turn grant or loan the funds to recipient developing countries. Finally, aid can be in the form of **technical assistance**, the provision of skilled individuals to augment national expertise, or **capital assistance**, the provision of finance or commodities for a variety of purposes discussed later in this chapter.

Foreign private saving consists of four elements. **Foreign direct investment** is made by nonresidents, typically but not always by multinational corporations, in the enterprises located in host countries; direct investment implies full or partial control of the enterprise and physical presence by foreign firms or individuals. **Portfolio investment** is the purchase of host country bonds or stocks by foreigners, without managerial control. This was a very important form of foreign investment in the nineteenth and early twentieth centuries, but has not been important since World War II. Portfolio investment may be reviving, however, as rich country investors show interest in emerging stockmarkets, especially in Asia. **Commercial bank lending** to developing-country governments and enterprises supplanted portfolio investment in importance for a time, but has itself waned with the debt crisis, discussed later in this chapter. Finally, exporting firms, their commercial banks, and official banks offer **export credits** to importing countries as a way of promoting sales by permitting delayed payment for imports, often at commercial interest rates.

---

2. The regional development banks include the Asian, African, and Inter-American Development Banks and others. Most of these are patterned on the World Bank.

TABLE 14–2   Net Resource Flows, 1970 and 1988

375

FOREIGN AID

	Billion U.S. dollars		Percent	
	1970	1988	1970	1988
Official development assistance[a]	8.1	51.3	43	51
Bilateral	7.0	40.0	37	39
Multilateral	1.1	11.3	6	11
Official nonconcessional finance	1.9	14.4	10	14
Bilateral	1.2	8.0	6	8
Multilateral	0.7	6.0	4	6
Export credits	2.1	3.0	11	3
Private finance	7.0	32.9	37	32
Direct investment	3.7	19.0	19	19
Bank lending	3.0	4.7	16	5
Total net resources	19.0	101.6[b]	100	100
(Percent of developing countries' GNP)	(3.9)	(3.3)		
Total net resources at 1988 prices[c]	61.6	101.6		

[a] Includes technical assistance, valued at more than $14 billion in 1988.
[b] The total for net resource flow differs from that in Table 14–1, line 7, although the concept is the same. Table 14–1 is based on estimates from the recipient countries' balance-of-payments accounts, whereas Table 14–2 is based on reports from the donor countries. Reconciliation of such balance-of-payments data between countries is notoriously difficult and subject to large margins of error.
[c] Deflated using the import unit value index for developing countries from International Monetary Fund, *International Financial Statistics Yearbook 1990* (Washington, D.C.: International Monetary Fund, 1990), pp. 136–37.
Source: Development Assistance Committee of the OECD, *Development Cooperation in the 1990s* (Paris: OECD, 1989), p. 150.

From 1970 to 1988, total net resource flows expanded by 60 percent in (1988) constant prices, a growth rate of 2.8 percent a year (Table 14–2). The net resource flow of $102 billion in 1988 was equivalent to 3.3 percent of gross domestic product for the low- and middle-income countries taken together, a decline from almost 4 percent in 1970. Net resource flows per capita in LDCs was roughly $26 per person in 1988. Concessional aid (ODA) made up half of all net resource flows in 1988 and was the most rapidly growing source of capital over the period. Private flows contributed almost a third of the total. Direct investment, which is the most discussed category of foreign private investment, accounted for over half of all private flows in 1988. However, during the intervening years commercial bank lending played a more important role: in the early 1980s it accounted for 70 percent of private resource flows, but it dried up as the debt crisis eroded international banks' profits and confidence.

FOREIGN AID

Historical Role

Foreign aid as now conceived is a product of the post-World War II era. Its roots are in the Marshall Plan, under which the United States transferred $17 billion over four years, equivalent to about 1.5 percent of U.S. GNP, to help rebuild Europe after the war. Two elements of the Marshall Plan were believed at the time to have been crucial for its success: an influx of financial capital from the United States and coordinated plans to employ it productively to rebuild Europe's devastated physical capital stock. This early manifestation of capital fundamentalism was reinforced by the Harrod-Domar view of growth economics, which emerged during the 1940s and centered on the role of investment in propelling economic growth (see Chapter 3).

The two decades after World War II saw the emergence of independent nations from Europe's colonies, especially in Asia and Africa. Encouraged by the success of Marshall Plan aid in rebuilding Europe, the United States took the lead in trying to help the newly emerging nations by providing that same element, capital, in the form of foreign aid, especially to countries that had development plans for investing the aid they received. Early aid programs also recognized that developing countries lacked certain kinds of skills and expertise, so donors also offered technical assistance programs, which supplied foreign experts in fields from economic planning to engineering to construction.

The motives behind the American aid programs of the postwar years were complex and ranged from the selfish to the generous. The security of the United States was the center of Congress's concerns in approving both the Marshall Plan and the Point IV program, under which President Truman began to shift U.S. attention and resources toward the less-developed countries. This meant "containing communism" around the perimeter of the Soviet bloc as well as trying to ensure access to raw materials needed for U.S. industry. Prosperity of both the United States and its allies required expanding trade and investment, also promoted by aid. It was believed that development would serve both security and economic interests by reducing instability and giving the emerging nations a stake in the capitalist world order. U.S. aid policy was also intended to encourage the new countries to maintain or adopt democratic political institutions and private-enterprise-based economies in the U.S. image. There was also a core of humanitarian concern for the welfare of the world's poor. Indeed the strength of the early aid programs depended on this mixture of nationalistic and altruistic motives, which drew political support from a wide spectrum of opinion. The context has changed over 40 years; the number of major donors has increased, and each donor has its own style and emphasis. Nevertheless, the menu of aims for most donors remains much the same: security, economic leverage, economic health, political evangelism, and humanitarianism.

In the early postwar years of aid, the United States, the United Kingdom and France were the most important contributors; the latter two contributed mainly to their former colonies. As the other industrial countries began to recover and prosper, however, some of them became important donors. The 18 industrial countries of the OECD now coordinate their programs through the Development Assistance Committee (DAC). Table 14–3 shows net official development assistance from these countries, including bilateral aid and contributions to multilateral organizations, from 1965 to 1988. Many members of DAC, including several not shown in the table, have increased their aid efforts substantially, as measured by the share of ODA in each country's GNP. Norway, Sweden, Denmark, and the Neth-

TABLE 14–3 Net Official Development Assistance (Disbursements) from DAC Countries to Developing Countries and Multilateral Agencies, 1965 to 1988

| Source | Percent of GNP | | Billion U.S. dollars 1988 |
	1965	1988	
Canada	0.19	0.49	2.34
France	0.76	0.72	6.87
West Germany	0.40	0.39	4.73
Italy	0.10	0.39	3.19
Japan	0.27	0.32	9.13
Netherlands	0.36	0.98	2.23
Sweden	0.19	0.87	1.52
United Kingdom	0.47	0.32	2.65
United States	0.58	0.21	10.14
Total DAC	0.48	0.36	48.17[b]
Index: real value[a]	100	184	

[a] Deflated by the unit value index of industrial country exports; IMF, *International; Financial Statistics Yearbook 1990*, pp. 132–133.
[b] Table 14–3 counts disbursements as they are made by the OECD countries to the developing countries and to multilateral agencies; Table 14–2 counts disbursements as they are received by the developing countries from both the bilateral and multilateral agencies. This difference in treatment explains the slight difference in total ODA for 1988.
Source: World Bank, *World Development Report 1990*, Table 19.

erlands had shares of 0.9 percent or more. Yet on the whole the aid effort of the DAC donors declined substantially. The main culprits were the United Kingdom and especially the United States, whose aid effort shrank from 0.6 to 0.2 percent of GNP over 23 years. Rapid economic growth has helped Japan to become as large a donor as the United States. Over this period, also, the multilateral agencies, especially the World Bank, become important dispensers of capital. By 1988, the multilateral share of official capital flows had reached 27 percent.

As the flow of aid expanded and more countries and multilateral agencies became important players, the economic development rationale for aid changed as well. During the 1950s the main economic goal was rapid growth of output and incomes, to be achieved by increasing the amount of domestic and foreign saving available for investment. By the 1960s the two-gap model, described in Chapter 6, augmented the Harrod-Domar perspective and foreign exchange became as important as capital. Human capital received emphasis beyond the recognized role of technical assistance and aid programs spread into education, health, and other human services. During the late 1960s and the 1970s aid programs began to incorporate goals other than the promotion of economic growth: income redistribution, poverty alleviation, satisfaction of basic needs, and rural development became motivators for the aid programs of most donors. But in the 1980s, the trends described in Chapter 5 led donors, particularly the World Bank, to focus more on macroeconomic stabilization and structural adjustment as goals of aid.

The 1988 total of official development assistance, $51 billion from Table 14–2, is equivalent to 1.7 percent of GDP for the low- and middle-income countries, or about $13 per capita. However, there are major and moderately systematic variations around this rather low average, as Table 14–4

TABLE 14–4 Net Receipts of Official Development Assistance by Selected Developing Countries, 1988[a]

Country	GNP per capita (dollars)	Net ODA		
		Million U.S. dollars	Percent of GNP	Dollars per capita
Low income				
Ethiopia	120	970	17	21
Tanzania	160	978	31	40
Bangladesh	170	1,592	8	15
Mali	230	427	22	54
Nigeria	290	120	0[b]	1
China	330	1,990	1	2
India	340	2,098	1	3
Pakistan	350	1,408	4	13
Kenya	370	808	9	36
Ghana	400	474	9	34
Sri Lanka	420	599	9	36
Indonesia	440	1,632	2	9
Middle income				
Bolivia	570	392	9	57
Philippines	630	854	2	14
Senegal	650	568	11	81
Egypt	660	1,537	4	31
Guatemala	900	235	3	27
Colombia	1,180	61	0	2
Mexico	1,760	173	0	2
Malaysia	1,940	104	0	6
Brazil	2,160	210	0	2
South Korea	3,600	10	0	0[c]

[a] Aid from all sources, including OECD, OPEC, former Soviet Bloc countries and multilateral institutions.
[b] In this column, 0 means less than 0.5 percent.
[c] In this column, 0 means less than 50 cents.
Source: World Bank, *World Development Report 1990*, pp. 216–217.

reveals. First, there is a strong tendency for aid to represent a higher fraction of GNP for poorer countries. The low-income countries received aid averaging 2.4 percent of GNP, whereas for the middle-income countries aid averaged less than 1 percent. And all but two of the 23 instances of ODA to GNP ratios over 10 percent were low-income countries. This suggests a strong tendency for donors to use scarce concessional aid in favor of the poorest countries.

The exceptions to this rule point to a second strong tendency. Among the low-income countries, five of the six most populous countries are the only ones to have aid-GNP ratios below 5 percent: China, India, Indonesia, Pakistan, and Nigeria. Without these five, the poorest countries receive aid equal to about 7 percent of GNP. Donors, faced with a choice of spreading their aid proportionally (to GNP or population) and thus having scant impact anywhere, or concentrating it where they can make a larger impact, choose the latter. Small countries thus get greater relative amounts of aid, but also become more dependent on the donors who provide it, than do large countries.

Finally, Table 14–4 includes some examples of countries that are favored for political and strategic reasons. Mali and Senegal benefit disproportionately, as do all Francophone African states, from France's generous aid program. Egypt, along with Israel, has been favored by the United States' involvement in the Middle East. During the 1950s South Korea, Taiwan, Pakistan, Turkey, and other allied governments were favored recipients of U.S. aid. Although the manifestations of politically inspired aid are strongest in these cases, they are present to some extent in many other countries.

Aid Institutions and Instruments

Bilateral aid donors usually plan and dispense loans and grants through an aid agency, such as the United States Agency for International Development (USAID), Britain's Overseas Development Administration (BODA), the International Development Agencies of Canada (CIDA) and Sweden (SIDA), and others. Most development assistance agencies deal with a wide range of aid instruments, both technical and capital assistance. Most of the capital aid is disbursed against specific projects, such as hydroelectric dams, roads, or rural development projects, and is called **project aid.** However, some bilateral agencies, including USAID, have made **program loans,** which finance general categories of imports and are conceived of as broad support for the balance of payments. **Structural adjustment loans,** made especially by the World Bank to support economic reforms as described in Chapter 5, are program loans. **Food aid** is a kind of bilateral program loan, since it provides commodities, mostly grains, that would otherwise have to be purchased with a country's own foreign exchange earnings.

The full range of motives of the donor countries, discussed above, is expressed in bilateral programs, which can easily be treated as extensions of donors' foreign policies. The establishment of multilateral institutions to dispense aid and the provision of these international agencies with a growing share of aid resources indicate that the donor countries give aid for reasons other than simple self-interest. It is true that the largest donors exercise considerable control over the World Bank and other multilateral agencies, though not over the United Nations agencies. Still the multilateral organizations are focused almost exclusively on development and shield recipients to a large extent from the foreign policy concerns of the individual industrial countries.

The main **multilateral aid** agencies and the amounts they disbursed in 1970 and 1988 are given in Table 14–5. The largest and most influential of these is the **World Bank** (International Bank for Reconstruction and Development, or IBRD), together with its affiliates, the International Development Association (IDA) and International Finance Corporation (IFC). Despite its leading role in the aid community, most of the capital supplied by the World Bank is not aid. The IBRD obtains its funds by borrowing on world capital markets at prevailing prime interest rates and relends to developing countries at slightly higher rates. It makes more capital available and at lower interest rates than could be obtained by the developing countries on their own. Its affiliate, the IFC, lends on commercial terms and takes minority equity positions in support of private foreign invest-

TABLE 14–5   Net Disbursements by Multilateral Aid Agencies, 1970–1988
(million U.S. dollars)

Agency	Concessional flows		All flows	
	1970–71	1988	1970–71	1988
World Bank and affiliates[a]	225	3,567	872	7,340
Inter-American Development Bank	219	134	323	1,227
African Development Bank	—	351	4	976
Asian Development Bank	3	660	32	1,258
European Economic Community	208	2,732	242	2,720
United Nations agencies	529	3,678	529	3,678
Other institutions	—	193	—	551
Total	1,184	11,315	2,003	17,750

[a] The World Bank group includes the International Bank for Reconstruction and Development, the International Development Association (IDA), and the International Finance Corporation (IFC).
Source: Development Assistance Committee of the OECD, *Development Cooperation in the 1990s,* p. 230.

ments. Only the IDA, which channels contributions from the richer member countries to the poorer countries on very soft terms, dispenses aid in the strict sense. Most World Bank and IDA loans have been for projects, but program loans have become increasingly important with the structural adjustment reforms during the 1980s. During the 1970s the World Bank became the world's leading center for research, information, and policy advice on economic development. In 1988 the World Bank group disbursed more than $7 billion, 41 percent of the total for all multilateral agencies.

The word "reconstruction" in the bank's title stems from its origin, at the Bretton Woods (New Hampshire) conference in 1944, when its first task was to help finance the reconstruction of war-torn European countries. The other institution founded at the conference was the **International Monetary Fund** (IMF), whose main charge was to reestablish an international system of national currencies in stable relation to each other, in support of a rejuvenated world trade system. The IMF played a significant role in the unprecedented expansion of world trade during the 1950s and 1960s. Although not primarily concerned with promoting development, IMF practices and resources have had a major effect on developing countries, and the Fund has increasingly turned its attention toward assisting LDCs by offering balance-of-payments support in a variety of ways. We have already seen in Chapter 5 how the IMF supports stabilization programs through **standby agreements** and **extended Fund facilities.** IMF loans and conditions have also featured prominently in the efforts of major debtor countries, especially in Latin America, to repay foreign loans, as will be discussed later in this chapter.

Each of the developing world's continents—Asia, Africa, and Latin America—has its own **regional development bank.** These each have separate "windows" that dispense hard and soft loans to member countries. Regional members and the major aid donors contribute to the capital of these banks, which also borrow on private capital markets to finance hard loans and receive contributions from aid donors for their soft loan windows. Most finance from the regional banks has been for projects. Other

multilateral donors include the European Economic Community and the
Arab countries of OPEC. The EEC originally concentrated its aid on former French colonies in Africa, but now spreads its assistance more widely, especially in Africa. Arab OPEC, which was especially active during the late 1970s and early 1980s when oil prices were high, concentrates its assistance on Islamic states.

The United Nations has the largest concessional program of the multilaterals, $3.7 billion of mostly technical assistance in 1988. This effort is coordinated by the United Nations Development Programme (UNDP), which makes grants to member countries. However, the specialized agencies of the United Nations, such as the UN Industrial Development Organization (UNIDO), International Labor Organization (ILO), and World Health Organization (WHO), among others, execute the technical assistance projects financed by UNDP.

Aid and Development

In a world of neoclassical growth, explained in Chapter 3, we can measure the contribution of aid and other foreign saving to development. In this model the role of foreign saving of all kinds is to augment domestic saving to increase investment and thus accelerate growth. If aid and other foreign saving added, say, 6 percent of GDP; if all of it went to additional investment; if the capital-output ratio were 3.0; and if capital's share of GNP were 50 percent; then the growth rate would be increased by 1 percentage point.[3] Or, in the two-gap world described in Chapter 6, aid would finance both more saving and higher imports, either of which could permit more rapid growth.

A glance at Table 14–4 shows that for some countries—Ethiopia, Tanzania, Bangladesh, Mali, Senegal, and others—foreign saving is a large fraction of GDP and could be contributing 1.5 percent or more to the growth rate in this simple neoclassical world. For countries like India, China, Indonesia, Mexico, and Brazil, foreign saving is a small fraction of GDP and could not have much impact on growth. In fact, there is no strong correlation across countries between aid receipts (as a share of GNP) and economic growth; this suggests the limitations of the neoclassical and two-gap models. Developing countries may of course lack some important complementary inputs to development, such as human skills, administrative capacity, infrastructure, economic institutions, and political stability, without which even high saving rates may not stimulate growth. In addition, some economists have argued that foreign aid may not contribute much to

---

3. From Equation 3–6 of Chapter 3, $g_Y = a + w_K g_K + w_L g_L + w_T g_T$. An increase in the growth of the capital stock dg_K would cause an increase in the growth of GNP; $dg_Y = w_K dg_K$. How much does foreign aid contribute to the growth of the capital stock? If all of it were invested, then $dg_K = S_f/K = (S_f/Y)(Y/K)$. We know that the aid share in GNP, S_f/Y, is .06 and capital-output ratio K/Y is 3, so $dg_K = .02$. If w_K, the share of capital income in GNP, is 50 percent, then this 2 percent increase in the annual growth of the capital stock adds $dg_Y = w_K dg_K = .5(.02) = .01$, or 1 percent, to the annual growth of income. In the Harrod-Domar model, where capital is the only input, its income share is 100 percent and foreign aid at 6 percent of GNP would add 2 percent a year to growth.

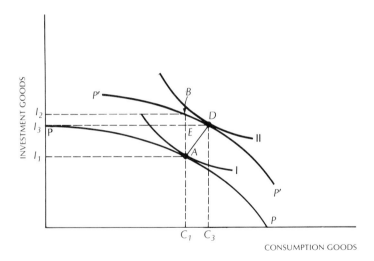

FIGURE 14–1 **Impact of Aid on Investment and Consumption.** Foreign aid totaling *AB* turns into actual new investment of only *AE*, because the country maximizes welfare on the new frontier *P'P'* at point *D*, not *B*. *P'P'* is not really a "production" frontier, but a "supply" frontier; see footnote 4.
Source: Adapted from Paul Mosley, "Aid, Savings and Growth Revisited," *Oxford Bulletin of Economics and Statistics* 42 (May 1980): 79–91.

additional saving or imports, but could be used instead to finance higher consumption or to reduce exports.

Figure 14–1 shows why these doubters are at least partly correct. A developing country, before it obtains aid, can produce consumption goods and capital goods along the production possibilities frontier *PP*. To simplify, the diagram ignores international trade. Community tastes are defined by a set of indifference curves, of which two, labeled I and II, are shown. Without aid the country's welfare is maximized if it produces and consumes at point *A*, where the indifference curve I is tangent to the frontier *PP*, with consumption at C_1 and investment at I_1. Now donor countries contribute an amount *AB* of aid. They intend that the full amount should be invested; this would raise total investment to I_2. However, the offer of aid *AB* in effect moves the production frontier outward from *PP* to *P'P'*.[4] With these added resources the country maximizes its welfare by producing at point *D*, the tangency between *P'P'* and indifference curve I_2. It consumes C_3 and invests I_3. Of the aid amount *AB*, *AE* (equal to I_3-I_1) has been invested, as intended by the donors, but *BE* (equal to I_2-I_3) has been consumed. If the country's tastes favored consumption over investment even more, then it would reach equilibrium at a point along *P'P'* to the southeast of *D* and would convert even more of its aid into consumption.

The diagram demonstrates that the amount of aid actually used to increase

4. The purist will worry about this shift in the production frontier. It is not production that has been increased, but the supply of goods through additional imports, financed by aid. Graphically this is equivalent to an outward shift in the frontier, in the same sense that additional income shifts the budget line outward for an individual consumer. Strictly speaking, however, the production frontier in Figure 14–1 remains *PP*.

investment rather than consumption will depend on production possibilities, community tastes, and other variables left out of the figure, such as trade. How can a country convert aid and other foreign saving, which is intended to be used for investment, into consumption? Some forms of foreign saving, such as program aid or commercial bank loans, are designed to provide finance for general purposes and thus deliberately give the recipient the kinds of choices demonstrated in Figure 14–1. Food aid, of course, is intended to increase or maintain consumption rather than investment. But even if all foreign saving were dispensed as project aid and targeted to specific investment projects, substitution would be possible. Project aid might, for example, be used for investments that the government or its private investors would have made even without aid. In that case resources are freed up for other purposes, including consumption. When aid finances projects that might not otherwise be implemented, a government may simply cut back on preferred projects because it wants to raise the share of consumption, for economic or political reasons. When substitutions of these kinds are possible, aid is called **fungible.**

Perhaps more important, a host of subtle influences of foreign saving on relative prices may also contribute to substitution. More capital in general could conceivably mean lower returns on investments and hence a greater tendency to consume in the recipient countries. More foreign exchange tends to lower its price (that is, to appreciate the exchange rate) and cause greater demand for imports, as intended by donors, but also creates a reduced incentive to produce for export, which is not intended. And food aid has a similar effect, lowering food prices because it satisfies part of domestic demand, and hence reducing the incentive for domestic farmers to produce grains and other foods. These influences could be overcome by countervailing government policies, but governments may not undertake such measures for a variety of reasons discussed in other chapters. In sum, the contribution of aid and other foreign saving to development is not that it provides specific amounts of additional investment, imports, or food. Rather, foreign aid provides additional purchasing power and thus gives recipient governments and citizens more room to choose between consumption and investment, more imports and less exports, more food consumption or less food production, and so forth.

Additional macroeconomic resource flows are not the only mechanism by which donors try to enhance development, however. Aid can have four other kinds of influence on a country's development. First, most capital assistance goes to specific projects. Donors frequently use project aid to give special attention to particular sectors or kinds of activities, in hopes of improving practices in those areas and initiating developments that eventually become self-sustaining. Investment in wheat and rice production was high priority for project aid during the late 1960s, for example, especially in Asia, whereas rural development projects were emphasized during the 1970s. It had become evident that neglect of rural investment had, in many countries, slowed economic growth and made it difficult to reduce poverty. Foreign assistance played a major role in spreading the Green Revolution, which delivered new seed varieties for wheat and rice— together with a "package" of inputs, including fertilizer, pesticides, and water—and made countries such as India and Indonesia much less vulnerable to famine and better able to promote widespread economic development. The World Bank reports that, of 112 rural development projects surveyed in 1989, 63 earned at least 10 percent a year; the overall rate of return was 17 percent.[5] Although horror stories about failed aid projects are common enough, these and other examples suggest that project assistance can have a beneficial impact.

A second avenue to influence development is **technical assistance.** In 1988, 27 percent of ODA financed the provision of experts in fields as diverse as agronomy, computer programming, economics, education, engineering, forestry, geology, law, management, medicine, and public health. Although the United Nations is perhaps the largest provider of technical assistance, all donors supply it to some extent. Foreign experts are sent to perform jobs for which local professionals are not qualified or are in short supply. Technical assistance is not always effective. In the best cases, however, expatriate professionals become agents of change when they put new systems in place, influence local professionals to try new or improved ways of performing tasks, and train local professionals.

The third route for aid to influence development is through **conditionality,** the attempt by aid donors to use their assistance as a lever to influence policy in recipient countries. Some conditions tied to assistance do not advance development. Donors offer aid to reward political friends and military allies and withhold it from those perceived as enemies. They tie aid funds to the purchase of goods and services in their own countries as a way of increasing their own markets for exports and of dampening the impact of aid on their own balance of payments. They channel it toward countries and institutions that adhere most closely to the donor's own views of economics and politics. These are perhaps the crassest uses of aid and they are generally confined to bilateral donors.

But donors, both bilateral and multilateral, also use aid to induce LDC governments to change their development policies in what donors believe to be the recipient's own best interests. Chapter 5 discussed donors' conditioning aid on economic reforms such as currency devaluation, market liberalization, changes in tax systems, adoption of new wage and income policies, adjustments in food and other agricultural prices, and many other policy actions. To the extent that host governments acquiesce to such changes, policy leverage may be as important a contribution of aid programs to development as the resource flows they finance. It is an open question, however, whether donors can do more than push governments in directions they already wish to go. If host governments wish to resist conditions attached to aid, they have ways of appearing to accept conditions, but then not implementing them fully; and donors have reasons to continue offering their aid even if conditions are not met.

The fourth way that aid influences development is the most diffuse but perhaps the most powerful. The international aid establishment directly

---

5. World Bank, "International Factors Reducing Poverty: Aid and Poverty," *World Development Report 1990*, p. 131.

and indirectly supports a large group of university scholars, professional consultants, aid administrators, and others, from both the industrial and developing countries, who conceive and eventually popularize new ways of thinking about development issues. This diverse group has, over time, influenced the way developing-country scholars and policymakers think about many issues including economic reform, trade strategy, fiscal policy, rural development, etc. Once this general and diffuse influence changes the minds of policymakers, foreign aid becomes far more effective in serving national development strategies because its basic premises are shared by recipients and donors.[6]

FOREIGN INVESTMENT AND THE MULTINATIONALS

Foreign direct investment accounted for 19 percent of the total net foreign resource flow entering developing countries in 1988 (Table 14–1), a recovery from only 8 percent in 1983, but below the 24 percent share in 1960. Although direct investment accounts for only a fifth of foreign resource flows, it generates much controversy. Its influence is magnified because foreign investment comes in a package that may include not only equity finance, but often much larger amounts of loan finance, management expertise, modern technologies, technical skills, and access to world markets. Indeed, it is often the nonfinancial elements of the investment package that are most desired by developing countries. Moreover, this package is controlled by multinational corporations, whose size and economic influence often match and sometimes outstrip that of the recipient country governments. Investment by a multinational corporation raises the spectre of interference by, and dependence on, foreign economic powers beyond the control of the host country. We shall examine the basis for these fears, and the potential benefits and costs of foreign investment, in this section.

Multinationals' Investment Patterns

The overwhelming proportion of direct foreign investment in third-world nations is done by **multinational corporations** (MNCs), or as they are also called **transnational corporations** (TNCs). A multinational is an enterprise that produces in more than one country and considers overseas operations to be central to its profitability. Multinational enterprises come in all sizes and from all regions of the world, but a relatively small number are dominant. In 1980 roughly 10,000 MNCs were in existence and exercised control over nearly 90,000 foreign affiliates.[7] But only 500 of these firms accounted for 80 percent of the world's stock of direct foreign investment in that year.

Most multinationals are based in the industrial countries: in 1985, 97 percent of the stock of foreign investment—$714 billion—was owned by rich

---

6. For a comprehensive review of the impact of foreign aid on development, see Robert Cassen et al., *Does Aid Work?* (London: Oxford University Press, 1986).
7. John Stopford, *The World Directory of Multinational Enterprises 1982–83* (Detroit: Gale Research Company, 1982), p. 2.

TABLE 14–6   Flows of Foreign Direct Investment, 1975–1985 (annual averages in billions of U.S. dollars)

Region or country[a]	Outflows from[b]		Inflows to[b]	
	1970–75	1980–85	1975–80	1980–85
Developed market economies	39.8	44.4	24.6	36.6
United States	17.1	8.6	7.9	19.2
United Kingdom	5.6	9.4	5.2	4.3
Australia	—[c]	—	1.3	2.2
France	1.8	2.5	2.1	2.1
Spain	—	—	1.0	1.8
Netherlands	3.8	4.0	1.3	1.4
Belgium and Luxembourg	—	—	1.2	1.1
Italy	0.4	1.7	0.6	1.0
West Germany	3.1	3.9	1.1	0.9
Japan	2.2	5.0	0.2	0.3
Developing countries	0.5	0.8	7.5	12.1
Brazil			1.8	2.0
Singapore			0.5	1.1
Mexico			1.0	1.1
Malaysia			0.5	1.1
China			—	0.8
Egypt			0.4	0.7
Colombia			0.1	0.6
Hong Kong			0.2	0.6
Argentina			—	0.5
Nigeria			0.2	0.4
Thailand			0.1	0.3
Indonesia			0.3	0.2
Chile			0.1	0.2
Tunisia			0.1	0.3

[a]Countries listed in declining order of investment inflows in 1980 to 1985.
[b]The differences in totals between outflows and inflows are due to differences in coverage.
[c]Not available.
Source: United Nations Centre for Transnational Corporations, *Transnational Corporations in World Development*, pp. 77, 504–507.

country investors. The largest suppliers of foreign investment are shown in Table 14–6. The decline in importance of the United States from the late 1970s to the early 1980s is notable, as is the rise of the United Kingdom and Japan. Since 1985, Japan's importance has increased further.

Most multinational investment is also directed toward other wealthy countries: in 1985, three-quarters of this stock of foreign assets was located in the industrial countries. The only exception to this pattern is Japan, which held nearly half of its overseas assets in developing countries. Of the $159 billion of private foreign assets located in developing countries, half was in Latin America and close to a third in Asia.[8] Table 14–6 tells the same story in terms of annual flows of foreign direct investment. Note the dominance of the United States as a host country to foreign investment: it absorbed almost two-fifths of the total flow in the early 1980s.

Contrary to popular belief, multinational investment in developing countries does not consist largely of manufacturing firms searching for cheap

8. United Nations Centre on Transnational Corporations (UNCTNC), *Transnational Corporations in World Development* (New York: United Nations, 1988), pp. 24–25.

foreign labor. Indeed, among the major investing countries, only Germany had more than a third of its developing-country assets in the manufacturing sector. Mining and modern services are the other main destinations ·for MNC investment, and both are capital-intensive sectors. Smaller multinationals from Korea, Taiwan, and Hong Kong and other middle-income countries do, however, invest overseas in export-oriented manufacturing in such labor-intensive industries as textiles, footwear, sporting equipment, and electronic assembly.

Characteristics of Multinationals

Not very long ago, the word "multinational" implied a giant, private, American manufacturing company with lots of overseas operations. Today, multinationals are a much more diverse group. Only 167 of the world's largest 500 companies were American in 1989, according to *Fortune* magazine; 111 of them were Japanese. Ten countries had at least ten entries in the top 500. Multinationals are not even necessarily from the industrial countries. Thirteen developing countries had companies in the top 500, including Korea (11 entries), India (6), Brazil (3), and Turkey (3). Nor are multinationals always private firms; the top 500 includes a number of giant, state-owned companies producing petroleum and steel, especially from the developing countries.

Nor are multinationals always large; small companies, especially in East and Southeast Asia, have been investing overseas for many years, as we have seen. The largest of the multinationals, however, are very large indeed, as Table 14–7 shows. Many multinationals have worldwide sales and assets that exceed the GDPs of some large developing countries. British Petroleum, the tenth largest MNC, had sales in 1989 only 20 percent less than the GDP of the tenth largest national economy, Thailand; the sales of Chevron, the twenty-fifth largest multinational, were more than twice the GDP of the twenty-fifth largest economy, Sudan.[9]

Benefits of Foreign Investment

Viewed as a **transfer of capital** from rich to poor countries, foreign direct investment—which includes investment by multinationals—is of secondary importance. Recall from Table 14–2 that direct investment was only 19 percent of total net resource flows in 1988, the same share as 20 years before. Equity financing has been dwarfed by debt financing of all kinds: for the developing countries as a whole, the stock of foreign direct investment was only a fifth the value of the stock of debt outstanding in 1985.[10]

Moreover, among developing countries there is a tendency for direct investment to flow toward countries with higher per-capita incomes, just the opposite of the tendency with foreign aid. Table 14–8 uses the stock of

9. Sales, a measure of gross output, is not comparable with GDP, a measure of value-added, or net output; and assets are a stock whereas GDP is a flow. Nevertheless, the size comparisons of Table 14–7 are indicative.

10. UNCTNC, *Transnational Corporations in World Development*, p. 129.

TABLE 14–7   The Size of Multinationals and of Developing-Country Economies, 1989
(billions of U.S. dollars)

Rank[a]	Company (Country)	Sales	Assets	Employees (1,000s)
1.	General Motors (U.S.)	127.0	173.3	775
10.	British Petroleum (U.K.)	49.5	51.0	120
25.	Chevron (U.S.)	29.4	33.9	55
100.	Enimont (Italy)	11.2	14.2	53
500.	DAF Trucks (Netherlands)	2.5	1.9	17
	Largest developing country MNCs:[b]			
20.	Samsung (South Korea)	35.2	28.4	177
47.	Daewoo (South Korea)	20.0	29.0	91
58.	Petrobras (Brazil)	16.4	16.1	68
65.	Pemex (Mexico)	15.3	42.3	165
76.	Petroleos de Venezuela	13.7	8.9	47
92.	Kuwait Petroleum	11.8	22.7	15

Rank	Country	GDP 1988		
1.	China	372.3		
5.	South Korea	171.3		
10.	Thailand	60.0		
25.	Sudan	11.2		
50.	Jamaica	3.2		

[a] Ranked according to sales.
[b] Rank in Fortune 500.
Sources: Fortune, July 30, 1990, pp. 263–328, and World Bank, World Development Report 1990, pp. 182–183.

TABLE 14–8   The Stock of Private Direct Investment per Capita in Developing Countries

Country	Year	Income per capita (U.S. dollars)	Population (millions)	Investment per capita (U.S. dollars)
Bangladesh	1978	90	85	1
India	1978	180	644	4
Tanzania	1978	230	17	10
Senegal	1978	340	5	63
Kenya	1983	340	17	50
Pakistan	1983	360	88	13
Nigeria	1978	560	81	49
Indonesia	1982	580	153	43
Egypt	1982	690	44	78
Philippines	1983	760	45	60
Thailand	1983	820	48	32
Colombia	1983	1,450	26	98
Malaysia	1983	1,840	15	556
Chile	1983	1,890	9	298
Mexico	1983	1,900	72	187
South Korea	1982	1,910	39	38
Brazil	1982	2,240	126	176
Argentina	1981	2,500	47	113
Hong Kong	1978	3,040	5	456
Singapore	1983	6,500	3	3,774

Source: Based on data from Vincent Cable and Bishakha Mukherjee, "Foreign Investment in Low-Income Developing Countries," in Investment in Development: New Roles for Foreign Capital? Theodore H. Moran et al., (Washington, D.C.: Overseas Development Council, 1986), pp. 88–89.

accumulated foreign direct investment per capita to indicate the importance of multinational finance to each host country. The table also shows a tendency for smaller countries to have higher per-capita stocks of direct investment, just as with aid, although there are important exceptions such as Brazil and Mexico. Multinationals tend to invest in higher-income countries because they have larger markets and better profit opportunities. But the higher incomes can also be a result of direct investment, which can exploit natural resources to the host country's advantage or bring other benefits that we discuss below.

The value of multinational investment lies not so much in the capital it provides as in a number of other potential benefits, including employment creation, technology transfer, technical and managerial skills, and access to world markets. The contribution of multinationals to **employment creation** in developing countries is not impressive. Of total employment in all sectors, multinationals account for less than 1 percent up to 6 percent in most developing countries. The contribution of MNCs to employment is more impressive in manufacturing alone; it ranges from 10 to 23 percent in Argentina, Bolivia, Brazil, and Colombia to over 50 percent in Singapore and Senegal.[11]

The issue is not gross employment, however, but net employment. How many jobs have been created by multinationals that would not otherwise have been created? The answer turns on a subsidiary question: Do multinational firms use more or less labor-intensive techniques than domestic firms? The spotty empirical evidence on this issue is hardly convincing one way or the other. To the extent that multinationals invest in sectors, such as petrochemicals and metals, that are inherently capital-intensive, they will employ relatively fewer workers per unit of investment than domestic firms that work in more labor-intensive industries. But the relevant comparison is between foreign and domestic firms in the same industries. Some studies find that foreign firms, wedded to capital-intensive techniques developed in their home markets where labor is expensive, tend to use these less-appropriate techniques in developing countries as well.[12] Yet there are also examples of multinationals using more labor-intensive techniques than comparable domestic firms. Much appears to depend on the extent of competition: when multinationals invest in domestic markets protected from domestic or foreign competition, they can afford to import capital-intensive production techniques. When they produce for export, however, or when they enter competitive domestic markets, competitive pressures force both multinationals and domestic firms to employ the lowest-cost techniques, and this frequently means more labor-intensive methods.[13] So job creation may depend as much on the host country's policies as on the multinationals' practices.

11. Ibid., p. 529.
12. In Figure 20–3 the foreign firm might choose technology T3 because at home it faces high wages (budget line B_rB_r), although in the developing country the relevant wage-rental ratio or budget line is B_pB_p and the appropriate technology is T2, which is more labor-intensive.
13. Joseph M. Grieco, ''Foreign Investment and Development: Theory and Evidence,'' in *Investing in Development,* Moran *et al.,* pp. 47–48.

The second major benefit expected from foreign investment is the **transfer of technology,** skills, and know-how. Because much of the world's research and development activity has been undertaken within large firms in North America, Europe, and Japan, firms from these areas are a potentially rich source of valuable information about innovative products, manufacturing processes, marketing methods, and managerial approaches. Smaller multinationals, particularly those from other developing countries, offer another kind of technological benefit: successful adaptation to local conditions of older technology from developed countries, and cost-saving innovations in small-scale manufacture. If this information is transplanted to host countries, innovation and adaptation can eventually become consistent with less future dependence on multinational investors.

For some kinds of operation, such as logging, many manufacturing activities, and open-pit mining, the acquisition of new information and methods by host country workers and supervisors requires only a basic educational background and a willingness to work in a modern, structured enterprise with clear standards for work schedules and work pace. But in other activities, particularly in natural-resource-based industries such as steel making, copper smelting, and chemical manufacturing, absorptive capacity depends on a locally available stock of more highly trained technical personnel such as chemical engineers, metallurgists, geologists, biologists, industrial economists, and experienced managers.

A few developing countries, such as India and Mexico, have trained relatively large numbers of technical industrial personnel and are able to absorb new technologies across a broad spectrum. Other countries have made strong efforts to train technical personnel specifically to take over important foreign-owned industries. Venezuela trained petroleum engineers and managers who now successfully run that sector; South Korea used its first chemical fertilizer plant, built and operated by a foreign firm, to train Koreans who soon were operating several other nationally owned fertilizer plants; and Malaysia became capable not only of operating its own rubber industry, but of conducting its own research on new species and methods of cultivation. Yet most developing countries do not have sufficient cadres of technically educated people to manage complex industries and only a few have the educational establishments needed to begin rectifying this shortage.

Perspectives on technology transfer differ markedly between multinationals and developing countries. The firms view their investments in the production of technology as a continuing process which should earn financial returns just as any investment would. Host countries, however, are concerned primarily with access to existing knowledge and, with some justification, regard past multinational investments in technology as sunk costs not requiring reimbursement. Public goods theory, as well as casual observation, tells us that multinationals will withhold information on technologies when they would not otherwise be able to appropriate the returns.

A third benefit sought from multinational investment is **managerial capacity,** without which access to technology is largely ornamental. To be sure, many developing countries have gifted entrepreneurs and innovators, including the market women in West African countries such as Ghana and Nigeria, clusters of industrialists in such Latin American cities as Monterey, Medellin, and Sao Paulo, the Gujaratis of India, and communities of Chinese and Indians who have long resided in developing countries from East Africa to Southeast Asia. Nevertheless, only a few developing countries possess sufficient numbers of managers capable of organizing and operating large industrial projects such as those undertaken by multinational firms, and virtually all are short of people with advanced training and experience in management. The number of MBAs and experienced managers in a single company such as IBM can rival the entire population of MBAs and other managers in even some well-endowed developing countries. Still, managers are created all the time in the most dynamic of the developing countries and the multinationals in particular employ and train them. The growth of MNCs from the developing countries themselves attests to their growing competence in management.

A fourth benefit is **access to world markets.** Developing countries capable of producing at competitive costs often find it difficult to penetrate foreign markets. Many multinationals, particularly in natural resources, chemicals, and other heavy industries, are vertically integrated, oligopolistic firms for which many transactions take place within the firm. In the early 1980s, over 60 percent of all imports by multinational manufacturers in the United States were from affiliates overseas, while almost 40 percent of exports were also within the firms.[14] Multinationals developed preferential access to customers by fashioning and adhering to long-term contracts in standardized products, such as petroleum, or by acquiring a reputation for delivering a specialized product of satisfactory quality on a reliable schedule, as in construction and engineering. Developing-country firms often require years to overcome such marketing advantages of the multinationals, although it is increasingly being done by firms in East Asia and elsewhere.

These benefits of multinational investment have for decades been made available to host countries only as investment **"packages"** incorporating equity capital (that is, ownership and control), management, technology, and marketing. During the early 1970s the Firestone Tire Company, for example, owned a rubber plantation and a tire factory in Ghana. It supplied the equipment and thus the technology for both facilities, along with financing and top management. Rubber was sold to its own tire plants, either in Ghana or the United States. Such investment packages have traditionally been offered on a "take it or leave it" basis, in the probably correct belief that the whole is more valuable than the sum of its parts, and also as a means of protecting the most crucial element, patented technology.

In recent years, developing countries have made some progress in "unbundling" the package to capture more of its benefits for themselves. Some multinationals have seen benefits in avoiding the risks of equity participation and maximizing the profits on sales of unbundled technology, management, or marketing access. Different contractual forms have been developed to transfer elements of the old package to host countries, includ-

---

14. UNCTNC, *Transnational Corporations in World Development,* p. 93. The ratios for Great Britain and Japan are lower, 27 percent, covering all industries.

ing joint ventures in which the foreign firm takes less than a majority partnership; agreements in the petroleum industry to share production rather than ownership; licensing of technology, as in the Korean automobile industry; management contracts in which a foreign firm runs the enterprise but may have little or no equity share; franchising of products and brands, as done by MacDonalds in the United States and worldwide; and "turnkey" projects that are handed over to the host country firm after being started up by a multinational, a form used in building electric power plants, for example. Another much-used route has been gradually to take over the management and ownership of existing foreign investments as the host country's capacities increase. Harvard economist Raymond Vernon has called this the **obsolescing bargain,** in recognition of the shift in negotiating strength that occurs once the foreign investment is in place and the host country increases its ability to operate the facility.[15] Through these and other means, industrializing countries such as Brazil, Mexico, India, Korea, and Taiwan have not only developed their own petrochemical industries, for example, but have themselves become suppliers of technology and management to less-advanced countries.[16]

Unbundling is not suitable in every case, however. Some countries have begun to reconsider arrangements in which multinationals make their profits on the provision of technology, management, or market access, but have little or no profit incentive to manage the firm productively and instead leave all the risks to the host country firms. This reconsideration is one factor that, together with growing burdens of foreign debt, has led developing countries to view multinational investment more tolerantly in recent years.[17]

Policies toward Foreign Investment

Host governments use a range of restrictions and incentives to capture as much as possible of the expected benefits from foreign investment, including performance requirements, local ownership requirements, restrictions on profit repatriation, monopoly privileges, and tax holidays. **Performance requirements** are generally tailored to fit each industry. Multinationals that assemble cars and other vehicles are often forced to increase annually the share of local content in each vehicle, for example, whereas those entering mining may commit themselves to future investments in domestic minerals processing. Policies that made foreign firms utilize local personnel are aimed not only at job creation but also at increasing absorptive capacity for the transfer of technology from multinationals. Indonesia has required foreign mining and petroleum companies to fill all unskilled jobs with Indonesians after three years, but only 75 percent of skilled and supervisory jobs, and 50 percent of technical and managerial personnel.

15. Raymond Vernon, *Storm over the Multinationals: The Real Issue* (Cambridge, Mass.: Harvard University Press, 1977), p. 151.

16. Charles P. Oman, "New Forms of Investment in Developing Countries," in *Investing in Development,* Moran et al., pp. 131–155.

17. UNCTNC, *Transnational Corporations in World Development,* p. 71.

Developing countries have tried to promote technology transfer by imposing standards requiring multinationals to import only the most advanced capital equipment rather than used machinery. But such measures work against other development goals because older equipment is likely to be more labor-intensive and less costly to operate. Ecuador has imposed special taxes on multinationals to finance government research and development, India has required firms to invest in local research and development activities, and other governments have simply pressured companies to undertake local research. One study cites 11 instances, primarily in Brazil and India, in which firms responded by establishing research and development facilities in the host country.[18]

Many host countries, particularly in Latin America and Southeast Asia, have made it mandatory for foreign investors to sell a specified share of equity, usually 51 percent, to local partners to form **joint ventures.** Through local ownership requirements, known as **saturation laws,** host governments hope to appropriate technology, limit the repatriation of profits, and maintain local control. Host countries assume that local joint-venture partners will become capable of matching technological and managerial capacities with foreign firms. However, many local joint-venture partnerships are pro forma arrangements involving local elites close to the centers of political power with little interest in business matters. And parent multinationals are often more reluctant to allow diffusion of technology to joint ventures than to wholly owned subsidiaries. Even if joint ventures do succeed in asserting greater national control over foreign investments, some analysts argue that such requirements may only divert scarce local resources to the multinational sector and also reduce the inflow of foreign capital, with little net gain to the host country. Raymond Vernon stresses that if local owners, in buying out their foreign partners, pay a price fully commensurate with the earnings they expect to receive, then the net effect is an export of scarce capital to the foreign multinational.[19]

Other common restrictions include ceilings on repatriation of profits to the parent corporation and stiff taxes on profit remittances. In Colombia profits remitted by a firm to a parent company abroad were at one time limited to 14 percent of the firm's Colombian investments; Brazil has at times limited remittances to 10 percent of registered capital. Other countries, such as Argentina and Ghana, with no explicit ceilings on profit repatriation, still limit repatriation through the administration of foreign exchange controls.

Restrictions on multinationals can increase the benefits to host countries only if they do not deter foreign firms from investing. To accompany these policy sticks, most developing countries also offer policy carrots, especially protection from competition and tax incentives. **Protection** includes tariffs and quotas to reduce imports of competing goods, and the outright grant of **monopoly control** over local markets. Monopoly positions in local

18. Jack N. Behrman and William A. Fischer, *Overseas R & D Activities of Transnational Corporations* (Cambridge, Mass.: Oelgeschlager, Gunn and Hain, 1980), pp. 107–109.
19. Vernon, *Storm Over the Multinationals*, p. 168.

markets are frequently sought and sometimes granted, for example by Kenya, Zambia, and, for a time, Indonesia to foreign rubber tire manufacturers. Because import protection and monopoly control create higher domestic prices and profits, they often result in higher direct transfers from host country consumers to the multinationals' foreign stockholders.

The transfer from local consumers to foreign stockholders is even higher if **income tax incentives** are used to induce investment by foreign firms. Although the variety of such incentives is almost limitless, the most common is **income tax holidays,** which exempt firms from paying taxes on corporate income, usually for three to six years. Most countries would otherwise tax profits at rates from 35 to 50 percent. During the heyday of these tax holidays, the postwar period through 1970, most multinationals investing in the developing world received tax exemptions. By 1980 tax holidays had virtually vanished for natural-resource investments, except in some Francophone countries in Africa, and were becoming less common in other sectors as well. Increasingly host countries have learned that, although such incentives may be valuable to the firms, they may serve little purpose other than the enrichment of foreign shareholders and governments, at the expense of the host government.

For tax holidays to help the multinationals, they must be creditable against income taxes due to their home country governments. Otherwise, if home countries tax firms on worldwide income, as all industrial countries except France do, then taxes foregone by the developing country would simply be transferred to tax revenues of the multinational's home country. Most industrial countries now permit their firms to take credit for tax holidays granted abroad through tax treaties negotiated between host and home country governments.

Still, there remains substantial doubt that developing countries do receive benefits commensurate with the costs of the tax revenues they forego. Tax holidays can only help the foreign investor if its project is profitable to begin with. Most studies conclude that income tax holidays have only marginal effects on multinational investment decisions, rewarding them for what they would have done in any case. This is especially true for firms intending to produce in protected domestic markets of the host countries. Export-oriented, labor-intensive, "footloose" industries, however, may be more sensitive to tax holidays and other incentives.[20] A prominent example is the electronics industry, which utilizes large amounts of unskilled labor to manufacture semiconductor chips, make integrated circuits, and assemble parts of products such as electronic calculators and computers. These firms operate largely in export processing zones in countries such as Malaysia, Thailand, and Ecuador. Electronics companies appear sensitive to differences in incentives offered by host countries, and developing countries have competed with each other in offering investment incentives and privileges to them. But even in this case, inducements like tax holidays proba-

20. Louis T. Wells, Jr., "Investment Incentives: An Unnecessary Debate," *The CTC Reporter* 22 (Autumn 1986): 58–60, and Steven Guisinger et al., *Investment Incentives and Performance Requirements* (New York: Praeger, 1985).

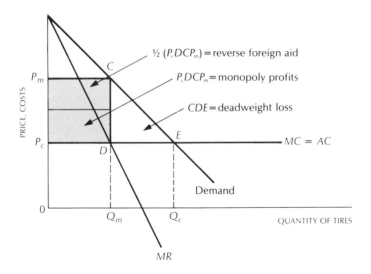

FIGURE 14–2 **Interaction of Incentive Policies.** A multinational subsidiary with monopoly rights and a tax holiday produces at Q_m instead of the competitive output Q_c. Consumers lose because they pay the monopoly price P_m rather than P_c. All monopoly profits P_cP_mCD are lost to the host country, until the tax holiday expires and the taxable portion of profits goes to the host country's treasury.

bly play a secondary role to more basic factors such as a stable source of low-cost, unorganized labor, decent living conditions for managers and engineers, reliable international transportation and communications facilities, and freedom from government regulation.

The combination of monopoly rights and tax holidays can result in large benefits to foreigners with little gain to host countries, as illustrated in Figure 14–2. Consider a multinational firm that has received monopoly rights to manufacture automobile tires for a developing country market and has also received a five-year tax holiday. For simplicity, assume the monopolist can produce at constant marginal cost MC and hence constant average cost AC. If the tire industry were a competitive industry consisting of many firms, or if imports were allowed into the country, then the supply curve of that industry would be identical to $MC = AC$. The price of tires would then be P_c, and the output of tires would be Q_c, the output that equates marginal cost with demand (average revenue).

A profit-maximizing monopolist, however, determines the level of output Q_m where marginal cost equals marginal revenue MR. Because Q_m is smaller then Q_c, it can be sold at a price of P_m, higher than the competitive price P_c. As a result, monopoly profits (rectangle P_cP_mCD) are generated, over and above "normal" (competitive) returns on capital. Consumers in the host country pay higher prices for fewer tires, and there is substantial economic waste (triangle CDE, the deadweight loss).[21] If the monopolist is a domestic firm, part of its profits will be taxed and there is a good chance that the after-tax portion will also remain available to the country. A for-

21. To interpret the meaning of triangle CDE, review Figure 12–1.

eign monopolist, however, is likely to repatriate its profits to the home country, and if it has a tax holiday, then all of the area $P_c P_m CD$ is lost to the country. After the tax holiday expires, tire consumers will continue to subsidize waste, but the host country treasury will at least receive a share of the monopoly profits.

If strong incentives to attract multinational investors can cost the host country more than it gains, what are the alternatives? One approach, described in Chapter 5, would be to open up the economy to foreign trade as well as foreign investment, reduce government intervention in the domestic economy, and rely on market forces both to attract foreign investors and to regulate their behavior. Where market forces alone are deemed inadequate and some kind of protection is employed, then investment incentives should be reserved for potential export industries where clear performance targets can be established and where profits depend on efficient operation. A study by economists Dennis Encarnation and Louis Wells lends support to this strategy. They performed social benefit-cost analyses on 50 foreign investment projects in a large Asian country, incorporating shadow prices and using the methods explained in Chapter 6. All the export-oriented projects had social rates of return above 10 percent, which they took to be the opportunity cost of capital. But in the four industries studied that were oriented to the protected domestic market, 30 to 70 percent of the projects were socially unprofitable, with rates of return below 10 percent. Moreover, the highest rates of failure were in the most heavily protected industries.[22]

Conflicting Objectives

Host countries thus try to derive from multinational investment the maximum benefits in terms of capital, technology, management, market access, and economic returns. Multinational investors have a variety of objectives that can be subsumed into two basic goals: global profits and long-term stability of the enterprise. In oligopolistic industries, companies may maximize joint profits of all firms in the industry, rather than of each firm separately, while maintaining stability to the extent possible. New enterprises are discouraged from entering the industry and established firms avoid intense competition that might substantially change their respective market shares. Multinationals in these industries evaluate projects in host countries for their contribution to the global profitability of the multinational and the stability of the firm and its industry.

Balancing these two goals has led MNCs to undertake projects in developing countries that would otherwise appear inexplicable. Oil multinationals have accepted contractual arrangements involving lower returns than received by competitors because they wanted to diversify reserves into new locations. A U.S. sulphur firm might enter copper mining in a developing country to diversify activity and insulate the firm better from the

---

22. Dennis J. Encarnation and Louis T. Wells, Jr., "Evaluating Foreign Investment," in *Investing in Development,* Moran, et al., pp. 61–85.

vagaries of the sulphur business. An established copper-mining MNC might respond by accepting less-favorable terms to mine copper in the same country, merely to protect its existing market share. Japanese companies often establish manufacturing subsidiaries in developing countries to protect the export markets they already have.

Such investments point to a fairly coherent pattern of defensive behavior by multinationals. Developing-country negotiators have increasingly recognized the importance of stability and other strategic considerations in multinational planning, which in turn has enhanced their ability to play off one firm against others. In the process many host countries have been able to curtail their use of generous inducements to invest, particularly tax incentives. Indonesia, for example, has not offered tax holidays to investors since 1985; instead it has used deregulation and export-promoting policies to attract foreign companies.

Despite inherently conflicting objectives between multinationals and host countries, the climate for foreign investment has improved over the last decade or so. As developing nations became independent after World War II and asserted their control over their economies, their relations with foreign investors became increasingly contentious. One indicator of conflict, the number of expropriations of foreign subsidiaries by developing countries, rose from an average of 11 per year in the early 1960s to 56 per year in the early 1970s. Since the mid-1970s, however, both sides have assessed the costs and benefits of foreign investment more realistically, and relations between multinationals and host countries have become less contentious. After 1975, there was a steady drop in the number of expropriations, which averaged less than three per year in the first half of the 1980s. The economic reforms of the 1980s have deregulated developing economies, opened them more to world trade, and thus made them more hospitable locations for outside investors. When multinational investments require contracts between investors and the government, as in natural-resource extraction and sometimes in heavy industry, terms have become more pragmatic and flexible and have provided for changing external circumstances. In manufacturing, host countries are concerned less about reducing foreign ownership and more about export performance and the utilization of local resources. Disputes, when they arise, are settled increasingly by international arbitration instead of confrontation.[23]

THE DEBT CRISIS

The two forms of foreign saving discussed so far—foreign aid and foreign direct investment—both require repayment by the recipient country. Although technical assistance and some capital assistance come as grants, most foreign aid is in the form of loans on soft terms, on which interest payments are relatively low and repayment of principal is spread over many years. Direct investment carries the obligation to permit repatriation of dividends, but these are only earned on profitable investments. Except in

23. UNCTNC, *Transnational Corporations in World Development*, pp. 313–329.

severely distorted economies, dividends should be self-financing. Three other forms of foreign saving have heavier burdens of repayment: export credits, portfolio investment, and commercial bank loans.

Commercial Borrowing

Of the three kinds of commercial borrowing, **export credits** have never accounted for much more than 10 percent of total net resource flows, and in recent years they have been even less important; **portfolio investment** has been accessible only to countries with virtually no problems in paying the interest and principal on their debt. It was the third form of commercial lending, **commercial bank loans,** that brought on the debt crisis of the 1980s. In the 1960s, commercial bank lending was a small if growing component of the resource transfer to developing countries. In 1970 it accounted for 16 percent of total net transfers (see Table 14–2). When OPEC raised prices in 1973–74 and again in 1979–80, the oil-producing states of the Middle East had large dollar surpluses to invest in world markets. One of their favorite investment outlets was bank deposits in the United States and Europe. The commercial banks, awash in petrodollars, had to find profitable lending outlets and took renewed interest in lending to developing countries, especially those in South America and East Asia.

By 1983, annual commercial bank lending to developing countries had grown tenfold from its 1970 level, which represented at least a threefold expansion net of inflation. In 1983 the net value of commercial bank loans accounted for 37 percent of total net resource flows and exceeded foreign aid as a source of finance. The stock of accumulated debt owed by developing countries to commercial banks had expanded 17 times to $335 billion, more than half of all LDC debt (Table 14–9). In effect, the commercial banks channeled petrodollars from the wealthy oil exporters to the middle-income developing countries, a constructive form of intermediation for which they were applauded at the time.

Table 14–9 Stocks of Long-Term Debt, All Developing Countries, 1970–1988 (billion U.S. dollars)

	1970	1983	1988
All sources	63	644	980
Official creditors	32	221	443
Multilateral	7	80	176
(World Bank)	(2)	(37)	(84)
Bilateral	25	141	267
Commercial banks	20	335	396

Source: World Bank, *World Debt Tables 1989–90,* Vol. 1, pp. 378–379.

The Repayment Crisis

In the early 1980s, borrowing countries, especially in Latin America, faced mounting debt and **debt service** (the payment of interest and principal). Latin

American countries' ratios of long-term debt to GNP rose from 18 percent
in 1970 to 25 percent in 1980 and exceeded 50 percent during the mid-1980s (Table 14–10). For Mexico, Argentina, and Chile, the **debt service ratio,** which compares payments of principal and interest with earnings on the exports of goods and services, also exceeded 50 percent.

These and other countries, not only in Latin America, began having difficulty generating sufficient government revenues and foreign exchange to service their debt. In the first half of 1982, eight countries had to reschedule their debt payments, compared with six reschedulings in 1981 and only three in 1978. In August 1982 Mexico declared a moratorium on the payment of interest on its foreign debt, and the debt crisis was in full cry. In 1985 there were 15 rescheduling packages and in 1987 more than 20 were concluded or negotiated. From 1983 to 1987, more than $300 billion of debt repayments had to be rescheduled.[24]

TABLE 14–10 Debt Ratios, Developing Countries, 1970–1988 (percent)

	1970	1980	1980–88 Max.	1988
All developing countries				
Long-term debt to GNP	14	21	43	37
Long-term debt to exports[a]	115	99	203	175
Total debt service to exports[a]	—	21	33	29
Latin America				
Long-term debt to GNP	18	25	54	42
Long-term debt to exports[a]	149	139	324	267
Total debt service to exports[a]	—	37	48	41
Debt service ratio[b] for:				
Argentina			80	65
Bolivia			60	35
Brazil			47	47
Chile			60	21
Mexico			54	46

[a]Exports of goods and services.
[b]Interest plus principal repayments as a percentage of exports of goods and services.
Source: World Bank, *World Debt Tables 1989–90,* Vol. 1, pp. 78, 94, and First Supplement.

Once it became clear that many debtors would be unable to meet their obligations, the commercial banks stopped making voluntary loans to the debtors. The only commercial lending that took place after 1982 came as part of elaborate refinancing agreements involving the IMF, World Bank, creditor governments, commercial banks, and debtor governments. Stabilization and structural adjustment packages, discussed in Chapter 5, were part of these agreements, providing official finance to underpin or substitute for commercial bank loans. The commercial banks would make additional loans to service payments on old loans, permit debtors to "capitalize" their interest payments by converting them into additional debt (on which

24. Rudiger Dornbusch, "Background Paper," in *The Road to Economic Recovery,* Twentieth Century Fund, Task Force on International Debt (New York: Priority Publications, 1989), pp. 29–30.

interest was charged), reschedule payments of principal, or employ some combination of these mechanisms to **restructure** debt. By these means, it was hoped, the debtors could quickly become solvent and the overexposed U.S. banks would not become insolvent. By the late 1980s, however, few banks were interested in further lending. From 1980 to 1982, private creditors sent more than $50 million a year of net resources into developing countries (measured in 1986 prices); in 1987 the net resource flow was negligible.[25]

The impact on the most indebted countries was severe. For a country to turn from being a net borrower into a net repayer of loans, it must reverse the beneficial effects of foreign saving inflows. Instead of investing more than it saves, a country must generate a surplus of savings to be used for repayment of debt. Instead of importing more than it exports, a repaying country must generate export surpluses because foreign lenders need to be repaid in dollars or other foreign currencies. Where net resource inflows once financed additional growth, net resource outflows from debtors will reduce growth; in Table 14–1, line 3 changes from a net inward transfer (imports exceed exports) to a net outward transfer of resources. If debtor governments find it difficult to raise more taxes or reduce noninterest expenditures, as most did, they typically resort to inflationary financing that further destabilizes the economy. Capital flight exacerbates the crisis, as domestic savers try to move their assets to more stable financial markets.

Over 1978 to 1981, a group of 15 heavily indebted countries managed to attract sufficient foreign saving to pay the interest and principal due on their debt and still import about $9 billion more of goods and nonfactor services each year than they exported. But from 1983 to 1988, the 15 countries were forced into a reverse transfer—exports exceeded imports—of almost $34 billion a year to service their debt.[26] From 1970 to 1981, these countries had enjoyed per-capita income growth of 2.7 percent a year, invested 25 percent of their GDP, and tolerated inflation of 39 percent a year on average. During the debt crisis, however, from 1982 to 1988, the same 15 countries suffered declines in per-capita income averaging 0.7 percent a year, were forced to reduce their investment to 18 percent of GDP, and inflated their economies by 149 percent a year.[27]

Sustainable Debt

Why did the debt crisis occur? Foreign borrowing, as we have seen, is an accepted part of economic development. Access to foreign saving permits countries to invest more than they can save and to import more than their export earnings would otherwise allow. If the additional investment and

25. World Bank, *World Debt Tables 1989–90,* Vol. 1, p. 10.

26. Annual average net outflows during the latter period were so much larger than the average net inflows of prior years because of the sharp decline in gross lending after 1982 noted above. Not only did countries have to repay their old debt, but they had to devote their own resources to purchase imports that had previously been financed by foreign borrowing.

27. Dornbusch, "Background Paper," p. 31.

imports are put to productive use, they should yield sufficient returns to pay the interest, dividends, and principal on the initial foreign inflows. Under these circumstances, continuing foreign borrowing and growing external debt can be sustainable and consistent with development.

We can determine the conditions for sustainable borrowing in terms of the **two-gap model** discussed in Chapter 6. Recall that foreign inflows can finance one of two possible gaps in an economy: (1) the foreign exchange gap, equal to imports (M) less exports (E) of goods and nonfactor services, or (2) the gap between investment (I) and domestic saving (S_d). Foreign borrowing can also finance a third gap, the government budget deficit. If the foreign exchange gap is binding, then foreign inflows help growth by increasing the amount of imports. In any period, the increase in debt due to this inflow is:

$$dD/dt = iD + M - E, \qquad [14–1]$$

where D is the stock of debt at any time, dD/dt is the change in the stock (the first derivative), and i is the average interest rate paid on all foreign inflows, including loans, equity, and grants. It is convenient to measure these flows in current dollars, the currency in which debt is conventionally measured. The simple differential equation can be solved under the following conditions: let E and M grow at the same exponential rate g_E, and find the long-run equilibrium conditions for sustainable foreign borrowing. In that case, the stock of debt will also grow exponentially at g_E, and in the long run the ratio of debt to exports will settle at

$$D/E = a/(g_E - i) \qquad [14–2]$$

where a is the ratio of the foreign exchange gap to exports, $(M - E)/E$, a constant under the assumption that imports and exports grow at the same rate.[28]

Equation 14–2 tells us that, for a given foreign exchange gap a, there is an equilibrium ratio of debt to exports that can be sustained. If g_E is greater than i, the gap can remain positive; this means that the country can continue to borrow and service its debt without a rise in its ratio of debt to exports. If the gap $(M - E)/E$ is 10 percent, the average interest rate is 7 percent (recall that grants and concessional loans have to be averaged in with commercial debt), and the growth of dollar earnings from exports g_E is 12 percent a year, then the ratio of debt to exports would settle at 2, which was about the average for the developing countries in the 1980s. If the growth of exports can be pushed above the growth of imports, the debt-export ratio would fall. If, on the other hand, the growth rate of exports were to fall below the interest rate, the only way to sustain debt would be to turn the foreign exchange gap into a surplus and begin repaying the debt,

28. Equation 14–1 is solved to yield Equation 14–2 by letting $D/D_o = E/E_o = M/M_o = e^{gt}$ and substituting into Equation 14–1, noting that $d(e^{gt})/dt = ge^{gt}$. Then Equation 14–1 becomes $g_E D = iD + M - E$, from which 14–2 can be readily derived. The result is given by Albert Fishlow, "External Borrowing and Debt Management," in *The Open Economy: Tools for Policymakers in Developing Countries,* Rudiger Dornbusch and F. Leslie C. H. Helmers, eds., (New York: Oxford University Press, 1988), pp. 220–221.

precisely what has happened in the high-debt countries of Latin America. The key to sustaining debt under a foreign exchange constraint, then, is the ability of the debtor to put the additional resources to productive use in export industries, either directly or indirectly.

A similar calculation can be made for the investment-saving gap. The differential equation is

$$dD/dt = iD + I - S_d = iD + vY - sY = iD + (v-s)Y, \qquad [14-3]$$

where Y is GNP, v is the investment share of GNP, and s is the propensity to save out of GNP. As with the foreign exchange gap, assume that both debt and GNP grow at the same exponential rate g_Y. Then the long-run equilibrium ratio of debt to GNP is

$$D/Y = (v-s)/(g_Y - i). \qquad [14-4]$$

In this case, if $v - s$ is 3 percent of GNP, i averages 7 percent on all foreign inflows, and the growth rate of GNP expressed in current dollars is 10 percent a year,[29] the debt to GNP ratio would settle at 1 and could be sustained at that level indefinitely. Although some countries reached debt to GNP ratios exceeding 1 during the 1980s, the Latin American debtors' ratios seldom exceeded 50 percent. From the saving-investment perspective, the requirement for sound debt management is to invest foreign saving in assets that are productive enough to boost the growth rate of GNP, and to adopt policies that reduce the share of consumption in GNP.

At one level, the issue of managing foreign loans and grants to yield high growth rates is simple. If the country behaves like an enterprise, it will borrow only if it can invest in projects that have rates of return above the cost of borrowing. Then loans can be serviced out of the earnings from those investments. For the country there is a further condition: that the project must earn or save sufficient foreign exchange to transfer payments of interest and principal in foreign currency. Seen this way, foreign resources should only be sought if there are productive foreign-exchange-earning investment opportunities for them.

This approach is too restrictive, however. The question for both lenders and borrowers is whether the economy as a whole can generate sufficient income and export growth to service debt on schedule. Concern over specific projects is one aspect of this problem. But it is secondary to the larger issue of sound macroeconomic management. If an economy has been well-managed and has proved itself able to use its resources productively and sustain growth over long periods, the role of foreign resources is to augment the entire investment menu. Precisely how these resources are invested is not important: additional loans are likely to be productively employed and serviced on schedule. Conversely, if an economy is poorly managed and unlikely to generate sufficient resources to service its debt, then precise targeting of loans toward specific projects, no matter how productive,

---

29. This is not as high as it seems. Remember we are measuring all quantities in current dollars, because that is the basis on which debt is serviced. If the real growth rate is 6 percent a year and the dollar rate of inflation is 4 percent a year, then the g_Y would be 10 percent a year.

is not much protection against default on those loans. Relevant issues of sound fiscal, monetary, and foreign exchange management of developing economies are discussed throughout this book.

Causes of the Crisis

Although there is nothing inherent in foreign debt to cause a repayments crisis, defaults occurred frequently in many Latin American and European countries during the nineteenth century and the 1930s. The crisis of the 1980s was the first since World War II, however. In this instance, several things appear to have gone wrong at once.

First, several of the borrowing countries were profligate with their resources and ignored principles of sound economic management. The oil shocks of 1973–1974 and 1978–80 caused major disruptions in every economy in the world: oil importers had to adjust to lower standards of living and oil exporters had to learn to manage massive new revenues productively. Facing plunges in income that sometimes threatened political stability, many governments tried to compensate by increasing spending and thus increasing budget deficits. Having thereby stimulated inflation, some of these governments compensated further by maintaining their exchange rates at overvalued levels. This restrained price increases for imports and exportable goods, but also discouraged export growth and encouraged capital flight. When recycled petrodollars became available through the commercial banks, governments grabbed at the chance to boost investment and prevent declines in consumption. Unfortunately, in many cases investments were wasteful and there was too much consumption. Resources were not channeled into investments that would eventually pay off the debts with a surplus for the host country.

Why did the banks lend to profligate governments? The gush of petrodollars left the banks highly liquid and seeking profitable outlets for their deposits. Lending to developing countries seemed to provide an outlet that had not been fully utilized in recent years. Because the debt was **sovereign,** i.e., it was guaranteed by governments, bankers apparently discounted the risk of default, even though history held many examples to the contrary. Once a few banks showed the way, others followed. And once the banks were heavily involved, further lending seemed a sensible way to keep debtor nations liquid enough to continue servicing earlier loans. Banks were encouraged by their own governments, especially the United States government, and the international agencies, all of whom hoped that the illiquidity of the early 1980s would disappear once the world economy recovered from its instability. Whatever the reason for the banks' persistence in lending, it is clear that neither they nor their governments foresaw the generalized debt crisis.

If debtor profligacy and creditor overindulgence were general causes of the crisis, instability of the world economy was its proximate cause. The unprecedented rises in oil prices have already been mentioned. During the latter 1970s, inflation in the United States reached double digits and the Federal Reserve Board tightened the money supply. The immediate consequence was that interest rates soared to a peak of 16 percent in 1981 before settling gradually into a range of 7 to 9 percent through the second half of the 1980s. Debtor countries had to pay the new rates if they had borrowed at flexible interest rates or if they had to refinance old loans now coming due, so their interest payments rose and became unpredictable. Tight money and fiscal stringency, especially in the United States, led to the world recession of 1981–82. Income in the industrial economies, having grown by more than 3 percent a year in the preceeding years, slowed to 2 percent growth in 1980–81 and declined in 1982. The recession shrunk the markets for debtor country exports and caused a decline in commodity prices, which fell by one-third in the early 1980s relative to the prices of manufactures. These external shocks would seem compelling reasons for the debt crisis, except that not all debtors suffered equally. South Korea and Indonesia are among the world's largest debtors, yet sound economic policies have enabled them to service their debt while continuing to grow throughout the 1980s. It took a combination of the deteriorating world economy, poor domestic management, and the myopia of the commercial banks to bring on the crisis.[30]

Escape from the Crisis

The debt crisis of the 1980s has become the debt problem of the 1990s. No longer does the stability of the world financial system seem threatened by debtor default. This is partly because debtors have for the most part decided that their interest lies in working out of their debt in cooperation with the creditors, their governments, and the international agencies. In part it reflects adjustment by the commercial banks, which have written off substantial portions of their outstanding loans to debt-ridden countries. However, the problem remains acute for the debtor countries, whose prospects for economic growth and political stability depend in part on an amelioration of their debt burdens.

It is important to separate two groups of highly indebted countries. The debt crisis has for the most part engulfed the overextended countries of Latin America and a few other middle-income countries such as the Ivory Coast, Morocco, the Philippines, and Poland. These countries got into difficulty because they borrowed heavily from commercial banks. Another set of low-income countries, mostly in Africa, also verge on bankruptcy, even though most of their foreign capital has been on very concessional terms. As an indicator of the difference between these groups, in 1988 the African countries were paying only 3.4 percent average interest on new inflows, which carried a grant element of 50 percent.[31] For the heavily indebted

---

30. On the causes of the crisis, see Dornbusch, "Background Paper," pp. 37–47, and John T. Cuddington, "The Extent and Causes of the Debt Crisis of the 1980s," in *Dealing with the Debt Crisis*, Ishrat Husain and Ishac Diwan, eds. (Washington, D.C.: World Bank, 1989), pp. 15–44.

31. The **grant element** of a concessional loan is the difference between the amount of the loan and the present value of the interest and repayments, discounted at a commercial market rate of interest. The softer the loan, i.e., the lower the interest rate and the longer the repayment period, the higher the grant element. A gift has a grant element of 100 percent.

middle-income countries, the average interest rate was 7.5 percent and the grant element only 14 percent. For the latter group, debt relief involves a complex mix of action by the aid agencies and the commercial banks. For the African debtors the problem resolves into one of net aid flows, whether received as debt relief or as new concessional finance, from the multilateral and bilateral donors.

Two extreme approaches to the Latin American debt crisis, though they have strong advocates, have been treated more as failures than as solutions by government and international agency officials. The first of these, advocated by Milton Friedman and other economists with faith in market-based solutions, is to let the commercial bank creditors and debtor governments, unassisted by any official intervention or finance, work out the solution. The banks would then face three alternatives, each of which would reduce their profits and could threaten insolvency: make concessions to the debtors in the form of debt relief or new loans on concessional terms; sell off their debt at market prices, about a third the nominal value; or try to collect and risk outright default. All these have been used to some extent, but mostly in conjunction with help from the international aid agencies. The banks' practice of writing down the value of their developing-country loans is an accounting method of anticipating losses by one of these measures. What attracts many economists to this approach is that the ultimate burden for poor loan decisions by bank management is borne by the shareholders of the banks.

The second radical approach is really the other side of the same coin: encourage the debtors to consider default or repudiation of their debt as a serious option. There has already been default in one sense, because interest payments have been missed, principal repayments have been rescheduled by virtually every Latin American country, and one government, Peru, put a cap on the share of exports it was willing to devote to debt service.[32] But, because lenders have been willing to capitalize missed interest payments by adding them to the loan principal, and to reschedule payments of principal, there has been no technical default and no repudiation of debt. The case for default is largely a benefit-cost calculation. Default has the immediate economic benefit of stopping the outflow of interest and principal. However, all inflows of new capital cease as well, and may not be resumed for many years; importers will have to pay cash in advance; creditors will try to seize foreign assets of the defaulting country; and some creditor governments may retaliate in political ways. In some cases debt obligations might become burdensome enough to make default worthwhile, but so far none of the major debtor governments has acted as if that were so.

Between these extreme solutions lies a range of mechanisms and programs to ameliorate the debt service burden. All programs of debt relief have centered on individual debtor countries. The participants include the debtor government; the international agencies, specifically the World Bank and IMF; the creditor governments, their treasuries, and aid agencies; and

---

32. Peru, with a debt service ratio of 29 percent in 1984, limited debt service payments to 10 percent of exports, beginning in 1988.

the commercial banks with loans to each debtor country. Each debt relief agreement requires a major negotiation among these parties, covering stabilization and structural adjustment programs, new aid and commercial credits, debt rescheduling, and a list of mechanisms for converting or retiring existing debt. Since 1989, the framework for debt relief has followed the plan outlined by U.S. Secretary of the Treasury Nicholas Brady. The most striking example of an agreement under the **Brady plan** is that with Mexico (see box).

Stabilization and structural adjustment programs, discussed in Chapter 5, are done under the tutelage of the IMF and World Bank, respectively, which provide substantial credits in return for the debtor country's adherence to a program of macroeconomic adjustments and microeconomic reforms. Stabilization and reform are crucial for resumed economic development in many countries. They contribute to debt reduction by helping to reduce deficits in the government budget and the balance of payments, to contain inflation, to stimulate savings, and to generate more resources for investment and debt service. The cost of debt service is borne by citizens of the debtor country in the form of reduced incomes, higher taxes and fees, reduced services from government, and other adjustments that reduce levels of consumption. The funds provided by the IMF, World Bank, and bilateral aid agencies are used to ease these burdens to some extent by financing imports and investment and, in some cases, by directly financing debt reduction. The cost of concessional finance from the multilateral and bilateral donors is borne ultimately by taxpayers in the industrial creditor countries.

The commercial banks at first entered these negotiations voluntarily, in the belief that relief in the form of new credits or rescheduled debt would stave off default until improvements in the world economy and better economic management enabled debtors to resume debt service. As this proved a false hope, banks became reluctant partners and increasingly pressed for official debt relief that would reduce their exposure to losses from developing-country debt. By the late 1980s the creditor governments and international agencies were encouraging the banks to use a number of mechanisms from a **menu** of debt reduction devices, including interest capitalization, debt rescheduling, buybacks, exchanges of claims, and debt-equity swaps—all sanctioned under the Brady plan.

Capitalization of interest converts current interest payments into additional principal, a way to decrease the debt service burden in the short run by increasing it in the long run. Interest is, of course, charged on the newly capitalized interest. **Rescheduling of principal** also puts off until tomorrow what debtors cannot service today. It can be done through debt negotiations or *de facto* through banks' choosing not to foreclose when a debtor does not pay the principal due. Sometimes rescheduling agreements involve improved loan terms for the debtor.

The major money markets of the world have active secondary markets in all kinds of debt, public and private, where creditors can sell their claims against debtors at a discount that reflects market expectations about repayment. At the end of 1989, the commercial debt of the 17 most heavily indebted countries sold on the secondary market at only one-third of its par value. A buyer of such paper pays $33 to obtain a promise of repayment of $100 plus interest, reflecting the buyer's expectation that the chances of repayment are only slightly better than 1 in 3. If the commercial banks believe the chances of repayment are less than 1 in 3, they may forego their claim of repayment, sell the loan on the secondary market, and realize a net loss of $67. Debtors, too, can purchase their own obligations on the secondary market and pay $33 to reduce the principal due by $100. Loan agreements normally prohibit borrowers from such **buybacks,** however, because they encourage debtors to default, drive down the price on the secondary market, and make it more advantageous to buy back their debt. As an indication of the intractability of the debt problem, buybacks have been placed on the menu of debt relief measures if approved by the creditor banks as an exception to the usual prohibition. Although buybacks can be highly advantageous to the debtor if the alternative is full repayment, it does require an immediate cash outlay in foreign exchange at a time when such resources are particularly scarce. Not all debtors are in a position to spend these resources, and it is not always advantageous to do so. In 1988, only $648 million of developing-country debt was repurchased on the secondary market.

An **exchange of claims** is the switch of one debt instrument for another. Banks offer to retire old debt in exchange for a new loan, with a reduction in the amount of principal or the rate of interest or both. In return, the debtor offers a more secure loan, usually involving some form of collateral, physical assets that can be claimed by the creditor in case of default. About $5 billion of debt was exchanged in this way in 1988.

Debt-equity swaps enable the debtor to pay the creditor in local currency, which can be used only for direct investment in the host country. A bank would accept cruzeiros in exchange for the retirement of a debt owed by Brazil and then lend these funds to companies that could use them to finance equity investments. The debtor government does have to raise funds on the domestic market, however; this could be inflationary, could squeeze out domestic private investors, or could require tax increases and expenditure reductions. Debt-equity swaps thus solve the problem of the foreign exchange constraint, but do not solve the budgetary constraint. Furthermore, many swaps have financed investments that might have been financed in dollars in any case and represent no net gain to the country. In 1988, $9 billion of developing-country debt was swapped for equity.[33]

When all forms of debt conversion are added up, the total was just over $20 billion in 1988. Yet the total long-term debt of developing countries was close to $1 trillion, and it was over $500 billion for the 17 most indebted countries alone, who continue to require 40 percent of their export earnings to service debt. The debt service problem is far from solved. The best hope

33. On the subject of debt relief measures, see Dornbusch, "Background Paper," pp. 67–101; Husain and Diwan, eds., *Dealing with the Debt Crisis,* "Introduction," pp. 1–11; Michel H. Bouchet and Jonathan Hay, "The Rise of the Market-Based "Menu" Approach and its Limitations," Ibid., pp. 147–158; and World Bank, *World Debt Tables 1989–90,* Vol. 1, pp. 21–31.

is that the magnitude of the problem can be whittled down by a buoyant world economy and an open trading system that provides export markets for the indebted countries; by sound economic management by their governments; by continued flows of new, concessional capital from the bilateral and multilateral agencies; and by constructive if self-interested approaches from the commercial banks.

The Mexican Debt Crisis

By far the two largest debtors in the developing world are Brazil and Mexico, each with over $100 billion of outstanding debt in 1989. It is ironic that Mexico should be so indebted, because in the latter 1970s it benefited from major increases in both oil production and rising oil prices. But the Mexican government, like other oil-exporting governments, spent the country's windfall profligately and borrowed heavily against the prospect of a continued oil boom. Chapter 15's discussion of "Dutch disease" explains why this behavior is typical of countries enjoying primary export booms. Mexican debt rose from 12 percent of GNP in 1975 to 53 percent in 1982, the very years that oil exports were booming. By 1982, Mexico's debt service ratio exceeded 50 percent. Despite the surge in resource flows from oil revenues and foreign borrowing, the Mexican economy actually grew faster, with less inflation, during the 17 years before the oil boom than it did during the boom, as Table 14–11 shows.

TABLE 14–11 **Mexican Growth and Inflation, 1955–1988 (percent per year)**

	1955–72	1973–81	1982–88
Income per capita	3.3	2.6	−2.2
Real wages	3.7	3.1	−5.9
Inflation	5	22	83

Source: Rudiger Dornbusch, "Mexico's Economy at the Crossroads," Journal of International Affairs 43, no. 2, (Winter 1990): 314.

When the newly elected government of President Miguel de la Madrid took over in 1982, its finance minister, Silvio Herzog, told creditors that the country could not meet interest payments on its debt. This announcement alarmed the creditor banks, which held about 70 percent of Mexico's debt, and international institutions, not only because of the large Mexican debt, but because other countries were likely to follow Mexico's lead. At the time, it seemed quite possible that debtor insolvency could lead to failures of major banks and a worldwide financial panic.

To stave off this disaster and help Mexico work out of its debt problem, the commercial banks, their governments, and the international agencies put together packages of debt rescheduling, new lending by all institutions, and economic austerity for the Mexican economy. Mexico's trade balance, excluding interest payments, turned from a net inward resource transfer of

4.3 percent of GNP in 1981 to a net outward transfer of 2.4 percent in 1988; its investment share of GNP fell from 28 to 21 percent. The results of this austerity are evident in Table 14–11: incomes fell and inflation accelerated. It was starkly obvious that the price of debt repayment would be deep reductions in the welfare of the Mexican people.

After six years of debt-induced retrenchment that seemed to offer no real relief to Mexico or its creditors, a new debt reduction package was negotiated among all parties in 1989, under the umbrella of the Brady plan. The commercial banks were offered a menu of options. They could (1) exchange existing debt for new bonds at a 35 percent discount, (2) exchange old debt for new bonds at the same value but a reduced interest rate of 6.25 percent, or (3) make new loans of at least 25 percent of the amounts due them, at market rates of interest over 15 years with a 7-year grace period when no principal would be due. In all cases, the new debt was to be considered "senior" to the old, with prior claims on payments, and the Mexican government was to pledge not to request rescheduling the new debt. Mexico was also permitted to purchase its own debt at the substantial discounts offered on the secondary market as long as it was current on its interest payments. Principal and interest payments on the new bonds were guaranteed by a $7 billion fund established by the IMF, the World Bank, and the Japanese government.

The new settlement was expected to decrease Mexico's net transfers of resources by $4 billion a year, 2 percent of GDP, and to reduce its outstanding debt by $8 billion, about 8 percent of Mexico's total debt. Announcement of the package had the immediate effect of causing a 20 percent fall in domestic interest rates, which could reduce the government's internal debt service requirements by up to 6 percent of GDP. An optimistic assessment is that debt relief, continued sound management of the economy, and Mexico's ongoing program of trade and investment deregulation will combine to restore confidence and attract back to Mexico some of the capital that fled to the United States and elsewhere with the onslaught of the debt crisis.[34]

---

34. Based on accounts by Rudiger Dornbusch, "Mexico's Economy at the Crossroads," *Journal of International Affairs* (43, no. 2) (Winter 1990): pp. 313–326, and World Bank, *World Debt Tables 1989–90*, Vol. 1, pp. 28 and 52–53.

PART 4

TRADE STRATEGIES AND DEVELOPMENT

15

Primary Exports and Growth

Every country trades with the outside world. The nature of that trade—the menu of goods that a country exports to other countries and imports from them—plays a central role in determining the character of development. Countries export commodities in which they enjoy a **comparative advantage,** as defined in the next section. This chapter discusses countries whose comparative advantage lies in primary commodities: food, agricultural raw materials, timber, metal ores, petroleum, and natural gas. The next two chapters describe development strategies that attempt to change comparative advantage from primary products to manufactures.

COMPARATIVE ADVANTAGE

Every country, regardless of size, ideology, or state of development, participates in international trade. Trade theorists have tried to explain why states trade and how they benefit from it largely under assumptions of **static conditions** that hold all domestic factors of production (land, other natural resources, labor, and capital) in fixed supply. The resulting **theory of comparative advantage** is rich in its implications about the gains from trade, the following among them: (1) Any country can increase its income by trading, because the world market provides an opportunity to buy some goods at relative prices that are lower than those which would prevail at home in the absence of trade. (2) The smaller the country, the greater this potential gain from trade, but all countries benefit to some extent. (3) A country will gain most by exporting commodities that it produces, using its abundant factors of production most intensively, while importing those goods whose production would require relatively more of the scarcer factors of production.

The first implication is a subtle one that requires elaboration. To simplify greatly, assume that two countries, which can be called Mexico and the United States, both produce only two products, vegetables and computers, and use only one factor of production, labor. Table 15–1 shows the labor days required to produce these products in each country.

TABLE 15–1 Production Costs and Comparative Advantage

	Mexico	United States
Labor-days to produce:		
Vegetables (1 ton)	5	4
Computers (1 unit)	30	20
Relative price (tons of vegetables per computer)	6	5

Notice that in this example it takes more labor days to produce either product in Mexico. Despite this, it is to the advantage of the United States to buy vegetables in Mexico, even though they can be produced at home with less labor, and to sell computers to Mexico in return. In the United States labor costs dictate that a computer sells for the equivalent of 5 tons of vegetables.[1] But if the United States sells one computer in Mexico, it can buy 6 tons of vegetables for consumption. So if labor is shifted from farming to manufacturing computers, U.S. consumers can eat more vegetables than if there is no trade with Mexico, while buying the same number of computers. Mexico, which has to produce 6 tons of vegetables to buy one computer in the home market without trade, is better off to switch its labor into producing more vegetables and selling them to the United States, where it only needs to trade 5 tons of vegetables for a computer and can save the other ton for its own consumption.

The important point of this example, and the core of comparative advantage, is that both countries can gain from trade whenever the **relative prices** of commodities in each country differ in the absence of trade. If the two countries do trade, then the relative price of vegetables in terms of computers would settle between 5 and 6, the two relative prices prevailing before trade. The final trade price, which can be called the world price, will settle closer to the initial price in the market of the country whose economy is larger. Thus small countries benefit more from trade because the gains are

1. If each ton of vegetables requires 4 labor-days to produce, then it takes 5 tons of vegetables to absorb the same labor as one computer, which uses 20 labor-days. This formula for calculating relative prices works in this oversimplified example because labor is the only input into production.

greater the more the pretrade relative price differs from the posttrade world

price. To see this, consider an extreme case in which the U.S. economy is so large that the posttrade price settles at the U.S. price before trade. Then the United States cannot gain from trade (nor can it lose), whereas Mexico would gain to the full extent of the price difference.

The theory of comparative advantage is posed here in the very simple form developed by David Ricardo during the nineteenth century: two countries, two goods, and only one factor of production, labor. Some of the complexities of the real world can be incorporated into the theory, however. A trading world of many countries can be handled by taking the home country, say Kenya, and treating the rest of the world as its trading partner. The complexities of many goods will be addressed in the next chapter. The theory was expanded to deal with two factors, such as labor and capital, by the Swedish economists Eli Heckscher and Bertil Ohlin during the first half of the twentieth century. Under certain conditions the Heckscher-Ohlin theory can be extended to include more factors of production and to yield another implication, that a country exports products that use its abundant factors of production more intensively and imports products that require relatively more of its scarce factors.

The implications of this more general approach to comparative advantage are encapsulated in Figure 15–1. In Chapter 6, where the production frontier was introduced, we divided the economy into production of X goods and Y goods, without being specific about the nature of those goods. In Figure 15–1, the economy of our *home country* is divided instead into **exportable goods,** such as rice, that are produced using relatively land- and labor-intensive methods, and **importable goods,** such as cloth, produced using relatively capital-intensive methods. As shown in the diagram, the home country is relatively well-endowed with land and labor, so the production frontier is skewed to the right; this depicts the country's greater

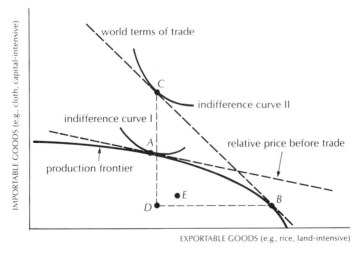

FIGURE 15–1 **Gains from Trade.** Before trade, a country both produces and consumes at a point like A. With trade, a country produces at a point like B and can increase its consumption of both goods and move to a higher indifference curve at C.

capacity to produce rice than cloth. The country's collective utility in consuming these goods is represented by the community indifference curves, also introduced in Chapter 6.

Without trade, the home country achieves its greatest utility by producing and consuming at point *A*, the tangency of the indifference curve I and the production frontier. The slope at *A* determines the domestic relative price of rice in terms of cloth. Assume that the rest of the world is better endowed with capital than with labor and land relative to the endowments of the home country and that world consumers have tastes broadly similar to those of the home country. Then on world markets the relatively higher production of cloth compared with the demand for cloth will drive its price lower than in the home country; and the relatively lower production of rice compared with the demand for rice will drive its price higher than in the home country. Since only relative prices matter, these two statements mean the same thing: in world markets the price of rice in terms of cloth will be higher than in the home country.

This difference in relative prices between the home country and the rest of the world presents an opportunity for the home country to improve its welfare through trade. **With trade** the country, taking advantage of its factor endowment, can produce more rice and less cloth and sell rice on the world market at the higher relative price, labeled the **world terms of trade** in Figure 15–1. In producing more rice the home country moves along the production frontier from *A* to *B*, where the terms-of-trade line is tangent to the production frontier. With rice to export, the country can then import cloth and consume more of *both* goods. The consumption point *C* is determined by the tangency of the terms-of-trade line with indifference curve II. The country now exports *BD* of rice and imports *DC* of cloth, given by the *trade triangle BCD*. As indifference curve II is above and to the right (northeast) of curve I, the country is better off with trade than without it.

This is a general result: Any country, whatever its size and stage of development, can benefit from trade in the way shown in Figure 15–1, from small countries like Ghana or Belgium to larges ones like China, India, and the United States. Large countries and others whose exports command a large share of world markets, such as Saudi Arabia in oil, Zambia in copper, or Sri Lanka in tea, may, in the process of expanding their trade, reduce the relative world price received for their exports. But even they still gain from trade if only their relative domestic prices would, in the absence of trade, differ from relative world prices.

Although every country can gain from trade, not all individuals or groups within each country share such gains. In the rice-cloth example of Figure 15–1, the producers of rice enjoy gains when trade is initiated because they sell more rice at a higher price. The consumers of cloth also gain from trade, because they can consume more at a lower price. But once trade begins, cloth manufacturers face competition from imports, and hence sell less cloth at a lower price than before, whereas rice consumers must pay higher prices. Comparative-advantage theory tells us that the gains outweigh the losses for the country as a whole, but that may be cold comfort to producers of cloth and consumers of rice. The losers from trade may share in the gains if suppliers of capital and labor to the cloth industry find it easy to shift into the production of rice or if mechanisms exist to transfer income from the gainers to the losers. In most countries, neither condition holds to a sufficient degree, especially in the short to medium term. Therein lies the seed of political opposition to policies that promote freer trade, even though all countries gain from it.

EXPORT CHARACTERISTICS OF DEVELOPING COUNTRIES

In their statistical analysis of cross-country patterns of development, economists Moises Syrquin and Hollis Chenery found that as incomes per capita rose from the neighborhood of $300 to $4,000 (in 1980 prices), the average export share of gross domestic product rose from 15 to 21 percent.[2] Size makes a considerable difference, however: for an average small country with a population of less than 25 million and income per capita of $700, exports of goods and services constituted about 25 percent of GDP, compared with only 15 percent for a typical large country with the same income. Large countries tend to export a smaller share of their total output because their larger markets can accommodate more industries economically, and they tend to have a greater diversity of resources that makes it possible to produce a wider range of goods.

Some sense of the wide variety of individual country characteristics can be had from column 3 of Table 15–2. Very large countries like China, India, Brazil, and Pakistan export a low share of gross domestic product, 6 to 14 percent. Oil-rich countries of any size export much more: 21 percent of GDP for Nigeria up to 55 percent for Libya, even during a period of relatively low oil prices. Smaller, nonpetroleum exporters show a wide range of export ratios, from 8 percent of GDP for Tanzania's diminished economy, 12 percent for war-torn and famine-stricken Ethiopia, and 17 percent for Colombia to more than 40 percent for such different countries as South Korea, an exporter of manufactures, Malaysia, a diversified exporter of primary products and manufactures, and Zambia, which exports little other than copper. Ratios as low as those for Tanzania and Ethiopia may be misleading, however, because they refer only to exports recorded through official channels. In Tanzania, a lively parallel (unofficial) market may be responsible for more exports than are registered in official markets. And in Colombia, substantial foreign exchange is earned by unrecorded narcotics transactions. When allowance is made for parallel market exports, it seems likely that all these countries export at least 20 percent of GDP.

Knowing the factor endowments of developing countries helps us explain the kinds of goods they export and import. Natural resources dictate the exports of the oil-rich countries of the Persian Gulf and elsewhere; copper exporters such as Zambia, Zaire, Chile, and Peru; and timber exporters,

2. Moises Syrquin and Hollis B. Chenery, *Patterns of Development, 1950–1983*, Washington, D.C., World Bank Discussion Paper No. 41, 1989, p. 20. Figures are for merchandise exports, excluding exports of services such as tourism, construction, etc.

TABLE 15–2   Export Characteristics of Selected Developing Countries, 1988

Country	Population 1988 (millions)	GNP per capita 1988 (U.S. dollars)	Export[a] share of GDP 1986–88 (%)	Major primary exports[b]	Share of col. 4 in merchandise exports, 1982–88 (%)
China	1,088	330	14[d]	Petroleum	9
India	816	340	6[e]	None	27[f]
Indonesia	175	440	24[c]	Petroleum	37[c]
Brazil	144	2,160	9[c]	Coffee, soy beans, iron ore	22
Nigeria	110	290	21[c]	Petroleum	97[g]
Bangladesh	109	170	6	Jute goods, raw jute	33
Pakistan	106	350	12	Cotton, rice	22
Mexico	84	1,760	18[c]	Petroleum	36
Philippines	60	630	24	Coconut products	9
Thailand	55	1,000	27[c]	Rice, rubber, tapioca	21
Egypt	50	660	16[c]	Petroleum, cotton	47
Ethiopia	47	120	12	Coffee, hides	81[c]
South Korea	42	3,600	41	None	7[f]
Zaire	33	170	67[g]	Diamonds	18[g]
Colombia	32	1,180	17[c]	Coffee, fuel oil	59
Tanzania	25	160	8[e]	Coffee, cotton	51[c]
Kenya	22	370	24[c]	Petroleum, tea, coffee	61
Peru	21	1,300	25[g]	Copper, fishmeal, petroleum, zinc, lead	56
Venezuela	19	3,250	23[c]	Petroleum	80
Malaysia	17	1940	63	Rubber, palm oil, wood, petroleum	42
Sri Lanka	17	420	25[c]	Tea, rubber, coconut	39
Ghana	14	400	18[c]	Cocoa, wood	60[c]
Saudi Arabia	14	6,200	37[c]	Petroleum	93[i]
Chile	13	1,510	29[e]	Copper	45
Ivory Coast	11	770	43[e]	Coffee, cocoa	51[c]
Guatemala	9	900	16[e]	Coffee, sugar	45[c]
Zambia	8	290	42	Copper	87
Bolivia	7	570	23[e]	Tin, gas, zinc, silver	73
Senegal	7	170	31[e]	Petroleum products, fish & shellfish, groundnuts & oil, phosphates	63[e]
Libya	4	5,420	55[h]	Petroleum	89[e]
Jamaica	2	1,070	56[c]	Alumina, bauxite, sugar	58

[a] Exports of goods and services.
[b] Commodities accounting for at least 5 percent of merchandise export revenues.
[c] 1985–1987.
[d] World Bank estimate for 1988; excludes factor services.
[e] 1984–1986.
[f] Primary commodity share of merchandise exports, 1988, as given by the World Bank; commodity breakdown not available.
[g] 1983–1985.
[h] 1980–1982.
[i] 1982–1984.

Sources: World Bank, *World Development Report 1990*, and International Monetary Fund, *International Financial Statistics Yearbook 1989.*

such as Malaysia and Ghana. Tropical climate may be considered a factor of production that helps to explain the exports of foods such as coffee, cocoa, bananas, and vegetable oils, and raw materials like rubber and cotton. Finally, abundant labor suggests the export crops that can be produced efficiently with labor-intensive manufactures such as textiles, clothing, and electronic components. The relative lack of both physical and human capital in developing countries indicates that they would gain by importing goods that use these factors intensively; such goods include most capital equipment and many intermediate products from the chemical, petroleum, and metals industries.

A standard description of a developing country would state that only one or a few primary commodities are responsible for most export earnings; many countries in Table 15–2 exhibit that characteristic. The extreme cases of export concentration include many of the major petroleum exporters, Ghana in cocoa, the Ivory Coast in cocoa and coffee, Colombia in coffee and cocaine (not a part of the official estimates!), Chile and Zambia in copper, and Jamaica in bauxite and alumina. Not surprisingly the very large countries show a much more diversified pattern. What may be surprising is that many of the primary-product exporters are highly diversified. In three of the cases shown—Bolivia, Malaysia, and Peru—no one product dominates, and at least four commodities each account for 5 percent or more of total earnings.

However suggestive the theory of comparative advantage may be for developing countries, it is only the beginning of an explanation of development through international trade. The theory fails to explain growth and structural change because it excludes growth in the stocks of productive factors, as well as improvements in the quality or productivity of those factors. The theory thus provides no mechanism to explain how economies evolve over time and change the composition of their output, their consumption, and their trade.

In order to understand how trade and development interact, one affecting the other, it is necessary to adopt an eclectic approach and use trade theory where it is useful but revert frequently to other kinds of analysis. The unifying theme is trade strategies: how different approaches to trade, favoring different types of exports and imports, lead to different kinds of economic development. The first such strategy, **primary-export-led growth** is examined in the balance of this chapter.

PRIMARY EXPORTS AS AN ENGINE OF GROWTH

Before the 1950s, it was conventional wisdom that the road to development could be traversed most rapidly by following comparative advantage, exporting foods and raw materials, raising per-capita income, and permitting structural change to take place as a consequence. The United States, Canada, Australia, and Denmark had become developed countries at least partly by following this path, and Argentina had gone quite far in that direction. Many countries in the third world, such as Colombia, Mexico, Ghana, Nigeria, Malaysia, and the Philippines, have undergone significant structural change as a consequence of primary exports, although these changes have propelled them only part of the way to development. Students of development, observing such cases, have noted three kinds of benefits to primary-export-led growth: improved utilization of existing factors, expanded factor endowments, and linkage effects.

Static models of the gains from trade start with a country that is not trading and show what happens when it is opened to trade. An isolated country, shut off from world markets, might have substantial amounts of land that is either idle or used in relatively unproductive ways. Recall the land-abundant, capital-short country of Figure 15–1. In that case all factors of production are fully employed without trade. However, by reallocating resources—producing and exporting more land-intensive goods, such as rice or cocoa, and importing more manufactures, such as cloth or chemicals—the country can consume more of both kinds of commodities and increase its welfare. The country moves along its production frontier, from A to B in Figure 15–1. Land, the abundant factor of production, is utilized more intensively with trade in the sense that its productivity (the yield per hectare) has risen as labor shifts from handicraft industries to agriculture or mining.

If, instead, the country has idle resources before trade begins, it can gain even more substantially from trade. This case is represented in Figure 15–1 by points D and E, within the production frontier. Trade may stimulate the economy so that all factors of production are utilized and the country, able to produce more of both goods, moves toward its frontier.

This static model of the gains from trade can, with imagination and some judicious simplification, be applied to the development of several countries. In the nineteenth century the United States and Canada had abundant land in relation to their endowments of labor and capital. Much of this land was idle, so both countries produced at points within their production frontiers. British demand for cotton and wheat enabled North America to bring this land into production and move toward the production frontier by growing cotton and wheat for export, while importing the manufactured goods it could not produce as efficiently as Britain.

Burmese economist Hla Myint has observed that when parts of Africa and Asia came under European colonization, the consequent expansion of their international trade enabled those areas to utilize their land or labor more intensively to produce tropical foodstuffs such as rice, cocoa, and oil palm for export. Myint applies Adam Smith's term **vent for surplus** to these cases (as well as the cases of surplus land in the Americas and Australia).[3] The concept implies that some land or labor is idle before trade and that trade enables these economies to employ either land or labor more fully.

However, when underutilized land or labor was vented as a result of colonization, as was typical during the nineteenth century, the gains from trade were often purchased at high cost to the indigenous population. Land which may have been idle or utilized at low productivity was frequently alienated from its occupiers, whether these were American Indians, the Kikuyu and other peoples of East Africa, or Javanese farmers. Colonizers also used taxation and coercion to keep plantations and mines supplied with low-cost labor in many parts of Africa and Asia. And especially in

---

3. Hla Myint, "The 'Classical Theory' of International Trade and the Underdeveloped Countries," *Economic Journal* 68 (1959): 317–337.

British India, the movement along a production frontier toward greater production for export often resulted in cheap imports to compete with traditional handicraft industries and the displacement of artisans and workers. The questions about colonization—which cannot be answered in this text—are whether the distribution of gains from trade favored native populations enough to compensate them for the losses they bore and whether colonial economies propelled indigenous people toward development or retarded their eventual progress.

Expanded Factor Endowments

Once the profitable opportunities in tropical agriculture or natural resources become apparent, foreign investment is likely to be attracted to the country, first to exploit the country's comparative advantage and, perhaps eventually, to invest in other sectors. The influx of foreign investors has been the familiar story in all mineral exporting industries and in many tropical products industries in which plantation agriculture was the rule: Standard Oil in Venezuela, British Petroleum in Iran, Anaconda in Chile, Alcoa in Jamaica, Lever Brothers and Firestone in West Africa, and United Fruit in Central America are only some of the more visible of scores of examples. Capital has frequently brought migrant labor to the mines and plantations, as occurred in Southern and West Africa, Malaysia, Sri Lanka, and many other places. Both foreign investment and migrant labor were of course prominent features in the development in the "new lands" of the Americas and Australia in the nineteenth century. The emergence of new lines of export production is also likely to open up many new profitable outlets for investment that foreign capital will not completely satisfy, whether in the export sector itself or in related industries. These opportunities represent an outward shift of the demand for domestic savings and should induce some supply response and further increase investment in the economy.

Thus the expansion of potential markets for primary products can lead to expanded supplies of foreign investment, domestic saving, labor, and skilled manpower to complement the fixed factors of production, land and natural resources. Not only does trade help an economy move toward its production frontier and then along it, but trade can also expand the frontier outward and enable the economy to produce more of all goods than before.

Linkage Effects

The notion of export-led growth implies some stimulus to other industries that would not otherwise expand. When the growth of one industry, such as textiles, creates sufficient demand for some input, such as cotton or dyestuffs, it may stimulate domestic production of that input. Hirschman coined the phrase **backward linkage** for this stimulus.[4] Backward linkages, which were described in Chapter 3, are particularly effective when the using industry becomes so large that supplying industries can achieve economies

---

4. Albert O. Hirschman, *The Strategy of Economic Development* (New Haven, Conn.: Yale University Press, 1958), Chap. 6.

of scale of their own, lower their production costs, and become more competitive in domestic or even export markets. The wheat industry worked this way in North America in the nineteenth century; it created sufficient demand for transportation equipment (especially railway rolling stock) and farm machinery that these industries became established in the United States. In Peru the rapid expansion of the fishmeal industry during the 1950s and 1960s led directly to the production of fishing boats and processing equipment. The boat-building industry became efficient enough to export fishing craft to neighboring countries, and the processing-equipment industry gave Peru a start on one kind of capital-goods production that can supply a wide range of food-processing industries.[5]

The linkage between food processing for export (rice, vegetable oils, tea) and a processing-equipment industry might well be repeated in other developing countries over time. Three conditions would contribute to such linkages. Production should initially take place in small units that use simple technology to give the fledgling equipment industry a chance to master production techniques and learn its trade by repetitive production. The export industry should grow steadily over time and thus promise a continuing market for its suppliers. And the export sector should be large enough to enable equipment manufacturers eventually to achieve scale economies. These conditions were met in fishmeal and can be met in several agricultural fields. But they are generally not satisfied in mining, which typically requires complex equipment for large-scale investments that must be implemented in the shortest time possible, conditions under which domestic infant industries are unlikely to thrive.

Linkages may also develop indirectly through the demand by income recipients for consumption goods. The **consumption linkage** is most likely to operate if a large labor force is paid wages above previous levels, creating a demand for mass-produced consumer goods like processed foods, clothing, footwear, furniture, radios, packaging materials, and so forth. The North American wheat industry, with its extensive endowment of land, high labor productivity, and egalitarian income distribution based on family farms, successfully stimulated local consumer goods industries. Neither plantation agriculture in Africa, with its large labor force but low wages, nor mining industries, which pay high wages but employ relatively few workers, are able to generate adequate demand to stimulate local consumer goods industries.

The provision of overhead capital—roads, railroads, power, water, telecommunications—for the export industry can lower costs and otherwise open opportunities for other industries. The classic example is the railroad in the nineteenth-century United States. Built to connect the East Coast with the grain-producing states of the Midwest, it lowered the costs of transporting both inputs and outputs for the manufacturing industry in the wheat-exporting region.[6] Harbors and rail and road networks built to facil-

---

5. Michael Roemer, *Fishing for Growth: Export-Led Development in Peru, 1950–1967* (Cambridge, Mass.: Harvard University Press, 1970).
6. Albert Fishlow, *American Railroads and the Transformation of the Antebellum Econ-*

itate the export of copper in southern Africa, cocoa and timber in Ghana, tea in India, and beef in Argentina have had similar effects on domestic manufacturing industries. Power projects that are made economically feasible by export industries, such as the Akosombo Dam in Ghana and the Guri Dam in Venezuela, provide cheap power that may encourage the domestic manufacturing industry. Primary export sectors may also encourage the development of local entrepreneurs and skilled laborers. The growth of the Peruvian fishmeal industry, with its many small plants, encouraged scores of new entrepreneurs and trained many skilled workers to operate and maintain equipment. These resources then became available for subsequent development. Rubber, palm oil, and tin production for export have encouraged entrepreneurs in Malaysia, and small-scale farming for export has proved to be an outlet for entrepreneurial talent in several African countries.

The best case for petroleum, mining, and some traditional agricultural crops is the **fiscal linkage;** this means simply that the large government revenues typically derived from these exports (as taxes or dividends) can be used to finance development in other sectors. Although a government is obviously better off with than without such a revenue source, its effectiveness in stimulating self-sustaining development in the rest of the economy depends critically on the kinds of programs and interventions that government undertakes.[7]

BARRIERS TO PRIMARY-EXPORT-LED GROWTH

Since the late 1950s some economists and many third-world leaders have argued that primary exports other than petroleum cannot effectively lead the way to economic development: markets for primary products grow too slowly to fuel growth, the prices received for these commodities have been declining, earnings are too unstable, and linkages do not work. We examine each of these arguments in turn.

---

omy (Cambridge, Mass.: Harvard University Press, 1965), and Robert W. Fogel, "Railroads as an Analogy of the Space Effort: Some Economic Aspects," in *Space Program: An Exploration in Historical Analogy,* Bruce Mazlish, ed. (Cambridge, Mass.: MIT Press, 1965).

7. The impact of export industries on economic development through various forms of linkages is the focus of a body of literature called **staple theory,** which tries to explain differing impacts by differing characteristics of production technologies. For examples of the genre, see Robert E. Baldwin, *Economic Development and Export Growth: A Study of Northern Rhodesia, 1920–1960* (Los Angeles: University of California Press, 1966); Douglass C. North, "Location Theory and Regional Economic Growth," *Journal of Political Economy* 63 (1955): 243–285; Roemer, *Fishing for Growth;* and Melville H. Watkins, "A Staple Theory of Economic Growth," *Canadian Journal of Economics and Political Science* 29 (1963): 141–158. Perhaps the ultimate expression of production characteristics and linkages as determinants of development patterns is the essay by Albert O. Hirschman, "A Generalized Linkage Approach to Development, with Special Reference to Staples," in *Essays on Economic Development and Cultural Change,* Manning Nash, ed. (Chicago: University of Chicago Press, 1977), pp. 67–98.

In a world of balanced growth, exporters of primary products could expect their exports to expand at the same pace as national incomes of the countries that import primary products, and they could also expect their own incomes to grow at that rate. Faster income growth for primary exporters would require structural changes such as import substitution. The world is not balanced in this way, however, and economists skeptical of primary-export potential have cited structural shifts in the industrial world that seem to condemn third-world primary exports to slower growth than industrial world incomes.[8] It is a common observation, known as **Engel's law,** that the demand for staple foods and beverages grows more slowly than income (see Chapter 3). For the industrial world the income elasticity of demand for foods is probably below one-half. Thus even if the growth in production of foodstuffs in the industrial world fell short of income growth, there is a *prima facie* case that its imports of foods would lag behind income growth. Technological change in manufacturing may also be working against the consumption of raw materials, as producers attempt to reduce costs by reducing wastage and otherwise raising the yield of finished products from a given input of raw material. Metal cans contain less tin, modern looms waste less cotton yarn, sawmills turn wood shavings into boards, and so forth. Concurrently, in affluent societies expenditures are expected to shift away from goods and toward services and further reduce the expected growth of material imports relative to income.

World Bank data confirm this gloomy picture. The share of nonfuel raw materials and food imports in total industrial-country imports has fallen substantially, from 39 percent in 1965 to about 19 percent in 1988. With import growth in the industrial world growing at 4.5 percent a year, imports of nonfuel raw materials and foodstuffs, valued in constant prices, appear to have grown by only 1.3 percent a year over almost a quarter century, too slow to fuel economic development in primary exporting countries.[9]

Despite the broad trend, there are likely to be encouraging prospects for some primary commodities and some primary exporting countries. Many of the raw materials now prominent in world trade were hardly on the scene at the turn of this century and thus have undergone substantial growth. The demands for petroleum, rubber, copper, aluminum, newsprint, plywood, and vegetable oils received substantial boosts from technological innovation or from high income elasticities of demand, the very factors cited against raw material exports. Several commodities have experienced substantial export growth rates since 1960: exports of sorghum, wheat, fish, soybeans, vegetable oils, oilseed cake and meal, alumina and aluminum, and nickel all grew by at least 5 percent a year from 1961 to 1982, valued at constant prices; timber and phosphate exports also grew rapidly until 1980.[10] Over the past 30 years, several small countries that are mainly exporters of pri-

8. An early and articulate proponent of this view is Ragnar Nurkse, *Equilibrium Growth in the World Economy* (Cambridge, Mass.: Harvard University Press, 1961), Chaps. 10 and 11.
9. World Bank, *World Development Report 1990*, Tables 14 and 15.
10. World Bank, *Commodity Trade and Price Trends, 1987–1988* ed. (Washington, D.C.: World Bank, 1988).

mary products have sustained periods of moderately rapid growth, including Botswana, Cameroon, Costa Rica, the Dominican Republic, Guatemala, the Ivory Coast, Kenya, Malawi, Malaysia, the Philippines, and Thailand.

With slower growth in the industrial countries, the impact of Engel's law, and materials-saving innovations, it seems unlikely that the developed countries will import enough tropical foods and raw materials to fuel an era of rapid development for the third world as a whole over the next few decades. Nevertheless, some commodities will face brisk demand growth and some countries will benefit substantially from producing such exports.

Primary-Export-Led Growth in Malaysia

When Malaysia achieved independence in 1957, it was close to the archetypical single-crop economy: rubber accounted for well over half its export earnings and about a quarter of Malaysia's gross domestic product. The second largest export, tin, earned between 10 and 20 percent of total export revenues. Neither commodity faced a bright future: demand for rubber was constrained by the availability of cheap synthetic substitutes, and the tin market was plagued by production exceeding likely demand. It would have been natural for the new country's planners to fall prey to the dominant export pessimism of the day and build a development strategy around import substitution.

But Malaysia enjoys a rich resource base with a relatively small population, and its development strategy was based on its comparative advantage. The country invested in research to reduce the costs of growing rubber and maintained its competitiveness with synthetic rubber. Measured relative to import prices, rubber export revenues fell by only 4 percent from 1960 to 1987. At the same time, Malaysia invested in planting oil palm and this new export grew by 15 percent a year in volume from 1960 to 1987. Petroleum exports grew by a steady 8 percent a year, and exports of logs and timber expanded by a total of 82 percent from 1960 to 1987. During this period, Malaysia also invested in manufacturing for export. Although primary products earned over 90 percent of export revenues in 1965, by 1988 manufactures had grown sufficiently to account for 45 percent of export revenues. Thanks to investments in both primary and manufactured exports, Malaysia's total export earnings, deflated by import prices (i.e., its income terms of trade, see next section) grew by 5.6 percent a year for almost three decades.

As a consequence of its investments in primary and manufactured exports, Malaysia has sustained rapid economic growth, over 6 percent a year from 1965 to 1988. Its per capita income of $1,900 puts Malaysia on a par with Brazil, Mexico, and Poland, even though in the mid 1960s its average income was close to that of Zambia and El Salvador. Although still dependent on exports for over 60 percent of its GDP, Malaysia's diversified export base, efficient production, and high income provide the resources for continued rapid development.[11]

11. Data are from the World Bank, *World Development Report 1990*, and the International Monetary Fund, *International Financial Statistics Yearbook 1990*.

An influential school of thought, led by Argentine economist Raul Prebisch and by Hans Singer of the University of Sussex,[12] has argued that not only will primary exports face sluggish growth of demand, but that, over the long run, prices received for these commodities will fall on world markets relative to the prices of LDC imports of manufactures from developed countries. The most commonly used measure of these relative prices is the commodity or **net barter terms of trade** T_n. T_n is a ratio of two indexes: (1) the average price of a country's exports (P_e), which can be approximated by dividing an index of export volume into an index of export revenue, and (2) the average price of its imports (P_m), determined for imports by the same method as P_e for imports. The commodity terms of trade rise if export prices rise relative to import prices.

Empirical tests of the Prebisch-Singer hypothesis reach ambiguous conclusions at best. In his 1950 monograph, Prebisch used data on the terms of trade for Great Britain from the 1870s to the 1930s that seemed to support his contention. Prebisch's data were imperfect, however, and inadvertently biased in favor of his hypothesis. In subsequent years, other economists have tried to replicate Prebisch's results, using different data sets and various periods of time, with conflicting results.[13] Recently, Georgetown University economist John Cuddington and associates have used improved data to measure the terms of trade for 24 primary commodities, excluding oil, for the period from 1900 to 1988.[14] Figure 15–2 shows the results. The net barter terms of trade for primary commodities fluctuated widely and suffered a precipitate drop in the early 1920s. Sophisticated econometric techniques show, however, that there has been no trend in these data—i.e., no decline—over 88 years. The Prebisch-Singer hypothesis cannot be sustained. If oil and other fuel prices were included in the index, and there is no obvious reason why they should not be, they would of course reinforce this conclusion.

Although the Prebisch-Singer hypothesis is properly addressed by looking at commodity data, it is the terms of trade for a country that really matters in its development. Figure 15–3 shows two different measures of the net barter terms of trade since 1954. When oil exporters are included, the terms of trade for developing countries rose dramatically after 1972.

However, the net barter terms of trade tells us little about income or welfare, which ought to be the basis for judging changes in the world trade conditions. A better measure of the income effect of price changes would be the **income terms of trade** T_i, which measures the purchasing power of

12. United Nations (Raul Prebsich), *The Economic Development of Latin America and its Principal Problems* (Lake Success, N.Y.: United Nations, 1950) and Hans W. Singer, "The Distribution of Trade between Investing and Borrowing Countries," *American Economic Review* 40 (May 1950): 473–485.

13. For a summary of these results, see Bela Balassa, "Outward Orientation," in *Handbook of Development Economics,* Vol. 2, Chenery and Srinivasan, pp. 1653–1659.

14. The numerator of T_n, P_e, is a geometric average of the price indexes for 24 nonfuel commodities; the denominator P_m is an index of unit values for manufactured goods. See John T. Cuddington and Carlos M. Urzua, "Trends and Cycles in the Net Barter Terms of Trade: A New Approach," *The Economic Journal* 99, no. 396 (June 1989): 426–442.

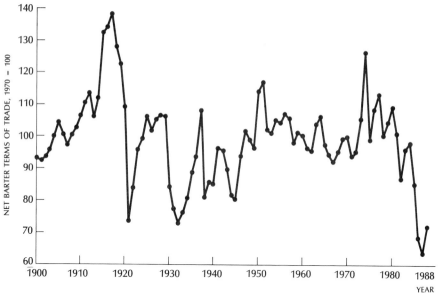

FIGURE 15–2   Net Barter Terms of Trade, Primary Commodities, 1900–1988. A geometric index for 24 commodities, excluding fuels, shows no trend over 88 years, despite wide fluctuations and a sharp drop in 1921.
Source: John Cuddington and Hong Wei, "An Empirical Analysis of the Prebisch-Singer Hypothesis: Aggregation, Model Selection and Implications," Working Paper No. 90-12, Economics Department, Georgetown University.

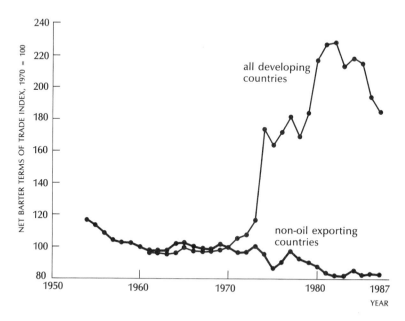

FIGURE 15–3   Net Barter Terms of Trade, Developing Countries, 1954–1988. For non-oil-exporting countries, the terms of trade show a decline of about 1 percent a year over the whole period. When all developing countries are included, there has been a dramatic rise in the terms of trade since 1972.
Source: International Monetary Fund, *International Financial Statistics Yearbook 1989.*

exports by comparing an index of export revenues with an index of import prices. This is equivalent to the net barter terms of trade multiplied by the volume of exports (Q_e), or $T_i = P_e Q_e / P_m = T_n Q_e$. If, for example, Zambia increases its copper exports and causes the world price to fall, but less than proportionately to the volume increase (that is, the absolute value of the demand elasticity for Zambian copper is greater than 1), then copper revenue will increase and, in the absence of import price changes, the income terms of trade will rise.[15] Assuming the resources shifted into copper production could not have produced goods or services of equal value in other sectors, Zambia would be unambiguously better off than before. For non-oil developing countries as a group, the income terms of trade rose almost 6 percent a year from 1954 to 1988.

Similarly, an increase in Zambia's copper production due to higher productivity may cause world copper prices to fall. But if the price decline is less than the percentage rise in the productivity (Z_e) of all factors engaged in production for export, the factors engaged in copper mining would be better off than before. The **single factoral terms of trade** T_s measures factor income relative to factor inputs and import prices, $T_s = (P_e / P_m) Z_e = T_n Z_e$. Note that a rise in either the income or single factoral terms of trade implies an improvement in income or welfare relative to that country's previous situation. But if, as is often the case, either index rises less than export volume, this also implies that exporting countries are sharing part of the potential gains with importing countries, as Prebisch and Singer suggest.

Should we have any theoretical expectations about future trends in the terms of trade? Pessimists can point to the sluggish growth in demand for primary products to argue that the terms of trade for these commodities will decline over time. More fundamentally, to the extent that developing countries increase their output of primary exports as a means of growing faster than the industrial countries, prices of their exports may be expected to fall relative to that of the industrial country exports, simply because the supply of LDC primary exports will be increasing faster than the demand for them.

Theoretical considerations can also lead to the opposite conclusion, however. Primary products are produced by factors in limited supply, particularly land, mineral deposits, and other natural resources. Although technological innovations can be expected to increase the productivity of these resources, they are not inexhaustible. If world income continues to grow, even slowly, it seems likely that eventually demand will grow faster than supply for many primary commodities. The prices of those commodities should then rise relative to the prices of manufactures, which are produced with labor and capital, the supply of which is expanding. Wood prices have been growing steadily, for example, and some have argued that the demand for energy resources is rapidly outstripping the discovery of new supplies.

---

15. The price elasticity of demand for the exports of any one country is $e_i = e_w / s_i$, where e_w is the worldwide price elasticity of demand for the commodity and s_i is the market share of the country. Even if e_w is quite low, say -0.3, if the country's market share is below 30 percent, which would be quite large, the price elasticity facing that country would be greater than (negative) one.

Fluctuating Export Earnings

429

BARRIERS TO
PRIMARY-
EXPORT-LED
GROWTH

Not only do the net barter terms of trade show a secular decline, they also fluctuate considerably, as is evident in Figures 15–2 and 15–3. Conventional wisdom has generally held that the instability in export earnings would be transmitted to the domestic economy and make domestic demand unstable and investment more risky. Uncertain access to imported materials, caused by fluctuating export earnings, intensifies investors' risks. Consequently, investment is discouraged and economic growth retarded. Observations on the structural characteristics of nonfuel minerals exporters—especially their heavy dependence on one or two mineral exports for government revenue—suggest that these countries may be severely hampered by earnings fluctuations.

Ghana—A Case of Arrested Development

At independence in 1957, Ghana was probably the richest country in Sub-Saharan Africa, with a per-capita income close to $500 (in prices of 1983). By 1983, its per-capita income had fallen to $340, below that of Kenya, Sudan, and Pakistan. Many things went wrong for Ghana in that quarter century, but the failure of export policy was crucial.[16] Like Malaysia, Ghana was a one-export country in the late 1950s: cocoa earned almost 60 percent of export revenues and represented almost a fifth of GDP. But in contrast to Malaysia, Ghana under its charismatic leader, Kwame Nkrumah, turned sharply away from its export base to invest in import substituting industries. In this it failed. Had export agriculture, forestry, and mining been maintained, Ghana might have earned sufficient revenues to make a gradual transition into import substitution. But so abrupt was the disinvestment in primary exports that cocoa exports halved in volume from the early 1960s to the mid-1980s, and other exports did not make up that deficit.

Ghana's failure to utilize its generous export base is made more vivid by the performance of its next-door neighbor, the Ivory Coast. With virtually the same resource base, the Ivory Coast invested enough to maintain its coffee exports and then diversified into cocoa (just as Ghana was disinvesting), wood, and other primary products. Over two decades, export volume more than doubled, and per-capita GDP grew to nearly twice that of Ghana, despite substantial immigration from less prosperous neighboring countries.[17]

Surprisingly, econometric tests of these propositions either fail to support them or prove the opposite: export instability seems positively correlated with investment and growth.[18] Trade economists Odin Knudsen and

---

16. On Ghana's development policies, see Michael Roemer, "Ghana 1950–1980: Missed Opportunities," in *World Economic Growth,* Arnold Harberger, ed. (San Francisco: Institute for Contemporary Studies, 1984), pp. 201–226.

17. World Bank, *World Development Report 1990* and *World Tables,* 1989–1990 ed.

18. For a summary of these tests, see Jere R. Behrman, "Commodity Price Instability and Economic Goal Attainment in Developing Countries," *World Development* 15, no. 5 (May 1987): 559–573.

Andrew Parnes have suggested that the permanent income hypothesis may help to explain why fluctuating earnings might not retard development. Income earners (and by extension, countries) count on some level of relatively certain annual income and try to maintain consumption patterns based largely on that *permanent* income. More of the uncertain, fluctuating component of income tends to be saved than is true for the permanent component. The more unstable total income is likely to be, the larger the fraction that income earners will save. Under this hypothesis about behavior, greater export instability forces residents (and governments) to save more than they otherwise would and hence to invest more.[19]

Most individuals and presumably most governments prefer situations of greater stability, other things being equal. If, as suggested by the permanent income hypothesis, greater variance of export economies leads to faster growth, then the preference for stable earnings (reduced variance) may force governments to choose slower growth as well, as depicted in Figure 15–4. Something like this model could explain the efforts expended by many developing-country governments to stabilize export earnings through producer price controls, international buffer stocks, or compensatory payments schemes, despite the implications of the permanent income hypothesis.

Curve *RR* represents the trade-off between export stability and economic growth in an economy, analogous to a production frontier with two goods, stability and growth. Indifference curves show the country's preference for lower variability and higher growth. A primary exporting country might be at *A* with high growth but high instability of export earnings.

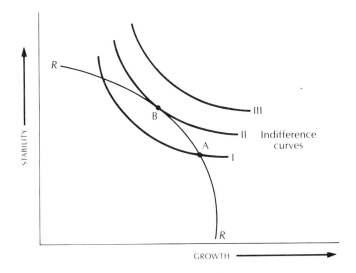

FIGURE 15–4 **Trade-Off between Export Stability and Economic Growth.** The curve *RR* represents achievable combinations of growth and stability. It can be viewed as a production possibilities curve. Countries will prefer points like *B* on a higher indifference curve, to points like *A*, even though growth is higher at *A*.

19. Odin Knudsen and Andrew Parnes, *Trade Instability and Economic Development* (Lexington, Mass.: Heath Lexington Books, 1975), pp. 81–128.

By reducing both instability and growth, shown as a move from A to B, the country could achieve a higher indifference curve and thus consider itself better off.

Commodity Agreements

Developing countries have made several attempts over the past two decades to **raise the prices** of specific export commodities. On of the proposals of the 1974 United Nations resolution on a "New International Economic Order" called for international **commodity agreements** that would both stabilize commodity prices and raise them. In order to raise export prices, it is necessary either to restrict output (that is, to shift the supply curve to the left) or to impose a common export tax. If world demand for the commodity is inelastic (i.e., the price elasticity is between −1 and 0), as is true for most tropical food exports, then restricting supply causes a more than proportional increase in price and an increase in total revenues to exporters. If, however, world demand is elastic, as may be true for meat, fish, dairy products, and many manufactured goods, then supply restrictions raise prices less than proportionally and revenues fall.

Output restriction works best when large majorities of both producing and consuming nations participate. The International Coffee Agreement, first negotiated in 1960, worked this way for a time. Export quotas were allocated to all producers, and most Western consuming nations agreed to buy only from producing members of the agreement. Exporters could sell to nonquota markets, such as Eastern Europe and most developing countries, at market prices that could be substantially lower than in participating countries.

Under certain conditions producers may be able to restrict demand and raise prices without the agreement of consumers. Among many unsuccessful attempts to accomplish this looms the one dramatic success, the Organization of Petroleum Exporting Countries (OPEC). From 1972 to 1982, OPEC raised oil prices from under $4 a barrel to over $30, a real increase (allowing for international inflation) of 240 percent. The slippage of OPEC prices after 1982 and the collapse in 1986 suggest the limitations of producer agreements, but does not detract from its dramatic accomplishments of the 1970s. This example has stimulated exporters of other commodities—especially minerals—to form their own **cartels,** as price-raising agreements among commodity producers may be called.

Attempts to raise world prices for primary exports are akin to a **zero-sum game** in which the gains of one group of countries (producers) are offset by the losses of another group (consumers and the foreign owners of capital). Even when developing-country exports are the object of price-raising agreements, potential losers include other LDCs that import these commodities. Developing-country importers of petroleum were among the hardest hit by OPEC's price-fixing cartel. There has been little consumer country support for the price-raising features of the NIEO, and the debate has instead centered on price stabilization, which can benefit both exporting and importing countries.

To **stabilize commodity prices** in world trade, it is necessary for some central authority—a large company, a private cartel, a single government, a cartel of producing countries, or an international agency—to intervene in the market, buy the commodity when prices are falling, and sell from its stocks when prices are rising. To do this, the authority must control a **buffer stock** and must have access to funds that can be used to increase that stock when necessary. The principle of stabilization is easy, but the application is fraught with difficulty. First, if predictions of future prices turn out to be higher than the actual average price, the authority will on balance buy more for the buffer stock than it sells and eventually may be unable to finance further purchases. Conversely a low prediction results in excessive sales, depleting and possibly exhausting the buffer stock.

Second, even if price forecasts are accurate, the authority must set floor and ceiling prices that it can maintain. Should speculators sense that the authority's resources are too limited, they can bid the price up or down, depending on whether stocks or finance are in short supply, to break through the ceiling or floor and make a certain profit. Finally, if buffer stocks lead to higher inventories of a commodity than would otherwise be held, this represents a real resource cost to someone. In the 1974 NIEO proposals the industrial nations were to bear this cost by financing a Common Fund, estimated to require $10 billion to support buffer stocks. Thus the eventual success of price-stabilizing agreements depends not only on whether the technical problems can be overcome, but also on the assessment of consuming nations about the costs to them of continued price fluctuations. In 1989, after 15 years of negotiation, a Common Fund was finally established, but it contained only about $300 million for buffer stocks, with the rest to be raised from commercial bank loans.

Stabilizing world commodity prices is not necessarily the same thing as stabilizing a particular country's export earnings. If one country's production is unstable because of variable weather, strikes, or other disruptions, then a stable world price can increase the variability of earnings.[20] An alternative with considerable appeal is to compensate directly for earnings fluctuations rather than to stabilize prices. Two such schemes are in existence: the Compensatory Financing Facility of the International Monetary Fund and the Stabex scheme operated by the European Community. Under the IMF facility countries can borrow to finance balance-of-payments deficits that are partially caused by a drop in export revenues below a five-year moving average. The EC scheme permits borrowing if a country's particular commodity export revenues, earned from the Community, fall below a four-year average. From 1983 to 1988,the IMF lent a total of $10 billion under its facility.

---

20. Jere R. Behrman, *Development, the International Economic Order and Commodity Agreements* (Reading, Mass.: Addison-Wesley, 1978). Chapter 3 provides an analytical treatment of commodity agreements and summarizes the conditions under which stable prices will stabilize or destabilize revenues.

Ineffective Linkages

It is a paradox of development that many economies have failed to develop despite booming primary export industries. One of the reasons for this is implicit in the previous discussion of **linkages:** backward, forward, and consumption linkages often fail to work. The petroleum industry and, with a few exceptions, the mining industry, generally remain **enclaves,** remote from other centers of production and ill-adapted to link with them economically. Neither backward linkages to suppliers of production materials and equipment nor consumption linkages are likely to work. In some instances railroads and ports built for the mines do aid other industries by lowering costs and stimulating investment, but examples of remote or specialized overhead capital can also be found. Liberia's rail and harbor link with its iron mines is poorly placed to stimulate agriculture or other industry, and the pipelines and tanker ports of the petroleum industry have no uses outside that sector. Some agricultural export sectors, particularly plantations in colonial Africa, also had few effective linkages, because they use few inputs and pay low wages. However, small-farm, labor-intensive agriculture typically does have effective linkages through transport and marketing services and consumer demand by farm families.

If petroleum and mining industries create few backward or consumption linkages, they can generate **forward linkages** to industries whose principal input is the export sector's output. Thus Venezuela is using its iron ore, natural gas, and hydroelectric power to produce steel, partly for export and partly for domestic use. If, and only if, the domestic steel is cheaper than imported steel, it may stimulate further forward linkages to steel-using industries like construction, transport equipment, processing equipment, and oil derricks. Other mineral and timber exporters are trying to exploit forward linkages and either substitute processed exports for raw materials or divert part of their raw materials into inputs for domestic industry.

Forward-linked industries are often encouraged through taxes or outright bans on the exports of primary products. Indonesia, for example, has banned the exports of logs and heavily taxed the exports of sawn wood to encourage the plywood and furniture industries. Because the price of the primary export is determined in world markets, export taxes and bans reduce the price of the primary commodity in the domestic market. Downstream industries then have a higher margin between the purchase price of the raw material and the export (or domestic) price of the processed good. Farmers, loggers, and miners are taxed to provide greater incentives for processors and manufacturing firms. This is one form of **protection** and is similar in its effects to protection against imports, the subject of the next chapter.

These **resource-based industrialization strategies** may succeed in expanding the industrial base and increasing the economic benefits derived from a natural resource. However, resource processing is no panacea for development. Most of the mineral-processing industries share with mining the characteristics of large scale, capital intensity, sophisticated technology, and high wages, so they tend to be extensions of the export enclave; they generate little employment and realize few linkages to the rest of the economy. Nor is there much diversification of risk in moving from crude to refined petroleum exports or from bauxite to aluminum.

Dutch Disease

Booming primary exports may fail to stimulate development for another, more pervasive reason, which has been labeled **Dutch disease.** This syndrome derives its name from the experience of the Netherlands after 1960, when major reserves of natural gas were discovered. The ensuing export boom and the balance-of-payments surplus promised new prosperity. Instead, during the 1970s the Dutch economy suffered from rising inflation, declining exports of manufactures, lower rates of income growth, and rising unemployment. The oil boom of the 1970s and early 1980s produced similar paradoxes in a number of countries, including Saudi Arabia, Nigeria, and Mexico. Economists began to realize that Dutch disease might be a very general phenomenon, applicable to all countries that "enjoy" export booms of primary commodities.[21] Because, as we shall see, it is the influx of foreign exchange that causes Dutch disease, the syndrome can also result from large inflows of foreign capital in any form. The import of gold and silver from the Americas, for example, may have helped to retard Spain's industrialization in the sixteenth century and a surge of investment to the United States probably helped to make its industries less competitive in the 1980s. How can this happen?

The key to this paradox is to understand (1) how export booms affect a country's **real exchange rate** and (2) how the real exchange rate, in turn, affects other industries. The **official or nominal exchange rate** is simply the price at which anyone holding foreign exchange, such as dollars, can convert it into local currency, say pesos in Mexico, naira in Nigeria, or rupiah in Indonesia. It is generally convenient to speak of this price or rate in local currency per unit of foreign currency, say pesos per dollar. The real exchange rate corrects the nominal rate for inflation. It is an index of prices, like the terms of trade, not a price itself. One formula for the real exchange rate is:

$$RER = R_o(P_w/P_d), \qquad\qquad [15\text{--}1]$$

where RER is an index of the real exchange rate, the value in the current period, say 1990, divided by the value in a base period, say 1985; R_o is an index of the official (nominal) exchange rate; P_w is an index of prices in world trade; and P_d is an index of domestic prices, either a wholesale or a consumer price index. When the real exchange rate rises—i.e., there are more pesos or naira or rupiah per dollar—there is **real depreciation** of the peso or naira or rupiah, because it takes fewer dollars to buy the same amount of pesos than before. When the RER falls, there is **real appreciation** of the currency because pesos are worth more in dollars than before. Offi-

21. Dutch disease has been analyzed from a theoretical standpoint by W. Max Corden and S. Peter Neary, "Booming Sector and Deindustrialization in a Small Open Economy," *Economic Journal* 92 (December 1982): 825–848. The application of this theory to developing countries is explored by Michael Roemer, "Dutch Disease in Developing Countries: Swallowing Bitter Medicine," in *The Primary Sector in Economic Development*, Matts Lundahl, ed. (London; Croom-Helms, 1985), pp. 201–26.

cial devaluations, which raise the peso price of dollars, cause the real rate to depreciate, at least initially. If domestic prices then increase more rapidly than world prices, however, the local currency appreciates in real terms.

To understand how the real exchange rate becomes the key to the Dutch disease paradox, begin with the impact of the real exchange rate on export industries other than the booming primary export industry. Table 15–3 demonstrates that, with a fixed nominal exchange rate, domestic inflation in excess of world inflation causes exporters' profits to decline: wages and the prices of domestic inputs rise faster than the price of exported output. This is, of course, the same thing as a real rate appreciation, since RER would fall in Equation 15–1. (The same reduction in profitability would follow from an appreciation of the nominal exchange rate, i.e., from lowering the peso price of a dollar.) If exporters' profits fall, they are likely to produce less for export, and this will reduce incomes and employment in export industries. Exporters' profitability could be restored by a nominal devaluation that offsets domestic inflation, as shown in the last section of Table 15–3.

Booming raw material exports cause just such appreciations of the real exchange rate as are illustrated in Table 15–3. This can occur in two ways. First, the influx of foreign exchange from higher export earnings creates a surplus of foreign currency, which tends to drive down its price in pesos, as would occur for any commodity. Unless the central bank tries to maintain the official exchange rate at its former level, this shift in supply causes the currency to appreciate in value.

Second, higher income from booming primary exports also spurs faster domestic inflation. It does this because the additional income creates greater demand for all goods and services in the economy. To the extent that this demand spills over into more imports, there is an outflow of foreign exchange

---

TABLE 15–3   Effects of Inflation and Devaluation on Exporters' Profits

Today: Exchange rate = 12 pesos per dollar; real exchange rate = 100

1. Exporter sells goods worth	$ 100,000
2. For which exporter receives local currency of	P1,200,000
3. Exporter's costs are now	P 900,000
4. Exporter's profits are	P 300,000

Three years later, after primary export boom: Cumulative domestic inflation 33% more than world prices; real exchange rate appreciated to 75

1. Exporter sells goods worth	$ 100,000
2. For which exporter receives local currency of	P1,200,000
3. Exporter's costs are now	P1,200,000
4. Exporter's profits are	P 0

Three years later, but with currency devalued by 33% to 16 pesos per dollar; real exchange rate restored to 100

1. Exporter sells goods worth	$ 100,000
2. For which exporter receives local currency of	P1,600,000
3. If exporter's costs—all domestic—are now	P1,200,000
4. Exporter's profits are	P 400,000
5. Which, deflated by 33% to year 1 prices, are again	P 300,000

but no inflation, because the price of imports is not much affected by demand in a single country. Economists call any good that is imported, or is likely to be imported, a **tradable.** Goods that are, or are likely to be, exported are also tradables. The price of any tradable is determined in world markets, not in the market of a single consuming or producing country, although very large consumers or producers of tradables have some influence on the world price. Tradables include most manufactures and many agricultural products.

Some of the new demand from the export boom will, however, go into goods that are produced domestically and not imported or exported, which economists call **nontradables.** Examples of nontradables include transportation, construction, electricity and other utilities, household and other personal services, and manufactures or farm products that are heavily protected and not subject to competition from imports.[22] Because there is a limited supply of nontradables, especially in the first months or years of the boom, the greater demand results in higher prices of nontradables, that is, in domestic inflation. From equation 15–1 and Table 15–3 we know that if domestic inflation exceeds world inflation, the real exchange rate appreciates (RER falls).

Now the paradox can be explained: Booming primary exports, by stimulating more rapid domestic inflation and thus causing the real exchange rate to appreciate, also render other exports less competitive and hence less profitable. Producers of tradables, both exporters and import competitors, face rising prices for their purchases of nontradable goods and services, including the wages of their workers. But they cannot charge higher prices because they compete with foreign producers, either as exporters or as import competitors. These farmers and manufacturers face a profit squeeze that will cause some of them to reduce production and employment. The boom in primary exports and nontradables is partly offset by a depression in tradable industries.

The depredations of Dutch disease are often fatal to development aspirations, as the example of Nigeria illustrates. But this is not necessarily so. Some countries have turned their resource windfalls into sustained development, as demonstrated by the case of Indonesia.[23] Determined governments can take several steps to allay the symptoms of Dutch disease.

The cure for Dutch disease depends on preventing or reversing real appreciation of the currency. In most cases this requires a devaluation of the currency—or, better, a series of small devaluations, called a **crawling peg**—by the central bank. Devaluation must be accompanied by stringent controls over budget expenditures by the government and by strong restraints over money creation by the central bank, both aimed at curbing inflation.

---

22. Whether a good is a tradable or a nontradable depends on whether the domestic price is affected by the world price or not. Because government policy can shield the domestic market from world market influences even for potentially tradable goods, as discussed in the next chapter, the distinction between tradables and nontradables can differ from country to country. See Appendix A for a more complete description.

23. World Bank economist Alan Gelb and associates have documented six cases of Dutch disease in *Oil Windfalls: Blessing or Curse?*. (New York: Oxford University Press for the World Bank, 1988).

In essence, the government **sterilizes** the revenues from the export boom by not spending them right away—i.e., by running budget surpluses—and by preventing commercial banks from turning increased foreign exchange reserves into more credit for the private sector. These are the same kinds of **stabilization measures,** introduced in Chapter 5 and explored in depth in Appendix A, that often must accompany market-based reforms.

As an extension of the stabilization program, the government needs to resist demands for profligate investments on new projects and expansions of existing services. Instead, it should save its new-found revenues until there is time to plan sensible, well-targeted projects with high returns. Some of the government windfalls can also be loaned to finance private-sector investments, once mechanisms for doing so have been established. Such an investment policy accomplishes two things. First, it harnesses export windfalls to finance sound, long-term development. Second, by delaying the new expenditures, government acts **countercyclically** and helps to stabilize the economy by spending less during the most inflationary period of the export boom and more after the boom has faded.

For reasons already discussed in Chapter 5, policies of restraint, essential to stabilization, are seldom popular and are often vigorously opposed by political pressure groups. Thus although the medicine for Dutch disease is easy to prescribe and essential for the patient's health, it is not often taken in sufficient doses to affect a cure.

Nigeria: A Bad Case of Dutch Disease[24]

In 1973 to 1974, the oil embargo imposed by Arab countries, followed by the activation of OPEC as an effective cartel, quadrupled the price of petroleum on world markets. In 1979 to 1980, the price doubled again, so that by the end of 1980 the terms of trade for oil exports, relative to the price of imports, was nearly 7 times the level in 1972. In Nigeria, higher export prices generated an oil windfall that added 23 percent to nonmining gross domestic product in the middle 1970s and again in the early 1980s.

Nigeria's political history has been marked by intense competition among ethnic groups—culminating in the Biafran war of the late 1960s—and one of the major battlegrounds of this strife has been the incidence of taxation and government expenditure. Under this kind of pressure, the Nigerian government spent all of its oil windfall. Public investment rose from 4 to 30 percent of nonmining GDP, and the average pay for civil servants was doubled in 1975. Much of the newfound revenue was squandered on wasteful projects. The second oil windfall only whetted fiscal appetites even more: from 1981 to 1984, the budget deficit averaged 12 percent of nonmining GDP.

Fiscal excesses exacerbated the tendency of export windfalls to create inflation. Prices rose while the central bank kept the nominal exchange rate fixed, so that by 1984 the real exchange rate had appreciated to nearly

---

24. This account is based on Henry Bienen, "Nigeria: From Windfall Gains to Welfare Losses?" in *Oil Windfalls*, Gelb, pp. 227–260.

3 times its level in 1970 to 1972. Over the decade ending in 1984, Nigeria's nonoil exports fell almost 90 percent in nominal terms, a classic if extreme symptom of Dutch disease.

Agriculture suffered worst. Because rural constituencies were politically weak, little of the oil windfall was invested in agriculture, whereas vast amounts were spent, and wasted, on infrastructure and industry. From 1973 to 1984, the quantity of agricultural exports fell by more than two-thirds, while agriculture output per capita and total calorie consumption per capita both declined. From 1972 to 1981, growth in nonmining GDP was a respectable 5.3 percent, but this was only 60 percent of the growth rate during the five years before the oil price boom. It can be argued that Nigeria might have been better off without its oil boom.

Indonesia: Finding a Cure[25]

Indonesia was both the poorest and the largest country in the world to receive substantial oil windfalls. At first, the oil boom affected Indonesia much as it did Nigeria. The 1973–74 boom added 16 percent to nonmining GDP and the 1979–80 price surge raised the windfall to 23 percent. Of the first windfall, the government itself spent more than 60 percent from 1974 to 1978, the real exchange rate appreciated an average 33 percent over its preboom level, a bit more than in Nigeria at that time.

Yet the outcome was very different in Indonesia. Throughout the boom period, government was required to balance its budget each year and, because all controls had been removed from foreign exchange transfers, stringent management of the money supply was necessary to protect foreign exchange reserves. These self-imposed restraints limited the impact of windfalls on inflation.

The Indonesian government adopted two policies that took advantage of oil windfalls for national development goals. First, investment in agriculture had a high priority, especially the goal of achieving self-sufficiency in rice production. Government financed irrigation systems, encouraged the adoption of new rice varieties, subsidized fertilizer and pesticide sales, provided credit to farmers, invested in rural health and education facilities, and built roads and other infrastructure in rural areas. By the mid-1980s, Indonesia was self-sufficient in rice and by 1982–83 its total food output per capita was a third above its 1970 level, a performance far above average for all developing and industrial countries over the period.

The second policy was to devalue the exchange rate enough to avoid real appreciation. Major devaluations were imposed in 1978, 1983, and 1986, after which the rate was managed flexibly to maintain its real value. At the end of the oil boom period in 1984, the Indonesian real exchange rate had been *depreciated* 8 percent from its 1970-to-1972 average. Consequently, over the period from 1971 to 1984, the quantity of nonoil exports grew by over 7 percent a year from 1972 to 1981 and nonmining GDP expanded by over 8 percent a year.

---

25. This account is based on Bruce Glassburner, "Indonesia: Windfalls in a Poor Rural Economy," in *Oil Windfalls*, Gelb, pp. 197–226.

Thus shrewd policy played a major role in affecting an early cure for incipient Dutch disease. The government's decisive action was made possible by its stability and longevity: the Suharto government came to power in 1966 and many of its key economic ministers remained in place for two decades. It and the previous government placed great stress on integrating the multitude of ethnic groups of this diverse country and avoided the conflicts over fiscal resources that paralyzed Nigeria. Moreover, the country had an important advantage over other oil exporters: its large labor force, nearly two-thirds of it working in rural areas in 1970, dampened any tendencies for surges in wages and thus in domestic prices throughout the oil boom.

Import
Substitution

The pursuit of static comparative advantage in primary exports has propelled a number of developing countries toward development. However,
comparative advantage is not immutable. The relative factor endowments
that dictate the export of primary products change with population growth,
degradation of natural resources, capital accumulation, education of the
labor force, the acquisition and adaptation of newer technologies, and other
processes. Most, though not all, countries' comparative advantage moves
with development away from land- and resource-intensive products toward
manufactures: to labor-intensive products first, then to capital-intensive
industries, and eventually to products embodying newer technologies. Just
as governments intervene to accelerate other development processes, they
almost universally attempt to hasten this natural shift of comparative
advantage toward a more industrial economy. This and the next chapter
dissect the two principal strategies employed to force the pace of changing
comparative advantage: import substitution and outward-looking development.

THE STRATEGY OF PROTECTION

Import substitution is the substitution of domestic production for imports
of manufactures. The strategy of import substitution is a well-trod path to
industrialization. It was taken during the nineteenth century by most of the
currently industrial countries as they followed the pathbreaker, England,

into the Industrial Revolution. In the newly independent United States, Alexander Hamilton's 1791 *Report on Manufactures* argued for tariffs to protect American manufacturers from cheap British imports, and President Thomas Jefferson unintentionally boosted American manufacturing by the politically inspired Embargo of 1807. Friedrich Lizst, the German economist, espoused protective tariffs as an instrument to industrialize Germany in the mid-nineteenth century. All the major European powers, including Russia both before and after the Communist revolution, and Japan marched down the road of protectionism to develop manufacturing as it became apparent that military strength depended on industrial growth.

In the third world, import substitution was first explored by Latin American countries when their primary export markets were severely disrupted, first by the Great Depression of the 1930s and subsequently by the breakdown of commercial shipping during World War II. Emerging from the war with fledgling industries, countries like Argentina, Brazil, Colombia, and Mexico began systematically to sustain these manufacturers by erecting tariffs and other barriers to competing imports from the United States. The export pessimism chronicled by Argentine economist Raul Prebisch, Hans Singer, and others reinforced protectionist sentiment, and Latin America developed import substitution regimes with a multitude of protective techniques that were later emulated by other developing countries. A few Asian countries, such as India and Turkey, also began to industrialize before World War II. But in most of Asia and Africa independence was the stimulus that induced countries to embark on the path of import substitution. By the 1960s import substitution had become the dominant strategy of economic development.

The underlying concept of import substitution is simple. First, identify large domestic markets, as indicated by substantial imports over the years. Then ensure that the technologies of production can be mastered by local manufacturers or that foreign investors are willing to supply technology, management, and capital. Finally, erect protective barriers, either tariffs or quotas on imports, to overcome the probably high initial cost of local production and make it profitable for potential investors in the target industries. This approach has generally meant that consumer goods industries—especially processed foods, beverages, textiles, clothing, and footwear—became the first targets for investment. Not only are these products manufactured with relatively standardized technologies easily accessible to LDC producers, but it was also believed that consumers could bear the higher costs of local production without disrupting development. The only other major category of manufactured import before industrialization began was capital goods. Increased investment was essential to development, however, and it was believed that the higher costs of capital equipment would discourage investors.

Infant Industries

Economists find much to criticize in the protective structures of both developing and industrial countries, as this chapter will make clear. But there are valid arguments that favor protective tariffs as a tool of development and center on the concept of an **infant industry.** A country wishing to hasten the shift of its comparative advantage toward industrialization may see opportunities in several lines of manufacturing to begin the process. Domestic capitalists, whether private or public, and their managers need to acquire a technology new to the country, whether this be the means to manufacture a product not previously made at home, such as the plastic material polyvinyl chloride, or a new process to produce familiar products at higher quality or lower cost per unit, such as a computer-controlled steel rolling mill. The products and technologies acquired by countries industrializing today have been manufactured and used by the more industrial countries for some time. So newly industrializing countries need only purchase technologies "off the shelf."

The managers and workers of the infant industry must then learn to use these technologies efficiently by the standards of the industrial countries. In some cases, this may require some engineering adaptation of the technology to suit local conditions. The learning process can take several years. Until these infant industries gain the necessary experience, however, they cannot manufacture profitably and sell at the price of competing imports. How, then, can such industries survive the years of learning until they can produce profitably at import-competitive prices?

One possibility is that private investors will finance the near-term losses if the prospects are good for long-term profits. In developing countries, however, domestic capitalists often appear to shun projects with long-delayed returns and capital markets are usually not sufficiently developed to assemble the funds of many savers into large, long-term loans for industry. The other alternative, almost universally employed, is that the government protects infant industries from competing imports by imposing tariffs or import quotas.[1] Although subsidies could accomplish the same thing and—for reasons explained in Chapter 17—are in many ways preferable to tariffs, they are seldom used in import substitution regimes.

To justify protection or a subsidy, an infant industry must eventually become capable of competing against imports in the home market, or, a stronger condition, as an export sector. This suggests a temporary tariff, one that declines towards zero as productivity increases and costs fall, or a declining subsidy. The subsidy has the advantage of clearly identifying the costs of starting the new industry, but the disadvantage of an additional burden on the government's revenue system. Most governments find it easier to impose tariffs, which make domestic consumers bear the cost instead. Even a temporary tariff or subsidy may not be justified if the eventual benefits to society of establishing the new industry, suitably discounted as explained in Chapter 6, do not exceed the costs of protection.[2] All too often

---

1. Williams College economist Henry Bruton takes a broad view of protection and extends infant-industry-like arguments to foreign investment, aid, and technical assistance; see his "Import Substitution," in *Handbook of Development Economics,* Vol. 2, Chenery and Srinivasan, pp. 1601–1644.

2. For a complete specification of the infant-industry argument, see Harry G. Johnson, "Optimal Trade Interventions in the Presence of Domestic Distortions, in *Trade,Growth and the Balance of Payments,* R. E. Caves et al., (Amsterdam: North-Holland, 1965), pp. 3–34.

these conditions are not met. The industrial landscape is littered with infants that never grew up and require protection indefinitely, from the petrochemical industry of Colombia to the textile industry of Kenya.

The infant-industry concept can be extended to include several industries at once and even to include all manufacturing. For example, a balanced-growth strategy of developing many industries simultaneously (see Chapter 3) might be started with a uniform protective tariff, declining over time.

Protective Tariffs

In the early stages of import substitution, when a protective tariff is placed on competing consumer good imports, not one but two significant aids are provided simultaneously to the potential manufacturer. First and obviously, the domestic price of the good, say cloth, will be raised above the world price. For the importing country the world price of imported cloth is the cost of the cloth landed at the port of entry, the c.i.f. (including costs, insurance and freight) or "border" price. With no tariff, the domestic price of cloth would settle at the world price. When a tariff is imposed, the domestic price must rise above the world price. If the home country's demand for imports does not affect world prices (i.e., the world supply is perfectly elastic) and if the tariff does not preclude imports altogether, then the domestic price will rise by the full extent of the tariff. Any potential manufacturer can charge anything up to the tariff-supported domestic price and still compete with imports, assuming his quality is comparable and domestic consumers do not prefer imports simply because they are foreign.

This effect of increased domestic price is called **nominal protection** and is depicted in Figure 16–1. At a world price P_w (equal to the border price, c.i.f.) consumers demand Q_1 of cloth and local producers find it profitable to produce only Q_2; the balance, $M_1 = Q_1 - Q_2$, is imported. If an *ad valorem* (i.e., a percentage) tariff t_o is imposed on imports competing with domestic cloth and if world supply is perfectly elastic, then the domestic price rises to P_d; this reduces the quantity demanded to Q_3 and increases domestic production to Q_4. Imports are thus reduced to $M_2 = Q_3 - Q_4$. The **protective effect,** given by the increase in domestic output from Q_2 to Q_4, entails a rent or **producers' surplus,** given by trapezoid a; and a **resource cost,** given by triangle b, because factors of production are diverted from more productive uses into import substitution for imported cloth. The government's tariff revenue is represented by rectangle $c = t_o P_w (Q_3 - Q_4)$. Consumers pay for protection by the loss of **consumer surplus,** equal to area $a + b + c + d$, generated by both the higher price and reduced consumption. Area $b + d$, two triangles representing welfare losses that are not compensated by gains to anyone, is called the **deadweight loss.** A prohibitive tariff would raise the domestic price to P'_d, at which point domestic demand equals domestic supply and no cloth is imported.

The second aid to domestic manufacture is that tariffs are typically *not* raised on the imported inputs required for production. If the textile manufacturer is to import cotton to spin into yarn and weave into cloth, then the manufacturer's concern is not only with the price of the cloth but with the

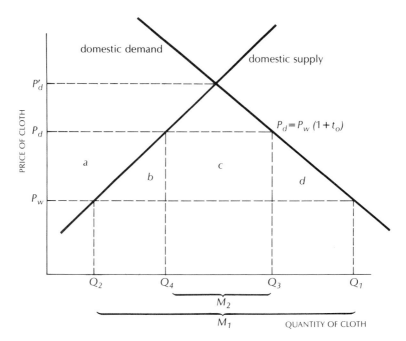

FIGURE 16–1 Nominal Tariff Protection. The imposition of a protective tariff t_o causes the domestic price P_d to rise above the world price P_w. Domestic production therefore increases. The resulting loss in consumers' surplus $(a+b+c+d)$ is offset by the gain in producers' surplus (a) and in tariff revenue for the government (c). The remaining areas b and d represent dead-weight losses.

margin between the cost of imported cotton (and other imported inputs, such as chemicals and dyes) and the sale price of finished cloth. It is within this margin that the manufacturer must pay wages, rents, and interest on borrowed capital and extract profit. The greater that margin, the more room there is to accommodate higher factor costs and the higher is the potential profit. This margin is the **value-added** measured **in domestic prices.** It can be increased by raising tariffs on competing imports of finished products, lowering tariffs on imported inputs, or both. This dual effect of the tariff structure is called **effective protection.**

To measure the concept of effective protection, it is necessary to compare two margins: first, the margin between the domestic, tariff-determined prices of inputs and outputs, or value-added measured at domestic prices, and, second, the same margin measured at world or c.i.f. prices, which is called **value-added at world prices.** The fraction by which the first margin exceeds the second is called the **effective rate of protection,** abbreviated ERP:

$$\text{ERP} = \frac{\text{value-added (domestic prices)} - \text{value-added (world prices)}}{\text{value-added (world prices)}}. \qquad [16\text{--}1]$$

To refine this further, note that value-added at domestic prices (V_d) is the difference between the potential domestic price (P_d) and the potential domestic cost of material inputs per unit of output (C_d). Further, the potential domestic price is equivalent to the world price (P_w) plus the increase permitted by the percentage (or *ad valorem*) tariff on competing imports (t_o), whereas potential domestic cost equals the cost at world prices (C_w) plus any increase permitted by the *ad valorem* tariff on imported inputs (t_i). The denominator, value-added at world prices (V_w), is the difference between the world price of competing imports and the cost of inputs, also valued at world prices (C_w). Given this, then,

$$ERP = \frac{(P_d - C_d) - (P_w - C_w)}{P_w - C_w} = \frac{P_w(1 + t_o) - C_w(1 + t_i) - (P_w - C_w)}{P_w - C_w}. \qquad [16-2]$$

$$ERP = \frac{P_w t_o - C_w t_i}{P_w - C_w}. \qquad [16-3]$$

As a last refinement, Equation 16–2 can be put in terms of a dollar of output by dividing the fraction through by P_w. The cost of an input for a dollar's worth of output, C_w/P_w, can be designated a, an input coefficient. If we then allow for several inputs, each with its own input coefficient a_i and its own tariff t_i, then the formula can be written:

$$ERP = (t_o - \Sigma a_i t_i)/(1 - \Sigma a_i). \qquad [16-4]$$

This formula can also accommodate subsidies on competing outputs and on inputs by treating them as negative tariffs.[3]

To illustrate the workings of effective protection, assume, using Equation 16–3, that $100 of cloth, valued at world prices, would require $60 of material inputs, such as cotton and chemicals, also valued at world prices. Value-added is $40 at world prices. If the government has imposed a uniform duty of 10 percent on both competing imports and imported inputs, then

$$ERP = \frac{100(.10) - 60(.10)}{100 - 60} = 0.10.$$

A uniform tariff, 10 percent in this case, yields an effective rate of protection of the same amount. If, however, in order to encourage investment in the textile industry, the government were to permit textile firms to import cotton and chemicals duty-free, then $t_i = 0$ and

$$ERP = \frac{100(.10)}{40} = 0.25.$$

Effective protection is 25 percent, or 2.5 times the nominal rate of 10 percent. If, instead, the input duty stayed at 10 percent but competing cloth imports were taxed at 20 percent, the ERP would rise to 35 percent. This latter case is illustrated graphically in Figure 16–2.

---

3. For a complete, although advanced, treatment of effective protection, see W. M. Corden, *The Theory of Protection* (London: Oxford University Press, 1971), especially Chaps. 2 and 3.

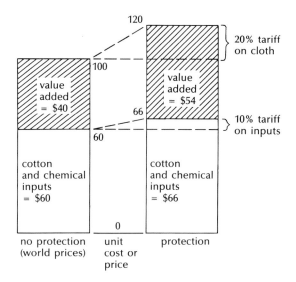

FIGURE 16–2. **Effective Protection.** With no tariffs, cloth is produced using inputs costing $60 and is sold in the domestic market at $100, the world price; value-added is $40. If cloth is protected with a 20 percent tariff but there is also a 10 percent tariff on cotton and chemical imports, the domestic sales price can rise to $120, inputs now cost $66, and value-added by domestic producers can rise to $54, which is 35 percent above value-added at free trade.

The implication of the third example is that, even though only modest nominal protection is provided, the domestic manufacturer enjoys a large margin of 35 percent over value-added at world prices. Taking advantage of the effective protection afforded by the tariff structure, the local manufacturers can earn extremely high profits, pay high wages, or simply accommodate inefficiencies and high costs substantially above those of foreign competitors. The higher is effective protection, the greater the incentive to establish the industry in the country, and the greater the economic costs of doing so. Note that the smaller is value-added in the industry (that is, the smaller is the denominator of Equations 16–3 or 16–4), the greater is effective protection for any given set of tariff rates. Thus superficial industrialization, such as the simple assembly of cars and trucks or the simple mixing of chemicals, can and usually does have especially high effective protection.

Tariff structures in most countries, including most industrial countries, are like those in the latter two textile examples: duties tend to escalate from low rates on imported industrial inputs to higher rates on imports of finished goods that compete with domestic manufactures. In fact the levels of protection in this hypothetical example are modest by world standards. It is common to observe effective protection of 100 percent or more in several industries in countries strongly pursuing import substitution. Not only is the level high, but there is a wide range of protective rates that result in severe discrimination against particular kinds of investment. The fairly typical pattern of protection is illustrated by the data in Table 16–1 for Bangladesh in 1984 and Brazil and the Philippines in the mid-1960s.

TABLE 16–1   **Effective Rates of Protection**

Sector	Bangladesh (1984)	Brazil (1966)	Philippines (1965)	Norway (1954)
Agriculture	13	46	33	34
Mining	—	−16	−9	−7
Manufacturing	114	127	53	9
Consumer goods[a]	na	198	72	29
Intermediate goods[a]	na	151	45	9
Machinery	10	93	24	18
Transport equipment	na	−26	−3	−6

[a] Aggregates for consumer goods and intermediate goods are simple, unweighted averages of constituent industry data.
na = not available.
Sources: For Bangladesh, Thomas L. Hutcheson and Joseph J. Stern, "The Methodology of Assistance Policy Analysis," Harvard Institute for International Development, Development Discussion Paper No. 226, April 1986, and for other countries, Bela Balassa et al., *The Structure of Protection in the Developing Countries* (Baltimore: Johns Hopkins Press, 1971), p. 55.

The average level of effective protection for manufacturing as a whole ranges from moderate (Philippines) to high (Brazil). However, the structure within manufacturing is widely skewed. Consumer goods are highly protected, at considerable cost to consumers of manufactures, and intermediate goods are comfortably protected, though at lower rates. The capital-goods industries, however, receive less protection because tariffs on capital goods are thought to discourage investors; rates are especially low in Bangladesh for machinery and in Brazil and the Philippines for transport equipment (which does not include automobiles, a consumer durable). As a consequence the incentive to invest in capital-goods production is less than in other manufacturing and the development of this sector typically lags behind the others. More damaging in terms of many development objectives, manufacturing as a whole enjoys a substantial advantage over agriculture, which faces effective rates of protection ranging downward from 46 percent to only 13 percent in these examples. In many countries, agriculture has negative effective protection.[4] These biases against investment in agriculture and in capital-goods industries are characteristic of import substitution regimes and have been partly responsible for the failure of import substitution to stimulate self-sustaining development. This biased protective structure is not unique to developing countries, as demonstrated by the figures for Norway in Table 16–1. However, extremes like the Bangladesh structure, especially the severe bias against agriculture, do seem confined to the third world.

Import Quotas

The protective effects of tariffs can also be achieved through restrictions on imports, known as **quantitative restrictions** (QRs), **quotas,** or **import**

---

4. A negative effective rate of protection can have two meanings. If the rate is small, it means that the industry faces high taxes on either its inputs or its own outputs, as is likely to be true for many primary-exporting industries. Alternatively, a very high negative ERP usually indicates that the industry is so inefficient that its inputs cost more in foreign exchange than its outputs are worth at c.i.f. prices; i.e., value-added is negative if measured at world prices! Then the denominator of Equation 16–3 or 16–4 becomes a small negative number.

licensing. For both the government and domestic manufacturers, import quotas have the advantage of permitting a known quantity of imports. With tariffs the quantity of imports depends on the elasticities of supply and demand, which are generally not known in advance. A quota that limits imports to the same quantity as a tariff would have most of the same effects. To see this, refer back to Figure 16–1. Instead of the tariff t_o, assume the government limits imports of cloth to the quantity, $M_2 = Q_3 - Q_4$. As with the tariff the domestic price would still rise to P_d, domestic production would rise from Q_2 to Q_4 and cause a resource cost measured by triangle b; consumption would fall from Q_1 to Q_3 and add the area of triangle d to the deadweight loss. But in two important respects the effects of import quotas differ from those of tariffs.

The first difference is that the government no longer collects tariff revenues. Instead the government issues licenses to a limited number of importers, giving them the right to purchase imports of cloth up to a total of M_2 in Figure 16–1. If the government were to sell these import licenses at auction, potential importers would be willing to buy these licenses for as much as $P_d - P_w$ per unit of imports. Then they could purchase each unit of imported cloth for P_w, the world price, and break even by selling it at the domestic price P_d. In that case the auction price for import licenses would just equal the tariff t_o that would have led to the same quantity of imports. Also, the government would collect the same revenue as under a tariff, rectangle c in Figure 16–1, in the form of fees for import licenses.

However, most governments do not auction import licenses, but give them free to a limited number of those importers who apply for them. Then although the importers pay only P_w for their imports, they can sell them at the domestic price, P_d in Figure 16–1, and keep for themselves a windfall profit of $P_d - P_w = t_o$. This rent—often called a **quota rent** or **premium**—can be substantial, so import licenses are valuable to their recipients. Much effort is expended and large bribes are offered to obtain import licenses, with consequences discussed later in this chapter.

The second difference between quotas and tariffs is that quotas can convert a single domestic manufacturer into a monopolist who can charge whatever price maximizes profits. Figure 16–3A depicts the market for a single domestic producer who is protected by a tariff t. Imports are available at the world price P_w plus the tariff tP_w. With infinitely elastic world supply, domestic consumers can buy all they want at the world price plus the tariff; $P_d = P_w (1 + t)$. The domestic producer, despite being the only local supplier, must compete with this price, which becomes the producer's marginal revenue schedule, so long as P_d is below the intersection of the marginal cost and demand curves. Consumers purchase Q_c while the domestic producer offers Q_p, an output that equates the producer's marginal revenue and marginal cost (point A). The balance $Q_c - Q_p$ is imported. Figure 16–3B depicts an alternative means of stimulating domestic production. Here, a quota replaces the tariff, as the government uses licensing to hold imports to the previous $Q_c - Q_p$ and leaves the domestic manufacturer with a residual demand (which must be drawn through the same point A) that can only be met from domestic production. With no further com-

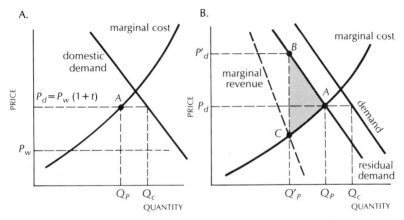

Figure 16–3 Protecting Domestic Monopoly: Tariff versus Quota. Part A depicts a monopolist protected by a tariff. The monopolist produces at the point (A) where marginal revenue equals marginal costs. The balance demanded is supplied by imports. In part B a quota is imposed to hold imports to the same level as part A. The domestic price rises and the economy suffers a deadweight loss.

petition from imports, the firm now faces a marginal revenue curve that is below the residual demand curve. It equates marginal revenue with marginal cost at point C, produces only Q_p, and charges P'_d in the captive residual domestic market. Hence, output and consumption fall, price rises, and society faces a deadweight loss (reduction of consumers' plus producers' surplus) given by shaded area ABC. Clearly, it matters a great deal whether protection is granted through tariffs that are not prohibitive or through equivalent import quotas.

Overvalued Exchange Rates

A third prop of the import substitution regime, the one that clarifies the biases of the entire system, is the **overvalued exchange rate.** There have been several definitions of the term "overvalued" in this context, but for purposes of understanding import substitution a simple explanation will do. In Figure 16–4, the schedules are **total revenue curves,** giving exporters' supply of and importers' demand for foreign exchange. In the absence of tariffs or quotas an exchange rate of r_e would just clear the market and thus be an equilibrium. If tariffs are imposed on imports, the demand curve shifts downward because importers are then unwilling to offer as much foreign exchange per unit imported. This lowers the peso-per-dollar rate for equilibrium to r_t. Often, however, the official exchange rate r_o is below both those levels. Because the peso price of the dollar is so low, import demand is high (M_d) and export supply is low (E_s): this creates a potential deficit in the current account of the balance of payments. To reduce the deficit, governments typically resort to import quotas and controls over all foreign exchange transactions. The rate r_o is considered **overvalued** in the sense that the dollar price of pesos (the reciprocal of that shown in the diagram) is too high to maintain equilibrium without controls and high tariffs; the peso rate r_o is therefore too low.

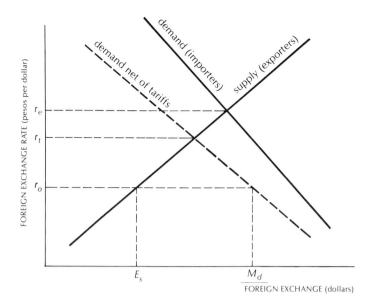

FIGURE 16–4 Overvalued Exchange Rate. The exchange rate r_o represents a common problem: it is too high in dollars per peso, or too low in pesos per dollar, to balance the demand for foreign exchange with the supply of foreign exchange without high protective tariffs, import quotas, and restrictions on other foreign exchange transactions.

Exchange rates become overvalued for a variety of reasons. The genesis of the problem is sometimes a boom in primary exports, which causes appreciate of the real exchange rate, as explained in the discussion of Dutch disease in Chapter 15. Also, as incomes rise with development and import demand increases, devaluation may be required to help stimulate the production of import substitutes and nontraditional exports and thus to maintain equilibrium in the balance of payments. Domestic inflation, which causes domestic prices and costs to rise faster than the world average, also requires devaluation to maintain the real exchange rate.

For much of the period after World War II, however, most governments maintained fixed exchange rates and were reluctant to risk the destabilizing political effects of devaluation. The exchange rate is one of the most pervasive prices in the economy, perhaps affecting more transactions than any other single price. To change it, especially by the large amounts sometimes required, means changing the relative wealth of influential segments of the population. Not only are the relative prices of imports raised, but in order to prevent domestic prices from rising as much as the currency is devalued, wages and other incomes must be restrained by government policy. Frequently it is the politically powerful who would lose by these measures, especially urban workers, middle-class professionals, the military, civil servants, the upper classes, and other whose consumption depends substantially on imports. For these reasons governments resist devaluation and, when they do undertake it, often devalue by too little in the face of growing demand and continuing inflation. Hence there has been a tendency for exchange rates to remain overvalued in the third world.[5] This tendency has been alleviated by the greater flexibility in exchange rates since 1971, but controlled rates at overvalued levels remain common in the third world.

A glance at Figure 16–4 shows that the overvalued exchange rate discourages exports. It does so by reducing the local currency payment for any given dollar amount of exports and hence reducing revenues and profits to domestic exporters, as demonstrated in Table 15–3 for exchange rate appreciation. But overvalued rates also encourage imports by keeping the peso payments lower than they should be, and this in turn is detrimental to import-substituting industries. How then is the overvalued rate consistent with import substitution regimes?

The answer lies in the triumvirate of exchange rates, tariffs, and quotas. Because the exchange rate is so low, import-competing industries depend heavily on high effective tariff protection and on quotas to shield them from cheap imports. Industries without such protection are unlikely to find it profitable to produce for either the home or the foreign market. Recall, then, the highly skewed protective structure presented in Table 16–1: consumer and intermediate goods manufacturing can overcome the overvalued exchange rate with their high effective rates of protection or with additional help from import licensing. But agricultural and capital goods manufacturing are exposed to import competition at the low local currency prices engendered by the overvalued exchange rate.

Outcomes and Problems

Import Substitution in General Equilibrium

The process of import substitution is represented in Figures 16–5, 16–6, and 16–7. Figure 16–5 depicts the imposition of uniform protective tariffs, say in 1965, when the country produces at point A and consumes at C under world terms of trade favorable to its export. Imposition of the tariff, presumed here to be a uniform one on all imports, swings domestic relative prices in favor of importable goods. Production moves towards point B where more of the importable and less of the exportable are produced. If the country is relatively small and does not affect world prices, trade can take place at the same terms of trade as before, so that consumption settles somewhere, such as point $E,$ along line $BD,$ drawn parallel to the terms-of-trade line. Consumption of both goods is lower than before the tariff, so consumers' well-being has been reduced. Both imports and exports have also fallen, as indicated by the line segment BE (the hypotenuse of the trade triangle, see Figure 15–1) which is shorter than $AC.$ Initially, this shift from free trade necessarily reduces both trade and consumers' welfare.

If protection successfully stimulates investment in infant industries and

---

5. The economic and political difficulties of devaluation make selective tariffs and quota restrictions even more appealing to governments, despite the allocative inefficiencies such measures entail.

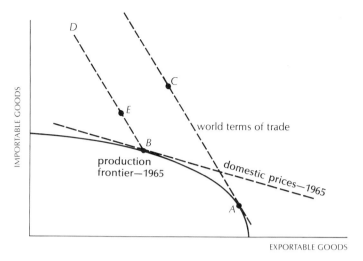

FIGURE 16–5 **Imposition of Protective Tariff (situation in 1965).** A protective tariff increases the relative domestic price of importables and induces a rise in their production from point *A* to point *B*. At first, consumption of both goods falls from point *C* to *E*.

subsequent growth is substantial, the production frontier will be pushed outward, as in Figure 16–6, and after several years consumer welfare will have increased. Over time, as more import substitutes become available, their relative domestic price is likely to fall, even if the protective tariff is maintained. So the 1990 domestic price line is drawn with a steeper slope than the 1965 line in Figure 16–5. In 1990, then, production takes place at a point like *F*, where the domestic price line is tangent to the new frontier, and consumption can take place at a point like *H*, somewhere along line *FG*, drawn parallel to the original world terms of trade (which are presumed not to have changed since 1965). In 1990 consumers are better off at *H* than they had been in 1965 at *C*, since they are on a higher indifference curve (not shown). There is also less trade than in 1965 (*FH* is shorter than *AC*). However, once the production frontier has been expanded, consumers' welfare could be improved still more by removing tariffs and reverting to the world terms of trade. Producers would then move along the 1990 frontier to point *I*, permitting consumption at a point to the northeast of *H*, on a still higher indifference curve. Trade would be increased compared with the situation a point *F*. This is the desirable result that attracts advocates of import substitution.

Too often, however, slow or arrested growth is the outcome of protective policies, as we shall see. In that case, shown in Figure 16–7, trade and consumer welfare may never reach their former levels. With slow growth, producers reach point *J* on the 1990 frontier, but consumption, at a point like *L*, remains below the original point *C*. Trade is reduced from its 1965 level. Here again consumption of both goods could be increased if the country reverted to world prices and moved production from *J* to *M* on the new frontier. Note that once import substitution has taken place, a return toward free trade can always improve welfare compared with both the protected position and the initial free trade position.

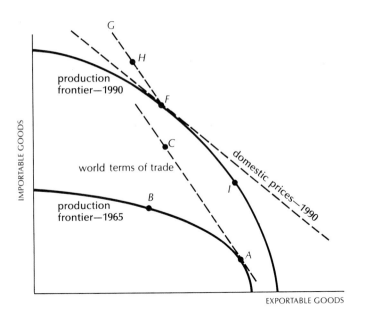

FIGURE 16–6   Import Substitution after Twenty-five Years of Rapid Growth, 1990. After twenty-five years of successful import substitution, the production frontier has been shifted outward sufficiently to enable the country to produce at point *F* and to consume at point *H*, on a higher indifference curve than at a point *C* before the imposition of a tariff.

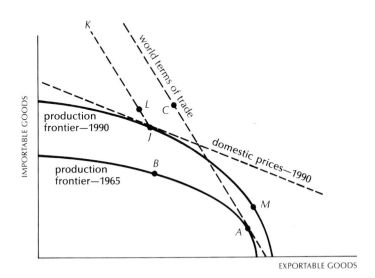

FIGURE 16–7   Import Substitution after Twenty-five Years of Slow Growth, 1990. If, instead, import substitution does not move the production frontier outward as substantially as in Figure 16–6, production will take place at a point like *J* and consumption, at *L*, will remain on an indifference curve lower than at the starting point *C*.

In both Figures 16–6 and 16–7, the **ratio of imports to national product** declines from 1965, before the tariff is imposed, to 1990.[6] This suggests that we use the ratio of imports to gross domestic product as an indicator of import substitution. Countries that have managed to use import substitution as a spur to economic growth, as depicted in Figure 16–6, should have a falling import ratio and sustained increases in GDP over a long period. Figure 16–8 gathers the evidence on import substitution for 36 countries from 1965 to 1988. Countries falling to the left of the line 00 have reduced the share of imports in GDP over nearly a quarter century. Countries falling above the horizontal line at 5 percent a year can be considered to have grown fairly rapidly.

Less than half the countries show a decline in the import-GDP ratio. Of these, only Kenya, Cameroon, Colombia, and the Ivory Coast grew at more than 5 percent a year, though Malawi, Panama, and Mexico were close. At best, these seven countries might lay claim to having been successful import substituters as depicted in Figure 16–6. Several countries with shrinking import ratios also exhibited slow growth, candidates for the case shown in Figure 16–7.

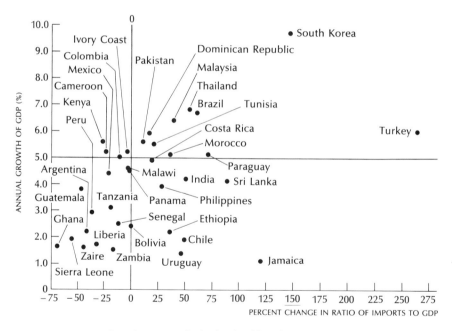

FIGURE 16–8   Growth and Import Substitution in Thirty-six LDCs, 1965–1988. A successful import-substituting country ought to have reduced its ratio of imports to GDP over the twenty-three years, and thus lie to the left of the vertical line 00, and to have grown relatively rapidly, and thus lie above the horizontal line at 5 percent a year.
Sources: World Bank, *World Development Report 1990,* and *World Tables,* 1989–1990 ed.

6. For this to be unambiguously true, national product must be measured at domestic, rather than world, prices. Since measures of national product are virtually always in domestic prices, this presents no problems in what follows.

Unfortunately, this simple picture may conceal as much as it reveals. Probably the most important single determinant of import levels is the level of exports, which is, for all countries, the largest source of foreign exchange to pay for imports. Some of the countries whose import ratios rose may have been able to increase export earnings while also substituting for imports in several industries. This is almost certainly the case for South Korea, Thailand, and Malaysia. Conversely, many if not most of the falling import ratios for those countries with low growth rates may have been caused, not by import substitution, but by falling export earnings.

Even where import substitution is taking place, part of the fall in import ratios is usually canceled by the new industries' own demands for imported inputs and by increased consumer demand for imports with rising incomes. Indeed, Moshe Syrquin and Hollis B. Chenery observe that as incomes (in 1980 prices) rise from $300 per capita to $4,000, there is a gradual but steady tendency for the import ratio to rise from 18 to 23 percent of GDP.[7] Because of these contradicting tendencies, we can only be confident of the story for those countries in the upper left quadrant of Figure 16–8, for whom import substitution led to satisfactory economic growth. Any further conclusions would require detailed, industry-by-industry, studies of import substitution.

Import Substitution in Kenya

Kenya is one of only four countries in Figure 16–8 whose GDP grew by more than 5 percent a year from 1965 to 1988 while its import to GDP ratio fell. This small, open economy provides an example of both the potential power and the structural difficulties of import substitution. Kenya's population of 23 million generated GDP of $370 per capita in 1988; this gave Kenya a total domestic market about 3 percent the size of India's and 16 percent the size of Colombia's domestic markets. Kenya exports goods and nonfactor services equal to 19 percent of its GDP, down from 31 percent in 1965. Still 31 percent of its GDP and over 60 percent of its exports come from agriculture, which has been relatively favored by policy compared with other African countries and most import-substituting regimes.

Yet Kenya pursued import substitution as a means of industrializing both before and especially after independence in 1963 and utilized high protective tariffs, quotas, and outright bans on competing imports to attract investors. Effective rates of protection ranged from slightly negative, especially on agricultural processing industries, to levels of 100 to 500 percent for chemical industries based on simple last-stage mixing and for the assembly of vehicles and consumer durables. After substantial liberalization in the early 1980s, about a third of imported items—many of them potential competitors with local industry—remained under highly restrictive import licensing. In 1960, Kenya imported over a third of its GDP. By the late 1980s, imports were down to 22 percent of GDP. From independence in

7. Moshia Syrquin and Hollis B. Chenery, *Patterns of Development 1950–1983*, World Bank Discussion Paper No. 41., Washington, D.C., 1989, p. 20.

1963 to 1988, GDP grew by 5.6 percent a year, with manufacturing lead-ing the way at over 7 percent a year. During the peak of import substitu-tion, from 1972 to 1983, the leading industries, with annual growth exceeding 10 percent, were canned vegetables, clothing, footwear, paper, printing, petroleum refining, rubber products, plastic products and vehicle assembly—all but the first being typical first-stage import substitution lead-ers. Also typical of import substitution, the import share of machinery and equipment more than doubled from 11 percent in 1965 to 24 percent in 1983, while the share for nonfood consumer goods fell from 18 to 7 per-cent.

By the end of the 1970s, it became generally recognized in Kenya that import substitution had run its course. The domestic market was too small to attract many more industries, manufacturing costs were generally too high to make manufactured exports feasible, and further backward integra-tion into intermediate goods would mean even higher costs for user indus-tries. During the early 1980s, economic growth slowed to just over 4 percent a year after its spurt of almost 8 percent a year from 1965 to 1973. Since 1980, Kenya has been shifting toward a more outward-looking policy for industry, along the lines described in the next chapter.[8]

Rents and Other Adverse Incentives

Underlying the protective regime is a set of incentives that reward political astuteness and **rent-seeking** (described in Chapter 5) more than economic competitiveness. Protective duties and access to low-cost inputs make the import-substituting firm profitable. Should the competitive positions of domestic firms be eroded by higher domestic costs of production, reduced prices of competitive imports, or competition from new or better quality foreign goods, the natural reaction of protected firms is to return to govern-ment for enhanced protection. This blunts the competitive instincts of entrepreneurs who, in the absence of government support, would have had to cut their own costs, improve quality, and thus raise productivity. Instead of facing reduced protection over time, as prescribed by infant-industry considerations, the enterpreneur can look forward to constant or rising protection, as needed, if political connections and support are maintained.

In this environment of government intervention the most successful managers are those who have political skills, who can bargain effectively with—or simply bribe—officials who administer import quotas and deter-mine tariff rates, or who have close ties with the political and bureaucratic elite. It is no accident that manufacturers usually locate their top execu-tives, if not the plant itself, in the capital city or that the executives spend much if not most of their time seeing government officials. Thus the wealthy and powerful succeed best and become reentrenched in their wealth and power. These tendencies exist in most political-economic regimes, but the

---

8. Data are from Central Bureau of Statistics, *Economy Survey 1990* (Nairobi: Government of Kenya Printer, 1990), and earlier issues; World Bank, *World Development Report 1990*; and unpublished reports.

adverse economic impacts seem accentuated when those regimes pursue an import substitution strategy.

Because import-substituting industry typically produces at high cost, it has little potential to penetrate export markets in the absence of large subsidies. Export subsidies have been part of several import substitution regimes: in Pakistan bonus vouchers were paid to exporters on nontraditional goods and gave them access to licensed imports that carried large quota premiums; in Colombia exporters were granted certificates entitling them to income tax reductions; in Ghana cash subsidy payments were offered; and in several countries exporters of nontraditional products have received access to controlled imports, tariff reductions on inputs, access to cheap credit, and so forth. In a few cases, notably Pakistan and Colombia, manufactured exports did respond to incentives. But for the most part these were weak measures. In the face of much stronger incentives to produce for the domestic market, and because of bureaucratic requirements that made it difficult to realize the proffered export incentives, such incentives often had only a marginal impact on exports. Moreover price incentives work against agriculture and discourage that potentially important source of new exports. Export diversification and growth are not consistent with the biases of an import substitution regime, but represent a very different approach to development, as will be seen in the next chapter.

Import substitution incentives also lead to potentially severe misallocations of national resources. The most serious of these affects foreign exchange. The overvalued exchange rate encourages the use of imported inputs, especially those on which duties are also low, and further widens the foreign exchange gap. If imported materials are cheap, users have less incentive to adopt practices or technologies that conserve their use, and in this sense scarce foreign exchange may be wasted. When the imports in question are capital equipment, on which duties are typically very low, investment is encouraged to be more capital-intensive than is desirable; this raises capital-output ratios, reduces the growth realizable from a given amount of saving, and limits employment creation. These effects are reinforced by the habit of legislating minimum wage rates (see Chapter 8) and of constraining interest rates (Chapter 13). The combined effects of typical import substitution policies on wages, interest rates, and capital-equipment imports can be substantial. Table 16–2 shows that the ratio of wages to

TABLE 16–2 Relative Costs of Labor and Capital under Import Substitution (changes in percent)

Country	Year(s)	Increase in labor costs due to wage policies	Reduction in annual capital costs due to trade, fiscal, and financial policies[a]	Increase in ratio of wages to annual capital costs
Argentina	1973	15	17 (8)	38
Pakistan	1961–64	0	76 (38)	316
Tunisia	1972	20	36 (30)	87

[a] Amounts in parenthesis are changes due to trade policy alone.
Source: World Bank, *World Development Report 1987*, p. 126.

annual capital costs was raised by 38 to 316 percent in Argentina, Pakistan, and Tunisia due to import substitution policies.

Salvaging Import Substitution

The obvious flaws of import substitution, coupled with the general shift toward market-regulated approaches to development, have led most economists to condemn—and many policy-makers to abandon—strategies of development that depend heavily on protection of domestic producers.[9] Yet industrialization is still a prime goal of most developing countries and is probably essential for most of them to sustain rising average productivity over extended periods. If domestic entrepreneurs, managers, and workers are to learn how to manufacture new products using new technologies, they require some form of protection from outside competition.[10] How can the failure of protection be reconciled with its continuing need?

Import substitution as often practiced has been **inward-looking**, as governments have seemed willing to promote domestic manufacturing almost at any cost to the rest of the economy. This attitude has led to the excesses of policy and the dead ends of industrialization described in this chapter. The infant-industry concept, the intellectual wellspring of import substitution, also provides the salvation of protection as a development tool: Protect only those industries that can eventually compete as exporters or as import substituters without protection and only if the initial costs of protection are fully compensated by the eventual benefits of domestic production. Use moderate and temporary subsidies or tariffs to achieve such protection, and never use quotas. Such a policy might be called **outward-looking** import substitution. The goal of international competitiveness implied by this approach strongly disciplines policymakers to avoid the worst excesses of inward-looking strategies. The next chapter describes how outward-looking strategies work.

9. Two excellent articles summarizing the experience of import substitution are John H. Power, "Import Substitution as an Industrialization Strategy," *The Philippine Economic Journal* 5 (1966): 167–204, and Henry J. Bruton, "The Import Substitution Strategy of Economic Development," *The Pakistan Development Review* 10 (1970): 123–146 [excerpts reprinted in *Leading Issues in Economic Development*, 3d ed. G. M. Meier, ed. (New York: Oxford University Press, 1976), pp. 747–752].

10. Henry Bruton provides a compelling statement of this necessity in his article for the *Handbook of Development Economics,* cited in footnote 1.

17

Outward-Looking Development

The inward-looking strategy of import substitution is one way to accelerate changes in comparative advantage. An alternative approach is an **outward-looking strategy** targeted directly at exporting manufactured goods. Although import substitution is a part of most outward-looking strategies, it is not an end in itself, but only a first step on the way to an internationally competitive industry. Outward-looking development has deep roots in neoclassical economics, but the strategy is defined as much by its practice in East Asia as by market-oriented theories of development. South Korea, Taiwan, Hong Kong and Singapore—variously called the *gang of four,* the *four tigers,* and, less colorfully but generically, the **newly industrializing countries (or economies),** have been the exemplars of outward-looking development. This chapter begins by defining outward-looking development and exploring its practice in East Asia. It then goes on to discuss protectionism in the industrial countries, which could thwart outward-looking strategies, and trade among the developing countries, which could enhance the strategy.

OUTWARD-LOOKING STRATEGIES

Outward-looking development is more than simply promoting manufactured exports. Countries such as Pakistan and Colombia have attempted, with some temporary success, to encourage the export of manufactures by embedding subsidies and other aids within basically inward-looking regimes.

As Chapter 16 explained, the lure of profits in protected domestic industries usually distracts investors from the tougher job of finding and competing in overseas markets. A government pursuing an outward-looking strategy has to turn the entire incentive system inside out and make it more profitable for firms to sell overseas than at home. Most economists have associated such outward-focused incentive regimes with the market economy, as defined in Chapter 5. Indeed, most of the market-based reforms described there are usually aimed at achieving an outward-facing posture. But in practice things are not so simple. The next section explains why.

Markets, Controls and Exports

The debate on market reforms has generally been couched in terms of dichotomous models: controlled, command, *dirigiste*, socialist, or Soviet-type economies versus liberal, market-based, capitalist, or mixed economies. In Chapter 5, however, we suggested five conditions that are essential to achieve market-based systems. Consider three of these: (1) goods must be available through market mechanisms, rather than through controls administered by government, (2) prices must reflect relative economic scarcities, and (3) there must be competition, either from within or from outside the domestic market. We can use these dimensions of market orientation to understand the outward-looking strategy of development.

Figure 17–1 categorizes a few countries and development strategies in terms of the first two dimensions: controls over the allocation of factors, goods and services versus distortions of market prices from relative scarcities.[1] Placement of particular countries on the graph is only a rough

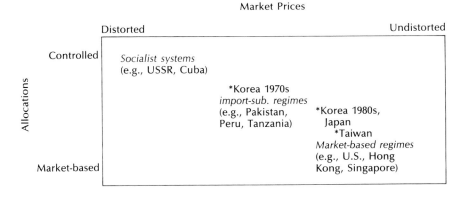

FIGURE 17–1 **Market Orientation and Strategy.** The neoclassical ideal of an outward-looking country would fall into the southeast corner, with few quantitative controls and mostly undistorted relative prices. But Korea, especially in the 1970s, and Japan, though strongly outward-looking, used government controls and accepted price distortions more than the most market-oriented regimes. Taiwan came closer to the market-oriented model. The relative placement of countries on this graph is intended to represent their strategies very approximately.

1. These two dimensions are not independent, because controls over quantities, such as import quotas, also contribute to price distortions. But the distinction is useful for our purposes even if not formally correct.

approximation of their comparative economic strategies. The neoclassical

ideal of an outward-looking policy regime lies in the southeast corner of the diagram, with few quantitative controls and little price distortion. However, the essence of outward-looking development is not the absence of market interventions or distortions; the essence is an incentive system that induces firms to seek export markets. Two of the most successful exporting countries, Japan and Korea, have at various times used nonmarket allocations and accepted or even encouraged price distortions. It is even possible for a Soviet-type regime in the northwest corner of Figure 17–1 to be outward-oriented, if it could use its controls to force firms into export markets and design pro-export incentives for its enterprises. Although some East European regimes made moves in this direction even before the demise of communism, none achieved great success as exporters.

Neoclassical economists naturally emphasize the market-oriented features of outward-looking regimes and pronounce these essential for success. They prescribe, not a bias towards exports, though that is acceptable, but rather a regime that is neutral in its treatment of exports, import-substitutes, and nontraded goods. In the neoclassical world, the market determines most allocations and prices, and the government is left to correct for the market failures described in Chapter 5. Hence private firms, governed by markets, determine what is produced for the home market and for export. In this world, the outward-looking strategy is simply the outcome of market forces. This prescription has dominated the literature on development for the past two decades and formed the basis for most programs of structural adjustment towards a more outward orientation.[2]

The examples of Japan and South Korea, however, have given rise to some dissenting voices, emphasizing the interventionist aspects of export-oriented regimes. In her recent study of South Korea, for example, economist Alice Amsden identifies **learning by doing** as the crucial achievement for countries borrowing existing technologies in order to industrialize in the twentieth century. Not only must economies adopt new technologies, but they must develop modern economic institutions such as corporations and capital markets. As we have seen in Chapter 16, protection is often essential to encourage such learning. In Japan and South Korea, governments protected fledgling industries, and thereby distorted prices, but also intervened to force the pace of technological adoption and learning and to push firms into export markets. This was done by controlling and subsidizing credit; paradoxically, by protecting most in the domestic market those firms that sold most overseas; and, in South Korea, by rewarding firms in various ways for meeting export targets while punishing those that failed.

---

2. Four prominent economists who strongly influenced thinking about inward versus outward strategies are Gustav Ranis, "Industrial Sector Labor Absorption," *Economic Development and Cultural Change* 21 (1973): 387–408; Anne O. Krueger, *Foreign Trade Regimes and Economic Development: Liberalization Attempts and Consequences* (Cambridge, Mass: Ballinger, 1978); Jagdish N. Bhagwati, *Foreign Trade Regimes and Economic Development: Anatomy and Consequences of Exchange Control Regimes* (Cambridge, Mass: Ballinger, 1978); and Bela Balassa, "The Process of Industrial Development and Alternative Development Strategies," *Essays in International Finance* No. 141, Princeton, N.J., International Finance Section, Economics Department, Princeton University, 1980.

Amsden sees such government "market-augmenting" management of the economy, down to the detailed guidance of investment decisions by firms, as the quintessence of twentieth century industrialization.[3]

Japan and South Korea demonstrate that carefully targeted government intervention can augment market mechanisms and force the pace of export-oriented industrialization. However, the more that intervention replaces or augments market mechanisms, the stiffer the requirements for success. Shrewd and incorruptible officials are needed to pick industrial "winners"—firms that will eventually compete successfully in world markets—and to permit "losers" to collapse. And firms, once chosen and cossetted by government, have somehow to be forced or induced to behave like competitive, profit-maximizing entities that continually pursue export markets. Few governments have sufficient numbers of trained and disciplined officials to carry out such a strategy. Moreover, interventions of this type lead directly to **clientelistic** relationships in which government officials and the private firms they assist become mutually dependent on each other's support. Then it is very difficult for officials to remain objective and disciplined in rewarding winners and punishing losers.[4]

The result, more often than not, has been the kind of rent-seeking, distorted, import-substituting regimes described in the previous chapter. Such regimes can engender learning, create new institutions, and promote industrialization. But they do so at a high cost to the state's welfare and with little prospect of attaining international competitiveness. Japan and South Korea have been important exceptions. For most countries, export-oriented industrialization seems to require a policy mix strongly oriented toward market mechanisms, albeit with market-augmenting interventions that are disciplined by infant-industry considerations. Taiwan, Hong Kong, and Singapore have been closest to this model. In the next pages we explore the main elements of outward-oriented policy regimes.

Protection Revisited

It may seem strange to return to the topic of protection in a chapter on export orientation, because exports cannot be protected as import substitutes can. However, protection is a relative concept. One line of production can be protected only if other lines are less-protected. Factors of production, especially investment in new capital, flow towards those industries that promise the highest rewards. If one or a few industries receive protection from external competition, they will attract investment in preference to others. But if all possible activities receive the same protection, none has an advantage over others and there is, in the only meaningful sense, no protection.

Furthermore, exports and even nontraded goods can be "protected" if

---

3. Alice Amsden, *Asia's New Giant: South Korea and Late Industrialization* (New York: Oxford University Press, 1989).
4. Howard Pack and Larry E. Westphal, "Industrial Strategy and Technological Change," *Journal of Development Economics* 22 no. 1 (June 1986): 87–128, describe the requirements for successful intervention, with special reference to South Korea.

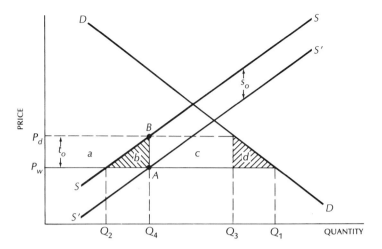

FIGURE 17–2 Equivalence of Tariffs and Subsidies. The domestic supply and demand curves for steel or textiles are SS and DD. At the world price of P_w, Q_1 would be consumed and Q_2 produced. A tariff t_o permits the domestic price to rise to $P_d = P_w(1 + t_o)$; consumption falls to Q_3 and production rises to Q_4 (see Figure 16–1). If, instead of a tariff, the steel industry were given an equal subsidy, $s_o = t_o$, the effective supply curve shifts from SS to $S'S'$. Domestic production is again at Q_4 and the producers receive the same price as with the tariff, $P_d = P_w(1 + s_o)$. However, consumers now purchase Q_1 instead of Q_3 and pay the world price P_w instead of P_d. The subsidy is the area P_wABP_d, paid by taxpayers instead of consumers. The deadweight loss is the shaded triangles b plus d under a tariff, but only triangle b under a subsidy.

we broaden the term to include, not only tariffs, but subsidies and other preferential treatment, which can provide the same relative profitability as tariffs. If textile production receives a 20 percent protective tariff while steel production receives a 20 percent subsidy, there is no change in their relative profitability. The only difference is that textile consumers pay for that industry's protection whereas taxpayers, through government, pay for the steel industry's protection. Figure 17–2 shows the equivalence of tariffs and subsidies.

Economists generally prefer the use of subsidies instead of protective tariffs because, as shown in Figure 17–2, consumers purchase more of a good under a subsidy whereas society pays no more for production than under an equivalent tariff. Thus welfare losses under a subsidy, triangle b, are smaller than those under an equivalent tariff, triangles b plus d.[5] Also, because subsidies usually appear in the government's budget and must be financed through taxation, there is an annual accounting for the costs of protection offered in this way. Government is, therefore, more restrained in conferring this kind of protection and is correspondingly more likely to adhere to infant-industry rules and keep protection moderate and short-lived.[6] In addition, subsidies can be more precisely targeted than protective

---

5. This ignores the additional distortions introduced when government tries to finance the subsidy by raising additional tax revenue.

6. But not necessarily. The United States and especially the European Community have subsidized their farmers for decades at rates that rival the effective rates protection provided for industry by import substitution regimes.

tariffs. Whatever the source of high costs—expensive capital, high wage rates, or lack of trained workers—subsidies can be paid to offset those costs. Protective tariffs, by contrast, can only compensate by raising the domestic price of output.

This broader view of protection, incorporating both tariffs and subsidies, is measured by the **effective rate of subsidy** (ERS), a concept derived from the effective rate of protection (ERP), defined in Chapter 16. The formula for ERS is similar to that for ERP (Equation 16–4) and its implications are the same. However, the ERS incorporates five elements, two of which are not in the ERP: (1) tariffs on imports competing with domestic output and on inputs, t_o and t_i, as under ERP; (2) subsidies on outputs and inputs paid directly to the industry, s_o and s_i (although not mentioned in Chapter 16, such subsidies ought to be included in Equation 16–4 as part of the ERP); (3) the premiums due to quota restrictions on imports, q_o and q_i (which could also have been included in the ERP of Equation 16–4); (4) relative subsidies in the form of preferential corporate income taxes that are lower than the average paid by other industries, s_t; and (5) relative subsidies in the form of below-average interest rates on loans, s_b. Because the last two elements are calculated as deviations from average rates of tax or interest, they can be either positive or negative for any industry, though for the entire economy they each must sum to zero. The formula for ERS, derived from equation 16–4, is

$$\text{ERS} = [t_o + s_o + q_o - a_i(t_i - s_i + q_i) + s_t + s_b]/(1 - a_i). \qquad [17\text{--}1]$$

The ERS is a comprehensive indicator of the extent to which protection affects the relative profitability of various industries. Under import substitution regimes, the ERS is expected to be highest for firms that compete with imports in the domestic market, as is true for the ERP. Under an outward-looking policy regime, however, import-substituting industries should not be favored over export industries; the ERS should be more uniform, with less variance among industries. Table 17–1 shows the ERS for six economies in the late 1960s. Argentina and Israel display the pattern typical of import-substituting countries: the ERS for export-oriented industries is much lower than that for industries selling primarily in the domestic market. By contrast, considering all industries, South Korea's regime is nearly neutral between exports and domestic sales, whereas Taiwan's is biased in favor of exports. Within manufacturing, Singapore and Taiwan have nearly neutral regimes, whereas South Korea shows a pro-export bias, the opposite of Argentina.

Table 17–1 captures the essence of outward-looking policies, which turn incentives inside out. Allowing for all impacts of policy, relative prices favor domestic firms less and export firms more. Neoclassical economists prefer that incentives be neutral and determined as much as possible by market mechanisms. But neutral or pro-export incentives can be achieved through market interventions and subsidies, as in South Korea, where government took a number of steps to favor exporters. Government-controlled banks loaned to export firms, especially large ones, at preferential interest rates, whereas other firms were forced to borrow in the informal credit

TABLE 17–1 **Effective Rates of Subsidy, 1969 (percent)**

	All industries		Manufacturing	
	Exports	Domestic sales	Exports	Domestic sales
Inward-looking:				
Argentina	−17	55	−29	116
Colombia	−12	−1	10	32
Israel	19	79	38	82
Outward-looking:				
South Korea	9	10	14	7
Singapore	1	8	−1	4
Taiwan	16	2	21	17

Source: Bela Balassa and Associates, *Industrial Strategies in Semi-Industrialized Countries* (Baltimore: Johns Hopkins Press, 1982).

market at higher interest rates. During the 1960s, when import controls were tight, export firms were given licenses for imported inputs in excess of their needs for export production; the balance would be used to produce for the highly profitable domestic market. Income taxes were lower for export firms, either through lower tax rates or informally, as tax authorities winked at tax evasion by firms meeting their export targets. And the South Korean government invested heavily in ports, roads, communications, and other infrastructure required by exporters. The measures used in South Korea are similar to policies employed in the import substitution regimes of other countries. But in South Korean a firm could not take advantage of market distortions unless it met stringent export targets; the capture of rents thus depended on export growth.

Exchange Rate Management

An outward-looking regime structures price incentives that encourage investors to create or enter export industries. Investors earn returns over several years and so must be assured that the incentive structure will continue in place for the long term. If investors perceive that the incentive system may swing against exports in the foreseeable future, they will be discouraged from developing export industries. This suggests that the tariff, subsidy, and tax rates should, if they are correctly structured, remain the same for long periods. If change is needed, as when tariff reform is essential or when infant industries are being protected temporarily, it should be done on a schedule that is published in advanced and adhered to strictly.

The exchange rate plays a central role in maintaining outward-oriented incentives. The **real exchange rate,** introduced in Chapter 15, is given as

$$RER = R_o P_w / P_d. \qquad [17-2]$$

RER is an index of the real exchange rate; R_o is an index of the official or nominal exchange rate, determined by the central bank; P_w is an index of world prices, generally taken to be a weighted average price in foreign currency of a country's imports; and P_d is an index of domestic prices, either a wholesale or consumer price index.[7] Recall from Table 15–3 how the appreciation of the real exchange rate through rapid inflation will reduce the profitability of any firm producing tradable goods, that is, exports or import-competing goods. It is precisely such real rate appreciation that haunts investors most, because the real exchange rate can be the most volatile price in the economy. If it does fluctuate widely, it makes profits less certain and reduces expected profitability of investments in exports.

Thus an important indicator of an outward-looking-policy regime is, first, that the exchange rate be set at a level that makes it profitable to invest in exports and, second, that the real exchange rate be maintained at a steady level over long periods. The central bank, which usually manages the exchange rate, has two instruments to do this. It can change the official exchange rate, and if the budget deficit is under control, it can restrict the rate of money creation to restrain domestic price inflation (see the Appendix). If domestic inflation can be kept no higher than the rate of world price inflation, the official exchange rate can be kept fixed. It is not always within the central bank's power to keep domestic inflation that low, however. To compensate for domestic prices that rise more rapidly than world prices, it will be necessary to devalue the official exchange rate periodically to maintain exporters' incentives.

For much of the period after World War II, governments tried to maintain fixed exchange rates. Devaluation was a rare and destabilizing event, one that often engendered stiff political opposition because it sharply raised prices of widely consumed commodities. In recent years many governments have depoliticized exchange rate management by resorting to more frequent and much smaller devaluations if price inflation required it. This technique of flexible exchange rate management, called a **crawling peg,** is a hallmark of an outward-looking policy regime. Figure 17–3 shows how the South Korean government managed its real exchange rate from 1963 to 1985, a long period during which investors learned to depend on the incentives implicit in the won-dollar exchange rate. After an initial sharp devaluation at the beginning of the period, the index was never permitted to fall more than 13 percent below its 1965 peak.

Although the real exchange rate is widely used, a more comprehensive indicator is the **real effective exchange rate** or REER. It incorporates both the real exchange rate and an index of nominal protection N:

$$\text{REER} = R_o N P_w / P_d. \qquad [17\text{--}3]$$

N and hence REER must be defined separately for exportables and importables. In the case of importables,

$$N_m = (1 + t_m + q_m)^t / (1 + t_m + q_m)^o, \qquad [17\text{--}4]$$

where t, s, and q are the average tariff, subsidy, and quota premium rates, respectively, on imports; the subscript m refers to imports; and the super-

---

7. The Appendix defines an alternative measure of the real exchange rate, the ratio of prices of tradable goods to prices of nontradables, or $R_o P_t / P_n$, with P_t in dollars and P_n in local currency. Both definitions have similar implications.

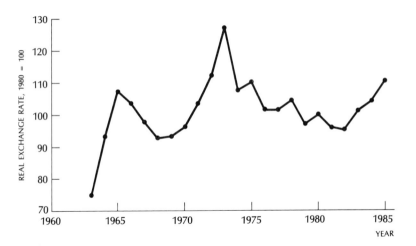

Figure 17–3 **Real Exchange Rate, South Korea, 1963–1985.** The government devalued the official won-dollar rate to compensate for domestic inflation that reached as high as 30 percent in some years and averaged over 15 percent from 1963 to 1980.
Source: Vittorio Corbo and Sang Woo Nam, "The Recent Macroeconomic Evolution of the Republic of Korea: An Overview," World Bank, Economic Research Department, Discussion Paper DRD 208, 1986.

scripts *t* and *o* refer to the current and base years. For exportables,

$$N_e = (1 - t_e + s_e)^t / (1 - t_e + s_e)^o, \qquad [17\text{--}5]$$

where t_e and s_e are the tax and subsidy rates on exports.

In reforming trade regimes to become more outward-looking, t_m and q_m are reduced via tariff reform and deregulation, whereas t_e is reduced and s_e may be increased to increase profits for exporters. Thus a reform would cause $REER_e$ to rise and $REER_m$ to decline. After an outward-looking reform, the policy goal is to ensure both that $REER_e$ not appreciate and that $REER_e$ stays in line with $REER_m$. Because the index N changes very little except during trade reforms, the real exchange rate RER is generally used instead of the more complex and harder to measure real effective exchange rate REER.

Factor Markets and Government Intervention

In the neoclassical version of the outward-looking strategy, relative scarcities of productive factors—land, natural resources, labor, and capital—are the guiding forces behind industrialization, as predicted by the Heckscher-Ohlin theory of comparative advantage (Chapter 15). In labor-surplus, capital-scarce countries, low market wages and high real interest rates dictate labor-intensive choices of both industries and technologies. All the Asian exporters, from Japan to South Korea to Bangladesh, started by exporting textiles, clothing, footwear, wood products, and other labor-intensive products; most of them still depend on such exports. As export and income growth leads to higher savings, and as education spreads and workers become more skilled, industrializing countries shift to new exports, such as steel, ships, machinery, automobiles, and electronics, that use more capital and more skilled workers, including engineers. South Korea and Taiwan have moved quite far along that path. Japan, of course, has gone beyond these products into goods embodying advanced technology.

Well-functioning labor and capital markets ought to generate such transitions automatically. The countries of East and Southeast Asia have, by and large, had labor markets in which wages reflected labor abundance and thus encouraged the first stages of labor-intensive, export-oriented industrialization. Government action to discourage strong labor unions played a hand in keeping wages low. Once the rapidly growing demand for workers absorbed the labor surplus, market wages began to rise. In South Korea this occurred in the late 1960s.

Some newly industrializing countries, however, have not been so pure about their capital markets. During the 1970s, the South Korean government in particular used its control of the major banks to channel credit at below-market interest rates to the large conglomerates or **chaebol** that it favored as vehicles to promote later-stage exports. Other, mostly smaller, firms were forced to borrow in the informal credit (**curb**) market, where interest rates reflected capital scarcity. Real interest rates on loans from banks were negative for several years during the 1970s, whereas curb market rates were 15 to 20 points above bank rates from 1965 to 1985.[8] This two-tiered credit market encouraged the transition into capital-intensive exports, such as steel, ships, and cars, more rapidly than the unaugmented market would have done.

This tendency was reinforced by the South Korean government's policies on technology and firm size. The initial spurt of labor-intensive exports such as textiles, clothing, footwear, and plywood took place in a large number of medium-sized firms. By the 1970s, however, the government was encouraging the *chaebol* to move into steel, ships, automobiles, electronics, chemicals, and other heavy export industries. All the weapons of state economic power were employed, including subsidized credit, preferential taxes, personal favors, and political sanctions. State firms were also employed as vehicles to obtain new technology, notably in the fertilizer, petrochemical, and steel industries, to train South Korean managers and engineers, and in some cases to spawn new firms once the technology had been mastered. Foreign firms were discouraged from entering these markets, where they would have had a competitive advantage. And, key to the entire strategy, government made it clear that the ability to export was the ultimate measure of success.[9] The push into heavy industries in the 1970s failed in many instances and was very costly to the economy, but did result in a range of new export industries and provided a base for reform and expansion in the 1980s. It also accelerated a tendency toward industrial concentration. In 1974 the five largest *chaebol* had combined sales of less than 12

8. Corbo and Nam, "The Recent Macroeconomic Evolution of the Republic of Korea."
9. These policies are described by Amsden, *Asia's New Giant,* and Pack and Westphal, "Industrial Strategy and Technological Change."

Taiwan stayed much closer to the market-based strategy than South Korea, a result of politics more than of economics. The Kuomintang government, exiles from China's mainland, did not wish to share political or economic power with the native Taiwanese, yet wished to encourage rapid development. A strategy that promoted the growth of small firms reconciled these two goals, and this in turn dictated dependence on market mechanisms.[11] From 1966 to 1981, the share of manufacturing workers employed by firms of less than 500 workers actually rose, from 65 to 72 percent; in South Korea, by contrast, the share employed in smaller firms fell from 74 percent to 59 percent. Some large industries were established, mostly controlled by the government or Kuomintang party, and some bank lending was subsidized and directed toward these firms. But the curb market was efficient in channeling credit to small firms, which were the principal exporters, and market allocations were always much more important than government intervention.[12]

OUTCOMES AND LIMITATIONS

Export Achievers

The export accomplishments of the four newly industrializing countries of East and Southeast Asia are summarized in Table 17–2. Over nearly a quarter of a century, all except Singapore enjoyed double-digit annual growth of exports in constant prices. Even Singapore's export growth was twice that of the average middle-income country—a group that contains most of the candidates for near future status as newly industrializing economies. Exports of all four Asian countries were a far higher share of gross domestic product than for the average middle-income country in 1988, and manufactured exports accounted for at least 75 percent of total export earnings. Three other countries of the region—Thailand, Malaysia, and Indonesia—are also shown in the table. They, too, have very open economies, as shown by their relatively high shares of exports in GDP, and are thought to be industrializing on the model of the four Asian tigers.[13] Though their export growth can be favorably compared with that of Singapore, it is clear from the table that Thailand, Malaysia, and Indonesia are much less-developed as exporters of manufactures.

10. Amsden, *Asia's Next Giant*, p. 116. The same caveat applies here as in the discussion of multinational firms in Chapter 14: sales and GNP are not comparable measures. But the large rise in this ratio is indicative.

11. Tun-jen Cheng, "Political Regimes and Development Strategies: South Korea and Taiwan." Gary Gireffi and Donald Wyman, eds. in *Manufacturing Miracles*, Princeton, N.J. (Princeton University Press, 1991).

12. Tyler Biggs and Brian Levy, "Strategic Interventions and the Political Economy of Industrial Policy in Developing Countries," in *Systems Reform in Developing Countries*, D. H. Perkins and M. Roemer, eds. (Cambridge, Mass.: Harvard University Press, 1991), pp. 365–401.

13. Although Indonesia's export share, 25 percent, is below the average for middle-income countries, it is quite high for a country of 175 million people. See Table 15–1.

TABLE 17–2   Export Performance, Seven Asian Outward-Looking Economies, 1965–1988

| Country | Growth of exports, (% per yr) | Share (percent) in 1988 | |
		Exports[a] in GDP	Manufactured exports in total exports[b]
South Korea	22.9	41	93
Taiwan[c]	17.3	n.a.	93
Hong Kong	10.3	136	91
Singapore	7.6	198	75
Thailand	9.5	34	52
Malaysia	6.1	67	49
Indonesia	7.3	25	29
Middle-income countries	3.6	27	68

[a]Exports of goods and nonfactor services.
[b]Commodity exports only.
[c]Data for Taiwan cover 1965 to 1987.
Sources: World Bank, World Development Report 1990, and Council for Economic Planning and Development, Republic of China, Taiwan Statistical Data Book 1989.

Some of the consequences of rapid export growth can be seen from Table 17–3. The most obvious is the impressive expansion of gross domestic product per person: more than 6 percent a year over almost a quarter century for the four tigers, and 4 percent a year for Thailand, Malaysia, and Indonesia. Thus the average South Korean has seen a nearly fivefold multiplication of annual income in little more than a generation, an unprecedented improvement in economic well-being. The rapid growth of value-added in manufacturing indicates that the outward-looking strategy has been associated with industrialization in all these countries, even though the three Southeast Asian economies remain important exporters of primary products.

TABLE 17–3   Growth Outcomes in Seven Asian Outward-Looking Economies, 1965–1988

| Country | Growth rate, in percent per year, of: | | | GDP share of saving[b] 1988 (%) |
	GNP per capita	Value-added in manufacturing	Total factor productivity[a]	
South Korea	6.8	16.9	4.1	38
Taiwan[c]	7.1	12.9	3.9	35
Hong Kong	6.3	—	2.9	33
Singapore	7.2	10.3	3.6	37
Thailand	4.0	9.7	2.5	26
Malaysia	4.0	10.0	2.5	36
Indonesia	4.3	12.4	3.0	25
All middle-income countries	2.3	6.7	0.8[d]	27

[a]Data are for 1963–1983, calculated according to the method reported by Dwight H. Perkins and Moshe Syrquin, "Large Countries: The Influence of Size," in Handbook of Development Economics, Vol. 2, Chenery and Srinivasan, p. 1737.
[b]Gross domestic saving.
[c]Data for Taiwan cover 1965 to 1987.
[d]Calculated for 1960–1982, for all countries reported in Perkins and Syrquin, "Large countries."
Sources: Same as Table 17–3, except total factor productivity (see note a).

In Chapter 3 we showed how the residual term of the sources-of-growth

equation can be interpreted as a measure of the increase in total factor productivity, the best overall indicator of a country's efficiency in achieving income growth. In Chapter 5 we suggested that, in outward-looking countries, competitive forces should result in the rapid growth of productivity. All seven countries listed in Table 17–3, however, have demonstrated far more rapid growth in total factor productivity than the average country over a twenty-year period. At the same time, five of them have saved and invested a larger share of income than is true for the typical middle-income country. From this sample of seven, it appears that outward-looking countries increase their growth rates both through faster accumulation of capital and through greater increases in productivity.

Advantages of Exports

What is it about export-led growth that conveys such advantages over import substitution? The answer to this questions dates back to Adam Smith who, in *The Wealth of Nations,* recognized that export markets would permit factories to produce more of any single item and thus to specialize more than if they produced only for the home market. Longer production runs reduce the setup costs of switching from one product to another, and specialization permits each firm to learn more about manufacturing its products more efficiently. International market competition provides the stimulus to do both.

In the two centuries since *The Wealth of Nations,* economists have embellished the case for export-led growth but not changed its essentials. During much of the twentieth century, innovations in both products and technologies led to plants that had to be large to be efficient (see Chapter 20). Thus in the production of chemicals, metals, automobiles, and other products, the ability to export can be a great advantage to countries with domestic markets that are small in relation to the economic size of a plant. If, as economists hypothesize, industrial productivity improves with practice, then learning by doing can be accelerated by more rapid growth of production, and exports provide an opportunity to increase output. Similarly, higher output combined with greater exposure to world markets enhances the opportunities to observe and adopt new technologies. University of Pennsylvania economist Howard Pack places these advantages in the context of dynamic allocative efficiency: When export markets exist, labor, capital, and even land can be moved rapidly from low- to high-productivity uses without encountering diminishing returns.[14]

When export-led growth is placed in the more comprehensive context of an outward-looking strategy, it has additional advantages. Internationally competitive domestic firms deliver goods to consumers at close to world prices, because home markets are not protected. As a corollary, even single-firm industries cannot exert monopoly power, because they face import

14. These and other observations on the advantages of exports can be found in Howard Pack, "Industrialization and Trade," in *Handbook of Development Economics,* Vol. 2, Chenery and Srinivasan, pp. 333–380.

competition. Because firms have learned how to earn profits in overseas markets, they put less effort into rent seeking, which in any case is severely circumscribed by the open economy. And rapid export growth means rapidly increasing capacity to import, with less danger of the economy running into a foreign exchange constraint.

Transferability to Other Countries

Can countries outside Asia benefit from outward-looking growth? Yes, and several already have done so. Portugal, Spain, and Greece, countries with many characteristics of LDCs, have benefitted from entry into the European Economic Community, discussed later in this chapter, whereas Turkey and Israel have also exported to Europe. Brazil was an export achiever in the 1960s and 1970s, a period that was undermined by unpayable debt and rapid inflation in the 1980s. Colombia has had some success with manufactured exports, and there are signs that Mexico is adopting an outward-looking strategy for the 1990s. In Africa, tiny Mauritius has become a haven for investors in simple export products, largely textiles and clothing. Only a few other African countries, such as Ivory Coast, Kenya, Seychelles, and Zimbabwe, have even approximated the strategy, and for the most part their modest success has been based on agricultural exports.

The worldwide trend toward market-based development was traced in Chapter 5. The economic and especially the political obstacles in the way of market reforms were discussed in that chapter; they apply fully to any radical shift from inward- to outward-looking development strategies. But, given such a shift, recent experience suggests that almost any country can benefit from export-oriented growth. Were all developing countries to adopt the strategy at once, world markets for several manufactured exports could be swamped and the benefits of export orientation would be reduced for each industry. Indeed, some have argued that today's newly industrializing economies face a much steeper path than did Japan or its Asian followers over the past 40 years, for reasons discussed in the next section. However, the rise of new export achievers, such as Thailand, Malaysia, and Indonesia, in the 1980s shows that opportunities do exist for some countries. And there seems little chance that all developing countries will shift to outward-oriented strategies at once. Even if they did, the consequent growth of markets within the developing countries would itself provide new export opportunities—a point also covered later in this chapter.

The precise shape of an outward-looking strategy, and the speed of transition, depends to some extent on a country's endowments. Large countries, such as China, India, Indonesia, or Brazil, have larger internal markets and could grow more rapidly without turning outward than smaller countries. But even for this group, outward orientation can be a powerful stimulus to growth, as shown by Indonesia and, for a time, by Brazil. China and India, because of their size, may face relatively price-inelastic demands for products in which they have a comparative advantage, particularly clothing, textiles, small motors, pumps, and other simple mechanical products. The threat of massive competition from these two giants is a specter that haunts smaller countries just starting their quest for new export markets. Smaller countries, however, have little scope for expansion in their home markets and are compelled to turn outward.

PROTECTION IN
THE NORTH

Countries with rich natural resource endowments, such as fertile land, vast tropical forests, rich mineral deposits, and an inviting climate, may find it more profitable to export the products of these resources for some time before turning to manufactures. For the most part, however, these resources are depleted with use and many of them do not lead inevitably to development, as noted in Chapter 15. Countries that harness resource revenues to outward-looking industrialization can sustain development beyond the exhaustion of their resource base, and at the same time diversify their export base away from the widely fluctuating prices of primary products. This is the route taken by Thailand, Malaysia, and Indonesia. It could be emulated by other primary exporters, but in many cases these countries could also gain a great deal by applying outward-looking principles to their agricultural and natural-resource industries before embarking on industrialization.

PROTECTION IN THE NORTH

As a group, the developing countries have become significant suppliers of manufactured goods. From 1970 to 1986, while the volume of all exports from developing countries rose by just two-thirds, the volume of manufactured exports multiplied 6 times, an annual growth rate of 12 percent a year. Most of these manufactured exports went to industrial market economies, which imported $125 billion of manufactures from developing countries in 1986 (see Table 17–4). Export products range from textiles, clothing, and footwear to wood paneling, machinery, electronics, chemicals, and automobiles. Developing-country exports of manufactures nearly doubled their share of total imports into developed countries from 1970 to 1986, but still accounted for only 12 percent. In clothing, however, developing country exports accounted for 47 percent of total industrial country imports.

The "New" Protectionism

The success of the newly industrializing countries of Asia and Latin America in penetrating northern markets for labor-intensive manufactures, together with Japan's export dynamism, has engendered a reaction popularly called the "new" protectionism. There is not much new about the motives behind this reaction: the northern countries are trying to stop the decline of aging industries that can no longer compete in world markets. In the United States and Europe industries such as textiles, clothing, footwear, chemicals, steel, and automobiles face increasing competition from less costly imports, often products of high quality, produced in Asia and Latin America. Lower wages in the newly industrializing countries are no longer offset by proportionately lower productivity, because of workers' learning by doing; managers, too, have learned how to operate industrial units more productively; and

TABLE 17–4   Exports of Manufactures from Developing Countries to Industrial Countries,[a]
1965–1986

	1965	1986
A. Value of exports (billions of US dollars)		
1. All exports (0–9)[b]	26.0	269.4
2. Manufactures (5–8)	3.8	125.4
a. Chemicals (5)	0.2	5.3
b. Machinery[c] (7)	0.1	39.4
c. Other (6 + 8)	3.5	80.7
1) Textiles (65)	0.7	7.8
2) Clothing (84)	0.3	24.3
B. Share of industrial-country imports (%)		
1. All commodities (0–9)	18.4	18.2
2. Manufactures (5–8)	6.6	12.2
a. Chemicals (5)	2.8	4.4
b. Machinery[c] (7)	1.3	7.9
c. Other (6 + 8)	12.0	19.6
1) Textiles (65)	10.7	18.2
2) Clothing (84)	22.9	46.7

[a] Market economies only, excluding socialist Asian and Eastern European countries and Cuba. (Socialist Asian countries are:
China, North Korea, Vietnam, Mongolia, Cambodia, and Laos.)
[b] Figures in parentheses give the standard industrial trade classification (SITC) for each group of commodities.
[c] Includes vehicles.
Source: United Nations, Yearbook of International Trade Statistics 1987, Vol. 1 (New York: United Nations, 1989), Special
Tables B and C.

in the case of steel and other resource-based products, some LDCs have ready access to raw materials and fuels that were exhausted long ago in the industrial countries. In these and other ways, comparative advantage has shifted toward the developing countries for a range of labor-intensive and resource-based manufactures once produced more efficiently in the industrial countries.

All countries would gain, in the manner described in Chapter 15, if production in these commodities moved to the south, while the north concentrated on temperate-zone farm products, more technologically sophisticated and more capital-intensive exports, and financial, communications, and professional services. Although all countries would gain in the long run, the readjustments require disinvestment from declining industries in the short run, which in turn means temporary unemployment for workers in those industries. Here is a classic example of the general good—widespread benefits among all consumers and the owners and workers of new export industries—being thwarted by the concentrated interests of a narrow range of losing groups—owners and workers of textile and steel mills, and clothing, footwear, and car factories. In the United States, the affected groups lobby members of Congress and often contribute generously to election campaigns. In Europe they work through political parties to write the protection of their specific interest into national policy and into the structure of the European Economic Community, which determines a common trade policy for its member countries. Any attempts to open world markets to freer trade must contend with these pervasive and effective political forces.

The motives for the "new" protectionism, then, are really both old and universal. It is the methods that are considered new. During the 1930s, protectionism was even stronger and more damaging than during the 1980s. The dominant method was high import tariffs. A series of negotiating rounds after World War II reduced the tariffs on most trade to very low levels, although tariffs on goods traded among industrial countries were cut more than goods exported principally by developing countries. In the United States, average tariffs, about 50 percent of import value in the 1930s, had been reduced to only 5 percent by 1985, about the same level as in Europe and Japan. The General Agreement on Tariffs and Trade (GATT) was established as a mechanism to negotiate and then to monitor multilateral tariff reductions. Tariffs under GATT are based on the **most-favored nation** (MFN) principle: all trading partners enjoy the lowest duty rate an importing country accords to any one of its trading partners.

With low tariffs and GATT rules, it became difficult to protect declining industries. Instead, starting in the 1960s, the United States and the EEC began to negotiate **voluntary export restrictions** (VERs) with trading partners, especially Japan and the newly industrializing countries, to restrict the export of sensitive goods such as textiles, cars, and steel. This new mechanism was added to more traditional **nontariff barriers** (NTBs) that are practiced by all countries. These include unilateral restrictions on the quantities of imports, as well as regulations affecting quality standards, packaging, labeling, health inspection, and so forth, established ostensibly to protect consumers but frequently utilized to protect competing domestic manufacturers.

Both VERs and NTBs act to reduce trade. The United States has been aggressively trying to pry open foreign markets and increase its exports by acting unilaterally against countries deemed to have been restricting imports from the United States. In 1988, Congress passed the Omnibus Trade and Competitiveness Act, containing a *Super 301* section that for the first time empowered the President to invoke broad punitive trade measures against any country found to employ unfair trade practices. Prior to 1988, retaliation was restricted to actions on specific products. The aim of Super 301 is to force negotiations that lead to an easing of restrictions against American exports. The principal target was Japan, but several developing countries, including South Korea and Taiwan, have been cited as possible candidates for retaliation, and Brazil and India have actually been named. Super 301 is a hybrid measure. It may work against protection and open a few markets for all countries. Yet it contradicts both the letter and spirit of GATT. Instead of seeking mutually beneficial reforms, negotiated multilaterally and open to all countries, Super 301 sanctions confrontational, unilateral actions taken in the interests of a single country.

The Costs of Protection

It is easy to generalize about the costs of protection: the theory of comparative advantage tells us that any divergence from free trade causes a loss to both trading partners. The losses to an economy from tariff protection of a single industry were illustrated in Figure 17–2 as the deadweight loss, the area of triangles *b* plus *d*. If the industry is protected by voluntary export restraints, the loss to the importing country can be greater. Recall in Figure 17–2 that under tariff protection, area *c* represents revenue to the government, which is not a loss to the country. But under voluntary export restraints, such as the Multifiber Arrangement protecting northern textile manufacturers or Japan's voluntary restriction on car exports to the United States, low-cost exporting firms can capture much or all of this revenue rectangle. Restrictive arrangements make it easy for exporting countries and firms to agree among themselves to share the protected export markets and to charge the higher domestic market prices, P_d in the diagram, even though they can export profitably at the lower world price P_w. This helps explain why such agreements are voluntary: the exporting countries and their firms can gain benefits otherwise accruing to the governments or consumers of the importing countries. Moreover, the result is a less competitive market in which exporters' profits are more stable. These agreements typically exclude potential new exporters, particularly those aspiring to follow the strategy of the newly industrializing countries.

Attempts have been made to estimate the cost to the United States and Canada of protecting jobs in the textile, clothing, auto, and steel industries.[15] The estimate for textile and clothing in the United States incorporates only the costs of tariff protection, that is, the area of the two triangles *b* plus *d* in Figure 17–2. In 1977, this cost was $80,000 per year for each job saved. In both Canada and the United States most workers who lose jobs in these industries find alternative jobs within a year and draw unemployment compensation while out of work. The net loss to these workers averaged $5,600 per person. Hence in the United States society paid $14 in higher-than-necessary costs and prices for every $1 of benefit to the workers whose jobs were saved. In Canada, where the estimate incorporated the higher costs of nontariff barriers, the ratio was $70 of costs to society for every $1 of net income saved by workers who held their jobs. And in the United States auto and steel industries in 1983, the cost of protecting one job was estimated to equal the wages of six workers. It would have been highly advantageous for the United States and Canada to import textiles, clothing, cars, and steel freely and to use a small portion of the resulting benefits to compensate the workers who lost their jobs.

But even these costs do not capture all the losses to importing countries from their own protection. Tariffs or NTBs reduce the volume of imports and keep the exchange rate at higher (overvalued) levels and thus make export industries less competitive in world markets. Reduced exports mean fewer jobs in those industries and some economists believe the net gain in jobs may be negligible. If so, the costs per job saved may, literally, approach infinity. In the United States during the mid-1980s, protection contributed to the overvaluation of the dollar which, in turn, made it more difficult to export farm products and to compete with Japan in electronics. This helped

---

15. World Bank, *World Development Report 1984*, p. 40, and *1987*, p. 152.

to put many farmers out of business and probably reduced potential
employment in electronics.

Why does such protection survive, even though the losses to society as a whole are far greater than the gains to protected labor and capital? The losses are widely spread across large populations of consumers, who may not always be aware of the costs. The smaller gains, in contrast, accrue to concentrated groups of workers, managers, and owners of protected industries, who are fully aware of these gains and fight vigorously to preserve them. The gains and losses from government interventions and market distortions are often distributed this way; this helps to explain why societies resist reforms.[16]

The costs to developing countries are also high. Protection limits their gains from trade and reduces potential growth for all the reasons that outward-looking strategies have proved superior to inward-looking ones. If Japan, Korea, and Mexico find they cannot expand their exports because of protection in the north, then India, Colombia, Kenya, and others will be discouraged from attempting to utilize exports to stimulate development. Countries facing large debt burdens will be unable to generate the foreign exchange to repay their loans, which will probably reduce the capital available to all developing countries (see Chapter 14). With the potential losses so high on both sides, it would seem natural that a way would be found to reduce protection and liberalize trade.

Multilateral Trade Reform

The various postwar negotiations to reduce tariffs were tedious and difficult, but successful. Negotiations to halt the new protectionism have been much more difficult. The most recent attempt to negotiate further trade liberalization has been the "Uruguay round," held under the auspices of the GATT. Negotiators from member countries have attempted to lower trade barriers on several fronts at once. First, in agriculture, the United States, Australia, and other exporters have tried to reduce agricultural subsidies, especially those paid by the EEC to farmers of grains and dairy products. Developing countries could benefit from an end to restrictions on imports of sugar, beef, and other products by the industrial countries. The World Bank estimates that restrictions on sugar and beef imports cost developing-country exporters over $12 billion in foreign exchange in 1983, more than half the total value of all industrial countries' aid programs that year.[17]

The second area for reform is textiles. The developing countries are hoping to phase out the Multi-Fiber Arrangement over a number of years and end the restrictions on world trade in textiles and clothing that have become more binding since their introduction in the 1960s. Third, the United States in particular has been pushing for an agreement that would lower restric-

16. A general statement of this problem is contained in Mancur Olsen, *The Rise and Decline of Nations* (New Haven, Conn.: Yale University Press, 1982).

17. World Bank, *World Development Report 1985,* p. 41.

tions on trade in services, including banking, insurance, telecommunications, transport, construction, tourism, and professional services. These industries are typically heavily protected in developing countries, who fear their domestic firms could not compete with foreign ones. Fourth, producers in the rich countries want developing countries to respect patents, trademarks, and other intellectual property rights that are strongly protected in Europe and North America. Piracy and counterfeiting have become common practice in developing countries, which have tried to avoid the higher costs of importing or manufacturing goods under patents and trademarks. The benefits of improved protection for intellectual property would accrue almost entirely to the wealthier countries whose citizens and corporations own the patents and trademarks. Finally, the developed countries are seeking to reduce the many barriers to investment by their firms in developing countries.[18]

At the heart of the negotiating process must be the acceptance by all countries, north and south, of the need for structural adjustment of their economies. In the industrial countries, the interests of exporters and consumers will have to prevail over those of declining, import-competing industries. This task will be easier if there are obvious gains to be made in exporting those items in which industrial countries now appear to have comparative advantage, especially some temperate-zone farm products, manufactures based on advanced technology, and services like finance and management consulting. But in these areas the southern countries themselves become protectionist. Brazil, aspiring to build its own capabilities, makes it difficult for U.S. firms to bid on telecommunications projects. Banking is one of the most protected industries throughout the world, and most countries favor their own nationals whenever professional services are considered. These are, of course, legitimate means to develop and add to human and technical capabilities by learning through doing. But trade is necessarily reciprocal. If northern countries are to show the political will to overcome the special interests favoring protection, southern economies will have to become more open to imports of many products and services in which they are not efficient and which they have been protecting. This is, of course, the essence of the outward-looking strategy of development.

INTEGRATION IN THE SOUTH

The developing countries, frustrated by their inability to gain wider access to industrial-country markets or to improve their terms of trade with these markets, have exhorted each other to form larger and more meaningful regional trade groups. In essence groups of developing countries would try to stimulate development by granting preferential access to each other's exports, placing relatively less emphasis on access to industrial-country markets. Table 17–5 shows that the value of trade among developing coun-

---

18. For a review of these negotiations, and of all the issues discussed in this section, see "A Survey of World Trade," *The Economist,* (Special Section, September 22, 1990).

TABLE 17–5   Trade among Developing Market Countries[a]

	1970	1986
A. Value of intra-LDC exports (US dollars billion)		
1. All exports (SITC 0–9)	10.8	117.0
2. Manufactures (5–8)	3.5	50.5
B. Share of intra-LDC trade in total LDC exports[b] (%)		
1. All exports (0–9)	19.7	27.7
2. Manufactures (5–8)	26.5	26.3

[a]Excludes Cuba and socialist countries in Asia.
[b]By current market value.
Source: United Nations, *Yearbook of International Trade Statistics 1987*, Special Tables B and C.

tries multiplied 11 times from 1970 to 1986; allowing for inflation, intrasouth trade more than tripled in real terms. For manufactured exports the quantity of intrasouth trade expanded fourfold over those 16 years. However, the share of manufactured exports in total developing-country exports did not change. Proponents of regional trade groups hope that greater economic integration among developing countries would increase the importance of intra-LDC trade to the benefit of all participants.

Three systems of trade arrangements can be defined, in increasing degree of economic integration. **Free-trade areas** eliminate tariffs among member countries, though each member is permitted to set its imports from the outside world. The European Free-Trade Association was a prominent example before it was largely absorbed in the European Economic Community. The Latin American Free-Trade Association is the largest current example. The trade agreement between the United States and Canada, should it eventually include Mexico, would become a North American free trade zone. Because members are typically free to set their own external tariffs, free-trade associations represent minimal cooperation and integration. **Customs unions** also eliminate tariffs among members, but go beyond free-trade areas by erecting a common external tariff against imports from the rest of the world. This is sometimes a stated aim of trade groupings, such as the Andean Pact among countries along the west coast of Latin America, but it has been difficult to achieve. The Preferential Trade Area of eastern and southern African countries, which began in 1984 to reduce internal tariffs for selected commodities, was intended to become a full-fledged customs union in the 1990s.

Common markets move several steps closer to full integration. In addition to free trade among members and a common external tariff, common markets either eliminate or substantially reduce restrictions on the movements of labor and capital among member states. They may go further to promote coordinated fiscal, monetary, and exchange-ratio policies and may cooperate in many others ways. Both the Central American Common Market and the East African Community had achieved important elements of economic integration until political differences among members destroyed each grouping. The European Economic Community (EEC) is the most integrated group in the world today. It has largely eliminated tariffs and customs procedures among its 13 member states. By 1992 there is to be harmonization of all taxes, fees, regulations, and procedures affecting trade among the 12. Discussions have been held for some time about a common monetary policy for the entire community and national currencies are already tied together at fixed exchange rates. Some European leaders have even talked optimistically about eventual political union.

Static Gains from Integration

Customs unions (which we use here as a shorthand for all regional preferential trading arrangements) may benefit their members by conveying **static gains,** in the form of a one-time improvements in resource allocations, and by offering **dynamic gains,** stimulating investment in production for export and linked industries. The traditional analysis of the static gains from customs unions makes the distinction between trade creation and trade diversion.

Trade is **created** when a new customs union, which lowers the duty on imports from all member countries, permits some member, say, country A, to export more to another, country B, by displacing production of country B's own industries. The import-competing industry in country B was presumably able to sell in the home market because the protective duty shielded it from the exports of more efficient, lower-cost industries in other countries. When the customs union lowers the duty on exports from other member countries, more efficient industries in those countries can then compete with country B's firms in their own markets. More is traded than before, hence the term **trade creation.** Although some producers in country B are disadvantaged by the change, presumably there are others that benefit from the lower duties in other member countries' markets, and of course consumers benefit from lower prices and wider selection. Gains from trade creation are analogous to gains from the opening of trade (see Chapter 15) except that they take place in the limited world of the customs union.

Because customs unions also discriminate against outside countries, they may cause **trade diversion** by permitting member country A to export more to country B and displace imports previously bought from a nonmember country. If before the union country B had a most-favored-nation tariff, i.e., all other nations were treated equally, then the outside country's exports must have been cheaper than those of country A, or else country B would have imported from country A in the first place. Once the union is formed, consumers in country B will buy from producers in country A at a lower cost to the consumers, because of the preferential tariff, but at a higher cost in foreign exchange to the country as a whole. Part of the revenue previously earned on imports from nonmember countries is now paid to exporters in country A, who are less efficient producers than their outside competitors.

From each member country's standpoint the customs union is beneficial if trade creation outweighs trade diversion. This is more likely to be the case if customs union partners have different relative resource endowments or if their consumers have different tastes, so that the members have a comparative advantage in the export of different commodities. For example, if Mexico, with a comparative advantage in vegetables and petroleum, were to join in a customs union with Colombia, with a comparative advantage in coffee and textiles (to oversimplify greatly), trade is likely to be created and both countries would benefit. But on the whole neighboring developing countries tend to export similar goods and there is a presumption that trade diversion would be large. In the East African Community, for example, much of the trade in manufactured goods came from industries, such as tire manufacturing in Kenya, that could not compete with the outside world. Tanzania and Uganda had to pay higher prices for these manufactures than if they had purchased from outside the market. Note that even if, on balance, trade creation within the union exceeds trade diversion, so long as there is some diversion nonmember countries are losers.

Dynamic Gains and Risks of Integration

Most advocates of customs unions among developing countries argue that the major gains are not static, but dynamic. Customs unions widen the market for industries in all member countries, with the attendant benefits noted earlier in this chapter. Economies of scale may be realized by some industries whose output would be too small if confined to the home market. One potentially important, if largely unimplemented, feature of the Andean Pact and the Association of Southeast Asian Nations (ASEAN) is the **complementation agreement,** under which large-scale infant industries are allocated to member countries. Then each member can benefit from, while each shares the costs of, starting industries such as petrochemicals, fertilizer, pulp and paper, vehicle manufacture, and basic metals.

Customs unions also increase competition among producers in the member countries. This can be especially important for large-scale industries that would otherwise monopolize home markets at efficient levels of output. But it can have a much more pervasive effect and sharpen entrepreneurial and managerial performance in all industries. Intensified competition is thought to have played a major role in stimulating European growth after the formation of the EEC and may have contributed to the temporary success of the Central American Common Market as well. One manifestation of increased competition is a characteristic pattern of trade in customs unions: much of the new trade is in similar or even identical products. Members will export canned foods, shoes, clothing, cosmetics, metal products, capital equipment, vehicles, and other products to each other. To some extent this represents specialization in fine detail; one textile firm narrows its products to concentrate on the few things it does especially well. To some extent it may represent more efficient subregional patterns of trade, a realignment to reduce transport costs once borders no longer serve as barriers. But a lot of the trade in similar goods may reflect greater competition and a wider range of choice for consumers. In any event, trade in similar goods certainly belies the trade creation approach, which predicts that countries will gain only if they export dissimilar goods.

These dynamic effects act over the long run to induce greater investment and hence accelerate growth within the customs union, and to restructure the economy toward exports of all kinds and toward industries that might otherwise have a difficult time getting started. Given these advantages, why are there so few examples of successful customs unions in the developing world? One major problem has been the distribution of the gains, whether static or dynamic. The East African Community illustrated this point. When it was functioning well, both Tanzania and Uganda believed that Kenya benefitted most from the resulting development of manufacturing. Kenya, which had moved faster to industrialize, was better able to take advantage of the customs union and exported more to its neighbors than it imported. Once Kenyan industries began to export, more investment flowed into Kenya to take advantage of the industrial infrastructure and the central location of Nairobi. Thus Kenya, and in particular the capital city of Nairobi, acted as a growth pole for the whole East African market. Growth poles are often considered desirable in developing countries, but not when the pole is outside one's own borders. The increasing concentration of gains in the more advanced members of common markets causes the less-advanced partners to resist integration, to avoid becoming backwaters. This contributed to the demise of the East African experiment and has helped to dampen the ardor of countries like Bolivia and Ecuador for the Andean Pact.

The concentration of gains—real or perceived—in the more-advanced member countries leads to political tensions that sometimes exacerbate the political problems among neighboring countries. Conversely, political disagreements among neighbors, which are probably inevitable, become much more dangerous when those neighbors are tied together in customs unions or other economic arrangements. Each partner, but especially the economically less-advanced ones, can use participation as a whip to threaten other partners if decisions are not taken in its favor. Political tensions among Uganda, Tanzania, and Kenya eventually destroyed the East African Community. Chile withdrew from the Andean Pact over political disagreements with Peru and other countries. The potential for such schisms always exists and substantially increases the risk a country takes when it enters an integration scheme. Certainly the country can reap substantial economic benefits from integration with its neighbors. But to achieve these gains it must develop its economy in ways that may not make much sense in the absence of a customs union. Malaysia might invest in a fertilizer plant intended to serve the ASEAN countries. But if the free-trade area does not develop, or if political arguments make it ineffective, Malaysia has considerably more fertilizer capacity than it can use, especially if it remains a high-cost producer. This kind of example, multiplied over several industries, could lead to serious dislocation and stagnation if the customs union breaks up.

Will the developing countries move toward greater trade with each other? The potential advantages are great, but so are the risks. To be successful, any integration plan must bring the promise of substantial additional investment in the foreseeable future and must provide for a broad and equitable distribution of the benefits of union. Member countries will have to be governed by leaders who recognize common interests and are prepared to

cooperate with their neighbors. Even this cannot rule out the risk of political change and future disagreements that cripple the union. The political
risks are reduced, however, the wider the membership of the union, so that
no single country can destroy the arrangement by withdrawing. Thus the
newly emerging Preferential Trade Area of eastern and southern Africa has
a better chance of avoiding crippling political conflicts than did the East
African Community.

Trading Blocs

Trading arrangements are changing rapidly in the 1990s. The Eastern European trading bloc, COMECON, has become a victim of political and economic reform in the Soviet Union and its former satellite countries. While
COMECON disintegrated was, its neighbor, the EEC, has been strengthening the ties among members. The United States, having entered a free-
trade agreement with Canada, now seeks to get Mexico to join a North
American free-trade area. Japanese trade, investment, and aid dominate
economic relations among the countries of East and Southeast Asia, and
create a *de facto* economic sphere of influence, though decidedly not a
formal trade arrangement. These newly emerging trading blocks may begin
to supplant the global, multilateral trading arrangements, governed by GATT,
that have guided international trade for almost five decades since World
War II. How will the changes affect developing countries?

The answer, of course, depends. The EEC has always granted preferential access to exports from its members' former colonies in Africa and
the Caribbean and has not been markedly more protectionist toward other
developing countries than the United States and Japan. Although some
observers see a more protectionist Europe emerging after 1992, it is far
from clear that internal harmonization will imply greater protection against
the outside world. If a North American free-trade zone does emerge, then
Mexico would presumably benefit from its easier access to this large market at the expense of other developing countries. The big losers would be
other Latin American countries, which may however be invited to join the
agreement, and the aggressive exporters of East and Southeast Asia, which
have depended heavily on the U.S. market. It is doubtful whether Japan
could replace the United States as an export destination for the latter countries. The populous countries of South Asia, notably Bangladesh, India,
and Pakistan, have not been prominently mentioned as candidates for
inclusion in any of the emerging blocs.

The possible emergence of three large regional trading blocs creates a
great deal of uncertainty for all countries. Until more is known about these
new trading arrangements, it is difficult to make reliable predictions about
their impact on world trade. The potential exists for substantial trade diversion and an unequal distribution of dynamic gains away from excluded
nations, toward those within the new trading agreements. The threat of
losses among many developing countries may be a spur to new arrange-

ments to stimulate trade among southern nations. It may alternatively give a boost to reforms in worldwide, multilateral trade under GATT or a successor organization and reduce the importance of trading blocs. The advantages of outward orientation for both developing and industrial countries argue in favor of multilateral trade reforms in preference to a strengthening of regional trading blocs, however organized.

PART 5

SECTORS

18

Agriculture

Understanding the nature of agriculture is fundamental to understanding development. The labor-surplus and neoclassical models presented in Chapter 3 dealt primarily with the nature of the relationship between the industrial and agricultural sectors. The problem of income distribution or extremes of poverty within developing nations discussed in Chapter 4 is substantially a question of how to do something about the rural poor. Nutrition, discussed in Chapter 10, is a question of food production and distribution. And the contribution of exports to development, as treated in Chapter 15, is for many countries a question of creating agricultural exports.

Much of this book has been about **rural development,** a term that refers to all those activities that affect the well-being of rural populations including the provision of basic needs, such as food, and the development of human capital in the countryside through education and nutrition programs. This chapter concentrates on problems that have a direct bearing on raising agricultural production and farmers' incomes. Indirect measures treated elsewhere in this book, even those as crucial as rural education, will be dealt with only in passing.

In a sense agriculture is simply one industry among many, but it is an industry with a difference. To begin with, the agricultural sector in a country at an early developmental stage employs far more people than all other industries and sectors put together—60 to 70 percent and more of the total work force are in agriculture in many of the poorer LDCs, including China and India. By contrast, agriculture in developed economies typically employs less than 10 percent of the work force (3 percent in the United States). Second, agricultural activities have existed for thousands of years, ever since humankind gave up hunting and gathering as its main source of food. Because of this long history the rural economy is often referred to as **tradition bound.** Generating electric power or manufacturing automobiles can only be done by means based on modern science and engineering, but crops are often grown using techniques developed hundreds or even thousands of years before the advent of modern science. And the rural societies in which traditional techniques are used often develop customs and attitudes that reinforce older ways of doing things and thus make change difficult.

A third characteristic of agriculture that separates it from other sectors is the crucial importance of land as a factor of production. Other sectors use and require land, but in no other sector does land play such a central role. The availability of cultivable land, whether relatively plentiful in relation to population, as in the Americas, or scarce, as in much of Asia, fundamentally shapes the kind of farming techniques that can be used. Closely related to the central role of land is the influence of weather. No other sector is as subject to the vagaries of the weather as is agriculture. Land, like the weather, differs from place to place so that techniques suitable in one place are often of little use elsewhere. The manufacture of steel must also adjust to differences in the quality of iron ore from place to place, and similar problems occur in other industries; but the basic techniques in much of manufacturing are similar, at least within and often between nations. In agriculture differences in soil quality, climate, and the availability of water lead to the production of different crops and different ways of raising a particular crop, not only within countries, but even within provinces or counties of a single country.

Finally, agriculture is the only sector that produces food. Humankind can survive without steel or coal or electric power, but not without food. For most manufactured products, in fact, there are substitutes, but there is no substitute for food. Either food must be produced within a country or it must be imported.

AGRICULTURE'S ROLE IN ECONOMIC DEVELOPMENT

Agriculture's role in economic development is central because most of the people in poor nations make their living from the land. If leaders are seriously concerned with the welfare of their people, the only ways they can readily improve the welfare for the majority is by helping to raise first the farmers' productivity in growing food and cash crops and second the prices they receive for those crops. Not all increases in farm output benefit the majority of rural people, of course. The creation of mechanized, large-scale farms in place of small, peasant farms may actually make the majority of the population worse off. Although it is a necessary condition, raising agricultural output is not by itself sufficient to achieve an increase in rural welfare. We shall return to this problem later.

Most developing countries must rely on their own agricultural sectors to produce the food consumed by their people, although there are exceptions. Nations with large natural-resource-based exports, such as Malaysia or Saudi

Arabia, have the foreign exchange necessary to import much of their food.

But most developing nations cannot rely so heavily on foreign exchange earnings to feed their populations.

Farmers in developing nations must produce enough to feed themselves, as well as the urban population. Hence, as the proportion of the urban population rises, the productivity of farmers must also rise. If productivity does not rise (and in the absence of food imports), the models in Chapter 3 make it clear that the terms of trade will turn sharply against the industrial sector, cut into profits, and eventually bring growth to a halt.

The agricultural sector's size is the characteristic that gives agriculture such an important role in the provision of factor inputs, notably labor, to industry and to the other modern sectors. With 70 percent or more of the population in agriculture, the rural sector is virtually the only source of increased labor power for the urban sector. Importation of labor is possible, and there is usually population growth within the urban sector itself, but neither of these sources is likely to be sufficient for the long-term needs of economic growth. If there are restrictions on the movement of labor out of agriculture, economic development will be severely crippled. Serfs in Russia through the mid-nineteenth century, for example, were tied to their lord's land by law and hence were not free to move to the cities and into industry. Thus Russian industry did not begin to grow rapidly until after the serfs were freed. Today such feudal restrictions are increasingly rare, but heavy indebtedness by a farmer to a landlord-moneylender often has the same effect as tying an individual to the land and thus making the individual unavailable to modern industry.

The agricultural sector also can be a major source of capital for modern economic growth. Some writers have even suggested that agriculture is the main or even the sole source of capital in the early stages of development, but this overstates agriculture's role. Capital comes from invested savings and savings from income. However, even in the poorest countries the share of agricultural income in national product is typically less than half of gross domestic project. Over half of GNP is therefore provided by nonagricultural sectors (industry and services), and these sectors are often important contributors to saving and hence to investment. Furthermore, whereas imports of labor seldom provide a large portion of the domestic labor force, imports of capital, whether in the form of aid or private investment, sometimes do contribute a substantial share of domestic capital formation without drawing on the agricultural sector at all. South Korea is a case in point, where capital formation in the early years of rapid growth was provided mainly by foreign aid and in later years was increasingly paid for from the profits of the industrial sector.

If one treats foreign exchange as a separate factor of production, agriculture has an important role to play in the supply of this factor as well. As indicated in Chapter 15, developing countries' comparative advantage usually lies with natural resources or agricultural products. In only a few cases is the export of manufactures or of services the principal source of foreign exchange for a nation in the early stages of modern economic growth. Thus, unless a nation is rich in natural resources, such as petroleum or copper, the agricultural sector will play a key role in providing foreign exchange with which to import capital equipment and intermediate goods that cannot be produced at home.

Finally, the farming population of a developing nation is, in some cases at least, an important market for the output of the modern urban sector. The qualification "in some cases" must be added because farm populations in some poor countries purchase very little from modern industry. This is particularly likely to be true where the distribution of income is extremely unequal, with most of the nation's income, land, and other wealth in the hands of a small urban and rural upper class. In that situation the rural population may simply pay taxes and rents to wealthy urban residents and subsist on whatever is left over. Even cheap cloth from urban factories may be beyond the means of a very poor rural population. If income is less unequally distributed, however, the rural sector can be an important source of demand for industrial products. If a large rural market exists, industries can continue to grow after they have saturated urban demand for their product without turning to foreign markets until they are better able to compete.[1]

Self-Sufficiency and Dwindling World Food Supplies

One important aspect of agriculture's role in development typically gets a great deal of attention from economic planners: the degree to which a nation wishes to achieve **food self-sufficiency.** Food self-sufficiency can take on several different meanings. At one extreme is the view that any dependence on foreign trade is dangerous to a nation's economic health, and dependence on food imports is simply one part of this broader danger. More common is the view that food is a basic or strategic good, not unlike military weapons. If a nation is dependent on others for food and hence for its very survival, the suppliers of that food will be in a position to bring the dependent nation to its knees whenever it suits the supplier nations' purposes. Others argue that population growth is rapidly eating into the world's food surpluses, and nations relying on food imports will soon find themselves paying very high prices in order to get what they need from the world's dwindling surplus.

The national defense argument for food self-sufficiency may be valid under certain specific circumstances. Since discussion of these circumstances would divert us into an analysis of complex international security issues, suffice it to say that the national defense argument is frequently used to justify policies that have little relationship to a nation's real security.

The issue of a dwindling world food surplus cannot be dealt with so eas-

---

1. There are a number of good studies that treat the role of agriculture in development, including John Mellor, *The New Economics of Growth* (Ithaca, N.Y.: Cornell University Press, 1976), and his *The Economics of Agricultural Development* (Ithaca, N.Y.: Cornell University Press, 1966); Bruce Johnston and Peter Kilby, *Agriculture and Structural Transformation* (London: Oxford University Press, 1975); and Lloyd Reynolds, *Agriculture in Development Theory* (New Haven, Conn.: Yale University Press, 1976).

TABLE 18–1   World Grain Exports (million metric tons)

Year	Exports
1962	85.34
1966	114.11
1970	113.34
1974	149.05
1978	191.02
1980	216.10
1985	224.49
1988	231.76

Sources: Food and Agricultural Organization, *Trade Yearbook 1972, 1976, 1978, 1987,* and *1989* (Rome: Food and Agricultural Organization, 1973, 1977, 1979, 1988, 1990).

ily. History does not support the view that world supplies of exportable food are steadily diminishing. Data on world grain exports are presented in Table 18–1. What these and other data indicate is that although the world grain export surplus and the corresponding size of the deficit in importing nations fluctuates, the overall surplus is growing, not declining. In 1972, for example, bad weather struck a wide part of the globe, including the Soviet Union, China, India, and Indonesia. The resulting surge in demand for grain imports drove prices up sharply in 1973, but prices fell again when production in these deficit areas recovered. The 1972 to 1973 "crisis" was not significantly different in magnitude from other weather-induced fluctuations of the past. After 1973 grain exports rose substantially and prices fell.

Those who speak of an impending world food crisis are implicitly or explicitly forecasting the future. Continued population growth is rapidly pushing people out onto the world's diminishing supply of arable land. In places like Africa's Sahel agriculture may already have developed beyond the capacity of the land to sustain it. The real issue, however, is not whether the world is running out of surplus land—it is—but whether yields on existing arable land can be raised fast enough to meet the needs of an increasing population with rising per-capita incomes. The problem is not one of biology. Research in the plant sciences has shown that yields per acre could be higher than even those of such advanced agricultural systems as Japan's. And most of the world produces food at levels per acre nowhere near those of Japan. Although there is some biological limit to the capacity of the planet earth to produce food, the planet is not remotely close to that limit today.

The real danger of a long-term food crisis arises from a different source. From a scientific point of view, the nations that could expand food output dramatically may not do so because of internal social and economic barriers to technical progress in agriculture. At the same time, because of economic reasons, the world's few food-surplus nations may not be able to continue to expand those surpluses. Thus it is possible that the world could face growing food deficits in importing nations that are not matched by rising surpluses in exporting nations. Under such circumstances, food prices would rise sharply, and only nations with large foreign exchange earnings could afford to continue to import sufficient food. Some of the poorest nations, including those where food imports make the difference between an adequate diet and severe malnutrition, may not have the foreign exchange earnings needed to maintain required imports. One must emphasize, however, that while the potential for a disaster of this kind is present, it is not today a reality; many economists believe it will never become a reality. A possible future world food crisis is a weak basis for a nation's economic planners to give a high priority to the development of agriculture.[2]

LAND TENURE AND REFORM

Before we focus on agricultural production, it is best to explore the problem of land, and the way it is owned and organized. Conditions of land tenure set the context within which all efforts to raise agricultural output must operate.

Patterns of Land Tenure

Land tenure and **land-tenure relations** refer to the way people own land and how they rent it to others to use if they choose not to cultivate it themselves. In Europe during the Middle Ages, for example, a local lord owned a piece of land and allowed the local peasants to cultivate it. In exchange for cultivating that land, the peasant family had to deliver a part of the harvest to the lord, and members of the peasant family had to perform labor services in the lord's castle. In most cases the peasant could not freely leave the land to seek work in the cities or with another lord. Peasants did flee, but the lord had the right to force them to return if they could be caught. Serfdom, as this system is sometimes called, was only a modest step up from slavery.

Serflike land-tenure relations prevail today in only a few remote and backward areas of the globe. The patterns that do exist, however, are diverse, as the following incomplete listing makes clear.

Large-scale modern farming or ranching usually refers to a large crop- or cattle-raising acreage which uses some hired labor but where many of the activities are highly mechanized. Many such farms are found in the United States, whereas much of Latin American agriculture is characterized by large modern farms that exist alongside small peasant plots.

Plantation agriculture is a system in which a piece of land is used to raise a cash crop such as tea or rubber, usually for export. Cultivation is by hired labor who are paid wages, and the plantation is run either by the owner or more frequently by a professional manager.

---

2. Works on the food self-sufficiency issue are numerous on both sides of the argument, including R. Barker, E. Bennagen, and Y. Hayami, "New Rice Technology and Policy Alternatives for Food Self-Sufficiency," in *Economic Consequences of the New Rice Technology,* International Rice Research Institute (Los Banos, Philippines: 1978), pp. 337–361; Richard Goldman, "Staple Food Self-Sufficiency and the Distributive Impact of Malaysian Rice Policy," *Food Research Institute Studies* 14, no. 3 (1975): 251–293; and Lester Brown, *By Bread Alone* (New York: Praeger, 1974).

Latifundia is a term used in Latin America and Europe to refer to large estates or ranches on which the hired labor still have a servile (master-servant) relationship to the owner.

Family farms or **independent peasant proprietors** own plots of land (usually small) and operate them mainly or solely with their own family's labor. This type of tenure is dominant in Asia and Africa and is important in Latin America as well.

Tenancy usually refers to a situation where an individual family farms a piece of land owned by a landlord to whom the farmer pays rent. Much of Asian agriculture is made up of either individual peasant proprietors or tenants.

Sharecropping is a form of tenancy in which the farmer shares his crops with the landlord.

Absentee landlords, who are particularly important in Asia and Latin America, tend to live in cities or other places far away from the land they own. Landlords who do live near their land may have little to do with it except to collect rents. Some resident landlords provide seeds and certain kinds of capital to tenants.

Communal farming is practiced in parts of Africa, where villages may still own some of their land jointly. Individuals and families may farm plots on communal land, to which they gain access by custom or by allocation from the community's leaders. Europe in an earlier period also had such common lands, which were used, among other purposes, as pasture for the village cows.

Collectivized agriculture refers to the kinds of agricultural systems found for the most part in the Soviet Union, China prior to 1981, and parts of Eastern Europe. Land, except for small family plots, is owned by a cooperative whose members are typically all or part of the residents of a single village. Management is by a committee elected by the villagers or appointed by government authorities, and members of the cooperative share in output on the basis of the amount of labor they contribute to it.

There are numerous variations within and among these categories, but this list gives some idea of the great range of land-tenure systems that exist in the developing world. The kind of land-tenure system existing in any given country or region has an important bearing on economic development for several reasons. To begin with, prevailing land-tenure arrangements have a major influence on the welfare of the farm family. A family farming only one or two acres of land that must turn over half its main crop to the landlord will not have much left over to feed itself or to invest in improvements. Such a heavy rent burden may seem harsh, but half and more of the farmers in some major countries, such as China and South Korea before land reform and parts of Latin America and India today, labor under comparable conditions or worse.

A second important impact of the land-tenure system is on the prevailing degree of political stability. Families that own the land they cultivate tend to feel they have a stake in the existing political order, even if they themselves are quite poor. Because they possess land they have something to lose from turmoil. Landless farm laborers and tenants who can be pushed off the land at the will of a landlord have no such stake in the existing order. The history of many nations with large landless rural populations is often one of periodic peasant rebellions. One such rebellion played a major role in bringing the Communists to power in China. Much of the history of modern Mexico has also been shaped by revolts of the landless.

Tenure and Incentive

Land-tenure systems also have a major impact on agricultural productivity. An individual proprietor who owns land knows that increased effort or skill that leads to a rise in output will also improve income. This result does not necessarily follow if the land is owned by someone else. Under sharecropping, for example, the landlord gets a percentage share, typically a half of any increase in output. If a tenant's rent contract is only a year or two in length, a rise in output may cause the landlord to threaten eviction of the tenant so that all or much of the increase in production can be captured through a rise in the rent. In some countries landlords have had to draw up land-rental contracts of many years or even a lifetime's duration, precisely because tenants otherwise would have no incentive to invest in improvements or even to maintain existing irrigation and drainage systems.

Farms with large numbers of hired laborers have an even more difficult incentive problem, compounded by a management problem. Farm laborers are paid wages and typically do not benefit at all in any rise in production. One way around this difficulty is to pay on a **piece-rate basis,** that is, to pay workers on the basis of the number of bushels of cotton or tea leaves they pick. But although this system works at harvest time, it is virtually impossible to pay on a piece-work basis for the cultivation of crops. A laborer can be paid by the acre for planting wheat, but it will be many months before it will be possible to tell whether the planting job was done well or carelessly. In a factory, elaborate procedures can be set up by management to check on the pace and quality of work performed. But work in a factory is much easier to reduce to a routine that can be measured and supervised than is work on a farm. There are a thousand different tasks that must be performed on a typical farm; and supervision, even in the hands of a skilled manager, is seldom a good substitute for a farmer motivated by the knowledge that extra effort will lead directly to a rise in income.

Incentives under communal farming suffer in a different way. Because the land is owned in common, each individual family has an incentive to use the land to the maximum extent possible, but no one has much of an incentive to maintain or improve the land because the benefits of individual improvement efforts will go not mainly to the individual but to everyone who uses the land. Economists call this the **public goods** or **free-rider** problem. Everyone agrees that a fire department is necessary if a town is to avoid conflagration, but few people would voluntarily pay what the fire department is worth to them. Instead they would pay little or nothing in the hope that their neighbors would pay enough to maintain the department, but of course their neighbors would not pay enough either. The usual solution to this problem is to turn payment over to the town government and allow that government to assess taxes on everyone in town on an equitable basis. Similar solutions are found in communal agriculture. Certain dates can be set aside when everyone in the village is expected to show up and work on a particular land improvement, such as repair of a fence with a neighboring village. But the incentive to work hard in a common effort relies heavily on community social pressure plus the inner goodwill of each individual. If farmers were saints, goodwill would do the job, but for better or worse, farmers are like the rest of us.

Collectivized agriculture has some of the incentive and management problems of both plantation and communal agriculture, but with important differences. Because the land is owned in common, the free-rider problem is present, but its impact is modified by paying everyone "work points" on the basis of the amount of work they actually do. At the end of the year the total number of work points earned by collective members is added up and divided into the value of the collective's output to determine the value of each work point. The individual therefore has a dual incentive to work hard. More work means more work points, and indirectly it leads to higher collective output and hence a higher total income for that individual.

The incentive issue posed by collective agriculture is whether the work-point system is an adequate substitute for the motivation provided on a family farm where increased output benefits a farmer's own family and only that family. The main problem with the collective system is that an individual can sometimes earn work points by claiming to have worked hard, when in fact that person was off behind a tree sleeping or leaning on a hoe. The solution to the leaning-on-a-hoe problem is to have the leadership of the collective check up on how hard members are working, but that can introduce the supervision or management problem found in plantation labor, namely that it is extremely difficult to supervise many agricultural activities. In general both the incentive and managerial problems worsen as the collective unit gets larger. In a unit of 20 or 30 families, the size of the Chinese production team in the 1970s, families can supervise each other and penalize laggards. But in a unit of several thousand families, the size of the Chinese commune in the late 1950s, family members have little incentive to pressure laggards to work harder because no single individual's work, however poorly done, will have much impact on the value of a neighbor's work points. If everyone in the collective thinks this way, of course, the output of the collective will fall. By 1981 the Chinese leadership had decided that even the 20- to 30-family collective unit created incentive and managerial problems, and they introduced reforms that returned Chinese agriculture to a system of family farming.

From an incentive and management point of view, therefore, the family-owned farm would seem to be the ideal system. The analysis so far, however, has left out one very important consideration: economies of scale. In agriculture economies of scale may exist because certain kinds of machinery can be used efficiently only on large farms. On small farms tractors or combines may be badly underutilized. Such considerations help explain why many Latin Americans feel that large-scale farming is the most appropriate way to increase agricultural production and exports. Economies of scale may also exist because large collective units are better at mobilizing labor for rural construction activities than are individual family farms. We shall return to the question of scale economies later. Here all we can conclude is that the question of the ideal type of rural land-tenure system has not been completely resolved.

Land Reform

The reform of land-tenure systems can assume many different forms. Typical measures found in many reforms, starting with the least radical, include:[3]

Reform of rent contracts ensures the tenure of a tenant farmer. Many tenants farm at the will of the landlord and can be easily removed at the end of a season. Laws requiring long-term contracts that restrict the landlord's right to remove a tenant can markedly improve the tenant's willingness to maintain and invest in the land, and also introduce a degree of stability into the family's life.

Rent reduction typically involves a ceiling on the percentage share of the crop that a landlord can demand as rent. If the percentage share is substantially below what prevailed in the past, the impact both on tenant welfare and the tenant family's surplus available for investment can be substantial.

Land to the tiller (the former tenant) **with compensation** to the landlord for loss of land is a measure that can take many different forms. A government can pass a law setting a ceiling on the number of acres an individual can own and so force individuals to sell all land over that limit. Or the reform law can state that only those who actually till the land can own it, and all other land must be sold. A key issue in this kind of reform is whether the former landlord receives full or only partial compensation for the land that must be sold.

Land to the tiller without compensation involves the most radical transformation of rural relations, except for the further step of collectivization. All land not cultivated by its owner is confiscated, and the former landlord receives nothing in return. Frequently in such reform the landlord may lose life as well as land.

The Politics of Land Reform

The main motive for undertaking land reform is usually political, not economic.[4] The politics that lead to reform are of two types. A society with a large tenant and landless laborer population that is controlled by other classes may find itself faced with increasing rural unrest. To keep this unrest from blowing up into a revolution, land reform bills are passed to reduce the

---

3. There are numerous studies of land reform. One of the best known practitioners was Wolf Ladejinsky. See Louis J. Walinsky, ed., *Agrarian Reform as Unfinished Business: The Selected Papers of Wolf Ladejinsky* (London: Oxford University Press, 1977).

4. Elias Tuma, *Twenty-six Centuries of Agrarian Reform: A Comparative Analysis* (Berkeley: University of California Press, 1965.)

burden on the peasantry and to give them a stake in continued stability. In the second type, land reform takes place after a revolution supported by the rural poor has occurred. The main purpose of reform in this case is to consolidate support for the revolution among the rural poor and to eliminate the economic base of one of the classes, the landlords, that was most opposed to the revolution.

The motive behind the Mexican land reforms of the twentieth century, for example, has been largely of the first type. Prior to the Mexican Revolution of 1911, land in Mexico had become increasingly concentrated in large haciendas ranging in size from 1,000 to over 400,000 acres. Although the revolution of 1911 was supported by those who had lost their land and other rural poor, those who took power after the revolution were largely from upper-income groups or the small middle class. This new leadership, however, had to deal with the continuing rural unrest that was often ably led by men such as Emiliano Zapata. To meet the challenge of Zapata and people like him, the Mexican government has periodically redistributed some arable land, most recently under the government of President Echeverria in the 1970s. Mexican land-tenure relations, however, continue to be characterized by large estates existing alongside small peasant holdings. Reform eliminated some of the more extreme forms of pressure for more radical change, but Mexican agriculture still includes a large, poor, and not very productive rural peasant class.

The Chinese land reform of the 1940s and early 1950s under the leadership of the Communist party was a reform par excellence of the second type. The Communist revolution had been built primarily on the rural poor, and the landlord class was one of the main pillars of support of the existing Kuomintang government. Prior to the reform some 40 percent of the arable land had been farmed by tenants who typically paid half their main crop to the landlord as rent. The landlord, whether resident in the village or absentee, contributed little or nothing other than the land. After the reform, and prior to the collectivization of agriculture in 1955 to 1956, land was owned by the tiller and the landlord received no compensation whatsoever. In fact many landlords were tried publicly in the villages and either executed or sent off to perform hard labor under harsh conditions.[5]

The Japanese land reform that followed World War II was different in important respects from the Chinese experience. Land reform in Japan was carried out by the U.S. Occupation forces. The Occupation government believed that the landlord class had been an important supporter of the forces in Japanese society that brought about World War II. Small peasant proprietors, in contrast, were seen as a solid basis on which to build a future democratic and stable Japan. Since the Americans had won the war, Japanese landlords were not in a position to offer resistance to reform, and a thoroughgoing reform was carried out. Compensation of landlords was provided for in legislation, but inflation soon had the effect of sharply reducing

5. Among the many studies on Chinese land reform are John Wong, *Land Reform in the People's Republic of China* (New York: Praeger, 1973), and William Hinton, *Fanshen* (New York: Vintage Books, 1966).

the real value of the amounts offered. As a result Japanese land reform also amounted to confiscation of landlord land with little compensation.[6]

A second feature of land reform efforts is that land reform legislation is extremely difficult to enforce in the absence of a deep commitment from the government. Most developing countries have some kind of land reform legislation on the books, but relatively few have experienced real reform. In some cases no serious effort is made to enforce the legislation. In other cases the legislation is enforced but has little effect because of legal loopholes.

India provides examples of both kinds of problems. In the Indian state of Bihar the government has awarded substantial tracts of land to the *harijan* (former untouchable) caste. But Bihar is a state where much of the real power rests in the hands of so-called "higher castes" that include many landlords, and these higher castes have forcibly prevented the *harijans* from taking over the land the government awarded to them. Elsewhere in India a law limiting the amount of land that can be owned by a single person has been enforced, but has had limited real effect. An individual with more land than allowed by law registers the extra land in the name of trusted relatives or associates. For truly enormous landholdings subterfuges of this kind may be impossible, but most landlords in India possess only several tens or a few hundred acres of land.

Land Reform and Productivity

The impact of land reform on agricultural productivity depends on what kind of system is being reformed as well as the content of the reform measures. Land reform has the greatest positive impact on productivity where the previous system was one of small peasant farms, with high rates of insecure tenancy (for example, one-year contracts) and absentee landlords. Under such conditions reform has little impact on cultivation practices since farms are small both before and after reform. Elimination of landlords also has little effect on productivity because they have nothing to do with farming. On the other hand, turning tenants into owners provides them with a greater incentive to invest in improvements. The Chinese, Japanese, and South Korean land reforms of the 1940s and 1950s were all essentially of this kind.

At the other extreme are reforms that break up large, highly efficient modern estates or farms and substitute small, inefficient producers. In many parts of the developing world, such as Mexico, Kenya, and Malaysia, large, highly mechanized estates using the most advanced techniques have grown up over time. The incentive problems inherent in the use of hired farm labor are at least partially overcome by the use of skilled professional estate managers. Often these estates are major suppliers of agricultural produce for export, and hence a crucial source of the developing country's foreign exchange. If land reform breaks up these estates and turns them over to

---

6. There are many studies of Japanese land reform, including R. P. Dore, *Land Reform in Japan* (London: Oxford University Press, 1959).

small peasant proprietors who know little about modern techniques and lack the capital to pay for them, the impact on agricultural productivity can be catastrophic. But there are also examples, as in the Kenyan highlands, where the breakup of large estates into small peasant holdings actually increased productivity, mainly because the small holdings were farmed much more intensively than the large estates. In between these two extremes are a myriad of variations with different impacts on productivity, both positive and negative.

Land Reform and Income Distribution

Land reform will have a major impact on the distribution of income in rural areas only if land is taken from landlords without compensation, or at least without anything close to full compensation. If former tenants are required to pay landlords the full market value of the land received, the society's distribution of wealth will be the same as before. The tenant will receive land together with a debt exactly equal to the value of the land, and hence the change in net wealth of the former tenants will be zero. The former landlord will surrender land but will acquire an asset of equal value in the form of a loan to the former tenant. Reform with full compensation may still be desirable on productivity grounds because of the advantages of owner rather than tenant cultivation, but initially at least the new owner will be just as poor and the new landlord just as rich as before. On the other hand, if the landlord is compensated with bonds paid for out of general tax revenues, the former tenant's income share may rise provided that the taxes to pay for this do not fall primarily on the tenant. The best-known successful land reforms have commonly involved little or no compensation for confiscated assets of landlords. Such was the case in Russia after 1917 and China after 1949, as well as in the Japanese and South Korean reforms after World War II.

This discussion of land-tenure relations and their reform sets the scene for the discussion of agricultural production and how it can be raised. Much of the analysis that follows will deal with subjects like agricultural research or the uses of chemical fertilizer. But it must always be kept in mind that behind the use of better techniques and more inputs there must be a land-tenure system that provides farmers with the incentive to introduce those techniques and inputs, and then use them efficiently.

Technology of Agricultural Production

The popular view of traditional agricultural systems is that they are made up of peasants who have been farming the same way for centuries. The implication is that traditional farmers are bound by custom and incapable of making changes that raise the productivity and efficiency of their efforts. Custom in turn is reinforced by values and beliefs often closely tied to religion. Change thus becomes doubly difficult because to make a change may involve rejection of deeply held religious beliefs. In this case only a revolution that completely overturns the traditional society and all it stands for holds out real hope for agricultural development.

Traditional Agriculture

Tradition-bound societies of this type do exist in the world, but the description does not fit the great majority of the world's peasant farmers. A great accumulation of evidence suggests that these farmers are efficient, that they have already made sensible—sometimes complex and subtle—adaptations to their environment and that they are willing to make further changes to increase their welfare if it is clear that an improvement will result without an unacceptable risk of crop failure and hence starvation.[7]

When traditional agriculture is described as "efficient," the word is used in the same way as it has been used throughout this book. Given existing technology, traditional farmers get the most output they can from available inputs or they get a given level of output with the smallest possible use of inputs. Foreign advisors, regardless of their background, have often had to relearn this fact, sometimes at considerable cost. With a little reflection it is hardly surprising that traditional agriculture tends to be efficient within the limits of traditional techniques. The central characteristic of traditional technology is that it changes very slowly. Farmers thus are not in a position to constantly respond to changing agricultural methods; instead, they can experiment over long periods of time with alternative techniques until just the right method for the given technology is found. Long periods of time in this context may refer to decades or even to centuries. If a slightly deeper method of plowing or a closer planting of seeds will raise yields per acre, for example, one or two more venturesome farmers are eventually going to give such methods a try. At least they will do so if they have plows capable of deeper cultivation. If the techniques work, their neighbors will observe and eventually follow suit. Given several decades or a century all farmers in the region will be using similar methods.

This example brings out a closely related characteristic of traditional agriculture. In addition to being efficient, traditional agricultural techniques are not stagnant; they have evolved slowly over time. That peasant farmers in a traditional setting are willing to change if the benefits from a change are clearly perceived has been demonstrated over and over again. Some of the best evidence in support of this willingness to change is that provided by responses to changes in prices. Time and again as prices of cotton or tobacco or jute have risen relative to other farm prices, farmers—even in some of the poorest nations in the world—have rushed to increase the acreage of these crops. And the reverse has occurred when prices have fallen.

Change in traditional agriculture has involved much more than responses to fluctuations in relative prices. Long before the advent of modern science and its application to farming, there were fundamental advances in all aspects of agricultural technology.

---

7. One of the clearest statements of this point has been made by Theodore W. Schultz, *Transforming Traditional Agriculture* (New Haven: Yale University Press, 1964). A classic field study making the same point, based on the author's work in Guatemala, is Sol Tax, *Penny Capitalism* (Chicago: University of Chicago Press, 1963).

Slash-and-Burn Cultivation

One of the most fundamental changes, of course, was the conversion of society from groups of hunters and gatherers of wild plants to groups of settled farmers who cleared and plowed the land. Initially settled farming often involved **slash-and-burn** methods of cultivation. In slash-and-burn agriculture, trees are slashed and fire is used to clear the land. The burnt tree stumps are left in the ground, and cultivation seldom involves much more than poking holes in the ground with a digging stick and dropping seeds into the holes. The original nutrients in the soil plus the nutrients from the burnt ashes make respectable yields possible for a year or two, after which most of the nutrients are used up, weed problems increase, and yields fall off drastically. Farmers then move on to slash and burn a new area; perhaps return they may to the first area 20 or 30 years later when the land has regained a sufficient level of plant nutrients. Slash-and-burn agriculture is thus often referred to as a form of **shifting cultivation** or **forest-fallow cultivation**. This system requires a large amount of land to support a small number of people. Today the system exists mainly in remote, lightly populated areas, such as in the mountains of Laos and in parts of Africa and the Amazon.

The Shortening of Fallow

The evolution from slash-and-burn agriculture to permanent cultivation in which a crop is grown on a piece of land once every year, can be thought of as a process of gradually shortening the period that land is left fallow. The term **fallow** refers to the time that land is left idle to allow the soil to reaccumulate the nutrients essential to successful cultivation. In Europe the shortening of fallow gradually took place during and after the Middle Ages, and annual cropping did not become common until the latter part of the eighteenth century. In China the evolution to annual cropping occurred at least a thousand years earlier. In both Europe and China the driving force behind this evolution was increased population pressure on the land.[8]

The elimination of fallow did not occur automatically or easily. Farmers had to discover ways to restore nutrients in the soil by rotating crops and by adding fertilizers such as compost and manure. Ploughs had to be developed to cultivate the land each year yet prevent it from being taken over by grasses. Each of these changes was at least as fundamental as many that have occurred in agriculture in the twentieth century. The difference is that these earlier changes took place over centuries rather than years.

Farming within a Fixed Technology

Once fallow was eliminated, increases in agricultural production could be obtained either by increasing yields on annually cropped land or by expanding onto previously uncultivated land. Where population pressure was partic-

---

8. Ester Boserup, *The Conditions of Agricultural Growth: The Economies of Agrarian Change and Population Pressure* (Chicago: Aldine, 1965), and Dwight H. Perkins, *Agricultural Development in China, 1368–1968* (Chicago: Aldine, 1969).

ularly severe several centuries ago, grain yields reached levels per hectare higher than those found in many parts of the world even today. In China, for example, two crops a year of rice or of rice and wheat were common before the sixteenth century. By the mid-nineteenth century in both China and Japan average rice-paddy yields per acre over large areas had passed 2.5 to 3 tons per hectare, whereas in India and Thailand as late as the 1960s average rice yields were under 1.5 tons per hectare. Hence, traditional agriculture was capable of achieving high levels of productivity per unit of land.

What separates traditional from modern agricultural development, therefore, is not the existence of technological progress or the sophistication of the techniques used. Traditional agriculture experienced substantial technological progress, and the techniques used in highly populated areas at least were as sophisticated as many so-called modern techniques found today. The difference between traditional and modern agriculture is in the pace and source of change. In traditional agriculture change is slow, whereas in modern agriculture it is rapid. And in modern agriculture scientific research produces most of the new techniques used, whereas in traditional agriculture new techniques were sometimes the result of the tinkering of individual farmers. At other times new inputs, such as improved seeds, were accidents of nature that led to a variety that produced higher yields or required a shorter growing season.

The principal problem of traditional agriculture, therefore, was that farmers worked most of their lives within a technology that changed very slowly. They could spend their energies raising the efficiency with which they used that technology, but the gains from higher levels of efficient use of a stagnant technique were limited. The improvements in technique that did occur happened over too long an interval of time to have anything but a marginal impact on rural standards of living.

Modernizing Agricultural Technology

Traditional agriculture can be modernized in two ways. The first is technological: specific inputs and techniques can be combined to produce higher agricultural production. Technological modernization deals with such issues as the role of chemical fertilizer and the relationship of fertilizer's impact to the availability of improved plant varieties and adequate supplies of water. These technological issues are the subject of this and the next section. The second approach to modernization concerns the mobilization of agricultural inputs and techniques in developing countries. How, for example, does a nation mobilize labor for rural public works or create institutes that will develop new techniques suitable to local conditions? These issues of mobilization and organization are the subject of the following part of this chapter.

There is no universally best technology for agriculture. All agricultural techniques must be adjusted to local soil and climatic conditions and to local factor endowments. Even in industry technology must be adapted to local conditions, but an automobile assembly plant in Ghana will look much

like one of similar size in Indonesia. In agriculture, local conditions are
fundamental, not secondary. Students from a developing country can be
sent to advanced nations to learn how to develop improved plant varieties
suitable to their country, but only occasionally will the plant varieties in
the advanced country be directly transferable.

Still, generalizations can be made about the characteristics of modern
agricultural technology. The technological development that occurs will
differ markedly depending on whether a nation has a large area of arable
land and a small declining rural population or a large rural population on a
very limited amount of land. The problem in the former is to get the most
output possible out of its limited rural labor force. The latter nation must
also raise labor productivity. The key to success depends primarily on
achieving rapid increases in the productivity of the land.[9] The fundamental
difference between these two strategies can be illustrated with a simple
diagram, Figure 18–1. As the figure makes clear, the United States and
Japan have pursued fundamentally different agricultural strategies, and most
other nations fall somewhere in between. In the United States labor productivity is extremely high but yields per hectare are well below those of
many nations, including more than a few in the less-developed category. In

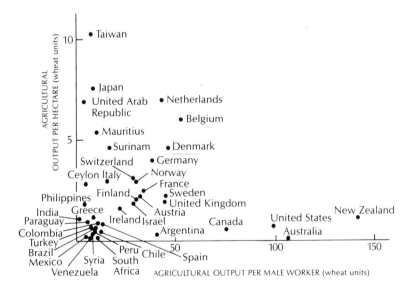

FIGURE 18–1   **International Comparison per Male Worker and per Hectare of Agricultural Land.**
The dot for the United States indicates that U.S. grain output per farm worker was nearly 100
tons of wheat or its equivalent but U.S. yields per hectare were only about 1 ton. Mauritius, in
contrast, had over 5 tons of output per hectare but little more than 10 tons per worker. Output
data in the diagram are 1957–1962 averages; and labor and land data are for the year closest
to 1960.
Source: Yujiro Hayami and Vernon W. Ruttan, *Agricultural Development: An International Perspective* (Baltimore: Johns Hopkins Press, 1971), p. 71.

9. The point is that innovation is induced by perceived needs. See Hans P. Binswanger and
Vernon W. Ruttan, *Induced Innovation: Technology, Institutions and Development* (Baltimore: Johns Hopkins Press, 1977).

contrast, Japanese labor productivity in agriculture is only a fraction of that in the United States, but land productivity is several times that of the United States.

The difference between the two strategies involves basically different technologies. These different technologies are often called the mechanical package (of technologies) and the biological package. The **mechanical package** refers to the use of tractors, combines, and other forms of machinery primarily as substitutes for labor that has left the farm for the cities. The **biological package** refers to raising yields through the use of improved plant varieties such as hybrid corn or the new varieties of rice developed at the International Rice Research Institute in the Philippines. Because of the dramatic effect on yields of some of these new varieties, the phenomenon is often referred to as the **Green Revolution.** But these new varieties raise yields only if they are combined with adequate and timely water supplies and increased amounts of chemical fertilizer. The basic production functions that describe these two packages therefore are fundamentally different. The isoquants of a production function representing the mechanical package indicate a high degree of substitutability (Figure 18–2), whereas the isoquants for the biological package are drawn in a way to indicate a

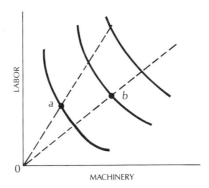

FIGURE 18–2 **The Mechanical Package Production Function.** The isoquants in this production function represent increases in agricultural output as one moves out from the point of origin (0). Movement from point a to point b represents a shift to the use of more machinery, which also involves a rise in agricultural output because machinery is a good substitute for labor.

high degree of complementarity (Figure 18–3). The L-shaped isoquants in Figure 18–3 indicate complementarity because only a limited number of fertilizer and water combinations will produce increases in grain output. Continual increases of only one input, such as fertilizer, will run into diminishing returns and then, where the curve flattens out, zero returns. Even with the biological package there is some substitutability but less than in the case of the mechanical package.

The Mechanical Package

To someone familiar with the cornfields of Iowa or the wheat fields of Nebraska and the Dakotas, mechanization means the use of large John

FIGURE 18–3 **The Biological Package Production Function.** The isoquants in this production function also represent increases in agricultural output as one moves out from the point of origin (0), but these isoquants, unlike those in Figure 18–2, indicate that there is little substitutability between inputs. An increase in fertilizer from point *a* to point *b*, for example, does not lead to a rise in agricultural output because the required increase in water supply to make the fertilizer effective has not occurred.

Deere tractors and combines, metal silos with mechanical loading devices, and numerous other pieces of expensive equipment. With such equipment a single farmer with one assistant can farm hundreds of acres of land. But mechanization can also occur profitably on farms of only a few acres. As labor becomes more abundant and land less so, the mechanical package becomes less important in relation to the biological package, but mechanization has a role to play even in poor, labor-intensive agricultural systems.

Mechanization of agriculture in labor-abundant developing nations is primarily a substitute for labor, just as in the labor-short U.S. Midwest. Even in nations such as China or India there are periods when the demand for labor exceeds its supply. When two rice crops are grown each year, for example, the first crop must be harvested, fields prepared, and the second crop transplanted—all within a matter of a few weeks. Transporting the harvest to market also takes an enormous amount of labor if goods must be brought in on carts hauled by men or animals, or as head loads by women, as is still the case in much of the developing world. One driver with a truck can do in a day what might otherwise take dozens of men and women several days to do. Nor can humans or animals working a hand pump or a water wheel move much water to the fields, however hard they work. A small diesel pump can move more water to higher levels than a large number of oxen turning wheels, and oxen cost more to feed than the pump costs to fuel.

Even when labor is extremely inexpensive, therefore, it can be economical to substitute machines for labor in some operations. Over the years manufacturers in Japan and elsewhere have developed whole lines of miniaturized machinery such as hand tractors and rice transplanters to meet this need, and these machines are in widespread use in the developing world. Not all mechanization in the developing world has been economic, however. Frequently tractors and other forms of farm machinery are allowed to enter a country duty free (when other imports have high tariffs) or are subsidized in other ways. Large farmers thus sometimes find it privately profitable to buy tractors and get rid of hired labor when, in the absence of subsidies, they (and the country) would be better off economically using laborers.

A major point of this discussion is that there is no one agricultural technology that is most efficient in all countries. The technology that produces a given level of output at the lowest possible cost in a nation with a low per capita income is likely to be very different from the technology that produces the same product at the lowest cost in a nation with a high per-capita income. The reason is straightforward. Labor in a nation with a low per-capita income is typically paid much lower wages than in the richer nation. Capital conversely is often less expensive in countries with a higher per-capita income.

How this works can be illustrated by adding **isocost** lines to Figure 18–2. This is done in Figure 18–4. The isocost lines (*ac* and *bd*) illustrate the various combinations of labor and machinery that can be purchased for a given sum of money, say $1,000 at prices prevailing for machinery and labor in that country. The line *bd* represents the relative costs of these inputs in a high per-capita income country where labor is expensive and capital relatively cheap. The line *ac* represents the situation in a poorer country where labor is inexpensive and capital is relatively costly. The objective for the efficient farmer is to produce the most output possible at a given cost (or to minimize the cost required to produce a given output). For the country with a low per capita income, that most efficient point is at *f* where its isocost line is tangent to the isoquant *efgh* of the production function. For the country with the higher per-capita income and the relatively expensive labor, in contrast, tangency is achieved at point *g* on that

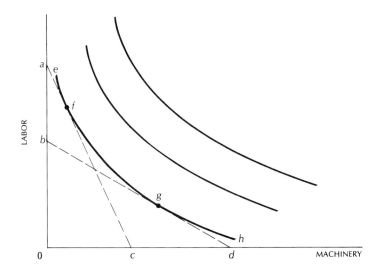

FIGURE 18–4 **Choices of Technology with Differing Costs of Capital and Labor.** The technology choices here are similar to those in Figure 18–2. Added are the isocost line for the high per-capita income country *(bd)* and the low per-capita income country *(ac)*.

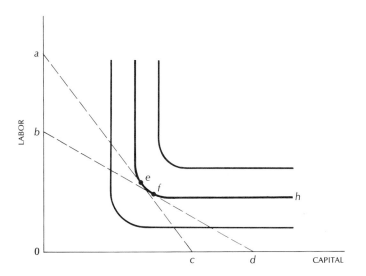

FIGURE 18–5   Choices of Technology with Differing Costs of Capital and Labor and Limited Substitutability between Capital and Labor. This figure is similar to Figure 18–4 except for the use of production function isoquants that indicate limited substitutability between capital and labor.

same isoquant. At point g the richer nation will use substantially more capital and less labor to produce the same level of output as will the poorer nation producing at point f.

In some cases, however, the capital-intensive technology will be superior regardless of the relative prices of capital and labor. An example would be the use of tube wells with power pumps to replace wells dug by hand with water obtained with a bucket and rope. The latter uses much more labor but saves little or no capital. This situation is illustrated in Figure 18–5. The isocost lines of both the high and low per-capita income countries, ac and bd, are tangent to the production isoquant at almost the same point (e is close to f). This situation where efficient substitutability is limited is also commonly found with respect to some elements in the biological package, to which we now turn.

The Biological Package and the Green Revolution

The main impact of the biological package is to raise yields. There is nothing new about using improved plant varieties in combination with fertilizers and pesticides to raise yields of rice or corn. The use of modern scientific laboratories to develop the new varieties dates back a half century and more. Only in the 1960s and 1970s, however, have the methods so successful in the industrialized countries been applied throughout the developing nations. The founding of the International Maize and Wheat Improvement Center (CIMMYT)[10] in Mexico and the International Rice Research Insti-

10. The acronym refers to the name in Spanish, *Centro Internacional de Mejoramiento de Mais y Trijo.*

TABLE 18–2   Estimated Area Planted in High-Yielding Varieties of Wheat and Rice in Asia
(in thousands of hectares)

Year	Wheat	Rice	Total
1965–66	9[a]	49[a]	59[a]
1967–68	4,123[a]	2,654[a]	6,777[a]
1970	11,098	36,718	47,816
1983	39,163	74,260	113,423

[a]These figures exclude China.
Sources: Dana G. Dalrymple, *Development and Spread of High-Yielding Varieties of Wheat and Rice in the Less Developed Nations*, U.S. Department of Agriculture, Foreign Agricultural Economic Report No. 95, 1976, p. 108, and Dana G. Dalrymple, "Development and Spread of High Yield Varieties of Wheat and Rice in Less Developed Countries," U.S. Agency for International Development, 8th ed. (forthcoming) as reported in Jack R. Anderson, "International Agricultural Research Centers: Achievements and Potential," Part III, Consultations Group on International Agricultural Research, August 1985, pp. 23–26.

tute (IRRI) in the Philippines marked the beginning of a truly international effort to develop high-yielding varieties of grain suitable to the tropical conditions found in so much of the developing world. National efforts preceded these international centers, and other international centers devoted to the problem of arid and semiarid developing areas have followed. The result has been a steady stream of new, high-yielding varieties of wheat and rice that have found increasing acceptance in Asia (see Table 18–2) and Latin America, and to a lesser degree in Africa. (See Chapter 16.)

A rapid increase in the use of chemical fertilizers in the developing world had accompanied the increased use of high-yielding and other improved varieties (see Table 18–3). Prior to World War II, modern chemical fertilizers were virtually unknown in the less-developed nations. By the 1970s they were in widespread use from Brazil to India. Unlike machinery, chemical fertilizers can be purchased in almost any quantity and even very small amounts help yields. Thus, chemical fertilizers are within reach of even quite poor peasants. The principal limitations on the greater use of chemical fertilizer have not been the conservatism of the peasants or their poverty, but the availability of supplies and the price at which these supplies have been sold. We will return to the price question later in this chapter.

TABLE 18–3   Consumption of Chemical Fertilizer in Less-Developed Countries
(in 1,000 metric tons of nutrient)

Year	Latin America	Far East[a]	Near East	Africa
1948/49–52/53 (annual average)	116.5	617.2	93.8	32.5
1961/62–65/66 (annual average)	609.7	1,839.3	379.3	192.2
1969/70	1,171.7	3,546.3	693.9	398.5
1979/80	6,720.0	9,473.0	2,831.0	1,142.0
1984	7,293.0	14,442.0	4,242.0	1,482.0
1988	8,807.0	19,237.0	5,019.0	1,694.0

[a]The Far East excludes Asian centrally planned economies.
Sources: Food and Agricultural Organization, *Production Yearbook 1970,* and *Fertilizer Yearbook 1984* (Rome: Food and Agricultural Organization), p. 121, and *1989*, pp. 88–89.

A key component of the biological package is water. Improved plant varieties using more chemical fertilizer lead to dramatically higher yields only when there is an adequate and timely water supply. In much of the U.S. Midwest rainfall provides all the water required and at the right time. In many parts of the developing world rainfall is often inadequate or comes at the wrong time. In much of India the difference between a good crop and a harvest failure still depends primarily on when the monsoon rains arrive and in what amount. As a result, efforts to raise yields in the developing world have often focused on measures to extend irrigation systems so that crops are less dependent on the vagaries of the weather.

Extending the irrigated acreage has often been seen as primarily a financial and an engineering problem. If a nation had enough money in the 1950s and 1960s (from aid or its own resources), it hired a group of engineers to build a dam to create a reservoir and canals to take water to the fields. As one dam project after another was completed, however, it became increasingly apparent that the irrigation potential of these systems was badly underutilized. Engineers could build the damns and the main canals, but they could not always get the farmer to build and maintain the feeder canals to the fields. Who should do the work, and who would reap the benefits of these canals, became entangled in the conflicting interests and local politics of rural society. Irrigation extension was as much a social, as an engineering and ecological, question.

More than anything else, the increased use of inputs from this biological package has made possible the steady, if unspectacular, expansion of agricultural output that has kept the food supply even with or a bit ahead of the rise in population (see Table 18–4). In the future, further development of improved varieties and expansion of irrigation systems, together with increased chemical fertilizer production, will remain the major contributors to higher yields. The main function of the mechanical package, in contrast, remains freeing labor from the burden of producing food so that it can do other, hopefully more productive, tasks. Whether those tasks will in fact be more productive depends on what is happening in the rest of the economy.

TABLE 18–4 **Food Production per Capita in Developing Countries**
(indices 1969 to 1971 = 100)

Year	All developing countries	Latin America	Far East[a]	Near East	Africa
1955	91	95	90	92	98
1960	95	95	95	98	102
1965	95	99	93	100	99
1970	101	102	102	99	100
1975	104	102	104	106	94
1980	108	108	105	104	89
1985	111	111	124	99	90
1988	117	115	132	109	96

[a] Does not include Asian centrally planned economies.
Source: Food and Agricultural Organization, *Production Yearbook 1971, 1980, 1981, 1984,* and *1989.*

Although the technology of increasing agricultural output is well-understood, the ways in which the relevant inputs can be mobilized are both complex and much less well understood. Some of the problems have already been touched on, both in the discussion of difficulties in expanding irrigation and in the earlier presentation of the relationship between land-tenure systems, individual incentives, and management difficulties. Here we shall discuss some of these issues further in the context of the agricultural production function. In brief the question is: What are the alternative ways a rural society can supply itself with the necessary amounts of labor, capital, and improved techniques?

Rural Public Works Projects

Mobilizing labor to raise crops is primarily a question of individual and family incentives. The main determinants of these incentives are the land-tenure system and the prices paid and received for agricultural inputs and outputs (treated later in this chapter). Mobilization of labor to create rural capital—roads, irrigation systems, and other parts of the rural infrastructure—is the topic of this section.

The creation of a rural infrastructure through the mobilization of rural labor has long been the dream of economic planners in the developing world. The idea is a simple one. In the off-season, labor in the rural sectors of developing nations is unemployed or underemployed. Therefore the opportunity cost of using that labor on rural public works projects is zero or near zero (although food consumption may go up for people doing heavy construction work).

To use this labor in factories, the factories must first be built, and that requires the use of scarce capital equipment. Furthermore, this equipment will lie idle when the rural workers return to the fields to plant and harvest their crops. No such problems exist, however, when off-season unemployed labor is used to build roads or irrigation canals. There is no need to buy bulldozers and other heavy equipment. If there is enough labor, shovels and baskets to carry dirt can accomplish much the same purpose, and farmers already have shovels and baskets or can easily make them. In the ideal situation, therefore, unemployed workers can first be put to work making crude construction tools, after which they can begin to create roads and canals. The end result is a major expansion in the rural capital stock at little or no cost to society other than the reduced leisure time of rural workers.

Effective implementation of rural public works programs using seasonally unemployed labor, however, has proved extremely difficult. The community development programs of India and elsewhere are widely perceived as failures. Time and again international aid agencies have started pilot public works projects, only to see the projects die quietly when aid money ran out. Of all the problems connected with the mobilization of unemployed rural labor, the most basic has been the lack of connection between those who did the work and those who reaped most of the benefits.

When an irrigation canal or a road is built, the main benefits that result take the form of higher yields on land near the canal or easier access to the market for crops grown on land near the road. Land distant from the canal or road receives fewer benefits or none at all. If the people who own the nearby land are also those who did the work constructing a road or canal, then there is a direct relation between effort and reward. Unfortunately, more often than not the people who do the work reap few of the rewards. The extreme case is when the land serviced by the new canal or road is owned by absentee landlords. Absentee landlords are never mobilized for rural public works projects. It is landless laborers and tenants who do all the work, and the landlords who benefit in the form of increased rents. Workers on such projects must be paid wages, and these wages tend to be higher than is justified by their productivity. Rural construction with crude tools is, after all, very low productivity work. If the wages paid exceed the benefits of the project, it is hardly surprising that these projects come to an end when government or aid agency subsidies run out.

Labor Mobilization in Chinese Communes

Even when land is owned by those who cultivate it, there is a problem of matching effort and reward. A typical project may require the labor of an entire village or several villages, whereas the benefits go primarily to farmers in only one part of the village. The Chinese solution to this problem was to collectivize agriculture by forming people's communes.[11] An entire village owned its land in common. People who participated in public works projects received work points based on the amount of effort expended just as if they had spent their time cultivating crops. When the project was completed the land in a part of the village would be more productive, but the higher productivity benefited the entire village. The gap between work and reward in effect had been closed.

The Chinese commune did make possible the more or less voluntary mobilization of large amounts of underemployed rural labor. Hills were leveled to create new fields, new reservoirs dotted the countryside, and roads reached deep into the countryside where only footpaths had existed before. But the Chinese ran into the work-reward problem in a different form. As the rural works projects became larger and larger, it became necessary to mobilize labor from two dozen villages, even though the benefits of the project went largely to only one or two of those villages.

The initial solution to this problem was to pool the land of all two dozen into a single commune. Then increased productivity on the land around a single village would be shared by all 24 villages, and workers in those

11. When China first collectivized agriculture (1955 to 1957), the Chinese called their rural collectives *producers' cooperatives,* but to simplify the discussion we refer to them as *communes.*

villages once again had an incentive to participate in the project. This larger commune, made up of two dozen villages, however, immediately ran into all the incentive and managerial problems common to large collective units. The result was that despite all the construction activity, or even because of it, Chinese agricultural output fell; and small collective units called *production teams* replaced the large communes as the basic agricultural management unit, although the latter continued to exist and to perform some functions.

Clearly the problem of mobilizing unemployed labor to build rural infrastructure is more difficult than economists and others first thought.[12] The complexity of successfully sharing the benefits is such that rural public works, though possible, are not the universal solution to the problem of rural development that some once thought them to be.

Rural Banks and Credit Cooperatives

A second approach to the problem of providing rural areas with sufficient capital for development is to establish rural banks or credit cooperatives that will lend to farmers. In traditional agriculture a farmer has only two sources of credit: members of the family and the local moneylender. Since the interest rates charged by moneylenders typically range from 30 or 40 percent to over 100 percent a year, a farmer goes to a moneylender only when desperate. Peasants do not borrow from moneylenders to buy more fertilizer or a new pump. Only rarely will such investments be productive enough to make it possible to pay off loans with exceedingly high interest charges.

There are numerous reasons why urban commercial banks do not move in and take over from the moneylenders. Because of their location, urban banks lack the knowledge and skills necessary to operate efficiently in rural areas. On the other hand, local moneylenders know the reliability of the people to whom they are lending and the quality of land put up as collateral. Individuals without land, of course, have difficulty getting money even from local moneylenders. Women in particular may have difficulty when they farm land registered in the name of an absent husband—a frequent occurrence in Africa and elsewhere.

Credit cooperatives set up by the small farmers are one potential solution to this problem. The idea is that each farmer is capable of saving a small sum, and if these sums are pooled, one or two farmers can borrow a substantial sum to buy a new thresher or pump. The next year it will be another farmer's turn, and so on. In the meantime those who put their money in the cooperative will draw interest, and thus be encouraged to save more. But this approach has flaws. Farmers' savings tend to be small, and hence the cooperatives tend to be financially weak. More seriously, farmers in

---

12. For a discussion of these problems in a number of developing economies, see S. J. Burki, D. G. Davies, R. H. Hook, and J. W. Thomas, *Public Works Programs in Developing Countries: A Comparative Analysis*, World Bank Staff Working Paper No. 224, February 1976.

developing nations have little experience relevant to the effective operation

and management of the cooperatives. In addition, economic, social, and political conflicts within the village may make it impossible to decide something as simple as who will get the next loan.

Because of these and other problems, the establishment of rural credit institutions usually requires significant injections of both money and personnel from outside the village, usually from the government. The entry of the government, however, does not necessarily or even usually solve the underlying difficulties. A common occurrence is for a rural credit institution to be set up with funds from the central government's budget. These funds are then lent to local farmers not only at rates far below those charged by private credit sources but at rates so low that each loan requires a subsidy from the government. Since the rates are low and the credit institutions are run by government personnel, local farmers with political clout have both the incentive and the means to grab the lion's share of the financing available. Corrupt bank officials may also skim off some of the funds, and corrupt officials are seldom among the poorer elements in the village. Equally or more serious is the fact that these loans are often never paid back, so that the new credit institution must be constantly resupplied from the central budget or go out of business. Too frequently the government personnel running the local bank or cooperative lack the will or the authority to make their clients live up to their contracts.

The problems involved in setting up effective rural credit operations can be overcome. States with well-trained banking personnel and a strong government administration capable of drawing up sensible procedures and enforcing them are certainly able to make rural credit institutions work.

Well-trained personnel and effective government administrators are in short supply in a great many developing nations, but this need not be an insurmountable barrier. The Indonesian state-owned Bank Rakyat Indonesia (BRI), for example, has revamped the incentive systems for its rural lending and savings mobilization personnel. The result has been a threefold rise in rural lending and an even larger increase in rural savings deposits— all happening at the same time that government subsidies to the BRI rural credit program were eliminated.

Extension Services

If one key to rapid progress in rural areas depends on the introduction of new inputs and new techniques, it follows that some of the most important rural institutions are those responsible for speeding the transfer of these new techniques to the farmers. **Extension services,** as these institutions are usually called, provide the key link between the research laboratories or experimental farms and the rural population that must ultimately adopt what the laboratories develop.

The key to the effectiveness of the extension worker is contact and trust. Rural education helps to increase the channels of contact, because if farmers can read, contact can be made through the written as well as the spoken word. Trust is necessary, because even if there is contact, the farmer may not believe what is read or heard. Trust, of course, depends not only on the extension worker's honesty or personality, but fundamentally, on the competence of the extension worker and of the research system. Giving a farmer bad advice that leads to crop failure is likely to close the channels of communication for some time. Making contact and establishing trust is further complicated because extension workers are usually men whereas those doing the farming, particularly in parts of Africa, are women.

These remarks are common sense, but they get at the heart of the failure of extension services in many developing countries. Frequently, training for the extension service is seen not as a way of learning how to help farmers but as a way of entering the government bureaucracy and escaping from the rural areas. Some extension workers are government clerks living in town and just as averse to getting their hands dirty as their colleagues in the tax collection bureau or the post office. Even when they do visit the farmers they are supposed to be helping, they know so little about how farmers really operate that they are incapable of pointing out genuinely useful new methods. Too often the extension worker visits the village, tells the farmers what is good for them, and departs; the farmers are left to guess as best they can whether the gain from using the new idea is worth the risk of failure.

At the other end of the spectrum are extension workers who are well-trained and who live in the villages and work closely with the farmers when new techniques are being introduced. Chinese communes in the 1960s and 1970s, for example, sent one of their members off for training on the condition that the individual would return to work for the commune. The same can happen in villages where family farms predominate, although the absence of the authoritarian controls found in China makes it more difficult in many places to guarantee that the individual sent will return. Another variation on this theme, tried by CIMMYT among others, is for the basic research to be carried out on farmers' fields rather than in separate experimental stations.

There is much that we do not yet know about the spread of advanced technology in agriculture, but an effective extension service is only a part of the picture. To a large degree, farmers learn from their neighbors. However, if one local farmer owns 30 acres and farms it with a large tractor and the neighboring farmers have only 5 acres and no tractors, the farmers with 5 acres may feel they have little to learn from the experience of their neighbor. More evidence is required, but technology appears to travel more rapidly when neighboring farms in a country or region are much alike. Extremes of inequality thus may impede technological progress as well as being undesirable on equity grounds.

As this discussion of mobilizing rural labor and capital and of accelerating the rate of technical advance makes clear, agricultural development in the less-developed countries is not solely a scientific or an engineering problem. It also depends on the quality of government administration at both central and local levels.[13]

---

13. A major study of these issues in the African context is by Uma Lele, *The Design of Rural Development: Lessons from Africa* (Baltimore: Johns Hopkins Press, 1975).

The Development of Rural Markets

One common theme in the preceding chapters has been the importance of avoiding major distortions in the structure of prices. Nowhere is an appropriate price structure more important than in the agricultural sector. But in agriculture as in other sectors there must first be a market before prices can have widespread effects. And in the rural areas of developing countries the existence of an effectively operating market cannot be taken for granted.

There are virtually no areas of the world today where subsistence farming in its purest form still exists. All farmers specialize to some degree and trade their surplus output on some kind of market. Economic development is usually accompanied by the increasing size and sophistication of this rural marketing network, and in turn that improved network has an important impact on productivity in agriculture. The key to an increasing role for the market is specialization, and specialization depends on economies of scale, low-cost transport, and acceptable risk.

Economies of scale are at the heart of specialization. If everyone could produce everything they needed at the lowest possible cost, there would be no need to turn over certain tasks to others. In fact economies of scale are pervasive. In the most advanced agricultural sectors such as the U.S. Midwest, farmers grow only one or two crops and rely on the market for all their other needs. In developing countries the single greatest barrier to taking advantage of these economies of scale is transport costs. The absence of good roads or of trucks to run on them can mean that it can cost as much to move a bulky commodity 50 miles as to produce it in the first place. In the United States wheat is turned into flour in large mills, and farmers buy bread in the local supermarket like everyone else. In developing countries only wheat destined for urban consumption is processed in large mills. In rural areas wheat is processed at home or in village mills, because to take the wheat to a large distant mill would be prohibitively expensive. In large parts of southern Sudan, to take an extreme but not uncommon example, there are no all-weather roads at all, and large regions are completely cut off from the outside world during the rainy season. Regions such as this cannot readily specialize in crops for sale in the cities or for export abroad.

In large parts of the developing world, therefore, improvements in the transport system and hence in marketing can have a major impact on agricultural productivity. Construction of an all-weather road system in South Korea in the 1970s, for example, made it possible for millions of Korean farmers to increase dramatically their emphasis on vegetables and cash crops destined for urban and export markets. Even the simple device of building paved bicycle paths connecting to the main road made it possible for Hong Kong farmers to expand their vegetable acreage. In the absence of refrigerated transport many vegetables spoil quickly, and hence it does not pay to raise them if too much time elapses between the harvest and their sale on the market. Furthermore, enormous amounts of labor are required if the vegetables must be carried every day on human backs across muddy fields. The ability to move the vegetables along a paved path on the back of a bicycle can make the difference between growing vegetables or concentrating on rice, which has to be moved to market only once a year.

Even when the transport system is adequate, farmers in developing countries may limit their dependence on the market because of the risk it entails. While cash crops can fail due to bad weather or pests, the principal risk from market dependence is that the price of the crop being raised will fall sharply by the time the farmer is ready to sell. For large farmers in advanced economies a fall in price of their main crop leads to a reduction in their income. If the fall is large enough, that farmer may be forced to borrow from a local bank to tide him over until prices rise again. Or he may merely have to draw from the family's savings account. In developing countries a fall in the price of a cash crop, particularly if food prices are rising simultaneously, may lead to a drop in a farm family's income to a level below that necessary to survive. Credit may tide the family over, but interest rates will be so high that once in debt, the farmer may never be able to pay off creditors and will lose the land put up as collateral. Most farmers in developing countries avoid becoming dependent on a single cash crop and instead devote part of their land to meeting their family's food requirements. Their average income over the long run might be higher if they planted all their land in cotton or tobacco, but they might not live to see the long run if one or two years of depressed prices wipe them out.

Governments can take measures to reduce both transport costs (by building roads) and risks (by guaranteeing prices and other similar measures), and thereby develop more efficient markets. But governments also can, and often do, take measures that inhibit the development of rural marketing. Governments around the world have seldom had a real understanding of the role of rural traders, of the numerous middle traders who make a marketing system work. Middle traders are seen as exploiters who get between the producer and consumer; they drive the price paid to the producer down and that charged to the consumer up, and reap huge monopoly profits. In response to political pressures from farmers, governments have often moved to take over the rural marketing system in order to improve its operation and eliminate the monopoly profits.[14] The temptation for governments to take this step is particularly strong where the middle traders are of a different race from the majority of the population, as is the case in much of Southeast Asia, where Chinese play a major role in marketing, and in East Africa, where descendants of nineteenth- and early twentieth-century Indian immigrants now control the wholesale and retail trade.

Although occasionally government involvement improves rural marketing, more often such involvement is based on a wrong diagnosis of the problem. The price at which a farm product is sold in the cities is markedly higher than the price paid to the farmer, but the difference has little to do with monopoly profits. The real cause is the high cost of transport and a generally rudimentary system of distribution and marketing. It is not that rural traders get paid so much, it is just that it takes so many of them to get the goods to market. When the government takes over it does not change this basic situation. For a high-cost, private rural trading network the gov-

---

14. The problems created by too much government interference in agricultural marketing in Africa are discussed in Elliot Berg et al., *Accelerated Development in Sub-Saharan Africa* (Washington, D.C.: World Bank, 1981).

ernment often substitutes an even higher cost bureaucratic control of the **517**
movement of goods.

AGRICULTURAL
PRICE POLICY

AGRICULTURAL PRICE POLICY

This discussion of agricultural development has stressed the central role of
institutional change such as land reform and the creation of effective rural
credit, marketing, and extension systems. It has also emphasized the
importance of government investment in infrastructure, notably in agricultural research. But the creation of new rural institutions can take a long
time. Needed changes in the land-tenure system, in particular, can be blocked
by powerful interests for decades and even longer. Nor can an agricultural
research system be created in a few years' time. New plant varieties suitable to local conditions may take a decade to develop. If the plant scientists
needed to carry out the research have not yet been trained, the process can
take longer.

The Multiple Role of Prices

There is one area, however, where government intervention has an immediate and often profound positive or negative impact. Most governments in
both industrialized and developing countries intervene in agricultural markets to set prices both for the rural producer and the urban consumer. How
they intervene can have a profound effect both on agricultural production
and on consumption. Specifically, the prices at which grain and other agricultural produce are bought and sold play three, and sometimes four, vital
roles: (1) The prices paid to farmers, and the relation of those prices to
prices farmers pay for key inputs, such as fertilizer, have a major impact
on what and how much that farmer can produce. (2) The prices paid to
farmers, together with the quantity of produce sold, are the primary determinants of farmers' cash income. (3) The prices at which agricultural products are sold in the cities are major determinants of the cost of living of
urban residents in developing countries. (4) Prices of agricultural products,
particularly in many African countries, are often controlled by government
marketing boards that manipulate them to earn profits for the government,
a slightly disguised form of taxation.[15]

Prices have a profound impact on agricultural production because most
farmers, even in very poor countries, are interested in raising their income.
While some hold that peasants grow particular crops or use particular inputs
because that is the way their grandfathers did it, study after study has shown
that when prices change, peasant farmers respond much like any profit-
maximizing businessperson operating in a world fraught with uncertainty.[16]

15. For a full discussion of the multiple role of prices, see C. Peter Timmer, Walter P.
Falcon, and Scott R. Pearson, *Food Policy Analysis* (Baltimore: Johns Hopkins Press, 1983).
16. The literature on farmer price responsiveness is large. See, for example, Hussein Askari
and John Cummings, *Agricultural Supply Response: A Survey of the Econometric Evidence*
(New York: Praeger, 1976), and Raj Krishna, "Agricultural Price Policy and Economic Devel-

If the price of cotton rises relative to, say corn, farmers will grow more cotton even in very traditional societies.

The most important price relationship from the standpoint of agricultural production is that between farm outputs and purchased inputs, notably chemical fertilizer. From the farmer's point of view it makes sense to use more chemical fertilizer so long as it increases the value of farm output by more than its cost. (This is simply a manifestation of the profit-maximizing rule that the use of a factor of production should be increased as long as the factor's marginal revenue product exceeds its marginal cost.) The simplest and most-effective ways of increasing rice yields are to raise the price of rice or to lower the price of chemical fertilizer, or both. As studies of rice production in Asia have shown, there is a clear relationship between the rice yield per acre in a country and the rice-fertilizer price ratio.[17] Other elements are also at work, but the role of prices is a primary influence. This basic point is illustrated with the diagrams in Figure 18–6.

Part A is a simple one-input–one-output production function. The production function is drawn to reflect diminishing returns. If we know the prices of both fertilizer and rice, we can easily derive the marginal cost and marginal revenue curves facing the individual farmer, as is done in part B.

If the price of fertilizer is lowered, the marginal cost curve will fall from MC_1 to MC_2 and rice production will rise from q_1 to q_2 as farmers maximize their profits at point b instead of point a by increasing the use of fertilizer. Similarly, a rise in the price from P_1 to P_2 while holding fertilizer prices constant will increase rice output from q_1 to q_3.

The Impact of Subsidies

One of the most persistent problems facing planners and politicians in the developing world is the conflict between urban consumers and rural producers over appropriate agricultural prices. Since food purchases account for at least half the budget of urban consumers in most developing nations, a substantial increase in the price of food will cut sharply into the income of all but the richest urban people. Even governments indifferent to the welfare of their poorer urban residents cannot ignore the political impact of major increases in food prices. From Japan in the 1920s to Zambia in the 1990s, food price rises have triggered massive rioting that has threatened the very existence of particular regimes. (This phenomenon is closely akin to—and often part of—the politically dangerous transition from controlled to liberalized economies discussed in Chapter 17.) Because political leaders themselves live in urban areas, and because urban residents are in a better position than rural villagers to threaten governments, many states attempt to hold food prices down even during periods of general inflationary pres-

opment," in *Agricultural Development and Economic Growth,* H. M. Southworth and B. F. Johnston, eds., (Ithaca, N.Y.: Cornell University Press, 1967).

17. Walter Falcon and C. P. Timmer, "The Political Economy of Rice Production and Trade in Asia," in *Agriculture in Development Theory,* L. Reynolds, ed. (New Haven: Yale University Press, 1975).

A.

B.

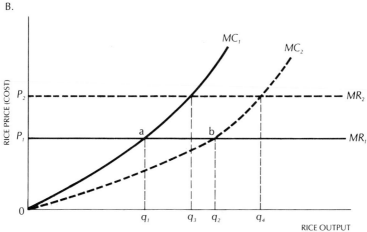

FIGURE 18–6 **Rice Production and the Rice-Fertilizer Price Ratio.**

sure. The result is depressed prices for farmers that reduce both farm income
and farm output.

Especially (but not exclusively) in some developed nations the political
power of the farmers is such that governments raise farm purchase prices
in order to gain rural support. Democracies that still have large or politically powerful rural populations are particularly likely to respond to these
pressures. The United States and Japan in the 1950s and 1960s, the EEC in
the 1960s, and South Korea in the late 1960s and early 1970s are examples.
The result is that prices are favorable to higher yields, but the income and
production benefits of the higher prices may not be equitably distributed.
In some countries it is richer farmers who market a high percentage of their
output and hence gain most from high prices. Small subsistence farms market little and hence gain little. In other nations, however, all farmers market
a high percentage of their crop and hence all gain from higher prices.

Where both urban and rural residents have considerable political influence, governments have sometimes tried to maintain both low urban food

prices and high farm purchase prices. Japan since World War II and South Korea and Mexico in the 1970s all pursued this dual goal. Since the government must pick up the resulting deficit arising from selling food at prices below what it cost to purchase, only governments with large resources or those willing to forego other high-priority goals can afford this policy. Thus there is no single right answer to how high prices to farmers should be. Ultimately the decision turns on political as well as economic judgments.

One common way to subsidize grain marketing is for the government to absorb the often substantial costs of moving grain from the farm to the urban retail market. Who benefits from this process depends on how the subsidy is handled. Several of the possibilities are illustrated in Figure 18–7, in which marketing costs are represented by the vertical distance between the farmer's grain supply curve and the retail supply curve facing urban residents. These costs are assumed to be a constant amount per unit of grain marketed. On a free market without subsidy, the retail price of grain on the urban retail market would be p_1 and the price received by farmers would be p_2. As this diagram indicates, if the subsidy goes to farmers, the result can be either a rise in grain storage or exports. If the subsidy goes to urban consumers, on the other hand, the excess demand will lead to a rise in imports.

It is not just foreign trade in grain that is affected by these subsidies. The cost of marketing must be borne by someone, and in these cases it will

FIGURE 18–7. **Effect of a Marketing Subsidy on Supply and Demand for Food Grains.** If farmers receive the marketing cost subsidy P_1P_2, then the farmer's price rises to P_1 and farm output rises from q_1 to q_2. Since food-grain supply now exceeds demand, the excess must either be stored or exported. On the other hand, if urban consumers are given the entire P_1P_2 subsidy, then the price paid by these consumers will fall to P_2 and their demand will rise from q_1 to q_3. The excess in demand will then have to be supplied from imports, or the government will have to ration the allocation of food grains to urban consumers.
Source: This diagram is a modified version of that in Timmer, Falcon, and Pearson, *Food Policy Analysis,* p. 198.

most likely be an expenditure item in the government's budget. Or the grain marketing authority may borrow from the central bank to cover its costs, but without the ability of ever paying the loan back. The macroeconomic effects of these subsidies can be substantial, particularly in countries where a large portion of marketed agricultural produce is subsidized.

Overvalued Exchange Rates

Because the high cost of large subsidies to government marketing boards becomes increasingly obvious to policymakers over time, steps are usually taken to eventually bring these costs under control even though the political cost can be high. There is another way of subsidizing urban consumers or rural producers, however, that has a less obvious effect on the government budget but a profound effect on the economy: the use of an *overvalued exchange rate* (see Chapter 16). The impact of an overvalued exchange rate on the grain market is illustrated in Figure 18–8. If, at an equilibrium exchange rate, the world price of grain is P_2, then domestic demand, represented by the curve *DD*, will be $0q_4$, and the domestic supply of grain will exceed demand by the amount q_4q_2. This excess could be either stored or exported. But if this nation's currency becomes overvalued, the world price of grain expressed in terms of domestic currency will fall from P_2 to P_1. Domestic food-grain supply, in this case, will fall to q_3, and the excess of demand at this price q_3q_1 will be made up with imports or by restricting urban demand through rationing. Thus, although this method of subsidizing urban consumers does not show up as an expenditure item in the govern-

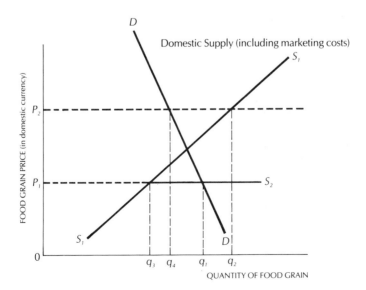

FIGURE 18–8. **The Grain Market with an Overvalued Exchange Rate.** If the world price of grain is P_2, then domestic demand (*DD*) will be q_4, and domestic supply (s_1s_2) will be q_2 and result in excess stocks for storage or export. With an overvalued exchange rate represented by P_1, however, domestic demand (q_1) exceeds domestic supply (q_3) and requires imports or rationing.

ment budget or a loss for the grain marketing board, it has a large negative impact on domestic agricultural production. Domestic agricultural production would fall from q_2 to q_3.

An undervalued exchange rate, of course, will have a positive impact on farm output, but poor urban and rural purchasers of food grain may be forced by high prices to reduce substantially their intake of food, and this may lead to malnutrition and worse. In developing nations the poor spend a high proportion—over 50 percent—of their budget on food. A price increase for food thus represents a sharp drop in income for these people. They can try to maintain food consumption by cutting back on other items in their budget, but these are usually necessities as well.

Agricultural price policies, therefore, have a profound effect on both agricultural production and on the standard of living and even the basic health of the poorer segments of a country's people. Since agricultural prices and the exchange rate are usually set by the government in developing countries, it is technically a simple matter to change these prices to reflect the objectives of the government. Price changes involve few of the institution-building or implementation problems connected with building an effective extension system or mobilizing labor for public works projects. Price changes, however, do involve readily apparent costs to those on the receiving end of higher prices. If these people are in a position of influence, the political barriers to effective price policy can be formidable.

19

Sustainable Development: Natural Resources and the Environment

As recently as the 1960s, economics textbooks typically presented air and water as prototypical "free" goods, available in limitless supply at a zero price. It is now well-understood that all natural resource endowments as well as environmental services must be interpreted as scarce resources and that underpricing them, whether by design or by default, has been a prime factor in the worldwide degradation of natural resources and the environment.

In economics, analysis is complicated by the fact that everything is connected to everything else. This is true with particular force of environmental and resource issues. As a result there is no satisfactory way to integrate these issues in a textbook on the economics of development; any format involves artificial divisions. For example, the pace and scale of environmental degradation is strongly related to problems of population growth and migration, discussed in Chapter 7. Chapter 4 deals with issues in human welfare, particularly poverty and income distribution. But ecological

524

SUSTAINABLE
DEVELOPMENT:
NATURAL
RESOURCES
AND THE
ENVIRONMENT
(Ch. 19)

calamities have often had catastrophic implications for poverty and income distribution; the reverse is also often true. In this chapter, fresh water and soils are treated as natural resources, while the uses of these resources in agriculture were covered in Chapter 18.

For expository purposes only, the discussion in this chapter is divided into two related topics: **natural resources** and the **environment**. Natural resources include a wide array of physical endowments provided by nature: soils, water, minerals, timber, and wild animals. Natural resources may be living (timber) or nonliving (fossil fuels). They may be **renewable** (wild animals) or nonrenewable (minerals). As the term is used here, "environment" means the natural systems that provide the underpinnings or the setting (or both) for human activity. These systems include not only forest ecosystems and watersheds, but geophysical systems such as meteorological systems and coastal systems.

SUSTAINABLE DEVELOPMENT

For the ecologists, economists, and biologists who understand the essence of resource scarcity, sustainable development is generally defined as the development path that maximizes the **long-term, net** benefits to humankind.[1] Sustainable development stresses not the need to limit development, but the need to develop in order to be able to conserve.[2] A sustainable development strategy allows drawing down on natural resource assets, and utilization of environmental services if that will produce greater long-term, net benefits (including income gains, employment, and reduction of poverty) than leaving resources in the ground or keeping the environment in pristine condition. It therefore makes conservation the helper of development and the guardian of the interests of future generations. The concept of sustainable development values preservation not for its own sake, but for its contribution to the welfare of present and future generations. Because sustainable development is focused on net benefits, it ensures that the cost of resource and environmental degradation values will not be undervalued (underpriced).

Sustainable development is an important concept for all societies. But poor people in developing countries are far more dependent on their soils, fisheries, and forests than are citizens of rich countries. Therefore, degradation of resources and environment is an even greater threat to living standards in developing countries. Fortunately for LDCs, sustainable development does not necessarily imply low rates of income growth. It does imply more efficient growth, however.

Development policies followed by many developing countries, often on the advice of foreign experts or lending institutions, have involved need-

---

1. For a systematic discussion of the history and practice of sustainable development, see William Ascher and Robert Healy, *Natural Resource Policy-Making in Developing Countries* (Durham, N.C.: Duke University Press, 1990). The above definition of sustainable development is set forth in detail on pages 5–10 of that volume.
   2. Ibid., p. 7.

less, and generally unintended, resource and environmental costs. Policies
intended primarily to service nonenvironmental goals (such as tax, exchange rate, credit, and food price policies) have often had major impacts on the environment.[3] The pursuit of agricultural, energy, urbanization, and industrial objectives can have significant implications for soil degradation, watershed management, water quality, coastal fishing, and survival of coastal reefs. But these costs have rarely been considered in the design and implementation of development projects. Greater attention to the environmental impact of development policies and development projects, then, may lead to more efficient resource use as well as to more equitably distributed growth. Measures that narrow the scope for natural resource waste and environmental damage then become good economics, good geology, and good social policy.

Natural Resources

Non-Renewable Resources Deposits of oil, gas, nickel, iron, and other minerals are examples of nonrenewable resources. This does not mean that the available stock of such resources is a quantity that remains fixed from decade to decade or century to century. Rather, higher resource prices that increase the value of reserves or technological improvements that lower extraction costs can and do convert rock into ore, and marginal sedimentary basins into commercially attractive fields that oil companies may spend billions of dollars on to bring into production. But in a zinc deposit once mined or an oil field once depleted, the extracted resources cannot be renewed by nature in the next thousand millennia if ever. In what follows, we discuss the special public policy problems and opportunities presented by the largesse or paucity of nonrenewable natural resources.

Mineral Resources and Growth We saw in Part 3 that for most nations capital accumulation involves a slow, and often painful, process involving austerity in domestic consumption, substantial inflows of foreign savings, or both. Many countries, however, have been favored by geological anomalies that have left sizable endowments of natural capital in the form of nonrenewable resource deposits. Such diverse countries as the United States, Canada, Australia, Kuwait, Saudi Arabia, Venezuela, and Chile have found sufficient natural capital within their borders to enable them to short cut the usually laborious and ordinarily lengthy processes of capital accumulation.

Many, but by no means all, countries with significant mineral endowments do have something to show from decades of extracting nonrenewable natural wealth, in the form of higher stocks of physical and human capital. Over at least the years 1973 to 1982, a period of relatively high oil prices, a few oil-producing countries outside the large Mideast oil-export-

---

3. For a discussion of how tax, credit, exchange rate, and food price policies have affected deforestation in the tropics, see Robert Repetto and Malcolm Gillis, eds., *Public Policies and the Misuse of Forest Resources* (New York: Cambridge University Press, 1988).

526

SUSTAINABLE
DEVELOPMENT:
NATURAL
RESOURCES
AND THE
ENVIRONMENT
(Ch. 19)

TABLE 19–1 Dependence on Oil and Natural Gas Exports and Real Average Annual GDP
Growth, 1980–1988

Low- and middle-income, capital-importing OPEC countries[a]	Fuel exports as a % of total exports for the year indicated		1980–1988 average annual GDP growth (%)
Algeria	1986	98	3.5
Ecuador	1984	70	2.0
Gabon	1983	79	−0.2
Indonesia	1986	56	5.1
Nigeria	1984	95	−1.1
Venezuela	1986	95	0.9
Mexico	1987	61	0.5
All low-income LDCs excluding India and China			2.0[b]
All middle-income LDCs			2.9[a]

[a] Data for Iran and Iraq are unavailable for the years in question.
[b] Low-income LDCs excluding China and India. With India and China included, average real GDP growth for all low-income nations was 6.4 percent for 1980 to 1988.
Sources: For 1981 oil exports, OPEC, *Facts and Figures: A Comparative Statistical Analysis* (Vienna: OPEC, 1981), p. 17, and for other years, United Nations, *1987 International Trade Statistic Yearbook* (New York: 1989), country tables. For 1980 to 1988, World Bank, *World Development Indicators 1990*, Table 2.

ing nations managed to convert booming resource exports into temporarily high income growth. These include Ecuador, Indonesia, and Malaysia, in all of which real GDP grew at a 6 percent annual rate or better. Growth in developing oil exporting nations declined sharply, however, in the period following the weakening in the world oil market from the end of 1982 to 1987. As can be seen in Table 19–1, only Indonesia and Algeria among LDC oil exporters managed to retain relatively high rates of GDP during the 1980s.

However, even during the period of the first two oil booms (1973 to 1982), most oil exporters did not turn mineral wealth into the beginnings of sustainable growth. Moreover, the postwar history of countries such as Bolivia, Chile, Zambia, and Zaire suggests countries exporting nonfuel minerals also encountered little success in deploying natural resource earnings in ways that fostered diversified, and hence more sustainable, economic growth. Table 19–2 shows that nonfuel mineral exporters tended to grow substantially more slowly than low-income nations in general and substantially more slowly than India and China. And among middle-income, nonfuel mineral exporters, only Morocco grew as rapidly as middle-income nations in general. But disappointing results are not exclusively a recent phenomenon. Chile, for example, has little to show for nearly a century of large-scale activity in the mining sector, first in the extraction of natural nitrates and later of copper; and Bolivia is still one of the poorest countries in Latin America after more than three centuries as a mining country *par excellence*.

Dependence upon nonrenewable resources for export earnings is marked for many of the relatively populous middle-income OPEC nations including Algeria, Nigeria, and Indonesia as shown in Table 19–1. For exporters of nonfuel minerals, listed in Table 19–2, hard minerals have typically accounted for more than 10 percent of GDP, more than 50 percent of total merchan-

TABLE 19–2 Nonfuel Mineral Exporters Dependence on Mining Exports and Annual Average GDP Growth, 1980–1988

Country	Share of mining in GDP for the year shown (%)		Share of nonfuel minerals in total exports (%)	1980–1988 average GDP growth (%)
Low-income countries				
Liberia	1986	9.5	65	−1.3
Mauritania	1984	13.4	52	1.6
Sierra Leone	1986	7.2	61	0.2
Togo	1981	8.8	51	0.5
Zaire	1975	22.7	59	1.9
Zambia	1986	8.5	93	0.7
All low-income countries' average annual growth				2.0[a]
Lower-middle-income countries				
Bolivia	1987	11.1	39	−1.6
Chile	1987	7.9	53	1.9
Guyana	1987	9.0	45	1.5[b]
Morocco	1987	3.7	43	4.2
Peru	1987	10.1	39	1.1
All lower-middle-income countries' average annual growth				2.6

[a]Figure excludes India and China.

[b]Figures are for 1973 to 1983 and are taken from World Bank, *World Tables 1983* (Baltimore: Johns Hopkins Press, 1984).

Sources: For share of mining in GDP, United Nations, *National Accounts Statistics: Main Aggregates and Detailed Tables, 1987* (New York: United Nations, 1990), country tables, Table 1.11; for export figures, United Nations, *1987 International Trade Statistics Yearbook,* country tables; and for 1980 to 1988 GDP figures, World Bank, *World Development Indicators 1990,* Table 2.

dise exports, or both. Thus we have to reject the conventional wisdom of the 1950s and 1960s, which held that countries with relatively rich natural-resource endowments would ordinarily be expected to achieve higher rates of economic growth than less well-endowed nations.

Energy Resources Energy from nonrenewable resources includes that derived from oil, coal, natural gas, and uranium. Nuclear power, obtained from enriched uranium, is an unimportant source of power for all but a very few LDCs. Other sources of **commercial** energy are renewable or inexhaustible in nature; in order of their relative importance in LDCs in 1988, they include hydroelectric power, geothermal energy, solar power, and wind power. Of this group, only water power was a significant source of commercial energy in LDCs in the late 1980s, particularly in Brazil, Chile, Colombia, Ghana, Zambia, and Zimbabwe. Studies by the World Resources Institute indicate that about 75 percent of electric power consumed in South America in 1987 was produced in hydroelectric plants, rather than oil- or coal-fired generating facilities. In Africa (excluding South Africa), however, the proportion supplied by hydropower was only one-third.[4]

Although virtually all energy consumed in transportation, electric power

4. World Resources Institute, *World Resources 1900–91* (New York: Oxford University Press, 1990).

528

SUSTAINABLE
DEVELOPMENT:
NATURAL
RESOURCES
AND THE
ENVIRONMENT
(Ch. 19)

generation, and residential and commercial use in the developed countries comes from commercial energy sources, developing countries also make substantial use of **noncommercial** energy sources, including animal dung, agricultural waste, and fuel wood. In large countries such as India, and even OPEC-member Indonesia in the mid-1970s, noncommercial energy use was almost as important as commercial energy. The share of noncommercial energy in overall LDC energy utilization has, however, been declining steadily since 1960, and this decline is expected to continue as nations develop.

A **resource reserve** is an identified deposit known to be recoverable with current technology under present economic conditions. Total world **proven** recoverable reserves of any resource are merely the sum total of all known deposits that can be recovered with reasonable certainty. Reserve figures are never precise, even for a particular deposit in a particular country, and published reserve figures by country often differ significantly according to whether they are derived from industry or government sources. Further, and more significantly, reserve estimates can change abruptly as resource prices change; at higher oil prices, for example, reserves are higher, as formerly submarginal deposits are converted into commercially attractive ones.

Table 19–3 portrays the distribution of proven hydrocarbon (crude oil, natural gas, and coal) energy reserves by region. Of these three energy resources, oil is the most prized, primarily because it can be transported most easily, through pipelines on land and in tankers on the oceans. In its

TABLE 19–3   Proven World Reserves of Energy in Oil, Natural Gas, and Coal, 1988
(in petajoules[a], share of energy reserves in percent in parentheses)

	Oil reserves	Natural gas reserves	Coal reserves	Total reserves
North America	230,285 (4.4%)	310,720 (7.1%)	5,622,779 (25.1%)	6,163,784 19.3%
Latin America	715,977 (13.8%)	260,228 (6.0%)	286,104 (1.3%)	1,263,309 (4.0%)
Western Europe	100,488 (1.9%)	221,388 (5.1%)	1,798,193 (8.0%)	1,120,069 (6.6%)
Middle East	3,236,551 (62.4%)	1,297,256 (29.8%)	0 (0.0%)	4,533,807 (14.2%)
Africa	314,025 (6.0%)	275,764 (6.3%)	1,826,124 (8.2%)	2,415,914 (7.6%)
Asia and Australasia	113,049 (2.2%)	264,112 (6.1%)	1,918,603 (8.6%)	2,295,764 (7.2%)
Centrally Planned Economies	473,131 (9.1%)	1,716,728 (39.5%)	10,906,690 (48.8%)	13,096,549 (41.1%)
Totals	5,183,506 (100.0%)	4,346,196 (100.0%)	22,359,494 (100.0%)	31,889,196 (100.0%)

[a]One petajoule = 23,883 metric tons of oil equivalent.
Source: World Resources Institute, *World Resources 1990–91,* Table 9.2, p. 145.

original state, natural gas can be shipped only via pipeline, and it can be shipped across oceans by tanker only when liquified in very expensive liquefication plants. But natural gas involves less severe environmental problems, because it burns more cleanly than oil, whereas oil ordinarily involves fewer pollution problems than coal. Coal, a resource with a high ratio of bulk to heat content, is also expensive to transport, particularly to overseas export markets.

Proven oil reserves are heavily concentrated in high-income OPEC countries in the Middle East (Table 19–3), whereas natural gas reserves were, and are located in economies that were centrally planned before 1988. Developed market economies had respectable shares of both oil and gas reserves, but poor nations in Africa and Latin America (aside from Mexico, Venezuela, and Ecuador) were virtually bereft of these energy resources. Proven world coal resources are also heavily concentrated in developed market economies and centrally planned economies. In terms of peta-joules, coal resources were roughly 2½ times greater than combined oil and gas reserves. (One petajoule is equal to 23,883 metric tons of oil equiva-lent.)

Production is, of course, related to reserves, though imperfectly. Two of the world's three largest petroleum and gas producers are not members of OPEC, and no developing country is a major coal producer. (See Table 19–4.) The world's first-ranking oil producer in 1989 was the Soviet Union,

TABLE 19–4   Major Producers of Crude Oil and Per-Capita Production, 1989

	Yearly production (million barrels)	Per-capita yearly production (barrels)
OPEC countries		
Saudi Arabia	1,802.7	128.8
Kuwait	567.6	283.8
Libya	409.9	97.6
United Arab Emirates	664.7	443.1
Iraq	1,050.5	59.7
Iran	1,075.7	22.1
Nigeria	584.4	5.3
Venezuela	627.1	33.4
Indonesia	446.4	2.6
Ecuador	101.8	10.1
Gabon	75.9	69.0
Western developed countries		
United States	2,795.2	11.3
Great Britain	641.7	11.2
Canada	569.8	21.9
Developing countries		
Mexico	954.8	11.4
Malaysia	203.3	12.0
Trinidad and Tobago	55.8	46.5
Egypt	311.0	6.2
Soviet Union	4,438.4	15.5

Sources: For 1989 production figures, *Oil and Gas Journal* 88, no. 7 (Feb. 12, 1990): 34, and for mid-1988 population estimates from which per-capita production figures have been derived (except for the Soviet Union), World Bank, *World Development Indicators 1990*, Table 1. A 1989 population estimate for the Soviet Union was obtained from *The World Almanac and Book of Facts 1990* (New York: 1990), p. 761.

530

SUSTAINABLE
DEVELOPMENT:
NATURAL
RESOURCES
AND THE
ENVIRONMENT
(Ch. 19)

followed by the United States and Saudi Arabia, which could at any time produce more than the United States if it so desired. Outside the broad expanses of the United States and the Soviet Union, the known geological anomalies that yield oil deposits have tended to occur in lightly populated countries in the Middle East, where annual production in several high-income OPEC members reaches 200 and even 400 barrels per capita per year. For middle-income LDCs, oil reserves are relatively modest, even among developing-country OPEC members. Per-capita production of oil in Canada was four times as high as in OPEC member Nigeria, and U.S. production per capita is almost 4 times that of OPEC member Indonesia.

Over the long run improvements in living standards within a country require steady advances in labor productivity. In turn enhanced productivity ultimately requires the replacement of human and animal power by electric power obtainable from such primary energy sources as oil and gas. World consumption of commercial energy across countries is even more skewed than world reserves and world production of commercial energy. The nation with the highest per-capita consumption of energy, Canada, uses 29 times more energy per person per year than the average for middle-income LDCs.

Nonfuel Minerals

Although developing countries are often considered to be a critical source of nonfuel minerals, in 1983 their share of annual world production exceeded 50 percent in only four metals: cobalt, chromite, copper, and tin. All except copper are relatively minor items in world trade when compared with petroleum. LDCs are also the leading producers of bauxite and phosphate. Developed industrial countries are the leading sources of world supply for lead, sulphur, nickel, and zinc. And for four of the minerals in Table 19–5, centrally planned economies, principally the Soviet Union and China, have a larger share in world production than developing countries.

Within developing countries, production of nonfuel minerals tends to be concentrated in less than a dozen nations. Brazil is far and away the leading producer of iron ore and is an important source of manganese and asbestos. Bolivia is a leading producer of both tin and tungsten, Indonesia the world's first-ranking producer of tin, and Zaire and Zambia the two principal sources of cobalt. After Chile, Zambia is also the second leading source of copper among LDCs. Over 80 percent of LDC production of bauxite comes from four developing countries—Jamaica, Guinea, Guyana, and Surinam—but even so, developed countries produce almost as much as these four.

RENTS AND RETURNS IN NATURAL-RESOURCE PROJECTS

Resource Rents

Commercial accumulations of nonrenewable resources are particularly valuable to countries because they involve potential surplus value over and

531

RENTS AND
RETURNS IN
NATURAL-
RESOURCE
PROJECTS

TABLE 19–5   Percentage Share of World Production of 10 Nonfuel Minerals, 1987,
Developed, Centrally Planned, and Developing Countries[a]

Mineral	Developed countries	Centrally planned countries	Developing countries
Bauxite	40.1	11.6	48.4
Copper ore	30.3	22.9	46.8
Iron ore	29.5	37.6	32.9
Lead ore	47.4	30.1	22.5
Manganese ore[b]	23.2	48.0	28.8
Nickel ore	41.8	26.4	31.8
Phosphate rock	32.8	30.6	36.6
Sulphur	50.4	35.1	14.5
Tin ore	9.1	26.1	64.7
Tungsten ore	10.2	74.5	15.3

[a] Rows may not add up to 100 due to rounding.
[b] Figures are for 1986.
Source: United Nations Conference on Trade and Development, UNCTAD Commodity Yearbook 1989 (New York: United Nations, 1989), pp. 262–365.

above the costs of labor and capital used to find and extract them. In resource economics this surplus value is called **rent**.[5] There are actually three types of rent associated with commercial resource deposits. First, **scarcity rent** is defined as any return accruing to any production factor in inelastic supply. Scarcity rents are not confined to natural resources; they can be received by sports figures blessed with extraordinary strength or speed, or by concert violinists possessing an unusual combination of musical skills and dexterity. Like natural resources, such talents are also scarce and in inelastic supply. Lacking these rare talents, the sports figures and violinists might be qualified only as security guards and music teachers. The earnings they receive in excess of salaries for security guards or teachers are called **rents.**

Geological processes do not produce large numbers of readily accessible deposits, nor do soil and climate conditions everywhere favor the rise of dense forests. Thus resources are scarce. Indeed, at any given time a particular natural resource is in perfectly inelastic supply. And ignoring exploration costs to keep the representation simple, the cost of a resource in the ground is zero, as it was left by nature at no cost to society. Because in the typical LDC situation government owns the property rights to natural resources, it may dispose of them as it sees fit.[6] Natural-resource firms will be prepared to bid for rights to extract the resource.

5. Advanced resource economics treatises show that resource rents depend on a complex set of relationships involving the time path of extraction, rate of interest, and risk. We present here a more prosaic, but still serviceable, view of rent.

6. Systems of property rights can and do have significant effects on the way a society uses resources, including nonrenewable resources. The United States is one of the few nations in the world in which property rights in minerals can be vested in private individuals. In all states, the owner of the right to surface land generally owns the title to the subsoil rights as well. While the federal government is a major landowner itself, particularly in the western states, most of the present known reserves of natural resources in the United States remain in private hands.

In the overwhelming majority of developing countries, subsoil rights are ordinarily separate from surface rights and may not be vested in individuals or private business firms. Rather,

532

SUSTAINABLE
DEVELOPMENT:
NATURAL
RESOURCES
AND THE
ENVIRONMENT
(Ch. 19)

To understand the nature of scarcity rent and to describe the other two kinds of rent, let us consider a mineral to be called monzanium. Assume initially that there is only one use for monzanium, say, in making ball bearings, and also assume that all monzanium deposits are of uniform size and quality (that is, they are homogeneous). Then, assuming a competitive market, the demand curve for monzanium deposits (*DD* in Figure 19–1) is the value of the marginal product schedule of monzanium in ball-bearing production. If, in 1980, monzanium deposits are very plentiful and easily accessible, then (ignoring exploration costs) *OD* deposits will be employed, and the government will receive no rents from firms that might bid for mining rights. But if monzanium is scarce relative to demand for it, and also in inelastic supply as shown by the supply curve in Figure 19–1, then each of the *OX* deposits available in 1980 will earn a "scarcity" rent equal to *OR*, consistent with *CD* deposits.

In the real world, however, resource deposits are not homogeneous; some deposits are of higher quality or can be more cheaply mined. Bidders for rights to extract monzanium will pay more for rights to the deposits of better quality. Let us assume two deposit qualities and indicate demand for poorer deposits as *DD* and demand for better deposits as D_1D_1. With the supply of monzanium still at *XX*, then OR_1 is the rent paid to each deposit of high quality and the lower-quality deposit will receive *OR* in rent. The rent *OR* may be viewed as a scarcity rent. The excess of OR_1 over *OR* is the second type of rent and may be called **differential resource rent,** to reflect the differential value of the higher quality deposit.

Two types of rent are therefore depicted in Figure 19–1: **scarcity rent,** due to the limited inelastic supply of a resource, and **differential rent,** due to the higher quality or lower extraction costs of some deposits relative to others. A third type of rent is often associated with natural-resource activities: **monopoly** (or **oligopoly**) **rent.** Historically, natural-resource extraction has been dominated by large multinational firms, several of which have had sufficient market power to affect world resource prices. For example, INCO of Canada until the late 1970s controlled enough of the international nickel market to set nickel prices. DeBeers of South Africa controlled virtually all the world's supply of uncut diamonds for nearly 50 years and clearly exercised monopoly power. Although the monopoly power of the natural-resource multinationals has eroded in recent years, there are still enough barriers to entry in modern, highly capital-intensive mineral and petroleum extraction to generate some monopoly rents, as shown in Figure 19–2.

Suppose that the mining of monzanium is dominated by a single profit-maximizing monopoly firm, or, almost the same, by a small group of oligopolists who attempt to maximize the joint profits of firms in the industry. If, for a monzanium deposit in any particular country, the resource can be extracted at constant marginal costs (a simplifying cost assumption), then average costs will also be constant, as represented in Figure 19–2 by hori-

---

natural resource deposits in most LDCs are defined, whether by constitutional or other legal means, as part of the national patrimony, wherein the state acts as either the trustee for, or the actual owner of, all natural resource endowments.

533

RENTS AND
RETURNS IN
NATURAL-
RESOURCE
PROJECTS

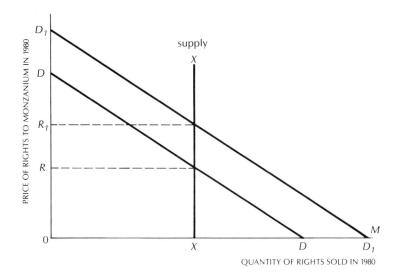

FIGURE 19–1 **Scarcity and Differential Rent for Monzanium Deposits.** Scarcity rent is depicted by OR and the differential rent (for higher quality deposits) is OR_1 minus OR.

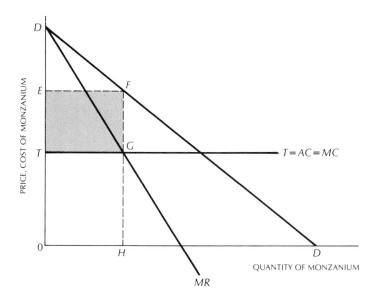

FIGURE 19–2 **Monopoly or Oligopoly Rent in the Monzanium Industry.** The shaded area $TEFG$ represents economic profit or the monopoly or oligopoly rent for monzanium.

zontal curve TT. As in any average cost curve depicted in microeconomics, included in AC is a "normal" return to capital, or simply the opportunity cost of capital.

If demand for monzanium is given as DD, we know that associated with any straight-line demand curve such as DD is a marginal revenue curve MR having exactly twice the slope of DD (which is merely the average-

534

SUSTAINABLE
DEVELOPMENT:
NATURAL
RESOURCES
AND THE
ENVIRONMENT
(Ch. 19)

revenue curve). Under these conditions then, the monopolist (or the joint-profit-maximizing oligopolists) will produce OH units of monzanium. This is the level of production that maximizes profit, since only at OH production does MC or producing monzanium equal MR from sales. Each unit of monzanium will sell for OE. Economic profit per unit is $OE - OT,$ or the excess return over per-unit average cost inclusive of a normal return to capital. Total economic profit is the shaded rectangle $TEFG$. This is identical to monopoly rent, defined as a surplus return over and above the costs of labor and capital used to extract the resource.

Rents, whether scarcity, differential, or monopoly, have a very special characteristic. By definition a rent is a return in excess of that required to attract factors of production to an activity. There are no laws, economic or otherwise, that can specify who has a "right" to rents arising from natural resources. The rents may accrue to investors in LDC resource projects; if they are multinationals, the rents will flow to stockholders abroad. Alternatively, the host LDC government may take steps to capture the rents through taxation or through direct involvement in the project. The central point, however, is that full capture of rents by the host country will not affect the behavior of the extractive firm, be it national or foreign. Only when government efforts go beyond the extraction of rents and impinge on the "normal" return to capital invested by the firm will the firm consider shutting down operations. That is, the government, through taxes or other devices, could appropriate 50 to 100 percent of the rents represented by the shaded area $TEFG$ in Figure 19–2 without affecting either the price or the production of the firm.

Public Policy and Rent Capture

If capture of rents in natural-resource activities in LDCs were as simple a matter as depicted above, many resource-rich countries would be substantially wealthier than at present. In fact, rents turn out to be easy to describe, but difficult to identify with any precision because modern extractive activity is a highly complex undertaking, in both an engineering and a managerial sense. Also, an accurate assessment of rent in oil and hard-mineral projects requires accurate delineation of reserves. Inasmuch as these are not always easily verifiable even with modern technology, magnitudes of potential resource rents in any project are never fully knowable.

Nevertheless, there have been enough lessons from natural-resource investments in the past few decades to allow one or two safe generalizations about rent and rent capture. First, experience around the world has shown that public policy toward nonrenewable resources that is not based on an appreciation of the existence of rents is **perforce** inimical to the interests of the society owning the resources. Second, public policies purporting to secure full capture of resource rents are not to be taken seriously, owing to the very considerable difficulties involved in identifying and collecting rents in any given project.

By now dozens of countries have learned these lessons, often only by trial and error. Over the period 1960 to 1990, the attitudes of developing-

535

RENTS AND
RETURNS IN
NATURAL-
RESOURCE
PROJECTS

country governments toward rent capture evolved steadily, and this has been reflected in both the design and execution of their policies toward natural-resource endowments. It is only a slight exaggeration to say that the prime objective of natural-resource policy in most LDCs only two decades ago was a very simple one: secure for the host country at least some share of resource rents from the exploitation of natural resources by the large multinational firms that then dominated the world resource picture. Attaining that modest goal depended almost entirely on tax policy. Employment, regional development, and other expected benefits from natural-resource development have historically been relatively insignificant in most LDCs, primarily because of the marked capital intensity of most extractive activity. (See the discussion of linkages in Chapter 15.) By the end of the 1960s, emphasis in many LDCs had shifted toward efforts to minimize the returns of the multinationals, and by the close of the 1970s, to the much sounder objective of maximizing net host country returns, which is not the same thing as minimizing multinationals' profits.

By the mid-1980s the changes in tax policy and tax administration sketched earlier had, in a number of LDCs, converted the natural-resource sectors into very significant revenue producers. Natural resources furnished between 5 and 15 percent of total central government receipts in Thailand, Colombia, Honduras, Panama, Peru, and the Philippines; between 15 and 25 percent in Chile and Malaysia; in excess of 25 percent in Ecuador, Mexico, Jamaica, Liberia, Zaire, and Zambia; and well in excess of 50 percent in Bolivia, Indonesia, Gabon, the Malaysian state of Sabah, Papua New Guinea, and New Caledonia.

Measures for facilitating host country capture of resource rents include **windfall** or **excess-profits taxes** and transfer of "free" equity shares in natural-resource projects to the governments involved. Such measures have met with a considerable degree of success. The percentage share of host country taxes in the value or resource production or in resource profits has been typically half again—and sometimes twice—the levels common in the early 1960s, except, in general, for uranium. This indicates a very marked tightening of terms available to investors.

Rising host country shares have been particularly evident in the case of oil. Host country shares of profits in oil were never much more than 10 to 15 percent before 1930. But by 1980 there were numerous instances in which this share had surpassed 80 percent. In 1980 Malaysia had managed to capture 80 percent of production and 98 percent of the profits in oil production. By 1990 even in countries that do not employ windfall profits taxes or windfall royalties in oil, the government's share in the value of oil produced was close to 70 percent. For many other non-OPEC producers, as well as some OPEC members like Indonesia, host country shares of between 75 and 85 percent of value and 80 and 90 percent of profits were common during periods of high oil prices such as 1979 to 1983.

Substantial changes also occurred in the taxation of tropical timber, but not until the latter part of the 1970s, after decades in which host governments seemed to overlook the presence of rents in timber. Tax adjustments by Indonesia and the Malaysian state of Sabah, the two dominant produc-

536

SUSTAINABLE
DEVELOPMENT:
NATURAL
RESOURCES
AND THE
ENVIRONMENT
(Ch. 19)

ers, from 1978 to 1980 resulted in sizable increments in revenues. The share of taxes in the gross value of timber exports doubled immediately to 29 percent in Indonesia and to 53 percent in Sabah.

Nonrenewable Resources and Sustainable Development

Tax and other policies for the capture of natural-resource rents play a critical role in the implementation of strategies for sustainable development. By their very nature, oil, gas, and mineral deposits per se cannot be expected to generate a sustainable yield for an indefinite period of time. A copper deposit once mined or an oil field once depleted is no longer capable of generating any positive returns, sustained or otherwise. Rather, sustainable development of exhaustible resources requires that they be utilized to produce the greatest long-term, net benefits to society. Sometimes this rule will mean that resources should be left where they are found because the resources are more valuable to society in their original, untouched state.

For instance, forested land containing extensive, low-grade copper deposits would not be mined if the value of the forested land in protecting the watershed exceeded the value of the copper that could be taken from the land. By the same token, a forest containing immense reserves of very high-grade tin resources would not be preserved as a wilderness. In this case, sustainable development policy would require society to draw down the natural resource endowment to finance acquisition of manufactured capital or to underwrite employment growth. Thus, sustainable development with exhaustible resources requires thinking about the possibilities for reconstituting the resource base; it means that we must think of the possibilities of converting part of the natural resource base into other forms of capital, to maintain or improve a country's income stream (and hence net wealth) over the long term.[7]

The necessary, but not sufficient, condition for this reconstitution is that the owner of the resource must capture the rents from the exploitation of the resource. One of the cornerstones of sustainable development strategies must be an effective policy for capturing rent from nonrenewable resources. Rents not captured cannot be reconstituted by the owner into useful physical capital (roads, water treatment plants) or human capital (an educated, healthy work force).

DEVELOPMENT AND THE ENVIRONMENT

It has long been recognized that development can have major effects on the environment. The concept of sustainable development goes well beyond this recognition to consider also the effects of the environment on development. Developing nations, including the environmentally devastated poor nations of Eastern and Central Europe, are faced with the task of coping not only with localized environmental problems generated primarily by local

---

7. See Ascher and Healy, "Natural Resource Policy-making," for a fully developed discussion of this point.

poverty, but also with global environment conundra having their origin chiefly in the wealthy industrialized nations. At the same time, some of the domestic environmental problems of developing states have major international implications on a significant scale. Consider the implications of tropical deforestation, a problem occurring almost wholly in developing nations.

By 1989, the area covered by moist tropical forest worldwide was less than 60 percent of the original extent of 13.6 million kilometers.[8] This means that an area of forest cover larger than the Soviet Union has disappeared, primarily since 1945. Worse, rates of tropical deforestation worldwide have accelerated over the past 10 years. Few analysts now doubt that the current annual rate of deforestation in the tropics is below 1.5 percent per year, a rate double that of the early eighties.[9] Worldwide loss of tropical forest has been one of the factors linked to global warming through the atmospheric accumulations of heat-trapping "greenhouse gases," especially carbon dioxide released from burnt-over cleared forests. Although skeptics argue over the scientific evidence on global warming, few argue that the risk can be ignored. The potential consequences include a rise in sea level that would accompany global warming and flood low-lying, sometimes populous lands; adverse consequences for world agriculture from shifting climate zones; and other threats we cannot anticipate, including those to human health.

But it is not necessary to invoke the specter of global warming to make a compelling case for slowing the present pace of tropical deforestation. The accelerating loss of tropical forest cover involves grave economic, ecological, and equity issues for developing nations, with or without greenhouse effects. Unfortunately, much of the international debate over measures for curtailing tropical deforestation has been conducted as if economic values are inherently in conflict with ecological and equity values.

Tropical deforestation is only one facet of the puzzle of the global environment. Other facets include acid rain, depletion of ozone in the upper atmosphere, disposal of nuclear wastes, depletion and pollution of water and air resources, loss of biodiversity, soil loss and soil degradation, and coastal degradation (including the destruction of coral reefs). Because acid rain and nuclear waste disposal are, at present, primarily problems originating in developed countries, and because developing nations have not been major factors in contributing to ozone depletion (but are nevertheless as much at risk as industrial nations), these quandaries will not be further treated here.

Other than tropical deforestation, the most urgent environmental dilemmas facing developing nations appears far less cosmic than say, ozone depletion and contamination from nuclear waste. But if not as cosmic, many are at a stage much more acute. Groundwater pollution from cadmium, mercury, and other heavy metals has threatened the health of such densely populated urban areas as Jakarta, Sao Paulo, Mexico City, and Silesia in Poland for over a decade.

Rural dwellers face groundwater contamination from runoffs of pesti-

8. Norman Myers, "Deforestation Rates in Tropical Forests and their Climatic Implications" (London: Friends of the Earth, 1989).
9. Ibid.

538

SUSTAINABLE
DEVELOPMENT:
NATURAL
RESOURCES
AND THE
ENVIRONMENT
(Ch. 19)

cides and fertilizers in at least a dozen developing countries, including such Eastern European nations as Bulgaria, where subsidized prices of these inputs have led to overuse. River and watershed pollution have made half of Poland's river mileage, including the Vistula, unfit even for industrial use.[10] So polluted with nitrates was the well water in the countryside in Czechoslovakia in 1989, that women with newborn infants were given priority access to bottled water for their infants. The most polluted air in the world is found in Prague, Seoul, Rio de Janeiro, Sofia, New Delhi, and Mexico City.[11] Watershed deterioration arising from deforestation has led to such heavy siltation of manufactured lakes for power projects that the useful life of many reservoirs has been slashed by 60 to 70 percent in Chile, the Philippines, Indonesia, and virtually every nation in Central America.[12] In the Philippines and several other nations, coral reefs and valuable coastal fishing areas are being destroyed by sediments coming from faraway upland forests converted to shifting cultivation. Elsewhere, reef systems are rapidly disappearing because of the mining of reefs for building materials (Maldives, Bali in Indonesia) or by the massive use of explosives to catch fish (Tanga in Tanzania). And the causes of coastal degradation are not limited to deforestation and mining of coral reefs. In several South American nations, mercury has long been used to concentrate gold from gold ore. Methyl mercury pollution has reached bays and coves in Brazil and Andean countries and resulted in human exposures hundreds of times above dangerous levels, with widespread neurotoxic effects. The short-term effects of such pollution on Indian populations is well-recognized; virtually nothing is known about the more insidious long-term effects.

Moreover, such problems are now appearing in clumps or clusters, especially in urban and industrial areas in the tropics and in low-income nations in Eastern and Central Europe. As a result, officials and environmental groups from Mexico City to Krakow to Jakarta and Bangkok have come to confront the grim possibility of environmental triage: with limited financial resources and expertise, not all, or even the most urgent, environmental dilemmas can be confronted. How does one choose which perils are to be dealt with first? How will decision makers be guided in selecting how many troops to shift to which environmental battlefield? What criteria will they use in these decisions? Should they invest in measures to reduce threats to human health for current generations, or should resources be concentrated on reducing the risks facing the next generation? Can the nutritional and health effects of the loss of employment for thousands of workers in polluting industries be ignored if these industries are shut down? Should saving the livelihoods of fishers be given a heavier weight than the livelihoods of pulp and paper workers in decisions to close plants discharging pollutants into the water? Should anyone attempt to do anything at all about already known cases of methyl mercury contamination, which lingers in bays for hundreds of years?

10. Tom Waters, "Ecoglasnost," *Discover* 11 (April 1990): 31.
11. *Health and Development* 1, no. 2, (Winter 1990): 17.
12. Jeffrey Leonard, *Natural Resources and Economic Development in Central America* [London: International Institute for Environment and Development (IIED) 1987], pp. 134–136.

These and milder forms of environmental triage involve economic, ecological, and equity issues of the most fundamental nature. Even if information about the severity of these problems were much better, and even if
we were more confident of what remedies could be applied, there would
still be little systematic basis for intelligent and humane choice in coping
with such a wide array of environmental dilemmas, particularly in nations
where many of the most serious environmental problems are rooted not in
the excesses of consumption, but in the exigencies of poverty.

Economic concepts can be helpful in improving the basis for these choices;
Economic and ecological tools together can help insure that the appropriate
questions about the environment will be asked and that the appropriate
answers are supplied for these questions. Before we try to find better answers
to better questions, it is essential that we identify as clearly as possible the
principal causes of environmental degradation in low and middle income
nations.

Causes of Environmental Degradation

No taxonomy of the causes of environmental degradation in poor nations
can be all-inclusive given the wide differences in incomes, cultures, institutions, climates, and resource endowments across over 100 developing
nations. The taxonomy offered here is by no means airtight and may require
significant modifications when applied to any single country.

The causes may be grouped into three broad categories, as long as it is
recognized that many environmental problems are outgrowths of two or
three interacting causes. These categories are (1) poverty, (2) ignorance,
and (3) institutional failure, including market failure and government failure. The taxonomy is used to provide two types of profiles of the role of
these three factors in environmental degradation in poor countries. The
first profile involves an issue cutting across dozens of countries: tropical
deforestation. The second profile examines, from the perspective of a single country (Indonesia), an array of rural and urban environmental problems caused by poverty, ignorance, institutions, and policies.

Tropical Deforestation

Poverty, without any question, is the most important cause of tropical
deforestation. In some tropical countries, poverty drives deforestation primarily by impelling shifting cultivation by rural peoples as well as by "shifted
cultivators," dislocated from cities to rural areas. In other countries, particularly in Africa, the role of poverty in deforestation is magnified by the
ever-more-desperate search for fuel wood by impoverished people. In Ghana
in 1983, for every tree harvested for lumber, nine were cut down for firewood;[13] this led to greater soil erosion, depletion of groundwater, and
declining agricultural productivity.

Ignorance spawns needless deforestation in two principal ways. First,

---

13. See Malcolm Gillis, "West Africa: Resource Management Policies and the Tropical
Forest," in *Public Policies and the Misuse of Forest Resources*, Repetto and Gillis.

540

SUSTAINABLE
DEVELOPMENT:
NATURAL
RESOURCES
AND THE
ENVIRONMENT
(Ch. 19)

the postwar, large-scale utilization of tropical forest land and timber resources began amidst virtually complete ignorance of the ecology of the tropical forest. It is now widely recognized that this ecology is fragile and complex, but otherwise not much ignorance about it has been dispelled. Little is known about such vital ecological issues as regeneration of cutover or cleared stands, flowering and fruiting in the natural forest, the role of forest animals in seed distribution, or conditions required for successful transplantation. Second, a high degree of ignorance remains regarding the effects of human encroachment on natural tropical forests. This is because information on the economic as well as the environmental impact of forest utilization is grossly incomplete and deeply flawed. As shown later, these flaws are particularly glaring in systems of national income accounting used by all nations. Consequently, there is a clear bias in decisions about forest utilization, in favor of activities most corrosive of the long-term value of tropical forest assets.

Institutional failure has been a third fundamental factor in environmental degradation generally, and tropical deforestation in particular. To economists, institutions are viewed in two principal ways. First, institutions can be the rules of the game governing decision making by individuals as producers, consumers, or voters. Second, institutions can be organizations, especially public organizations or agencies affecting the operation of the economy. Institutions affect individual and social choices by shaping incentives, by influencing the availability of information and resources, and by establishing the basic rules of social transactions.[14] Economic institutions are the principal focus here. They include systems of property rights, contract systems and markets, including those for capital, goods, and labor markets, all of which mediate the interaction of supply and demand. They also include public economic organizations such as government departments, state-owned firms, and banks. In some instances, environmental problems can be traced directly to the failure of such institutions.

Consider first the failure of systems of property rights in natural forests and rules of land tenure for disturbed forests. Throughout the tropics, central governments have appropriated property rights to vast areas of forest from local peoples. About 80 percent of closed forest area in developing countries is owned by government,[15] rather than by local people most knowledgeable about forest ecology and most sensitive to the economic and social benefits of maintaining the productive services (wood, nonwood forest products) as well as protective services (regulation of runoff, control of floods, and erosion and provision of animal and plant habitat) of intact or lightly perturbed forests. Since central governments in many developing nations have generally lacked the means (and often the interest) to enforce forestry regulations in remote regions, local peoples have often been pow-

14. For an overview of modern institutional analysis as applied to economic development, see Norman Nicholson, "The State of the Art," in *Rethinking Institutional Analysis and Development Ostrom, Feeng, and Picht,* (San Francisco: Institute of Contemporary Studies Press, 1990.) See also Brian Van Arkadie, "The Role of Institutions in Development," in *Proceedings of the World Bank Annual Conference on Development Economics,* 1989.

15. Repetto and Gillis, *Public Policies and the Misuse of Forest Resources,* p. 16.

erless to resist opening up access to the forest for virtually uncontrolled exploitation. The forest then becomes an **open access** or **common property** resource, to which everyone has free access. This institutional arrangement leads to what has become known as the "tragedy of the commons,"[16] a phenomenon present in the degradation of almost all common property, including the atmosphere and the oceans. What is owned by everyone is owned by no one, so that incentives to conserve and improve common property are absent or extremely weak.

Institutions of land tenure impinge on the tropical forest in other ways. For example, in Ecuador, Brazil, and the East Malaysian state of Sarawak, destruction of natural vegetation is usually a prerequisite for formal tenure in a colonized parcel. Even where property rights to the forest are well-defined and can be held by local peoples, the rights are often insecure, so that farmers will not make improvements or protect the soils of cleared land. And even secure property rights to forest area may not be transferable through sale, lease, or bequest.[17] If property rights are not transferable, then incentives for conserving the resource are greatly diminished because the owner of a nontransferable property right faces sharply diminished prospects for recovering the costs of any investments made to protect the value of the resource.

Fortunately, some tropical governments have begun to pay greater attention to the common-property problem and to the role that well-defined, secure, and transferable property rights can play in reducing deforestation and other forms of environmental degradation. It is important, however, to note that solutions to common property problems do not necessarily imply shifting land rights in forests from governments to individuals. For example, in February 1990, Colombia announced that it would award land rights to half the Colombian Amazon region to local Indian groups. The land will be transformed from common property status to communal property status. The latter type of land right is well-defined, transferable, and enforceable; the former is not.

Market failure is the most studied form of institutional failure leading to environmental degradation. Markets for environmental services—clean air and water, soil conservation, preservation of climate—do not exist, are incomplete, or function poorly. We have seen how open access, insecure rights, and nontransferable rights to forest land can promote deforestation. But market failures also arise from the sources identified in Chapters 5 and 12: monopoly and oligopoly power, externalities, and public goods. The last two sources of market failure also figure in tropical deforestation. Deforestation, whether caused by land clearing for agriculture or by logging, also involves sizable external costs in the form of diminished watershed protection, soil erosion and sedimentation, and increased vulnerability of the forest to disastrous fires. These costs can run into billions of dollars for

16. The historical basis for the term "tragedy of the commons" relates to the fate of common grazing grounds in Medieval England. Common fields were set aside for animal grazing. All property owners had free access to grazing, so severe overgrazing resulted.

17. Countries such as the Ivory Coast and the Central African Republic allow property rights in timber concessions to be transferable. But in Cameroon and several other tropical nations, transfer of such rights is expressly forbidden.

542

SUSTAINABLE
DEVELOPMENT:
NATURAL
RESOURCES
AND THE
ENVIRONMENT
(Ch. 19)

a particular country. The most striking recent example of external costs arising from logging took place in Malaysia and Indonesia in 1983.

Market Failure and Forest Fires

Between January and May of the drought year of 1983, a great fire spread over millions of acres of moist tropical forest in northeastern Borneo, in the Malaysian state of Sabah and the Indonesian province of East Kalimantan. This conflagration was both a cause and a consequence of very wide-scale deforestation. On the Indonesian side of the island of Borneo, an area the size of Belgium was burned, on the Malaysian side, perhaps half as much was burned. Standing timber valued at over $5 billion was destroyed in Indonesia alone.

The fire raged with an intensity never before seen in the region. In the severe droughts that occurred before 1983, very little of the forest in Sabah or East Kalimantan had been disturbed; fires that were started tended to burn at very low temperatures and never reached the canopy. Large-scale logging on the island began only in the late 1960s. Destruction from the fire was particularly severe in logged-over areas. Indeed, in East Kalimantan, the unlogged forest escaped major damage. The principal reason was that in logged-over areas there was a great amount of dead wood and other combustible ground litter (in logging on Borneo, up to 50 percent of the residual stock left after logging is destroyed or damaged.) The fires thus burned at very high temperatures. Damage was slight in undisturbed forest areas as relatively low volumes of dead wood and other ground litter prevented fires from generating enough heat to ignite large trees.

Logging after 1968, then, predisposed the natural forest to catastrophic fires, a large external cost that was not reflected either in the prices paid by loggers for logging rights or in the prices paid by consumers for wood products. Even if the governments that owned the forests had recognized the risks of greater forest vulnerability from logging, even if they had wanted to charge a price for wood high enough to cover these costs, there was no way for the market to value them. Market failure thus led to ecological calamity.

The concept of public goods is helpful in understanding another aspect of market failure leading to excessive tropical deforestation. The productive and protective services, or benefits, provided by intact tropical forests are of two types: divisible and indivisible. Divisible benefits include the potential value of wood available from logging, or the value of nonwood forest products (resins, meat, pharmaceutical compounds, nuts, etc.) for local forest people and national and world markets. These benefits are internalized to firms and individuals and are rival in nature, as defined in Chapter 12.

But the protective services provided by intact tropical forests have characteristics of pure public goods, in that the benefits are neither divisible nor appropriable by any single person. The benefits instead are indivisible: no one can be excluded from enjoying them whether they pay for them or not. Moreover, the benefits are nonrival: consumption of these services by any one person or groups of people does not diminish the possibilities for consumption by others. Examples include the stabilization of local climate, maintenance of pools of genetic materials, watershed protection, and regulation of runoff. Many of these benefits are localized to one region of a country and sometimes in smaller nations to an area as large as the entire country.

Some of the services provided by forests even have international dimensions. Forest endowments in the tropics have significant effects on stabilization of global atmosphere and on rainfall patterns over wide areas. Agriculture, medicine, and even some aspects of industry all over the world depend in varying degrees on the richness of known genetic resources in tropical forests, which contain at least 50 and perhaps 80 percent of all species on earth.[18] Thus, certain characteristics of intact tropical forest may be seen as pure public goods open to all global citizens, independently of who pays for them. To the extent that citizens in nontropical countries derive such benefits, they may be called *free riders*.

Those in industrial countries who ride free on the tropical forests include owners and employees of wood product, pharmaceutical, and cosmetic enterprises based on tropical forest resources, and Americans and Europeans who benefit from the climatic, water, and wildlife protection provided by the forest. Worldwide interests are clearly furthered when Brazil, Indonesia, or Gabon take measures to curb deforestation or set aside new areas in park and forest reserves. It is therefore apparent that the constituency for tropical conservation is worldwide. But since most of this constituency consists of free riders, and since free riders cannot be excluded from these benefits (so long as they last), they have little incentive to offer to pay for them, quite apart from the fact that they may be unaware they are partaking of them. Consequently, market failure leads to an undersupply of financial support for reducing deforestation.

The role of **policy failure** in tropical deforestation may rival that of market failure. A battery of government policies, including those adopted for worthy objectives, have played a large and hitherto unappreciated role in creating economic incentives that have aggravated the extent and severity of deforestation in the tropics. These include both forestry and nonforestry policies.

Government forestry policies, including royalty and timber concession policies, have grossly underpriced the wood resources of the tropical forest. This has resulted in unmistakable signals to loggers, ranchers, and agriculturalists that natural forest resources are cheap and may be freely wasted. Nonforestry policies are policies that, intentionally or not, have a significant impact on forest utilization, but which are primarily intended to further nonforest objectives. Such policies include tax, trade, monetary, exchange rate, and food policy. Tax policies have subsidized deforestation by offering large income tax incentives for investments in logging, timber-processing, and land-clearing activities for estate crops and cattle ranching.

18. Myers, ''Deforestation Rates in Tropical Forests and Their Climatic Implications.''

544

SUSTAINABLE
DEVELOPMENT:
NATURAL
RESOURCES
AND THE
ENVIRONMENT
(Ch. 19)

Timber booms in the Philippines (1950 to 1970), West Malaysia (1960 to 1975), East Malaysia and Indonesia (1967 to 1980) were particularly fueled by generous income tax exemptions for logging and for processing plants, as well as by sales of timber from government-owned land at prices well-below market.[19]

Financial policies involving credit subsidies have added to perverse incentives for forest investments in Ghana, the Philippines, and especially Brazil. Artificially low interest rates available for logging activities and for forest-clearing projects for large-scale cattle ranching have by themselves produced very powerful incentives for destruction in the Brazilian Amazon. When coupled with general tax subsidies, the incentives for very large-scale forest clearing have proven irresistible, so that intrinsically uneconomic cattle ranches in the tropics, particularly in Latin America, have generated large profits for investors.

Environmental Degradation in Indonesia

With 180 million people, two-thirds of whom live on densely populated rural lowlands in Java, and a per-capita income of around $500, Indonesia presents a large array of examples of environmental problems traceable to poverty, ignorance, institutional failure, and policy failure and to interactions among these causes. We chose Indonesia to illustrate these problems, not because its environmental problems are extreme, but because they are so common to many developing countries. Indonesia is also now doing more to correct these problems than many countries, north and south. This is apparent in several recent policy reforms affecting the pricing of energy, fertilizer, and pesticides and in strong policy measures undertaken to attack the principal cause of environmental degradation in most developing countries: poverty.

Poverty has been a major cause of river pollution, the degradation of coral reefs in Bali, the extinction of the Java tiger, and especially deforestation. Shifting cultivation driven by poverty has been the leading cause of deforestation in Indonesia, as it has been across Africa.

Consider river pollution. In 1978 a foreign company was discharging noxious wastes into a river in West Java. Despite strong pressure either to close the plant or to curtail drastically its discharges, an explicit decision was made not to close the plant. This was done not so much to protect 150 jobs, but because closing the plant would have had no effect at all on water quality. This was because the river flowed through areas densely populated by very poor families. Household wastes and the by-products of cottage industries had already so polluted the river that no benefit would have resulted from closing the plant. Sacrificing the plant's 150 jobs for no ecological benefit would have been bad economics, and bad income distribution policy as well. The solution to this environmental problem lies first in the reduction of poverty, not in environmental policy per se.

---

19. Repetto and Gillis, *Public Policies and the Misuse of Forest Resources.*

Coral reefs surround and protect a large part of Sanur beach on eastern Bali, a tourist mecca. Bali is very densely populated, and even a tourist boom has not eradicated severe poverty. Groups of poor families have long harvested coral between the reef and the beach. As in the Maldives, the coral is used as a binding agent in making a particular form of very durable cement for building construction. As a result of coral harvests, the reef is being slowly destroyed and the beaches, coastal ecology, and thousands of jobs in tourism threatened. Many foreign experts have recommended the construction of seawalls to protect the threatened beaches from erosion, a solution that works no better in Bali than it works on the east coast of the United States.[20] Others have advocated banning the harvest of coral. But this would result in a loss of livelihood affecting perhaps 4,000 people. If coral gathering is banned, how will these people survive? Is a job in the tourist industry worth more than two or three jobs in coral gathering? This is both an economic and ethical question. And what if the degradation of the reef is now so advanced that it is too late to save it by prohibiting coral harvests? This is a difficult ecological question.

Finally, consider the virtual extinction of the Java tiger. Habitat for these beasts has been severely constricted over the past half century, by population pressure and poverty-driven uplands fuel-wood harvests. It is extremely doubtful that any mating pairs survived through 1989. Similar problems beset wildlife in Africa.

Ignorance, or better said, the absence or inaccessibility of good scientific and ecological information, underlies many severe environmental problems in developing countries.

The case of the Bali coral reefs illustrates one interaction between ignorance and poverty. Ignorance prevents us from knowing whether the prohibition of coral harvests at this stage would come in time to save the reefs. Ignorance about key determinants of the fragile ecology of tropical forests prevents Indonesia and other countries from knowing how to utilize the products and services of the natural forests in a sustainable way. Some tropical countries, fortunately not Indonesia, do not even keep statistics on the value of production and exports of the nonwood forest products that can be harvested without cutting down trees.

Worldwide scientific ignorance of ocean ecology has led in many countries to regulations that have allowed over-fishing in formerly rich fishing grounds. This was also long the case in Indonesia, where limits on catches in the Indonesian economic zone were not even formulated for years. That, combined with intrusions of foreign fishing vessels into Indonesian territory, has resulted in a sharp curtailment of annual catches, particularly in northeast Indonesia.

Sumatra, an island larger than the state of California, contains a wealth of animal life. The Sumatran tiger is seen by many as not only a valuable attraction for tourists, but also an important predator of the wild pigs that destroy farmers' crops. Once numerous throughout a wide range on the island, the tiger is becoming increasingly scarce. Over the past two decades,

---

20. Orrin Pilkey, "The Engineering of Sand," *Journal of Geological Education* 37 (1989): 308–311.

546

SUSTAINABLE
DEVELOPMENT:
NATURAL
RESOURCES
AND THE
ENVIRONMENT
(Ch. 19)

thousands of families from densely populated areas of Java and Bali have been resettled in Sumatra under the government sponsored transmigration program. The government provides transportation, land sites, and subsidies for families resettled under the program, designed to alleviate population pressure and therefore poverty in Java and Bali and to give poor transmigrants a new start in life. Unfortunately, government officials responsible for selecting new transmigration sites chose several sites that were directly in the migration paths used habitually by the Sumatran tiger, but this information was never made available to them. When a tiger enters a village, particularly one with many children, the tiger tends to be destroyed. Here, lack of information, as well as the poverty that the transmigration program attempts to overcome, may help lead to the tiger's extinction.

In Indonesia, as elsewhere, environmental problems arise from interactions among poverty, ignorance, and policies. From 1972 to 1984, the government heavily subsidized the consumption of kerosene and other fuels. Part of the justification offered for the kerosene subsidy was to benefit poor rural dwellers; part of the justification was ecological. It was known that much of the erosion in Java was caused by fuel-wood harvests on mountain slopes inhabited by very poor families. It was thought that by heavily subsidizing kerosene, poor families would have less incentive to gather firewood for cooking. This justification for the program rested on the mistaken belief that rural families used kerosene primarily for cooking. No one had ever done any research on kerosene used in rural areas. But it turned out that rural families used kerosene predominately for lighting, rarely for cooking.[21] As a result, the kerosene subsidy may have protected about only 20 thousand hectares of land per year from the ravages of fuel-wood harvest. As a forest conservation program, the kerosene subsidy involved a cost of U.S. $77,000 per year for each hectare protected. The most complete replanting program for cutover areas in Java involved costs of $1,000 per acre. The subsidy, then, was bad economics and bad ecology.

Finally, some hydroelectric projects in Indonesia have been designed under the assumption that reservoirs would have a useful life of 75 to 100 years. This assumption was also founded on ignorance regarding the rate of siltation expected with continued population growth and deforestation. Particularly in Java, with its hundred million people, erosion from deforestation and cassava planting on hillsides has caused rivers to silt up so badly that many formerly perennial rivers are now annual ones. As a result, some reservoirs may be useless for power generation purposes in only two or three decades.

Institutional Failure

Institutional failure is common to virtually all aspects of developing economies. Institutions of property rights and land tenure contribute materially

---

21. Malcolm Gillis, "Indonesia: Public Policies, Resource Management and the Tropical Forest," in *Public Policies and the Misuse of Forest Resources,* Repetto and Gillis, pp. 82–83.

to deforestation in Indonesia for many of the same reasons as described

earlier for Latin America and other countries. In addition, prior to the 1980s, the Ministry of Mines granted mining concessions to firms in environmentally sensitive forest areas without informing the Ministry of Forestry. Even remedies for deforestation have been hindered in institutional flaws in public organizations. In Indonesia in the mid-1970s, a massive and expensive "regreening program" for the heavily populated island of Java failed because of a virtual absence of institutional cooperation and consultation between the Ministry of Agriculture and the Ministry of the Interior. Hundreds of thousands of seedlings were delivered by the Agriculture Department at dozens of locations in Java, where they rotted because local officials reporting to the Ministry of the Interior, and responsible for distributing the seedlings to farmers, did not know where to pick them up.

In urban areas, the workings of institutions conspired to yield unintentional environmental damage. Contamination of local drinking water by such heavy metals as mercury and cadmium in Jakarta and other large cities could become one of the most serious health issues in Indonesia. But for decades, no government agency had clear responsibility for monitoring water quality. And even though a new agency, the State Ministry for the Environment, was created in 1978 to deal with such problems, it has a professional staff smaller than the environmental quality staff of most middle-sized U.S. cities.

Government policies, by themselves, and in interaction with poverty, ignorance, and institutions have led to the significant environmental degradation in many countries, including Indonesia. These damages have been principally the outgrowth of policies intended to promote nonenvironmental goals, not the results of misguided environmental policies per se or deliberate attempts to degrade the environment.

Government policies in the 1980s contemplated resettlement of 1 million families from densely populated Java to the outer islands. The ultimate objective was to relocate 15 million more people before the year 2000. Eighty percent of the settlements were to be within primary forests. Reaching the program's objective by the year 2000 would have required the clearing of nearly 30 million more acres of forest land. At that rate, annual losses in forested area due to the transmigration program would surpass all other sources of deforestation combined.

Other policies have brought sizeable unintended environmental damages in their wake. This has been particularly true for subsidy policies for pesticides, fuel, and, some say, fertilizer.

From 1976 through 1987, heavy subsidies were offered for pesticide use, especially pesticides to combat an insect called the brown-leaf hopper, which preys on rice—the major staple in the Indonesian diet. Even after pesticide prices were increased by 100 percent in 1986, the subsidy per liter was still two-thirds the retail price; this led to very heavy applications by farmers. Not only did the runoff of chemicals from pesticide use pose a serious threat to health, but this very expensive subsidy was counterproductive. Many of the pesticides had the effect of wiping out the insect predators that consumed pests, while the pests themselves multiplied. This was the case

548

SUSTAINABLE
DEVELOPMENT:
NATURAL
RESOURCES
AND THE
ENVIRONMENT
(Ch. 19)

with the brown-leaf hopper, which destroyed thousands of hectares in many years between 1976 and 1987, and often in areas where pesticide application was heaviest.

Fertilizer subsidies, common to dozens of countries, are also heavily used in Indonesia. As late as 1987, fertilizer subsidies were nearly one-third of farmgate prices, and this was after drastic subsidy reductions in 1986. Partly as a result of this subsidy, before 1986 Indonesian farmers used 3 times as much fertilizer as did farmers in Thailand and the Philippines. The World Bank has argued that not only has excessive application of fertilizer over long periods failed to improve soil fertility, but runoffs have, particularly in the presence of high rates of deforestation, begun to result in potentially sizable environmental damages. We will return to this point.

The kerosene subsidy, described above, had unintended effects on air pollution for many years. Because kerosene can be burned in diesel engines, heavy subsidies on kerosene require heavy subsidies on diesel fuel. Otherwise, diesel vehicle owners will, as in Pakistan and Indonesia in the 1970s, use kerosene for fuel and foul the air even more then would be the case if they used diesel fuel. And heavy subsidies on diesel fuel lead to strong incentives to choose diesel engines in motor fleets, unless gasoline is also subsidized. For most of the period 1972 to 1984, all motor fuels were therefore subsidized heavily. By 1980, the economic costs of these subsidies amounted to 4.5 percent of GDP.[22] As a result, incentives to conserve fuel were weak, and the air in major cities, especially Jakarta, was badly fouled.

Over the past decade, however, Indonesia has begun to tackle these problems; important positive lessons can be drawn from the Indonesian environmental experience. By 1986, the fuel subsidies had been reduced to virtually nothing, and 57 types of pesticides were banned for use on paddy crops.[23] In addition, subsidies on fertilizer were sharply reduced. Environmental and biological arguments played a role in reversing these policies, but economic arguments were also used to show why these policies failed to produce the desired results for agriculture and income distribution. Economic arguments were deployed to illustrate the great size of the cost of these subsidies. These are just a few examples of how good economics can be placed in the service of good ecology.

ECONOMIC POLICY REFORM AND THE ENVIRONMENT

Three immediate changes in policies and programs affecting natural resources and the environment offer hopeful prospects for promoting sustainable development. They are: (1) greater stress on the role of prices in resource conservation, (2) incorporation of environmental accounting within national income accounting frameworks, and (3) appropriate use of discount rates in infrastructure projects affecting the environment.

---

22. Malcolm Gillis "Energy Demand in Indonesia," Cambridge, Mass., HIID Development Discussion Paper No. 9, April 1980.
23. Presidential Instruction No. 3, November 5, 1985.

The Role of Prices

549

ECONOMIC
POLICY REFORM
AND THE
ENVIRONMENT

Chapter 5 noted that some economists, particularly those of the structuralist school in Latin America, take a pessimistic view of supply and demand elasticities; they believe them to be so small that the economy will not respond, or not respond quickly, to changes in relative prices needed to accomplish a given shift in resources. Neoclassical economists, although agreeing that short-term elasticities are generally much lower than medium- or long-term ones (see Chapter 11), believe that most supply and demand elasticities are high enough over the medium to the long term to base reforms on market rules. We have stressed the efficacy of markets in promoting income growth and reducing poverty throughout this book. Similar arguments apply to many, but by no means all, environmental problems.

The pessimistic view of elasticities lost adherents steadily over the past two decades and was apparently swept away in Eastern and Central Europe by the Revolution of 1989. But the demise of this view has been much slower worldwide for policies affecting the environment than for agricultural, credit, foreign exchange, and other economic policies. As late as 1973, governments as well as oil companies, both in industrial and developing countries, routinely published projections of oil consumption based on the assumption of a near-zero price elasticity of demand for energy. In the influential report of the **Club of Rome** in the early 1970s, the role of prices in resource conservation was almost nonexistent. Curtailment of heavy subsidies on the use of gasoline and kerosene in Indonesia, Colombia, Bolivia, and Venezuela were delayed for years by false claims that prices would have little impact on energy use.

Unwillingness to concede a role for prices in promoting conservation and protecting the environment has not been confined to developing nations. While it should not be surprising that the role of prices was largely ignored in the Soviet Union prior to 1989, egregious examples persist in the United States as well (see boxed example).

U.S. Rangeland and U.S.S.R. Water Resources

In the U.S. West, ranchers graze cattle and sheep on 70 percent of the 367 million acres of public land. Overgrazing has left what may be a lasting imprint on government-owned arid rangelands. As late as 1986, grazing fees charged for cattle on government-owned lands were, according to the General Accounting Office, set at one-fourth to one-fifth of the fair market value of grazing on private rangelands in the West. Artificially low grazing fees naturally led to overgrazing and contributed first, to "cowburnt" pastures, second, to accelerated desertification in the West, and third, to the destruction of wildlife habitat, including the salmon beds in parts of Idaho.

In the Soviet Union, near-zero prices were charged for irrigation water taken for cotton growing from the Syr Darya and Amy Darya rivers flowing into the Aral Sea. Consequently, water was wasted profligately in irrigation, and the Aral Sea, once larger than West Virginia, was reduced in area by fully 40 percent from 1951 to 1989. The immediate economic costs of

550

SUSTAINABLE
DEVELOPMENT:
NATURAL
RESOURCES
AND THE
ENVIRONMENT
(Ch. 19)

the resultant steep loss of biological productivity of the sea has included the disappearance of the commercial fish catch with its 60,000 jobs and the poisoning of the cotton lands by salt storms. Environmental consequences have included powerful dust storms arising from overdried areas of land surface, as well as distinct alterations in temperature and moisture conditions over a wide area adjacent to the sea. In the future, the sea could dry to a residual brine lake. Sadly, virtually none of the dozen or so schemes discussed in publications by western and Soviet scientists to preserve the Aral Sea make any mention of the role that higher prices for irrigation water might play in water conservation.

Both in the case of publicly owned rangelands in the United States and of the Aral Sea, higher prices for grazing fees and water, respectively, could have forestalled much of the environmental damages that have already occurred.

Nowhere in environmental policies has the role of prices in conservation been more neglected than in those policies affecting the utilization of tropical forests. In virtually all countries governments as owners have consistently sold wood resources at prices well below their **commercial,** not to mention their social value; this has encouraged accelerated timber harvests. Timber royalties (prices charged by the owner for logs harvested) have typically been small fractions of the wood value. Taxes on wood products, especially those used in local sawmills and plymills, have been even less substantial than royalties. License fees, or charges based on the size of the timber concession areas, have also been low in virtually all tropical nations. In Brazil and other countries where forests have been cleared for ranches, incentives for land clearing have extended well beyond artificially low land prices. Interest rates for investments in land clearing have been subsidized heavily, and subsidies, rather than taxes, have been applied to income from cattle operations.

Moreover, virtually no costs of environmental degradation have been included in the prices charged to loggers or to plantation operations requiring large-scale land clearing. Although not all of these costs are easily measured, some are. Relatively good documentation of the loss of agricultural productivity from the removal of forest cover, in the form of erosion and siltation, is now available, and could form the basis for taxes on logging and land clearing high enough to cover these costs.

The appropriate use of prices for securing environmental goals often requires innovative use of taxes, whether to raise prices on the extraction of resources or to increase prices paid by consumers for goods and services involving significant external costs of production or consumption. Taxes on environmentally damaging activities can stimulate far-reaching changes in industrial processes, in patterns of resource extraction, and in consumer behavior. Indeed the viability of sustainable development depends critically on the use of environmental taxes to conserve natural resources and fulfill pollution abatement goals. Development can be sustainable only if economic progress can be reconciled with environmental protection. This reconciliation, in turn, requires that considerations of resource efficiency and environmental protection must be fully integrated (internalized) into the decisions of firms and households throughout the economy. When an investor chooses a production technique, the prices paid for equipment should reflect the external costs of any environmental damage associated with production; when buying gasoline, a consumer should pay the full environmental costs involved in auto emissions. Environmental taxes are critical for making all prices reflect environmental costs.

The Role of Resource Accounting

The system of national income accounts in use by virtually all countries suffers from several flaws that have serious implications for prospects for sensible environmental policies: the system (and the way it is normally used) greatly distorts the role of natural resources in economic processes. These distortions have several important dimensions. First, in measuring income and in formulating economic policy, economists and policymakers rely on the major aggregates published in national income accounts, compiled in accordance with the System of National Accounts (SNA) of the United Nations. The SNA emphasizes Gross Domestic Product (GDP), which is primarily a measure of market activity. The SNA framework is defective on a number of counts in its treatment not only of natural resources, but of manufactured capital as well. The SNA does not provide for measures such as net domestic product (NDP), which takes account for depreciation of manufactured capital. In addition, the SNA framework does not recognize natural resources as economic assets, not does it take into account the consumption of natural capital.[24] Consequently, the protective services provided by these assets are not valued, whereas the additional expenditures forced on society by the loss of these services are valued. As a result, there is an asymmetry in the way we measure, and therefore the way we think about, the value of natural resources. This asymmetry gives rise to patently anomalous and uneconomic practices. On the one hand, government expenditures for cleaning up a catastrophic oil spill in Alaska **add to** the nation's gross national product, even though the affected waters and sea life are severely harmed by the spill. Moreover, the SNA provides the wrong signals about the benefits of "defensive" environmental expenditures by private firms: any outlays to reduce or avoid environmental damage are netted out of the final value-added.

On the other hand, under the SNA, a country could exhaust all its forest resources and, in the process, silt up its rivers and harbors, but measured national income would not be reduced as these resources vanished. But a country that year after year draws down its assets that happen to take the form of natural resources by mining, drilling, or logging may enjoy high rates of GNP growth for long periods, even in the absence of any new

24. For extensive discussions of these problems, see Yusuf Ahmed, Alah El Serafy, and Ernst Lutz, ed., *Environmental Accounting for Sustainable Development*, (Washington, D.C.: World Bank, 1990), and Ernst Lutz and Mohan Munasinghe, "Accounting for the Environment," *Finance and Development* 28 (March 1991): 19–25.

552

SUSTAINABLE
DEVELOPMENT:
NATURAL
RESOURCES
AND THE
ENVIRONMENT
(Ch. 19)

investments in sustaining the stock of these natural assets. Under prevailing systems of natural income accounting, the economy's health would appear robust during the drawdown. And even in the few countries that do calculate NDP, inconsistent treatment of manufactured and natural capital remains. The liquidation of manufactured assets shows up in the natural income accounts decline; the liquidation of productive assets provided by nature would show up as economic growth.

This defective system of information provides false signals to policymakers that discouraged the implementation of policies that could lead to sustainable development. Clearly then, a high premium should be placed on the incorporation of concepts of environmental accounting in the national income accounting frameworks of all nations, developing or otherwise. A promising first attempt to supplement traditional national income accounts to reflect resource depletion has been made in Indonesia. There, one study indicates that nearly half of that nation's rapid economic growth in the 1970s was generated not by sustainable productivity increases, but by drawing down natural endowments of oil, soils, and forests.[25]

The point is not that it is inherently wrong to draw on natural resource assets to finance economic growth. But there seems to be something palpably wrong in using systems of accounting that ignore the very real economic costs of the utilization of natural resources and the degradation of air, water, and soil resources. The incorporation of environmental accounting concepts as integral parts of existing systems of national income accounts would be supportive of economic and ecological goals of all societies. To do this will require resolution of a number of challenging empirical questions, not the least of which is the valuation of the flows of services from environmental assets. In the meantime, deficiencies in national income accounting systems will result in continued overestimation of the development potential of nations, to the detriment of the interest of future generations.

Appropriate Use of Discount Rates

The concept of net present value (NPV), introduced in Chapter 6, lies at the core of the economic analysis of private- as well as public-sector investment projects. For public-sector projects, the choice of an appropriate social discount rate is critical for any investment decision guided by the NPV criterion.

Environmental critics have attacked the net present value criterion on a number of grounds. First, it is correctly argued that public projects for protecting or preserving the environment typically involve net benefits extending over several decades. An example would be the creation of a nature reserve in a threatened tropical forest. Use of a 10 percent discount rate, not uncommon in private investment analysis in recent years, would mean that a million dollars in benefits 35 years from now would be worth only $500 in net present value today. The World Bank uses 10 percent for

---

25. Robert Repetto et al., "Natural Resource Accounting for Indonesia," (Washington, D.C.: World Resources Institute, May 1987).

its projects, and Inter-American Development Bank uses 12 percent. At a
2 percent discount rate, however, the same million dollars would have a
present value of about $500,000 today. Given these vast disparities, some
economists argue that much lower discount rates should be used for public
sector investments affecting natural resource conservation. Some environmental critics, including economists, have gone even further and argued
for a discount rate of zero for long-lived public projects, particularly environmental projects, for at least two reasons. First, the use of the net present value criterion can discourage conservation altogether, and, second,
it may lead to irreversible actions such as global warming or species extinction. Indeed some economists have contended that the use of any positive
discount rate is inappropriate for any project affecting future generations:
a half century ago, for example, the influential British economist
A. C. Pigon called discounting "ethically indefensible."

It is possible however, to show that the net present value criterion and
the discount rate are not always the tools of enemies of the environment.
Perhaps as much damage has been done in recent years to natural resources
and the environment by discount rates that have been too low, rather than
too high—the opposite of the usual claim made by opponents of discounting. To understand this assertion, consider tropical forests. The overwhelming proportion of tropical forests are owned by governments, and a
very sizable share of forest destruction in such countries as Brazil, Gabon,
and Thailand has been attributable to large-scale government infrastructure, electric power, and resettlement projects with putative benefits
stretching over several generations. The lower the discount rate, the more
attractive these forest-encroaching projects appear to the current generation of policymakers. At zero rates of discount, the case for these public
projects can easily be made compelling. The higher the discount rate, the
less economical they are perceived.

Particularly within the past decade, dozens of government projects have
made large incursions in the tropical forest. The $4 billion Trans-Gabon
railway completed in the 1980s was intended primarily to open up over 4
million hectares of previously unaccessible forest land. In Sarawak, vast
areas of tropical forest would be submerged by a planned $3.3 billion proj-
ect involving two dams planned for the Rajang River Valley. As a result,
83 percent of the population above the catchment areas would have to be
resettled into other forest areas. These "shifted cultivators" might be
expected to cause additional deforestation from shifting cultivation. In
Thailand, the lower northeast region was covered by undisturbed forest as
late as 1973. But then the area was made accessible to loggers and shifting
cultivators when the government constructed a major highway; the result
was the destruction of 1 million hectares of forest land in only four years.
The transmigration, or resettlement, program of the Indonesian government, underwritten for so long by the World Bank, was responsible for 4
to 5 times as much deforestation as was logging in the mid-1980s. In Brazil,
several huge hydroelectric projects, including the $4 billion Tucurui proj-
ect, have submerged vast areas of forested land. Tucurui alone has flooded
2,160 square kilometers. In all of these cases, higher, not lower discount

554

SUSTAINABLE
DEVELOPMENT:
NATURAL
RESOURCES
AND THE
ENVIRONMENT
(Ch. 19)

rates in cost-benefit analysis of the projects would have been in the interest of conservation.

Those critical of the use of the net present value criterion in social cost-benefit analysis may have also helped to redirect attention away from a much more fundamental problem in all decision making affecting ecology and the environment. Good economics requires that all real costs and all real benefits, tangible and intangible, be considered in decision making on public projects. Undervaluation of future costs and overvaluation of future benefits in infrastructure projects encroaching on tropical forest endowments have played major roles in decisions by governments and aid donors to proceed with many of these large infrastructure projects. Siltation in hydroelectric projects in deforesting areas provides a sobering example. Unexpectedly high rates of siltation have led to massive unforeseen costs in hydroelectric projects and to sharp constriction in not only the estimated life of dam projects by in power production during the shortened life of such projects, in Brazil, India, the Dominican Republic, and many other countries. In the Philippines, operational lives of major hydropower reservoirs have been cut by half or more by siltation. Mistakes in forecasting future costs and benefits in such projects were not a consequence of the use of discounting in cost-benefit analysis per se, but of the use of poor quality scientific information regarding erosion and siltation over the affected watersheds. When a dam has a projected life of 50 years and heavy siltation reduced that life to 7, the choice of a high or low discount rate may become almost inconsequential in decisions to undertake the project.

These considerations argue for the reform of public investment policies affecting the environment, but care must be taken to avoid throwing out the baby with the bath water. Dispensing with discounting of future returns could hardly be justified for public environmental projects alone. And dispensing with discounting for all public projects would clearly invite massive waste of scarce tax monies required for a variety of critical social needs, particularly in the poorest nations. On the other hand, we might expect an entire society to have a lower discount rate than that appropriate for private sector projects, if only because of greater continuity and great capacity for pooling risks across society, relative to an individual firm.

Moreover, many argue that a decision to conserve natural resources is reversible; a decision to exploit them is not. This consideration seems to support the use of discount rates in resource conservation projects affecting present as well as future generations that are lower than those approximating long-term interest rates, such as those used by the World Bank, the Inter-American Development Bank, and many governments. But the economic, ecological, and ethical arguments for zero discount rates in projects where benefits extend beyond the current generation have yet to be convincingly made.

Conclusion

This chapter does not contend that sustainable use of natural resources and the environment is a matter that can be fully settled by economic determinancy. It does contend, however, that powerful economic arguments can be mustered in favor of the sharp curtailment of natural resource waste and environmental degradation. The economic arguments have hardly been used by environmentalists. This is been doubly unfortunate, since ecological and ethical arguments for curtailing environmental degradation often have not been communicated to policymakers with short-time horizons in the language most intelligible to them: the short-run as well as long-run economic costs of ecological degradation. Inasmuch as government policies have, directly and indirectly, been responsible for a sizeable share of environmental degradation, then these policies must be reformed in short order. Economic arguments are essential for reinforcing biological and ethical arguments if this is to occur.

Industry

The concept of development and the process of industrialization have often been treated as synonymous, ever since the Industrial Revolution enabled Britain to raise its industrial production by 400 percent over the first half of the nineteenth century.[1] From then until the present the dominant criterion for development has been the rise in per-capita incomes brought about largely by industrialization. Earlier chapters, especially those in Parts 1 and 4, have focused on the relation between development and industrialization. This chapter emphasizes aspects not covered in depth elsewhere.

INDUSTRY AS A LEADING SECTOR

From Chapter 3's discussion of cross-country patterns, we know that higher shares of gross domestic product generated by industry are closely associated with rising income per capita. Figure 20-1 shows this pattern for manufacturing value-added in 1988 for 22 large countries (with populations over 25 million) and 21 small ones. In making such cross-country comparisons, economists conventionally segregate large from small countries. Nations with larger markets are able to develop a wider range of industries sooner in their development because they can take advantage of scale economies[2]

---

1. E. J. Hobsbawm, *The Pelican Economic History of Britain,* Vol. 3, *Industry and Empire* (Baltimore: Johns Hopkins Press, 1969).
2. The concept of *scale economies* is explained later in this chapter.

A. Large Countries

B. Small Countries

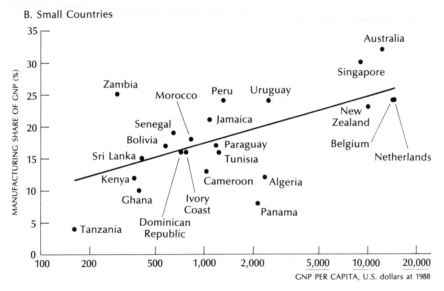

FIGURE 20–1   **Manufacturing Share of GDP, Large and Small Countries, 1988.** Large countries (with populations over 25 million) are, on average, more industrialized than small ones at the same incomes. In both cases, however, there is a strong tendency for manufacturing value-added to rise as a share of GDP as average income rises.
Source: World Bank, *World Development Report 1990*, pp. 178–83.

within the domestic market. Hence we expect large countries to industrialize faster than small ones.

Both tendencies are evident in Figure 20–1. At any level of income per person, the average for large countries, determined by the regression line, is higher than for small countries. Yet for both sets of countries, there is a strong correlation between industrialization and average income. On average for large countries, as income quintuples from $300 to $1500 per person, manufacturing value-added rises from 17 to 23 percent of GNP. In an average small country undergoing the same change in income, the manufacturing share rises from about 12 to about 20 percent of GNP. A country with per-capita income growing at 3 percent a year would take 54 years to make this transition.

But wide variations are evident. The regression lines in each scatter diagram explain half or less of the variation in country experience. The heavy dependence of Indonesia, Cameroon, and Algeria on mineral exports is evident from their low manufacturing share, but mineral-rich countries like Bolivia, Zambia, Jamaica, and Peru lie above the regression line, at least partly because they process their minerals before export. Both import substituters (the Philippines and Argentina) and outward-looking economies (South Korea, Singapore, and Thailand) are above the regression line. Of the industrial countries shown, only West Germany and Australia lie above the regression line; this suggests that manufacturing shares may indeed decline at very high average incomes.

Cross-country patterns imply that value-added in manufacturing ought to grow more rapidly than GDP in the typical developing country. This prediction is borne out by World Bank data. For the low- and middle-income countries as a whole, over the period from 1965 to 1988, manufacturing grew by 7.4 percent a year, compared with 5.3 percent a year for GDP. This average pattern is observed in most individual countries, too: of 44 developing countries for which data are available over 1965 through 1988, manufacturing grew at least 1 percent a year faster than GDP in 23 countries and lagged behind GDP by at least 1 percent a year in only 5.

Chapter 3's discussion of patterns of industrialization and Chapter 16's discussion of import substitution suggest that the process of industrialization requires the **backward integration** from predominantly consumer goods industries towards producer goods industries. This progression is evident in cross-country comparisons of the value-added shares among branches within the manufacturing sector. The study summarized in Table 20–1 shows that the GDP share of the "early developing" branches of manufacturing—food, textiles, clothing, and leather—changes little with further growth. These industries employ relatively simple technologies, and the income elasticity of demand for their output is lower than for other industries. Most of the above-average growth of manufacturing is supplied by the producer goods (and consumer durable) branches, including the so-called basic or heavy industries: pulp and paper, chemicals and rubber, basic metals, and metal products.

Linkages

If manufacturing generally and early developing branches of manufacturing in particular are to lead economic development, they ought to have more **backward linkages** than other sectors, in the sense described by Albert Hirschman and introduced in Chapter 3. There have been several attempts to measure linkages. Those used by Pan Yotopoulos and Jeffrey Nugent

TABLE 20–1   Structure of Manufacturing (share of GDP per capita, cross-country average
over 1950–1983)

Branches of manufacturing	GDP per capita, 1988 U.S. dollars[a]		
	350	1,200	5,000
Early industries[b]	6.8	8.3	7.8
Middle industries[c]	3.3	5.3	6.5
Late industries[d]	1.8	5.3	10.2
Total manufacturing	11.9	18.9	24.5

[a]Converted from 1980 prices using the U.S. wholesale price index.
[b]Consumer goods industries, such as food, textiles, clothing, and leather.
[c]Intermediate goods, such as chemicals and nonmetallic minerals.
[d]Investment goods (e.g., machinery), some intermediates (e.g., paper), and consumer durables.
Source: Moises Syrquin and Hollis B. Chenery, "Three Decades of Industrialization," The World Bank Economic Review 3, no. 2 (May 1989): 145–81.

seem as easy to understand and useful for our purposes as any.[3] Not surprisingly, linkage formulas depend on input-output tables, which are constructed to display linkages within an economy. A **direct backward linkage** for any industry j is measured as

$$L_{bj} = \sum_i a_{ij}, \qquad [20\text{–}1]$$

where L_{bj} is the index of backward linkage and a_{ij} is the Leontief (input-output) coefficient defined in Chapter 6. Thus a measure of backward linkage for any industry is simply the sum of its domestic input coefficients. If, for example, the textile industry adds value equal to 30 percent of its output, and imports inputs equivalent to another 15 percent of output, its backward linkage index L_b would be 55 percent, the share of domestically purchased inputs ($100 - 30 - 15 = 55$).

Those who recall Chapter 6 will immediately recognize that this index captures only the direct links. But if textile production stimulates cotton growing, might not cotton in turn stimulate fertilizer production? It is easy to incorporate these indirect effects by summing the direct plus indirect coefficients of the Leontief inverse, designated r_{ij},[4] to get

$$L_{tj} = \Sigma r_{ij}, \qquad [20\text{–}2]$$

where L_{tj} is an index of direct plus indirect or **total backward linkages** from the jth industry.

There is an analogous simple measure of **direct forward linkages:**

$$L_{fi} = \sum_j X_{ij}/Z_i, \qquad [20\text{–}3]$$

where L_{fi} is the forward linkage index for the ith industry, X_{ij} is the output

3. Pan A. Yotopoulos and Jeffrey B. Nugent, "A Balanced-Growth Version of the Linkage Hypothesis: A Test," *Quarterly Journal of Economics* 87 (May 1973): 157–171; reprinted in their text, *Economics of Development: Empirical Investigations* (New York: Harper & Row, 1976), pp. 299–306.
4. The Leontief inverse matrix is explained in footnote 3 of Chapter 6.

of the ith industry that is purchased by each jth user industry (the row of the input-output table), and Z_i is the production of good i for both intermediate and final use.

Yotopoulos and Nugent have used input-output tables for five developing countries (Chile, Greece, Mexico, Spain, and South Korea) to measure the linkage indexes for 18 industries. The results are shown in Table 20–2. For leather, the next-to-last column tells us, for example, that for each additional dollar of leather goods produced, production of all inputs must rise by $2.39. A high index indicates that expansion of the industry will stimulate production in other sectors of the economy. Manufacturing industries dominate the upper ranks of Table 20–2 on the basis of both direct and total backward linkages. The early-developing sectors—leather, clothing, textiles, and food and beverages—represent four of the first five branches ranked by total backward linkages. Primary industries, utilities, and services are low on both lists. Hence an unbalanced-growth strategy should, to stimulate investment in other sectors, begin with the early-developing industries and then move to chemicals and metal products. Advocates of import substitution strategies find sustenance in these findings.

But what do these indices really mean? Should a country base its development strategy on them, even if rapid growth is the principal goal? These particular measurement formulas have been attacked for several reasons, many of them sound ones. But alternative and more-complicated formulations give similar rankings anyway. The real issue is whether a mechanical

TABLE 20–2   Sectoral Linkage Indexes and Rankings in Five Less-Developed Countries[a]

	Direct forward linkage index (L_f)	Rank	Direct backward linkage index (L_b)	Rank	Total backward linkage index (L_t)	Rank
Leather	0.645	4	0.683	2	2.39	1
Basic metals	0.980	1	0.632	5	2.36	2
Clothing	0.025	18	0.621	6	2.32	3
Textiles	0.590	8	0.621	7	2.24	4
Food and beverage manufactures	0.272	16	0.718	1	2.22	5
Paper	0.788	3	0.648	3	2.17	6
Chemicals and petroleum refining	0.599	7	0.637	4	2.13	7
Metal products and machinery	0.430	13	0.558	9	2.12	8
Wood, furniture	0.582	9	0.620	8	2.07	9
Construction	0.093	17	0.543	10	2.04	10
Printing	0.508	10	0.509	12	1.98	11
Other manufactures	0.362	15	0.505	13	1.94	12
Rubber	0.453	12	0.481	14	1.93	13
Minerals (nonmetallic)	0.870	2	0.517	11	1.83	14
Agriculture	0.502	11	0.368	15	1.59	15
Utilities	0.614	6	0.296	16	1.49	16
Mining	0.638	5	0.288	17	1.47	17
Services	0.378	14	0.255	18	1.41	18

[a]Chile, Greece, South Korea, Mexico, and Spain.
Source: Yotopoulos and Nugent, "A Balanced-Growth Version of the Linkage Hypothesis," Table 2, p. 163.

summing up of input-output coefficients for one country really tells us anything about the dynamic processes of growth in another country. The textile industry, which ranks high in Table 20–2 according to its total backward linkage coefficient, may well require inputs of cotton and synthetic fibers. But whether this additional demand will lead to new investment in farming and chemicals depends on many conditions, none of them reflected in the index. Can cotton be grown in the country at all and if so, at what cost? It might remain cheaper, and to the country's advantage, to import cotton and use the land to grow more profitable crops. If cotton is already being grown and exported, can output expand to accommodate the textile plant or would it simply divert exports? Reduced exports would of course cancel the backward linkage effect.

The potential linkage back to synthetic fibers raises additional issues. Petrochemical industries are subject to substantial economies of scale (discussed later in this chapter), and it would take a considerable expansion of the textile industry to justify the very large investment in petrochemicals. If protection is used to keep out imports of synthetic fibers, the textile industry itself would suffer higher costs and perhaps lose its impetus to expand, as explained in Chapter 16. However, it is also possible that some infant supplier industries may have the potential to reduce costs over time— learning by doing—if they are given a chance.

The requirements for effective forward linkages from manufacturing are even more stringent. To continue the example, textiles have a large forward linkage index, primarily to the clothing industry. But does domestic cloth stimulate the clothing industry? It can if textiles can be produced at costs below the world price of imported cloth. Otherwise the user industry is better off importing its input. If clothing manufacturers are forced, through tariffs or import controls, to take more expensive domestic cloth, this would discourage, rather than stimulate, the forward linkage.

The static linkage indices can help direct attention to potential linkages, but detailed studies are required to consider all the relevant conditions and to pinpoint the ways in which investment in one industry will lead to investment in others. These studies may well show that some manufacturing sectors can lead growth in certain countries. But some of the references cited in Chapter 15 demonstrated that certain primary sectors also generate effective linkages, and there is no overwhelming case favoring manufacturing on this ground.

Urbanization

Since the Industrial Revolution, urbanization and industrialization have moved in tandem. England started the nineteenth century with 30 percent of its people living in cities and ended the century with an urban population share of over 70 percent.[5] The trend towards urbanization with industrial development is evident today in cross-country comparisons, depicted in Figure 20–2. Although there is considerable variation among countries at

5. Hobsbawm, *Industry and Empire,* Fig. 13.

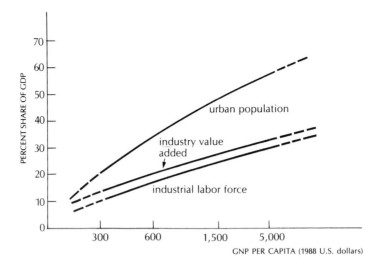

FIGURE 20–2 **Industrialization and Urbanization: Cross-Country Comparisons, 1965.** Cross-country comparisons indicate that as GNP per capita rises from $300 to $1,500 in 1988 prices, on average industrial value-added grows from 14 to 28 percent of GDP while the urban population increases its share of total population somewhat faster, from 20 to 51 percent in a typical country.
Source: Chenery and Syrquin, *Patterns of Development,* pp. 36, 50, and 55.

any income level, the association between development and urbanization is nevertheless unmistakable.

What causes this apparently inexorable urban growth as industrialization proceeds? Several **external economies** (see Chapter 5) benefit manufacturing firms in urban settings. Large populations reduce the firms' cost of recruiting labor of all kinds, but especially skilled workers and technicians. Moreover, in cities workers usually find their own housing, so firms do not have to provide it, as they might in rural areas or small towns. **Infrastructure,** including industrial sites, electricity, water, sewage, roads, railroads, and in many cases ports, is provided by government in the cities at costs that reflect substantial scale economies. Health and education facilities are also more highly developed in the cities.

Each firm also benefits from the **economies of agglomeration** that result from the presence of many other firms, because a wide range of necessary inputs and services becomes available. Manufacturers can reduce transport costs and shipping delays if they locate near their suppliers. They also benefit from the proximity of repair and other industrial services. Financial markets cluster in cities where domestic and international communication facilities are available and cheap. Manufacturers need access to banks and other financial institutions. They also need the city's communications to stay in touch with distant suppliers and markets, especially export markets. When the city in question is a national capital, manufacturers may locate there to gain ready access to government officials who control investment licenses and incentives, import allocations, and a myriad of other policy and administrative devices that affect the profitability of the firm. Finally, the strong preferences of capitalists, managers, and technicians for the amenities of large cities can be a significant reason for locating there.

Once a city is established, its large market creates reinforcing attractions. Distribution costs are minimized when the firm locates near its largest market. If the costs of shipping output weigh heavily in a firm's costs, and especially if they are more important than the costs of transporting inputs, firms will be pulled toward cities. This attraction is particularly strong in developing countries, where intercity and rural-urban transport networks are sparse or costly. In developed countries, where transport networks are dense and efficient, manufacturing tends to be more footloose and seeks out advantages like cheap labor with less regard for transport costs.

But urbanization has its costs, as the residents of every large city in the world observe daily: overcrowding, unsanitary conditions, displacement of rural migrants, crime. These too have been features of industrialization for two centuries. During the first half of the nineteenth century, London and the other growing cities of Britain were dismal places:

> Smoke hung over them and filth impregnated them . . . the elementary public services—water supply, sanitation, street-cleaning, open spaces, and so on—could not keep pace with the mass migration of men into the cities, thus producing, especially after 1830, epidemics of cholera, typhoid and an appalling constant toll of the two great groups of nineteenth-century urban killers—air pollution and water pollution, or respiratory and intestinal disease. . . . New city populations . . . pressed into overcrowded and bleak slums, whose very sight froze the heart of the observer.[6]

Migrants to the large cities of the third world probably do not have to put up with conditions as bad as those of early nineteenth-century London, but cities like Calcutta, Lagos, and São Paulo contain large slums with many of the same kinds of problems.

Although urban infrastructure can be provided at lower cost than the alternative of providing the same services in small, scattered towns, infrastructure is still the largest direct cost of urbanization. A study of cities and towns in India conducted in 1967 estimated that the capital cost of infrastructure provided for manufacturing industry was $820 for every $1,000 of incremental value-added in manufacturing, or about $1,400 per employee (converted to 1988 prices) in a city of 1 million. Only about a quarter of this is due to construction in the industrial area itself. The balance serves the residential area, so can generally be interpreted as the capital cost of supporting workers in the city. If capital costs are amortized at 10 percent a year and maintenance costs ($600 per employee) are added, it would appear that cities provide manufacturers with annual infrastructure services costing 13 percent of the value-added in manufacturing.[7]

Industrializing cities become magnets for rural workers seeking jobs at higher wages, a pervasive third-world phenomenon explored in Chapter 8.

6. Hobsbawm, *Industry and Empire*, p. 86.
7. Stanford Research Institute et al., *Costs of Urban Infrastructure for Industry as Related to City Size in Developing Countries: India Case Study* (Menlo Park, Calif: Stanford Research Institute, 1968).

Despite the risks of unemployment and congested living conditions, urban life may still be attractive to many rural dwellers, relative to the opportunities available at home. The costs of congestion are external diseconomies: each new migrant will benefit on average, but in so doing, reduces the well-being of all others, even if only slightly. The social costs are high, however, because this marginal reduction in well-being must be added up for all residents of the city.

No government feels comfortable with crowded cities, and many have attempted to stem the flow of migration. Over the long run this can best be done by encouraging rural development as actively as industrialization, using the wide range of land tenure, investment, price, incentive, and other policies described in Chapter 18 and elsewhere in this text. A complementary approach is to encourage the dispersal of new industries to smaller cities through the provision of infrastructure, incentives, and controls over location. Spreading investment reduces congestion and may also reduce the cost of migration. Migrants will have shorter average distances to travel, so more of them can search for jobs without a commitment to permanent residence in cities remote from their homes. The decentralization of industry also has complementary benefits for agriculture; it distributes urban markets and manufactured supplies more widely among the farming population.

Industrial dispersion does have costs, however. Infrastructure costs may be greater in small towns, which have not provided as much of the basic facilities as large cities. The study of urban infrastructure in India cited earlier (see footnote 9), showed that in a town of 50,000, infrastructure for industry costs 13 percent more than in a city of 1 million, allowing for both capital and recurrent costs. No measurements were made for larger cities, in which economies of scale are evidently exhausted and congestion may well raise the unit cost of infrastructure. To this must be added the higher costs of transport and other infrastructure required to connect dispersed industrial locations.

Even with this wider network of transport and communications in place, private firms—and society—incur higher costs of hauling freight (both their material inputs and their final outputs) if they do not locate in the most efficient place; of communicating with suppliers, customers, and financial institutions, not to mention government officials; and of waiting with idle facilities while parts and repair specialists from distant places arrive to fix broken equipment. Whether the benefits of dispersal justify the costs will depend on the circumstances. Costs will be lower if the population is already dispersed, if several urban centers and connecting infrastructure already exist, and if the new sites have obvious advantages, such as nearby raw materials or abundant water.

INVESTMENT CHOICES IN INDUSTRY

Chapter 3 introduced the proposition that, because factors of production can be substituted for one nother in many production processes, economies were able to conserve capital and get more growth out of a given amount

of saving. Chapter 8 used the same analytical device—the neoclassical production function—to demonstrate that policies to make labor less expensive and capital more expensive could move producers toward investments that employ more labor and less capital for a given level of output. But is there enough variance in production techniques to make such policies effective in conserving capital and creating more employment for a given amount of production? For industry, the answer is yes.

Choice of Technique

Table 20–3 illustrates the choice of technology for a single industry, textile weaving. Three alternative technologies are included: an older, semi-automatic loom, (T-1); a more modern, fully automatic, high-speed loom (T3); and an intermediate technology (T2). More alternatives could have been shown, including handloom weaving, which is still used in some Asian countries. As expected, the three technologies show increasing capital intensity, in the sense that the ratio of capital to output rises, and decreasing labor intensity. The treatment of Chapter 8 has been augmented by the consideration of other operating costs, including rental of space, power, and differential wastage of the main output, yarn. In many cases modern

TABLE 20–3 Choice of Technology in Textile Weaving

A. Inputs (per million yards of shirting)	Alternative technology[a]		
	T1	T2	T3
1. Equipment cost ($1,000)	80.0	200.0	400.0
2. Labor (person-years)	22.0	11.0	5.0
3. Other costs ($1,000/year)[b]	11.4	9.3	6.7

B. Factor costs	Rich Country	Poor Country
1. Real interest rate (% p.a.)	5.0	10.0
2. Present-value factor (20 years)[c]	12.46	8.51
3. Wages ($1,000/year)	15.0	1.5

C. Present value of costs ($1,000)[d]	Alternative technology		
	T1	T2	T3
Rich country			
1. Capital charges	80	200	400
2. Wages	4,112	2,056	935
3. Other costs	142	116	83
4. Total	4,334	2,372	1,418
Poor country			
1. Capital charges	80	200	400
2. Wages	280	140	64
3. Other costs	97	79	57
Total	457	419	521

[a]Technologies are: T1—semi-automatic loom, T2—intermediate technology, and T3—fully automatic, high-speed loom.
[b]Includes cost of space, power, and wastage of yarn, all of which vary depending on the technology. Excludes the common cost of yarn in the finished product.
[c]Present value of $1 per year for 20 years at the interest rate shown in B1.
[d]Wages and other costs discounted at appropriate interest rate over 20 years using present value factor in B2.
Source: Adapted from data in Howard Pack, "The Choice of Technique and Employment in the Textile Industry," in Technology and Employment in Industry, A. S. Bhalla ed. (Geneva: International Labour Office, 1975), pp. 153–174.

equipment conserves both energy and material inputs and lowers production costs.

Analysis of the choice of technology is conveniently done using project analysis as described in Chapter 6. Revenues and costs, including the cost of investment, can be discounted over the life of each technology and the technology with the highest net present value chosen as the most economic. In Table 20–3, it is assumed for simplicity that all techniques produce cloth of equal quality and value, so revenues are not brought into consideration. Instead, the present value of costs is minimized.

Part B of the table presents indicative factor costs for a rich country and a poor one: workers in the rich country are paid 10 times the wage of those in the poor one, whereas the real interest rate in the poor country is twice that of the rich one. Under those conditions, investors in the rich country would minimize costs by choosing the most modern looms, largely because these require so much less labor. Investors in the poor country should select the intermediate technology. However, should the annual wage in the poor country be $1,000 a year instead of $1,500, which is a realistic possibility, the oldest and most labor-intensive technology would minimize costs. Figure 20–3 represents these technological choices as a production isoquant

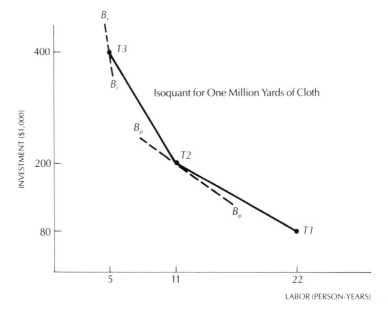

FIGURE 20–3 **Technological Choice in the Weaving Industry.** Three alternative weaving technologies T1, T2, and T3 are taken from Table 20–3. Each represents a different ratio of capital to labor. Because the industry, or even a single firm, is able to use any combination of technologies, production could take place at all combinations of labor and capital along *T1T2* and along *T2T3*. Thus an isoquant can be traced from *T1* to *T2* to *T3*. The slopes of the budget lines, B_rB_r and B_pB_p, represent the ratios of wages to capital charges for the rich and poor countries, respectively. They indicate that costs will be minimized for the rich country by using the most capital-intensive technology T3, whereas the poor country should use intermediate technology T2. Were wages in the poor country only slightly lower relative to capital costs, it might well find the most labor-intensive technology T1 to be optimal.

similar to those of Figures 3–2 and 8–3, only in a form more realistic for alternative technologies in single industries.

The range of technologies represented in Figure 20–3 is realistic for the weaving industry in a developing country. The scope for technological choice in this industry can be indicated by the range of capital-labor ratios from the most to the least capital-intensive technology. The capital-labor ratio of technology T3 is 22 times that of technology T1. The study from which these figures are taken gives a similar range for cotton spinning, whereas cement block-making in Kenya alone exhibits a ratio of 11:1.[8]

Even if the scope is narrowed to a choice between the appropriate technology (T2 for the poor country in Figure 20–3) and the most capital-intensive alternative (T3), there is a wide range of technologies available in several industries; for shoe manufacturing, the most capital-intensive technology has a capital-labor ratio 2.8 times that of the appropriate technology; for cotton weaving the ratio is 4.3; for cotton spinning, 7.3; for brickmaking, 13.8; for maize milling, 3.3; for sugar processing, 7.8; for beer brewing, 1.5; for leather processing, 2.3; and for fertilizer manufacturing, 1.1.[9]

The cumulative impact of the choice of more labor-intensive technologies can be considerable. In one indicative experiment, Howard Pack, an American economist who specializes in the choice of technology, assumes that each of the nine industries listed in the previous paragraph receives $100 million of investment. If all of this were spent on the most capital-intensive technology, it would generate employment of 58,000 and value-added of $364 million a year. But if invested in the appropriate technology instead, the same investment would create over 4 times the employment (239,000) and 71 percent more value-added ($624 million).[10]

Despite the advantages to be gained in both output and employment from using appropriate, more-labor-intensive methods in developing countries, we observe many industrial plants using processes that are too capital intensive. Several possible explanations for this were given in the discussion of the employment problem of Chapter 8 and elsewhere in this text: market prices of productive factors typically do not reflect true factor scarcities (opportunity costs or shadow prices) and so distort technology choice; more labor-intensive methods are usually embodied in older models of equipment, frequently available only in used machinery, which may be difficult to learn about, obtain, and maintain; newer equipment may manufacture products of higher quality and value; or managers may not be skilled in handling large labor forces. These factors are often exaggerated. In any case, most of them can be incorporated in present value calculations that reveal least-cost technologies.

These factors probably do not explain the wide range of technologies, many of them apparently inappropriate, that can be observed in a single country or in similar countries. There may be two further explanations for

8. Howard Pack, "The Choice of Technique and Employment in the Textile Industry," p. 169, and Frances Stewart, "Manufacture of Cement Blocks in Kenya," in *Technology and Employment in Industry*, Bhalla, p. 221.

9. Howard Pack, "Aggregate Implications of Factor Substitution in Industry Processes," *Journal of Development Economics* 11, no. 1 (August 1982): 7.

10. Ibid., p. 10.

this. First, different firms can face different factor prices. Foreign firms usually have access to cheaper capital than domestic companies can obtain, so their optimal choice of technology is more capital intensive. (However, this may be countered by the multinational firm's greater knowledge of, and easier access to, machinery using older techniques, some of which may be in use in older plants of the same company.) Among domestic companies, small firms, with limited access to formal capital markets, may have to pay more for their capital than large firms. Similarly, small firms may escape both unionization and minimum-wage laws, and so are able to employ workers at lower costs. In Indonesia, Australian economist Hal Hill observed four textile-weaving technologies in operation, with a capital-output ratio for the most modern looms over 200 times that for traditional handlooms. Two of these technologies represented least-cost choices for their firms. Surprisingly, these were the two most capital-intensive. But when shadow prices were used, only the more labor-intensive of the two techniques remained appropriate.[11]

Second, investors may purchase inappropriate equipment because they and their managers have a strong bias towards the most modern machinery and the highest possible quality of output, with less emphasis on profitability and other economic considerations. Harvard management expert Louis Wells has called this the behavior of "engineering man."[12] If the characteristics of management constrain the choice of technology, the selection may be technique T3 in Figure 20–3, even though the budget line indicates the choice of technique T2. Such non-economic behavior is more likely to prevail in highly protected, monopolistic situations, where a decision to produce at less than minimum cost will not threaten the firm's existence. State-owned enterprises are particularly prone to inefficiencies of this type.

Economies of Scale

In decisions about alternative technologies, **economies of scale** may be a crucial consideration. It has been observed by economists at least since Adam Smith that for many kinds of production, larger facilities may be able to produce at lower unit costs than small ones. For example, steel produced in a mill designed for 2 million tons a year might cost 15 percent less than steel produced in a mill designed for only 1 million tons. As the scale of output rises, the potential average cost falls. (However, if the larger mill produces only 1 million tons, its average cost is likely to be higher than the small mill, because the small one was designed for lower output and the large one was not.) Readers familiar with the theory of the firm will recognize the concept of **long-run average cost,** the potential unit cost of output when plant size is variable. If the long-run cost curve declines over a range

11. Hal Hill, "Choice of Technique in the Indonesian Weaving Industry," *Economic Development and Cultural Change* 31, no. 2 (January 1983): 337–54.

12. Louis T. Wells, Jr., Economic Man and Engineering Man: Choice of Technique in a Low-wage Country," in *The Choice of Technology in Developing Countries,* C. P. Timmer et al., eds. (Cambridge, Mass.: Center for International Affairs, Harvard University, 1975), pp. 69–94.

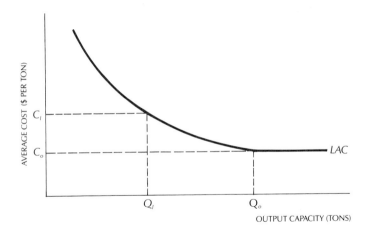

FIGURE 20–4 **Economies of Scale.** The long-run average cost curve *LAC* shows the average cost for plants designed to produce at any capacity. Average cost falls as capacity rises up to Q_0, sometimes called the *minimum efficient scale* (MES). Q_1 is half of Q_0. The percentage by which C_1 exceeds C_0 is a measure of the economies to be gained by building plants to a larger scale.

of output relevant to the plant in question, as depicted in Figure 20–4, there are economies of scale.

Scale economies arise for a number of reasons. (1) Some costs, such as research and design efforts or start-up costs, may be fixed over a wide range of output. (2) The amount and cost of materials used in capital equipment will rise with output, but not always in proportion. For example, the capacity of a boiler is related to its volume, which for a sphere varies as the cube of its radius, whereas the material used to build it is related to its area, proportional to the square of the radius. (3) The amount of inventories and other working capital does not rise proportionally to output. (4) Greater scale permits greater specialization of both workers and equipment (the point emphasized by Adam Smith), which in turn permits higher productivity. (5) Larger production runs reduce the number of times equipment must be set up or readjusted for each run. For example, a plant that produces two or more products with one machine, such as metal cans of different sizes, could be run more efficiently once it has enough volume to produce each on a separate machine and reduce set-up costs. (6) Larger producers may be able to obtain quantity discounts when they procure inputs. These economies all apply to individual plants. At the level of the firm, further economies may arise in management, transport, marketing, and finance as more plants are added.

These cost savings can be quite important in manufacturing certain products. Table 20–4 presents data on the scale economies measured for several industries in the United Kingdom in 1969. The **minimum efficient scale** (MES) is defined as a plant large enough so that no further economies can be gained by building a larger facility, Q_0 in Figure 20–4. The first column of the table gives the percentage by which average cost would be greater if a plant were built to only half the MES, compared with a plant built at the

TABLE 20–4   Economies of Scale in Manufacturing in the United Kingdom, 1969

Product	% increase in average cost for plant capacity = half the MES[a,b]	MES[a] as % of UK market
Bread	15	1
Beer	9	3
Footwear	2	0.2
Dyes	22	100
Sulphuric acid	1	30
Polymers	5	33
Cement	9	10
Steel (integrated)	8	80
Machine tools	5	100
Electric motors	15	60
Automobiles (one model)	6	50
Bicycles	small	10
Diesel engines	4	10
Domestic appliances	8	20

[a] Minimum efficient scale defined as the output beyond which average costs cease to decline (Q_0 in Figure 20–4) or beyond which no larger plants have been built.
[b] As a percent of the average cost of production for a plant producing at minimum economic scale.
Source: C. F. Pratten, *Economies of Scale in Manufacturing Industries* (London: Cambridge University Press, 1971).

MES, or $100 (c_1 - c_0)/c_0$ from Figure 20–4. In practice, if the largest plant in existence does not exhaust potential scale economies, investigators often take that output as the MES until a larger plant is built and its costs measured.

Some of the cost increases in column 1 (for plants half of MES) are significant: 8 to 22 percent for bread, beer, dyes, cement, steel, electric motors, and domestic appliances. However, this is not very meaningful unless we know how large a MES plant is relative to the national market. In the cases of bread and beer in Britain, the second column shows that economies of scale are exhausted at outputs that are very small relative to total consumption, so it is possible to have many plants of sufficient scale. For dyes, steel, electric motors, and automobiles, however, a plant of minimum efficient scale would (in 1969) have met at least half British demand. This suggests that as manufacturers of these products pursue profits through cost savings, output is likely to become concentrated in a few firms, even in markets as large as Britain's.

No developing country has an internal market as large as Britain's. In 1988 the total gross national product of the largest LDC, China, was just over half that of the United Kingdom; Brazil's GNP was less than half Britain's, and India's only a third. The largest African economy is Nigeria's with a GNP only 4 percent that of Britain.[13] For medium to large third-world economies, then, only industries with negligible scale economies (footwear, sulphuric acid, and bicycles in the table) or with a very small

13. Gross national product is only a rough approximation of market size, especially for specific products. Both income per capita, which helps to indicate the per-capita demand for individual commodities, and population should be included separately in a more comprehensive measure of market size.

MES (bread, beer, and footwear) can be accommodated efficiently in a

competitive domestic market. For the other industries in the table, large size and significant cost savings imply that plants built to serve the domestic market will have no domestic competition, produce at high cost, or both.

The characteristics of these large-scale industries shed light on the industrialization process. All are producer goods or consumer durables. The industries in which small countries face the greatest disadvantages, those with large economies at large outputs, are in chemicals (dyes and, to a lesser extent, polymers), basic metals (steel), capital equipment (electric motors and, to a lesser extent, machine tools), and consumer durables (automobiles and appliances). Thus the nondurable consumer-goods industries develop early at least in part because economies of scale are not much of a barrier, except in the very smallest countries. And the barrier to backward integration, noted in discussing import substitution (Chapter 16), can also be blamed in part on economies of scale.

Despite the existence of scale economies it may be efficient to build small plants in developing countries. A steel plant, for example, should be built when it can produce at a cost below the price of imported steel. This may happen long before the market grows to accommodate a steel mill of minimum efficient scale. Economic size is only one of the factors that bears on efficiency. All the others mentioned earlier in this text—productivity, opportunity cost of capital and labor, availability of raw materials and complementary inputs, managerial skills, market organization—also affect the outcome and may outweigh the effects of scale economies. Techniques such as project appraisal (Chapter 6) can be employed to analyze the impact of all these elements on profitability.

Moreover, the domestic market is not the only possibility. The "virtuous circle," through which export markets make it possible to attain scale economies, which in turn increase export competitiveness, was one of the forces behind Britain's Industrial Revolution. Indeed if a domestic industry in a small LDC were efficient enough to compete with foreign plants at any given output, then scale economies would not matter: the home industry could export enough to achieve any scale desired. Developing countries like South Korea and Brazil have achieved scale economies, even in industries like steel and automobiles, with the help of export markets. Economic integration among developing countries may help other countries to do the same.

Small-Scale Industry

Although economies of scale require large plants in some branches of production, there are many other industries in which small- and medium-scale firms can compete effectively with large ones (see Table 20–4, above). This is especially true in developing countries, where many widely used manufactured items—including most food and tobacco products, textiles, clothing, footwear, furniture and other wood products, cement blocks, bricks, tiles, and various simple metal products—are commonly made in smaller firms.

It has often been argued that LDC governments should promote small-scale industry as either a complement or an alternative to large-scale modern manufacturing. India, probably the postindependence leader in planning for large-scale industrialization, has also pursued small-industry development with vigor, a legacy of Gandhi's famous advocacy of small units using traditional technologies. China's use of small-scale rural industry in support of local self-reliance is equally well-known. E. F. Schumacher, author of *Small is Beautiful,* founded a movement of small-industry enthusiasts.[14] Over the years, very few development plans have failed to pay homage to the goal of small-industry development.

Advocates of small-industry promotion promise a wide range of benefits, including accelerated employment creation, income generation for the poor, dispersal of economic activity to small towns and rural areas, and mobilization of latent entrepreneurial talent. They have also argued that support for small enterprise and the **informal sector** (see Chapter 8) will create a wider base of political support for capitalism and free-market policies.[15]

Shortly we will assess the potential of small industry to realize these hopes, but first we need to consider what "small industry" really means. There are several different ways to classify manufacturing plants by scale, none perfect. Classifying by the number of workers employed has the advantage that data are widely available. Units with one to four workers (usually a proprietor and family members) may be classified as **cottage shops,** whereas larger plants can be divided into small enterprises (sometimes 5 to 19 workers), medium enterprises (20 to 99), and large enterprises (100 or more), respectively. Such distinctions are arbitrary. In a large country, or a small industrial one, a plant employing 200 workers would be considered small. Moreover, when plants are classified by other criteria, such as capital invested or technology used, they may shift into different categories.

Cottage shops and small enterprises employ one-half to three-quarters of all manufacturing sector workers in many low-income countries. Their share in manufacturing value added is likely to be much lower, however, usually about one-fourth of the total. This marked discrepancy between the employment share and the value-added share shows that value-added per worker is much lower on average in small plants than in large ones. In part, this reflects the greater labor intensity of small plants.

Since low-income countries typically have abundant labor but little capital, most economists would expect labor-intensive technologies to be efficient in these settings. By this line of reasoning, the fact that small firms are usually more labor-intensive is sometimes taken to mean that they are more efficient than large firms. As part of the informal sector, small firms may be exempted from, or escape the enforcement of, taxes, minimum wage laws, employment codes, and other regulations that raise the costs of larger firms. They may also lack access to subsidized loans, foreign exchange at overvalued (cheap) rates, and controlled imports, which artificially lower

14. E. F. Schumacher, *Small is Beautiful* (London: Sphere Books, 1974).
15. See Hernando de Soto, *The Other Path* (New York: Harper & Row, 1989), and P. N. Dhar and H. F. Lydall, *The Role of Small Enterprises in Indian Economic Development* (Bombay: Asia Publishing House, 1961).

the costs of larger firms. It has been theorized that this freedom from many

sources of factor-price distortion may induce small firms to use resources
more efficiently than large firms. Alternatively, however, they might simply use all resources less efficiently—capital, labor, and material inputs.
Attempts to measure the relative efficiency of different size plants in industries where large and small firms coexist have generally been unable to
reach firm conclusions.[16] Such comparisons face many difficulties in any
case, not least the fact that product quality may differ greatly between large
and small firms. Although cottage shops make cheap plastic sandals, for
example, large plants may produce shoes of higher quality.

As a country develops, the average size of its industrial plants tends to
rise as implied by Table 20–5. This rise is associated with the expansion of
markets, which permits a few firms in some industries to expand and realize economies of scale and thereby beat out their smaller competitors. A
related factor is declining transportation and communication costs, which
facilitate the integration of national markets and permit goods to be manufactured in least-cost locations and then shipped to their final markets. Thus
the "natural monopoly" conferred on smaller local firms by high transportation costs and poor communication begins to break down. Industrialization also tends to narrow productivity and wage differentials among units
of different sizes, a condition for the efficient allocation of resources.

The presence of many small firms in most poor countries—and the many
people who depend on them for a living—does not necessarily mean that
government should promote or subsidize small-scale industry. Most of the
cottage shops and small enterprises in low-income countries probably have
little capacity for enterprise growth. They typically provide a living for the
proprietor and a few family members at a standard above that of peasant
farmers but below that provided by efficient modern firms. Like small family farms, most of these "livelihood enterprises" survive as long as no
better economic opportunities present themselves, then gradually disappear as the modern sector of the economy develops and workers move on
to higher-productivity employment. Only a few small- and medium-scale
enterprises have the potential to modernize themselves, upgrade their

TABLE 20–5 **Share of Small Establishments in Total Manufacturing Employment, 1980s
(percent)**

GNP per capita ($)	Distribution of employment by size class (%)			
	1–4 workers	5–19	20–99	100+
$100–$500	64	7	4	25
$500–$1,000	41	12	10	37
$1,000–$2,000	11	13	14	61
$2,000–$5,000	8	11	17	64
Over $5,000	4	6	20	70

Source: Tyler S. Biggs, "Firm Transformation in the Tropics," forthcoming.

16. Ian M. D. Little, Dipak Mazumdar, and John M. Page, Jr., *Small Manufacturing Enterprises* (New York: Oxford University Press for the World Bank, 1988). They also claim to
detect a tendency for medium-sized firms to be most efficient.

technologies, and compete successfully with larger firms. To do so, they must usually define some niche of excellence. The small firms that do survive in industrial countries tend to be just as capital-intensive and high-tech as larger firms in the same economy and to differ from them only in degree of specialization.

Can the promotion of small-scale industry deliver the benefits promised by its advocates? Let us examine the evidence on each of the claims noted earlier.

Small plants are generally more labor-intensive than large ones, although there are many labor-intensive large firms as well. Labor intensity contributes to equity in countries where income is very unequally distributed and people often have difficulty finding remunerative employment. The amount a worker earns is more important than merely having a job, however, and the level of pay is ultimately linked to productivity. In small industries in the poorest countries, labor productivity is low and most jobs in small firms provide little more than a chance to share in the general poverty. Government policy should aim not just at raising employment but at helping firms of all scales to develop new markets, adopt new technologies, and raise labor productivity. This is more likely to occur in medium-scale firms than in very small ones.

The claim that small-scale industry promotes regional decentralization also needs considerable qualification. Although it is true that many small firms are located in rural areas and small towns, these tend to be traditional "livelihood enterprises" that are likely to lose out in the process of industrialization. Keeping them alive through subsidization might increase equity, but at a high cost to efficiency and long-term growth. Modern small firms, in contrast, cluster in large cities, perhaps even more densely then large firms. Large firms are more self-sufficient and rely on economies of scale to lower production costs. Small firms, however, depend more on **economies of agglomeration** generated by proximity to firms engaged in similar or complementary activities. Most small producers need access to intermediate material inputs and thus prefer to be close to ports and other transport facilities. They are less likely than large firms to train their own workers, so they benefit from being near urban growth centers where skilled workers are located.

Small-scale industry does indeed serve as a breeding ground for potential entrepreneurs. Most societies have actual or potential entrepreneurs in farming, retail trading, transportation, and other small-scale activities. Small-scale industry represents a feasible step for these entrepreneurs, who would be blocked from entering manufacturing if large amounts of credit and the ability to manage large-scale enterprises were essential. Small enterprises can sometimes be developed in imitation of earlier entrants and so require less-innovative entrepreneurs. Some small firms have the potential to grow to medium or even large enterprises. It is important, however, not to yield to romanticism. Statistically, very few small firms even survive over long periods of time, let alone grow up to be medium or large enterprises. The rate of business failure is high among small firms in all countries.

Government can assist by providing a legal system, supporting financial and other institutions, and market-based policies that permit successful enterprises to flourish and require unsuccessful ones to meet market pressures or give way to more efficient alternatives. Most governments can begin by eliminating the many facets of policy that discriminate against small firms. Controlled imports and subsidized credit seldom reach small firms, whereas licensing requirements, health regulations, zoning restrictions, and other measures are often used actively to discourage small enterprises, especially those operating in the informal sector. In the kind of market-based, outward-looking regime described in Chapter 17, small firms should thrive if they have the economic advantages claimed for them by the advocates of small-scale industrialization.

Even in a deregulated, market-oriented economy, however, many feel that small industry needs special help from government to overcome some of its initial handicaps. A fairly standard package of services is used to provide this assistance.[17] It includes credit, usually provided through a small-industry development bank or similar institution; technical advice, organized along the lines of an agricultural extension service; training programs for managers and skilled workers; help in setting up procurement and marketing channels; and industrial estates that provide sites with infrastructure and a focal point for the assistance package. The idea behind this kind of package is to help inexperienced entrepreneurs over their early hurdles, introduce them to regular marketing channels, and eventually make them self-reliant.

However, the package is expensive and often ineffective. It requires government agencies to make contact with numerous and varied individual entrepreneurs and to offer assistance tailored to their specific needs and thus draws heavily on the government's limited managerial and technical resources. Firms served by these programs often find the advice they receive unhelpful and the places in industrial estates that they are offered poorly located or too expensive. Many have failed to repay their loans, and this has sometimes resulted in the bankruptcy of the specialized lending institution. At best, the expense and complexity of small-industry assistance programs limits their outreach to a small fraction of target firms. Nor is it clear that government agencies have the skills and nimbleness required to help small entrepreneurs deal with market situations. Thus this approach is no substitute for general economic policies that permit small operators to do what they do best.

Rural Small Industry in China

The Chinese have done what appears to be difficult in market economies: they have established modern small factories in rural centers to supply farm inputs, equipment, and consumer goods to communes and other rural customers.[18] Several conditions encouraged the emergence of local facto-

17. See Eugene Staley and Richard Morse, *Modern Small Industry for Developing Countries* (New York: McGraw-Hill, 1965).
18. This account is based on the report of the American Rural Small-Scale Industry Dele-

ries. China's rural transport and marketing system is poorly developed, so that rural communities are isolated from urban centers of production. Centralized planning and control of industrial goods intensifies this isolation, because communes wanting fertilizer or trucks must apply to authorities located in urban centers—a process that entails long delays and may not prove successful. It is in the communes' interest for their regions to become self-reliant in agricultural inputs to avoid these delays, and it is also in the planners' interest if local materials, capital, and labor can be used, so that other industrial priorities are not sacrificed. Local industry has the additional advantages of bringing modern technology directly to the countryside and of helping to narrow the economic and social gap between farm and city.

Despite the success of the small-industries program, Chinese planners apparently have only limited goals in mind. The program is not conceived as a generator of off-farm employment; rather, there is concern that rural factories will draw needed workers away from the communes. Nor is rural industry expected to replace modern, urban industry. "Walking on two legs" means that both must be pursued, and self-reliance implies that rural factories must not divert resources from large-scale, urban ones. Self-reliance also suggests that regional equality is not a prime goal of the program, because wealthier regions with more resources, especially savings, are likely to do better than poor ones. However, rural-urban equality is probably served by the program. Finally, it should be recognized that China is a huge, densely populated country. The rural counties in which self-reliant factories are based have populations greater than many of the countries in the third world. And the "small" factories—of 50 to 600 employees—are also large by the standards of most developing countries.

Industry and Development Goals

This and previous chapters, which have examined industry from several perspectives, point toward a consensus on the role that industry can be expected to play in development. Industrialization is not a panacea for underdevelopment. But two of its strengths are essential for any development program. As suggested by the Lewis-Fei-Ranis two-sector model (Chapter 3), greater productivity in industry is a key to increased per-capita income. And manufacturing provides a much larger menu of possibilities for efficient import substitution and increasing exports than is possible with primary industries alone.

Industrialization and rural development must proceed in tandem. Industry can supply agriculture with inputs, especially fertilizer and simple farm equipment, that raise farm productivity. If outward-looking policies have been followed and manufacturing is efficient, these inputs may be supplied more cheaply than imports. The relationship is reciprocal, because agriculture supplies raw materials for manufacturing, such as cotton and other

---

gation, *Rural Small-Scale Industry in the People's Republic of China* (Berkeley: University of California Press, 1977), Chap. 1. Dwight Perkins led the delegation.

fibers, rubber, or tobacco. Agriculture and industry also provide reciprocal consumer-goods markets. If agricultural incomes grow in egalitarian fashion—which may require land reform and broad-based rural development—then manufacturing will enjoy a wide and growing market for its consumer goods, one that may enable it to achieve scale economies in both production and marketing. Similarly, the growth of urban incomes, stimulated by industrial expansion, should provide a continuing stimulus to agricultural output and productivity through increasing demand for food. The key to growing food demand is expanding employment and improved urban income distribution.

Industry cannot by itself generate sufficient jobs to absorb the growing number of workers or to equalize income distribution, especially in the poorest countries. Liberalized economies, with reduced controls and market prices closer to scarcity values, can help to arrest the tendency toward capital intensity and inappropriate, modern technologies in manufacturing and thus to raise job creation in industry. A renewed emphasis on small industry may also help. Moreover, to the extent that intermediate or innovative technologies are needed to save capital and create more jobs relative to output, an innovative, efficient capital-goods industry is an essential part of a development strategy. But in the final analysis much of the burden for employment creation and income equalization will lie outside industry, in agriculture and the services.

Industry has rightly been seen as a key to another goal of many developing countries: reduced dependence. If a country wants the capability of doing without imports of essential commodities, it must develop both in integrated industrial structure and a productive agriculture. If it wishes to exclude foreign political and cultural influence, it must learn to operate its manufacturing plants without foreign help. Much of the discussion about reduced dependence really is about increasing autarky or self-sufficiency; this implies that a country must produce everything it needs. But an alternative goal suggests the capability of producing a wide variety of goods efficiently enough to trade them on world markets and obtaining some goods overseas when it is advantageous to do so. This leads to the outward-looking strategy discussed in Chapter 17.

Behind these considerations lurks a hidden development goal: industrialization for its own sake. Despite advice from many quarters to temper their protective and other industrial policies and instead to promote greater efficiency, employment, and equity, many governments continue to establish the most modern, capital-intensive industries available. This cannot be attributed entirely to misguided policy. The desire to have modern industry may be as great for a country as the desire for a radio or car can be for an individual. To the extent that modern manufacturing is a goal in itself, the best that development economists can do is to point out how much could be accomplished with alternative policies and measure the costs of industrialization in terms of other goals that remain to be achieved.

Appendix: Adjustment in a Small, Open Economy

In Chapter 5 we identified macroeconomic stabilization and structural adjustment as essential reforms for a large number of countries trying to resume economic development in the 1990s. Many economies became unbalanced because of unstable world market conditions, including: sharp rises in oil prices during the 1970s, then equally precipitate declines in the mid-1980s; rising world inflation during the 1970s, followed by tight money, rising interest rates, and the ensuing world recession in the early 1980s; and wide swings in the major exchange rates throughout the two decades. Some governments managed their economies shrewdly enough to overcome—and even to benefit from—these changing conditions. But a larger number of developing countries were unable to cope and several governments made the situation worse by running unsustainable deficits in their budgets, allowing the balance of trade and current payments to deteriorate, accumulating unserviceable debt, expanding the money supply to accommodate rising inflation, and intervening in markets to counteract the effects of profligate macroeconomic management. Stabilization programs, funded by the IMF, are intended to reduce the macroeconomic imbalances and curb the inflation that resulted from poor economic policies. Structural adjustment programs, supported by the World Bank, are designed to free markets from controls and adjust relative prices to reflect economic scarcities.

This appendix treats the problems of adjustment from two complementary perspectives.[1] We first employ the tools of trade theory—production frontiers and community indifference curves, utilized in Part 4—to show how both macroeconomic stabilization and relative price adjustments are inextricably linked in achieving a balanced economy. We then adopt a Keynesian perspective—introduced in Chapter 6 and used in Part 3—to explore the approaches that can be used to reduce macroeconomic imbalances and curb inflation.

ADJUSTMENT IN THE AUSTRALIAN MODEL

Developing economies have two features that are central to understanding how macroeconomic imbalances occur and can be corrected. First, they are **open economies,** in that trade or capital flows across their borders in sufficient quantity to influence the domestic economy, particularly prices and the money supply. Most economies are open in this sense, though openness is a matter of degree. Some countries—China in the 1970s, the Soviet Union until recently, Cuba, Burma, and Albania—have been so heavily protected and regulated that they might not qualify as open.

Second, these are **small economies,** meaning that neither their supply of exports nor their demand for imports has a noticeable impact on the world prices of these commodities and services. Economists call these countries **price takers** in world markets. Though a number of developing countries can exert some influence over the price of one or two primary exports in world markets, they almost never affect the price of goods they import and for macroeconomic purposes it is usually adequate to model even these countries as price takers.

These two qualities—smallness and openness—are the basis for the **Australian** or **dependent economy model** of an economy.[2] In Chapters 15 and 16 we used general equilibrium models to describe comparative advantage (Figure 15–1) and economic growth through import substitution (Figures 16–5 to 16–7). In those models the two goods were importables and exportables. The Australian model lumps importables and exportables together as **tradables** and distinguishes these from all other goods and services, called **nontradables.** We used this specification in Chapter 15's discussion of Dutch disease.

---

1. For this appendix, "adjustment" refers to both stabilization and structural adjustment, although only some elements of each are considered here.
2. It is called the "Australian" model because it was developed by Australian economists including W. E. G. Salter, "Internal Balance and External Balance: The Role of Price and Expenditure Effects," *Economic Record,* 635, no. 71 (August 1959): 226–238; Trevor W. Swan, "Economic Control in a Dependent Economy," *Economic Record* 36, no. 73 (March 1960): 51–66; and W. Max Corden, *Inflation, Exchange Rates and the World Economy* (Chicago: University of Chicago Press, 1977). Australia is considered a small, open economy.

Tradable goods and services are those whose prices within the country are determined by supply and demand on world markets. Under the small-economy assumption, these world market prices cannot be influenced by anything that happens within the country and so are **exogenous** to the model (determined outside the model). **Nontradables** are goods and services, such as transportation, construction, retail trade, and household services, that are not easily or conventionally bought or sold outside the country, usually because the cost of transporting them from one country to another is prohibitive or because local custom inhibits trade. Prices of nontradables are therefore determined by market forces within the economy. Nontradable prices are thus **endogenous** to the model (determined within the model).

Tradables and **traded** goods or services are not necessarily the same thing. All exported goods are tradables because domestic producers must sell them at world prices. Goods that are imported, even if they bear tariffs, are also tradables. But, paradoxically, imports become nontradables if their supply is limited by import quotas or other nontariff barriers, so the price of imports on the domestic market is set by domestic supply and demand instead of the world price (see Figure 16–2 for one demonstration of this). Similarly, a good that might be imported under most circumstances, say clothing or steel, could be rendered nontradable if tariffs were so high that no imports actually entered the country and domestic market forces controlled prices. It is even possible for a nontraded good to be treated as a tradable, if government (or a private monopolist) controls the price at world market levels. In Indonesia, for example, rice is only occasionally imported or exported, but the official domestic price tracks the world price, averaged over several years. In all cases where goods that are or might be traded are instead treated as nontradable, or where nontraded goods are treated as tradable, the cause is some policy intervention that inhibits price-setting market mechanisms.

Figure A–1 depicts equilibrium under the Australian model.[3] The vertical axis represents nontradables (N); the horizontal axis takes both the exportables and the importables of previous diagrams (Figures 15–1 and 16–5 to 16–7) and treats them together as tradables (T). The production frontier shows the menu of possible outputs of the two kinds of goods, N and T. The community indifference curves show consumer preferences between consumption of tradables and nontradables. Equilibrium is at point A, the tangency of a consumer indifference curve and the production possibility frontier. This tangency determines the relative price of tradables in terms of nontradables; $P = P_t/P_n$. The slope of the relative price line P_1 gives this price in Figure A–1. (Recall that in previous diagrams, with exportables and importables, the relative price was the world terms of trade.) The value of income (GNP) or expenditure is Y_a, the intersection of price line P_1 from point A to the X-axis.[4]

3. The presentation in this section follows the more complete treatment of the Australian model in Richard E. Caves, Jeffrey A. Frankel, and Ronald W. Jones, *World Trade and Payments: An Introduction* (Glenview, Ill.: Scott, Foresman / Little, Brown, 1990), Chap. 19. For a more advanced presentation based on algebra and phase diagrams, see Rudiger Dornbusch, *Open Economy Macroeconomics*, 2nd ed. (New York: Basic Books, 1989), Chap. 6.

4. The quantity of T-goods is valued at T_a. The quantity of N-goods is N_a, which can be

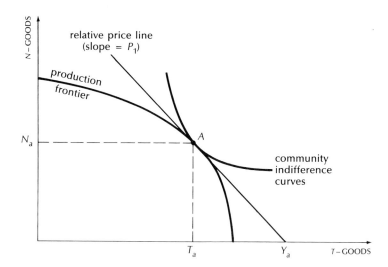

FIGURE A–1 Equilibrium in the Australian Model. With equilibrium at point A, the tangency of the production frontier and a community indifference curve, the country produces and consumes T_a of tradables and N_a of nontradables. The relative price P is an alternative and potentially useful measure of the real exchange rate (see text). National income measured in tradable prices is Y_a.

The relative price P is an alternative measure of the **real exchange rate** and is one of the important innovations of the Australian model. In Chapters 15 and 17 we defined the real exchange rate index as $RER = R_o(P_w/P_d)$, a composite index of prices that measures the incentives for exporters (or import substituters) given by the nominal exchange rate and the rates of world and domestic inflation. In the Australian formulation, the price of tradables in the home market P_t replaces $R_o P_w$ in the earlier definition, and the price of nontradables P_n replaces the overall domestic price level P_d which incorporated both tradable and nontradable prices. The Australian formulation of P is a more precise and potentially more useful definition of the real exchange rate, with similar implications: when P rises, tradables become more expensive relative to nontradables, so the incentive to produce tradables increases and the incentive to consume tradables decreases.[5] Thus a rise in P is the same as a rise in RER, a depreciation of the real exchange rate, and should work to improve the balance of trade, which is defined as:

$$B_t = E - M = \text{production of exportables and importables}$$
$$- \text{ domestic consumption of exportables and importables}$$

---

valued at $N_a(\Delta T/\Delta N) = N_a(Y_a - T_a)/N_a = Y_a - T_a$. So the value of both goods is $T_a + Y_a - T_a = Y_a$. (Note that $\Delta N/\Delta T = P_1$.)

5. In the Australian model, P_t is the price of tradables on the domestic market, so it incorporates any protective tariffs, taxes, and subsidies on tradables. In the real exchange rate RER, the term P_w is the price in world markets, excluding domestic taxes. Thus the Australian version P is more akin to the real effective exchange rate, defined in Equation 17–3. $REER = R_o N P_w/P_d$, where N, the nominal protection index, accounts for tariffs, taxes, and subsidies. Note, however, that N also includes the quota premium q_m. If imports are subject to quota, they become nontradable in the terms of the Australian model, as explained above.

B_t = production of tradables – domestic consumption of tradables. [A–1]

In Figure A–1, with the economy in equilibrium, consumption of each good is equal to production, so the balance of trade is zero.

The relative price of tradables to nontradables is potentially more useful than the RER because it separates out prices (P_n) that are under the influence of monetary and fiscal policy, as well as market forces, within the country from prices (P_t) that can be changed only by adjustments of the nominal exchange rate.[6] In practice, however, it is difficult to measure P, because the division between T and N goods is not always clear. Moreover, national governments have not begun to collect price series that segregate tradables and nontradables; this makes it difficult to keep continuous time series on the relative price P.

As the next step toward understanding adjustment within the open economy model, consider what happens if there is an exogenous increase in expenditure, which would move the relative price line P outward in Figure A–2, so that the value of expenditure (measured in T-goods) moves from Y_a to Y_b. The rise in expenditure could result from a rise in government expenditure in excess of revenues; expenditure in excess of income (dissaving) by consumers; or a spurt in foreign currency inflows, whether from overseas borrowing, foreign direct investment, or foreign aid.

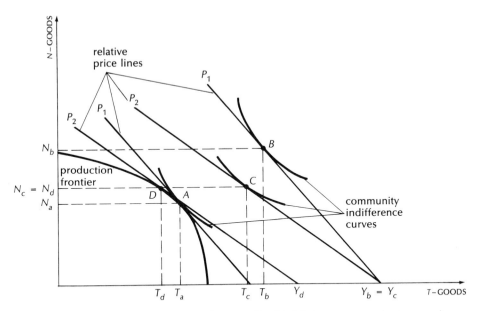

FIGURE A–2 Rise in Expenditure under the Australian Model. An exogenous rise in expenditure causes the price and budget line P_1 to shift outward to a transitory consumption equilibrium at B. Excess demand for N-goods ($N_b - N_a$) causes an inflationary rise in P_n and hence a downward rotation of the relative price to P_2. Consumers now satisfy their preferences at C, whereas producers shift along the production frontier to D. The excess demand for N has been eliminated, but the trade deficit ($T_c - T_d$) remains large.

6. Trade policy can also influence the price of tradables. A rise in tariffs, for example, raises the domestic price of importables. This effect is captured by both the relative price of tradables in the Australian model and by the term N in the real effective exchange rate.

If the shift in expenditure does not change relative prices, there would be a shift to a transitory equilibrium at a point such as B, where consumption of tradables T_b and nontradables N_b both exceed production, which remains at T_a and N_a. The excess demand for nontradables $(N_b - N_a)$ cannot be sustained very long. Nontradable goods might be supplied from inventories for a time, but services cannot be stored. Because demand exceeds supply, the price of nontradables P_n will rise. (Remember P_t is determined in world markets and cannot change in the home country unless there is an exchange rate adjustment.) As P_n rises, the relative price of tradables P rotates downward to a price like P_2 in the diagram, with a new equilibrium for consumers at point C. (Note that the value of expenditure Y_c remains the same as Y_b.) At the same time, producers shift out of tradables into nontradables along the production frontier, from A to D, in response to the rise in the relative price of N goods. With consumption at C and production at D, the inflationary excess demand for N-goods has been eliminated $(N_t = N_d)$. However, the trade gap $(T_c - T_d)$ remains large and gross expenditure (Y_c) exceeds gross product (Y_d). A trade gap can be sustained as long as foreign capital inflows continue to finance it or until the country's foreign reserves run out.

Dutch disease was first diagnosed by the Australian school, and some aspects of it can be seen clearly in Figure A–2. Consider the horizontal axis to represent all tradables except the booming export sector, which is considered to be an economic enclave and therefore outside this model. Then the shift in expenditure can be due to an improvement in the price of exports from the booming sector. Recall from Chapter 15 that, under Dutch disease, the real exchange rate appreciates when the rising demand for nontradables causes a rise in their price, precisely what has been shown in Figure A–2 as the rotation of P_1 to P_2. Another symptom of Dutch disease is the decline in the production of traded goods, caused by the appreciation of the real exchange rate; in the diagram, the move of production from A to D, caused by the decline in P, is precisely this. With Dutch disease, however, there is a trade deficit only because we excluded booming sector exports from the diagram; when these are counted, there is no trade deficit.

To understand stabilization under this model, let us start from the final point of equilibrium in Figure A–2, consumption at C and production at D, which have been translated to Figure A–3. Assume the balance-of-trade deficit is not sustainable. How can stabilization be achieved? Assume that policymakers aim first to eliminate the trade deficit by reducing expenditure, the rise of which caused the problem in the first place. (We discuss how they would do this in the next section.) With prices remaining at P_2 in the absence of a change in the exchange rate, the economy would have to settle at a point like E in Figure A–3, where (1) production and consumption of tradables are equal $(T_d = T_e)$ and (2) consumer preferences are satisfied by a tangency of P_2 and an indifference curve. If consumer tastes are even approximately *homothetic*, that is, neither good is strongly preferred to the other as incomes change, this tangency cannot take place along the production frontier. With homothetic preferences, tangencies between indifference curves and the P_2 line take place along a ray from the origin,

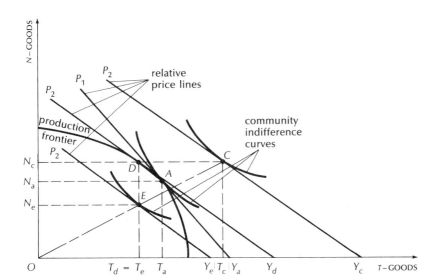

FIGURE A–3   **Adjustment under the Australian Model.** Reductions in expenditure, in the absence of any change in relative prices, move the economy from C to E, where trade is balanced and consumer preferences are satisfied. But there is unemployment of resources because potential production of N-goods N_d exceeds consumption N_e. Devaluation of the real exchange rate from P_2 back to P_1 is needed to regain the full-employment tangency at A.

O, to point C. But along the production frontier the same tangency at D is above the ray OC. The two conditions are, however, satisfied at a point like E, which is inside the frontier. But at E, there is unemployment because, although consumption of tradables is balanced with production, consumption of nontradables (N_e) is less than potential production (N_d).

The cost of stabilization is high at E because policymakers used only one instrument, reduction in expenditure, to achieve balance in both the T- and N-goods markets; put another way, they used expenditure reduction alone to balance trade and maintain full employment. If a second policy instrument is used, however, it would be possible to achieve a balance of production and consumption in the markets for both T- and N-goods. Seen through the lens of the Australian model, the goal is to achieve (or to regain) a tangency between the production frontier and a community indifference curve. We know from Figure A–1 that this takes place at point A, also shown in Figure A–3.

To regain point A, it is necessary to shift the relative price from P_2 to P_1, the original real exchange rate. This real devaluation of the exchange rate could be achieved in either of two ways. If the price of N-goods is flexible, then the excess supply of N-goods ($N_d > N_e$) would work through market forces to reduce P_n and thus raise $P = P_t/P_n$. Alternatively, if rigidities in the economy are likely to prevent prices from falling rapidly enough, as is often the case, then the authorities could devalue the exchange rate; this will drive up the domestic price of tradables P_t and raise the real exchange rate from P_2 back to P_1.

The lesson of this model is that, to achieve stabilization and full employment, policymakers are likely to need two kinds of policies, reduction in aggregate expenditure and a change in relative prices. Devaluation of the currency is the most obvious way to achieve the latter, but changes in taxes and subsidies, as well as deregulation of markets, could also be part of the package. Expenditure reduction and devaluation are part of the standard IMF stabilization package. Devaluation, tax and subsidy policy, and deregulation are part of most World Bank structural adjustment packages, which aim to move production towards tradable goods (*D* to *A* in the figures) and consumption away from tradables (*C* to *A*).

MACROECONOMIC POLICY INSTRUMENTS

The policy issue facing many developing countries during the 1980s was (and remains) that of escaping macroeconomic instability represented by points like *B* and *C* in Figure A–2: a large trade deficit, frequently (though not necessarily) accompanied by inflationary demand for nontraded goods. In the Australian model of Figure A–2, which only represents real variables, there is no way to show monetary phenomena and continuing inflation. Hence within the model the excess demand for nontradables shown at point *B* cannot continue; temporary inflation (a rise in P_n) realigns supply and demand for *N*-goods automatically, and then inflation ceases. But in actual economies, governments can—and often do—continue to increase the money supply enough so purchasing power exceeds the value of goods supplied and so perpetuate inflation.

We have shown how a move to stabilize a small, open economy—a move from *B* or *C* to *A* in Figure A–3—requires both a reduction in expenditure (from Y_c to Y_a) and a change in relative prices (from P_2 to P_1). There are a number of ways to shift relative prices, from deregulating markets to using taxes and subsidies. In small, open economies, devaluation of the exchange rate, discussed in Chapter 13 and in Part 4, is a particularly powerful tool. Here, we concentrate on measures to reduce expenditure, to drive the economy from point *C* to a new position on or within the production frontier.

The policy instruments available to reduce expenditure are implicit in the national income accounting identity

$$Y = C + I + E - M, \qquad [\text{A--2}]$$

which was encountered in a slightly different form in Equation 6–8. The symbols have the same meanings as in Chapter 6: gross national product, consumption, investment, exports and imports of goods and nonfactor services, respectively. For our purposes, here it is useful to transform this identity into an equation for the foreign balance B_f:

$$B_f = E - M = Y - (C + I). \qquad [\text{A--3}]$$

Note that B_f is the surplus on current account, the negative of foreign saving (called *F* in Chapter 6); for an economy at point *C*, $B_f < 0$. It is clear from Equation A–3 that to reduce its deficit on current account (to raise

B_f), a country must cut back consumption, investment, or both. The other possibility, raising output (Y), is not likely in the short term for an economy producing at point D, because it is already producing at full capacity and new investment takes time to become productive.[7]

To find the policy levers implicit in Equation A–3, we need to break out some of its components:

$$B_f = Y_p + T - (C_p + C_g + I_p + I_g). \qquad [A–4]$$

where T is taxes paid to government, Y_p is after-tax income left to the private sector, and the items in parentheses are the private and government components of consumption and investment. These components can be regrouped:

$$B_f = (Y_p - C_p) - I_p + T - (C_g + I_g)$$
$$B_f = S_p - I_p + B_g. \qquad [A–5]$$

where S_p is private saving and B_g is government's budget balance, positive for a surplus.[8] An improvement in the foreign balance requires an increase in private saving, a decrease in private investment, and/or a decrease in government's budget deficit.

Policymakers have a variety of instruments to achieve the required cuts in expenditure. **Private saving** could be increased by increases in interest rates and by incomes policies that shift earnings toward groups with higher marginal saving rates (see Chapter 11). Neither effect is likely to be strong, however, especially in the short run, and the required incomes policy would work against lower-income groups. **Private investment** is more amenable to interest rate policy and to supporting monetary policies that would slow the growth of private credit from the banking system (Chapter 13). Freeing interest rates and permitting them to rise to market-determined levels is crucial to the capital-deepening strategy discussed in Chapter 13 and is a central feature of many stabilization and structural adjustment packages. An important long-run monetary reform is to develop money market instruments that give the central bank greater flexibility in influencing the market conditions that determine interest rates and hence private saving and investment.

The **government budget deficit** receives more attention than private saving and investment in both IMF and World Bank packages. It is more readily controlled by government, at least in principle, and has in many cases been a prime cause of inflation and trade deficits. When foreign borrowing has been used extensively, much of it often goes into government expenditure. Tax reform, discussed in Chapter 12, is essential to raise tax revenue in many developing countries, but generally it cannot be accomplished in the few months to a year in which stabilization must take place. Some increase in tax rates and more effective enforcement may help to reduce

---

7. In this national income model we have abandoned the distinction between tradables and nontradables, although these could be broken out if needed: E and M consist mostly of tradables, whereas C and I can be divided into their tradable and nontradable components.

8. The government budget balance could be written $B_g = S_g - I_g$, where $S_g = T - C_g$ is government saving.

the deficit, but the scope for this is often limited. Hence the greater burden falls on reductions in expenditure, and the issue is where to cut.

The largest expenditures are typically salaries of government employees, the provision for interest and principal repayments on public debt, and government investment. Reducing government salaries or, more drastically, government employment are politically dangerous measures; yet a few governments have managed to do one or the other. Defaulting on debt is even more drastic, as discussed in Chapter 14. Governments typically look toward purchases of materials and equipment (e.g., paper, educational materials, medicines, fuel, vehicles), and especially toward investment projects, to meet expenditure targets of stabilization programs. These kinds of reductions tend to make government less efficient in delivering services; to slow down the long-run development of infrastructure, health, education, and other government services; and, to the increasing concern of policymakers and aid donors, to jeopardize the living standards of the poorest in society.

A popular target for deficit reduction is the subsidies—explicit and implicit—paid from government to its state-owned corporations. The swing toward market-based development has convinced many governments to **privatize** their corporations by selling shares, or entire companies, to private owners. Those corporations that remain under government control are increasingly being denied cash subsidies or subsidized credit, and are thereby forced to become profitable or go bankrupt. These measures, though they contribute to stabilization, are more properly considered long-run structural adjustments.

Although fiscal management is crucial to adjusting the economy, stabilization does not necessarily require a balanced budget. It all depends on the required foreign balance and the balance that can be achieved between private saving and investment, as can be seen from Equation A–5. If the aim is to achieve balanced trade, for example, and private investors are trying to spend more than private savers are willing to finance, then government will have to run a surplus to achieve overall balance. But if private saving exceeds private investment, government can afford to run a deficit without destabilizing the economy. The foreign balance need not be zero for stability, either. For those developing countries that are not heavily indebted, we expect there to be a sustainable deficit on trade, financed by foreign aid and investment, as discussed in Chapter 14. Much of this inflow of foreign saving typically does go into the government budget to finance deficits, generally deficits caused by government development (investment) expenditures. For heavily indebted countries, however, the trade balance has to be positive in order to service debt, and this is likely to require a surplus in the government budget as well.

Note, also, that any given improvement in the budget balance requires more in additional taxes than it does in expenditure cuts. This is because taxes reduce private disposable income (Y_p in Equation A–4), which determines saving:

$$S_p = f(Y_p) = f(Y - T). \qquad [A\text{--}6]$$

Thus part of any tax increase comes out of private saving and does not contribute to the required improvement in the overall balance between saving and investment.

Behind these approaches to expenditure reduction is **monetary policy.** In Chapter 13, we introduced the monetary identity, $MO = DC + IR$, or

$$\Delta MO = \Delta IR + \Delta DC, \qquad\qquad [A-7]$$

where MO is the money supply, IR is international reserves, and DC is domestic credit. With a foreign deficit, international reserves are likely to be declining and causing a fall in the money supply, which helps to correct any inflationary tendencies in the economy. The trouble comes with domestic credit, which consists of credit from the commercial banks to the private sector and to government:[9]

$$\Delta DC = \Delta DC_p + \Delta DC_g. \qquad\qquad [A-8]$$

The excess demand for goods in either the tradables or nontradables markets causes private agents to seek more credit from the banking system ($\Delta DC_p > 0$). To the extent that government funds a deficit and gets the banks to finance it, $\Delta DC_g > 0$. Thus a reduction in the government deficit reduces expenditure directly and simultaneously eases the pressure for monetary expansion. (Government borrowing from the nonbank private lenders does not create additional domestic credit, but does switch liquidity from private lenders to the government; this is sometimes called **crowding out** of private investment.) An independent central bank may try to swim against this tide by using the various means described in Chapter 13 to contain the growth in credit and the money supply. But most central banks in developing countries are under the thumb of the finance ministry and are not able to resist demands for credit expansion. The IMF makes it clear through the conditions on its stabilization packages that the central bank must restrain growth of domestic credit or the government will forfeit IMF loans (and any other finance tied to IMF conditions).

Thus at the core of stabilization packages in developing countries are three essential components: reduced government deficits to cut back aggregate expenditure, restraint by the central bank in monetary and credit management to control inflation, and devaluation to switch expenditures away from tradables and to switch production into tradables. Other components may be helpful, even important to stabilization, but these three form the irreducible core to most adjustment packages. They work together, complementing and reinforcing one another.

9. Here we use DC_p and DC_g to avoid confusion with the consumption variables, C_p and C_g.

Bibliography and Additional Readings

CHAPTER 1. INTRODUCTION: WORLDS APART

World Bank, *World Development Report* (New York: Oxford University Press, annual).

CHAPTER 2. STARTING MODERN ECONOMIC GROWTH

Obstacles to Development

Alexander Gerschenkron, *Economic Backwardness in Historical Perspective* (Cambridge, Mass.: Harvard University Press, 1962).
W. W. Rostow, *Stages of Economic Growth,* 2nd ed. (New York: Cambridge University Press, 1971, 1st ed., 1960).

Imperialism

Paul Baran, *The Political Economy of Growth* (New York: Monthly Review Press, 1957).
Celso Furtado, "The Brazilian 'Model' of Development," in *The Political Economy of Development and Underdevelopment,* Charles K. Wilber, ed. (New York: Random House, 1979) pp. 324–333.
Keith Griffin and John Gurley, "Radical Analyses of Imperialism, the Third World, and the Transition to Socialism," *Journal of Economic Literature* 23, no. 3 (September 1985).
Merilee Grindle and John Thomas, "Policy Makers, Policy Choices, and Policy Outcomes: The Political Economy of Reform in Developing Countries," in *Reforming Economic Systems in Developing Countries,* Dwight Perkins and Michael Roemer, eds. (Cambridge, Mass.: distributed by Harvard University Press, 1991), pp. 81–114.

Dwight H. Perkins and Michael Roemer, eds., *Reforming Economic Systems in Developing Countries* (Cambridge, Mass.: distributed by Harvard University Press, 1991).

Alan Hodgart, *The Economics of European Imperialism* (New York: W. W. Norton & Company, 1977).

Karl Marx, *Das Kapital* (1867).

Joan Nelson, "Comparative Perspectives: The Politics of Economic Adjustment in Developing Nations," Washington, D.C., Overseas Development Council, 1988.

Robert I. Rhodes, ed., *Imperialism and Underdevelopment: A Reader* (New York: Monthly Review Press, 1970).

Historical Heritage and Economic Development

Keith Hart, *The Political Economy of West African Agriculture* (New York: Cambridge University Press, 1982).

Albert O. Hirschman, "Ideologies of Economic Development in Latin America," in *A Bias for Hope* (New Haven, Conn.: Yale University Press, 1971).

Anthony G. Hopkins, *An Economic History of West Africa* (New York: Columbia University Press, 1973).

E. S. Mason, Mahn Je Kim, Dwight H. Perkins, Kwang Suk Kim, and David C. Cole, *The Economic and Social Modernization of the Republic of Korea* (Cambridge, Mass.: Harvard University Press, 1980).

D. H. Perkins, ed., *China's Modern Economy in Historical Perspective* (Stanford, Calif.: Stanford University Press, 1975).

CHAPTER 3. GROWTH AND STRUCTURAL CHANGE

The Harrod-Domar Model

Evsey Domar, "Capital Expansion, Rate of Growth and Employment," *Econometrica* (1946): 137–147.

———, "Expansion and Employment," *American Economic Review* 37 (1947): 34–55.

Roy F. Harrod, "An Essay in Dynamic Theory," *Economic Journal* (1939): 14–33.

The Changing Structure of Output

Hollis B. Chenery, Sherman Robinson, and Moshe Syrquin, *Industrialization and Growth: A Comparative Study* (London: Oxford University Press, 1986).

Hollis B. Chenery and Moises Syrquin, *Patterns of Development, 1950–1970* (London: Oxford University Press, 1975).

Hollis B. Chenery and Lance J. Taylor, "Development Patterns: Among Countries and Over Time," *Review of Economics and Statistics* 50 (November 1968): 391–416.

Edward F. Denison, *Accounting for United States Economic Growth, 1929–1969* (Washington, D.C.: Brookings Institution, 1974).

Irving Kravis, Alan Heston, and Robert Summers, *International Compar-*

isons of Real Product and Purchasing Power (Baltimore: Johns Hopkins Press, 1978).

Dale Jorgenson, Frank Gollop, and Barbara Fraumeni, *Productivity and U.S. Economic Growth* (Cambridge, Mass: Harvard University Press, 1987).

Simon Kuznets, *Economic Growth and Structure* (New York: W. W. Norton & Company, 1965).

————, *Modern Economic Growth* (New Haven, Conn.: Yale University Press, 1966).

Dwight H. Perkins and Moshe Syrquin, "Large Countries: The Influence of Size," in *Handbook of Development Economics* Vol. 2, Hollis B. Chenery and T. N. Srinivasan, eds. (Amsterdam: North-Holland, 1989).

W. W. Rostow, *Theorists of Economic Growth from David Hume to the Present* (London: Oxford University Press, 1990), Part III.

Moshe Syrquin, "Patterns of Structural Change," in *Handbook of Development Economics* Vol. 1, Hollis B. Chenery and T. N. Srinivasan, eds. (Amsterdam: North-Holland, 1988).

Two-Sector Models

J. C. Fei and Gustav Ranis, *Development of Labor Surplus Economy* (Homewood, Ill.: Richard Irwin, 1964).

Dale W. Jorgenson, "Testing Alternative Theories of the Development of a Dual Economy," in *The Theory and Design of Development,* I. Adelman and E. Thorbecke, eds. (Baltimore: Johns Hopkins Press, 1966).

W. Arthur Lewis, "Economic Development with Unlimited Supplies of Labor," *The Manachester School* 22 (May 1954): 139–191.

————, *The Theory of Economic Growth* (Homewood, Ill.: Richard Irwin, 1955).

Balanced versus Unbalanced Growth

Albert O. Hirschman, *The Strategy of Economic Development* (New Haven, Conn.: Yale University Press, 1958).

Ragnar Nurkse, *Problems of Capital Development in Underdeveloped Countries* (New York: Oxford University Press, 1953).

Paul N. Rosenstein-Rodan, "Problems of Industrialization of Eastern and Southeastern Europe," *Economic Journal* (June–September 1943), reprinted in *The Economics of Underdevelopment,* A. N. Agarwala and S. P. Singh, eds. (New York: Oxford University Press, 1963).

CHAPTER 4. DEVELOPMENT AND HUMAN WELFARE

Concepts and Measures

Gary S. Fields, *Poverty, Inequality and Development* (London: Cambridge University Press, 1980).

Charles R. Frank, Jr., and Richard C. Webb, eds., *Income Distribution and Growth in the Less-Developed Countries* (Washington, D. C.: Brookings Institution, 1977).

Arnold Harberger, "Basic Needs versus Distributional Weights in Social Cost-Benefit Analysis," *Economic Development and Cultural Change* 32, no. 4 (April 1984): 455–477.

Morris David Morris, *Measuring the Condition of the World's Poor. The Physical Quality of Life Index* (Elmsford, N.Y.: Pergamon Press for the Overseas Development Council, 1979).

Dudley Sears, "The Meaning of Development," in *The Political Economy of Development and Underdevelopment,* Charles K. Wilber, ed. (New York: Random House, 1973).

Amartya K. Sen, *On Economic Inequality* (New York: W. W. Norton & Company, 1973).

Richard Szal and Sherman Robinson, "Measuring Income Inequality," in *Income Distribution and Growth in the Less-Developed Countries* (Washington, D.C.: Brookings Institution, 1977), pp. 491–533.

United Nations Development Program, *Human Development Report* (New York: Oxford University Press, 1990).

Wouter van Ginneken and Jong-goo Park, eds., *Generating Internationally Comparable Income Distribution Measures* (Geneva: International Labor Office, 1984).

Patterns of Inequality and Poverty

Irma Adelman and Cynthia Taft Morris, *Economic Growth and Social Equity in Developing Countries* (Stanford, Calif.: Stanford University Press, 1973).

*Irma Adelman and Sherman Robinson, *Income Distribution Policy in Developing Countries. A Case Study of Korea* (Stanford, Calif.: Stanford University Press, 1978).

Montek S. Ahluwalia, "Income Inequality: Some Dimensions of the Problem," in *Redistribution with Growth,* Hollis Chenery et al., eds. (New York: Oxford University Press, 1974), pp. 3–37.

———, "Inequality, Poverty and Development," *Journal of Development Economics* 3 (1976).

Gary S. Fields, "Changes in Poverty and Inequality in Developing Countries," *The World Bank Research Observer* 4, no. 2 (July 1989): 167–185.

Simon Kuznets, "Economic Growth and Income Inequality," *American Economic Review* 45, no. 1 (March 1955).

Jacques Lecaillon et al., *Income Distribution and Economic Development. An Analytical Survey* (Geneva: International Labor Office, 1984).

Christian Morrisson, "Income Distribution in East European and West European Countries," *Journal of Comparative Economics* 8 (1984): 121–138.

Gustav F. Papanek and Oldrich Kyn, "The Effect on Income Distribution of Development, The Growth Rate and Economic Strategy," *Journal of Development Economics* 23 (1986): 55–65.

Theories of Inequality and Poverty

William R. Cline, "Distribution and Development: A Survey of the Literature," *Journal of Development Economics* (1975): 359–400.

W. Arthur Lewis, "Economic Development with Unlimited Supplies of Labor," *The Manchester School* 22 (1954).

Strategies for Growth with Equity

Hollis Chenery et al., *Redistribution with Growth* (London: Oxford University Press, 1974).

Giovanni Andrea Cornia, Richard Jolly, and Frances Stewart, eds., *Adjustment with a Human Face*, 2 vol. (Oxford: Clarendon Press, 1987).

International Labor Office, *Employment, Growth and Basic Needs: A One-World Problem* (New York: Praeger, 1977).

John Mellor, *The New Economics of Growth: A Strategy for India and the Developing World* (Ithaca, N.Y.: Cornell University Press, 1976).

Rati Ram, "The Role of Real Income Level and Income Distribution in Fulfillment of Basic Needs," *World Development* 13, no. 5 (May 1985): 589–594.

T. N. Srinivasan, "Development, Poverty and Basic Human Needs: Some Issues," *Food Research Institute Studies* 16, no. 2 (1977): 11–28.

Paul B. Trescott, "Incentives versus Equality: What Does China's Recent Experience Show?" *World Development* 13, no. 2 (February 1985): 205–217.

CHAPTER 5: GUIDING DEVELOPMENT: MARKETS VERSUS CONTROLS

The March toward Markets

Bela Balassa, "Exports and Economic Growth: Further Evidence," *Journal of Development Economics* 5, no. 2 (1978): 181–89.

Jagdish Bhagwati, *Foreign Exchange Regimes and Economic Development: Anatomy and Consequences of Exchange Control Regimes* (Cambridge, Mass.: Ballinger Press, 1978).

Henry J. Bruton, "The Import Substitution Strategy of Economic Development," *The Pakistan Development Review* 10 (1970): 123–146.

Anne O. Krueger, *Foreign Exchange Regimes and Economic Development: Liberalization Attempts and Consequences* (Cambridge, Mass.: Ballinger Press, 1978).

———, "The Political Economy of Rent-Seeking," *American Economic Review* 64, no. 3 (1974): 291–303.

Ian M. D. Little, *Economic Theory, Policy, and International Relations* (New York: Basic Books, 1982).

———, Tibor Scitovsky, and Maurice Scott, *Industry and Trade in Some Developing Countries* (London: Oxford University Press, 1970).

Ragnar Nurkse, *Equilibrium Growth and the World Economy* (Cambridge, Mass.: Harvard University Press, 1961).

Theodore W. Schultz, *Transforming Traditional Agriulture* (New Haven, Conn.: Yale University Press, 1964).

Hans W. Singer, "The Distribution of Trade between Investing and Borrowing Countries," *American Economic Review* 40 (1950): 470–485.

Moshe Syrquin and Hollis Chenery, "Three Decades of Industrialization," *The World Bank Economic Review* 3, no. 2 (1989): 145–181.

United Nations (by Raul Prebisch), *The Economic Development of Latin America and its Principal Problems* (Lake Success, N.Y.: 1950).

BIBLIOGRAPHY
AND
ADDITIONAL
READINGS

Armeane M. Choksi and Demetrius Papageorgiou, eds., *Economic Liber-alization in Developing Countries* (New York: Blackwell, 1986).

Sebastian Edwards and Sweder van Wijnbergen, "Disequilibrium and Structural Adjustment" *Handbook of Development Economics,* Vol. 2, Hollis B. Chenery and T. N. Srinivasan, eds. (Amsterdam: Elsevier, 1989).

Tony Killick, ed., *The Quest for Economic Stabilization: The IMF and the Third World* (London: Heinemann, 1984).

Janos Kornai, *The Road to a Free Economy* (New York: W. W. Norton & Company, 1990).

Juan Antonio Morales and Jeffrey D. Sachs, "Bolivia's Economic Crisis," in *Developing Country Debt and the World Economy,* J. D. Sachs, ed. (Chicago: University of Chicago Press, 1989), pp. 57–79.

Joan M. Nelson, et al., *Fragile Coalitions: the Politics of Economic Adjust-ment* (Washington D.C.: Overseas Development Council, 1989).

———, "The Political Economy of Stabilization: Commitment, Capacity and Public Response," *World Development* 12, no. 10 (1984): 983–1006.

Mancur Olson, *The Rise and Decline of Nations* (New Haven, Conn.: Yale University Press, 1982).

Dwight H. Perkins, "Reforming China's Economic System," *Journal of Economic Literature* 26, no. 2 (June 1988): 601–645.

——— and Michael Roemer, *Reforming Economic Systems in Developing Countries* (Cambridge, Mass.: Harvard University Press, 1991).

Jeffrey D. Sachs, "The Bolivian Hyperinflation and Stabilization," *Amer-ican Economic Review* 77, no. 2 (May 1987): 279–83.

Paul Streeten, "Structural Adjustment: A Survey of the Issues and Options," *World Development* 15, no. 12 (December 1987): 1469–1482.

*Lance J. Taylor, *Varieties of Stabilization Experience: Toward Sensible Macroeconomics in the Third World* (Oxford: Clarendon Press, 1988).

Raymond Vernon, ed., *The Promise of Privatization: A Challenge for American Foreign Policy* (New York: Council on Foreign Relations, 1988).

John Williamson, ed., *IMF Conditionality* (Washington, D.C.: Institute for International Economics, 1983).

World Bank, *Accelerated Development in Sub-Saharan Africa* (Washing-ton, D.C.: World Bank, 1981).

———, *World Development Report 1989* (New York: Oxford University Press, 1989) (on financial systems reform).

CHAPTER 6. PLANNING MODELS

Keynesian Models

*Jere Behrman and James Hanson, *Short-term Macroeconomic Policy in Latin America* (Cambridge, Mass.: National Bureau of Economic Research, 1979).

*Hollis Chenery and Alan Strout, "Foreign Assistance and Economic Development," *American Economic Review* 56 (1966): 679–733.

*Ronald McKinnon, "Foreign Exchange Constraints and Economic Development," *Economic Journal* 74 (1964): 388–409.

*Lance J. Taylor, "Theoretical Foundations and Technical Implications," in *Economy-wide Models and Development Planning*, C. R. Blitzer et al., eds. (London: Oxford University Press, 1975): 33–109.

*————, *Macro Models for Developing Countries* (New York: McGraw-Hill, 1979).

Jan Tinbergen, *Economic Policy: Principles and Design* (Amsterdam: North-Holland, 1956).

————, *Central Planning* (New Haven, Conn.: Yale University Press, 1976).

Interindustry and General Equilibrium Models

Hollis Chenery and Paul Clark, *Interindustry Economics* (New York: Wiley, 1959).

*Kemal Dervis, Jaime de Melo, and Sherman Robinson, *General Equilibrium Models for Developing Countries* (London: Cambridge University Press, 1982).

*Robert Dorfman, Paul Samuelson, and Robert Solow, *Linear Programming and Economic Analysis* (New York: McGraw-Hill, 1958).

Graham Pyatt and Erik Thorbecke, *Planning Techniques for a Better Future* (Geneva: International Labor Office, 1976).

*Sherman Robinson, "Multisectoral Models," in *Handbook of Development Economics*, Vol. 2, Hollis B. Chenery and T. N. Srinivasan, eds. (Amsterdam: North-Holland, 1989): 885–947.

Project Appraisal

*Arnold Harberger, *Project Evaluation: Collected Papers* (Chicago: Markham, 1974).

*I. M. D. Little and James A. Mirrlees, *Project Appraisal and Planning for Developing Countries* (New York: Basic Books, 1974).

Michael Roemer and Joseph J. Stern, *Cases in Economic Development* (London: Butterworths, 1981).

———— and ————, *The Appraisal of Development Projects* (New York: Praeger, 1975).

*United Nations Industrial Development Organization (P. Dasgupta, S. Margolin, and A. Sen), *Guidelines for Project Evaluation* (New York: United Nations, 1982).

CHAPTER 7. POPULATION

A Brief History of Human Population

Lester R. Brown, *In the Human Interest* (New York: W. W. Norton, 1974).

Carlo Cipolla, *The Economic History of World Population*, 7th ed. (New York: Barnes & Noble, 1978).

The Demographic Future

Thomas W. Merrick, "World Population in Transition," *Population Bulletin* 41, no. 2 (January 1988): 8–16.

*Gary Becker, *A Treatise on the Family* (Cambridge, Mass.: Harvard University Press, 1981).

John C. Caldwell, "Toward a Restatement of Demographic Transition Theory," *Population and Development Review* 2, nos. 3–4 (September–December 1976): 225–255.

Richard Easterlin, "Modernization and Fertility: A Critical Essay," in *Determinants of Fertility in Developing Countries,* Vol. 2, R. Bulatao and R. Lee, eds. (New York: Academic Press, 1983), pp. 562–586.

Michael S. Teitelbaum, "Relevance of Demographic Transition Theory for Developing Countries," *Science* 188 (May 2, 1977): 420–425.

Analyzing the Effects of Rapid Population Growth

Nancy Birdsall, "Economic Approaches to Population," in *Handbook of Development Economics,* Vol. 1, Hollis B. Chenery and T. N. Srinivasan, eds. (Amsterdam: North-Holland, 1988), pp. 477–542.

Ester Boserup, *The Conditions of Agricultural Growth* (Chicago: Aldine, 1965).

Colin Clark, "The 'Population Explosion' Myth," *Bulletin of the Institute of Development Studies* (Sussex, England, May 1969).

———, "The Economics of Population Growth and Control: A Comment," *Review of Social Economy* 28, no. 1 (March 1970).

Ansley J. Coale and Edgar M. Hoover, *Population Growth and Economic Development in Low-Income Countries: A Case Study of India's Prospects* (Princeton, N.J.: Princeton University Press, 1958).

Geoffrey McNicoll, "Consequences of Rapid Population Growth: An Overview and Assessment," *Population and Development Review* 10, no. 2 (June 1981): 177–240.

Mark Perlman, "Population and Economic Change in Developing Countries: A Review Article," *Journal of Economic Literature* 19, no. 1 (1981): 74–82.

Rati Ram and Theodore W. Schultz, "Life Span, Savings, and Productivity," *Economic Development and Cultural Change* 27, no. 3 (April 1979): 394–421.

Julian Simon, *Theory of Population and Economic Growth* (Oxford: Blackwell, 1986).

———, *The Ultimate Resource* (Princeton, N.J.: Princeton University Press, 1981).

Population Policy

Nick Eberstadt, "Recent Declines in Fertility in Less Developed Countries and What 'Population Planners' May Learn from Them," *World Development* 11, no. 1 (March 1985): 113–138.

"Fertility and Family Planning Surveys: An Update," *Population Reports* ser. M, no. 8, Johns Hopkins Press, September–October 1985.

W. Parker Mauldin and Bernard Berelson, "Conditions of Fertility Decline in Developing Countries, 1965–75," *Studies in Family Planning* 9, no. 5 (1978).

National Academy of Sciences, *Population Growth and Economic Devel-*

opment: Policy Questions (Washington, D.C.: National Academy Press, 1986).

Ronald G. Ridker, ed., *Population and Development: The Search for Selective Interventions* (Baltimore and London: Johns Hopkins Press for Resources for the Future, 1976).

World Bank, *World Development Report 1984* (New York: Oxford University Press, 1984), pp. 51–206.

CHAPTER 8. LABOR'S ROLE

Analyzing Employment Issues

George A. Akerlof and Janet L. Yellen, eds. *Efficiency Wage Models of the Labor Force,* (London: Cambridge University Press, 1986), "Introduction," pp. 1–21.

Albert Berry, "The Labor Market and Human Capital in LDCs," in *Surveys in Development Economics,* Norman Gemmell, ed. (Oxford: Blackwell, 1987), pp. 205–235.

Albert Berry and R. H. Sabot, "Unemployment and Economic Development," *Economic Development and Cultural Change* 33, no. 1 (October 1984): 99–116.

Henry J. Bruton, "Economic Development and Labor Use: A Review," *World Development* (December 1973): 1–22.

Peter Gregory, "An Assessment of Changes in Employment Conditions in Less Developed Countries," *Economic Development and Cultural Change* 28, no. 4 (July 1980): 673–700.

International Labor Office, *Towards Full Employment* (Geneva: International Labor Organization, 1970).

Lawrence F. Katz, "Efficiency Wage Theories: A Partial Evaluation," *NBER Macroeconomics Annual 1986* (Cambridge, Mass.: National Bureau of Economic Research, 1986): 235–276.

Dipak Mazumdar, "The Urban Informal Sector," *World Development* 4, no. 8 (August 1976): 655–679.

Mark Rosenzweig, "Labor Markets in Developing Countries," in *Handbook of Development Economics,* Vol. 1, Hollis B. Chenery and T. N. Srinivasan, eds. (Amsterdam: North-Holland, 1989), pp. 713–762.

Joseph E. Stiglitz, "Economic Organization, Information and Development," in *Handbook of Development Economics,* vol. 1, Chenery and Srinivasan, pp. 93–160.

Labor Reallocation

Jagdish Bhagwati and Martin Partington, *Taxing the Brain Drain: A Proposal* (Amsterdam: North-Holland, 1976).

John R. Harris and Michael P. Todaro, "Migration, Unemployment and Development: A Two-Sector Analysis," *American Economic Review* 60 (March 1970): 126–142.

Ragnar Nurkse, *Problems of Capital Formation in Underdeveloped Countries* (Oxford: Blackwell, 1957, first published in 1953).

Jeffrey G. Williamson, "Migration and Urbanization," in *Handbook of Development Economics,* Vol. 1, Chenery and Srinivasan, pp. 425–465.

BIBLIOGRAPHY
AND
ADDITIONAL
READINGS

Henry Bruton, "Technology Choice and Factor Proportions Problems in LDCs," in *Surveys in Development Economics,* Norman Gemmell, ed. (Oxford: Blackwell, 1987), pp. 236–265.

S. J. Burki et al., "Public Works Programs in Developing Countries: A Comparative Analysis," World Bank Staff Working Paper No. 224, February 1976.

Edgar O. Edwards, ed., *Employment in Developing Nations* (New York: Columbia University Press, 1974).

Richard Jolly et al., *Third-World Employment: Problems and Strategy* (Harmondsworth, England: Penguin, 1973).

Howard Pack and Larry E. Westphal, "Industrial Strategy and Technological Change. Theory versus Reality," *Journal of Development Economics* 22 (1986): 87–128.

Lyn Squire, *Employment Policy in Developing Countries: A Survey of Issues and Evidence* (New York: Oxford University Press for the World Bank, 1981).

Frances Stewart, "Technology and Employment in LDCs," in *Employment in Developing Nations,* Edwards, pp. 83–132.

Susumu Watanabe, "Exports and Employment: The Case of the Republic of Korea," *International Labour Review* 106, no. 6 (December 1972): 495–526.

Louis T. Wells, "Economic Man and Engineering Man: Choice of Technology in a Low-wage Country," in *The Choice of Technology in Developing Countries: Some Cautionary Tales,* C. Peter Timmer et al., eds. (Cambridge, Mass.: Harvard University Center for International Affairs, 1975), pp. 69–93.

Larry E. Westphal, "Fostering Technological Mastery by Means of Selective Infant-Industry Protection," in *Trade, Stability, Technology and Equity in Latin America,* Simon Teitel, ed. (New York: Academic Press, 1982), pp. 255–279.

Larry E. Westphal, Linsu Kim, and Carl J. Dahlman, "Reflections on the Republic of Korea's Acquisition of Technological Capability," in *International Technology Transfer: Concepts, Measures, and Comparisons,* Nathan Rosenberg and Claudio Frischtak, eds. (New York: Praeger, 1985), pp. 167–221.

Lawrence White, *Industrial Concentration and Economic Power in Pakistan* (Princeton, N.J.: Princeton University Press, 1974).

CHAPTER 9. EDUCATION

Importance of Education

George Psacharopoulos and Maureen Woodhall, *Education for Development: An Analysis of Investment Choices* (New York: Oxford University Press, 1985).

Theodore W. Schultz, "Investment in Human Capital," *American Economic Review* 51 (January 1961): 1–17.

World Bank, *World Development Report 1980* (New York: Oxford University Press, 1980).

M. Blaug, R. Layard, and M. Woodhall, *Causes of Graduate Unemployment in India* (Harmondsworth, England: Penguin, 1969).

Martin Carnoy, "Rates of Return to Schooling in Latin America," *Journal of Human Resources* (Summer 1967): 359–374.

Russell Davis, "Planning Education for Development," Harvard Institute for International Development, Development Discussion Paper No. 60, June 1979.

World Bank, *Primary Education. A World Bank Policy Paper* (Washington, D.C.: World Bank, 1990).

Education's Role in Development

Mark Blaug, "The Empirical Status of Human Capital Theory: A Slightly Jaundiced Survey," *Journal of Economic Literature* 14, no. 3 (September 1976): 827–855.

M. Boissiere, J. B. Knight, and R. H. Sabot, "Earnings, Schooling, Ability, and Cognitive Skills," *American Economic Review* 75, no. 5 (December 1985): 1016–1030.

Philip H. Coombs with Manzoor Ahmed, *Attacking Rural Poverty: How Nonformal Education Can Help* (Baltimore: Johns Hopkins Press, 1974).

Ronald Dore, *The Diploma Disease. Education, Qualification and Development* (Berkeley: University of California Press, 1976).

Philip J. Foster, "The Vocational School Fallacy in Development Planning," in *Education and Economic Development,* C. A. Anderson and M. J. Bowman, eds. (Chicago: Aldine, 1966), pp. 142–163.

Paolo Freire, *Pedagogy of the Oppressed,* translated from the Portuguese by Myra Bergman Ramos (New York: Seabury Press, 1970).

Robert H. Haveman and Barbara L. Wolfe, "Schooling and Economic Well-Being: The Role of Nonmarket Effects," *Journal of Human Resources* 19, no. 3 (1984): 377–407.

Arthur Hazlewood et al., *Education, Work, and Pay in East Africa* (Oxford: Clarendon Press, 1990).

Ivan Illich, *Deschooling Society* (New York: Harper & Row, 1970).

Emmanuel Jiminez, "The Public Subsidization of Education and Health in Developing Countries. A Review of Equity and Efficiency," *World Bank Research Observer* 1, no. 1 (January 1986): 111–129.

John B. Knight and Richard H. Sabot, *Education, Productivity, and Inequality. The East African Experience* (New York: Oxford University Press for the World Bank, 1990).

Herbert S. Parnes, *Forecasting Educational Needs for Economic Development,* Mediterranean Regional Project (Paris: Organisation for Economic Cooperation and Development, 1962).

George Psacharopoulos, "Education and Development: A Review," *World Bank Research Observer* 3, no. 1 (January 1988).

———, "Returns to Education: A Further International Update and Implications," *Journal of Human Resources* 20, no. 4 (1985): 583–604.

T. Paul Schultz, "Education Investments and Returns," in *Handbook of Development Economics,* vol. 1, Hollis B. Chenery and T. N. Srinivasan, eds. (Amsterdam: North-Holland), pp. 543–630.

Theodore W. Schultz, "The Value of the Ability of Deal with Disequilibria," *Journal of Economic Literature* 13, no. 3 (September 1975): 837–846.

Jan Tinbergen and H. C. Bos, "A Planning Model for the Educational Requirements of Economic Development," in *Econometric Models for Education* (Paris: Organisation for Economic Cooperation and Development, 1965).

World Bank, *Financing Education in Developing Countries. An Exploration of Policy Options* (Washington, D.C.: World Bank, 1986).

CHAPTER 10. HEALTH AND NUTRITION

Health in the Third World

Samuel H. Preston, "The Changing Relationship between Mortality and Level of Development," *Population Studies* 29, no. 2 (July 1975): 231–248.

———, *Mortality Patterns in National Populations, with Special Reference to Recorded Causes of Death* (New York: Academic Press, 1976).

Amartya Sen, "More than 100 Million Women Are Missing," *The New York Review of Books* (December 20, 1990): 61–66.

United Nations Childrens Fund (UNICEF), *The State of the World's Children 1984* (New York: Oxford University Press, 1984).

World Bank, *Health Sector Policy Paper,* 2nd ed. (Washington, D.C.: World Bank, 1980).

Effects of Health on Development

Jere R. Behrman and Anil B. Deolalikar, "Health and Nutrition," in *Handbook of Development Economics,* Vol 1., Hollis B. Chenery and T. N. Srinivasan, eds. (Amsterdam: North-Holland), pp. 631–711.

Richard Feuchem et al., *Water, Health and Development: An Interdisciplinary Evaluation* (London: Tri-Med Books, 1974), Chap. 9.

Selma Mushkin, "Health as an Investment," *Journal of Political Economy* 70, no. 5, part 2 (Supplement, October 1962): 129–157.

Barry M. Popkin, "Nutrition and Labor Productivity," *Social Science and Medicine* 12 (1978): 117–125.

Nicholas M. Prescott, "Schistosomiasis and Developmpent," *World Development* 7, no. 1 (1979): 1–14.

C. Peter Timmer, "Food Policy, Food Consumption, and Nutrition," Harvard Institute for International Development, Development Discussion Paper No. 124, October 1981.

Burton Weisbrod and Robert E. Baldwin, "Disease and Labor Productivity," *Economic Development and Cultural Change* 22, no. 3 (1974): 414–435.

Malnutrition

Jere R. Behrman, Anil B. Deolalikar, and Barbara L. Wolfe, "Nutrients: Impacts and Determinants," *The World Bank Economic Review* 2, no. 3 (September 1988): 299–320.

Alan Berg, *The Nutrition Factor: Its Role in National Development* (Washington, D.C.: Brookings Institution, 1973).

———, *Malnutrition. What Can Be Done? Lessons from World Bank Experience* (Baltimore: John Hopkins Press for the World Bank, 1987).

Alan Berg and James Austin, "Nutrition Policies and Programs: A Decade of Redirection," *Food Policy* 9, no. 4 (November 1984): 304–312.

Thomas T. Poleman, "Quantifying the Nutritional Situation in Developing Countries," *Food Research Institute Studies* 18, no. 1 (1981): 1–58.

Shlomo Reutlinger, "Malnutrition: A Poverty Problem or a Food Problem?" *World Development* 5, no. 8 (1977): 715–724.

Shlomo Reutlinger and Marcelo Selowsky, *Malnutrition and Poverty: Magnitude and Policy Options,* World Bank Occasional Papers No. 23, Baltimore, Johns Hopkins Press, 1976.

Amartya Sen, "Ingredients of Famine Analysis: Availability and Entitlements," *Quarterly Journal of Economics* 96, no. 3 (August 1981): 433–464.

C. Peter Timmer, Walter P. Falcon, and Scott R. Pearson, *Food Policy Analysis* (Baltimore: Johns Hopkins Press, 1983).

World Bank, *Poverty and Hunger. Issues and Options for Food Security in Developing Countries* (Washington, D.C.: World Bank, 1986).

Medical Services

Frederick Golladay and Bernhard Liese, "Health Problems and Policies in Developing Countries," World Bank Staff Working Paper No. 412, August 1980.

James Kocher and Richard A. Cash, "Achieving Health and Nutritional Objectives within a Basic Needs Framework" (Harvard Institute for International Development, Development Discussion Paper No. 55, March 1979).

Michael Lipton, *Why Poor People Stay Poor: Urban Bias in World Development* (Cambridge, Mass.: Harvard University Press, 1977).

Chapter 11. Capital and Saving

Sources of Saving

International Monetary Fund, *Government Financial Statistics Yearbook 1989* (Washington D.C.: International Monetary Fund, 1990).

Raymond F. Mikesell and James E. Zinser, "The Nature of the Savings Function in Developing Countries: A Survey of the Theoretical and Empirical Literature," *Journal of Economic Literature* 11, no. 1 (March 1973): 1–26.

Stanley Please, "Savings Through Taxation: Reality or Mirage?" *Finance and Development* 4, no. 1 (March 1967): 24–32.

Alan Tait, Wilfred Gratz, and Barry Eichengreen, "International Comparisons of Taxation for Selected Developing Countries," *International Monetary Fund Staff Papers* 26, no. 1 (March 1979): 123–156.

Vito Tanzi, "Quantitative Characteristics of Tax Systems in Developing Countries," in *Modern Tax Theory for Developing Countries,* David Newbery and Nicholas Stern, eds. (forthcoming).

Determinants of Private Savings

Ranadev Banerji, "Small-Scale Production Units in Manufacturing: An International Cross-Section Overview," *Weltwirtschaftliches Archiv* 114, no. 1 (1978).

Angus Deaton, "Saving in Developing Countries: Theory and Review," *Proceedings of the World Bank Annual Conference on Development Economics,* Washington, D.C., World Bank, 1989.

Robert H. Frank, "The Demand for Unobservable and other Non-Positional Goods," *American Economic Review* 75 (March 1985).

Fortune Magazine, "World Business Directory," various issues 1980–1990.

Nicholas Kaldor, "Problems Economicas De Chile," *El Trimestre Economico* 26, no. 102 (April–June 1959): 193, 211–212.

Philip Musgrove, "Income Distribution and Aggregate Consumption Function", *Journal of Political Economy* 2, no. 88 (June 1980): 504–525.

Constantino Lluch, Alan Powell, and Ross Williams, *Patterns in Household Demand and Savings* (New York: Oxford University Press, 1977).

F. Modigliani, R. Brumberg, and A. Ando, "Life Cycle Hypothesis of Savings: Aggregate Implication and Tests," *American Economic Review* 52, no. 3 (1963).

Roger S. Smith, "Factors Affecting Saving, Policy Tools and Tax Reform: A Review," *International Monetary Fund Working Paper* No. 89/47, May 23, 1989, Table 2.

International Mobility of Capital and Domestic Saving Mobilization

Ranadev Banerji, "Small-Scale Production Units in Manufacturing: an International Cross Section Overview," *Weltwirtschafliches Archiv* 114, no. 1 (1978).

Jeremy Greenwood and Kent Kimbrough, "Capital Controls and the World Economy," *Canadian Journal of Economics* 19, no. 2 (1986): 111–116.

Arnold Harberger, "Vignettes on the World Capital Market," *American Economic Review* 70, no. 2 (May 1980): 331–337.

Larry Summers, "Issues in National Savings Policy," *National Bureau of Economic Research Working Paper* No. 1710, Cambridge, Mass., September 1985.

CHAPTER 12. FISCAL POLICY

Expenditure Policies and Public Saving

Anita Bhatia, "Military Expenditures and Economic Growth," Washington, D.C., World Bank, 1987.

Malcolm Gillis, "Tacit Taxes and Sub-Rosa Subsidies," in *More Taxing Than Taxes,* Richard Bird, ed. (forthcoming).

Peter Heller, "Underfinancing of Recurrent Development Costs," *Finance and Development* 16, no. 1 (March 1979): 38–41.

Norman Hicks, "Expenditure Reductions in Developing Countries," Washington, D.C., World Bank, 1988.

Alfred H. Saulniers, "Improvements in Public Enterprises in Francophone Africa," in *Public Enterprises at the Crossroads,* John Hearth, ed. (forthcoming).

R. P. Short, "The Role of the Public Enterprises: An International Statistical Comparison," IMF, Dept. Memo 83/34, Washington, D.C., 1983.

J. Alm, R. Bahl, and M. Murray, "Tax Base Erosion in Developing Countries," *National Tax Journal* (forthcoming).

Richard Bird, and Oliver Oldman, eds., *Readings on Taxation in Developing Countries*, 3rd ed. (Baltimore: Johns Hopkins Press, 1975).

John F. Due, "Some Unresolved Issues in Design and Implementation of Value-Added Taxes," *National Tax Journal* 42, no. 4 (December 1990): 383–398.

———, *Indirect Taxation in Developing Economies* (Baltimore: Johns Hopkins Press, 1970).

——— and Raymond Mikesell, *Sales Taxation: State and Local Structure and Administration* (Baltimore: Johns Hopkins Press, 1983).

Dwight R. Lee and Richard B. McKenzie, "The International Political Economy of Declining Tax Rates," *Natural Tax Journal* 42, no. 2 (March 1989): 79–87.

Malcolm Gillis, "Tacit Taxes and Sub-Rosa Subsidies," in *More Taxing Than Taxes,* Richard Bird, ed. (forthcoming).

———, ed., *Tax Reform in Developing Countries* (Durham, N.C.: Duke University Press, 1989).

———, "Federal Sales Taxation: Six Decades of Experience," *Canadian Tax Journal (January–February 1985).*

——— and Charles E. McLure, Jr., "Taxation and Income Distribution: The Colombian Tax Reform of 1974," *Journal of Development Economics* 5, no. 3 (September 1978): 237, 249.

International Monetary Fund, *Government Finance Statistics Yearbook 1989* (Washington, D.C.: International Monetary Fund, 1990), country tables.

Richard A. Musgrave et al., *Fiscal Reform in Bolivia: Final Report and Staff Papers of the Bolivian Mission on Tax Reform* (Cambridge, Mass.: Harvard Law School, International Tax Program, 1981).

Oliver Oldman, and Daniel M. Holland, "Measuring Tax Evasion," paper presented at the Fifth Annual General Assembly of the Inter-American Center of Tax Administration, Rio de Janiero, May 17, 1971.

Joseph A. Pechman, ed., *World Tax Reform: A Progress Report* (Washington, D.C.: Brookings Institute, 1988), "Introduction," p. 13.

Robert Repetto and Malcolm Gillis, eds., *Public Policies and the Misuse of Forest Resources* (New York: Cambridge University Press, 1988), "Conclusions," Chap. 10.

Carl Shoup, "Choosing Among Types of VAT," in *Value-Added Taxation in Developing Countries,* M. Gillis, C. Shoup, and Gerry Sicat, eds. (Washington, D.C.: World Bank, 1990).

Joseph Stiglitz, *Economics of the Public Sector* (New York: W. W. Norton,1985).

Harvey Rosen, *Public Finance* (Homewood, Ill.: Richard Irwin, 1985).

Alan A. Tait, *Value-Added Tax* (Washington, D.C.: International Monetary Fund, 1988), Chap. 1.

Vito Tanzi, "Quantitative Aspects of Tax Systems in Developing Countries," in *The Theory of Taxation for Developing Countries,* David Newberry and Nicholas Stern, eds. (London: Oxford University Press, 1987).

World Bank, *World Development Report 1988.*

BIBLIOGRAPHY AND ADDITIONAL READINGS

Richard M. Bird and Luc Henry DeWulf, "Taxation and Income Distribution in Latin America: A Critical View of Empirical Studies," *International Monetary Fund Staff Papers* 20 (November 1975): 639–682.

Alejandro Foxley, Eduardo Aninat, and J. P. Arellano, *Redistributive Effects of Government Programs* (Elmsford, N.Y.: Pergamon Press, 1980), Chap. 6.

Malcolm Gillis, "Micro and Macroeconomics of Tax Reform: Indonesia," *Journal of Development Economics* 19, no. 2 (1986): 42–46.

Charles E. McLure, Jr., "Taxation and the Urban Poor in Developing Countries," *World Development* 5, no. 3 (1977): 169–188.

Donald R. Snodgrass, "The Fiscal System as an Income Redistributor in West Malaysia," *Public Finance* 29, no. 1 (January 1974): 56–76.

CHAPTER 13. FINANCIAL POLICY

The Role of Finance in Development

Anand G. Chandavarkar, "Monetization of Developing Economies," *International Monetary Fund Staff Papers* 24, no. 3 (November 1977): 678–679.

International Monetary Fund, *International Financial Statistics,* various issues, 1970–1990.

Ronald I. McKinnon, *Money and Capital in Economic Development* (Washington, D.C.: Brookings Institution, 1973).

Edward Shaw, *Financial Deepening and Economic Development* (New York: Oxford University Press, 1973).

Inflation and Savings Mobilization

Yaw Ansu, "Comments," in *World Economic Growth,* Arnold C. Harberger, ed. (San Francisco: Institute of Contemporary Studies, 1984).

Arnold C. Harberger, "A Primer on Inflation," *Journal of Money, Credit and Banking* 10, no. 4 (November 1978): 505–521.

Albert O. Hirschman, *Journeys Toward Progress: Studies of Economic Policy-making in Latin America* (New York: Twentieth Century Fund, 1963), pp. 208–209.

Michael Roemer, "Ghana, 1950 to 1980: Missed Opportunities," in *World Economic Growth,* Arnold C. Harberger, ed. (San Francisco: Institute of Contemporary Studies, 1984), pp. 201–230.

George M. von Furstenberg, "Inflation, Taxes, and Welfare in LDCs," *Public Finance* 35, no. 2 (1980): 700–710.

Interest Rates and Saving Decisions

Charles Beach, Robin Broadway, and Neil Bruce, "Taxation and Savings: Some Life-Cycle Estimates for Canada," Queens University Working Paper Series, August 1985.

Michael J. Boskin, "Taxation, Savings and the Rate of Interest," *Journal of Political Economy* 8b, no. 2, part 2 (April 1978): 3–27.

Alberto Giovanni, "The Interest Elasticity of Savings in Developing Countries," *World Development* 11 (July 1983): 601–608.

Larry Summers, "Capital Taxation and Capital Accumulation in a Life-Cycle Growth Model," *American Economic Review* 71 (September 1981): 533–544.

Colin Wright, "Savings and The Rate of Interst," in *The Taxation of Income from Capital,* Arnold C. Harberger and Martin Bailey, eds. (Washington, D.C.: Brookings Institution, 1969).

Financial Development

Sebastian Edwards, "Stabilization with Liberalization: An Evaluation of Chile's Experiment with Free-Market Policies 1973–1983," *Economic Development and Cultural Change* 27 (September 1985): 224–253.

Sergio Pereira Leite, "Interest-Rate Policies in West Africa," *International Monetary Fund Staff Papers* 29, no. 1 (March 1982): 48–76.

Ronald I. McKinnon, "Financial Liberalization and Economic Development: A Reassessment of Interest Rate Policies in Asia and Latin America," *International Center for Economic Growth Ocassional Paper* No. 6, San Francisco, 1988.

Steven C. Leuthold, "Interst Rates, Inflation and Deflation," *Financial Analysis Journal* (January–February 1981): 28–51.

World Bank, *World Development Report 1989.*

Monetary Policy and Price Stability

Arnold Harberger, "A Primer on Inflation," *Journal of Money, Credit and Banking* 10, no. 4 (November 1978): 505–521.

———, "The Inflation Syndrome," paper presented in the Political Economy Lecture Series, Harvard University, March 19, 1981.

Anne O. Krueger, *Exchange Rate Determination* (New York: Cambridge University Press, 1983), pp. 123–136.

John Williamson, *The Open Economy and the World Economy* (New York: Basic Books, 1983), pp. 238–241.

CHAPTER 14. FOREIGN AID, INVESTMENT, AND DEBT

Concepts and Magnitudes

Development Assistance Committee on the OECD, *Development Cooperation in the 1990s* (Paris: OECD, 1989).

International Monetary Fund, *Balance of Payments Yearbook 1990,* Vol. 2 (Washington, D.C.: International Monetary Fund, 1989).

———, *International Financial Statistics Yearbook* (Washington, D.C.: International Monetary Fund, annual).

United States Agency for International Development, *Congressional Presentation* (Washington, D.C.: annual).

World Bank, *World Debt Tables* (Washington, D.C.: World Bank, annual).

Robert L. Ayres, *Banking on the Poor* (Cambridge, Mass.: MIT Press, 1984).

Robert Cassen et al., *Does Aid Work?* (London: Oxford University Press, 1986).

Jonathan Eaton, "Foreign Public Capital Flows," in *Handbook of Development Economics,* Vol. 2, Hollis B. Chenery and T. N. Srinivasan, eds. (Amsterdam: North-Holland, 1989): 1305–1386.

Joint Ministerial Committee of the Boards of Governors of the World Bank and the International Monetary Fund, *Aid for Development: The Key Issues* (Washington, D.C.: 1986).

Paul Mosley, "Aid, Savings and Growth Revisited," *Oxford Bulletin of Economics and Statistics* 42 (May 1980): 79–91.

Foreign Investment and the Multinationals

Jack N. Behrman and William A. Fischer, *Overseas R & D Activities of Transnational Corporations* (Cambridge, Mass.: Oelgeschlager, Gunn and Hair, 1980).

Fred C. Bergsten, Thomas P. Horst, and Theodore H. Moran, *American Multinationals and American Interests* (Washington, D.C.: Brookings Institution, 1978).

Eliana Cardoso and Rudiger Dornbusch, "Foreign Private Capital Flows," in *Handbook of Development Economics,* Vol. 2, Hollis B. Chenery and T. N. Srinivasan, eds. (Amsterdam: North-Holland, 1989): 1387–1439.

David Goldsborough, "Foreign Direct Investment in Developing Countries," *Finance and Development* (March 1985).

Steven Guisinger et al., *Investment Incentives and Performance Requirements* (New York: Praeger, 1985).

G. K. Helleiner, "Transnational Corporations and Direct Foreign Investment," in *Handbook of Development Economics,* Vol. 2, Hollis B. Chenery and T. N. Srinivasan, eds. (Amsterdam: North-Holland, 1989): 1441–1480.

Theodore H. Moran, ed., *Multinational Corporations* (Lexington, Mass.: Lexington Books, 1985).

——— et al., *Investment in Development: New Roles for Foreign Capital?* (Washington, D.C.: Overseas Development Council, 1986).

John Stopford, *The World Directory of Multinational Enterprises 1982–1983* (Detroit: Gale Research Company, 1982).

United Nations Centre for Transnational Corporations (UNCTNC), *Transnational Corporations in World Development* (New York: United Nations, 1988).

Raymnond Vernon, *Storm over the Multinationals: The Real Issues* (Cambridge, Mass.: Harvard University Press, 1977).

Louis T. Wells, Jr., "Investment Incentives: An Unnecessary Debate," *The CTC Reporter* 22 (Autumn 1986): 58–60.

The Debt Crisis

Rudiger Dornbusch, "Background Paper," in *The Road to Economic Recovery,* Twentieth Century Fund, Task Force on International Debt (New York: Priority Publications, 1989).

———, "Mexico's Economy at the Crossroads," *Journal of International Affairs* 43 no. 2 (Winter 1990): 313–326.

Albert Fishlow, "External Borrowing and Debt Management," in *The Open Economy: Tools for Policymakers in Developing Countries,* Rudiger Dornbusch, F. Leslie C. H. Helmers (New York: Oxford University Press, 1988): 187–222.

Ishrat Husain and Ishac Diwan, eds., *Dealing with the Debt Crisis* (Washington, D.C.: World Bank, 1989).

Carol Lancaster and John Williamson, eds., *African Debt and Financing* (Washington, D.C.: Institute for International Economics, 1986).

Jeffrey Sachs, "The LDC Debt Crisis," *NBER Reporter* (Winter 1986): 15–16.

CHAPTER 15. PRIMARY EXPORTS AND GROWTH

Comparative Advantage

Richard E. Caves, Jeffrey A. Frankel, and Ronald W. Jones, *World Trade and Payments: An Introduction.* 5th ed. (Boston: Little, Brown, 1990).

Gerald M. Meier, *International Trade and Development* (Westport, Conn.: Greenwood Press, 1975).

Moises Syrquin and Hollis B. Chenery, *Patterns of Development, 1950–1983* (Washington, D.C.: World Bank, 1989).

United Nations, *Yearbook of International Trade Statistics* (New York: United Nations, annual).

John Williamson, *The Open Economy and The World Economy* (New York: Basic Books, 1983)

Primary Exports as an Engine of Growth

Robert E. Baldwin, *Economic Development and Export Growth: A Study of Northern Rhodesia, 1920–1960* (Los Angeles: University of California Press, 1966).

Albert Fishlow, *American Railroads and the Transformation of the Antebellum Economy* (Cambridge, Mass.: Harvard University Press, 1965).

Robert W. Fogel, "Railroads as an Analogy to The Space Effort: Some Economic Aspects," in *Space Programs: An Exploration in Historical Analogy,* Bruce Mazlish, ed. (Cambridge, Mass.: MIT Press, 1966).

Albert O. Hirschman, "A Generalized Linkage Approach to Economic Development, with Special Reference to Staples," in *Essays on Economic Development and Cultural Change,* Manning Nash, ed. (Chicago: University of Chicago Press, 1977): 67–98.

Stephen R. Lewis, "Primary Exporting Countries," In *Handbook of Development Economics,* Vol. 2, Hollis B. Chenery and T. N. Srinivasan, eds. (Amsterdam: North-Holland, 1989): 1541–1600.

Hla Myint, "The 'Classical Theory' of International Trade and the Underdeveloped Countries," *Economic Journal* 68 (1959): 317–337.

Douglass C. North, "Location Theory and Regional Economic Growth, *Journal of Political Economy* 63 (1955): 243–285.

Michael Roemer, *Fishing for Growth: Export-Led Development in Peru, 1950–1967* (Cambridge, Mass.: Harvard University Press, 1970).

Melville H. Watkins, "A Staple Theory of Economic Growth," *Canadian Journal of Economics and Political Science* 29 (1963): 141–158.

Barriers to Primary-Export-Led Growth

Bela Balassa, "Outward Orientation," in *Handbook of Development Economics,* Vol. 2, Hollis B. Chenery and T. N. Srinivasan, eds. (Amsterdam: North-Holland, 1989): 1645–1689.

Jere R. Behrman, "Commodity Price Instability and Economic Goal Attainment in Developing Countries," *World Development* 15, no. 5 (May 1987): 559–573.

———, *Development, The International Economic Order and Commodity Agreements* (Reading, Mass.: Addison-Wesley, 1978).

John T. Cuddington and Carlos M. Urzua, "Trends and Cycles in the Net Barter Terms of Trade: A New Approach," *The Economic Journal* 99 (June 1989): 426–442.

Jagdish N. Bhagwati, ed., *The North-South Debate* (Cambridge, Mass.: MIT Press, 1977).

W. Max Corden and S. Peter Neary, "Booming Sector and Deindustrialization in a Small Open Economy," *Economic Journal* 92 (December 1982): 825–848.

Alan Gelb et al., *Oil Windfalls: Blessing or Curse?* (New York: Oxford University Press for the World Bank, 1988).

Odin Knudsen and Andrew Parnes, *Trade Instability and Economic Development* (Lexington, Mass.: Heath Lexington Books, 1975).

Ragnar Nurkse, *Equilibrium Growth in the World Economy* (Cambridge, Mass.: Harvard University Press, 1961).

Michael Roemer, "Dutch Disease in Developing Countries: Swallowing Bitter Medicine," in *The Primary Sector in Economic Development,* Matts Lundahl, ed. (London: Croom-Helms, 1985).

———, "Ghana 1950–1980: Missed Opportunities," in *World Economic Growth,* Arnold Harberger, ed. (San Francisco: Institute for Contemporary Studies, 1984), pp. 201–226.

———, "Resource-based Industrialization: A Survey," *Journal of Development Economics* 6, no. 6 (June 1979): 163–202.

Hans W. Singer, "The Distribution of Trade Between Investing and Borrowing Countries," *American Economic Review* 40 (May 1950): 470–485.

United Nations (Paul Prebisch), *The Economic Development of Latin America and its Principal Problems* (Lake Success, N.Y.: United Nations, 1950).

World Bank, *Commodity Trade and Price Trends* (Washington, D.C.: World Bank, annual).

CHAPTER 16. IMPORT SUBSTITUTION

The Strategy of Protection

Bela Balassa et al., *The Structure of Protection in the Developing Countries* (Baltimore: Johns Hopkins Press, 1971).

Robert E. Baldwin, "The Case Against Infant Industry Protection," *Journal of Political Economy* 77 (1969): 295–305.

Henry Bruton, "Import Substitution," in *Handbook of Development Economics,* Vol. 2, Hollis B. Chenery and T. N. Srinivasan, eds. (Amsterdam: Elsevier, Science Publishers, 1989): 1601–1644.

*W. M. Corden, *The Theory of Protection* (London: Oxford University Press, 1971).

*Thomas L. Hutcheson and Joseph J. Stern, "The Methodology of Assistance Policy Analysis," Harvard Institute for International Development, Development Discussion Paper No. 226, April 1986.

Harry G. Johnson, "Optimal Trade Interventions in the Presence of Distortions," in *Trade, Growth and the Balance of Payments,* R. E. Caves et al. (Amsterdam: North-Holland, 1965):: 3–34.

Anne O. Krueger, "Trade Policies of Developing Countries," in *Handbook of International Economics,* Vol. 1. R. W. Jones and P. B. Kenen, eds. (Amsterdam: North Holland, 1984): 519–569.

Outcomes and Problems

Henry J. Bruton, "The Import Substitution Strategy of Economic Development," *The Pakistan Development Review* 10 (1970): 123–146.

Albert O. Hirschman, "The Political Economy of Import Substitution," *Quarterly Journal of Economics* 82 (1968): 1–32.

I. M. D. Little, Tibor Scitovsky, and Maurice Scott, *Industry and Trade in Some Developing Countries* (London: Oxford University Press, 1970).

John H. Power, "Import Substitution as an Industrialization Strategy," *The Philippine Economic Journal* 5 (1966): 167–204.

CHAPTER 17. OUTWARD-LOOKING DEVELOPMENT

Outward-Looking Strategies

Alice Amsden, *Asia's New Giant: South Korea and Late Industrialization* (New York: Oxford University Press, 1989).

Bela Balassa, "The Process of Industrial Development and Alternative Development Strategies," *Essays in International Finance* No. 141, Princeton, N.J., International Finance Section, Economics Department, Princeton University, 1980.

———, "Outward Orientation," in *Handbook of Development Economics,* Vol. 2, Hollis B. Chenery and T. N. Srinivasan, eds. (Amsterdam: North-Holland, 1989): 1645–1689.

Jagdish Bhagwati, *Foreign Exchange Regimes and Economic Development: Anatomy and Consequences of Exchange Control Regimes* (Cambridge, Mass.: Ballinger, 1978).

Vittorio Corbo and Sang Woo Nam, "The Recent Macroeconomic Evolution of the Republic of Korea: An Overview," World Bank, Economic Research Department, Discussion Paper DRD 208, 1986.

Anne O. Krueger, *Foreign Trade Regimes and Economic Development: Liberalization Attempts and Consequences* (Cambridge, Mass.: Ballinger, 1978).

Deepak Lal and Sarath Rajapatirana, "Foreign Trade Regimes and Economic Growth in Developing Countries," World Bank *Research Observer* 2, no. 2 (July 1987).

Howard Pack and Larry E. Westphal, "Industrial Strategy and Technological Change," *Journal of Development Economics* 22, no. 1 (June 1986): 87–128.

Gustav Ranis, "Industrial Sector Labor Absorption," *Economic Development and Cultural Change* 21 (1973): 347–408.

Robert Wade, *Governing the Market: Economic Theory and the Role of Government in East Asian Industrialization* (Princeton, N.J.: Princeton University Press, 1990).

Outcomes and Limitations

Tyler Biggs and Brian Levy, "Strategic Interventions and the Political Economy of Industrial Policy in Developing Countries," in *Systems Reform in Developing Countries*, D. H. Perkins and M. Roemer, eds. (Cambridge, Mass.: Harvard University Press, 1991): 365–401.

Tun-jen Cheng, "Political Regimes and Development Strategies: South Korea and Taiwan," in *Manufacturing Miracles*, Gary Gireffid and Donald Wyman, eds. (Princeton, N.J.: Princeton University Press, 1991).

Charles R. Frank, Kwang Suk Kim, and Larry E. Westphal, *Foreign Trade Regimes and Economic Development: South Korea* (New York: Columbia University Press, 1975).

Helen Hughes, ed., *Achieving Industrialization in East Asia* (Cambridge, U.K.: 1988).

Lawrence J. Lau, ed., *Models of Development: A Comparative Study of Economic Growth in South Korea and Taiwan* (San Francisco: Institute for Contemporary Studies, 1990).

Howard Pack, "Industrialization and Trade," in *Handbook of Development Economics*, Vol. I, Hollis B. Chenery and T. N. Srinivasan, eds., (Amsterdam: North-Holland, 1989): 333–380.

William G. Tyler, *Manufactured Export Expansion and Industrialization in Brazil* (Tubingen, W. Germany: J. C. B. Mohr, 1976).

Protection in the North

Jaleel Ahmad, "Prospects of Trade Liberalization Between Developed and Developing Countries," *World Development* 13 (September 1985): 1077–1086.

Diane P. Berliner, Kimberly Ann Elliot, and Gary Hufbauer, *Trade Protection in the United States; 31 Case Studies* (Washington, D.C.: Institute for International Economics, 1986).

Jagdish Bhagwati, *Protectionism* (Cambridge, Mass.: MIT Press, 1988).

"A Survey of World Trade," *The Economist*, (Special Section, September 22, 1990).

United Nations, *Yearbook of International Trade Statistics* (New York: United Nations, annual).

Integration in the South

*Martin Carnoy, "A Welfare Analysis of Latin American Economic Union: Six Industry Studies," *Journal of Political Economy* 78 (1970): 626–654.

Harry G. Johnson, *Money, Trade and Economic Growth* (London: Allen & Unwin, 1962), Chap. 3.

Alistair I. MacBean and P. N. Snowden, *International Institutions in Trade and Finance* (London: Allen & Unwin, 1981), Chaps. 8–10.
*Pan A. Yotopoulos and Jeffrey B. Nugent, *Economics of Development: Empirical Investigations* (New York: Harper & Row, 1976), Chap. 19.
Jacob Viner, *The Customs Union Issue* (New York: Carnegie Endowment for International Peace, 1950).

Chapter 18. Agriculture

Agriculture's Role in Economic Development

Bruce F. Johnston and Peter Kilby, *Agriculture and Structural Transformation* (London: Oxford University Press, 1975).
John Mellor, *The New Economic Growth* (Ithaca, N.Y.: Cornell University Press, 1976).
———, *The Economics of Agricultural Development* (Ithaca, N.Y.: Cornell University Press, 1966).
J. W. Mellor and B. F. Johnston, "The World Food Equation: Interrelations among Development, Employment, and Food Consumption, *Journal of Economic Literature,* no. 22 (1984).
J. Mohan Rao, "Agriculture in Recent Development Theory," *Journal of Development Economics,* no. 22 (1986).
Lloyd Reynolds, *Agriculture in Development Theory* (New Haven, Conn.: Yale University Press, 1976).
T. W. Schultz, *Transforming Traditional Agriculture* (New Haven, Conn.: Yale University Press, 1964).
Erik Thorbecke, ed., *The Role of Agriculture in Economic Development* (New York: Columbia University Press, 1969).
C. Peter Timmer, "The Agricultural Transformation," in *Handbook of Development Economics,* Vol. 1, Hollis B. Chenery and T. N. Srinivasan, eds. (Amsterdam: North-Holland, 1988).
World Bank, *World Development Report 1982* (New York: Oxford University Press, 1982).

Self-Sufficiency in Food

R. Barker, E. Bennagen, and Y. Hayami, "New Rice Technology and Policy Alternatives for Food Self-Sufficiency," in *Economic Consequences of the New Rice Technology,* International Rice Research Institute (Los Banos, Philippines: 1978), pp. 337–361.
Lester Brown, *By Bread Alone* (New York: Praeger, 1974).
Richard Goldman, "Staple Food Self-Sufficiency and the Distributive Impact of Malaysian Rice Policy," *Food Research Institute Studies* 14, no. 3 (1975): 251–293.

Land Reform

Ronald P. Dore, *Land Reform in Japan* (London: Oxford University Press, 1959).
William Hinton, *Fanshen* (New York: Vintage Books, 1966).
Elias Tuma, *Twenty-six Centuries of Agrarian Reform: A Comparative Analysis* (Berkeley: University of California Press, 1965).

Louis J. Walinsky, ed., *Agrarian Reform as Unfinished Business: The Selected Papers of Wolf Ladejinsky* (London: Oxford University Press, 1977).

John Wong, *Land Reform in the People's Republic of China* (New York: Praeger, 1973).

Technology of Agricultural Production

Hans B. Binswanger, "Agricultural Mechanization: A Comparative Historical Perspective," *World Bank Research Observer* 1, no. 1 (January 1986).

——— and Prabhu Pingali, "Technological Priorities for Farming in Sub-Saharan Africa," *World Bank Research Observer* 3, no. 1 (January 1988).

——— and Vernon W. Ruttan, *Induced Innovation: Technology, Institutions and Development* (Baltimore: Johns Hopkins Press, 1978).

Ester Boserup, *The Conditions of Agricultural Growth* (Chicago: Aldine, 1965).

Dana G. Dalrymple, *Development and Spread of High Yielding Wheat Varieties in Developing Countries* (Washington, D.C.: Agency for International Development, 1986).

Yujiro Hayami and Vernon W. Ruttan, *Agricultural Development: An International Perspective* (Baltimore: Johns Hopkins Press, 1971).

Dwight H. Perkins, *Agricultural Development in China, 1368–1968* (Chicago: Aldine, 1969).

Theodore W. Schultz, *Transforming Traditional Agriculture* (New Haven, Conn.: Yale University Press, 1964).

Sol Tax, *Penny Capitalism* (Chicago: University of Chicago Press, 1963).

Mobilization of Agricultural Inputs

S. J. Burki, D. G. Davies, R. H. Hook, and J. W. Thomas, *Public Works Programs in Developing Countries: A Comparative Analysis,* World Bank Staff Working Paper No. 224, February 1976.

Uma Lele, *The Design of Rural Development: Lessons from Africa* (Baltimore: Johns Hopkins Press, 1975).

Dwight H. Perkins and Shahid Yusuf, *Rural Development in China* (Baltimore: Johns Hopkins Press, 1984).

Agricultural Price Policy

Hussein Askari and John Cummings, *Agricultural Supply Response: A Survey of the Econometric Evidence* (New York: Praeger, 1976).

Elliot Berg et al., *Accelerated Development in Sub-Saharan Africa* (Washington, D.C.: World Bank, 1981).

Walter P. Falcon and C. Peter Timmer, "The Political Economy of Rice Production and Trade in Asia," in *Agriculture in Development Theory,* L. Reynolds, ed. (New Haven, Conn.: Yale University Press, 1975).

Raj Krishna, "Agricultural Price Policy and Economic Development," in *Agricultural Development and Economic Growth,* H. M. Southworth and B. F. Johnston, eds. (Ithaca, N.Y.: Cornell University Press, 1967).

C. Peter Timmer, Walter P. Falcon, and Scott R. Pearson, *Food Policy Analysis* (Baltimore: Johns Hopkins Press, 1983).

Natural Resources and the Environment

William Ascher and Robert Healy, *Natural Resource Policy-Making in Developing Countries* (Durham, N. C.: Duke University Press, 1990).

Robert Repetto and Malcolm Gillis, eds., *Public Policies and the Misuse of Forest Resources* (New York: Cambridge University Press, 1988).

World Resource Institute, *World Resources 1990–91* (New York: Oxford University Press, 1990).

Development and the Environment

Yusuf Ahmed, Alah Elseraty, and Ernst Lutz, eds., *Environmental Accounting for Sustainable Development* (Washington, D.C.: World Bank, 1990).

Malcolm Gillis, "Indonesia: Public Policies, Resource Management and the Tropical Forest," in *Public Policies and the Misuse of Forest Resources,* Robert Repetto and Malcolm Gillis, eds. (New York: Cambridge University Press, 1988).

————, "West Africa: Resource Management Policies and the Tropical Forest," in *Public Policies and the Misuse of Forest Resources,* Repetto and Gillis.

————. "Energy Demand in Indonesia," Cambridge, Mass., Development Discussion Paper No. 9, April 1980.

Jeffrey Leonard, *Natural Resources and Economic Development in Central America* [London: International Institute for Environment and Development (IIED), 1987].

Ernst Lutz and Mohan Munasinghe, "Accounting for the Environment," *Finance and Development* (March 1991).

Norman Myers, "Deforestation Rates in Tropical Forests and their Climate Implications" (London: Friends of the Earth, 1989).

Norman Nicholson, "The State of the Art," in *Rethinking Institutional Analysis and Development,* Ostrom, Feeng, and Picht (San Francisco: Institute of Contemporary Studies, 1990).

Orrin Pilkey, "The Engineering of Sand," *Journal of Geological Education* 37 (1989).

Robert Repetto et. al., "Natural Resource Accounting for Indonesia," (Washington, D.C.: World Resources Institute, May 1987).

Tom Waters, "Ecoglasnost," *Discover* 11 (April 1990): 31.

CHAPTER 20. INDUSTRY

Industry as a Leading Sector

E. J. Hobsbawm, *The Pelican History of Britain,* Vol. 3, *Industry and Empire* (Baltimore: Penguin, 1969).

David S. Landes, *The Unbound Prometheus: Technological Change and Industrial Development in Western Europe from 1750 to the Present* (London: Cambridge University Press, 1969).

Stanford Research Institute et al., *Costs of Urban Infrastructure for Indus-*

try as Related to City Size in Developing Countries: India Case Study (Menlo Park, Calif.: Stanford Research Institute, 1968).

Moises Syrquin and Hollis Chenery, "Three Decades of Industrialization," *The World Bank Economic Review* 3, no. 2 (1989): 141–181.

Pan A. Yotopoulos and Jeffrey B. Nugent, "A Balanced-Growth Version of the Linkage Hypotheses: A Test," *Quarterly Journal of Economics* 87 (1973): 157–171.

Investment Choices in Industry

American Rural Small-Scale Industry Delegation, *Rural Small-Scale Industry in the People's Republic of China* (Berkeley: University of California Press, 1977).

Ranadev Banerji, "Average Size of Plants in Manufacturing and Capital Intensity," *Journal of Development Economics* 5 (1978).

P. N. Dhar and H. F. Lydall, *The Role of Small Enterprises in Indian Economic Development* (New York: Asia Publishing House, 1961).

Hal Hill, "Choice of Technique in the Indonesian Weaving Industry," *Economic Development and Cultural Change* 31, no. 2 (January 1983): 337–354.

International Labor Office, *Employment, Income and Equality: A Strategy for Increasing Productive Employment in Kenya* (Geneva: International Labor Office, 1972).

Ian M. D. Little, Dipak Mazumdar, and John M. Page, Jr., *Small Manufacturing Enterprises* (New York: Oxford University Press for the World Bank, 1988).

Alan S. Manne, ed., *Investments for Capacity Expansion: Size, Location and Time Phasing* (Cambridge, Mass.: MIT Press, 1967).

Howard Pack, "Aggregate Implications of Factor Substitution in Industry Processes," *Journal of Development Economics* 11, no. 1 (August 1982).

———, "The Choice of Technique and Employment in the Textile Industry," in *Technology and Employment in Industry,* A. S. Bhalla, ed. (Geneva: International Labor Office, 1975).

C. F. Pratten, *Economies of Scale in Manufacturing Industry* (London: Cambridge University Press, 1971).

E. F. Schumacher, *Small is Beautiful* (London: Sphere Books, 1974).

Eugene Staley and Richard Morse, *Modern Small Industry for Developing Countries* (New York: McGraw-Hill, 1965).

Hernando de Soto, *The Other Path* (New York: Harper & Row, 1989).

William F. Steel, *Small-Scale Employment and Production in Developing Countries: Evidence from Ghana* (New York: Praeger, 1977).

Frances Stewart, "Manufacture of Cement Blocks in Kenya," in *Technology and Employment in Industry,* A. S. Bhalla, ed. (Geneva: International Labor Office, 1975).

Louis T. Wells, Jr., "Economic Man and Engineering Man: Choice of Technique in a Low-wage Country," in *The Choice of Technology in Developing Countries,* C. P. Timmer et al., eds. (Cambridge, Mass.: Center for International Affairs, Harvard University, 1975), pp. 69–74.

Jeffrey Williamson, "Regional Inequality and the Process of National Development: A Description of Patterns," *Economic Development and Cultural Change* 13 (1965): 3–45.

Richard E. Caves, Jeffrey A. Frankel, and Ronald W. Jones, *World Trade and Payments: An Introduction* (Glenview, Ill.: Scott, Foresman / Little, Brown, 1990), Chap. 19.

*W. Max Corden, *Inflation, Exchange Rates and the World Economy* (Chicago: University of Chicago Press, 1977).

*Rudiger Dornbusch, *Open Economy Macroeconomics,* 2nd ed. (New York: Basic Books, 1989), Chap. 6.

W. E. G. Salter, "Internal Balance and External Balance: The Role of Price and Expenditure Effects," *Economic Record* 35–71 (August 1959): 226–238.

Trevor W. Swan, "Economic Control in a Dependent Economy," *Economic Record* 36–73 (March 1960): 51–66.

Index

two-gap model 135